PRODUCING VEGETABLE CROPS

Fourth Edition

PRODUCING

JOHN M. SWIADER, Ph.D.

Associate Professor of Horticulture
University of Illinois

GEORGE W. WARE, Ph.D.

Associate Director
Agricultural Experiment Station
The University of Arizona

VEGETABLE CROPS

J. P. McCOLLUM, Ph.D.

Late Professor of Plant Physiology
University of Illinois

INTERSTATE PUBLISHERS, INC.
Danville, Illinois

PRODUCING VEGETABLE CROPS

Fourth Edition

Prior Editions: 1968, 1975, 1980

Order from

Interstate Publishers, Inc.
510 North Vermilion Street
P.O. Box 50
Danville, IL 61834-0050
Phone: (800) 843-4774
FAX: (217) 446-9706

Library of Congress Catalog Card No. 91-72369

ISBN 0-8134-2903-X

1 2 3
4 5 6
7 8 9

To *Peg, Eileen, James,* and *Bill*, who have spent count-less hours in lively discussion debating the morpholog-ical and taxonomical differences between turnips and rutabagas

JMS

——————

To my wife,	my children,	and my grandchildren,
Doris	*Cindy*	*John*
	Lynn	*Karyn*
	Sam	*Ashleigh*
	Melanie	*Lauren*
	Julie	*Matthew*

GWW

DISCLAIMER CLAUSE / STATEMENT OF WARRANTY

PREFACE

Olericulture, the study of vegetable production, is a subject of enormous scope. It involves the integration of a wide spectrum of disciplines that cut across soil science, plant physiology, biochemistry, horticulture, agronomy, plant pathology, entomology, and genetics. Although many of the principles of growing vegetables are generally applicable, they may vary materially in different sections of the country, depending upon economic, environmental, and edaphic factors. As new technologies and developments become available, cropping systems and production practices change. Many principles and practices that were common a few years ago may no longer be current.

Producing Vegetable Crops, Fourth Edition, deals with the principles, production practices, management, and handling of vegetable crops. The purpose of this text is to provide complete, reliable, up-to-date information on the various phases of vegetable production in a systematic and convenient manner. Intended as a comprehensive text for vegetable production courses, the book is written in such a way that it can also be used by extension workers, commercial growers, and home gardeners. Although the information is discussed primarily from the perspective of commercial production, much of the material is also applicable to the home vegetable garden.

The book is organized into several broad areas. Chapters 1 through 11 deal with basic information and fundamental principles pertinent to vegetables in general. Chapters 12 through 28 discuss the specific vegetable crops and the cultural practices and technology used in their production; detailed information is presented for over 60 specific crops that are of commercial significance in the U.S. In addition, *Producing Vegetable Crops* includes separate chapters on controlled environment production (Chapter 29) and home vegetable gardening (Chapter 30).

The fourth edition incorporates significant changes and technical advances that have taken place in vegetable production since publication of the previous edition in 1980. These include new developments in vegetable genetics and breeding (e.g., new genes for high sugar sweet corn, all-male asparagus hybrids, gynoecious and parthenocarpic cucumbers), the use of new techniques for seed enhancement and crop establishment (e.g., seed priming and gel seeding), and new methodologies and practices in plant culture (e.g., polyethylene mulches, spun-bonded fiber row tunnels, high-density plantings, etc.). Chapter 11, "Biotechnology and Genetic Engineering: New Directions in Agriculture," which is a new chapter, discusses the new plant biotechnology (tissue and cell culture, protoplast fusion, recombinant DNA) that is being used to improve vegetable quality, increase yields, and decrease the use of pesticides in vegetable production.

Also included are considerable new material and increased emphasis in the areas of plant growth and development. This is a significant change from the previous edition and is designed to provide the reader with a better understanding of vegetable growth and the factors affecting it. The underlying theme throughout the book is that in order to grow vegetables successfully, one must know how vegetables grow. When a basic understanding of vegetable growth and development is acquired, many of the practices and principles of vegetable production follow logically.

We have used the latest information obtained from state agricultural experiment stations, the U.S. Department of Agriculture, university and private vegetable scientists, processors, growers, and other industry-related sources. Graphs and tables have been updated, and many new photographs and illustrations have been added.

The chapters are complete in themselves, but cross references are made to avoid repetition and to supply additional information. As much as possible, the production practices in the vegetable chapters are discussed in order of seasonal sequence. Due to continuous revisions and restrictions on their use, specific pesticide recommendations for pest control are not included in this book. Rather, such information can be obtained from extension vegetable specialists at state agricultural experiment stations throughout the U.S. A listing of these is in the Appendix.

The Latin plant names (binomials) used in this book conform generally with *Hortus Third* (Macmillan Publishing Co., 1976). The U.S. system of weights and measures (pounds, acres, Fahrenheit temperatures) has been used throughout the book because most commercial growers in the U.S. have not changed over to the metric system. A conversion table of U.S. measurements to metric units is provided in the Appendix. Selected references are provided at the end of each chapter for further study. A brief glossary containing nomenclature pertinent to vegetable production precedes the Index.

The authors express thanks to their colleagues for their valuable information and suggestions. Thanks are also extended to the individuals, companies, and organizations that provided the photographs, illustrations, and data used in the various chapters. Wherever possible, acknowledgement has been given for their contributions. Credit is also due to the U.S. Department of Agriculture for supplying most of the current production statistics used throughout the text.

The authors are especially thankful for the contribution of the following authors: Dr. R. D. Morse, Chapter 3; Dr. F. J. Sundstrom, Chapters 5 and 22; W. H. Shoemaker, Chapters 8 and 19; and Dr. E. L. Kerbel, Chapter 10. The authors also offer their sincere thanks to Elaine Cornwell for her excellent typing of the numerous tables in the manuscript. Finally, the authors express gratitude to Interstate Publishers, Inc.; and in particular to Ron McDaniel for his patience and assistance throughout this endeavor and to Pat Ward for her expertise in editing and proofing the revision.

John M. Swiader
George W. Ware

The current authors of *Producing Vegetable Crops* wish to acknowledge the valuable contributions to previous editions by the late George W. Ware, Sr., some of which remain as part of this book.

CONTENTS

Page

PREFACE   vii

Chapter

1 — The Vegetable Industry   1

2 — Classifying Vegetables   29

3 — Plant Growth and Development   39
        by R. D. Morse

4 — Breeding and Improving Vegetables   55

5 — Crop Establishment: Transplanting
        and Direct-Field Seeding   69
        by F. J. Sundstrom

6 — Soil Management and Fertilization   95

7 — Weed Management in Vegetables   119

8 — Irrigating and Mulching   133
        co-authored by W. H. Shoemaker

Chapter			Page

9 — Controlling Insects and Diseases — 151

10 — Postharvest Handling of Vegetables — 171

    by E. L. Kerbel

11 — Biotechnology and Genetic Engineering:
New Directions in Agriculture — 197

12 — Perennial Crops — Asparagus, Rhubarb,
and Globe Artichokes — 209

13 — Garden Beans — Snap Beans, Lima Beans, and
Other Beans (Scarlet Runner Beans, Cowpeas,
Asparagus Beans, Catjang Beans, Garden Soybeans,
Fava Beans, Garbanzo Beans, Mung Beans) — 233

14 — Cole Crops — Cabbage, Broccoli,
Cauliflower, and Related Crops
(Brussels Sprouts, Kohlrabi,
Chinese Cabbage) — 255

15 — Root Crops — Carrots, Beets, and Related
Vegetables (Horseradish, Parsnips, Radishes,
Rutabagas, Turnips, Jerusalem Artichokes) — 279

16 — Celery — 309

17 — Cucumbers — 323

18 — Lettuce and Other Leafy Salad Vegetables
(Endive-Escarole, Chicory) — 341

19 — Melons — Muskmelons, Watermelons,
and Honeydews — 361

    by W. H. Shoemaker

20 — Onions and Related Alliums
(Garlic, Leek, Chives, Shallots) — 381

21 — Peas — 405

Chapter			Page

22 — Peppers 421

        by F. J. Sundstrom

23 — Potatoes 435

24 — Spinach and Other Leafy Vegetable
Greens (Collards, Kale, Chard, Mustards,
New Zealand Spinach, Dandelions) 459

25 — Sweet Corn 477

26 — Sweet Potatoes 495

27 — Tomatoes 513

28 — Other Vegetables — Eggplants, Pumpkins and
Squashes, Okra, Salsify, Celeriac,
Florence Fennel, Orach, Parsley 537

29 — Controlled Environment Vegetable
Production 555

30 — Home Vegetable Gardening 575

APPENDIX 589

GLOSSARY 601

INDEX 611

1

THE VEGETABLE INDUSTRY

Vegetable production is a dynamic and major segment of the U.S. economy. The task of producing vegetables for a growing population with changing food habits is complex. Vegetable growers in the U.S. produce an ever-expanding selection of food choices covering hundreds of traditional and specialty vegetables.

The U.S. vegetable farmer continues to be one of the most efficient producers of quality crops. Relative to other parts of the world, U.S. consumers spend a very small portion of their disposable income on food. Each year, vegetable output efficiency continues to show gains. U.S. farmers are now producing two times more per worker-hour than in 1970, and eight times more than in 1940. Never before have so many people been so well fed by so few as in this country today.

Commercial vegetable production is one of the most diverse, least subsidized, and financially successful components of U.S. agriculture. Although accounting for about 1% of the nations's harvested cropland, the vegetable sector generates 15% of all U.S. crop cash receipts and accounts for $1 billion in agricultural exports. The vegetable sector alone generates nearly a tenth of all agricultural net cash income in the U.S. It provides the raw ingredients for a vast network of activity through the rest of the U.S. economy, including processing, wholesaling, transporting, retailing, and merchandising.

Commercial vegetable production is a highly speculative endeavor in which success and failure are narrowly separated. It has developed into a highly mechanized and computerized industry requiring special managerial and technical skills to meet the competition of other foods. With the increasing demand for farm-fresh produce and new alternative specialty crops, vegetables also play a major role in improving the income of small farmers and are a source of additional family income.

1

HISTORY

The growing of vegetables has been practiced for centuries. Many vegetable species were used for medicinal purposes long before they became important food crops after years of plant improvement.

The American colonial families were largely self-supporting, growing vegetables for a major part of their food supply. Root cellars were common in many areas for the storage and winter use of crops. With the industrial expansion that began about 1865, a marked change occurred in vegetable production. Concentrated populations became largely dependent upon special producers for their food supply, and as a result, commercial production of vegetables developed near population centers. This practice persisted until about 1910, when production gradually shifted to specially adapted areas having favorable climates with long growing seasons and where relatively cheap labor was available.

For a period following 1920, vegetable production increased more rapidly than other types of crop production. This was due to improved facilities for production, processing, and distribution; to educational and promotional programs dealing with the importance of vegetables in the diet; and to rising purchasing power and changing food habits.

In the late 1950's, with the start of the federal interstate highway system and improvements in refrigeration technology, commercial production began to shift from eastern and northern regions to the South and West. In response to consumer demand, a large variety of fresh vegetables became available throughout the year.

During the 1960's and 1970's, major advances in harvest mechanization of vegetables and improvements in bulk handling, partly in response to labor shortages, revolutionized the processing industry, and significantly increased production efficiency. This trend continued in the 1980's with emphasis on self-propelled implements and increased automation of product handling in production and marketing.

SCOPE AND IMPORTANCE

The vegetable industry contributes significantly to the national economy. For the period 1987–1989, the annual farm value of thirteen selected vegetable crops (asparagus, broccoli, carrots, cauliflower, celery, cucumbers, honeydew melons, lettuce, onions, peas, snap beans, sweet corn, and tomatoes) reported by the U.S. Department of Agriculture (USDA), and including potatoes and sweet potatoes, was approximately $7.1 billion (Table 1.1). For the first time, total vegetable crop cash receipts exceeded $10 billion in 1989.

Along with the farmer's role, many businesses and millions of people are involved in processing, transporting, and marketing, and in manufacturing and supplying machines, seed, fertilizer, pesticides, packaging, and related materials. Extensive educational, supply, and maintenance services are associated with the commercial vegetable industry. Private and public research activities are heavily involved with vegetable production, and are expanding into new fields, such as biotechnology and genetic engineering (see Chapter 11).

Table 1.1. Harvested Acreage, Production, and Value for Selected Vegetable Crops, and Potatoes and Sweet Potatoes, in the U.S. (average of 1987–1989)[1]

Crop	Harvested Acres	Production	Value
		(tons)	*($1,000)*
Vegetables & melons[2] . . .	2,508,275	24,947,806	4,923,596
Fresh market	(1,131,800)	(12,257,350)	(3,896,609)
Processing	(1,376,475)	(12,690,456)	(1,026,987)
Potatoes	1,268,033	18,432,150	2,033,135
Sweet potatoes	89,600	583,650	161,362
Total	3,865,908	43,963,606	7,118,093

[1]Source: USDA. 1990. *Vegetables 1989 Summary.* National Agricultural Statistics Service (NASS), Agricultural Statistics Board.

[2]Fresh market includes asparagus, broccoli, carrots, cauliflower, celery, honeydews, lettuce, onions, sweet corn, and tomatoes; processing includes asparagus, broccoli, carrots, cauliflower, cucumbers, green peas, snap beans, sweet corn, and tomatoes.

U.S. Commercial Statistics (1987–1989)

The U.S. commercial vegetable crop, along with potatoes and sweet potatoes, was harvested from about 3.9 million acres. Production averaged 12.7 million tons for processing vegetables, 12.3 million tons for fresh market crops, 18.4 million tons for potatoes, and 0.6 million ton for sweet potatoes (Table 1.1). Harvested acreage was fairly evenly split among processing vegetables (36%), fresh market vegetables and melons (29%), and potatoes (33%). In terms of farm value, fresh market vegetables and melons accounted for 55% of the total, with a value of almost $3.9 billion. Processing vegetables and potatoes were valued at $1.03 billion (14%) and $2 billion (29%), respectively.

It should be noted, however, that the statistics in Table 1.1 do not include several major vegetables, such as beets, cabbage, muskmelons, lima beans, peppers, spinach, and watermelons. With a value estimated to approximate around $1 billion, these crops also contribute significantly to the commercial vegetable industry. The U.S. Department of Agriculture discontinued data collection on these crops after 1981, due to concern about data reliability. Many fruit and vegetable growers shift in and out of these crops to supplement their income, making it difficult to accurately identify and survey production.

Principal Vegetable Crops

Eleven vegetables are grown primarily for fresh market (Table 1.2). These are Brussels sprouts, celery, eggplants, escarole, garlic, honeydews, lettuce, muskmelons, onions, green peppers, and watermelons. Twelve crops (asparagus, broccoli, cabbage, carrots, cauliflower, cucumbers, potatoes, snap beans, spinach, sweet corn, sweet potatoes, and tomatoes) are produced commercially for both processing and fresh market. Lima beans, beets, and green peas are grown almost totally for processing, primarily for canning and freezing.

The acreage, production, and value of vegetable crops change according to increasing population, changing food habits, and corresponding demand. Potatoes lead all crops in production, harvested acreage, and value. Tomatoes rank second in total production, followed by lettuce, sweet corn, and onions. In terms of output, the leading fresh vegetable crops (excluding potatoes) are lettuce, onions, and tomatoes. The leading processing vegetables (excluding potatoes) are tomatoes, sweet corn, and snap beans.

Principal Areas of Production

A great majority of commercial vegetables are grown in a few states. Nearly every state produces some supplies of summer fresh vegetables. Due in part to the increase in out-of-season fresh vegetables, much of the fresh market production has shifted to the West, South, and Southwest. California accounted for approximately half of the harvested acreage, production, and value of fresh vegetables and melons (Table 1.3). Other leading states for fresh vegetables, in order of total output, are Florida (12%), Arizona (6%), Texas (4%), Oregon (4%), Washington (3%), New York (3%), Colorado (3%), and Michigan (3%).

The leading states for processing vegetables are California, Wisconsin, Minnesota, Oregon, Washington, and Ohio. These states produced approximately 85% of the tonnage on 71% of the acreage. Although California is second to Wisconsin in processing acreage, it is first by a wide margin in production, accounting for 58% of the U.S. crop.

Because of the relatively high- or low-unit values of different vegetables, some states have large acreages with comparatively low values. For example, Wisconsin

Table 1.2. Harvested Acreage, Production, and Value for Fresh Market and Processed Vegetables and Potatoes in the U.S. (average of 1987–1989, except where noted)[1]

Vegetable	Harvested Acres	Production		Value
		Fresh Market	Processed	
		(tons)	*(tons)*	*($1,000)*
Asparagus	99,753	72,700	48,350	145,812
Broccoli	117,633	489,400	140,823	269,279
Beans, snap[2]	230,220	4,127,050	714,603	119,872
Beans, lima[3]	50,820	—	61,270	25,137
Beets[3]	13,340	—	205,370	9,659
Brussels sprouts[3]	5,400	36,450	—	15,706
Cabbage[3]	93,870	942,450	208,880	158,209
Carrots	100,250	1,039,900	411,000	286,122
Cauliflower	65,533	318,000	66,883	197,619
Celery	34,407	959,100	—	232,620
Cucumbers[2]	117,557	307,150	643,240	125,217
Eggplant[3]	3,900	35,950	—	10,411
Escarole[3]	7,840	50,150	—	16,227
Garlic[3]	15,200	98,800	—	33,816
Honeydews	29,900	252,700	—	68,905
Lettuce	235,747	3,559,200	—	997,733
Muskmelons[3]	86,350	594,500	—	161,133
Onions	128,410	2,329,050	—	473,761
Peas, green	296,300	—	419,110	97,235
Peppers, green[3]	55,500	274,700	—	123,732
Potatoes[4]	1,268,033	18,432,150	—	2,033,135
Spinach[3]	71,490	59,350	164,850	44,617
Sweet corn	584,690	776,750	2,745,457	399,698
Sweet potatoes	89,600	583,650	—	161,362
Tomatoes	438,570	1,736,200	8,167,360	1,509,638
Watermelons[3]	184,500	1,135,800	—	149,757

[1]Source: USDA. 1990. *Vegetables 1989 Summary*. National Agricultural Statistics Service (NASS), Agricultural Statistics Board.

[2]Harvested acreage, production, and value data for 1987–89 are for processing only; the USDA discontinued reporting fresh market data in 1981; fresh market production statistics are for 1980.

[3]Data are for commercial crops for 1980; the USDA discontinued reporting data in 1981. (Source: USDA. 1981. *Agricultural Statistics*. Statistical Reporting Service)

[4]Statistics combined for fresh market and processed.

is second in total harvested acreage in the U.S. but ranks ninth in farm value. Florida, which has 28% less commercial vegetable acreage than Minnesota, has a farm value 10 times greater than Minnesota. Both Wisconsin and Minnesota grow mainly processing vegetables, where unit value is relatively low. Florida produces primarily for fresh market, so unit value is high, resulting in total farm receipts of over $0.75 billion.

Table 1.3. Leading U.S. States in Harvested Acreage, Production, and Value for Commercial Vegetable Crops (average of 1987–1989)[1, 2]

State	Harvested Acreage			Production		Value
	F. Market[3]	Processed[4]	Total	F. Market[3]	Processed[4]	
				(tons)	*(tons)*	*($1,000)*
Alabama	7,200	2,400	9,600	29,750	3,607	10,895
Arizona	63,330	—	63,330	773,350	—	270,166
Arkansas	1,030	4,910	5,940	12,500	12,973	11,379
California	540,930	252,830	793,760	6,484,400	7,362,097	2,384,455
Colorado	20,630	1,850	22,480	346,800	20,963	74,452
Connecticut . . .	4,130	—	4,130	13,850	—	5,231
Delaware	—	19,660	19,660	—	58,263	7,212
Florida	137,400	6,400	143,800	1,471,400	39,963	752,963
Georgia	4,400	3,230	7,630	100,800	10,493	18,687
Hawaii	630	—	630	5,700	—	4,756
Idaho	7,570	29,240	36,810	210,750	190,803	51,331
Illinois	5,510	61,890	67,400	19,250	262,729	33,903
Indiana	1,800	16,230	18,030	9,850	195,493	23,653
Iowa	—	7,130	7,130	—	51,750	3,541
Louisiana	360	695	1,055	2,000	2,050	1,982
Maryland	2,750	15,260	18,010	19,250	74,430	19,277
Massachusetts . .	7,930	350	8,280	38,500	6,207	19,548
Michigan	55,630	52,330	107,960	317,900	325,310	125,532
Minnesota	4,170	195,250	199,420	33,100	755,040	67,703
New Jersey . . .	19,930	10,580	30,510	88,700	62,193	39,039
New Mexico . . .	9,000	—	9,000	162,600	—	39,551
New York	47,380	66,510	113,890	353,350	250,933	137,330
North Carolina . .	6,170	26,310	32,480	27,700	91,590	27,219
Ohio	18,440	21,340	39,780	107,950	414,153	67,431
Oregon	24,150	96,830	120,980	423,050	572,483	153,442
Pennsylvania . . .	21,370	13,300	34,670	90,950	57,683	40,454
South Carolina . .	3,630	12,210	15,840	62,650	40,127	31,434
Tennessee	3,800	5,620	9,420	31,800	10,033	18,207
Texas	51,930	20,030	71,960	438,300	86,710	150,604
Utah	1,800	2,340	4,140	39,250	8,123	6,850
Virginia	5,100	3,350	8,450	59,000	14,160	36,636
Washington . . .	49,100	99,400	148,500	386,450	546,700	158,575
Wisconsin	4,600	317,000	321,600	96,450	1,133,980	124,717
Other states . . .	—	12,000	12,000	—	29,417	5,441
U.S.	1,131,800	1,376,475	2,508,275	12,257,350	12,690,456	4,923,596

[1]Source: USDA. 1990. *Vegetables 1989 Summary.* National Agricultural Statistics Service (NASS), Agricultural Statistics Board.

[2]Fresh market crops include asparagus, broccoli, carrots, cauliflower, celery, sweet corn, honeydews, lettuce, onions, and tomatoes; processed crops include asparagus, broccoli, carrots, cauliflower, cucumbers, green peas, snap beans, sweet corn, and tomatoes.

[3]Includes processing total for dual-usage crops (asparagus, broccoli, carrots, cauliflower).

[4]Excludes processing total for dual-usage crops (asparagus, broccoli, carrots, cauliflower).

In recent years, some of the U.S. vegetable production has shifted to other countries. Many large U.S. operators have decreased their domestic operations and expanded foreign plantings in Mexico and Central America. Workers are available to farmers in these other countries at a much lower wage than in the U.S., providing a decided advantage that is difficult to offset.

Per Capita Vegetable Use

The total per capita use of commercially produced fresh and processed vegetables, excluding potatoes and sweet potatoes, increased from 179 pounds in 1970–72 to 201 pounds in 1988 (Table 1.4).

Table 1.4. U.S. Annual per Capita Utilization of Commercial Vegetables, 1970–88[1]

Year	Grand Total	Vegetables[2]				Potatoes	Sweet Potatoes
		Total	Fresh	Canned	Frozen		
		(pounds per person)					
1970–72	302.7	179.0	70.9	94.9	13.2	118.7	5.0
1973–75	299.6	176.9	73.7	89.1	14.1	117.8	4.9
1976–78	307.9	181.3	75.7	91.1	14.5	121.6	5.0
1979–81	302.3	181.2	79.6	87.3	14.7	115.9	4.8
1982–84	302.9	180.5	84.1	81.2	15.2	117.4	5.0
1985–87	326.5	197.9	93.9	87.4	16.6	123.8	4.8
1988	332.3	200.6	100.3	82.8	17.5	127.3	4.4

[1]Source: USDA. 1989. *Vegetables and Specialties Situation and Outlook Yearbook.* Economic Research Service (ERS), TVS–249.

[2]Fresh includes asparagus, broccoli, carrots, cauliflower, celery, honeydews, lettuce, onions, sweet corn, and tomatoes; canned includes asparagus, carrots, green peas, pickling cucumbers, snap beans, sweet corn, and tomatoes; frozen includes asparagus, broccoli, carrots, cauliflower, green peas, snap beans, and sweet corn.

After several decades of more demand for processed vegetables than fresh market produce, per capita use of fresh and processed vegetables was equally split in 1988. Since 1970, the trend has been a steady increase in the use of fresh (+42%) and frozen products (+33%), and less demand for canned vegetables (-13.0%). This trend started in the early 1970's as consumers began substituting fresh vegetables for canned vegetables. As a result, per capita canning use has generally declined since 1971, when it reached a peak of 98 pounds. Tomatoes are the only canned vegetable maintaining consumption levels of the mid-1970s. The upward trend in use of frozen vegetables has resulted from the consumer's perception that frozen produce is nearly equivalent to fresh vegetables in quality.

Total per capita utilization of all crops, including potatoes and sweet potatoes, has increased 10% in the last two decades, from 303 pounds in 1970–72 to 332 pounds in 1988. Potatoes remain the most popular crop, followed by tomatoes, lettuce, and sweet corn (Table 1.5). However, unlike many vegetables, potato utilization has experienced a general shift away from fresh produce and an increase in the processed forms, due mainly to increased popularity of frozen products in the fast-food market.

Table 1.5. U.S. per Capita Utilization of Selected Vegetables and Potatoes, 1974 – 88[1]

Commodity	1974–76	1977–79	1980–82	1983–85	1986–88
			(pounds per person)		
Asparagus					
fresh	0.41	0.30	0.33	0.42	0.63
canned	0.54	0.38	0.35	0.30	0.30
frozen	0.22	0.19	0.12	0.09	0.13
total	1.17	0.87	0.80	0.81	1.06
Broccoli					
fresh	0.95	1.24	1.87	2.62	3.77
frozen	1.05	1.30	1.39	1.44	2.10
total	2.00	2.54	3.26	4.06	5.87
Carrots					
fresh	6.59	5.69	7.15	7.69	8.15
canned	0.98	1.05	0.88	0.90	0.91
frozen	2.65	2.61	2.39	2.50	2.36
total	10.22	9.35	10.42	11.09	11.42
Cauliflower					
fresh	0.91	1.08	1.52	2.03	2.77
frozen	0.62	0.70	0.86	0.91	0.90
total	1.53	1.78	2.38	2.94	3.67
Celery					
fresh	7.20	7.24	7.71	7.42	7.27
Corn					
fresh	7.88	7.50	7.29	7.60	7.10
canned	12.88	13.34	11.66	11.10	10.83
frozen	5.87	7.02	7.38	8.60	7.93
total	26.63	27.86	26.33	27.30	25.86
Cucumbers					
pickles	—	5.93	—	—	5.20
Snap beans					
canned	4.73	5.30	3.68	4.27	3.70
frozen	1.43	1.40	1.49	1.68	1.63
total	6.16	6.70	5.17	5.95	5.33

(Continued)

Table 1.5 (Continued)

Commodity	1974–76	1977–79	1980–82	1983–85	1986–88
	(pounds per person)				
Green peas					
canned	2.85	2.84	2.61	2.15	1.97
frozen	1.93	1.81	1.69	1.93	1.80
total	4.78	4.65	4.30	4.08	3.77
Honeydews					
fresh	1.10	1.47	1.70	2.00	2.50
Lettuce					
fresh	23.75	25.78	26.00	25.70	26.60
Onions					
fresh	15.00	16.10	15.50	18.19	17.63
Tomatoes					
fresh	12.13	12.80	13.33	14.91	17.30
canned	62.96	61.94	60.98	64.10	63.00
total	75.09	74.74	74.31	79.01	80.30
Potatoes					
fresh	50.60	50.52	47.09	47.41	48.30
canned	2.08	2.19	1.87	1.79	1.80
frozen	36.96	41.88	38.02	41.00	45.20
other process . . .	30.80	27.89	26.90	28.19	28.15
total	120.44	122.48	113.88	118.39	123.45

[1]Source: USDA. 1989. *Vegetables and Specialties Situation and Outlook Report.* Economic Research Service (ERS), TVS–248.

Lettuce consumption has declined after reaching a peak period in the late 1970's and early 1980's when salad bars in restaurants and fast-food establishments grew in popularity. The largest percentage increases in vegetable consumption (1974–88) have occurred in broccoli and cauliflower. This has resulted from consumer demand for vegetables that are high in vitamins and fiber. The consumption of celery and sweet corn has tended to remain relatively constant, while that of carrots, onions, and tomatoes has increased, and snap beans and peas has decreased. In future years, changes in vegetable utilization patterns are likely to continue as changes occur both within the industry and in society.

Exports-Imports

Of the large volume of commercial vegetables produced in the U.S., significant quantities of fresh and processed produce are exported annually throughout the world. For the period 1985–88, the U.S. exported approximately 1 million tons of vegetable produce (Table 1.6). This is down from a peak quantity of 1.4 million tons during 1980–84.

Table 1.6. Export, Import, and Trade Balance for Major U.S. Vegetables, 1970 – 88[1]

Year	Exports	Imports	Trade Balance	
	(1,000 tons)	(1,000 tons)	(1,000 tons)	($1,000,000)
1970–74	850.5	945.5	–95.0	–51.5
1875–79	1,386.0	1,196.0	190.0	–44.0
1980–84	1,436.5	1,690.0	–253.5	89.0
1985–88	1,103.0	2,361.5	–1,258.5	–400.3

[1]Source: USDA. 1989. *Vegetables and Specialties Situation and Outlook Report*. Economic Research Service (ERS), TVS–248.

Potatoes, lettuce, and sweet corn are the leading export crops, followed by tomatoes, onions, melons, and celery (Table 1.7). By far, the most important export market is Canada, which imports large quantities of potatoes, lettuce, fresh tomatoes, onions, celery, carrots, cabbage, peppers, asparagus, green beans, cucumbers, and melons. Substantial quantities of vegetables are also exported to western Europe, eastern Asia, and some Latin American countries. Since 1985, there has been a sizeable increase in the export of frozen potato and sweet corn products to Japan and other Pacific rim countries.

The U.S. is also a large importer of fresh and processed vegetables. About 85% of all vegetables imported into the U.S. come from Mexico. Many of these consist of warm-season crops, such as eggplants, tomatoes, peppers, cucumbers, muskmelons, and watermelons, grown in the winter. Recently, Mexican exports of vegetables to the U.S. have expanded to include cool-season crops such as asparagus, broccoli, cauliflower, celery, and lettuce.

Canada is the second largest supplier of vegetables to the U.S., shipping large quantities of table and seed potatoes, carrots, and variable amounts of cucumbers (pickles), lettuce, tomatoes, and other vegetables. Israel, Spain, Italy, and Portugal export significant quantities of processing tomatoes to the U.S.

Since 1970, the quantity and value of vegetables imported into the U.S. has generally exceeded exports, resulting in a deficit trade balance for many U.S. crops. Much of this is due to duties and quotas, and other barriers, imposed on U.S. produce by other countries. If agricultural trade agreements can be worked out removing many of the restrictions on importing U.S. vegetables, U.S. producers have the capability of increasing exports substantially.

Table 1.7. Export and Import of Selected U.S. Vegetables (average of 1985 – 88)[1]

Crop	Export		Import	
	F. Market	Processed	F. Market	Processed
	(1,000 pounds)	*(1,000 pounds)*	*(1,000 pounds)*	*(1,000 pounds)*
Artichoke	—	—	—	19,674
Asparagus	9,848	1,153	12,886	3,002
Beans, snap	—	7,923	—	5,263
Broccoli	25,919	—	8,960	71,414
Brussels sprouts . . .	—	—	—	3,230
Carrots	30,382	4,748	57,269	6,143
Cauliflower	17,028	—	7,299	22,930
Celery	59,117	—	10,917	—
Cucumbers (pickles) .	—	12,656	—	6,842
Lettuce	159,297	—	14,579	—
Melons[2]	73,684	—	338,311	—
Onions	90,864	—	166,190	6,667
Peas, green	—	14,825	—	25,782
Potatoes	53,008	139,975	217,713	46,046
Tomatoes	72,832	39,904	444,976	164,474
Sweet corn	15,964	141,959	5,268	7,846
Total	607,943	363,143	1,284,368	389,313

[1]Source: USDA. 1989. *Vegetables and Specialties Situation and Outlook Yearbook.* Economic Research Service (ERS), TVS–249.

[2]Includes muskmelons, watermelons, and other melons.

TYPES OF VEGETABLE GROWING

There are several different types of vegetable-growing operations. These range in complexity from small garden patches of vegetables, in which the crops are taken to local markets or sold at small roadside stands, to large factory farms that are highly organized and mechanized, in which crops are sold under strict contractual requirements for volume, quality, and packaging.

Market Gardening

The market garden industry involves the intensive production of a wide assortment of vegetables near large population centers. Crops are marketed at roadside stands, "pick-your-own" operations, farmers' markets, and local food stores. Market proximity is the most important factor, although markets do not necessarily have to be local. Acreages tend to be on a small scale, usually less than 100 acres.

A wide variety of crops may be grown, with crop selection based on demand. However, in some areas, many market gardeners, who originally grew a large variety of vegetables under intensive and very expensive conditions, have been forced to change their farming styles to meet competition from specially adapted distant areas. These gardeners no longer grow many kinds of vegetables but instead produce those crops that can be most profitably grown to supply and supplement the demand in their respective localities.

Truck Farming

Increased demand for vegetables throughout the year, rapid transportation, and uniform refrigeration facilities have led to the production of special crops in relatively large quantities for distant markets. Truck farming is more extensive and specialized than market gardening and is the most important kind of modern vegetable industry. The location of producing regions is determined primarily by climatic factors and soils favoring the culture of special crops, rather than market proximity.

Growers tend to specialize in one or a few crops, with much of the produce being shipped to terminal produce markets or other wholesalers. Large areas for vegetable production in the West, South, and Southwest have been developed in truck farming regions and are major suppliers of fresh vegetables in the U.S. during the winter and spring months.

Production for Processing

Vegetables for processing are usually produced on a more extensive scale than those grown for fresh market and are frequently grown in rotation with field crops. Processors generally contract for tonnage, with certain limitations on quality, at a market price lower than for fresh vegetables. Because of the necessity of low-cost production, the industry is located in areas of favorable climate and lower costs.

Maximum mechanization is necessary to minimize production costs. Growers are normally located within economical hauling distance of the processing plants and are required to invest in expensive harvest machinery, although some processors may provide specialized harvesting equipment. Most processors employ field representatives who work closely with growers throughout the growth of the crop.

Controlled Environment Production

Controlled environment production (CEP), including greenhouse production, is a total concept of modifying the natural environment for optimum plant growth. Control of air, light, temperature, humidity, composition of atmosphere, and nutrients makes it possible to grow some vegetables in unfavorable environments year-round. CEP is one of the most intensive forms of agriculture known and presents one of the greatest challenges in the production of vegetable crops.

Investment and production costs are substantial, especially energy costs for heating and cooling. Limited market demand for relatively high-priced fresh vegetables, together with increased importation of vegetables from Mexico during winter months, has limited the overall growth in this type of production. CEP is discussed more fully in Chapter 29.

Vegetable Seed Production

The production of vegetable seed is a specialized and highly technical business. The industry is located mostly in the West where climatic conditions are favorable for proper curing and disease control. Although relatively few growers produce their own seed, they should be aware of some of the practices and problems involved in seed production and handling.

Home Gardening

In colonial days, the home garden was the principal source of fresh food supply for a large part of the population. Today, however, home gardening is more of a recreational hobby, although it can still be a considerable source of vegetable production (especially in rural areas). Growing vegetables at home complements commercial vegetable production, and very few home gardens become involved on a commercial basis. Home gardening is discussed in more detail in Chapter 30.

PHYSICAL FACTORS AND REQUIREMENTS

Climatic Requirements

Climate is the most important factor in commercial vegetable production. The main vegetable-growing regions of the U.S. have developed as a result of climatic conditions favorable to certain crops during the season in which they are grown. Now that transportation is generally available to all regions of the country, it is possible to grow a vegetable in any area that is best suited to it.

Of the various climatic factors, temperature is probably the most important in determining the location of vegetable-growing areas. Atmospheric humidity is also very important for some crops. For example, watermelons are extensively grown in southern areas of the U.S., such as Florida and Louisiana, whereas muskmelon production is restricted to more arid areas, such as Arizona and California, where temperatures are high but humidity is low. Rainfall is very important for the production of vegetables where irrigation is not used. In many areas of the eastern U.S., vegetables can usually be successfully grown without irrigation because of favorable rain distribution during the growing season.

Just about all vegetable regions at long distances from market are important because of suitable climatic conditions for the production of crops at the specific time they are grown. The vegetable-growing regions of the South and Southwest, and parts of California, are important because the climate in these areas permits production during winter and spring when other regions cannot produce vegetables. These regions have become important, in spite of the long hauls and transportation costs to major midwestern and eastern markets. The area around Salinas, California, is the most important summer lettuce-producing area in the U.S. because of the relatively low summer temperatures. Despite transportation costs, this region and a few others in the West control the lettuce market in the large cities of the Midwest and East.

Soil Requirements

While climate largely determines the vegetable-growing regions, soil characteristics are important in selecting specific locations. Soil requirements vary for different vegetables. For example, muck soils are highly desirable for onions, celery, and lettuce. Soil preferences for vegetable crops are discussed in Chapter 6, and in the chapters on specific crops.

Transportation Requirements

The earliest development of commercial vegetable production in the South and some other areas was largely confined to places that provided waterways for boat transportation to major markets. For many years, railroads delivered the bulk of the vegetables to market. With the introduction of commercial refrigeration in 1886 and the subsequent development of the refrigerator car, vegetable production spread to distant areas providing the most suitable climatic conditions.

Improved farm-to-market roads and the development of the super highways introduced the motor truck as a major means of transportation of vegetable produce. With the improvement in size, speed, and refrigeration, truck transportation has continued to increase with resulting economy and promptness of vegetable shipping. Further improvements in road, water, rail, and air transportation, along with advances in refrigeration and packaging, will continue to stimulate vegetables production in areas with the most favorable growing conditions. Transportation factors are discussed in more detail in Chapter 10.

Personal Factors

Successful vegetable production depends to a considerable extent on the expertise, aptitude, and "philosophy" of the individual grower.

Vegetable crops require a high level of management. Some farmers adapt themselves easily to vegetable growing and the exacting requirements of intensive vegetable production. Other growers may not have the patience for the daily activities of intensive vegetable production, preferring to grow a crop that has a wider planting and harvesting range. Where farms are large enough, many growers prefer to raise crops that can be handled entirely by machine instead of vegetables which require more hand labor but give a higher unit return.

MARKETING

Marketing has long been a term loosely associated with promotion, selling, and advertising. Simply defined, *marketing* is the performance of services required to move commodities from the farms into the possession of customers, in the form, at the time, in the place, and at the price desired.

Vegetables, for the most part, are moderately to highly perishable and are some of the most difficult commodities to market. After harvest, special handling, storage, and processing are usually required to prepare these products for the consumer (see Chapter 10, "Postharvest Handling of Vegetables").

Marketing Objectives

Marketing decisions and activities must be oriented to the customer who is purchasing the products or services. The objectives of a good marketing program are: 1) to supply a product at a reasonable cost that the consumer wants and needs; 2) to move the product with the least loss of quality to consumers; 3) to provide sales appeal by attractive and convenient packaging; 4) to keep marketing costs at a minimum, and thereby, 5) provide fair prices to both producers and consumers.

To meet these objectives, successful marketing requires an organization capable of bringing the product to the consumer profitably. Commercial vegetable growers strive to meet these objectives by growing quality crops that people want, and at a price they are willing to pay.

Marketing Services and Procedures

Marketing services and procedures are expensive and complicated and, depending on the particular market outlet, are performed more and more by specialists, and less and less by producers. The complex marketing responsibility has given rise to a vast marketing industry, which employs millions of people and requires extensive technological and physical facilities.

Agricultural marketing services include assembling, grading and standardizing, storing, packaging, processing, transporting, financing, advertising, risk-sharing, and wholesaling and retailing. The number and type of treatments vary with the particular product. Some of these operations may be performed more than once in the marketing process, while others, such as storing, processing, and packaging, may not be involved with certain vegetables. Growers who relinquish all of or some of the marketing phase of production to specialists must also be willing to earn a smaller share of the consumer's dollar in return for the various marketing services received.

Market Outlets

In planning for vegetable growing, commercial growers must find an outlet for their product. Regardless of the commodity or acreage involved, without a well-planned market for the crops being produced, profitability may be unlikely.

Commercial vegetable growers may choose from several different market outlets. These include large-scale fresh vegetable production for distant markets, contracting with processors, and various kinds of direct marketing aimed at local markets. Individual growers may sell their products in more than one market.

Each type of market outlet has certain characteristics and requirements that growers must take into account when determining the best way to sell their crops. The suitability of the different outlets varies considerably, depending on such factors as grower resources (capital, labor, land, equipment), crops grown, grower expertise, volume produced, grower marketing ability (including sales responsibility), proximity to market, and level of harvesting and handling involved.

Market opportunities and availability enter into production decisions. Even before growers begin to plant, marketing processes and decisions such as crop selection, planting schedules, kinds of cultivars to grow, and postharvest handling must be worked out.

Fresh Market — Direct to Consumers. Selling directly to consumers has become increasingly important in recent years. Consumers like to buy vegetables directly from farmers because of the freshness, vine-ripe quality, and price advantage.

Direct marketing is an important outlet for many major producers, as well as a method of supplementing income for small operators and part-time farmers. Selling directly to consumers offers the opportunity for diversification and production of high-value crops by small growers, permitting them to be competitive in the marketplace. By selling directly to consumers, growers can minimize packaging and handling costs and eliminate shipping and "third-party" fees.

Direct market crops are sold at roadside stands, farmers' markets, and customer pick-your-own operations. Large acreages are not required, and no preplanting marketing arrangements are usually made. The grower is responsible for the production, harvesting, handling and delivery of the product (except for pick-your-own operations) and assumes all sales responsibility. As with all fresh produce, there is a strict requirement for product quality.

Fresh Market — Direct to Retailers. Retailers, such as independent supermarkets and local farm stands, deal directly with growers who can supply fresh-picked produce according to a prearranged schedule. Large supermarket chains generally purchase directly from growers who deliver to their warehouses.

Grower responsibilities generally include planting schedules, harvesting, cleaning and grading, precooling and icing, and product delivery. There are strict requirements for quality, including freedom from insect and disease damage, and particularly for satisfactory shelflife. This last factor often will require some type of precooling to remove field heat from the produce as soon as possible after harvest. Usually the grower assumes a portion of the sales responsibility.

The larger retailers normally require assurance of product availability and some product packing. Large acreages are not necessarily required, although it is usually the larger growers and cooperative marketing groups who can best sell directly to chain stores. They can supply uniformly packaged, precooled, high-quality vegetables in sufficient quantities.

Fresh Market — Direct to Wholesalers. A significant portion of the fresh produce in the U.S. is marketed by growers to wholesale agencies or commission houses at terminal produce markets. These markets are located in most major cities, and include such notables as the South Water Market in Chicago and the Hunt's Point Market in New York (Figure 1.1).

Although the major food chains get a sizeable portion of their produce directly from growers, the terminal market is still the main source of vegetables for restaurants, businesses, institutions, and many independent retail stores. The advantage of terminal markets is that buyers can see produce quality and price from across the U.S. in a side-by-side comparison (Figure 1.2). Vegetables of varying sizes and grades can be marketed easier through the terminal market system.

Growers bring in their vegetables to the market, where commission buyers sell the produce on consignment, with a certain percentage of the sale price charged as a commission fee. The wholesalers usually buy in large volumes, such as car lots or truck lots, and then sell in smaller quantities to buyers from chain stores, grocery stores, restaurants, hotels, and various institutions.

Crops are usually grown under the terms of some formal agreement between grower and handler that covers sales of the product. Grower responsibilities and product quality requirements are normally the same as those for marketing through retailers, except that wholesalers may require more product packing than with retailers. Standardization of pack and conforming to market requirements is essential. Product delivery depends on the terms in the marketing agreement.

This type of product marketing generally requires large acreages, and growers may need to show the necessary resources. Concentration of production of a few kinds of crops is usually necessary in this kind of outlet.

Figure 1.1. Terminal produce markets, such as the South Water Market in Chicago, are located in most major cities, where commission buyers sell the products for growers each day.

Figure 1.2. Fresh produce from around the country is displayed and marketed at terminal produce markets.

Grower Cooperatives. Marketing cooperatives are associations and groups of farmers who work together to market their products collectively and directly to wholesalers, retailers, and the general public. Through economic integration and coordination of commodity marketing systems, cooperatives enhance the growers' bargaining power.

Grower membership is voluntary and generally open to anyone who can benefit from the services provided. The cooperative may perform only the grading and packing operations, or it may also perform sales, replacing the wholesaler. Other grower requirements are similar to the wholesale fresh market. Of nearly 7,700 agricultural cooperatives in the U.S., approximately 4,750 are marketing cooperatives, 2,775 are supply cooperatives, and 175 perform related services.

Processing. Growing vegetables for processing usually involves advanced contracts for production, at a predetermined price, for an agreed-upon volume of produce or acreage. The terms of the contract, including prices and grower responsibilities, vary with commodity and processor (see next section). Prices are normally based on yield and quality, and the processor assumes all sales responsibility.

Large acreages are usually needed, and growers may be required to show the necessary resources and expertise. Processors have strict requirements for product appearance, pesticide residues, and freedom from insect and disease damage. The grower must be located within economic hauling distance of the processing plant. The product is usually delivered in bulk and then graded and sorted by the processor.

Growing vegetables for processing has the advantage of limited risk, but returns are usually modest and opportunity is limited by the availability of outlets in a particular area.

Specialty Vegetables. In recent years, specialty vegetables have become increasingly important. These are generally minor crops that include ethnic vegetables and gourmet vegetables. Most are non-traditional crops such as globe artichokes, endive–escarole, green leaf and radicchio chicories, fancy lettuce, arugula, mustard, kale, shallots, leeks, fresh herbs, and a wide assortment of oriental vegetables, including snow peas (won tou), radishes (lopo), Chinese cabbage (pak-choi and pe-tsai), Chinese broccoli (gai lohn), and yard-long beans (chiang tou). Specialty vegetables can also be traditional crops grown in non-traditional ways, such as organically grown and miniature vegetables.

Specialty crops are well suited for small acreages, since their potential value is high, ranging from $4,000 to over $20,000 per acre. This makes them especially attractive to small growers, allowing them to be competitive in the marketplace with larger volume producers.

Marketing demands are very exacting. Buyers want quality and are willing to pay for it. Specialty vegetables, which currently account for a very small percent of vegetable supply, command a large price premium over conventional vegetables. Most speciality crops are highly perishable, which limits competition from distant locations. Market volume for specialty crops is relatively small and limited. Only a small amount of produce is in demand at any one time, so the market can be easily saturated. Increases in production and number of growers can quickly fill the market and depress prices.

Other Market Outlets. Numerous other market outlets, varying in size and complexity, are available to commercial vegetable growers. These include restaurants, ranging from single independent stores to large fast-food chains, schools, businesses, hospitals, and government institutions such as prisons and military bases. In truck farming areas, local shippers and truckers may buy from growers at growing and shipping points.

Contractual Production of Commercial Vegetables

Vegetable growers today are more specialized than ever and generally consider themselves as either fresh market or processing vegetable producers. Vertical integration (processors or dealers are also growers) is more common in vegetables grown for fresh market than in processing crops. Subsequently, contracting activities in commercial vegetable production are more important for processing vegetables than for fresh market crops.

Today, just about all vegetable processing production is conducted under some type of contractual arrangement, and processing vegetable growers no longer rely on open market outlets. This serves the processor's interest as well as the grower's, because it allows the processor to specify the cultivars to be grown, production practices, and planting and harvest dates. Generally, cultivars best suited for processing are often not the best ones for fresh market sales, which greatly reduces the opportunity for dual marketing.

Specifications set forth in contracts vary widely among crops, areas, and processors. Price arrangements are indicated in nearly all contracts, either as a specific price arrangement or in terms of how the price is calculated. Many different specifications for cultivars, seed, fertilizers, cultural practices, harvesting, and crop grading may be involved in contracts. Many contracts provide some labor, equipment, materials, or financing terms for such items. Nearly all contracts call for processors' field technicians for advice, counsel, and inspection.

Shifting Marketing Requirements

Supply, consumption, and markets interact constantly in the vegetable industry. The introduction of a technological change such as quick-freezing started a chain of events that affected almost every part of the vegetable industry. New areas increased production, while others stood still or declined. New marketing channels, embodying new firms with different buying, selling, and handling practices, entered into the industry, taking a share of the market from established firms handling fresh and canned vegetables.

When consumers increase the demand for one product at the expense of other products, the market structure is influenced, and the demand for the services of some firms increases while the demand for others decreases. Such a change in consumer demand for the products of different areas affects not only growers in those areas but also marketing firms and transporting agencies.

The tendency for more vegetables to be merchandised by large retailers has increased the demand for large supplies of vegetables, graded and packed uniformly. This has placed the small grower at a disadvantage compared to the large grower in a specialized region of production.

THE CHANGING VEGETABLE INDUSTRY

The management and operations performed in producing vegetables have changed materially in the last several decades. Labor requirements for most crops have declined significantly, while yields have increased. In addition to production and marketing decisions, growers today are confronted with social issues, ranging from public concern about pesticide residues on food and effects on environmental quality to new government policies on immigration and farm labor.

Number and Size of Farms

The number of vegetable farms (not including potatoes and sweet potatoes) involved in some type of commercial vegetable production has decreased steadily from about 280,000 in 1954 to almost 61,000 in 1987 (Table 1.8). In comparison,

Table 1.8. U.S. Census Report for Number, Harvested Acreage, and Value of All Farms Reporting Vegetable Sales, 1987[1,2]

Year	Number of Farms	Harvested Acres	Net Cash Value
			($1,000)
1954	279,606	3,739,994	645,095
1964	131,653	3,333,772	987,378
1974	78,566	3,124,257	2,837,640
1982	69,109	3,330,637	4,145,446
1987	60,819	3,467,563	4,698,013

[1]Source: U.S. Department of Commerce. 1987. *1987 Census of Agriculture.* Bureau of the Census, AC87–A–51.

[2]Data are for asparagus, artichokes, green lima beans, snap beans, beets, broccoli, Brussels sprouts, Chinese cabbage, cabbage, carrots, cauliflower, celery, chicory, collards, cowpeas, cucumbers, daikon, eggplants, endive, escarole, garlic, honeydews, kale, lettuce, mustard greens, dry onions, green onions, okra, parsley, green peas, hot peppers, green peppers, pimientos, pumpkins, radishes, rhubarb, shallots, spinach, squash, sweet corn, tomatoes, turnips, turnip greens, watercress, watermelons, mixed, and other vegetables.

harvested acreage remained relatively constant over that period, indicating that the average size of individual farms has increased substantially. Based on data from the *1987 Census of Agriculture*, the average size of a vegetable farm in 1987 was approximately 57 acres; 38% of the operations were less than 5 acres, 50% between 5 and 99.9 acres, and 12% of the farms 100 acres and above.

California, Arizona, Texas, Florida, and Wisconsin have the highest numbers of large growers, although there are extensive operations in many states. Some produce a diversity of vegetables, while others concentrate on a few crops. By virtue of their collective size, large growers tend to make a disproportionate impact on the industry as a whole.

Increased Vegetable Productivity

Vegetable yields per acre have been increasing as a result of many factors. Plant breeders have developed new and better producing cultivars; more fertilizers and better methods of application and placement are used; chemicals used to control weeds, insects, and diseases are highly effective; improved machines and equipment that enable growers to perform tasks at the optimum time with a minimum of plant damage have been developed; irrigation of vegetable acreage has increased even in the humid areas of the East; and improved farm and market transportation has enabled vegetable production to shift to areas of more suitable climates.

Preharvest labor requirements have dropped sharply, largely as a result of precision planting and the application of selective herbicides. Precision planting and new seeding technologies, which increase seed germination ability (see Chapter 5), have reduced the need for thinning in direct-seeded crops such as carrots, lettuce, and onions and to a lesser degree with cabbage, broccoli, and cauliflower. The use of selective herbicides (see Chapter 7) has provided effective weed control, eliminating costly repetitive hand weeding and hoeing operations.

Mechanization of Harvest

The hand harvesting of most vegetable crops is a very labor-intensive operation, often requiring over 50% of the total annual labor input. Growers generally use hand labor as long as it is available at a reasonable cost. Mechanical harvesting is generally used when hand labor is unavailable or not practical, or when appreciable savings result. For example, the bush bean harvester replaces about 70 hand pickers. For some crops, e.g., staked tomatoes, mechanical harvest is not feasible.

Most processing vegetables are mechanically harvested. In contrast, relatively few fresh market crops can be successfully machine-harvested. Crops such as beans, carrots, green peas, potatoes, and radishes are harvested almost entirely by machine (Table 1.9). Others, such as broccoli, cauliflower, lettuce, melons, green peppers, and eggplants, are picked almost entirely by hand. Those process-

Table 1.9. Vegetable Crops Mechanization Status in the U.S.[1]

Crop	Harvest		% Mech. Harvest in 1979
	Hand	Mech.	
	— (worker-hours/acre) —		
Asparagus	150	10	1
Beans, lima	50	2	90
Beans, snap	75	3	90
eets	80	15	90
Broccoli	80	no	0
Brussels sprouts	150	60	75
Cabbage	20	3	10
Carrots	120	10	98
Cauliflower	80	no	0
Celery	150	15	20
Cucumbers	150	5	16
Eggplants	160	no	0
Lettuce, head	50	no	0
Lettuce, leaf	75	no	0
Muskmelons and honeydews	50	no	0
Onions, dry	80	25	50
Onions, green	300	no	0
Peas, green	100	2	100
Peppers, green	200	no	0
Potatoes	200	20	99
Potatoes, sweet	200	40	40
Pumpkins	30	2	70
Radishes	300	1	99
Spinach	40	5	80
Squash, summer	40	no	0
Squash, winter	30	2	na
Sweet corn	30	4	80
Tomatoes	50	10	55
Watermelons	25	no	0

[1]Source: Brown, G. K., D. E. Marshall, B. R. Tennes, D. E. Booster, P. Chen, R. E. Garrett, M. O. O'Brien, H. E. Studer, R. A. Kepner, S. L. Hedden, C. E. Hood, D. H. Lenker, W. F. Miller, G. E. Rehkugler, D. L. Peterson, and L. N. Shaw. 1983. *Status of Harvest Mechanization of Horticultural Crops.* Amer. Soc. Agric. Eng., St. Joseph, Missouri.

ing vegetables that cannot be harvested mechanically may gradually disappear from the market or be produced in outside areas where hand labor is plentiful and less expensive.

Mechanization often requires a large capital investment. When a grower changes from hand harvesting to machine harvesting, the flexibility to change from one crop to another may be lost, and sometimes a whole new scheme of vegetable production must be developed.

Generally, machine harvesting requires higher plant populations, concentrated maturity, and more efficient bulk handling systems. Crops usually are precision planted, and stand establishment is critical. Weed control takes on added importance, since weed seeds and plant debris can interfere with harvest operations.

Although mechanization has done much to increase the efficiency of production and handling of vegetables, in many cases it has also increased damage to crops.

Labor Management

From the standpoint of labor, vegetable production is perhaps the most unstable and critical of all farm industries in the U.S. Unlike most field crops, many vegetables mature unevenly and require repetitive pickings. Many crops are harvested mechanically, but for some vegetables, mechanization of harvesting is not feasible, and labor requirements remain high.

The seasonality of growing and harvesting precludes the year-round employment of workers for vegetables only. In many vegetable production areas there are too few local workers to meet the demand. California's annual requirement alone is estimated in the range of 150,000 to 200,000 workers. In 1956, as many as 445,000 Mexican nationals, commonly known as "Braceros," supplemented the domestic work force in the U.S. The program was terminated in 1964, cutting off a large labor source.

Producers depend upon the migration of large numbers of workers from one area to another to take care of peak labor requirements during critical production and harvest periods. Lettuce growers in New York employ workers from Puerto Rico for much of their field labor during a three-month summer harvest period. These workers follow the lettuce season starting in the winter in Arizona, New Mexico, and Florida and work their way to New Jersey prior to coming to New York. In some regions, the seasonal progression of production from the Gulf Coast and Mexico northward to Canada overlaps, increasing the demand for farm laborers.

The application of mechanization to some crops and not to others has produced gaps in the northward sequence of vegetable harvest requiring seasonal farm labor. For example, workers in Texas may have to wait for July and August to pick tomatoes and cucumbers (pickles) in Michigan, Illinois, and Wisconsin, as there may not be sufficient work after the fresh market harvest is over in the spring and early summer season in Texas.

Today, the majority of seasonal farm workers in the U.S. are either Mexican-Americans who are U.S. citizens from Texas, or Mexican nationals. Large numbers of Mexicans have entered the U.S. without proper immigration documents, making them illegal or unauthorized workers.

A major change in the farm labor market in the U.S. occurred in 1986 with the passage of the the Immigration Reform and Control Act. Under the rules of this act, illegal non-resident farm workers could apply for legal status as "special agricultural workers" (SAWs), on the basis of farm work done in the U.S. in 1985–86. Employers who knowingly hired illegal aliens became subject to stiff penalties. The organization of this labor, along with federal and state legislation requiring minimum wage, housing, and safety standards, has had a marked effect on the industry, resulting in substantially higher labor costs.

While some labor efficiencies have been achieved, the vegetable industry still has uneven labor requirements throughout the year. At least for the foreseeable future, the commercial vegetable industry will continue to depend upon large seasonal labor resources during critical periods of growing and harvesting.

Food and Environmental Safety

Water quality and pesticide residues on vegetables are major health issues facing the vegetable industry in the 1990's. In recent years, vegetable growers have seen an increasing number of pesticides removed from the market with no replacement materials.

For 40 years, widespread use of pesticides and fertilizers has helped growers meet the demand for a large quantity and variety of relatively inexpensive and attractive vegetable products. However, today, public and government concerns about food and environmental safety are changing pesticide and fertilizer usage in vegetable production. Consumers want to know what the health risks are from low amounts of pesticide residues found in vegetables.

Much of the emphasis is on groundwater pollution, as nonpoint source pollutants from agriculture have caused major contamination problems of groundwater sources. Fertilizers and animal wastes are principal sources of high nitrate concentrations in groundwater in many agricultural regions. Some agricultural chemicals continue to cause serious groundwater pollution problems years after their application. Investigators have found an increasing number of locations where insecticides and herbicides occur in groundwater, even though these chemicals have not been used for years.

As a result of this concern for groundwater quality and the environment, the U.S. Department of Agriculture initiated a program to study low-input, renewable cropping systems. This program, generically known as "LISA" (low-input sustainable agriculture), attempts to use low-impact technologies to reduce growers' dependance on certain kinds of purchased inputs in ways that may increase profits; reduce environmental hazards from heavy fertilization, pesticides, and monocropping systems; and ensure a more sustainable agriculture for the future.

Some of the low-input technologies include biological control of weeds and insects, use of living mulches and green manures, increased use of animal manures to replace commercial fertilizers, and soil rehabilitation with cover crops and cereal / legume rotations. Many of these practices are already employed by vegetable growers, including both organic and conventional farmers. Although some parts of the LISA system may work well for many small farmers who operate on marginal lands, there is disagreement on whether these practices can be successfully incorporated into mainstream commercial vegetable production. Presently most of the low-input practices have been based on small-scale demonstrations, and research is needed to test this system under large-scale, intensive vegetable operations.

Agricultural Biotechnology

As a result of a wide range of new technologies that use genetic manipulation of crops, growers are likely to see new products developed during the 1990's that are safe for both the consumer and the environment. Biopesticides that are biodegradable and which do not threaten groundwater or cause residue problems are expected to replace some of today's synthetic chemicals. Genetically engineered disease-resistant plants, along with herbicide-resistant seeds and plants that allow crops to remain undamaged when a field is sprayed, will give growers new options in pest control and cultivar selection.

Biotechnology will have an impact on other areas of vegetable production, including genetic modification of soluble solids and ripening characteristics in tomatoes, frost-inhibiting bacteria, and virus-resistant potatoes. These new plant technologies have considerable implications for crop improvement in commercial vegetable production and are discussed in more detail in Chapter 11.

INFORMATION ON VEGETABLE PRODUCTION

Information concerning vegetable production is continuously changing, as new discoveries in vegetable pest control, plant breeding, nutrition, processing, marketing, handling, and general production practices are made. Keeping up with these and getting the new information out to growers, processors, distributors, consumers, and other persons interested in vegetable production is no easy task.

The U.S. Department of Agriculture publishes a vast array of information on many aspects of the production, marketing, consumption, and utilization of food crops, including vegetables. Likewise, state experiment stations (see Appendix) and many commercial industries and organizations publish general and specific information on the many areas of producing, handling, and marketing of vegetables. Many of these publications are free upon request.

SELECTED REFERENCES

TEXTBOOKS ON VEGETABLE PRODUCTION

Lorenz, O. A., and D. N. Maynard. 1988. *Knott's Handbook for Vegetable Growers*, 3rd ed. John Wiley & Sons, Inc., New York.

Nonnecke, I. L. 1989. *Vegetable Production*. Van Nostrand Reinhold, New York.

Pierce, L. C. 1987. *Vegetables: Characteristics, Production, and Marketing*. John Wiley & Sons, Inc., New York.

Thompson, H. C. and W. C. Kelly. 1959. *Vegetable Crops*, 5th ed. McGraw-Hill Book Co., New York.

Yamaguchi, M. 1983. *World Vegetables*. AVI Publishing Co., Westport, Connecticut.

PERIODICALS WITH INFORMATION ON VEGETABLES

American Vegetable Grower. Meister Publishing Co., Willoughby, Ohio (monthly).

The Great Lakes Vegetable Growers News. Sparta, Michigan (monthly).

The Grower. Shawnee Mission, Kansas (monthly).

The Packer: The National Weekly Business Newspaper of the Fruit and Vegetable Industry. Shawnee Mission, Kansas (weekly).

Vegetables and Specialties Situation and Outlook Report. USDA, Economic Research Service, Washington, D.C. (twice yearly).

Western Grower and Shipper. Costa Mesa, California (monthly).

2

CLASSIFYING VEGETABLES

Some system of classification of vegetables and their cultivars is essential for the person interested in *olericulture*, the study of vegetable production. Vegetables number in the hundreds and comprise an extensive group of plants that vary in physiological complexity, morphological characteristics, growth habits, life cycles, and cultural and climatic requirements. Within this wide range of diversity, no two vegetable species are exactly alike. Some are very similar, and it is obvious that they are related, while others are very different. Each year, the information base for vegetable production is being continually increased by additional research. For convenience, as well as necessity, some orderly method with which to systemize or categorize the vast amount of material being accumulated on the numerous vegetable food plants is needed.

There are many ways to classify vegetable crops, but because of the wide diversity among species, a generally acceptable system is almost impossible to define. Any system of classification must depend on how the classification is to be used. The systems used in this chapter are intended to reflect similarities for general cultural needs and management practices, and include botanical relationships, edible plant parts, temperature requirements for optimum growth, and plant life cycles.

CLASSIFICATION BY BOTANICAL FAMILY

The botanical classification is one of the most common systems for categorizing vegetables. Based largely on morphological characteristics, primarily flowers and fruits, it groups vegetables into classes, families, genera, and species.

All vegetables belong to the class of plants known as Angiospermae, having seeds produced in a carpel, or ovary. They may be further grouped into subclasses Monocotyledoneae and Dicotyledoneae, having one or two cotyledons (seed leaves), respectively. Most vegetables belong to the Dicotyledoneae, with the primary exceptions being asparagus, sweet corn, yams, and onions and related crops.

The broadest grouping of plant classification at which more definitive similarities between different members become apparent is the family. Plants in the same botanical family are closely related morphologically, sharing certain characteristics of flower, fruit, and sometimes leaf. In many cases, morphological similarities carry over into common growth requirements, and vegetables in the same plant family have similar cultural practices, as well as many of the same insect and disease pests.

The genus is the classification below the family and consists of individuals that have even more characteristics in common than in the family. The basic unit of plant classification is the species, which is made up of plants that have many characteristics in common, including common ancestry and the ability of interbreeding freely.

Sometimes a group of plants within a species can be sufficiently different to warrant unique names to distinguish them from one another, so that a classification below that of species is given and is known as a variety. In horticulture, there are varieties that have persisted under cultivation and have retained their distinguishing features when reproduced (either sexually or asexually). These are known as cultivars, and in seed catalogs the specific name is usually set off by single quotation marks. The botanical classification for the tomato cultivar 'Jet Star' is shown as follows:

> Division—Spermatophyta (plants bear seeds)
> Class—Angiospermae (seeds enclosed)
> Subclass—Dicotyledoneae (two cotyledons)
> Family—Solanaceae (nightshade family)
> Genus—*Lycopersicon*
> Species—*Lycopersicum*
> Cultivar—'Jet Star'

Table 2.1 represents the botanical classification for the most commonly grown vegetables. The classification, which conforms closely to *Hortus Third* (Bailey and Bailey, 1976), groups the various vegetable crops alphabetically by family within Monocotyledoneae and Dicotyledoneae.

Table 2.1. Botanical Classification of Vegetables[1]

I. Monocotyledoneae	
Amaryllidaceae — Amaryllis Family	
Allium Ampeloprasum (Porrum group)	Leek
Allium Cepa (Aggregatum group)	Shallot, multiplier onion
Allium Cepa (Cepa group)	Onion
Allium Cepa (Proliferum group)	Egyptian onion
Allium fistulosum	Welsh onion, Japanese bunching onion
Allium sativum	Garlic
Allium Schoenoprasum	Chive
Dioscoreaceae — Yam Family	
Dioscorea alata	White yam
Dioscorea Batatas	Chinese yam
Gramineae — Grass Family	
Zea Mays var. *indentata*	Dent corn
Zea Mays var. *indurata*	Flint corn
Zea Mays var. *everta*	Popcorn
Zea Mays var. *saccharata*	Sweet corn
Liliaceae — Lily Family	
Asparagus officinalis	Asparagus
II. Dicotyledoneae	
Chenopodiaceae — Goosefoot Family	
Atriplex hortensis	Orach
Beta vulgaris (Cicla group)	Chard
Beta vulgaris (Crassa group)	Beet
Spinacia oleracea	Spinach
Compositae (or Asteraceae) — Sunflower Family	
Artemisia dracunculus	Tarragon
Chichorium Endivia	Endive, escarole
Chichorium Intybus	Chicory, radicchio
Cynara cardunculus	Cardoon
Cynara Scolymus	Globe artichoke
Helianthus tuberosus	Jerusalem artichoke
Lactuca sativa	Lettuce
Taraxacum officinale	Dandelion
Tragopogon porrifolius	Salsify
Convolvulaceae — Morning-glory Family	
Ipomoea aquatica	Water spinach
Ipomoea Batatas	Sweet potato
Cruciferae (or Brassicaceae) — Mustard Family	
Armoracia rusticana	Horeseradish
Brassica hirta	White mustard
Brassica juncea	Leaf mustard
Brassica Napus (Napobrassica group)	Rutabaga
Brassica Napus (Pabularia group)	Siberian kale
Brassica nigra	Black mustard

(Continued)

Table 2.1 (Continued)

Cruciferae (or Brassicaceae) — Mustard Family (continued)	
Brassica oleracea (Acephala group)	Kale, collard
Brassica oleracea (Alboglabra group)	Chinese kale
Brassica oleracea (Botrytis group)	Cauliflower
Brassica oleracea (Capitata group)	Cabbage
Brassica oleracea (Gemmifera group)	Brussels sprouts
Brassica oleracea (Gongylodes group)	Kohlrabi
Brassica oleracea (Italica group)	Broccoli
Brassica oleracea (Tronchuda group)	Tronchuda cabbage
Brassica Rapa (Chinensis group)	Chinese cabbage (leafy), pak-choi
Brassica Rapa (Pekinensis group)	Chinese cabbage (heading), pe-tsai
Brassica Rapa (Perviridis group)	Spinach mustard
Brassica Rapa (Rapifera group)	Turnip
Brassica Rapa (Ruvo group)	Broccoli raab
Lepidium sativum	Garden cress
Nasturtium officinale	Watercress
Raphanus sativus	Radish
Cucurbitaceae — Gourd Family	
Citrullus lanatus	Watermelon
Cucumis Melo (Inodorus group)	Honeydew melon, casaba
Cucumis Melo (Reticulatus group)	Muskmelon, Persian melon
Cucumis Melo (Cantalupensis group)	Cantaloupe
Cucumis sativus	Cucumber
Cucurbita maxima	Winter squash, pumpkin, turban squash
Cucurbita mixta	Cushaw squash, pumpkin
Cucurbita moschata	Winter butternut squash, pumpkin
Cucurbita Pepo var. *Pepo*	Pumpkin, acorn squash, marrow
Cucurbita Pepo var. *Melopepo*	Bush summer squash, pumpkin
Luffa aegyptiaca	Sponge gourd
Momordica charantia	Bitter melon
Sechium edule	Chayote
Euphorbiaceae — Spurge Family	
Manihot esculenta	Cassava, yuca
Leguminosae — Pea or Bean Family	
Cicer arietinum	Garbanzo bean
Glycine Max	Soybean
Phaseolus coccineus	Scarlet runner bean
Phaseolus limensis	Lima bean
Phaseolus limensis var. *limenanus*	Bush lima bean
Phaseolus lunatus	Sieva bean (butter bean)
Phaseolus lunatus var. *lunonanus*	Bush sieva bean
Phaseolus vulgaris	Snap bean (green, dry)
Phaseolus vulgaris var. *humilis*	Bush snap bean (kidney bean)
Pisum sativum	Garden pea
Pisum sativum var. *arvense*	Field pea
Pisum sativum var. *macrocarpon*	Edible-podded pea
Vicia Faba	Fava bean (broad bean)
Vigna mungo	Black bean
Vigna radiata	Mung bean
Vigna unguiculata	Cowpea

(Continued)

Table 2.1 (Continued)

Leguminosae — Pea or Bean Family (continued)	
Vigna unguiculata subsp. *cylindrica*	Catjang bean
Vigna unguiculata subsp. *sesquipedalis*	Asparagus bean (yard-long bean)
Vigna unguiculata subsp. *unguiculata*	Black-eyed pea
Malvaceae — Mallow or Cotton Family	
Abelmoschus esculentus	Okra
Polygonaceae — Buckwheat Family	
Rheum Rhabarbarum	Rhubarb
Rumex Acetosa	Sorrel
Rumex Patientia	Dock
Solanaceae — Potato or Nightshade Family	
Capsicum annuum var. *annuum*	Pepper (bell, cayenne chili, red)
Capsicum frutescens	Pepper (tabasco)
Lycopersicon Lycopersicum	Tomato
Lycopersicon Lycopersicum var. *cerasiforme* . .	Cherry tomato
Lycopersicon pimpinellifolium	Currant tomato
Physalis pruinosa	Husk tomato
Solanum Melongena var. *esculentum*	Eggplant
Solanum tuberosum	Potato
Tetragoniaceae — Carpetweed Family	
Tetragonia tetragoniodes	New Zealand spinach
Umbelliferae — Parsley Family	
Anthriscus cerefolium	Chervil
Apium graveolens var. *dulce*	Celery
Apium graveolens var. *rapaceum*	Celeriac
Daucus Carota var. *sativus*	Carrot
Foeniculum vulgare	Fennel
Pastinaca sativa	Parsnip
Petroselinum crispum	Parsley
Petroselinum crispum var. *tuberosum*	Turnip-rooted parsley
Valerianaceae — Valerian Family	
Valerianella locusta	Corn salad

[1]Classification conforms closely with *Hortus Third*.

CLASSIFICATION BY EDIBLE PART

A botanical classification alone is not sufficient in classifying vegetables. The members of the same botanical family may be grown for different plant parts. For example, some members of the Umbelliferae are grown for their foliage (celery, parsley), while others are grown for their fleshy roots (carrots, parsnips). In the Solanaceae, tomatoes and peppers are grown for their mature fruits, eggplants for their immature fruits, and potatoes for their underground tubers. Production and handling practices for vegetables grown for different parts are likely to differ considerably, although within each group similar cultural requirements and handling procedures would generally apply. The classification in Table 2.2 is based on the edible plant parts, including root, stem, leaf, flower part, immature fruit, and mature fruit.

Table 2.2. Partial Classification of Vegetables by Edible Part

A. Root

Beets	Horseradish	Salsify
Carrots	Parsnips	Sweet potatoes
Cassava	Radishes	Turnips
Celeriac	Rutabagas	

B. Stem

Asparagus	Kohlrabi	Yams (tubers)
Jerusalem artichokes (tubers)	Potatoes (tubers)	

C. Leaf

Brussels sprouts (buds)	Dandelions	Onions (bulbs)
Cabbage	Endive	Parsley
Celery (petioles)	Garlic (bulbs)	Rhubarb (petioles)
Chard	Kale	Spinach
Chicory	Leeks (leaf base)	Turnips
Chinese cabbage	Lettuce	Watercress
Chives	Mustards	
Collards	New Zealand spinach	

D. Immature Flower Part

Broccoli	Cauliflower	Globe artichokes

E. Immature Fruit

Cowpeas (seeds)	Okra	Soybeans (seeds)
Cucumbers	Peas (seeds)	Summer squash
Eggplants	Podded peas	Sweet corn (seeds)
Lima beans	Snap beans	

F. Mature Fruit

Muskmelons	Pumpkins	Watermelons
Peppers	Tomatoes	Winter squash

CLASSIFICATION BY TEMPERATURE REQUIREMENT AND HARDINESS

A classification based on the temperature requirement for optimum growth and development is valuable in determining which crops may be planted in a given region and at what time during the year. In this classification (Table 2.3), vegetables are grouped into the categories cool-season and warm-season. The subgrouping into hardy, half-hardy, tender, and very-tender is based on the ability of young plants to withstand frost, and to a lesser extent, on the ability of seed

Table 2.3. General Classification by Temperature Requirement and Hardiness

Cool-Season Crops		Warm-Season Crops	
Hardy	**Half-Hardy**	**Tender**	**Very-Tender**
Asparagus	Beets	Cowpeas	Cucumbers
Broccoli	Carrots	New Zealand spinach	Eggplants
Brussels sprouts	Cauliflower	Snap beans	Lima beans
Cabbage	Celery	Soybeans	Muskmelons
Chives	Chard	Sweet corn	Okra
Collards	Chinese cabbage	Tomatoes	Peppers
Dandelions	Chicory		Pumpkins
Garlic	Globe artichokes		Squash
Horseradish	Endive		Sweet potatoes
Kale	Lettuce		Watermelons
Kohlrabi	Parsnips		
Leeks	Potatoes		
Mustard	Salsify		
Onions			
Parsley			
Peas			
Radishes			
Rhubarb			
Rutabagas			
Spinach			
Turnips			

to germinate at low temperatures. Those classified as hardy will generally tolerate moderate frost without injury, while those classified as tender are susceptible to damage during cold weather. The very-tender crops are easily damaged by light frost.

Cool-season vegetables make optimum growth under cool and moderate temperatures, and seeds germinate reasonably well in cool soils. These crops can withstand light to moderate frost; some of them, notably rhubarb and asparagus, can even endure winter freezing. Vegetables in this group are the ones generally planted earliest in the spring, and again later in the season for fall and winter harvest. The cool-season crops include mostly vegetables grown for their edible stems, leaves, immature flower parts, and roots (garden peas are the exception, being grown for their seeds). In comparison to their warm-season counterparts, the cool-season vegetables are usually more shallow rooted, and plant size is generally smaller. Except for the potato, cool-season vegetables are usually stored near 32°F after harvest.

The warm-season vegetables make optimum growth under mean monthly temperatures of 65–86°F. Their growth is usually checked when the air is cool, and injury or death results if they are frosted. The warm-season crops are mostly grown for their fruits, the exceptions being sweet potato and New Zealand spinach, which are grown for their roots and leaves, respectively. Within the tender and very-tender groups, there is considerable variation in the soil temperature necessary for seed germination. Many warm-season vegetables are subject to postharvest chilling injury when stored at temperatures between 32 and 50°F. Among warm-season vegetables, sweet corn is the only one stored at 32°F after harvest.

CLASSIFICATION BY LIFE CYCLE

Another classification of importance to vegetable growers is based on life span, and it groups vegetables into annuals, biennials, and perennials (Table 2.4). Although grown as annuals, many vegetables are actually biennial or perennial in habit. Asparagus, rhubarb, and globe artichokes are some of the few vegetables commercially grown as true perennials. Tomatoes, peppers, eggplants, potatoes, and sweet potatoes are perennials in their native tropical environments but are grown as annuals for vegetable production in temperate regions. The biennial crops are marketed for their vegetative parts (except for broccoli and cauliflower) and are grown as annuals. Especially sensitive to low temperatures, these vegetables can be induced to flower and produce seedstalks prematurely if exposed to periods of low temperatures during their early development (see Chapter 3).

Table 2.4. Partial Classification of Vegetables by Life Cycle

A. Perennial

Asparagus	Garlic	Potatoes
Chicory	Globe artichokes	Rhubarb
Chives	Horseradish	Sweet potatoes
Dandelions	Lima beans (large-seeded)	Tomatoes
Eggplants	Peppers	Watercress

B. Biennial

Beets	Celery	Leeks
Broccoli	Chard	Onions
Brussels sprouts	Chinese cabbage	Parsley
Cabbage	Collards	Parsnips
Carrots	Kale	Rutabagas
Cauliflower	Kohlrabi	Turnips

C. Annual

Broccoli	Muskmelons	Snap beans
Cauliflower	Mustard	Soybeans
Cowpeas	New Zealand spinach	Spinach
Cucumbers	Okra	Squash
Endive	Peas	Sweet corn
Lettuce	Potatoes	Watermelons
Lima beans (small-seeded)	Pumpkins	

Numerous other methods can be used for classifying vegetables. Some of these include minimum, maximum, and optimum temperatures for germination; method of propagation (seeds or asexual); depth of rooting; water requirements; fertilizer requirements; tolerance to salts and boron; optimum soil pH ranges; response to photoperiod in relation to flowering, bulbing, and tuberization; and length of season (short growing period or long growing period).

SELECTED REFERENCES

"Anonymous". 1980. *Seed for Today.* Asgrow Seed Company, Kalamazoo, Michigan.

Bailey, L. H., and E. Z. Bailey. 1976. *Hortus Third.* Macmillan, New York.

Bailey, L. H. 1974. *Manual of Cultivated Plants,* 14th ed. Macmillan, New York.

Fernald, M. L. 1950. *Gray's Manual of Botany.* American Books, New York.

Lorenz, O. A., and D. N. Maynard. 1988. *Knott's Handbook for Vegetable Growers,* 3rd ed. John Wiley & Sons, Inc., New York.

Minges, P. A. 1976. *Botanical Classification of Vegetables.* Cornell University, VC 413.

Smith, P. G., and J. E. Welch. 1964. Nomenclature of vegetables and condiment herbs grown in the United States. *Proc. Amer. Soc. Hort.* Sci. 84:535–548.

Stace, C. A. 1989. *Plant Taxonomy and Biosystematics,* 2nd ed. E. Arnold, London.

Thompson, H. C., and W. C. Kelley. 1957. *Vegetable Crops,* 5th ed. McGraw-Hill Book Co., New York.

3

PLANT GROWTH
AND
DEVELOPMENT

R. D. Morse*

Economic yield of vegetables and other food plants is defined as the weight per plant (plant yield in pounds / plant) and weight per unit area (crop yield in tons / acre) of the edible portion of the plant. *Biological yield,* or productivity, refers to the production of biomass, which includes the economic yield plus all remaining supporting structures (roots, leaves, and stems) not used for consumption. The ratio of economic yield to the biological yield constitutes the *harvest index* and is a measure of the inherent efficiency of the plant and the crop systems to accumulate or partition the products of photosynthesis into economic yield. Over the years, the harvest index and crop yield have generally improved for many crops through practices which favor growth and development of the edible part at the expense of the nonedible portions.

Most vegetables crops are fast-growing annuals or biennials or perennials grown as annuals. Maximum yield of the economic portion of vegetables depends on supplying the crop with the correct amount and balance of growth inputs such as carbon dioxide, water, mineral nutrients, heat (temperature), and light. The balance or relative proportion of growth inputs (growth factors) varies throughout the life of the plant and ultimately determines crop yield.

*Associate Professor of Horticulture, Virginia Polytechnic Institute and State University

Any input that is sufficiently out of balance to disrupt or limit the desired pattern of plant growth and development is said to be limiting and generally decreases crop yield. How much crop yield is decreased depends on the level of deficiency or the excess of the limiting factor and its duration and when it occurs. The grower's challenge, therefore, is to understand the factors that limit plant growth and development of crop yield and to keep them in desirable amounts and proportions throughout the life of the plant.

GROWTH FACTORS

To grow and produce optimum yields, the vegetable plant must be supplied with chemical (food) energy, heat (optimum temperature), and a balance of water, nutrients, and growth regulators.

Chemical Energy

Photosynthesis. All living cells obtain their energy from oxidizable fuels called foods. These food molecules are chemically very diverse. Complex food substances such as carbohydrates, fats, proteins, and related materials are synthesized from simple manufactured compounds such as glucose, which in turn were formed from the simpler substances CO_2 and water through the process of photosynthesis in living green cells.

Respiration. In contrast to photosynthesis, respiration is essentially an energy-releasing reaction. The potential chemical food energy originating through photosynthesis is transformed into various kinds of kinetic energy as well as being used in all growth and development stages of plants and animals. In this way, the light-energy reserve built up in crop plants through photosynthesis becomes available not only for the growth and development of crops but for all humankind.

Net Photosynthesis. The difference of photosynthesis minus respiration is termed *net photosynthesis.* Net photosynthesis is simply a measure of the total photosynthesis of the plant less any respiration which occurred during its growth. Further, any factors that limit net photosynthesis limit plant productivity; thus, there is considerable interest among crop physiologists to increase plant productivity by either decreasing respiration or increasing photosynthesis.

Since plant productivity (biological yield) can be equated with net photosynthesis, many research workers have attempted to relate biological and economic yields with rates of net photosynthesis when these rates were measured for isolated leaves or leaf sections over a short duration of time (hours). However, generally there is no discernible relationship between yield and these net photosynthetic rates because numerous factors interact throughout the entire growth and development of plants that ultimately influence the final yield.

The banker's statement "what will eventually determine the net worth of an individual is not necessarily the size of his/her net salary, but how much of this money is wisely saved or reinvested into productive enterprises" is equally applicable in the plant's attainment of crop yield. Regardless of the net photosynthetic rates, high yields would only be expected from those plants which utilize the products of photosynthesis in a timely and efficient manner. The grower must therefore supply growth inputs and utilize the best cultivars, planting dates, and production practices to maximize net photosynthetic rates as well as to obtain the optimum pattern of growth and development.

Temperature

The optimum temperature range is defined as the range within which maximum photosynthesis and normal respiration take place throughout the life cycle of the plant and within which the highest marketable yields are obtained. Diurnal temperatures — alternating day and night temperatures — favor increased yields. Higher day-time temperatures followed by lower night-time temperatures are nature's 24-hour diurnal cycle of utilizing the sun's energy for making abundant substances during the day and utilizing them for making new growth and in storage during the night. With all vegetable crops, the optimum day temperature range is higher than the optimum night temperature range, indicating that the optimum temperature range for photosynthesis is higher than the optimum temperature range for cell division and cell elongation.

Most of the cell division and production of protoplasm for vegetable crop plants is made at night. Within the optimum range, the rate of cell division and growth is in general proportional to temperature; comparatively high rates will take place within the upper half, and moderate rates will take place within the lower half. For optimum yields, night temperatures in the upper half of the optimum range are preferred during the vegetative phase of plant growth, while temperatures in the lower half are preferred during the reproductive phase. In addition, the quality of vegetable crops is generally improved when development of the edible part occurs in the lower half of the optimum night temperature range. At relatively low temperatures, this rate of cell division and growth is slow and sugars tend to accumulate, and plants develop less fiber and strong flavors, such as pungency in onions and crucifers. At relatively high temperatures, growth is rapid, and sugars, instead of accumulating, are used in respiration and growth.

When plants are grown at temperatures either above or below the optimum night temperature range, net photosynthesis is decreased, resulting in decreased yields and quality. Flower initiation and fruit set are often affected at non-optimal temperatures.

In addition to influencing yield and quality, temperature can also affect the rate of plant development. For many vegetables, including peas, sweet corn, broccoli, and tomatoes, the concept of *heat units* is used to make predictions of crop maturity. The concept of heat units was introduced in the 1940's as an effort to facilitate harvest scheduling. It is based on the principle that the quantity of heat, not days from planting, determines when a crop will mature.

Heat units (sometimes called degree days) are calculated as the deviation of the daily mean temperature from the base or minimum temperature for growth. The base temperature is usually defined on a physiological basis as the lowest temperature at which plant development will proceed. The standard base temperatures for vegetables varies considerably with crop species, ranging from 35°F for onions to 60°F for eggplants. The minimum temperature for tomatoes is 50°F; thus, on a day with a maximum temperature of 78°F and a minimum of 58°F, the mean temperature would be 68°F, providing 18°F of heat units toward tomato maturity. If the daily mean is lower than the base temperature, no heat units are accumulated. The harvest date can be ascertained by an accounting of cumulated heat units (CHU's).

Commercial growers and processors find the heat-unit system very valuable in handling their crops. In addition to predicting crop maturity, heat units can also be used to schedule planting dates for a desired succession of harvests. For this purpose, the grower uses historical temperature averages to predict the date on which the number of heat units required for a specific cultivar to mature will have accumulated. Precision is gained when temperature records are taken near the planting area.

The use of CHU for determining planting dates has often been criticized since temperature is only one of many factors that influence plant growth and maturity. Some recognized limitations of the heat-unit concept include: 1) Soil temperature has a very significant effect on plant growth, especially seed germination and early growth. Organic and plastic mulches tend to influence soil temperature more than air temperatures, thus affecting the CHU needed. 2) Differences in day-night (diurnal) shifts, photoperiodic effects, and the differential effects of temperature on various stages of plant growth affect the accuracy of the CHU system. 3) Rate of plant growth may not be equally affected by all temperatures above the minimum. To account for different growth-rate responses to temperature, numerous methods of calculating CHU's have been devised, especially when temperatures exceed the maximum for growth.

Nutrients and Water

The supply of nutrients and water influence growth and yield in many ways other than their direct contribution to the photosynthetic processes.

Most mineral absorption by plants occurs near the apexes of young roots. The older roots develop layers impervious to water and are relatively ineffective in the absorption of ions. The absorbing areas of roots have to be in contact with the immobile or adsorbed ions such as K^+ or $H_2PO_4^-$ to absorb them from the soil. Young plants with limited root systems are inefficient absorbers of these ions and usually require high fertility to make optimum growth. A discussion of the sources, functions, and application of the essential nutrients is briefly covered in Chapter 6.

Succulent vegetables are very high in water content, with lettuce having about 95% moisture. To maintain succulence and tenderness, the plant usually requires a continuous supply of water throughout its development. Large losses of water occur from plants because of the structure of leaves. They consist essentially of layers of photosynthetically active cells, well supplied with vascular elements and encased in a fairly waterproof but perforated layer, the epidermis. The wet surfaces of the mesophyll cells evaporate large quantities of water into the inter-cellular spaces. Since the open stomates occupy from 1 to 3% of the surface of a leaf, they offer little resistance to the diffusion of water to the atmosphere. Under conditions of high humidity and still air, net loss from the leaf is greatly diminished, but with low humidity and turbulent air, water vapor is quickly removed from the leaf surface, greatly increasing the rate of transpiration.

Even with the soil well supplied with moisture, a plant may become deficient during the middle of a bright, warm day. As a result, guard cells of leaves become flaccid and stomates close, restricting CO_2 uptake as well as loss of water and thus decreased photosynthesis. As plants become more deficient in moisture, stomates may remain closed for longer periods during the day. Cell division and enlargement are dependent upon plant turgidity. If a plant loses water, even though not wilted, the rate of growth is reduced, and the products of photosynthesis may accumulate even with reduced photosynthesis.

Water is absorbed by young roots primarily by osmotic forces. The soil forms a reservoir which alternately is filled and depleted. When the soil is filled and the free water removed by percolation, it is held at approximately 0.1–0.3 bar water tension and is said to be at *field capacity*. Soil moisture held between field capacity and 1.0 bar is easily removed by roots, but as the soil becomes progressively desiccated, absorption by roots becomes more difficult. Finally, at approximately 15 bars, the rate of absorption by the plant roots will be so slow that the plant will remain wilted and will eventually die if water is not added. The soil water content at this stage is called the *permanent wilting percentage*. Moisture retained in the soil between the field capacity and the permanent wilting percentage is said to be usable by plants and as such is called *available water*. Water held at tensions greater than 15 bars is unavailable to most plants. Soils vary widely in their available water-holding capacity. It is low in coarse-textured soils and relatively high in fine-textured soils. The soil moisture content at both the field capacity and permanent wilting percentage increases as the soil changes from coarse-textured to fine-textured; however, with changes in the soil texture, the moisture content at field capacity increases more rapidly than that at the permanent wilting percentage, thus accounting for the sizeable increase in available soil moisture in the fine-textured soils.

Growth Substances

Growth hormones are known to be involved in many plant responses. They may be classified roughly as auxins, gibberellins, cytokinins, and inhibitors.

The auxin indole-3-acetic acid is generally distributed in plants. It is known as the growth hormone and is vitally involved with cell elongation, proliferation, and differentiation. Many plant responses, such as apical dominance, phototropism, geotropism, and root initiation can be traced to auxin. Its content in plants is controlled by the enzyme indole acetic acid oxidase. Some of the synthetic auxins such as 2,4-D are much more active than the plant auxin primarily because they are not readily metabolized by plant enzymes.

Applied gibberellins have been shown to cause dramatic responses in stem elongation of plants. These growth substances are natural constituents of plants and are known to participate in the endogenous control of growth activities and a variety of developmental activities, including dormancy, flowering, and responses to light and temperature. Dwarfness in some plants has been shown to be due to a deficiency of gibberellin.

The cytokinins include a diverse group of growth substances. Unlike auxins and gibberellins, they are nonacidic and relatively immobile. Cytokinins are apparently necessary for cell growth and differentiation but also have other interesting physiological roles. Detached leaves treated with cytokinins stay green longer and retain their proteins. Constituents tend to accumulate in areas where cytokinins are applied, indicating a mobilizing effect.

In addition to growth-promoting substances, plants also contain inhibitors. These are associated with such plant responses as restricted growth, dormancy, abscission, and senescence. The inhibition of growth during fruiting is an important factor in reproduction. Dormancy is important during periods unfavorable for growth and for storage. Dormant buds of the potato have been found to be high in inhibitors which decrease when dormancy is broken. Abscission seems to be a protective mechanism of plants and is enhanced by abscissic acid and ethylene, both of which are associated with senescence.

The use of chemicals to control certain phases of growth has become important in the production of many crops. The control of fruit setting, fruit ripening, sex ratios, sprouting in storage, dormancy, and weeds are a few of the many uses.

GROWTH INPUTS AND QUALITY

Proper application and timing of growth inputs directly affect the quality of the edible product. Yield and quality often compete for the available plant food energy (products of photosynthesis), and a grower must often choose which component (yield or quality) is most important. In many cases, however, cultivars and grower practices that will provide an acceptable compromise between yield and quality can be selected. Conversely, faulty grower practices may cause severe limitations in one or more growth inputs, resulting in drastic reductions in both yield and quality. Although detailed examples and physiological explanations of this principle are reserved for more advanced texts, three conclusions can be drawn:

1. In general, both the market and the eating quality of vegetables are closely correlated with yield. Recommended cultural practices that permit normal plant growth will generally result in desirable yield and quality. Conversely, serious imbalances in growth inputs often result in poor quality and yield. Water or nitrogen shortages will generally reduce both quality and yield of most vegetables. Excess nitrogen during early plant growth can delay fruit set, which limits fruit size (quality) and yields of many crops because the duration of the yield-producing phase is too short for optimum growth. Weed problems which limit light and space and may limit water and nutrients generally result in low yields of non-marketable produce. Excessive infestation of insects and / or diseases can reduce plant growth, resulting in poor yields and quality.

2. Situations may arise or the grower may select cultivars and / or cultural practices that favor high quality (size, protein or sugar content, etc.) at the expense of yield. Cultivars that tend to accumulate high sugar contents and / or practices such as reducing water and nitrogen during the latter part of the yield-producing phase will produce high-quality fruit; however, the yield will be reduced. Wide spacing and / or fruit thinning may give large fruits for specialty markets, but the total yield potential is reduced.

3. Situations may arise or the grower may select cultivars and / or cultural practices that favor high yields at the expense of quality. Abundant water or nitrogen during the yield-producing phase will frequently increase yields; however, the sugar content and other quality characteristics may be reduced. Frequently the quality, especially the size and appearance, of high-yielding cultivars is inferior to that of low- to moderate-yielding cultivars.

PATTERNS OF PLANT GROWTH AND DEVELOPMENT

The growth and development of vegetables can be divided into two distinct, though overlapping, phases — vegetative and reproductive. Although all species have both vegetative and reproductive phases, some vegetables are products of the plant's growth in the vegetative phase (leaves, stems, buds), while others are products of growth occurring predominantly in the reproductive phase (fruit, seed, and storage organs). A basic knowledge of the differences between these two phases as they relate to crop yield and quality is important for the student or farmer involved with vegetable production.

How close the actual yield obtained by a farmer in any given situation approaches the potential yield of a crop under ideal conditions depends on the degree to which the desired patterns of development are achieved. The desired pattern of growth and development for most vegetable crops is 1) uninterrupted, rapid crop growth leading to a predetermined vegetative biomass possessing the structural and productive potential for high crop yields, followed by 2) differentiation (fruit set, tuber or bulb initiation, etc.) and growth of yield-producing organs using the already prepared vegetative plant.

With the vegetative-type species, such as lettuce and spinach, the crop is harvested prior to reproductive growth (flowers and fruit) and major crop losses can result when premature flowering occurs before the crop plant reaches desirable harvest size and quality. The plants should therefore be maintained in an active vegetative state by providing a continuous supply of growth inputs and avoiding any unnecessary stress that could trigger premature onset of flowering and fruiting. With crops in which the edible parts are predominantly developed during the reproductive phase, such as tomatoes and muskmelons, yield and quality depend upon the achievement of a desirable vegetative structure, an adequate growing environment and time (duration) that would allow the plant's yield potential to be realized.

The Vegetative Phase — Carbohydrate Utilization

The vegetative phase includes seed germination and growth of the primary supportive structure. Germination of a seed begins with the imbibition of water. The embryo is stimulated to activity with the radicle beginning to elongate. It pushes through the seed coat weakened by enzymes. Cell division in the apex produces new cells for the developing root and also for the root cap, which prevents injury to the young root as it penetrates the soil. Growth activity in the shoot growing point follows that in the root, the shoot of each kind of seed having its particular method of penetrating the soil. The food reserves in the seed should be sufficient to last until photosynthesis is established.

Growth in the vegetative phase is associated with three important processes: cell division, cell enlargement, and initial stages of cell differentiation. Large quantities of carbohydrates are required for all three processes. Thus, the plant utilizes carbohydrates for growth in the vegetative phase, and the rate of plant growth and ultimately the size of the edible part (lettuce head, celery stalk, etc.) are dependent upon the daily availability of carbohydrates (net photosynthetic rate) as well as the inherent plant growth potential — i.e., the plant's capacity to divert or reinvest its net photosynthetic gain into new photosynthetically useful plant parts (leaves and supporting structures). Although a continuous source of carbohydrates through photosynthesis is obviously essential for optimum yields, the plant growth potential generally determines plant productivity (plant size) more than the rate of net photosynthesis.

The eating quality of the vegetative types is also influenced by plant growth rate. A relatively rapid, steady growth in which nearly all the available carbohydrates are used for new growth results in succulent, tender, crisp produce. Conversely, a relatively slow, non-uniform, stressed growth, in which some of the available carbohydrates are used to thicken and mature existing tissues, results in woody, hard, off-flavor produce.

Factors limiting the development of plant growth potential may be genetic or environmental. Thus, vegetable growers should select cultivars that have high growth potentials and are well adapted to local climates. Growers can maximize the chance of obtaining the inherent high plant growth potential and marketable crop yield potential of these cultivars by 1) planting at the proper time to allow growth during a period when the environment is most favorable for photosynthesis and net assimilation rate; 2) establishing the crop at the proper spacing and density to assure maximum development of marketable edible parts per acre (marketable crop yield); 3) selecting and preparing soils that are well drained and friable to optimize root growth and nutrient uptake; 4) supplying adequate, but not excessive levels of water and nutrients throughout the life of the crop; 5) maintaining healthy, photosynthetically efficient plants through the judicious use of recommended pest-control systems; and 6) using mulches and row covers to alter soil temperature, conserve water and nutrients, and control weeds.

The Reproductive Phase — Accumulation or Storage of Carbohydrates

Relatively little cell division occurs during the reproductive phase. Several important processes are associated with the reproductive phase: 1) the maturation and thickening of tissues and fibers laid down during the vegetative phase; 2) production of plant growth regulators necessary for the development of flower-bud primordia; and 3) development of flower buds, flowers, fruit, and seed, or the development of storage organs (bulbs, storage roots, tubers, etc.). Although some of the available carbohydrates are used for continued growth and thickening of the vegetative structures, most are accumulated in the fruit, seed, or storage organs.

With the reproductive-phase crops, there is a gradual transition from the vegetative to the reproductive phases; however, the plant processes are never totally reproductive and a vegetative-reproductive balance occurs with every crop. The reproductive-phase vegetables can be divided into two distinct groups: 1) those which have dominance of the vegetative phase during the first part of the growing season and dominance of the reproductive phase during the latter part and 2) those which have dominance of the vegetative phase during their first period and a relatively equal balance of vegetative and reproductive during the second period. The first group includes determinate fruit crops (main axis terminates in a flower bud) such as sweet corn and certain cultivars of tomatoes and beans and crops grown for their storage organs (bulbs, storage roots, tubers, and fleshy roots). The second group includes the indeterminate fruit crops (main axis remains vegetative and flowers form on auxiliary buds) such as bell peppers, cucurbits, eggplants, and certain cultivars of tomatoes and beans.

The vegetative and reproductive phases can be altered by environmental conditions and cultural practices. Temperature and light are two important environmental factors that affect the duration and pattern of crop development.

Temperature and Vernalization. The yield potential of a reproductive-type vegetable crop is dependent upon the size of the vegetative structure and the level to which the vegetative parts have been conditioned for reproduction. Plants grown under optimum diurnal temperatures will develop a large, rigid plant structure that is physiologically prepared (conditioned) for optimum utilization of the products of photosynthesis to set, develop, and mature high yields of fruit and storage organs.

Many of the vegetative-type crops may be induced to prematurely flower when the young plants are exposed to temperatures below the optimum night temperature range. The biennials and some annuals are subject to this low-temperature induction of flowering, termed *vernalization* (Table 3.1). The premature appearance of a flower stalk in vegetables, called *bolting*, can cause substantial yield loss, particularly in crops such as celery that require little cold exposure. Bolting is a problem that occurs frequently in winter production areas and occasionally in the North. Under favorable temperatures, the normal edible parts of the quantitative annuals (lettuce, sprouting broccoli, cauliflower, spinach, Chinese cabbage, etc.) and the biennials (cabbage, carrots, celery, onions, etc.) are harvested for consumption prior to flower initiation. These same plants, however, will prematurely bolt and flower before they reach marketable size when the seedling plants are subjected to temperatures somewhat below the optimum

Table 3.1.   Flowering Response of Vegetable Crops to Exposure to Low Temperature (Vernalization)

Classification[1]	Vegetable Crop
No exposure needed to induce flowering	Snap beans, lima beans, sweet corn, Irish potatoes, tomatoes, peppers, cucumbers, muskmelons, water-melons, pumpkins, squashes, sweet potatoes, eggplants, garden peas (Ecvs),[2] asparagus
Quantitative (preferential)	Cauliflower, sprouting broccoli, lettuce, radishes, spinach, Chinese cabbage, kohlrabi, turnips, garden peas (Lcvs),[2] endive (Ecvs), chicory (Ecvs)
Obligate (qualitative)	Beets, cabbage, carrots, celery, Swiss chard, collards, kale, leeks, onions, parsley, parsnips, rutabagas, Brussels sprouts, overwintering cauliflower (heading broccoli), endive (Lcvs), chicory (Lcvs)

Vegetable crops flower during periods of moderate to warm weather. However, with many vegetable species, flower initiation requires (obligate) or is hastened by (quantitative) exposure of the plant to a period of cool weather. With most of these crops, flower initiation does not occur during the chilling period, but only after the plants are exposed to higher temperatures following chilling. Normally, to be effective the vegetable plants that respond to chilling should be partly developed (physiologically mature) before they receive the cold period. Most of them are not greatly affected by the cold if they are too small. The chilling period should average below 45°F (7°C) and continue for 2–8 weeks. The cooler the temperature, the shorter the period of exposure.

[1]*Obligate* — Absolute requirement for vernalization and will not flower without the crops' minimum chilling needs. *Quantitative* — Optional requirement for low temperature treatment. Hence, flowering is hastened or promoted by a cool weather period but will occur in unvernalized plants (i.e., plants not exposed to cool weather).

[2]Ecvs — Early-maturing cultivars. Lcvs — Late-maturing cultivars.

range, i.e., between 40° and 50°F for 4 to 8 weeks, depending on the species and cultivar.

Light and Photoperiod. The intensity of light and the relative length of the light and dark periods can dramatically affect the pattern of crop development and yield. The light intensity available to a leaf varies considerably and is influenced by 1) the season of the year, 2) latitude, 3) elevation, and 4) shading (clouds, humidity, plant density, etc.). As with temperature, light has an optimum range for growth, and this favorable light range varies with the crop species. Within this range, assuming there are no other limiting factors, the rate of net photosynthesis is high and there are abundant carbohydrates available for growth. Outside the optimum light range, net photosynthesis is reduced and growth and yield decline.

Table 3.2. Flowering Response of Vegetable Crops to Photoperiod

Classification[1]	Vegetable Crop
Day neutral	Asparagus, cucumbers, muskmelons, watermelons, squashes, pumpkins, tomatoes, peppers, eggplants, cabbage, broccoli, cauliflower, Brussels sprouts, kohlrabi, potatoes, garden peas (Ecvs)[2], snap beans, lima beans, lettuce ("Great Lakes" types), onions
Long day[3] (short night)	Spinach (O)[4], endive (O), chicory (O), beets, radishes, parsnips, carrots, celery, garden peas (Lcvs)[2], lettuce ("Grand Rapids" types), Swiss chard, Chinese cabbage, turnips
Short day (long night)	Sweet potatoes (O), sweet corn

[1]Day neutral — No preferential photoperiod for flowering. Long day — Flower only if photoperiod is equal to or exceeds threshold (obligate), or flower best under relatively long days (quantitative, or preferential). Short day — Flower only if photoperiod is equal to or less than threshold (obligate), or flower best under relatively short days (quantitative, or preferential). Obligate plants will not flower without being exposed to their critical or threshold daylength. With quantitative plants, flowering is hastened or promoted by exposure to their preferential photoperiod (either short or long days), but flowering will occur in nonpreferential photoperiods (either long or short days).

[2]Ecvs — Early-maturing cultivars. Lcvs — Late-maturing cultivars.

[3]Some species such as many of the *Brassica* crops (cabbage, broccoli, cauliflower, Brussels sprouts, and kohlrabi) are preferential long day with plants that have not been exposed to a low-temperature treatment (unvernalized plants). Thus, with these unvernalized *Brassica* plants, bolting and flowering tends to occur more readily under long days than short days. After these plants are vernalized, photoperiod has no effect on flowering.

[4]With the long-day and short-day plants, all species listed are quantitative except for those marked with an "O" (obligate).

The length of the light and dark period affects plant growth and development in two ways: 1) determines the relative amount of carbohydrates or net photosynthetic products made by all crops and 2) regulates the time of flower bud formation of many crops and the time of initiation of storage organs of such crops as onions, garlic, Irish potatoes, and sweet potatoes. Long daylengths result in high rates of net photosynthesis, favoring high growth and yield potentials. This explains, at least partially, why high marketable yields of many vegetable crops are achieved in the northern latitudes during the summer months. The importance of daylengths to net photosynthesis means that vegetable growers should plant early to be able to benefit from the long days of June.

The relative length of day and night influences the initiation of flowers and storage organs with many vegetable crops. Plant development reactions to daylength are called *photoperiodism* or photoperiod responses. Vegetative species vary considerably with regard to their photoperiodic response to flowering or formation of storage organs (Tables 3.2 and 3.3). For example, spinach flowers and onions initiate a bulb only when a critical or threshold daylength is reached. At the threshold daylength or longer, spinach plants flower and onion plants bulb; such species are called *obligate* long-day plants. For each obligate long-day species, the plant remains vegetative and fails to flower or set storage organs until its threshold photoperiod is reached. The length of the threshold photoperiod may vary considerably among cultivars within a given species such as onions. Other species such as carrots flower more profusely under relatively long photoperiods than short days. Such species are referred to as *quantitative* (preferential) long-day plants, since flowering is not prevented under short photoperiods. Sweet potato cultivars only flower at a specific daylength or shorter and are referred to as *obligate* short-day plants. Sweet corn flowers and Irish potato sets tubers best

Table 3.3. Formation of Underground Storage Organs of Vegetables in Response to Photoperiod

Classification[1]	Vegetable Crop
Day neutral	Carrots, beets, turnips, radishes
Long day (short night)	Onions (O)[2], Garlic (O)
Short day (long night)	Potatoes, sweet potatoes, yams, cassavas

[1]Day neutral — No preferential photoperiod for storage organ formation. Long day — Develop storage organs only if photoperiod is equal to or exceeds threshold (obligate) or develop storage organs best under relatively long days (quantitative or preferential). Short day — Develop storage organs only if photoperiod is equal to or less than threshold (obligate), or develop storage organs best under relatively short days (quantitative, or preferential).

[2]O — Obligate photoperiodic requirement. All species listed as short day are quantitative.

under relatively short photoperiods and thus are considered to be quantitative (preferential) short-day plants with regard to these responses.

The majority of vegetable crops are classified as day-neutral. These crops will flower or form storage organs under either long- or short-day photoperiods (Tables 3.2 and 3.3).

The yield of photoperiodic plants (plants in which formation of flowers or storage organs is affected by the relative length of day) can be profoundly influenced by daylength. Photoperiodic response also varies among cultivars of the same crop species. Thus, for photoperiodic crops, daylength must be considered an essential growth input, and regional and local adaptation of species and cultivars is required.

Since the relative rate and duration of growth in each phase of plant development directly affect crop yield, the grower can adjust cultural practices and manipulate the environment and thus alter the pattern of plant growth and development to favor increased yield and / or quality. Methods of manipulating crop growth and development are briefly discussed under the heading "The Vegetative Phase" and are discussed in more detail throughout the remainder of this text.

SELECTED REFERENCES

Benjamin, L. R., and J. J. Wren. 1978. Root development and source — sink relations in carrot (*Daucus carota* L.). *J. Exp. Bot.* 29:425–433.

Black, M., and Jack Edelman. 1971. *Plant Growth*. Heineman Educational Books, Ltd., London.

Board, J. E. 1985. Yield components associated with soybean yield reduction at nonoptimal planting dates. *Agron J.* 77:135–140.

Borthwick, H. A., and S. Hendricks. 1981 Effects of radiation on growth and development. *Encyl. Plant Physiol.* XVI, 220.

Carlson, P. S. (ed.). 1980. *The Biology of Crop Productivity*. Academic Press, New York.

Crookson, R. K., J. O'Toole, R. Lee, J. L. Ozbun, and D. H. Wallace. 1974. Photosynthetic depression in beans after exposure to cold for one night. *Crop Sci.* 14:457–464.

Dickson, M. H., and R. Petzoldt. 1989. Heat tolerance and pod set in green beans. *J. Amer. Soc. Hort. Sci.* 114:833–836.

Ewing, E. E. 1978. Critical photoperiod for tuberization: a screening technique with potato cuttings. *Amer. Potato J.* 55:43–53.

Ewing, E. E., and P. F. Wareing. 1978. Shoot, stolon, and tuber formation on potato (*Solanum tuberosum* L.) cuttings in response to photoperiod. *Plant Physiol.* 6:348–353.

Gardner, F. P. 1985. *Physiology of Crop Plants*. Iowa State University Press, Ames.

Halvey, A. H. (ed.). 1985. *CRC Handbook of Flowering* (Vols. I, II, III, IV). CRC Press, Inc., Boca Raton, Florida.

Hay, R. K. M., and A. J. Walker. 1989. *An Introduction to the Physiology of Crop Yield*. John Wiley & Sons, Inc., New York.

Hughes, D. L., J. Bosland, and M. Yamaguchi. 1983. Movement of photosynthates in muskmelon plants. *J. Amer. Soc. Hort. Sci.* 108:189–192.

Lasley, S. E., and M. P. Garber. 1978. Photosynthetic contribution of cotyledons to early development of cucumber. *HortScience.* 13:191–193.

Leopold, A. C., and P. E. Kriedemann. 1975. *Plant Growth and Development*, 2nd. ed. McGraw-Hill Book Company, New York.

Liu, P., D. H. Wallace, and J. L. Ozbun. 1973. Influence of translocation on photosynthetic efficiency of *Phaseolus vulgaris* L. *Plant Physiol.* 52:412–415.

Loewy, A. G., and P. Sickevitz. 1963. *Cell Structure and Function.* Holt, Rinehart & Winston, Inc., New York.

Nerson, H., R. Cohen, M. Edelstein, and Y. Burger. 1989. Paclobutrazol—a plant growth retardant for increasing yield and fruit quality in muskmelon. *J. Amer. Soc. Hort. Sci.* 114:762–766.

Perry, K. B., T. C. Wehner, and G. L. Johnson. 1986. Comparison of 14 methods to determine heat unit requirements for cucumber harvest. *HortScience* 21:419–423.

Rudich, J., E. Zamski, and Y. Regev. 1977. Genotypic variation for sensitivity to high temperature in the tomato: pollination and fruit set. *Bot. Gaz.* 138:448–452.

Symposium: Chemical regulation of plant processes. 1969. *HortScience* 4:101–116.

Symposium: Environmental factors affecting vegetable production. 1971. *HortScience* 6:22–36.

Symposium: Increasing the biological efficiency of vegetable crops. 1978. *Hortscience* 13:671–686.

Symposium: Potassium in horticulture. 1969. *HortScience* 4:33–48.

Symposium: The role of phosphorus in plant growth. 1969. *HortScience* 4:309–324.

Symposium: Yield: a challenge for all seasons. 1988. *HortScience* 23:32–47.

Tesar, M. B. (ed.). 1984. *Physiological Basis for Crop Growth and Development.* Amer. Soc. Agron., Madison, Wisconsin.

Van Overbeek, J. 1966. Plant hormones and regulations. *Science* 152:721.

Widders, J. E., and H. C. Price. 1989. Effects of plant density on growth and biomass partitioning in pickling cucumbers. *J. Amer. Soc. Hort. Sci.* 114:751–755.

4

BREEDING AND IMPROVING
VEGETABLES

In vegetable production there is a continuous demand for superior vegetable cultivars with attributes that increase both crop productivity and quality. These include maximum early and total yields, better uniformity and vigor, multiple-disease resistance, different maturities, adaptation to different climatic zones, tolerance to drought stress, concentrated fruit set, increased nutrient content, extended postharvest life, and adaptability to mechanization. For example, tomato cultivars that have square-shaped fruit with firm flesh and concentrated set have been developed for machine harvest. Supersweet and sugary-enhanced sweet corn hybrids have been produced that have dramatically more sugar in their kernels and greatly extended storage life. Many potato cultivars now being grown are resistant to late blight (*Phytophthora infestans*).

Crop improvement is possible because plants differ in their heritable characteristics. For most cultivar improvement, conventional breeding methods are based largely on the principles of Mendelian genetics. The development of new and improved cultivars has resulted from sexual hybridization followed by selection. Hybridization, or crossing two or more sources, often results in new and superior combinations of characters. Selection usually follows hybridization to isolate the superior combinations that may occur.

However, in the attempt to get as many desirable characteristics as possible combined in a cultivar, vegetable breeding becomes very complicated. Vegetable breeders need to know how genes that control plant development are passed from parents to progenies. Today, as a result of recent advances in laboratory techniques and new knowledge of cell physiology and molecular biology, new

55

technology, commonly referred to as *biotechnology*, is being used to complement traditional breeding techniques for the purpose of crop improvement. This includes cell culture, protoplast fusion, recombinant DNA, micro-injection, and somaclonal variation. These and other new technologies are discussed in detail in Chapter 11.

CELLS, CHROMOSOMES, AND GENES

An organism, plant or animal, consists of cells, each of which contains a nucleus and other organelles embedded in cytoplasm. Within the nucleus is a number of rod-shaped bodies, the chromosomes. These contain the basic genetic information of the cell, DNA or deoxyribonucleic acid. The molecules of DNA occur in the form of double strands of intertwined helixes. The individual molecules are long, linear aggregates of four basic building blocks called *nucleotides*. The order in which the nucleotides occur in the chain determines the specific genetic information carried. The DNA molecule acts as a template from which a related molecule called RNA (ribonucleic acid) is formed. The RNA acts as a messenger which migrates from the nucleus to the cytoplasm and determines the many kinds of proteins produced. Proteins with specific catalytic properties are called *enzymes*. These control the numerous chemical reactions of the cell and thereby regulate the development of the organism.

The chromosomes carry the genes or factors that determine heritable characters of the individual. These characters are the attributes which identify an individual and result from the expression of one or more genes as modified by the environment.

The chromosomes are distinguishable only when the cells are undergoing division. Cells of the same species have the same number of chromosomes, occurring in pairs. Every chromosome in the cell has an exact duplicate in size, shape, and composition. In cells of different species, however, the number, size, and appearance of the chromosomes may vary considerably.

During plant growth and asexual reproduction, cell division in the shoot and root tips, axillary buds, leaf primordia, and vascular cambium is by *mitosis*. In this process, each individual chromosome divides longitudinally, resulting in two chromosomes that are identical to each other. When the cell divides, one member of each pair goes to each daughter cell. The two resulting daughter cells have the same number of chromosomes that were in the mother cell. For example, each body cell of the onion (*Allium Cepa*) contains eight pairs or sixteen chromosomes. At cell division, during growth of the plant, these sixteen chromosomes split longitudinally, with each daughter cell receiving the same number and composition of chromosomes as the mother cell.

In the flower, another type of division known as *meiosis*, or reduction division, occurs in mother cells prior to the formation of the germ cells (sperm and eggs). In meiosis, daughter germ cells, or gametes, are produced that have one set (one chromosome of each pair) of chromosomes which occurred in the parent. Instead of each chromosome dividing, the pairs meet at the middle of the cell; then the members of each pair move to opposite ends, and two cells are formed in which the number of chromosomes is reduced to one-half that of the body cells (Figure 4.1). When different gametes recombine at fertilization, the original chromosome number is restored. In the process, varying degrees of chromosome rearrangement may occur, resulting in genetic variation.

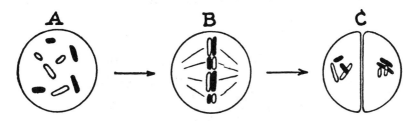

Figure 4.1. The mother cell (A) contains four pairs of chromosomes. Those colored black have been derived from the male parent, the white from the female parent. Preparatory to reduction division (B), members of a pair meet at the center of the cell. In (C), members of a pair have moved away from each other, and a wall has formed between. Note that the chromosomes derived from the male or female parent do not remain together.

The genes are distributed along the chromosomes like beads on a string, each with a definite position or locus. During cell division, when the chromosomes divide lengthwise, all genes also divide, so that the two daughter cells have the same genic complex as the parent cell.

In most chromosomes there are probably hundreds of genes, all tending to remain together as a unit. Genes belonging to the same chromosome are said to be linked, and collectively they are known as a linkage group. A plant has as many linkage groups as it has pairs of chromosomes. When certain genes are linked, the characters they express will also be linked.

Not only are the chromosomes in pairs but also the genes on them are in pairs, arranged in the same lineal order. Genes that occupy the same position on homologous chromosomes (pairs of individual chromosomes) and affect the same trait are termed *alleles*. If both members of a pair of genes are alike, the plant is homozygous for that allele. When the alleles are different, the plant is heterozygous.

Allelic genes can be dominant or recessive to each other. A dominant gene causes a certain characteristic to be expressed whether the plant is homozygous or heterozygous. A recessive gene has to be present in both alleles before a recessive character can be expressed.

FLOWERS, POLLINATION, AND FERTILIZATION

Most species of vegetables have four whorls of floral organs consisting of sepals, petals, stamens, and pistils; although some may lack one or more whorls (Figure 4.2). From the standpoint of breeding, only the stamens and pistils are important. The stamen, or male part, contains within its mature anther a yellowish powder called pollen that produces the sperm. The pistil, or female part, has an ovary at its base (Figure 4.3) which contains one or more small, white, kidney-shaped objects called ovules that contain the eggs.

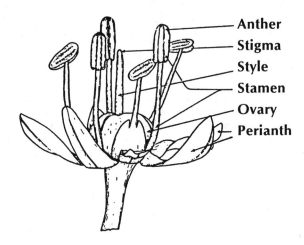

Figure 4.2. Onion flower. Inner whorl of stamens has burst open.
(Source: *Truck-Crop Plants*, McGraw-Hill Book Co.)

Flowers containing only stamens are referred to as *staminate*, or male, those with only pistils are *pistillate*, or female, and flowers with both pistils and stamens are known as *hermaphroditic*, or perfect. When making crosses, a breeder must distinguish male from female, and whether they occur in the same flower, in different flowers of the same plant (*monoecious*), or in different plants (*dioecious*). In addition, other types of flower combinations can occur; muskmelons can have perfect and staminate flowers on the same plant (*andromonoecious*). Most vegetable crops have perfect flowers, and in only a few species (spinach and asparagus) are the sexes on different plants (Table 4.1).

Figure 4.3. Zucchini is a monoecious plant with separate female *(left)* and male *(right)* flowers on the same plant; note the developing fruit as part of the female flower.

The transfer of pollen from the anther to the stigma is called *pollination*. Self-pollination occurs when pollen is transferred from the anther to the stigma of the same flower or from one flower to another of the same plant. Cross-pollination occurs when the transfer is from one plant to another. Most vegetable crops are cross-pollinated to various degrees. In beets, cabbage and related crucifers, chicory, mustards, potatoes, radishes, rhubarb, sweet potatoes, and turnips, the plants are self-incompatible (self-sterile) so cross-pollination is usually complete. At the other extreme are peas, beans, lettuce, and tomatoes, in which self-pollination is the rule.

The technique a breeder uses to make a pollination will vary with the structure and the normal mode of pollination of the flower and whether self- or cross-pollinations are being made. The flower structure should be studied to determine the size, shape, and position of the anthers and stigmas, and blooming habit. It is important to know the time of flower opening and receptivity of the

Table 4.1. Vegetable Breeding and Reproduction Characteristics[1]

Crop	Chromos. No.	Prop. Method	Life Cycle	Flower Struct.[2]	Compat- ibility	Pollen Vector	Prop. of Outcross.[3]
Artichokes	34	Veg.	Peren.	P	SF	Insects	H
Asparagus	20	Sex.	Peren.	D	SF	Insects	C
Beans	22	Sex.	An.	P	SF	Insects	S
Beets	18	Sex.	Bien.	P	SI	Wind	C
Cabbage group	18	Sex.	Bien.	P	SI	Insects	C
Carrots	18	Sex.	Bien.	P	SF	Insects	H
Celery	22	Sex.	Bien.	P	SF	Insects	H
Chicory	18	Sex.	Bien.	P	SI	Insects	C
Corn	20	Sex.	An.	M	SF	Wind	H
Cucumbers	14	Sex.	An.	M	SF	Insects	H
Eggplants	24	Sex.	An.	P	SF	Insects	M
Endive	18	Sex.	Bien.	P	SF	Insects	H
Lettuce	16	Sex.	An.	P	SF	Insects	S
Melons	24	Sex.	An.	M	SF	Insects	H
Mustards	20–36	Sex.	An.	P	SI	Insects	C
Okra	72	Sex.	An.	P	SF	Insects	H
Onions	16	Sex.	Bien.	P	SF	Insects	H
Peas	14	Sex.	An.	P	SF	Insects	S
Peppers	24	Sex.	An.	P	SF	Insects	M
Potatoes	48	Veg.	Peren.	P	SI	Insects	C
Pumpkins, squashes . .	40	Sex.	An.	M	SF	Insects	H
Radishes	18	Sex.	Bien.	P	SI	Insects	C
Rhubarb	44	Veg.	Peren.	P	SI	Wind	C
Spinach	12	Sex.	An.	D	SF	Wind	C
Sweet potatoes	90	Veg.	Peren.	P	SI	Insects	C
Tomatoes	24	Sex.	An.	P	SF	Insects	S
Turnips	20	Sex.	Bien.	P	SI	Insects	H
Watermelons	22	Sex.	An.	M	SF	Insects	H

[1]Courtesy, J. A. Juvik, University of Illinois.

[2]P (perfect), D (dioecious), M (monoecious).

[3]H (high), C (complete), S (self), M (moderate).

stigma. As a general rule, the stigma is receptive shortly before the flower naturally opens. However, with certain vegetables, such as onions and celery, the pollen of an individual flower may shed 2–4 days before the stigma is receptive. The reverse may be true in other species.

The length of time a stigma remains receptive varies considerably and may be markedly affected by environmental factors such as temperature and humidity. The stigmas of most species remain receptive 1–2 days on the average, but as a general rule, the best results are obtained when pollination is not delayed. The longevity and viability of pollen varies considerably with different species. Pollen for certain species, such as tomatoes, can be successfully stored for relatively long periods under proper temperature and humidity.

VARIATION

It is rare that two plants are exactly alike, no matter how uniform the cultivar to which they belong appears en masse. The variations between plants may be of two types: those caused by the environment and those caused by differences in the genic makeup of the chromosomes. Variations caused by a difference in environmental factors such as moisture, temperature, and light are not inherited. The main effect of these factors primarily is on the size of the plant or its parts.

Variations originating in the genic material of the chromosomes are heritable. They may arise in several ways: as a recombination of characters, change of a single gene, change of several genes, loss or gain of a portion of a chromosome, or loss of an entire chromosome or whole sets of chromosomes. Although in many cases they may be deleterious, variations provide plant breeders with the raw material in developing new cultivars.

In addition to naturally occurring variations, changes in genes and chromosomes can be induced by various artificial means. Hereditary modifications can be brought about by radiation (X-rays, gamma rays, thermal neutrons, ultraviolet rays) and by chemicals (ethyl dimethyl sulfate). For example, tomato plants that normally have twelve pairs, or twenty-four chromosomes can, be treated with the chemical colchicine, resulting in a doubling of the chromosome number to forty-eight. Plants with more sets of chromosomes than the normal two (diploid) are called polyploids. The tomatoes with four sets of chromosomes are called tetraploids. Plants with three sets of chromosomes are called triploids, and are obtained by crossing a tetraploid with a diploid. The hybrid seedless watermelon, which is a triploid, is obtained this way. The triploid, which is sterile and seedless, is grown commercially by interplanting it with a normal diploid line that serves as a pollinator necessary for fruit set.

Polyploids can sometimes be recognized by their increased size and more luxuriant growth, although this is not always true. Artifically induced tetraploids tend to be less fertile than their diploid parents. Generally, tetraploids have not proved directly useful for most vegetable crops but have been used successfully in some flowers such as snapdragons and marigolds to increase flower size.

HYBRIDIZATION AND SELECTION

Crop improvement through plant breeding is accomplished primarily by hybridization and selection and the combination of the two. Hybridization, or crossing two or more parent lines (or sources), often results in new and superior combinations of characters. Selection usually follows hybridization to isolate the superior combinations that may occur.

Hybridization

Hybrids in vegetable production are important for a number of reasons including improved uniformity and earlier maturity, higher yields, enhanced processing characteristics, increased disease resistance, and extended field and storage life. Hybrid vigor, or heterosis, refers to the increase in vigor shown by the progeny as compared to either parent. It is commonly found when two inbred lines are crossed (Figure 4.4).

Figure 4.4. Comparative yields of the hybrid onion 'Granex' (center) and its two parent lines; hybrid vigor is associated with higher yields of the progeny as compared to that of either parent.

Extensive commercial use is made of F_1 hybrids, or the first generation following a cross. Many combinations are usually made and tested to find the ones best suited to the conditions under which they are to be used. Certain characteristics, such as the seedless condition in watermelons, are possible only in hybrids. Hybridization also allows precise control over the hybrid cultivars through control of the parent lines. Table 4.2 lists various vegetable species in which commercial F_1 hybrids are available.

However, hybrid seed may not always be the best choice when price is weighed against other factors. Hybridization is costly, and indiscriminate crossing of plants should be avoided. One should always have a clear-cut objective before starting to make crosses between plants. If not, much effort can be wasted. The natural sources of variation should be adequately explored before hybridizing.

Certain situations make the production of hybrid seed economical. Any condition that aids in the separation of the male and female elements of a flower or plant will help provide a method for making economical crosses between plants. For example, the monoecious flowering habit in corn separates the female

Table 4.2. Vegetable Crops in Which Commercial Hybrids Are Available

Asparagus	Chinese cabbage	Spinach
Beets	Cucumbers	Squashes
Broccoli	Eggplants	Sweet corn
Cabbage	Muskmelons	Tomatoes
Cauliflower	Onions	Watermelons
Carrots	Peppers	

ear from the male tassel. An inbred line can be made essentially female by removing the tassel before it sheds pollen. Crossing the detasseled line with a pollinator line will result in the desired cross, provided the two lines are isolated from other corn plantings.

Another means making hybrid production easier is provided by conditions of male sterility. Certain inherited factors bring about sterility within the male parts of the flowers which effectively make the flower and plant female. If some means are provided to transfer fertile pollen from another line, hybrid seed can be easily and economically produced. Male sterility has been found in nearly every kind of vegetable. The production of hybrid seed in onions is based upon the use of male sterility. Methods of using male sterility are being worked out to produce hybrids in such crops as beets, carrots, squashes, sweet corn, tomatoes, eggplants, and peppers.

Selection

Following hybridization, the desirable genotypes must be recognized and saved. Selection is effective only when differences are heritable. Variation is not created by selection, but rather, existing desirable variation may be collected and concentrated by selection. Frequently, selections may be back-crossed to one of the parents for several generations. This is done to incorporate some desirable feature such as disease resistance into an otherwise desirable cultivar lacking this one character. The various selection techniques used by vegetable breeders differ depending on the method of reproduction of the plant. These are discussed in the next section.

BREEDING METHODS

The specific method of breeding used depends upon the crop and the objectives sought. For the purposes here, vegetable crops can be divided into four groups: 1) those naturally self-pollinated, 2) those naturally cross-pollinated, 3) those often or partially cross-pollinated, and 4) those vegetatively propagated.

Space does not permit an extensive discussion of the breeding methods and objectives for all the crops in each group.

Vegetables Naturally Self-pollinated

This group includes beans, peas, lettuce, and tomatoes. Self-pollination is not absolute, as some crossing usually occurs. In this group, little if any loss of vigor is caused by inbreeding that results from self-pollination. Essentially homozygous or pure lines are developed in a few generations because self-pollination is such an intensive form of inbreeding. Selection within a pure line is therefore likely to be ineffective. In old or unselected cultivars an opportunity exists for increased variability arising from mixtures, mutations, and natural crossing. Consequently, the chances of obtaining improvement by selection are much greater from old than from new cultivars.

The two general methods of selection used in self-pollinated vegetables are mass selection and pedigree selection. With mass selection a fairly large number of desirable plants with relatively similar characteristics are selected and maintained in bulk without testing the progenies separately. The selected lot is usually compared with the original cultivar. Mass selection is most useful in dealing with characters that are not modified greatly by environment because the effects of heredity and environment are not separated. Under certain conditions it is possible to obtain quicker results from mass selection than from pedigree selection, since uniformity for one character may be obtained with less danger of altering other varietal characteristics. Rapid changes in varietal type are not usually made with mass selection. A form of mass selection called *roguing* is commonly used to maintain a stock or cultivar by eliminating undesirable or inferior plants. As a general rule, seed stocks of self-pollinated crops are easy to maintain true to type by isolation and selection.

The pedigree system of selection may be superior to mass selection as more rapid progress may usually be expected. Selection of the most desirable genotypes is based on progeny performance. It is, however, more expensive and requires fairly extensive record-keeping. In practice, the single-plant selections are kept separate, and the progenies are grown out for evaluation. The original selections from a variable population will isolate many pure lines, within which further selection is not likely to be effective. The main problem is to find which pure lines are the best. Further selection of lines is usually based on a pedigree method using the performance of the whole row. Many of the lines are discarded for one reason or another, reducing the number of lines to be tested the next generation. By the sixth to tenth generation, the lines derived from single-plant selections will be essentially homozygous for more than 95% of their genes.

When controlled hybridizations are made to produce new sources of variation and to obtain new combinations, some form of selection is begun as soon as segregation of characters occurs. Pedigree selection is most commonly used and mass selection is seldom used following hybridization.

Within self-pollinated crops, hybrid vigor is commonly found when different pure lines are crossed. Since self-pollination is the general rule, inbreeding is unnecessary to obtain pure lines in this group of plants.

The economic feasibility of using hybrids in self-pollinated crops depends on the cost of producing hybrid seed in relation to the improvements in plant performance (e.g., increased yields). Since most self-pollinated crops produce a relatively small amount of pollen, which is not transferred by wind or insects to any significant degree, hand-pollination is most likely necessary. If many seeds are produced by each hand-pollination and if few seeds are needed per acre, it is usually more feasible to use hybrids. For example, with tomatoes a relatively large number of seeds may be obtained in each fruit by hand-pollination, and the increased yields justify hybridization. With crops like peas and beans, hand-pollination is difficult, and relatively small numbers of seeds are produced per pollination.

Plants Naturally Cross-pollinated

Vegetable crops that are cross-pollinated include the crucifers (cabbage, cauliflower, rutabagas, turnips, and radishes); root crops such as carrots, beets, parsnips; and other vegetables including onions, sweet corn, spinach, asparagus, and rhubarb. Most of these crops have perfect flowers, and pollen is largely transferred by wind and insects. Sweet corn is monoecious, and asparagus and spinach are dioecious. The monoecious and dioecious conditions are responsible for a very high degree of cross-pollination. Most crops that are highly cross-pollinated tend to lose vigor with inbreeding.

The development of true-breeding cultivars may be accomplished by selecting naturally occurring plants with desirable characteristics. Mass selection is often preferable to pedigree selection because cultivars can be obtained that are relatively uniform for observable characteristics but still retain vigor. The "Danish" type of cabbage (Chapter 14) used in eastern regions was originally developed by this method. If pedigree selection is used with controlled pollination, these crops ordinarily lose so much vigor by inbreeding that the strains developed are seldom directly useful.

Combinations of pedigree and mass selection are sometimes used. This method is useful in dealing with characters that are modified greatly by environment. After a generation or two of pedigree selection, a fairly large number of selected lines should be massed to regain vigor. This method has been used successfully with onions and carrots.

Variation may be produced by controlled hybridization in much the same manner as with self-pollinated crops. Frequently, natural crossing will provide abundant recombinations of characters within existing cultivars. If specific characters are missing in a cultivar, they may be incorporated through appropriate controlled crosses.

Breeding methods for improvement of dioecious crops have not received much study. Mass selection has been the most common method. Since the sexes are separated into different plants, they cannot be closely inbred. Brother-sister or sibling mating is the closest form of inbreeding. Dioecious plants usually lose vigor on sibbing. Occasionally plants can be found in some crops of spinach and asparagus that have both sexes on the same plant. These plants can then be inbred. As indicated above, F_1 hybrids are commercially available for spinach and asparagus and can increase yields by more than 50% in these crops.

Plants Partially Cross-pollinated

Eggplants, peppers, celery, and those in the cucurbit family (squashes, pumpkins, muskmelons, cucumbers, and watermelons) are sometimes classified as being partially cross-pollinated. The amount of crossing will vary depending upon the environment. The breeding methods employed will vary depending upon the amount of crossing and the loss in vigor resulting from self-pollination. Generally, most of these crops do not lose as much vigor with inbreeding as might be expected. Care must be taken in producing seed from these plants in order to maintain purity of stocks and cultivars. Hybrids of summer and winter squashes, cucumbers, muskmelons, watermelons, and eggplants are commercially available. Pepper hybrids are appearing on the market. For most of the vegetables in this group, male sterility has been found and is the basis for the economical production of hybrid seed.

Plants Vegetatively Propagated

Vegetable crops propagated chiefly by vegetative means include asparagus, potatoes, sweet potatoes, globe artichokes, rhubarb, garlic, and horseradish. In the breeding of vegetatively propagated crops, if one plant is found with desirable characteristics, an indefinite number of plants that are identical to the selected plant can be obtained. Selection among plants propagated by vegetative means will not be effective.

In some crops favorable mutations may occur quite frequently. Some, such as red skins on white potato tubers, are easily recognized. Much of the improvement in the sweet potato has been the result of selection of favorable mutations. In the Puerto Rican cultivar of the sweet potato, the mutation rate is fairly high, with one mutation occurring in about every 7,000 plants. Nonflowering cultivars of sweet potatoes have been induced to flower by grafting a small portion of the growing point on certain species of morning-glory, to which it is closely related. It is now possible to make crosses among any of the varieties of the sweet potato. As with the potato, desirable seedlings can be maintained indefinitely by vegetative propagation.

SELECTING CULTIVARS

The performance of a cultivar is the result of the interaction between its genetic potential, environment, and culture. Since growing and marketing conditions vary widely throughout the U.S., every cultivar is not appropriate for every location. In choosing cultivars, growers should consider climate (temperature, rainfall, humidity), soil (type, fertility, drainage), cropping season (winter, spring, summer, fall), culture (spacing, mulching, irrigation, fertilizer treatment), time of planting, harvest method, intended market use (processing, fresh market, storing), and disease resistance. These factors are likely to have a great deal of influence on crop performance and maturity for different locations. Therefore, when selecting early and late cultivars, growers should interpret days to maturity carefully.

Growers should consult current catalogs and trade publications for promising cultivars. The latest results of cultivar field evaluations are published by agricultural experiment stations of state universities. In addition, growers may perform their own cultivar evaluations, to judge the potential of new cultivars for their area, use, and market.

In spite of great effort to produce new cultivars, many old ones with obvious shortcomings are still being used. A well-known cultivar may still be in demand even though others are superior. To introduce a new cultivar and have it accepted, the plant breeder must combine in it as many new desirable characters as possible. It must have wide adaptability and be significantly better in some aspect than others that are already available. One cultivar with limited demand is seldom profitable. Rather, a cultivar that has received special publicity, such as an All-American award, or has some exceptional character, such as disease resistance, is more likely to be commercially produced. New cultivars of vegetables are constantly being developed by plant breeders, and older ones discarded.

SELECTED REFERENCES

Bassett, M. J. (ed.). 1986. *Breeding Vegetable Crops*. AVI Publishing Co., Westport, Connecticut.

Bliss, F. A., R. E. Stronsider, L. M. Pike, N. L. Innes, and E. J. Ryder. 1984. The role of public and private plant breeders in horticultural crop improvement. *HortScience* 19:797–811.

Watts, L. 1980. *Flower and Vegetable Plant Breeding*. Grower Books, London.

Welsh, J. R. 1989. *Fundamentals of Plant Genetics and Breeding*. Krieger Publishing Co., Melbourne, Florida.

5

CROP ESTABLISHMENT: TRANSPLANTING AND DIRECT-FIELD SEEDING

F. J. Sundstrom*

Successful crop establishment depends on many factors, the most important of which is seed quality. If poor-quality seed is used, then regardless of good cultural practices, crop production efforts are likely to be inefficient and unprofitable. The quality and yield of the harvested crop can be no better than that of the quality of the seed from which it was grown. In this light, seed quality should never be taken for granted, and growers should acquire the highest-quality seed available.

Environmental factors such as light, soil moisture, and temperature all interact to influence crop establishment. Although complete control of these factors cannot be achieved, it is possible by careful planning and preparation to assure that the environment will be generally favorable for rapid seedling growth and development.

Direct-seeding and transplanting technology is more advanced now than it was a few years ago. The use of hybrid vegetable seed is common today; thus, seed costs are no longer only a fraction of the total production costs. This fact often justifies the additional cost of transplanting. Most hybrid vegetable seed is of high vigor, but the seed of some hybrids, such as the seedless watermelon do

*Associate Professor of Horticulture, Louisiana State University

69

not have good vigor, and transplanting this crop is recommended. If crop production for an early market is the goal, cool temperature stress effects on germination must be considered. Conversely, some cool-season crops must be germinated under temperatures that are far above optimum. Many crop establishment
options are available to growers, and decisions concerning direct seeding and
transplanting are no longer as straightforward as in the past.

SEEDS AND SEED TECHNOLOGY

SEED QUALITY CHARACTERISTICS

Commercial seed should: 1) be "true-to-type," 2) have a high germination
percentage, 3) have high vigor, 4) have no dormancy, 5) be free of foreign matter,
and 6) have no disease or insect contamination.

"True-to-type" refers to the genetic purity of the seed. Any cultivar that is still
actively segregating or producing variant individuals is not marketed. Crop genetic
purity is maintained in part by use of a four-generation production scheme.
Genetic purity is maintained by production of each generation under strict guidelines. Isolation is used to prevent undesired cross-pollination and mechanical
mixing of different seeds during harvest. Minimum isolation requirements have
been established by the Association of Official Seed Certifying Agencies (AOSCA)
for each seed class to assure satisfactory genetic purity standards. Each generation
is then identified by a specific colored labeling tag. The following progeny classes
have been established:

1. *Breeder's seed.* Breeder's seed is produced under the direct supervision
   of the plant breeder and is the initial source of the cultivar.

2. *Foundation seed.* Foundation seed is the progeny of the breeder's seed
   and is handled to maintain the highest degree of purity. It is sometimes
   produced under contract by a foundation seed organization and is labeled
   with a white tag.

3. *Registered seed.* Registered seed is the progeny of foundation seed and
   is intended to be used for the production of certified seed. This class of
   seed is sometimes not maintained, and in such cases certified seed is
   produced directly from foundation seed. Registered seed is labeled with
   a purple tag.

4. *Certified seed.* Certified seed represents the final product of the certification program. It is produced either by the seed company itself or by

certified seed growers in volumes necessary for commercial sale to crop producers. It is also produced under strict guidelines so that the vegetable producer who is purchasing this seed can be assured of a satisfactory level of genetic purity and quality. Certified seed produced in a particular state must be certified (based on field inspection and laboratory testing) by that state's certification agency and then labeled with a blue tag.

Production and marketing of high-quality seeds are regulated in each state by a state seed certification program, sometimes recognized as "Crop Improvement Associations." Each state program, coordinated through the AOSCA, is designated by law (the Federal Seed Act of 1939) to certify seeds. Members of these associations include seed growers and commercial seed companies who are involved and interested in the production of certified seed. Standards of seed quality used by both federal and state seed testing laboratories are defined by the Association of Official Seed Analysts (ASOA). Such terms as *germination, pure seed, other crop seeds, inert matter,* etc., as well as the official "Rules for Testing Seeds," are defined and outlined by the ASOA.

Depending on the crop, certified or blue tag seed is generally labeled with at least the following information: 1) cultivar name, 2) lot number and / or origin, 3) purity (usually ±99%), 4) germination percentage, 5) date of the germination test, 6) amount of inert material (not generally a problem with vegetable seed), and 7) identification of any disease or insect control treatments.

Treatment of seeds with chemical protectants (primarily fungicides) has become a standard practice since the 1960's. Most vegetable seeds are treated in order to: 1) disinfect the surface of the seed from seed-borne fungi, 2) protect the seed from soil-borne fungi in the seedbed, and 3) systematically protect the seedling from damping-off organisms. By law, seed companies must identify the use of any chemical seed protectants and provide the proper antidote on the seed package.

Most seed companies now voluntarily size vegetable seed. Seed sizing serves two purposes. First, it allows selection of larger, generally more vigorous seeds from smaller individuals within a given lot. For example, larger (heavier) corn seed germinates faster, with more uniformity, and with subsequent faster crop maturity and total yield. And second, it provides greater seed size uniformity required by many advanced precision seeders. Sweet corn seed is often sized on the basis of a round or flat kernel to allow the grower to select the correct seed plate for some vegetable seeders.

Barring unusual circumstances, growers should purchase high-quality certified seed from a reputable seed company or seed dealer. Seed purchased from "feed and seed" stores or supply houses is sometimes improperly handled and stored. Seed is occasionally stored in rooms that are not climate-controlled, and high heat and humidity may significantly reduce seed vigor. At times, seed not sold from the previous year is improperly marketed without re-testing germination.

Seed germination should be tested the year the seed is sold. Germination testing can be done in the laboratory in petri dishes or in rolled germination towels, or it can be done in the greenhouse in flats filled with soil. A germination test will indicate seed germination percentage and rate (germination rate can be used as a measure of seed vigor). If necessary, the viability of those seeds that did not germinate may be measured to determine seed dormancy. Seed companies will not market any seedlots with dormancy or substandard vigor or germination.

HYBRID VS. OPEN-POLLINATED CULTIVARS

Plant breeders at universities, seed companies, and the U.S. Department of Agriculture (USDA) have improved crop performance by developing hybrid cultivars of many vegetable crops. A hybrid cultivar is the product of controlled pollination between two or more genetically distinct parental inbred lines (see Chapter 4). To produce hybrid seed, a breeder must manually cross these inbred lines each year. Such an effort is time-consuming and expensive, but the resulting hybrid normally possesses characteristics (such as increased cold, heat, or disease tolerance) superior to those of either of its parents. One particularly important characteristic of many hybrids is that of improved crop uniformity. The success of crop mechanization efforts is often dependent upon hybrid crop uniformity.

Open-pollinated (OP) cultivars are either self- or cross-pollinated species. Strict artificial isolation is essential to maintain genetic purity, because fertilization

Figure 5.1. Isolation cages used in a commercial plant breeding operation.

with the pollen of another cultivar will have disastrous consequences. Crops and / or cultivars may be isolated by distance, by maturity or planting date differences, or by use of isolation cages (Figure 5.1). Because maintenance and seed production of these cultivars only requires isolation, the seed of OP cultivars is much less expensive than hybrid seed. On-farm trials comparing the performance of OP and hybrid cultivars will provide growers with the information needed to choose the best cultivars for their needs.

SEED PERFORMANCE

The seed germination percentage listed on the seed label does not always represent the proportion of seed that will germinate and emerge in the greenhouse or field. Seed companies and seed-testing labs germinate seed under near-optimum conditions to measure germination. Realizing this, most seed companies understate on the label the germination percentage measured in the lab or greenhouse in order to provide the grower with a more realistic estimate of field germination.

Seed germination and subsequent seedling emergence are dependent on seed vigor. The International Seed Testing Association (ISTA) has defined *vigor* as "the sum total of those properties of the seed which determines the potential level of activity and performance of the seed or seed lot during germination and seedling emergence." To simplify, vigor is rapid, complete, and uniform seed germination. Specific laboratory tests are used to objectively determine seed vigor. Proper seed production in the field, upgrading (eliminating low-vigor seeds), and sometimes vigor enhancement techniques, all monitored by the seed company, contribute to seed and seedling performance in the seedbed.

SEED ENHANCEMENT

Seed enhancement research is now yielding many commercial successes. Basically, the objective of this work is to improve seed vigor, particularly under stressful germination conditions. One manner used for years by gardeners to shorten the time between sowing and seedling emergence is called *chitting*. This involves: 1) germination of seeds under ideal conditions until radicle (root) emergence and 2) carefully sowing / transplanting in a moistened media in the field to avoid radicle breakage or desiccation. The primary drawback to chitting is that this technique does little to improve germination uniformity or vigor.

Today, therefore, seed researchers use a technique referred to as *os-*

moconditioning or *priming* to improve seed and seedling vigor, as well as to improve germination rate, uniformity, and total germination percentage. Basically this treatment involves seed imbibition in a temperature-controlled, dilute, aerated solution of an organic or inorganic osmoticum. The concentration of this solution (the identity, concentration of the osmoticum, as well as the method of imbibition, is often proprietary) controls both the rate and amount of water imbibed by the seed. The concentration of the solution is such that there is not quite sufficient free water available for the seed to complete germination (measured by radicle emergence). The seeds are allowed to imbibe water in this aerated solution for such time that upon removal, all the seeds will have exactly the same moisture content. During this slow imbibition period, seed metabolism is stimulated, and during subsequent germination and seedling development, vigor is significantly improved. Occasionally, plant growth regulators are also used alone, or in combination with an osmoticum, to stimulate germination. A properly enhanced seed will generally germinate faster, more completely and uniformly than an untreated seed, particularly under temperature or moisture stress.

The success of such research has led to the development of numerous commercial products. Most major U.S. vegetable seed companies now offer enhanced seed products. Because these seeds have been imbibed and then re-dried, seed handling and storage must be carefully monitored. For this reason, seed companies will sell such seed with a special disclaimer. This is not to discourage use of such products but rather to indicate the special care required to assure maintenance of high vigor. The commercially enhanced products currently on the market will perform admirably if these special precautions are carefully followed.

Another option available to growers is the use of coated or pelleted seed (Figure 5.2). When coated, small-seeded vegetables such as tomatoes, can be handled and singulated in precision seeders much more efficiently. Technology has made great strides since the time when coating involved placing a relatively thick layer of diatomaceous earth, montmorillonite clay, sand, etc., with a binder around seeds to increase size and shape uniformity. For example, full-coated lettuce seeds were once formulated at a ratio of 50 parts clay to 1 part seed. Now, ratios have decreased with new mini-coatings to 10:1. Some pelleting materials are designed to instantly split after coming into contact with moisture. This prevents any problems with oxygen availability to the germinating seed or difficulties with the radicle emerging through the pelleting material.

Pelleted seeds have the additional advantage of increased pestilence protection when fungicides and / or insecticides are incorporated into the coating material. It is possible to coat the seed, apply the fungicide or insecticide, then coat once again. This process permits the use and concentration of materials that ordinarily would be phytotoxic, because the first layer of coating material acts as

Figure 5.2. Coated seed *(right)* can be handled more effectively than raw seed *(left)* by modern precision seeders.

a protectant to the seed. Furthermore, the outer coating layer makes seed handling much less hazardous. With today's technology, seeds that have temperature- and light-dependent dormancies, such as lettuce and endive, can be treated with growth regulators to overcome these dormancies, osmoconditioned to promote germination rate and vigor, and ultimately pelleted with fungicides and / or insecticides for successful direct-field precision seeding. Commercial coatings have been primarily developed by commercial seed companies, and their composition is proprietary. An example of the economics of using coated seed is given as follows:

> *Economics of Coated Seed.* If a grower normally sows 0.5–0.75 pound (approximately 300,000 seeds) of raw lettuce seed per acre, only 3.5 ounces (approximately 90,000 seeds) of coated seeds per acre, 210,000 fewer seeds per acre, would be needed. Assuming coated seed costs $0.43 per 1,000 seeds, it will cost $38.70 per acre for seed. Assuming raw seed costs $0.10 per 1,000 seeds, it would cost $30.00 per acre for seed. The increased cost of pelleted seed is only $8.70 per acre, or about the price of one carton of lettuce. Due to the use of coated seed, estimated savings on thinning alone is easily as much as $200 per acre.

Use of enhanced (coated or uncoated) seed is particularly appropriate when a grower is attempting to germinate seed under stressful environmental conditions. Enhanced seeds will germinate under conditions that untreated seeds will not. Establishment of a crop by direct-field seeding is therefore possible in conditions where, in the past, transplanting was essential. Use of these products, however, is expensive. On-farm trials will provide invaluable information as to their suitability in a particular grower's operation.

Another area of technological research that may afford exciting future opportunities is the production of synthetic seeds. Starting with disease-free plant tissue, somatic embryos are produced aseptically in vitro. The embryos can be removed from the culture media and encapsulated in synthetic gels that replace the endosperm (food reserves) and seed coat of a normal seed. Chemicals for protection against pestilence can be incorporated within this gel. The process of applying tissue culture and genetic manipulation to create commercial products has sparked the development of a number of biotechnology firms. These firms hope to capitalize patentable techniques to market superior cultivars and propagation methods.

SEED GERMINATION

A seed physiologist defines *germination* as the emergence of the radicle through the seed coat. A grower defines *germination* as the emergence of the seedling through the soil. Whatever the definition, good seed germination and seedling emergence require high-quality seed and the proper environment. Environmental factors necessary for seed germination are: 1) moisture, 2) oxygen, 3) favorable temperature, and sometimes 4) light.

Water is a basic requirement for seed germination. In their resting, or "quiescent," stage, seeds contain very little moisture. Low moisture maintains low seed metabolic activity necessary for proper storage. Upon contact with adequate soil moisture, seed metabolism accelerates and the physiological activities necessary for embryo cell elongation and division are initiated.

Vegetable seeds vary in the amount of soil moisture required for germination. Soil moisture availability can be described by the terms *field capacity* and *permanent wilting percentage*. Table 5.1 shows the response of various vegetable seeds to different levels of soil moisture. Although not indicated in the table, it should be noted that excessive soil moisture (greater than 40%) can be detrimental to the germination of some crops, especially beans and peas.

As seeds begin to germinate, seed respiration increases. If soil moisture levels are excessive, anaerobic conditions can occur, and seed respiration and subsequent germination can be retarded. Generally, this problem is greater in heavy-

Table 5.1. Effect of Soil Moisture on Germination of Vegetable Seed[1]

1. **Seeds germinate well in soils with moisture at permanent wilting percentage to field capacity**

cabbage	onions	sweet corn
carrots	peppers	tomatoes
cucumbers	radishes	turnips
muskmelons	squashes	watermelons

2. **Seeds germinate best in soils with intermediate moisture content to field capacity**

beans, lima	endive
beans, snap	lettuce
beets	peas

3. **Seeds germinate only when soil moisture is near field capacity**

celery

4. **Seeds germinate best at lower soil moisture contents**

New Zealand spinach
spinach

[1]Source: Doneen, L. D., and J. H. MacGillivray. 1943. Germination (emergence) of vegetable seeds as affected by different soil moisture conditions. *Plant Physiology* 18:524–529. In: Harrington, J. F., and P. A. Minges. 1954. *Vegetable Seed Germination*, University of California Agric. Ext. Leaf. 7–54.

textured soils, but it can occur in any situation where there is inadequate soil drainage. Not only can flooding severely reduce germination, but it also can wash shallow-sown seeds from the seedbed. Raised seedbeds are commonly used both for drainage and for furrow irrigation purposes.

Temperature requirements for seed germination vary among vegetable crops. Table 5.2 lists minimum and maximum temperatures, in addition to the optimum range and specific optimum temperature for major vegetable crops. It is important to realize that although seeds will germinate at the listed minimum and maximum temperatures, germination rates and percentages will be less than satisfactory. Cool-season vegetables will generally germinate at temperatures close to 32°F, while warm-season crops require temperatures above 59°F for satisfactory germination.

Two important vegetable crops express a high-temperature–induced seed dormancy called *thermodormancy*. Many celery and lettuce cultivars will not germinate at temperatures above 79° and 86°F, respectively. This natural crop protection mechanism prevents germination and subsequent seedling development under unfavorable growing conditions. High soil temperatures in the field can be lowered, particularly in desert growing regions, by the use of overhead irrigation. Growth regulator seed treatment with ethylene and kinetin will over-

Table 5.2. Soil Temperature Conditions for Vegetable Seed Germination[1]

Crop	Minimum	Optimum Range	Optimum	Maximum
	(°F)	(°F)	(°F)	(°F)
Asparagus	50	60–85	75	95
Beans, snap	60	60–85	80	95
Beans, lima	60	65–85	85	85
Beets	40	50–85	85	95
Cabbage	40	45–95	85	100
Carrots	40	45–85	80	95
Cauliflower	40	45–85	80	100
Celery	40	60–70	70[2]	85[2]
Chard, Swiss	40	50–85	85	95
Corn	50	60–95	95	105
Cucumbers	60	60–95	95	105
Eggplants	60	75–90	85	95
Lettuce	35	40–80	75	85
Muskmelons	60	75–95	90	100
Okra	60	70–95	95	105
Onions	35	50–95	75	95
Parsley	40	50–85	75	90
Parsnips	35	50–70	65	85
Peas	40	40–75	75	85
Peppers	60	65–95	85	95
Pumpkins	60	70–90	95	100
Radishes	40	45–90	85	95
Spinach	35	45–75	70	85
Squashes	60	70–95	95	100
Tomatoes	50	60–85	85	95
Turnips	40	60–105	85	105
Watermelons	60	70–95	95	105

[1]Compiled by J. F. Harrington, Department of Vegetable Crops, University of California, Davis.

[2]Daily fluctuation to 60°F or lower at night is essential.

come this dormancy, and breeders have now introduced some hybrid cultivars of both crops that will tolerate higher germination temperatures.

Some celery and lettuce seeds require light requirement for germination. If moisture, oxygen, and temperature requirements have all been satisfied, sunlight (or incandescent light) is required for germination to proceed. These light sources are rich in red wavelengths (ca. 650 nm) that are sensed by a protein pigment found in the seed embryo called *phytochrome*. This pigment exists in two forms: one inhibits germination, and the other promotes germination. If light is very weak, then far-red wavelengths (ca. 750 nm) predominate, phytochrome will be converted to the biologically inactive form, and the seed will be dormant. These events are important to crop producers because if celery or lettuce seeds are sown too deep (±1 inch), the seeds will likely become photodormant. For this reason, in the greenhouse, seeds are frequently not sown directly in the media, but rather on top, and then covered with wet burlap or cheesecloth to keep the seeds moist. Not all celery and lettuce cultivars are light-sensitive, but even light-insensitive cultivars become light-sensitive if they are exposed to high temperatures for several days. Growth regulator treatments (such as gibberellic acid) are used commercially to satisfy the light requirement of these seeds, circumventing many potential germination difficulties and allowing the seed to be pelleted.

SEED STORAGE

Generally, most vegetable seed will store well under favorable conditions for at least a year (Table 5.3). Even when stored under the best conditions (i.e., low temperature and humidity), seed quality cannot improve.

Table 5.3. Length of Time Seeds May Be Expected to Retain Their Vitality[1]

Kind of Vegetable	Years	Kind of Vegetable	Years
Asparagus	3	Onions	1
Beans	3	Parsley	2
Beets	4	Parsnips	1
Brussels sprouts	4	Peas	3
Cabbage	4	Peppers	3
Carrots	3	Pumpkins	4
Cauliflower	4	Radishes	4
Celery	5	Rutabagas	4
Cucumbers	5	Spinach	4
Eggplants	5	Squashes	4
Endive	5	Sweet corn	1
Kale	4	Tomatoes	3
Lettuce	5	Turnips	4
Muskmelons	5	Watermelons	5
Okra	2		

[1]When stored under favorable conditions, seed of the age indicated (from harvest not from time of purchase) should be viable. Seed is often good much longer, but specific lots may not survive as long.

Typical home refrigeration temperatures (ca. 41°F) are sufficient for good seed storage. Seed moisture will equilibrate with the humidity of the surrounding atmosphere. A relative humidity of ca. 60% at a temperature ca. 77°F (as would often be found within a home) is very adequate to dry most vegetable seeds to a moisture of ca. 10%. At this moisture level, most vegetable seeds can be safely stored under refrigeration for at least 1 year. Stable storage moisture and temperature conditions are important because severe fluctuations in storage temperature or moisture are harmful to seed vigor.

STAND ESTABLISHMENT

Crops may be established in the field by the use of transplants, or "plugs," or by the use of pregerminated or raw seed. Whatever method is used, it is important to realize that a complete crop stand is an economic necessity. Production costs of fertilizing, cultivating, spraying, etc., are greater on a per plant basis when working with an incomplete stand. Greatly overseeding in the field is no longer a feasible alternative to assure a satisfactory stand. The high cost of seed and thinning makes this practice uneconomical.

TRANSPLANTING

Perhaps the best manner to assure a complete stand of seed-propagated crops is by the use of transplants, or "plugs." When very expensive hybrid seed is used, transplants become more economically attractive. Crops such as celery and lettuce are very often transplanted due to seed germination difficulties. Other vegetable crops are not propagated by true botanical seed. Examples of some asexually propagated vegetables include artichokes, garlic, horseradish, potatoes, and sweet potatoes.

Growers often use transplanting to 1) extend a short growing season for a late-maturing crop, 2) improve land-use efficiency, 3) substantially save on the cost of expensive hybrid seed, or 4) force crop production for an early market. Western U.S. vegetable growers may transplant crops to reduce irrigation costs. A direct-seeded tomato crop in the West requires about 2.5 acre-feet of water per season, while a transplanted crop uses only 1.5 acre-feet. As water and energy costs continue to rise, this water savings becomes more important. Early-season weed control is more manageable when transplants are used, and thinning costs and damages are completely eliminated. Crop uniformity can also be improved in some crops. For example, the number of times a field of cauliflower must be harvested can be reduced from seven to three. With increasing overseas competition, many vegetable growers are now under greater pressure to provide a specific product, for a specific market, and at a specific time. Sometimes, transplanting is the only manner in which they are able to accomplish this.

Growing Transplants

Virtually all commercially produced transplants are grown in heated and ventilated greenhouses. Most transplants are grown in trays or flats; however, a relatively small bare-root transplant production industry still exists in the southeastern U.S., producing primarily peppers and tomatoes. These plants are grown in raised beds, pulled, packed, and often shipped to northern growing regions. The only advantage of using bare-root transplants is that they are generally less expensive than container-grown plants.

Until recently, container vegetable transplant production was limited to growing seedlings in "Todd" expanded polystyrene planter flats or a facsimile (Figure 5.3). Today, many vegetable transplants are grown in a plug production system, very similar to bedding plant production. Plug or plug trays differ from planter flats primarily in cell size (Figure 5.4). Typical planter flats are identified by the dimensions of the cell size. A "080" or "175" means that each side of the square cell measures 0.80 or 1.75 inches, respectively. Plug trays are identified by the number of cells per flat, starting at 33 and increasing to 648.

The use of plug technology has decreased production costs per seedling and has facilitated greater transplant mechanization. As a result, the acreage of vegetables established by transplanting is increasing. Plug culture differs from planter flat production due to the very small volume of the plug media used. Since the volume of the media (generally peat-based) is very limited, it must be very uniform in texture, and well-mixed if any nutrients or lime has been added. Because of the size of the plug, the possibility of moisture stress is very great. The plug can dry out quickly, yet it can also be saturated very easily as well. For this reason, as in the bedding plant industry, some commercial plug growers use mist rooms for

Figure 5.3. Todd planter flats illustrating size and shape of cells with pepper transplants.

Figure 5.4. Plug trays with varying cell sizes and shapes. (Photo: courtesy of Blackmore Transplanter Co., Ypsilanti, Michigan)

seed germination. These rooms are constantly "fogged" with microscopic water particles to maintain a relative humidity of 100%, temperature is very accurately monitored, and high intensity artificial lighting is provided. This system is much different from a typical greenhouse mist system. The seed is mechanically placed on top of the media (Figure 5.5) rather than buried to assure that soil anaerobiosis is not a concern. After germination, seedlings are carefully adapted to a greenhouse environment for further development. Plug plants may be transplanted when only two or three true leaves have developed. The smaller the plug volume, the less time a seedling can remain in the tray. One of the great advantages of using plugs is that transplanting can be completely mechanized (Figure 5.6). The business of custom operations that produce the plug and subsequently transplant it to the field is increasing.

More traditional transplant production involves seedling production in flats with much larger cell sizes. Cells are still mechanically seeded, but flats are set at final spacing in the greenhouse for germination and production of a finished transplant. Larger cells do not necessitate as much care in regard to moisture availability, and they permit seedlings to remain in the flat until they achieve traditional transplant size (five or six true leaves). Most cells, modules, or plugs are inversely tapered and open at the bottom (Figure 5.3). This type of cell results in an "air-pruning" of the taproot, which encourages good lateral root development and orientation. Planter flats are utilized in semi-automatic transplanters such as the one shown in Figure 5.7. These transplanters require operators to pick the seedlings from the trays and drop them through a chute into the bed. Planting

Figure 5.5. This automatic plug seeder can be adjusted to precisely place one seed of virtually any size and shape at a specific depth in each cell. (Photo: courtesy of Blackmore Transplanter Co., Ypsilanti, Michigan)

Figure 5.6. Automatic transplanter; after plug trays are placed on the conveyer, no additional hand labor is necessary for transplanting.

Figure 5.7. Semi-automatic mechanical transplanter unit. These single units are mounted on a tool-bar behind a tractor, and operators pull transplants from trays and drop them down rotating cups. (Photo: courtesy of Mechanical Transplanter, Holland, Michigan)

depth and in-row spacing are accurately controlled, and seedlings are firmly packed into the soil by press wheels.

Because the seedling taproot is "air-pruned" in plug and seedling trays, the pruned taproot is unable to penetrate the soil profile as deeply. Root foraging for water and nutrients deep in the soil profile is therefore reduced. This situation is commercially important if irrigation is not available. For example, watermelons produced on deep, light-textured soils without irrigation should be direct seeded because transplanted crops are more susceptible to possible water stress.

Often, seedling performance depends on transplant cell size. Although there are subtle crop differences, generally transplants grown in larger cells produce greater early crop yields. If the length of the growing season is not limited, cell size does not affect total crop yields. When early crop yield is an objective, large cell sizes should be used. Based on the difference in the number of plants per square foot of greenhouse bench space, the cost of producing seedlings in large cells is greater.

Hardening

Before any transplant (cool- or warm-season crop) is removed from the near-optimum conditions of a greenhouse and set in the field, it should be adapted to the harsher field environment by "hardening." Hardening involves a treatment which slows or retards seedling growth before transplanting. Physiologically, hardening 1) reduces growth rate, 2) thickens the cuticle, 3) increases the waxy covering (bloom) on the leaves of certain crops, 4) increases the percentage of dry matter, 5) increases the percentage of water-holding colloids, 6) decreases the percentage of freezable water, and 7) develops anthocyanins (pink pigments) in the stems, petioles, and veins. Hardening increases the adaptability of the transplant to field conditions which may include excessively cool or warm temperatures, water stress, wind, pestilence, etc. Generally, hardening is imposed anywhere from 7 to 14 days prior to transplanting by withholding moisture, and / or reducing temperature. Hardening should not involve any treatment such as nutrient stress that may reduce the rate of photosynthesis. If plants are grown when temperatures are high, hardening is accomplished by withholding water. If one is growing a biennial such as cabbage, celery, or onions, lower temperatures during hardening may induce vernalization and promote premature flowering. Biennial crops should be hardened only by reducing water.

Hardening reduces seedling growth rate and allows an accumulation of carbohydrates within the tissue. This increase in carbohydrates and the corresponding increase in percentage of dry matter within the seedling is beneficial, as these carbohydrates serve to effectively drop the point at which the tissue will freeze (which is particularly important in cool-season crucifers). In addition, the carbohydrates are needed as an energy source for seedling root regeneration following transplanting. When a seedling is transplanted, damage to the root system is inevitable. Those areas of the root system that are most affected are the tender root tips, the very portion of the root that is vital for moisture and nutrient absorption. Stored carbohydrates within the foliage are therefore used for necessary root regeneration activities.

Transplanting Success

The adaptability of vegetables to transplanting varies widely between crops (Table 5.4). Transplanting success depends on how rapidly a plant is able to regenerate those areas of the root system that were damaged by transplanting. The more quickly a plant is able to absorb adequate moisture and nutrients, the greater are its chances of survival. Crops such as crucifers, peppers, and tomatoes are able to form adventitious roots which greatly improve the survivability of transplants. Others, such as the cucurbits, have a rapid rate of root suberization, a process that prevents root hair and lateral branch-root formation in older root tissues. The inability to form lateral branch roots and root hairs substantially reduces soil moisture and nutrient absorption. If root suberization occurs in a very

Table 5.4. Relative Ease of Transplanting Vegetables[1]

Easy	Moderate	Require Special Care[2]
Beets	Celery	Cucumbers
Broccoli	Eggplants	Muskmelons
Brussels sprouts	Onions	Summer squashes
Cabbage	Peppers	Sweet corn
Cauliflower		Watermelons
Chard		
Lettuce		
Tomatoes		

[1]Source: Lorenz, O. A., and D. N. Maynard. 1988. *Knott's Handbook for Vegetable Growers*, 3rd ed. John Wiley & Sons, Inc., New York.

[2]Containerized transplants are recommended.

young plant, as it does in cucurbits, seedlings are not easily transplanted successfully. If transplanting becomes necessary, such crops should be set in the field at a very early age. Products such as peat pots, Jiffy 7's, paperpots, etc., which are transplanted with the seedlings and later decompose in the soil, can be used to minimize root damage to such tender crops. These products, however, do not easily lend themselves to mechanization.

Seedlings grown in cells or modules can be transplanted more successfully than bare-root seedlings, because roots of cell-grown seedlings suffer significantly less damage during transplanting. Pulling a plant from the seedbed is itself very damaging compared to removing a seedling from a plug tray. The entire root system of bare-root plants is susceptible to damage during transplanting, whereas a much smaller proportion of the roots of a plug are exposed to injury. Nevertheless, commercial growers continue to use bare-root transplants each year, and it appears that this market will exist for some time.

Additional factors that influence the success of transplanting are transplant age, seedling reproductive development, and field environment. As seedlings grow older, the rate of root replacement decreases. If flower bud development begins, root replacement is also suppressed. Normally, seedlings are started in the greenhouse anywhere from 4 to 8 weeks prior to anticipated transplanting. When plugs are grown, this time may be reduced; when transplants are grown in large cells, this time may be slightly increased. The cost of transplant production is directly related to the length of time required to grow them. If seedlings must be held in the greenhouse longer than anticipated, the current stage of plant development should be maintained without reducing the photosynthetic rate. Care should be taken not to over-harden plants, which may delay maturity and in some instances even reduce crop yields.

Clipping or pruning transplants for size control should be avoided at all costs.

Plant pruning removes tissue carbohydrates and results in diminished root regenerative capabilities. Pruning should be practiced only for flower or flower bud removal. When this is necessary and it is impractical to simply de-bud the plants, then plants should be clipped as far in advance of transplanting as possible to allow partial regeneration of removed foliage and restoration of carbohydrate reserves.

If possible, transplanting should be done as early in the morning or as late in the afternoon as feasible. High mid-day temperatures are obviously detrimental. Furthermore, relative humidity is generally higher in the early morning and late afternoon, reducing transplant desiccation. Water should be supplied immediately following transplanting. Normally a starter fertilizer solution is applied from tanks on the transplanter or tractor at the time of transplanting. The importance of the starter solution cannot be overemphasized. Starter solutions with greater concentrations of phosphorus rather than nitrogen or potassium (e.g., 10-50-10) are preferable. Phosphorus has been demonstrated to be critical in stimulating early crop root development.

DIRECT-FIELD SEEDING

Sowing seed directly in the field seedbed is the most economical manner of establishing a crop, provided seed germination and emergence are satisfactory. Of course, very often seed germination and seedling emergence are not satisfactory for a great number of reasons. This situation has led to the development of innovative methods of handling the seed with the objective of obtaining consistently complete and uniform stands.

Proper seedbed preparation is the first step in successful direct seeding. The bed must be straight, level, and free of large clods, debris, and weeds. It is possible to overwork a seedbed and almost completely destroy the soil structure. In such instances, soil pore space may be severely reduced, and any precipitation or overhead irrigation may result in serious soil crusting that will impede seedling emergence. The seedbed should only be worked to sufficiently assure that seed placement can be accurate.

Some vegetables have notoriously weak seedlings. Carrot and onion seedlings are very susceptible to soil crusting and weed competition. Soil crusting can be alleviated by the use of anticrustants such as phosphoric acid and vermiculite. These materials are applied on top of the seedbed, covering the seed to prevent soil compaction and to enhance seedling emergence. Other seeds are particularly sensitive to soluble salts. Legume crops are intolerant of high salt concentrations in the seedbed and are therefore easily damaged by improper fertilizer placement or the use of high-salt, low-quality irrigation water. Surface, as well as subsurface, water supplies should always be tested for soluble salts, sodium, carbonates, and bicarbonates. If these are found to be excessive, it is possible to alter bed shape to reduce salt concentrations in the root zone (Figure 5.8).

Figure 5.8. Modified bed shape reduces salt buildup in the crop root zone, as well as increases daytime soil temperatures. The additional use of hotcaps ensures an early-season harvest.

Modification of bed shape can also be used to increase early-season soil temperatures to enhance seed germination and to hasten crop maturity. Simply orienting the beds in an east-west direction, sloping to the south, will increase the angle of incidence of sunlight striking the beds, and soil temperatures (at a 0.5-inch depth) will be significantly higher (ca. 10°F in late afternoon) than on flat beds.

Soil moisture has a great influence on soil temperatures in the seedbed. Heavy-textured soils hold moisture closer to the soil surface for a longer period of time than do light-textured soils. Since air warms faster than water, temperatures in the bed will be much warmer during the day in light-textured or drier fields. This situation, as well as superior drainage characteristics, makes light-textured soils ideal for early-season crop production. Good field drainage is mandatory for successful seed germination and crop production. The timing and amount of precipitation cannot be controlled, but field drainage characteristics can be improved. Adequate field drainage will reduce the risk of flooding and enable some degree of soil moisture control, critical for successful seed germination.

Seeding Dates

The date for planting various vegetable crops in the field is dependent on the geographic location, crop hardiness, length of the growing season, and time required for the crop to mature. The dates of the average last and first frosts in the U.S. are given in Figures 5.9 and 5.10, respectively. For seeding recommendations for specific crops and areas, it is advisable to consult local agricultural extension personnel. These individuals will also be able to provide specific crop cultural information and recommend cultivars, planting densities, etc., that are very geographically dependent.

Seeding Methods

There are three manners to direct seed a vegetable crop in the field. One may 1) drill, 2) precision seed, or 3) plant to a stand. Perhaps the best example of drilling is to recall the function of a grain drill. It places seed so thickly in the bed that adjacent seeds are touching. Drilling is expensive and generally impractical today because of seed and thinning costs.

The last method of seeding places one seed at every point in the bed where one plant is desired. This method is risky because incomplete germination and / or emergence, pestilence, etc., can result in an economically unacceptable stand.

The seeding method most frequently utilized in the vegetable industry today is precision seeding. Precision seeders are able to accurately place seeds in the bed at a pre-set spacing and depth. Precision seeders overseed to assure a satisfactory stand, but in-row seed spacing is sufficiently great (unlike drilling) that thinning damage to plants remaining in the bed is almost eliminated.

There are a variety of manners that vegetable seed may be precision planted. Some of these include 1) precision seeders that utilize seed plates, perforated belts, a vacuum, or small cups or spoons; 2) plug-mix seeders; and 3) fluid drilling seeders. The standard vegetable seeder that utilizes seed plates and has been used by the industry for the last 50 years may be referred to as a precision seeder in certain circumstances. It is possible with these planters to sow large-seeded vegetables such as legumes, okra, and sweet corn with some degree of depth control. The difficulty with these planters is with seed singulation by the seed plate, which often gets clogged or drops multiple seeds unless seed size and shape are very uniform.

In addition, older vegetable seeders are not able to achieve the depth control necessary for small-seeded vegetable crops. Seeds as small as the head of a pin often do not have the necessary stored food reserves to germinate and develop seedlings with sufficient vigor to emerge at excessive depths. If the seed is sown at too shallow a depth however, high soil temperatures may damage or kill the

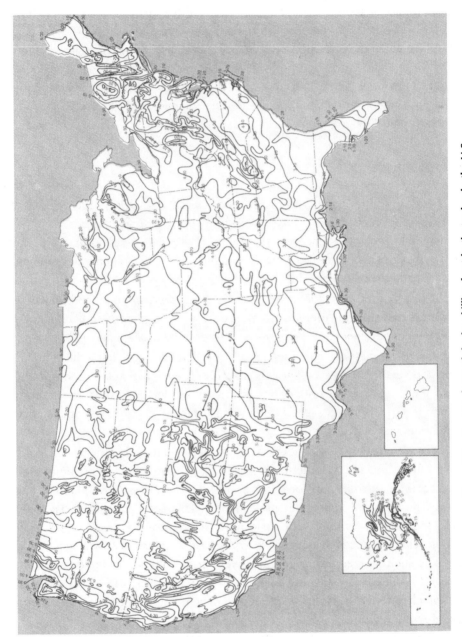

Figure 5.9. Average dates of the last killing frost in the spring in the U.S.

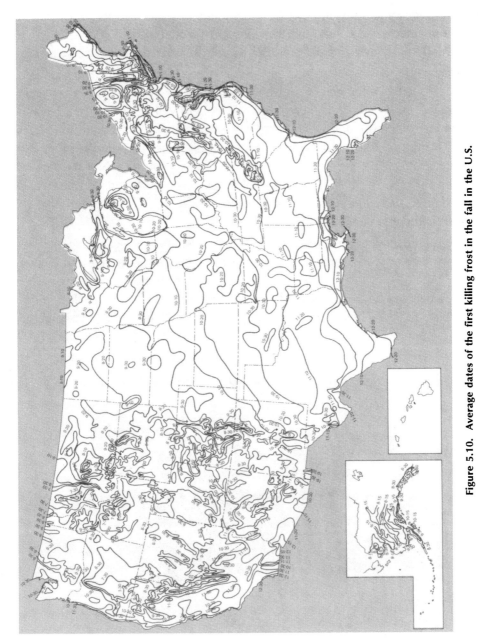

Figure 5.10. Average dates of the first killing frost in the fall in the U.S.

emerging seedling. Precision vegetable seeders permit excellent depth control, which is utilized by many growers in seasonal crop production. For example, in spring broccoli production, seeds are sown almost on top of the ground where they take advantage of warmer soil temperatures to germinate. In the fall, when soil temperatures are much higher, seeds are planted deeper (0.5–0.75 inch) where soils are cooler and soil moisture is more available.

The primary difference between modern precision seeders and standard vegetable seeders is the manner in which they singulate the seed. Some precision seeders use interchangeable, perforated rubber belts with specific hole sizes and shapes for each crop, and when necessary, even for each crop cultivar. Others use a vacuum to hold seeds against holes in a disc. This is a very fast method, which can effectively handle unusually shaped seeds. Some of the others use a gear-driven wheel of small, interchangeable cups or spoons to individually lift and drop single seeds. It is easy to understand why uniformly sized and shaped pelleted seed are in such demand.

Plug-mix seeders are quite different from customary precision seeder because they drop seeds, mixed in a peat-based media, in hills in the bed (Figure 5.11). There are advantages and disadvantages to this method. The strong points are 1) seeds can be pregerminated (with emerged ca. 0.25-inch radicles) under favorable conditions before seeding in the bed, 2) seedlings develop and emerge

Figure 5.11. A plug-mix seeder using a heated punch to burn holes through plastic mulch to plant tomato seeds. (Photo: courtesy of S. Kostewicz, University of Florida)

in the favorable conditions within the plug (for example, without crusting), and 3) seedlings are protected against early-season herbicide injury. The weak points of this method of seeding are 1) seed number within each plug can only be estimated (by mixing a certain weight of seeds with a known volume of media), 2) seeds are uniformly mixed within the media and individual seed depth in the bed cannot be precisely controlled, 3) the peat-based porous media has a tendency to dry very quickly unless wetting agents are used, or unless it is covered, for example, with vermiculite, and 4) more than one seedling per hill may emerge, so thinning can be quite laborious, damaging, and expensive. For these reasons, plug-mix seeding is normally used only with crops such as tomatoes and cucumbers where multiple plants per hill are acceptable.

Fluid drilling is similar to plug-mix seeding. A water-soluble gel rather than a peat-like media is used to disperse seeds. The concept is almost the same as with plug-mix seeding. Seeds are pregerminated under favorable conditions, and ungerminated seeds are removed before being incorporated into the gel. The gel, with seeds, is extruded through a pump either intermittently in hills or continuously in a band in the bed. The seedlings which develop and emerge in the gel have the same advantages as plug-mix seeding. Fluid drilling, however, is not limited to hill culture. It is important to note that if seeds are pregerminated before incorporation in the mix or gel, both plug-mix seeding and fluid drilling allow the grower to plant only germinated seed. This tremendous advantage, coupled with a favorable initial environment for seedling development, has allowed direct-field seeding of some vegetables under conditions where it would be otherwise ill-advised. Although both seeding methods are currently being employed in the U.S., many growers have had difficulty justifying the additional expense of these precision seeders, and as a result, their use is currently limited.

With the availability of precision seeders and transplanters today, the method of crop establishment selected by the vegetable grower should be coordinated with specific cropping conditions. Large-seeded crops may be successfully precision seeded with only slight modifications of old vegetable seeders. Vegetables with very small and irregularly shaped seed may require coating and may need to be seeded with a more technologically advanced belt, spoon, or vacuum-type precision seeder. Seeding under stressful temperatures or in soils of unusual tilth (such as marl soils) may require the use of plug-mix or fluid-drilling equipment. Small seeds of inherently low vigor, and / or very specific germination requirements may necessitate germination in a seedling or plug tray in the greenhouse prior to being transplanted. Growers forcing crop production for a specific market window may need to consider transplanting, regardless of seed germination characteristics. Recent agricultural engineering and horticultural research efforts have provided vegetable growers with an array of crop establishment alternatives.

It is important that the individual growers make an informed decision as to the suitability of a particular system for their specific needs.

SELECTED REFERENCES

Bewley, D. J., and M. Black (ed.). 1985. *Seeds: Physiology of Development and Germination.* Plenum Press, New York.

Copeland, L. O., and M. B. McDonald. 1985. *Principles of Seed Science and Technology.* Burgess Publishing Co., Minneapolis, Minnesota.

Hartman, H. T., and D. E. Kester. 1975. *Plant Propagation: Principles and Practices,* 3rd ed. Prentice-Hall, Inc., Englewood Cliffs, New Jersey.

Justice, O. L., and L. N. Bass. 1978. *Principles and Practices of Seed Storage.* USDA Agric. Handbook No. 56.

Lorenz, O. A., and D. N. Maynard. 1988. *Knott's Handbook for Vegetable Growers,* 3rd ed. John Wiley & Sons, Inc., New York.

McDonald, M. B., and W. D. Pardee. 1985. *The Role of Seed Certification in the Seed Industry.* Crop Sci. Soc. Amer. Spec. Pub. No. 10, Madison, Wisconsin.

Sims, W. L., M. P. Zobel, D. M. May, R. J. Mullen, and P. P. Osterli. 1979. *Mechanized Growing and Harvesting of Processing Tomatoes.* Univ. of California, Div. Agric. Sci. Leaf. 2686.

Stefferud, A. 1961. *Seeds: The Yearbook of Agriculture, 1961.* USDA, Washington, DC.

6

SOIL MANAGEMENT
AND FERTILIZATION

Traditionally, the best soils and high rates of fertility have been accorded vegetable crops in order to achieve top quality and optimum yields. Vegetables, for the most part, have relatively limited root systems and are fast-growing. They therefore require high levels of soil fertility maintained throughout most of their growth. Vegetable growers must depend on chemical fertilizers and organic materials along with crop rotation to supply the nutrients essential to their crops.

Quality in vegetables depends primarily on tender, succulent growth. The best quality of leafy vegetables results when growth is rapid and continuous, which requires soils with a continuous supply of available nutrients and moisture. Crops such as peas and cauliflower must develop quickly while weather conditions are favorable. Most seed- and fruit-producing vegetables cease growing at the time of fruit set, and subsequent yields are dependent upon the amount of growth before fruiting. Nutrient stress at critical stages of crop development can interrupt growth, causing irreparable damage to both crop yield and quality.

VEGETABLE SOILS

The best soils for growing vegetables are well drained, fairly deep, and relatively high (3–5%) in organic matter. They have good physical condition, or structure, with ample nutrient- and water-holding capacity. Vegetable soils should be uniform and free of compacted layers that can reduce root penetration and restrict gas exchange and water infitration. Proper fertilization, drainage, pH control, and cultivation practices are essential for all soils used for vegetable production.

Selecting Soils

For certain situations, some types of soils may be better than others. In general, sandy loams and silt loams are preferred for most vegetable production. They possess most, if not all, of the above characteristics, and through proper soil management can maintain their high levels of production.

When earliness is of more importance than total yield, sandy soils and light sandy loams are best. These soils are well drained and aerated, drying out and warming up rapidly in the spring. They can be worked soon after a rain or irrigation without danger of soil compaction. This last factor is an important advantage for fresh market farmers who irrigate right up to harvest to keep vegetables fresh and turgid. However, sandy soils are usually low in nutrient and moisture retention and require irrigation and extra fertility practices to produce commercial yields.

Loams and silt loams are preferred when large yields are more important than earliness and moisture is likely to become limited. These soils have good water retention and are relatively free from leaching. They have high base exchange capacities and will absorb and hold large quantities of nutrients. Consequently, phosphorus and potassium can usually be applied sufficiently before planting to supply the crop during its full development.

Clays and heavy soils are not usually well adapted for intensive vegetable production because of poor aeration and consequent poor nutrient liberation and root growth. They may, however, be used advantageously for late crops started during warm, dry weather. If worked when wet, these soils will compact severely.

Well-drained muck soils are used for many leafy vegetables and for some root and bulb crops. The muck forms a very fine seedbed for excellent germination and emergence for small-seeded vegetables. These and other organic soils provide good moisture-holding capacity and can supply a relatively large amount of nitrogen for annual crop growth. However, muck soils tend to warm up slowly in the spring and are not conducive for most early plantings. These soils are very light and subject to wind erosion any time they are fallow. A good drainage system is important to remove water from the soil in the spring and after a heavy rain. To deal with some of these disadvantages, several cultural practices have been widely adapted to muck soils; these include the use of raised beds, fall cover crops, and subirrigation to control the water table.

Topography and Drainage

Soils with only a slight grade will generally have good air and water drainage, making them desirable for growing vegetables. When soils of moderate to steep grades are used, measures should be adopted to conserve soil and moisture. These include no-till planting, terracing, contour cultivation, and strip cropping.

Flat land may have no erosion problem, but it can have drainage and leaching problems. If the subsoil is loose and permits ready drainage, no provision for drainage need be made; but, if the subsoil is tight, and water tends to stand on the land, a drainage system pays big dividends. Properly installed tile is best because it permits free use of the land, although open ditch drainage is better than none. Care must be taken to prevent overdrainage because excessive leaching and lack of moisture may result.

Leaching is greatest during periods when the land is not in use, especially in the winter. During these periods, some sort of cover crop may be used to absorb nutrients as they are liberated and to hold them for use by the next crop.

Southern and southeastern exposures are preferred for early spring and fall crops. A sunny slope dries and warms earlier in the spring than a northern exposure.

PREPARING THE SOIL

Whether from transplants or from seeding directly in the field, successful stand establishment requires a planting bed with soil in good tilth (physical condition). The soil should be free of trash, clods, and any other debris that can interfere with seed germination and plant root growth. The soil surface should be loose and open, with a minimum of crusting (a form of soil compaction) after a rain or irrigation. Tilling excessively or overworking the soil to form a fine seedbed can damage the structure of the soil's upper portion, causing it to quickly dry out.

Breaking

Land should be loosened 6–8 inches for vegetables. If the soil has never been plowed more than 6 inches, care should be taken to bring up only about an inch of subsoil at a time, especially if the subsoil is fine-textured. Growers sometimes use deep plowing (at least 12 inches) to aid in disease control. By deep plowing, they hope to put fungus-causing spores, such as sclerotinia in lettuce, beyond the reach of tillage tools and the plant root system.

Fall plowing has advantages in regions of winter freezing, but in the South its value is questionable because of leaching and erosion of sloping soils, which do not freeze much in the winter. However, if level loamy soils are plowed deeply, and especially if a covering of coarse organic matter is turned under, the losses from leaching and erosion will generally not be great and probably will be more than offset by the following advantages: 1) improved physical conditions, resulting from alternate wetting and drying and light freezing; 2) reduction in insects, because of exposure to the weather; 3) rotting of organic materials in contact with the soil, thereby increasing the humus and liberating nutrients; and 4) relieving the pressure of spring work by making it possible to work the soil earlier in the spring.

Spring plowing should not be done too far in advance of planting unless heavy cover crops are turned under. Special care must be used to avoid working the soil when it is too wet. If the soil crumbles readily after being pressed in the hand, it is dry enough to plow; but if it retains its form, the land is too wet for breaking.

Finishing

Vegetables with small seeds require a fine seedbed free of trash for even seeding and uniform germination. Plowed land must be disced well, usually in both directions, before planting. A harrow and float are commonly used to follow the discings for final seedbed preparation. A wide variety of harrows are used; the most popular types are spike-tooth and spring-tooth harrows. Cultipackers and rollers also break up clods and smooth the surface for planting. If vegetables are planted on raised beds, power bedders or a set of disc tillers followed by a bed shaper are used to make the beds.

ORGANIC MATTER

Through good management, most vegetable soils can maintain their high level of productivity. Many low-producing and marginal soils may be improved by sound management practices that involve a combination of tillage, cultural practices, cropping systems, and soil treatments. Central to any soil management program is the maintenance of soil organic matter through the use of manures, sod, and cover crops.

Organic matter constitutes the active or "living" component of the soil, affecting physical and chemical properties. It consists of plant and animal residues in various stages of decomposition and acts as a storehouse for nitrogen, sulfur, and phosphorus. Organic matter increases the cation exchange capacity of the soil and serves as a buffer for chemical reactions.

Organic matter functions as a granulator of soil particles, promoting better soil structure. It increases the porosity of heavy soils, which, in turn, increases water absorption and lessens water runoff, leaching, and erosion. The increased porosity also causes greater aeration, which favors the right kind of bacteria for nutrient liberation and direct chemical oxidation processes. On the other hand, organic matter will help keep sandy soils from becoming too porous. The dark color imparted by organic matter increases heat absorption, aiding the soil to warm up quickly, provided that the amount of water present is not excessive.

However, the use of fresh organic matter too close to the planting time of vegetables may cause problems including 1) burning from rapid decomposition, 2) formation of excessively aerated layers and pockets, which interfere with water movement, 3) locking up of available nitrogen by decomposition bacteria, 4) mechanical interference to plowing and cultivation, and 5) formation of toxic organic compounds, under certain anaerobic and non-colloidal conditions. If air and moisture are favorable and sufficient time is allowed, these difficulties are usually overcome. The addition of lime, if needed, and nitrate will aid in cases of nitrogen deficiency.

Soils differ considerably in their organic matter content. In the semiarid climate of the West, soil organic matter content is quite low, usually less than 1%. In eastern regions, and in areas of higher rainfall, vegetation is more abundant, and organic matter levels in soils may range upwards to 10–15%, although 3–5% is more common.

In most mineral soils used for vegetable production, organic matter breaks down quickly from oxidation as a result of intensive cultivation and frequent irrigation. The other major loss of organic matter from soils is crop removal. Growers try to maintain soil organic matter levels by the use of green-manure crops, sod rotations, cover crops, animal manures, and mulches and composts. Unfortunately, in most cultivated soils, any long-term increase in soil organic matter would be highly unlikely. Soils such as peats and mucks are inherently high in organic material and generally do not require special practices to maintain their organic matter content.

Maintaining Organic Matter with Green-Manure and Cover Crops

Green-manure crops are grown during the same season as a cash crop and are plowed under before they mature. At this stage, plants contain the highest amount of nitrogen plus adequate moisture for rapid decay. Green vegetation incorporated into the soil rots much more quickly than dry material. When vegetation is allowed to dry out before it is turned under, nutrients are transformed to less available forms. Long exposure to oxidation in the weather may result in some loss of nitrogen. Common green-manure crops are sweet clover, soybeans, sudan grass, and a mixture of peas and oats.

Perhaps the best system for maintaining soil organic matter levels is a rotation that includes the extended use of a legume or grass sod. Leaving the soil undisturbed for an extended period under a sod will minimize organic matter oxidation and may cause some accumulation from root disintegration. Including grasses and legumes in a rotation once every 3 years not only helps maintain organic matter but also promotes good structure and friability of the soil.

Although green manures and sod rotations are probably the cheapest and most effective ways to maintain organic matter and secure nitrogen, they are not always feasible. Production and marketing decisions, land availability, and financial conditions may dictate when or what rotations to use. For a grower located on a limited area of land, it may be economically prohibitive to take the land out of production for any extended period by growing sod or green-manure crops.

When rotations and green-manure crops are not feasible, fall-seeded cover crops may be used. The cover crops are planted after harvest and are turned under in the early spring, in time so as not to interfere with planting. Seeding cover crops in the fall is a common practice on sandy soils that are subject to blowing. Generally, grasses are used as cover crops because they are easily started and form a nonerosive surface which quickly prevents leaching. Rye is almost universally used as a winter cover by farmers, but there is some question as to its value for the southern vegetable growers, because it is difficult to kill and hinders early gardening. In many cases in the southern states, vegetables are grown in the late fall and early spring, and cool-season crops are grown during January and February so that rye would be of little value. Oats make a good cover if sown in the fall, but this crop is subject to winter injury.

Various methods are employed in the planting of cover crops. A seed drill has the advantage of planting at uniform depth and rate and saves unnecessary operations. The hand-broadcast method is uncertain and requires more seed for satisfactory coverage.

Maintaining Organic Matter with Animal Manures

If animal manure can be secured cheaply, it is one of the best materials for maintaining the organic content of the soil as well as a good source of nitrogen. Usually, it is advantageous to use fresh manure in the fall and well-rotted manure in the spring. Fresh and straw manures may cause damage if used too near planting time.

Decomposed manure that has been well cared for is valuable because it has no burning effects and can be applied just ahead of the crop. It offers less mechanical interference to plant roots and equipment and generally produces more uniform action throughout the soil mass than fresh manure. If excessive leaching has been stopped, it will have a high percentage of total nutrients and usually contains more phosphorus in relation to nitrogen than fresh manure, thus furnishing a more balanced nutrient supply. The decomposition process destroys or reduces weed seed germination.

If applied far enough in advance of the crop, fresh and straw manures have several important advantages over rotted manure: 1) fewer nutrients are lost through decomposition and leaching, 2) more bacteria are added to the soil, 3) more energy is provided for bacteria, resulting in a much greater liberation of nutrients through solvent action, and 4) buffer effects are greater.

The rate of manure application varies greatly with the land, the crop, the cost of manure, and the kind of manure. Often 30–40 tons, especially of the straw mix of cow manure, are not excessive. Many experiment stations have shown that light applications supplemented by commercial fertilizers, especially phosphate, are more economical than manure alone. Chicken manure should be put on very lightly and far enough from the plants to avoid burning. Broadcasting of manure is best, except in the case of widely spaced hills of cucurbits or melons.

In many cases, animal manures are rather expensive and difficult to secure, especially for a market gardener who keeps no livestock. However, with tractors replacing animals on the farm, more crop residues are available for maintaining soil organic matter.

CONSERVATION TILLAGE — "NO-TILL"

Conservation tillage systems, such as "no-till" culture, have become accepted practices in the production of corn, soybeans, and other non-irrigated agronomic crops. Vegetables traditionally have required more intensive management, and conservation tillage methods are not used to any great extent. Depending on the crop, a grower may use as many as six different tillage operations in a growing season.

There are, however, certain situations where conservation tillage may be used. No-till systems offer the advantages of moisture conservation and erosion control, making it possible to grow vegetables on sloping, highly erodible soils. The mulch, or plant residue, that is left on the surface acts as a barrier, protecting the soil against the impact of rain drops. The surface mulch also reduces moisture evaporation and helps retain moisture under drought conditions. Reducing tillage trips across the field protects the soil structure from breakdown and compaction under heavy equipment use.

When vegetables are grown under no-till culture, the seed is planted in previously undisturbed soil by means of a heavy special planter equipped to plant through a surface residue in firm soil. Proper planting is critical to ensure uniformity of emergence and yield, and seeding depth must be carefully adjusted according to the surface mulch and soil moisture content. Fertilizers and pesticides must be applied to the soil surface or in the narrow, tilled area of the row. Without cultivation, weed control is dependent on herbicides. This is critical if no-till culture is to be successful. Weeds growing at planting are killed with a contact herbicide. Annual summer weeds are controlled with herbicide combinations.

Early spring plantings generally do not lend themselves to no-till systems because cool soil temperatures and wet conditions that occur with this type of culture slow germination and increase the incidence of seedling diseases. The potential for insect and disease problems is greater with no-till than with conventional systems because no-till culture gives pests a stable environment for development. Previous crop residues can hinder mechanical harvesting of vegetables.

SOIL REACTION (pH)

The soil reaction, or pH, is a measure of the acidity or alkalinity of a soil. The pH scale ranges from 1 to 14; a pH value of 7.0 is neutral, values below 7.0 are acid, and those above 7.0 are alkaline.

Most vegetable crops on mineral soils grow best in a pH range of 5.5–7.0 (Figure 6.1). However, if the proper amounts and ratios of nutrients for the crop are maintained, and other elements, such as aluminum, are not present in high concentrations, the optimum pH growth range can be expanded to 5.0–8.0. On muck soils, or highly organic soils, a pH of 5.0–6.0 is best. Sometimes potatoes may be grown in a soil with a pH of about 5.0 in order to avoid serious damage from scab disease. Cabbage may also be grown in soil with a pH slightly above 7.0 to reduce incidence of club root.

In eastern growing areas of the U.S. and in most humid regions, many soils are naturally acid or become acid under present soil management systems. The most common cause of acidity in vegetable soils is the use of chemical fertilizers, specifically, ammonium containing N fertilizers. Bacteria in the soil convert ammonium ions to nitrate ions, releasing hydrogen into the soil solution. Other factors resulting in increased soil acidity are the decomposition of organic matter and calcium removal by crops or leaching.

In western growing areas and in arid climates, the soil pH is usually neutral or alkaline. This results from a lack of significant leaching and the accumulation of basic cations such as calcium, magnesium, potassium, and sodium.

Optimum pH levels are very important for vegetable fertility, because nutrient availability is determined by the level of soil acidity or alkalinity (Figure 6.2). In acid soils, potassium, calcium, and magnesium may be deficient, and the availability and uptake of phosphorus is reduced. Minor elements such as aluminum and manganese are more soluble at low pH and may become toxic. Also,

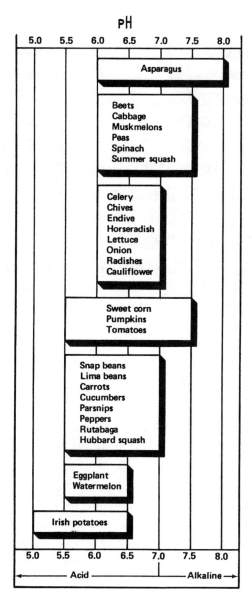

Figure 6.1. Optimum pH ranges for vegetable crops. (Source: Gerber, J. M., and J. M. Swiader. 1982. *Liming Vegetable Crops.* University of Illinois Coop. Ext. Ser. Hort. Facts VC–18–82)

microbial activity in the soil is hindered in acid soils, thus restricting the decomposition of plant residues and the mineralization of organic nitrogen. In alkaline soils with a pH above 7.4, deficiencies of such micronutrients as iron, manganese, zinc, and boron are most likely to occur. At high pH levels (above 9.0), excess sodium can retard the growth of some crops.

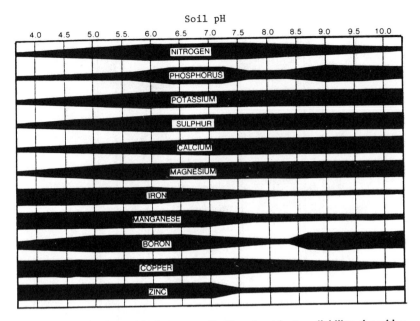

Figure 6.2. The relationship between soil pH and nutrient availability; the wider the band, the greater the availability.

LIMING

Liming neutralizes excess soil acidity and also supplies calcium and magnesium. Soil pH tests indicate the soil acidity but do not show the amount of lime needed to adjust soil pH to a specified value. This is determined by the lime index or buffer pH.

The amount of lime needed to raise the pH a given amount will vary, depending on the soil type, organic matter content, degree of reaction present, reaction desired, and liming material used. Heavy clay soils require more lime than light sandy soils. If soil pH tests indicate strong acidity, it is usually advisable to apply lime in several smaller rates rather than in one large application. For most vegetable soils, 4 tons per acre is the maximum amount of lime that is practical to apply at one time.

Liming Materials

Several types of lime are generally used for vegetable crops (Table 6.1). Liming materials having the highest total oxide content and the finest particle size will neutralize soil acidity most rapidly per unit weight of material used. However, fine lime breaks down rather quickly, and applications may have to be made more frequently to maintain the desired soil pH.

Table 6.1. Types of Liming Materials

Material	CaO Content	MgO Content	Solubility
	(%)	*(%)*	
Calcite	50–56	1–4	Very high
Magnesian	39–42	5–15	Moderate
Dolomite	30	20	Low – moderate
Hydrated lime	60	12	High

Calcitic or high-calcium lime should be used where soil pH and calcium are low and magnesium is high. This material is generally more soluble than other types of ground limestone and corrects soil acidity rapidly. Magnesian or hi-mag lime is intermediate in solubility and should be used where pH, calcium, and magnesium are low. Dolomitic lime is recommended where magnesium is particularly low. This is the least soluble of the materials, and too much magnesium is much more likely to cause harmful effects than too much calcium. Hydrated lime reacts more rapidly than other types of lime but is expensive and difficult to use, since it can burn plants. Liquid lime or fluid lime is a water suspension of finely ground limestone. There is generally no difference in the rate of activity of liquid lime over dry limestone, provided both materials are ground to the same fineness.

Lime should be mixed in the top 3-4 inches of soil. A commercial lime spreader is best for making application, although a shovel can be made for small areas. A grain drill can also be used, when light applications are made.

VEGETABLE NUTRITION

Sixteen chemical elements, known as nutrients, are required by vegetable crops to maintain life and growth. Three of the sixteen elements (carbon, hydrogen, and oxygen) are supplied primarily from air and water. The remaining thirteen are normally absorbed by plant roots. Very often, the soil levels of these nutrients are inadequate to support optimum growth, and they must be supplied by fertilizers.

Primary Plant Nutrients

Nitrogen, phosphorus, and potassium are the major fertilizer nutrients, since they are required in relatively large quantities and are most often lacking in vegetable soils.

Nitrogen is a vital component of protoplasm, chlorophyll molecules, nucleic acids (DNA and RNA), and amino acids, from which proteins are made. Nitrogen builds up the vegetative portions, producing large, green leaves, and is also necessary for filling out fruits. If it is present in large amounts in relation to other elements, it can cause excessive vegetative growth and succulence, and can seriously delay fruiting.

Phosphorus is necessary for cellular metabolism and is utilized by the plant in the storage and transfer of radiant energy to chemical energy through energy-rich linkages (ATP and ADP). Phosphorus stimulates early growth and root production and promotes maturity and seed development. It is especially essential in fruit production. The plant will be stunted and the fruit will fail to set if phosphorus is inadequate, especially if nitrogen is high.

Phosphorus is an immobile element in soils, and soon after application becomes absorbed on the clay particles and does not remain in solution. Consequently, roots must come in direct contact with the fertilizer, so phosphorus is often applied in bands at the time of planting to provide high concentrations near the roots of young plants (see "Starter Solutions" under "Methods of Application").

Potassium is important in the formation and translocation of carbohydrates and therefore is especially important for root and tuber crops (particularly potatoes) and in the formation of rigid stems in celery and rhubarb. It is also important in disease resistance, cell division, and water relations. Potassium enhances fruit size and quality and has been shown to influence ripening in tomatoes.

Secondary Plant Nutrients

Calcium, magnesium, and sulfur are generally described as secondary plant nutrients since they are not deficient as often as nitrogen, phosphorus, and potassium, and because their plant contents tend to be lower than the primary elements. In many vegetable soils, calcium and magnesium are naturally plentiful and are the dominant cations.

The main function of calcium in the plant is maintaining the structure of membranes and cell walls. It is also believed that calcium counteracts toxic effects of organic acids in the plant and the harmful effects of too large amounts of other elements such as magnesium, sodium, and boron.

Most vegetable crops need relatively small amounts of calcium, and "true" deficiencies of this nutrient are uncommon since most agricultural soils are relatively abundant in this element. The major requirement as a fertilizer usually occurs on very acid soils where lime is needed. This is most common in vegetable regions of the Midwest and Southeast. However, in some areas of the West, the decreased use of well water and increased irrigation with project water has created a greater need for calcium on some crops. Project water, which originates as snow-melt and mountain runoff, contains very small amounts of calcium, compared to many well waters that can contain enough calcium to supply crop needs. In areas such as these, where calcium may be needed, but there is no need to increase soil pH, gypsum (calcium sulfate) should be used.

There are times, however, when calcium deficiencies occur in vegetables even though the actual amount of calcium in the soil is quite high. These are most often caused by other factors, such as water stress and environmental influences that restrict the movement of calcium to specific sites within the plant, most commonly fruits and growing points. In reality, these are not true deficiencies that affect the whole plant, but are localized areas of calcium stress in the plant, and are generally referred to as calcium disorders. The list of these calcium-related disorders in vegetable crops is quite long and includes blossom-end rot in tomatoes, peppers, and watermelons, tipburn in cabbage and lettuce, cavity spot in carrots and parsnips, blackheart in celery, and internal browning in Brussels sprouts. Soil application of calcium may not alleviate the problem; foliar applications of calcium (as calcium nitrate or calcium chloride) are usually more effective.

Magnesium is essential to plant growth since it comprises the central position in the chlorophyll molecule, making it vital to photosynthesis. Much of the magnesium in plants functions as an enzyme activator for a wide diversity of reactions. Magnesium is most likely to be deficient in vegetables grown on acid sandy soils in areas of moderate to high rainfall or when large amounts of calcitic limestone or potassium have been applied. A magnesium deficiency may occur in carrots, celery, tomatoes, and spinach. Dolomitic limestone can be applied on acid sandy soils that need both magnesium and lime, or magnesium sulfate (epsom salts) may be used when magnesium is low but lime is not needed.

Sulfur is needed by most vegetable crops in about the same quantities as phosphorus and is an essential component in proteins. Among vegetable crops, crucifers have perhaps the highest sulfur requirement.

In many vegetable growing regions, environmental sources of sulfur supply a major portion of plant sulfur requirements. These sources include mineralized organic matter, atmospheric sulfur released from emissions of fossil fuels and returned to the soil in rain water, and sulfur impurities in fertilizers and pesticides. Annual precipitation deposits of sulfur can range from 1 to over 100 pounds per acre. In recent years, however, this source of sulfur, along with that from fertilizer by-products, has diminished considerably with increased environmental controls of emissions and increased use of high-analysis fertilizers. This has led to speculation that sulfur deficiencies may develop in the next 5–15 years.

The need for sulfur would most likely occur in sandy soils or in soils low in organic matter located upwind from urban industrial centers. Either elemental or sulfate forms of sulfur fertilizers can be used on vegetable crops, although sulfate forms are more readily available to the plant. For most crops, an application of 10–30 pounds per acre of sulfur should correct a sulfur deficiency.

Micronutrients

The elements boron, copper, manganese, iron, zinc, and molybdenum are classified as essential micronutrients because they are required for proper plant growth, although in relatively small amounts. Even though their requirements are relatively low, micronutrients are just as essential for plant growth as the larger amounts of primary and secondary nutrients. A micronutrient deficiency can be just as limiting and reduce yields just as much as a deficiency of any of the major nutrients.

Vegetables show a wide range of response to micronutrients, and a micronutrient deficiency usually occurs only in specific crops. If the soil is low or deficient in a certain micronutrient, response to application of that micronutrient would likely occur if the crop has a high requirement for that micronutrient (Table 6.2). For example, boron is the most widely deficient micronutrient in vegetable crops, and beets, broccoli, cauliflower, celery, and turnips are particularly susceptible to a boron deficiency. However, in certain situations, crops may respond to micronutrient fertilizers, even though their requirements may be low to moderate.

Very often problems that arise in micronutrient nutrition in vegetables result from low availability and not from the soil micronutrient content. In general, deficiencies of most micronutrients are accentuated by five situations: 1) strongly

Table 6.2. Relative Response of Selected Vegetable Crops to Micronutrients[1]

Vegetable	Iron	Manganese	Zinc	Copper	Boron	Molybedenum
Asparagus	M[2]	L	L	L	L	L
Beans	H	H	H	L	L	M
Beets	H	H	M	H	H	H
Broccoli	H	M	—	M	M	H
Cabbage	M	M	—	M	M	M
Carrots	—	M	L	M	M	L
Cauliflower	H	M	—	M	H	H
Celery	—	M	—	M	H	L
Cucumbers	—	M	—	M	L	—
Lettuce	—	H	—	H	M	H
Onions	—	H	H	H	L	H
Peas	—	H	L	L	L	M
Potatoes	—	H	M	L	L	L
Radishes	—	H	—	M	M	M
Spinach	H	H	—	H	M	H
Sweet corn	M	M	H	M	L	M
Tomatoes	H	M	M	M	L	M
Turnips	—	M	—	M	H	M

[1]Source: Vitosh, M. L., D. D. Warncke, and R. E. Lucas. 1973. *Secondary and Micronutrients for Vegetables and Field Crops.* Michigan State University Coop. Ext. Ser. Bull. E–486.

[2]Relative response: low (L), medium (M), high (H).

weathered soils, 2) coarse-textured soils, 3) soils high in pH, 4) highly organic soils such as peats and mucks (especially for copper), and 5) soils inherently low in organic matter.

Perhaps the single most important factor determining micronutrient availability in vegetable soils is soil pH (Figure 6.2). The availability of boron, copper, manganese, zinc, and iron decreases as pH increases. Molybdenum is an exception, and its availability increases as pH increases. For vegetable crops, maintaining soil pH between 6.0 and 6.8 is best, both to avoid a deficiency and to avoid toxicity from excess micronutrient solubility.

When present in the soil at higher than optimum concentrations, or when applied in excessive amounts, some micronutrients (most commonly boron and manganese, but sometimes zinc and copper) can have adverse effects on plant growth. Sensitive vegetables, such as snap beans and cucumbers, can be damaged from residual carry-over of boron applied to previous crops.

Micronutrients should be applied to vegetables only on competent advice or where experience has proven their application to be necessary. Soil and plant tissue tests will aid in diagnosing a micronutrient deficiency, although these are not always reliable. In most situations, either soil or foliar applications can be used to correct a micronutrient deficiency. Plant response is quicker with foliar application, but crop injury is more likely from fertilizer misuse.

FERTILIZING VEGETABLE CROPS

Commercial fertilizers are added to a soil for the purpose of directly increasing the amounts of nutrients available to plants. They are not added to improve physical conditions or to make soil reserves available. Manures and lime do more than simply add nutrients and, for this reason, often produce better results than commercial fertilizers alone. However, manures and lime cannot be depended on to provide enough available nutrients in soils with low reserves; and even in fertile soils, organic materials and lime may cause improper nutrient ratios. Commercial fertilizers are necessary to furnish limiting elements in the most economical manner and to maintain proper ratios of the nutrients for the particular crop (Figure 6.3).

Fertilizer Analysis, Formula, and Ratio

Any substance that can supply nutrients to growing plants should be considered as a fertilizer. Animal manure, ammonium nitrate, bone meal, compost, and superphosphate are all examples of fertilizer materials, although the amount of nutrients supplied may differ. Plant response and economics should dictate the

Figure 6.3. Celery grown on sandy soil in Florida; plants on left received well-balanced fertilizer regime, while those on right were unfertilized.

form of fertilizer used. If animal manure is available and can be spread easily, it makes an excellent fertilizer. However, when fertilizer must be purchased, more nutrients for the least amount of money are usually found in a bag of commercial inorganic fertilizer, such as the 5-10-10 and 10-20-20 formulations.

The grade, or analysis, of a fertilizer should always be printed on the bag, such as 5-10-5. These numbers represent respectively the total nitrogen (N), available phosphorus (expressed as P_2O_5), and water-soluble potassium oxide or potash (K_2O) content of the fertilizer in terms of percent by weight. For example, a 100-pound bag of 5-10-5 would contain 5 pounds of nitrogen, 10 pounds of P_2O_5, and 5 pounds K_2O. From the standpoint of economy, the higher the analysis, the more economical the fertilizer; a 10-20-10 fertilizer furnishes more nutrients per dollar than a 5-10-5. However, the high-analysis fertilizers are a little more difficult to distribute evenly and are more likely to burn on contact with seeds or plants; other than this, they are as good as the low-analysis fertilizers.

Fertilizer ratio differs from analysis in that it expresses the fertilizer in the relative proportions of one element to another, usually in terms of nitrogen. For example, 5-10-5 is the analysis, but 1-2-1 is the ratio. Therefore, as in this case, the ratio simply indicates that there is twice as much available phosphorus as nitrogen and the same amount of soluble potassium as nitrogen.

The formula indicates the quantity and composition of the various ingredients or compounds that are mixed together in a ton of the fertilizer. For a standard vegetable fertilizer with an analysis of 5-10-10, the formula may read: 365 pounds ammonium sulfate (21% N), 484 pounds calcium nitrate (15.5% N), 667 pounds triple superphosphate (45% P_2O_5), and 484 pounds potassium chloride (62% K_2O). When choosing fertilizers, one should know the formula, the rate of avail-ability of the nitrogen, and the effect the compounds have on soil reaction.

Fertilizers

The composition of various fertilizers is shown in Table 6.3. Nitrogen and potassium fertilizers should be used with caution since there could be some danger of injury from high salt levels when placed in close contact with seeds and roots. Vegetables such as beans, carrots, and onions are particularly salt-sen-sitive and can easily be injured by banding high fertilizer rates.

As indicated earlier, ammonium-based fertilizers will generally leave an acid residue, while nitrate materials are mostly basic (ammonium nitrate is slightly acid). Anhydrous ammonia contains the highest percentage of nitrogen of any fertilizer and is the cheapest source of nitrogen. It is commonly used for preplant applica-tions. However, free ammonia is toxic to vegetables, especially seedlings, and it should not be placed near seeds or roots.

Many vegetable growers prefer to use urea (a high N solid fertilizer produced by reacting ammonia with carbon dioxide under pressure) or nonpressure nitro-gen solutions (aqueous solutions of nitrogen salts, most commonly mixtures of ammonium nitrate and urea). These materials, along with diammonium phosphate (DAP), are safe when broadcast but can cause injury when banded on alkaline soils. Granular ammonium nitrate and nitrogen solutions are most often used for sidedressed nitrogen applications. Problems from fertilizer injury are more likely to occur on light-textured soils than on silt loams or clays.

Organic materials, such as cottonseed meal, linseed meal, castor-oil meal, blood tankage, fish tankage, and guano, are neutral in their effect on soil reaction. The high cost of organic carriers and their slow availability tend to make them impractical in most situations for use in commercial production.

Methods of Application

Broadcasting. Scattering the fertilizer on the soil surface, either by hand or by machine, followed by incorporation with a plow or disk is the most common method of application used. Usually 50–60% of the recommended nitrogen and all of the phosphorus and potassium (except on sandy soils) are broadcast. Broadcasting fertilizer too far ahead of planting on sandy soils, however, can cause leaching losses of nitrogen and sometimes potassium. Since the fertilizer is inti-mately mixed with a large volume of soil, there is also an opportunity for increased phosphorus fixation on alkaline or very acid soils.

Table 6.3. Typical Composition of Fertilizer Materials

Organic Material	Nitrogen	Phosphorus	Potassium
	(% dry wt.)	(% dry wt.)	(% dry wt.)
Bat guano	10.0	1.8	1.7
Blood	13.0	0.9	0.8
Blood and bone	6.5	3.1	—
Bone, black	1.3	6.6	—
Bone meal, raw	3.0	6.6	—
steamed	2.0	6.6–14	—
Castor bean meal	5.5	0.9	0.8
Cattle manure (dried)	1.5	2.0	1.2
Chicken manure (dried)	3.5	2.0	2.6
Cottonseed meal	6.0	1.3	0.8
Fish meal	10.0	3.8	—
Garbage tankage	1.5	0.9	0.6
Horn and hoof meal	12.0	0.9	—
Seaweed (kelp)	0.2	0.1	0.6
Sewage sludge	1.5	0.6	0.3
Activated sewage sludge	6.0	1.3	0.1
Tankage	9.0	2.6	—

Inorganic Fertilizer	Total N	Available P_2O_5	Water-soluble K_2O
	(%)	(%)	(%)
Nitrogen materials			
Ammonium nitrate	33.5–34	—	—
Ammonium nitrate-sulfate	30	—	—
Monoammonium phosphate	11	48	—
Ammonium phosphate-sulfate	16	20	—
Ammonium phosphate-nitrate	27	12	—
Diammonium phosphate	16–18	46–48	—
Ammonium sulfate	21	—	—
Anhydrous ammonia	82	—	—
Aqua ammonia	20	—	—
Calcium ammonium nitrate solution	17	—	—
Calcium nitrate	15.5	—	—
Calcium cyanamide	20–22	—	—
Sodium nitrate	16	—	—
Urea	45–46	—	—
Urea formaldehyde	38	—	—
Urea ammonium nitrate solution	28–32	—	—
Phosphate materials			
Single superphosphate	—	18–20	—
Triple superphosphate	—	45–46	—
Phosphoric acid	—	52–54	—
Superphosphoric acid	—	76–83	—
Potash materials			
Potassium chloride	—	—	60–62
Potassium nitrate	13	—	44–46
Potassium sulfate	—	—	50–53
Sulfate of potash-magnesia	—	—	22–26

Banding. Although broadcasting is necessary when soil tests call for large amounts of fertilizer, small amounts can be applied more efficiently in a band. The fertilizer is placed 2 inches to the side and 2 inches below the level of the seed in the row at planting. This is especially effective when phosphorus is added to either cold or calcareous soils. Also, since banding places the fertilizer close to the plant roots where it is needed, less nitrogen and potassium are likely to be lost through leaching. When applied in a band, rates of nitrogen and potassium combined generally should not exceed 80–100 pounds per acre because of possible injury to roots.

Sidedressing. A sidedressing is an application of fertilizer (usually nitrogen, and sometimes potassium on sandy soils) during the season, 6–10 inches from the base of the plant, and lightly incorporated into the soil. The purpose of sidedressing is to supply additional nutrients during growth of the crop (Figure 6.4). Although fertilizer nutrients are needed for early growth, the greatest quantities of nutrients are usually taken up during the second half of the season. On sandy soils, much of the nitrogen fertilizer applied at planting may be leached out before it can be used by the plant.

Figure 6.4. Vegetables on sandy soils are commonly sidedressed with liquid nitrogen solutions.

Starter Solutions. Water-soluble and liquid fertilizers high in phosphorus, and usually containing some nitrogen and potassium, are used to stimulate the growth of young transplants. The solution is directly applied to the roots at planting and provides nutrients in a highly available form. The use of starter fertilizers should be considered standard practice for plantings made early in the season in cool, wet soils. Starter fertilizers are used commonly with tomatoes, peppers, melons, and cole crops (cabbage, broccoli, cauliflower). Typical starter fertilizers include 9-45-15, 10-52-8, and 16-32-16, but any water-soluble fertilizer high in phosphorus will do.

Foliar Fertilization. Plant leaves are able to absorb and utilize nutrients sprayed directly on them. This method of application has had the greatest use with nutrients required in only small amounts and when a quick plant response to fertilization is desired. Nutrients required in large amounts such as nitrogen, phosphorus, and potassium are usually added to soil rather than foliage because sufficient amounts of these nutrients needed for plant growth applied to leaves may damage vegetation due to leaf burn.

Fertigation. Applying fertilizers with irrigation water has been in practice for about 30 years. The advent of center-pivot, lateral-move, and solid-set sprinkler systems has made fertigation a practical system for uniform application of fertilizers. Multiple small applications are used to increase fertilizer efficiency, and as a precaution against burning foliage, especially from nitrogen fertilizers. When used in conjunction with drip irrigation, growers benefit from the reduction in water consumption and from greatly increased efficiency of fertilizer use.

This method requires considerable management input, including calibration of irrigating equipment, operation of the sprinkler system, check valves, and safety equipment. Fertigation and foliar application are useful methods to supplement normal soil application.

DETERMINING FERTILIZER REQUIREMENTS

Due to strict requirements for produce quality, and for marketing reasons, fertilizer recommendations for vegetable crops usually are in excess of crop removal requirements. For example, nitrogen recommendations for sweet corn commonly exceed yield requirements and are designed to keep the husk green to allow marketing of the fresh product. Potassium recommendations in tomatoes are made to assure uniform ripening of fruits. In both cases, lower fertilizer rates would likely not affect yields but could sharply reduce market quality.

Soil Testing

Vegetable crops are fertilized on the basis of annual soil tests, along with soil type, crop requirements, field history, and good judgement based on experience. Standard tests for vegetable soils include pH, lime index, soil cation exchange capacity, soluble salts, available phosphorus, exchangeable potassium, calcium, and magnesium, and the percent base saturation. Special tests are also available to determine organic matter and some micronutrients (boron, manganese, and zinc). Tests for nitrogen are highly variable and are of little value in estimating the true nitrogen status of the soil.

Separate soil tests should be made for every field that differs in color, slope, drainage, or previous fertilization and cropping. Each sample should represent no more than 2–4 acres and should consist of several subsamples collected at random locations throughout the field. Samples are collected from the top 6–8 inches in the late fall when the soil is relatively dry but not frozen.

Determining Fertilizer Rates

Soil test results indicate the relative levels (very low, low, medium, high, very high) of plant-available phosphorus and potassium in the soil. The vegetable crops are divided into five categories according to their phosphorus and potassium requirements. These, along with the amounts of phosphorus and potassium to apply for each soil fertility level, are shown in Table 6.4. For example, if the soil test indicates that the relative levels of phosphorus and potassium are medium and low, respectively, the fertility recommendation for lettuce would be 100 pounds P_2O_5 per acre and 200 pounds K_2O per acre.

Phosphorus and potassium fertilizer recommendations are usually given in the oxide form of each element because most fertilizer grades are listed, sold, and discussed by the trade in this way. Some fertilizer is recommended even for soils testing high, in order to maintain adequate levels of fertility. A home garden may be treated as if all crops were in the highest fertilizer requirement category.

Since soil tests for nitrogen are of little value, the nitrogen recommendations (Table 6.5) are based on the needs of the crop, field trials, and yield potential. Previous cropping, the presence of decomposable residues, soil type, and leaching should also be considered when one is determining the amounts of nitrogen to apply. If the season is cool and wet, or the soil is poorly drained, additional nitrogen may be necessary. Light-colored soils usually have less than 2.5% organic matter and require higher nitrogen rates than dark-colored soils, where organic matter contents can range from 3% to over 10%.

Table 6.4. **Phosphorus (P$_2$O$_5$) and Potassium (K$_2$O) Requirements for Vegetables on Mineral Soils Related to Soil Test Results[1]**

Soil Test Results	Fertilizer Requirement				
	(lbs P$_2$O$_5$ per acre)				
Phosphorus					
Very low	250	250	200	150	100
Low	250	200	150	100	100
Medium	200	150	100	50	50
High	100	50	50	50	0
Very high	0	0	0	0	0
	(lbs K$_2$O per acre)				
Potassium					
Very low	350	300	250	200	150
Low	300	250	200	150	100
Medium	250	200	150	100	50
High	150	100	50	50	0
Very high	50	50	0	0	0
	Vegetable				
	Celery Eggplants Rhubarb Tomatoes[3] Asparagus[3] (cutting bed)	Cucumbers[3] Broccoli Brussels sprouts Cabbage Cauliflower Horseradish Melons[3] Peppers Squashes[3] Pumpkins[3] Tomatoes[2] Asparagus (new bed)	Cucumbers[2] Lettuce Onions Melons[2] Pumpkins[2] Squashes[2] Spinach Sweet corn Asparagus[2] (cutting bed)	Beets Carrots Parsnips Radishes Turnips	Beans Peas

[1]Timing and placement will vary with the specific crop.

[2]Phosphorus requirement only.

[3]Potassium requirement only.

Table 6.5. Nitrogen Requirements for Vegetable Crops on Mineral Soils

Crop	N Requirement (lbs. per acre)[1]	
	Dark-colored Soils	Light-colored Soils
Asparagus	50	100
Beans	40	75
Beets	75	100
Broccoli	100	150
Cabbage	100	125
Carrots	75	100
Cauliflower	100	150
Celery	150	200
Cucumbers	75	125
Eggplants	75	125
Horseradish	50	100
Lettuce	80	120
Muskmelons	75	125
Onions	80	100
Parsnips	75	100
Peas	30	45
Peppers	75	125
Potatoes	120	180
Pumpkins and winter squash	75	125
Radishes	30	50
Rutabagas and turnips	50	80
Spinach	80	120
Summer squash	75	100
Sweet corn	80	120
Sweet potatoes	50	75
Tomatoes (processing)	60	100
(market)	100	150
Watermelons	75	125

[1]Timing and placement of N fertilizer will vary with the specific crop.

SELECTED REFERENCES

In addition to the references listed below, information on specific fertility recommendations for vegetable crops may be obtained from commercial production guides published by the cooperative extension service of the various state universities.

California Fertilizer Association. 1985. *Western Fertilizer Handbook*, 7th ed. Interstate Publishers, Inc., Danville, Illinois.

Gerber, J. M., and J. M. Swiader. 1982. *Liming Vegetable Crops*. Univ. of Illinois Coop. Ext. Ser. Hort. Facts VC-18-82.

Lorenz, O. A., and D. N. Maynard. 1988. *Knott's Handbook for Vegetable Growers*, 3rd ed. John Wiley & Sons, Inc., New York.

Maynard, D. N. 1979. Nutritional disorders of vegetable crops. *J. Plant Nutrition* 1:1–23.

Maynard, D. N. 1979. Seventy-five years of progress in the nutrition of vegetable crops. *HortScience* 14:355–358.

Minotti, P. L. 1975. Plant nutrition and vegetable crop quality. *HortScience* 10:54–56.

Mortvedt, J. J. (ed.). 1977. *Micronutrients in Agriculture*. Soil Sci. Soc. Amer., Madison, Wisconsin.

Olson, R. A., T. J. Army, J. J. Hanway, and V. J. Kilmer (eds.). 1971. *Fertilizer Technology and Use*. Soil Sci. Soc. Amer., Madison, Wisconsin.

Shear, C. B. 1975. Calcium-related disorders of fruits and vegetables. *HortScience* 10:361–365.

Tisdale, S. L., and W. L. Nelson. 1985. *Soil Fertility and Fertilizers*, 4th ed. Macmillan, New York.

Traynor, J. 1980. *Ideas in Soil and Plant Nutrition*. Kovak Books, Bakersfield, California.

Vitosh, M. L., D. D. Warncke, and R. E. Lucas. 1973. *Secondary and Micronutrients for Vegetables and Field Crops*. Michigan State Univ. Coop. Ext. Ser. Bull. E-486.

7

WEED MANAGEMENT
IN VEGETABLES

Weeds pose one of the most serious threats to vegetable production in the U.S., causing millions of dollars in losses as a result of lower yields, poorer quality, and reduced efficiency and higher production costs (Table 7.1). In cultivated vegetable crops, weeds regularly appear, almost immediately after soil tillage and to a lesser extent throughout the remaining growing period. Each farm, as well as each crop area within a farm, may reveal unique weed problems. In many less developed countries more worker-hours are spent on weeding crops than any other cropping practice activity.

The successful management of weeds requires an integrated program that includes chemical and nonchemical methods. Some control methods entail the physical destruction of weeds. Other methods aim to establish a vigorous crop that competes effectively with weeds. The decision on which methods to use depends on the weed pressure, labor availability, environmental concerns, marketing opportunities, and the particular weed and crop species.

WEEDS

The first step of weed management in vegetable crops begins with an understanding of the growth habits and biology of weeds. Each grower must know or develop information on the specific weed problems likely to be encountered in a particular crop planting.

Table 7.1. Estimated Average Annual Losses of Vegetables in the U.S. due to Weeds[1]

Vegetable Crop	Losses from Potential Production		
	Reduction	Quantity	Value
	(%)	(tons)	($1,000)
Broccoli	13	60,900	22,403
Cabbage	10	97,300	13,629
Spinach	19	9,550	3,834
Carrots	12	86,600	14,415
Onions	9	275,000	40,102
Potatoes	7	1,400,000	105,980
Lettuce	8	569,350	91,512
Tomatoes	10	207,600	154,457
Green beans	10	22,100	10,165
Sweet corn	11	82,200	22,320
Cucumbers	12	44,200	17,395
Muskmelons	10	60,150	12,967
Watermelons	9	232,350	16,016
Total		3,147,300	525,195

[1]Source: Chandler, J. L., A. S. Hamill, and A. G. Thomas. 1984. *Crop Losses due to Weeds in Canada and the United States.* Weed Science Soc. Amer., Champaign, Illinois.

Weed Classifications

Weeds can be divided into three general groups: grasses, which include crabgrass, foxtails, barnyardgrass, and wild proso millet; sedges, such as yellow nutsedge; and broadleaf weeds, such as pigweed, purslane, and common milkweed (Table 7.2). In grasses and sedges, growth comes from a meristem located at or near the soil surface, while in broadleaf weeds, growth can be initiated from both apical and lateral meristems.

Weeds can also be grouped according to their life cycle: annual, biennial, or perennial. The most serious problem weeds for vegetables are generally the summer annuals such as barnyardgrass, giant foxtail, purslane, and common lambsquarter, which complete their life cycle during the summer. Winter annual weeds (e.g., wild mustard, chickweed), which complete their life cycle when most vegetables are not planted, are usually not a problem, except with fall-planted vegetables (e.g., cole crops) and perennial crops (e.g., asparagus). Annual weeds reproduce mainly by seeds, and the aim in their successful management is to prevent their seed production.

Biennial weeds, such as wild carrot and wild parsnip, have a 2-year life cycle and are usually not a problem in annual vegetable crops. They occur primarily in reduced tillage or perennial crops and should be controlled in the first year as seedlings, before their seeds germinate the following spring.

Table 7.2. **Common Weeds in Vegetable Crops**

Broadleaves		
Annuals	**Biennials**	**Perennials**
Cocklebur	Common burdock	Canada thistle
Common lambsquarter	Evening primrose	Common milkweed
Common purslane	Wild carrot	Dandelion
Common ragweed	Wild parsnip	Field bindweed
Chickweed		Hemp dogbane
Galinsoga		Horsenettle
Giant ragweed		
Groundsel		
Jimsonweed		
Morning-glory		
Mustards		
Nightshade		
Pennycress		
Redroot pigweed		
Shepherds purse		
Smartweed		
Velvetleaf		

Grasses and Sedges	
Annuals	**Perennials**
Barnyardgrass	Johnsongrass
Fall panicum	Quackgrass
Foxtails	Wild garlic
Goosegrass	Yellow nutsedge
Crabgrass	
Shattercane	
Wild proso millet	

Perennial weeds, such as Canada thistle, field bindweed, johnsongrass, and yellow nutsedge, live more than 2 years and remain in fields until they are killed. Although they usually start from germinating seeds, many perennial weeds propagate and spread largely by asexual means (rhizomes, stolons, or tubers), making them difficult to control. Some perennial weeds may lose their leaves, while the stems of others may die back to the ground each winter. Managing perennial weeds requires a combination of mechanical and chemical methods, but even then their control may be difficult. It is usually best just not to use fields with perennial weed problems.

Weed Competition

Vegetables and weeds have the same basic requirements for growth and development. Weeds compete effectively with vegetables for water, nutrients, sunlight, carbon dioxide, and space. They usually dominate because of their more aggressive growth habit (Figure 7.1). The period from emergence until approximately 4 weeks later is a critical time for competition, especially for small-seeded crops like carrots and lettuce. Weeds can also harbor insects and disease. Carrots may be attacked by the carrot weevil which uses wild carrots as an alternate host. Onion thrips can live in ragweeds and wild mustards.

Figure 7.1. Weed competition is particularly severe in crops such as onions which are poor competitors.

Some weeds affect vegetable growth by releasing toxic or growth-inhibiting substances into the soil. This is known as *allelopathy* and is a form of weed competition. For example, leachates from common lambsquarter can significantly reduce the growth of tomatoes. For about 90 weed species some type of allelopathic potential has been reported.

In addition to yield reductions, poorer-quality crops are produced where weeds are present. Muskmelons grown where weeds are present are smaller and remain green longer than those produced in weed-free plots. Due to competition for water, blossom end-rot in tomatoes is more severe in fields infested with nightshade than in weed-free fields. A negative effect on vegetable quality can also occur from physical damage due to weeds or contamination of the harvested crop with weed seeds or parts. This is particularly troublesome for mechanically harvested crops used for processing. Increased expense in harvesting because of heavy weed populations can cause substantially higher production costs. Very often, vegetables faced with serious uncontrolled weed infestations are not harvested.

MECHANICAL AND CULTURAL CONTROL

Vegetable growers today must rely on sound, well-established mechanical and cultural practices for a good part of their weed control. In the past, the tendency was for growers to do less cultivating and to depend more on herbicides for weed control. This has changed, and today nonchemical weed management methods are of increasing importance due to public and industry concern with pesticides impacting the environment by leaching into groundwater sources, as well as from residues on food.

In addition, many older herbicides are no longer available. There are also many weed problems in vegetable crop production that cannnot be effectively solved with available chemicals. For these reasons, weed management should include nonchemical practices to combat and reduce weed problems. The modern vegetable grower should use chemical weed killers where practical and only as a supplement to good cultural and mechanical practices.

Plowing and Rotary Hoeing

Thorough working of the land prior to seeding or planting will kill many small weeds that have just germinated. Primary tillage operations prior to planting are particularly effective against perennial weeds. Moldboard plowing will destroy emerged annual weeds. Rotary hoeing is used with large-seeded vegetable crops such as sweet corn, beans, and peas and should be done after the weeds germinate but before they emerge. Once the crop germinates or transplants have been established, row cultivation is the most effective mechanical method in controlling weeds.

Cultivating

Cultivation, or intertillage of crops, is a very old agricultural practice that is used primarily to control weeds that emerge between rows of crops (Figure 7.2). It is most effective when weeds are breaking through the surface, since at this time weeds are not well established and merely breaking the soil surface will destroy them.

Frequent cultivations will be needed when conditions are favorable for the germination of weed seeds, such as after a rain or after the application of irrigation water. If cultivated when too wet, most classes of soils, except sands and loose peats and mucks, will bake on drying. If allowed to dry, the surface will have already become baked and hard and will not crumble when broken up. The best

Figure 7.2. Cultivation is used to control weeds that grow between the rows of snap beans.

time to cultivate after a rain or after the application of water is when the soil is dry enough to crumble, but not so dry as to break into lumps.

Shallow cultivation is preferable to deep cultivation to minimize damage to crop roots. Some vegetable growers in the past practiced deep cultivation when the plants were small, with the idea that breaking of the roots near the surface would result in greater development of the crop roots. Experimental evidence indicated that this was a mistake and that destroying the surface roots did not make the roots go deeper. On the contrary, deep cultivation might bring a fresh supply of weed seeds to the surface where they could germinate.

Cultivation close to the crop row can be very destructive, causing significant root damage and uprooting of plants (Figure 7.3). Where high plant populations are grown for single-harvest cropping, rows may be too close for tillage, and weeds normally must be controlled with herbicides.

Hand weeding and hoeing may be used to supplement other weed control practices, and are most effective in the row where weeds are close to the crop plants. In order to avoid damaging shallow roots, hoeing should remove weeds at the soil surface. Hand weeding and hoeing are labor-intensive and costly, and for most commercial vegetable production, they are practiced as little as possible.

Cultivating Effects on Soil Moisture and Temperature

Other benefits of cultivation include conservation of moisture and lower soil

Figure 7.3. Damage to sweet corn can result from close cultivation.

temperatures through the formation and maintenance of a soil mulch. By destroying weeds, cultivation usually results in moisture conservation. The formation of a soil mulch prevents or decreases surface runoff and slows the movement of water to the soil surface where it evaporates. Working the soil surface also increases aeration, which promotes biological and other chemical changes in the root environment.

However, under certain conditions, cultivation can also result in moisture loss. In general, when the soil is cultivated soon after a rain of 0.5 inch or less, moisture is likely to be lost because evaporation is hastened by exposing more surfaces to the drying action of air. Moisture may also be lost if cultivation is done when a mulch is already present. The mulch is deepened, and moist soil from below is brought to the surface where moisture is lost by evaporation.

It is often believed that cultivation increases the absorption and retention of heat. This is because heat is used in the evaporation of water. If this was the only factor involved, working the soil would raise the temperature when it resulted in conserving soil moisture and would lower the temperature when cultivation increased the loss of moisture. In fact, many studies have shown that during the growing season, cultivation reduces the soil temperature. The compactness of the surface of an uncultivated soil most likely accounts for its higher temperature, since a compact surface layer is a better heat conductor than a loose, dry layer.

Cultivation for the purpose of conserving moisture or reducing soil temperatures does not always increase yields. Destruction of roots by improper cultivation may more than offset the benefits from either conserving moisture or lowering soil temperatures. In general, the effects of cultivation on soil moisture and temperature are probably small and normally of little practical significance. Except for the purpose of controlling weeds, there is generally no justification for cultivating vegetable crops at regular intervals. Not only is unnecessary cultivation an added expense, but very often it is also injurious.

Cultivating Implements and Tools

Vegetables are cultivated by all types of equipment that are used for cultivating other intertilled crops. Special garden tractors and hand cultivators are also used in certain situations. Hand cultivators of the wheel-type hoe are used mainly for cultivating small growing crops produced intensively and for home gardens. Tractor cultivators range in size from the small garden tractor to the large four-wheel–drive farm tractor. Generally, the heaviest tractors are not well suited for cultivating most vegetables. Some of the medium-sized farm tractors are satisfactory for cultivating potatoes, cabbage, tomatoes, and other crops grown in rows far enough apart to give ample space for wheels.

Various types of attachments are used on cultivators. The sweep and the blade are efficient in controlling weeds between the crop rows and are less destructive to roots than the shovel and teeth attachments. Rotary hoe attachments are excellent for cultivating within the row over the plants when they are small.

Rotation

Vegetables are commonly grown in rotation with field crops such as corn, soybeans, and wheat. By rotating fields among different families of crops, growers can sometimes avoid problems with weeds since a wider spectrum of herbicides is generally available for use in agronomic crops than with vegetables. Weed problems that cannot be controlled in vegetable crops may be curbed with herbicides applied to field crops in the rotation. Rotation is often used in vegetables to prevent the buildup of common weeds, such as purslane. Cover crops such as barley, rye, sorghum, and alfalfa are especially competitive with weed species and can be either rotated with vegetables or used as fall cover crops.

When planning a rotation system between vegetables and field crops, growers should consider the potential threat of herbicide carry-over. Herbicide persistence, which is required to provide season-long weed control in field crops, can lead to injury in subsequent crops, since many vegetables exhibit extreme sensitivity to many commonly used herbicides. Environmental factors such as low temperatures, dry soils, and high soil pH all decrease microbial degradation of herbicides and increase the likelihood of herbicide carry-over. Problems with herbicide carry-over can usually be avoided through careful selection of herbicides and crop rotations. Bioassays and laboratory residue analyses are common practices used by growers to identify and prevent potential carry-over problems.

Mulching

Properly applied organic and synthetic mulches can be useful in managing weeds. Fine-grained organic mulches applied 1–2 inches deep prevent light penetration to germinating weed seeds and reduce weed growth. Organic materials must be free of weed seeds and other noxious pest organisms. Unfortunately, most organic materials are difficult to apply over large areas and are best suited for specialized situations and the home garden.

Black and opaque synthetic plastic films are easy to apply by machine and will prevent weed growth. They are most useful to control weeds in warm-season crops, such as tomatoes, peppers, muskmelons, and watermelons, due to their added ability to increase soil temperatures (see Chapter 8). Clear plastic materials do not control weeds and must be used in combinations with selective herbicides to avoid weed problems. In practice, most mulches, whether organic or synthetic, control only annual weeds and are largely ineffective against perennial weeds.

Other Nonchemical Strategies

A general rule in weed management is not to plant vegetable crops on land with a history of weed problems, especially perennial weeds. In fields where weed problems may exist, growers should select competitive crops such as peas, potatoes, and cabbage and avoid poorly competitive vegetables such as onions and carrots. Growers should use cultivars adapted to their area.

Balanced fertility and effective insect and disease management will provide for vigorous, healthy crops that are more competitive against weeds. In combination with proper row spacings and plant densities, well-grown crops will provide an effective canopy cover that will shade out late emerging weeds.

CHEMICAL CONTROL

Although in many instances mechanical and cultural practices may be sufficient for weed control, they are generally time-consuming and require a large expenditure of both mechanical and human energy. Perennial weeds are usually difficult to control with nonchemical measures but can often be effectively suppressed with herbicides. Along fence rows and irrigation ditches, where cultivation is not feasible, herbicides can be successfully applied. Weedy areas, formerly not recommended for vegetable crops, may be used with the proper application of herbicides.

For certain crops, such as snap beans, weeds between the rows can be controlled by cultivation, while weeds within the row are controlled with herbicides. In other cases (green peas), the rows are too close together for mechanical control and herbicides must be used.

Herbicides

The age of modern chemical weed control began in 1944 with the introduction of the auxin-type synthetic plant growth regulator 2,4-D (2,4-dichlorophenoxyacetic acid). Today, chemical weed suppression is still the primary method of weed control in commercial vegetable production.

Herbicides can be classified as either selective or nonselective. Selective herbicides will kill a specific group of weeds and not harm other plants. Certain herbicides control only grasses, while others control only broadleaf weeds. For example, 2,4-D when used on sweet corn will kill broadleaf weeds such as carpetweed, dandelion, and wild mustard but will not harm grasses, including the crop. Nonselective materials, such as paraquat, will kill all or most types of vegetation. The vast majority of herbicides used on vegetable crops are selective in nature.

Herbicides can also be categorized by their chemical structure (e.g., triazines, dinitroanilines, acetanilides) and mode of action (i.e., photosynthesis inhibitors, meristematic inhibitors, amino acid synthesis inhibitors). After they are applied, herbicides are translocated from the point of absorption to their specific site of action. This may be in the roots or in above-ground parts of the plant. Contact herbicides, such as paraquat, normally are applied to the foliage and will kill all vegetative matter they contact. A knowledge of herbicide mode of action is important for proper selection of materials and application methods to develop an effective and safe chemical weed control program.

For most vegetable crops, there are usually several choices of herbicides available, depending on crop species, soil type, climate, and weed species. Growers must make their choice based on their specific situation. Identifying the weeds present and knowing the weed history of the site will allow the grower to select the herbicide that will give the best results. In some cases, there may be very few, sometimes only a single herbicide, to treat a crop. Some herbicides have very specialized use and may be limited to one crop. These limit grower flexibility in crop rotation, since herbicide residue from one crop may carry over and damage the following crop.

When selecting a herbicide the grower must also consider potential environmental hazards. Information on environmental hazards is contained on the herbicide label.

Herbicide Application

Herbicides used to control weeds in vegetable crops can be applied as 1) preplant, 2) preemergent, and 3) postemergent treatments. Preplant herbicides are applied before the crop is planted. In preplant-incorporated (PPI), the herbicide is applied before the crop is planted and worked into the soil to place it in the root zone of germinating weed seeds. Preemergent herbicides (PRE) are applied to the soil surface after the crop is planted but before the emergence of either the weed or crop seedlings, or both. Postemergent treatments are applied after the emergence of the crop plant.

Most vegetable herbicides are applied PPI or PRE (Table 7.3). The advantage of PPI herbicides is that they are in contact with soil moisture and usually do not require immediate rain or irrigation for activation, while PRE herbicides usually need a small amount of moisture to kill weeds. PPI application is used with volatile herbicides to prevent their escape to the atmosphere. Postemergent herbicides generally have foliar action, and their effectiveness (penetration and action) is usually greater when both the temperature and the relative humidity are high (Table 7.4).

Herbicides may be applied in a number of different ways. Broadcast treatments are uniform applications to an entire area (Figure 7.4). Foliar treatments are applied directly to leaves. Band treatment is the application of herbicide to a

Figure 7.4. Broadcast application with a boom sprayer is commonly used with preemergent and preplant-incorporated herbicides.

Table 7.3. Effectiveness of Preplant-incorporated and Preemergent Herbicides on Weeds[1]

Herbicide	Barnyardgrass	Crabgrass	Fall Panicum	Foxtails	Quackgrass	Common Lambsquarter	Common Purslane	Common Ragweed	Galinsoga	Mustards	Nightshade	Prostrate Spurge	Redroot Pigweed	Smartweeds	Velvetleaf	Yellow Nutsedge
Atrazine	G[2]	F	P	G	G	E	E	E	G	E	E	G	E	E	F	F
Naptalam	P	P	P	P	P	G	F	F	F	F	P	P	G	G	G	P
Chloramben	F	F	P	F	P	E	G	G	F	F	G	G	E	G	F	P
Diethatyl	G	G	G	G	P	F	F	P	G	P	G	F	G	F	P	F
Benefin	E	E	E	E	P	F	G	P	P	P	P	P	G	P	P	P
Cyanazine	G	G	F	G	P	E	E	E	G	G	G	G	F	E	P	P
Prometryn	F	G	F	F	P	E	G	G	F	G	G	G	E	F	F	F
Clomazone	G	E	G	G	P	G	E	G	F	F	P	F	P	G	E	P
Ethalfluralin	E	E	E	E	P	G	G	P	P	F	F	P	G	G	P	P
DCPA	E	G	G	E	P	F	F	P	P	P	P	F	F	P	P	P
Napropamide	E	E	E	E	P	P	G	P	P	P	P	P	G	P	P	P
Metolachlor	E	E	E	E	P	F	F	P	G	P	G	G	G	F	P	F
EPTC	E	E	E	E	G	G	P	F	F	F	F	P	G	F	F	G
Oxyfluorfen	P	F	P	F	P	G	E	G	G	G	G	F	E	G	G	P
Diuron	E	F	F	E	P	E	E	E	G	G	G	F	E	E	F	P
Pronamide	F	F	P	F	G	F	G	F	P	P	P	F	P	F	P	P
Alachlor	E	E	E	E	P	F	G	F	G	P	G	G	E	F	P	F
Metribuzin	G	F	G	G	P	E	E	E	E	E	P	G	G	E	G	P
Linuron	G	F	F	E	P	E	G	E	G	G	G	G	G	G	F	P
Bensulide	E	E	E	E	P	P	P	P	P	P	P	P	G	P	P	P
Simazine	E	F	F	E	F	E	E	E	G	E	E	G	E	E	F	P
Pendimethalin	E	E	E	E	P	G	F	P	F	P	P	G	G	F	F	P
Pyrazon	F	F	F	F	P	E	G	G	P	G	G	F	G	G	P	P
Propachlor	E	E	E	E	P	F	G	F	G	P	G	G	G	F	P	P
Cycloate	E	E	F	E	P	F	F	F	F	P	P	P	G	P	F	F
Terbacil	G	G	G	G	F	E	G	G	G	E	G	F	G	G	G	P
Norflurazon	E	E	E	E	F	F	F	G	G	E	F	G	F	G	F	F
Oryzalin	E	E	E	E	P	G	G	F	F	F	F	F	G	F	P	P
Butylate	E	E	E	E	P	P	P	P	F	P	P	P	F	P	F	G
Pebulate	E	E	F	E	P	F	P	P	F	P	P	P	F	P	P	G
Trifluralin	E	E	E	E	P	F	F	P	P	P	P	P	G	P	P	P

[1]Source: Zandstra, B. H. (ed.). 1990. *North Central Weed Control Guide for Vegetable Crops.* Michigan State Univ. Coop. Ext. Ser., North Central Regional Pub. 330.

[2]E (excellent), G (good), F (fair), P (poor); weed control will vary with soil type and weather.

narrow strip, most often directly over the crop, with mechanical weed control methods used in the aisles. Directed sprays are applied to a particular portion of the plant and are used most often when the crop is susceptible to the herbicide.

Some herbicides can be effectively applied either as granules or as sprays.

Table 7.4. Effectiveness of Postemergent Herbicides on Weeds[1]

Herbicide	Barnyardgrass	Crabgrass	Fall Panicum	Foxtails	Quackgrass	Common Lambsquarter	Common Purslane	Common Ragweed	Galinsoga	Mustards	Nightshade	Prostrate Spurge	Redroot Pigweed	Smartweeds	Velvetleaf	Yellow Nutsedge
Atrazine	G[2]	G	F	G	G	E	E	E	G	E	G	G	E	E	G	G
Bentazon	P	P	P	P	P	G	G	G	G	G	F	P	P	E	G	G
Cyanazine	G	F	G	G	G	G	G	G	G	G	G	G	F	G	F	P
Bromoxynil	P	P	P	P	P	E	P	G	G	G	G	P	F	G	G	P
Prometryn	F	F	F	F	P	E	G	E	G	G	G	G	E	F	F	P
2,4–D	P	P	P	P	P	E	P	E	G	G	E	E	E	E	F	P
Oxyfluorfen	P	P	P	P	P	F	E	G	F	F	G	P	E	F	G	P
Pyridate	F	P	P	F	P	G	P	F	G	F	G	G	G	F	F	P
Metribuzin	F	F	F	G	P	E	E	E	E	E	P	G	G	E	G	P
Linuron	F	F	F	G	P	E	G	E	G	G	G	G	E	E	F	P
Paraquat	E	E	E	E	E	E	E	E	G	E	E	G	E	E	G	G
Glyphosate	E	E	E	E	E	E	E	E	E	E	E	E	E	E	E	F
Terbacil	F	P	F	P	P	E	E	G	G	E	G	G	G	G	F	P
Phenmedipham	P	P	P	P	P	G	G	G	G	G	F	F	P	G	P	P
Clopyralid	P	P	P	P	P	P	P	G	G	P	P	P	P	F	P	P
Stod. solvent	E	E	E	E	F	E	E	P	F	E	E	F	E	E	P	F

[1]Source: Zandstra, B. H. (ed.). 1990. *North Central Weed Control Guide for Vegetable Crops.* Michigan State Univ. Coop. Ext. Ser., North Central Regional Pub. 330.

[2]E (excellent), G (good), F (fair), P (poor); weed control will vary with soil type and weather.

In general, sprays provide more precise placement and better distribution, as well as the best weed control. Herbicides are usually applied to vegetable crops with ground applicators, although in some specific instances, fixed-wing or helicopter aircraft may be used.

Considerations in Herbicide Effectiveness

The effectiveness of a herbicide often depends on the care exercised in following the directions for its use. The rate and timeliness of application, soil type, cultural practices, weather conditions, type of crop, and weed species should be considered. Rates are usually lower on sandy or low organic matter content soils, and higher on heavier or organic soils. Soil pH can markedly influence herbicide performance, and many herbicides may not work well in acid soils. Herbicides to be incorporated should not be applied to rough, cloddy soils, because the herbicides will likely be distributed unevenly as the clods break up. A well-prepared seedbed provides the best conditions for herbicide performance.

Herbicide combinations may be used in lieu of single herbicide applications to increase the control spectrum on some hard-to-control weed species. It is important that labels and instructions indicate the approval of the specific mixture being used. When an unfamiliar chemical is used, a small test trial plot should be treated before the herbicide is extensively applied.

Proper timing of application relative to weed and crop growth is important to control weeds and to avoid crop injury. Weeds are controlled easier as seedlings than in later growth stages. Also, crop species are usually more tolerant to herbicides as they mature.

Herbicides are generally not recommended for the home garden because of the wide variety of crops at different stages of development in a relatively small area. The use of any material and method depends upon registration of the herbicides by federal and state agencies. A herbicide should not be used unless the label states that it is cleared for the intended purpose. Due to the constant introduction of new chemicals and materials, and to changes in herbicide labels, no specific herbicide recommendations are included here. For the most up-to-date information on herbicides, growers should contact their state extension specialists.

SELECTED REFERENCES

Anderson, W. P. 1983. *Weed Science: Principles*. West Publishing, St. Paul, Minnesota.

Ashton, F. M., and A. S. Crafts. 1981. *Mode of Action of Herbicides*, 2nd ed. John Wiley & Sons, Inc., New York.

Crafts, A. S. 1975. *Modern Weed Control*. Univ. of California Press, Berkeley, California.

Duke, S. O. (ed.). 1986. *Weed Physiology*, Vols. 1 and 2. CRC Press, Inc., Boca Raton, Florida.

Fedtke, C. 1982. *Biochemistry and Physiology of Herbicide Action*. Springer-Verlag, New York.

Fischer, W., and A. Lange. 1978. *Grower's Weed Identification Handbook*. Univ. of California Div. Agric. Sci. Handbook 4030.

Klingman, G. C., F. M. Ashton, and L. J. Noordhoff. 1982. *Weed Science: Principles and Practices*, 2nd ed. John Wiley & Sons, Inc., New York.

Masiunas, J. B. 1990. *Weed Management Guide for Commercial Vegetable Growers*. Univ. of Illinois Coop. Ext. Ser. Cir. 907-90.

Odland, T. E., R. S. Bell, and J. B. Smith. 1950. *The Influence of Crop Plants on Those Which Follow*. Rhode Island Agric. Exp. Sta. Bull. 309.

Putnam, A. R., and W. B. Duke. 1978. Allelopathy in agroecosystems. *Ann. Rev. of Phytopath.* 16:431–451.

Ross, M. A., and C. A. Lembi. 1985. *Applied Weed Science*. Burgess Publishing Co., Minneapolis.

Zandstra, B. H. (ed.). 1990. *North Central Weed Control Guide for Vegetable Crops*. Michigan State Univ. Coop. Ext. Ser. North Central Regional Pub. 330.

8

IRRIGATING
AND
MULCHING*

IRRIGATING

In order for vegetable crops to grow successfully, large quantities of water, either as rain or as irrigation, are needed. Unfortunately, in most areas in the U.S. where vegetables are grown, rainfall is either inadequate or too inconsistent for optimum vegetable production. Many regions may receive adequate rainfall during the year, but the rain does not occur when crops need it the most.

Irrigation is the only reliable means of assuring adequate water supply for successful commercial vegetable production. All vegetables in California, Arizona, and New Mexico are irrigated in some form or fashion, and a large percentage of crops grown in other western states are fully or partly irrigated. Not only is irrigation important in arid and semi-arid regions, but it is also important in humid regions. With the high costs of production, growers cannot afford losses in crop quality or yields due to insufficient water.

WATER REQUIREMENTS

During the production of a crop, water is lost from plants mostly from

---

*This chapter co-authored by W. H. Shoemaker, Horticulturist, University of Illinois

transpiration and by evaporation from soil and accumulations on plant surfaces. The sum of these losses is called *evapotranspiration*, and together with the water retained by the plant (about 85–96% of the total plant weight), makes up the consumptive water use. For some crops, up to 400–600 pounds of water will be required to produce 1 pound of dry matter.

A crop's water requirement may also include water expended for other purposes, including leaching, frost protection, crop cooling, seed germination, and other reasons. Part of this water can be supplied by water previously stored in the soil, growing season precipitation, and groundwater within reach of the roots. Water which is not supplied by any of these sources must be supplied from irrigation during the growing season. In California, it takes 23 gallons of irrigation water to produce 1 pound of lettuce, 33 gallons for 1 pound of carrots, 39 gallons for 1 pound of cucumbers, 61 gallons for 1 pound of spinach, 51 gallons for 1 pound of muskmelons, and 122 gallons for 1 pound of sweet corn on the cob.

The water requirement for most crops is affected by many natural and management factors. Natural factors include soils, topography, and climate (temperature, precipitation, solar radiation, and wind). Management factors include water supply, water quality, planting date, crop species and cultivar, irrigation scheduling, fertility, plant spacing, cultivation, and pest control. Plant species and cultivar determine rooting depth and length of growing season. Management factors can usually be controlled, although many are interrelated with natural factors.

Critical Periods of Water Use

Vegetables require a fairly constant supply of soil moisture throughout the growing season. Water stress early in their production can delay maturity and reduce yields. Water shortages later in the growing season, especially during maturation, can severely decrease quality, even though yields may not be affected.

In general, vegetables grown for their foilage require uniform moisture throughout their development, while those grown for fruits and seed require the largest amounts during fruit set and maturation (Table 8.1). Root, tuber, and bulb crops need water the most during the period of enlargement of these parts. The same holds true for plants such as cabbage and lettuce that develop heads. For solanaceous crops (tomatoes, peppers, and eggplants) and cucurbits (melons, cucumbers, squashes, and pumpkins), water stress during anthesis can result in poor pollination, which can severely reduce fruit yield and quality. Moisture stress or moisture fluctuations during fruit development may cause fruits to crack. Crops such as beans, peas, and corn, which are grown for their fresh or dry seeds, pods, or ears, need adequate moisture at the time of flowering (or tasseling), fruit set, and fruit development. Moisture stress during anthesis can cause flowers to abort

Table 8.1. Critical Periods of Water Use in Vegetable Crops

Crop	Critical Period
Broccoli, cabbage, cauliflower, lettuce	Head development
Beets, carrots, radishes, turnips	Root enlargement
Sweet corn	Tasseling and ear development
Cucumbers, eggplants, melons, peppers, tomatoes	Flowering, fruit set, and fruit enlargement
Beans, peas	Flowering and pod development
Onions	Bulb development
Potatoes	Tuber initiation and tuber enlargement
Asparagus	Fern development

in beans and peas and can result in incomplete tipfill in sweet corn from inadequate pollination. During fruit development, water stress can cause malformed pods and ears.

Bad timing or too much irrigation can reduce yields and quality. Excessive moisture in combination with high nitrogen levels can overstimulate vegetative growth in solanaceous crops and cucurbits, severely delaying maturity. For processing crops such as pumpkins and potatoes, excessive amounts of water late in the season can decrease total solids and dry matter in fruits and tubers, resulting in poor quality and low product recovery.

Soil Moisture

For determining the amount and frequency of irrigation, the soil type, texture, and depth should be checked, since this information is used to ascertain the soil water-holding capacity or field capacity (FC). This is the quantity of water that the soil will hold against the pull of gravity and represents the upper limit of available water. The difference between the actual available moisture in the soil and the FC indicates how much water to supply. The actual available soil moisture can sometimes be estimated by feel but can be more precisely determined by instruments such as tensionmeters, neutron probes, or meters for measuring electrical resistance.

Measurement of soil moisture levels, however, provides only indirect measurements of plant water status. Generally, irrigation should begin when 40% of the FC is removed from fine-textured soils, and 60% is removed from sandy soils. There should be no delay in supplying water. Research and experience show that with many crops a damaging water shortage may exist before the plants exhibit outward signs of water stress.

Water Frequency and Amount

The frequency of water application depends on the total supply of available moisture to the roots and the rate of water use, which is influenced by factors such as rainfall, plant age, rooting depth, soil type, and rate of evapotranspiration; the latter depends on crop cover, temperature, humidity, and wind. For most vegetables in humid regions, from 1 to 2 inches of water per week is needed during their active growing season. However, under hot, dry, windy conditions, 2–3 inches of water may be needed per week. In arid regions, vegetables may require up to 4 inches of water per week.

When plants are young, the rate of water use is low. Later in the season, as the crop canopy size increases, daily water use increases because there is more transpirational surface from growth, but the depth of rooting is also greater. Generally, less frequent irrigations will be needed later in the season, but at each irrigation, more water will be required. Light, frequent irrigations are usually not recommended, except at the early seedling stage, when the plant has a limited root system.

A consumptive water-use curve for dry bulb onions grown in Arizona is presented in Figure 8.1. The figure contains estimates of seasonal use (23.3 inches), semi-monthly use, and soil moisture depletion. Peak water use rate occurs

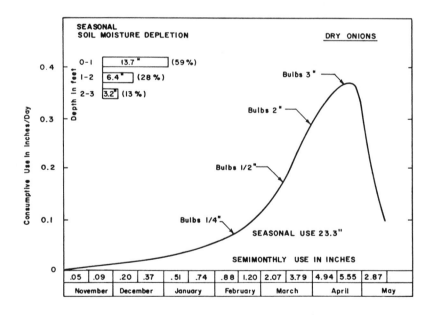

Figure 8.1. Mean consumptive water use for dry bulb onions at Mesa, Arizona. (Source: Erie, L. J., O. F. French, D. A. Bucks, and K. Harris. 1982. *Consumptive Use of Water by Major Crops in Southwestern United States.* USDA ARS Consv. Res. Rpt. No. 29)

during the period when the bulb increases in size from 0.25 to 3 inches. Seasonal moisture depletion in the soil down to 3 feet is shown by bar graphs in the upper lefthand corner of the figure.

Rooting depth is an important factor affecting the crop's water requirement and the frequency of irrigation. Not only does it determine the depth of the soil profile that roots can utilize as a water source, but it also influences the irrigation depth. Vegetables such as celery, lettuce, potatoes, and sweet corn are shallow-rooted, and it is necessary to keep the available soil moisture in the surface foot of soil, especially for the first part of the growing season. Onions are very shallow-rooted, and available water must be maintained in the surface 6–10 inches throughout the growing season.

Water requirements per irrigation application for shallow-rooted crops are small, but the frequency of application may be high. Shallow-rooted vegetables should not go more than 4–6 days without water, either as rainfall or irrigation, in sandy soils, and 10–12 days in clay soils (Table 8.2). Deep-rooted vegetables such as tomatoes and melons require less frequent irrigations, but more water is needed at each irrigation. When applying water, the grower should add enough to increase the soil moisture content in the rooting zone to field capacity.

Table 8.2. Relative Frequency and Amount of Irrigation Water for Vegetable Crops as Affected by Soil Type and Rooting Depth

Rooting Depth	Sandy Soil		Loam Soil		Clay Soil	
	Irrigation Interval	Application Rate	Irrigation Interval	Application Rate	Irrigation Interval	Application Rate
	(days)	*(in.)*	*(days)*	*(in.)*	*(days)*	*(in.)*
Shallow (0–2 ft.)	4–6	1–2	7–10	2–3	10–12	3–4
Medium (0–4 ft.)	7–10	2–3	10–15	3–4	15–20	4–5
Deep (0–6 ft.)	10–12	3–4	20–30	4–5	30	5–6

As discussed, water requirements for vegetable crops are likely to vary, depending on natural and management factors. However, for maximum production, a crop requires a fairly definite amount of water during the growing season. Table 8.3 presents information on water requirements in selected vegetable crops according to rooting depth.

Table 8.3. Depth of Rooting and Amount of Irrigation Water Needed for Vegetable Crops in California[1]

Rooting Depth	Water Needed for Crop (in.)			
	12	12–17	18–24	30–40
Shallow (<2 ft.)	Lettuce (winter) Spinach	Broccoli Brussels sprouts Cabbage Cauliflower Onions (early)	Lettuce Potatoes Onions (late) Sweet corn	Celery Potatoes (summer)
Medium (2–4 ft.)	Peas (winter)	Cucumbers Pole beans Snap beans Turnips	Beets Carrots Eggplants Peas (fall) Peppers Summer squash	
Deep (4 ft. or more) . .		Artichokes Lima beans Watermelons	Asparagus Muskmelons Parsnips Pumpkins Winter squash Sweet potatoes Tomatoes	

[1]Source: Doneen, L. D., and J. H. Macgillivray. 1956. *Suggestions for Irrigating Commercial Truck Crops.* Univ. of California Agric. Exp. Sta. Leaf. 9938.

IRRIGATION METHODS

Surface Irrigation

Surface irrigation, as the name implies, is the practice of spreading water over the surface of the land. Two systems — flood irrigation and furrow irrigation — are common. In flood irrigation, water is released into fields that are very level, with only slight contour, and which have border ridges of soil to contain the water. Usually, a thorough saturation (3–4 inches) is applied, reducing the number of required irrigations. Salts which can accumulate on the surface are leached into the subsoil, making this method well suited for arid regions.

With furrow irrigation the crops are grown on beds with furrows (6–8 inches deep) between them (Figure 8.2). Water is allowed to flow down the furrows, from either supply ditches or portable pipe. This method is more suitable than flood irrigation in fields that are not level, provided they have a constant slope. A modification of furrow irrigation, known as surge irrigation, was developed in the 1980's. Using portable pipe with electronically controlled gates, water is allowed to flow down alternate rows only as far as it can be uniformly applied. Then the other row is irrigated. As the first row soaks up water, the soil surface

Figure 8.2. Sprinkler irrigation is generally more efficient than furrow irrigation, though the furrow system still remains the most economical and most widely used in western growing areas.

closes up, allowing the next surge of water to pass. The result is more uniformity of water application between the beginning and end of the furrow.

When the initial cost of wells, pumps, and other equipment is not so large, surface irrigation requires only a modest investment. If the supply of water is limited, this method is well adapted to irrigating large areas, since water loss from evaporation is considerably less than in some other systems. Among the disadvantages are the necessity for constant attention, the tendency for soils to crust, and the large loss of water by seepage in supply ditches.

Sprinkler Irrigation

Approximately 33% of irrigated ground in the U.S. is sprinkler-irrigated. Several different systems are used, including center-pivot and linear-move systems, traveling guns, portable pipe, solid-set pipe, and wheel-roll systems. In all of these, water under pressure is dispersed above the ground.

Center-pivot and linear-move systems are characterized by having a main water line that is carried on top of mobile towers (Figure 8.3). Nozzles to disperse the water are evenly spaced along the main conduit, often at the end of drops. With center pivots, one end of the main is stationary and the main turns around the pivot point, similar to the hands of a clock. Linear-move systems simply advance the main at an even pace across the field in a swath pattern. Both are able to irrigate large areas with a single pass and are best suited for large fields with no more than three or four crops. However, maintenance demands are considerable.

Traveling guns resemble large sprinkler nozzles on a rolling cart. Water is carried to the gun by a hose and pumped through a reel which winds up the hose as the water is being applied. The guns can wet a pattern of up to 600 feet in diameter. The system is well suited to fields that are long and narrow or irregular

Figure 8.3. Center-pivot systems can range in size, covering from 20 acres to over 100 acres. (Photo: courtesy of Valmont Industries, Valley, Nebraska)

in shape, as well as to small operations. The main drawback is the low efficiency of application. However, the low initial cost of the system makes it a reasonable option in some cases.

Portable pipe and solid-set pipe consist of a pipe system laid out in the field to carry water to a grid of sprinklers. A solid-set system is permanently installed, whereas a portable pipe system is temporary and can be moved or rearranged at any time. Solid-set systems are generally limited to perennial crops because they can be a serious impediment to cultural operations. However, they can reduce labor inputs if a cultural system can be devised around it. Portable pipe is usually made of a light-gauge aluminum, from 2 to 12 inches in diameter, with risers and sprinklers at each joint. It is labor-intensive but can be rearranged and easily moved. About 1 worker-hour per acre is required for a portable pipe system, compared to about 10–15% as much labor for most mechanically moved systems. If labor is not a problem, portable pipe is the most flexible of sprinkler systems.

Wheel-roll systems are used more often in sod production but can be used in vegetables. A pipe with sprinklers is mounted on wheels, which carries it through the field, applying water as it goes. A hose carries water from a main to the system. This system is restricted by the height of the plants and works best with short crops.

Sometimes a combination of systems may be used. In the Southwest, growers often use portable pipe sprinkler irrigation to germinate lettuce. The wet soil provides a softened soil cap which is easily penetrated by the small seeds during germination. The sprinkler irrigation also has a cooling effect on the soil, increasing seed germination under high temperatures. After the crop has emerged and is growing well, irrigation is changed to the traditional furrow method.

Trickle (Drip) Irrigation

Trickle or drip irrigation is characterized by operation under low-pressure (6–20 psi), point-source application, slow application, and high efficiency. Water is carried through plastic tubes or tapes and released through emitters that regulate the amount and rate of water applied. The slow rate of application accommodates infiltration rates, increasing efficiency. Because of the low pressure and volume, operating costs are reduced. Other advantages include: 1) the ability to fertilize or apply pest control materials through the system, 2) irrigation of crops during cultural operations, 3) no wetting of plant material, 4) adaptation of automated control systems, and 5) greater ease of coordinating foliar pest control with irrigation schedules. Some disadvantages of this method include a tendency for emitters to become clogged with debris and algal and fungal growth, and a possible salt buildup around the perimeter of wetting patterns in arid climates. The cost of installation and material is moderate, but it is higher than for conventional furrow irrigation.

Two major types of drip systems — lightweight tapes and heavy-gauge tubing — are available. The plastic tape is approximately one-third the cost of the tubing but does not last as long. Either can be laid on the surface or buried, which facilitates cultural practices and increases longevity.

Trickle systems have been used successfully for years in arid regions but are also feasible in many humid areas and in home gardens. Recent research in south Texas has shown trickle irrigation to increase yields of tomatoes, peppers, onions, muskmelons, and watermelons by 15–25%, and with water savings of more than 50%, compared to conventional furrow irrigation.

Subirrigation

In subirrigation, water is added in such a way that it permeates the soil from below. Subirrigation requires an abundance of water, a sandy loam topsoil through which water will move freely by capillary attraction, and an impervious subsoil which will hold the water. At the same time, adequate drainage is necessary. The large amount of water required and the great expense involved in the laying of tile pipes (if any such structures are needed) are disadvantages. Advantages include the maintenance of an undisturbed soil mulch and lack of trouble from soil baking. In actual practice, subirrigation is sometimes difficult, justifying considerable investigation of existing soil conditions and the water supply before such a system is installed.

SOURCES OF WATER

Water for irrigation may be obtained from streams, lakes, wells, springs, and municipal sources. Virtually all states have laws and regulations pertaining to the use of water for irrigation. These should be known and understood before any irrigation system is designed. Local state water conservation offices can be of assistance.

In the past, when water was obtained from flowing wells or springs, or diverted from streams and lakes, the costs of water application were relatively low. This is still true for many areas of the East and Southeast, but the situation has changed considerably in other regions of the U.S. In the West and Southwest, the expense of applying water to the land has increased dramatically in recent years. The costs of irrigating vegetable crops in the Sacramento and San Joaquin valleys of California have quadrupled, going from $160 an acre for 2 acre-feet of water to $400 an acre (note: an acre-foot is approximately 326,000 gallons). This is due in part to urban competition for water sources and 5 years of below average rainfall in northern California where winter mountain snows supply the water to southern growing areas.

When powerful pumps are required to raise the water, initial expenses are high. The cost of drilling a well and installing a pump and motor, as well as building a reservoir for temporary storage, can amount to a substantial investment. If water has to pumped uphill to the field, the costs can double what a gravity-feed would cost.

Water Quality

The agricultural suitability or quality of irrigation water for vegetable crops is determined by the concentration and composition of dissolved salts in the water supply. The concentration of salts in the water can increase soil salinity to the point where the osmotic pressure of the soil solution in the root zone makes it very difficult for plants to extract water. Consequently, crops subjected to excessive salt levels show many of the same symptoms as in a drought, including wilting and impaired growth. Vegetables differ considerably in their sensitivity to salts. Crops such as beans, carrots, and onions are very susceptible to high salt levels and will suffer large yield reductions if irrigated with saline (high salt) water. At the other extreme are asparagus, beets, and spinach, which are tolerant of salts and can be successfully grown when saline water is used for irrigation.

There are several elements found in natural waters that can be toxic to plants, with the most common ones being chloride, sodium, and boron. Leaf burn caused by sodium and chloride may occur in some crops with sprinkler irrigation when the humidity is low and the evaporation rate is high. Beans, onions, and Jerusalem artichokes are highly sensitive to boron and will experience significant yield reductions if boron concentrations exceed 1 ppm in irrigation waters. In contrast, asparagus and beets are tolerant of boron and will grow quite well at relatively high boron levels in the water supply.

Problems with water quality are usually less in humid climates than in arid and semi-arid regions, where high concentrations of dissolved ions and salts frequently occur in water used for irrigation. Depending on water management practices, environmental conditions, and species tolerances, these could become toxic to plant growth. For most vegetable production, irrigation water with a salinity content less than 480 ppm (total dissolved solids), sodium below 3.0 SAR (adjusted sodium adsorption ratio), boron less than 1 ppm, and chloride below 100 ppm, would be considered excellent (Table 8.4).

Other components of water quality include bicarbonate, nitrate, and pH. Bicarbonate ions in water can be a problem in some areas, primarily from their adverse effect on soil permeability. With overhead sprinkler irrigation, a white deposit of calcium carbonate may form on the leaves and fruit. Although this is not detrimental to plant growth, it can render harvested crops unattractive, and in some cases unmarketable. In some areas, high nitrate concentrations in irrigation water are becoming major environmental and consumer health concerns.

Table 8.4 outlines some water quality guidelines for vegetable production. Some flexibility should be considered, depending on crop, soil characteristics, irrigation methods, and local climate.

Table 8.4. Qualitative Classification of Irrigation Water[1]

	Water-Quality Problems		
	None	**Increasing**	**Severe**
Salinity TDS (ppm)[2]	Less than 480	480–1,920	More than 1,920
Boron (ppm)	1.0	1.0–2.0	2.0–10.0

Sodium (adj SAR, ppm)[2]
    Root absorption . . . . . .
    Foliar applied . . . .
	Less than 3.0
	Less than 70
		3.0–9.0
		70
			More than 9.0
			—

Chloride (ppm)
    Root absorption . . . . . .
    Foliar applied . . . .
	Less than 70
	Less than 100
		70–345
		100
			More than 345
			—

Bicarbonate (ppm)	Less than 40	40–520	More than 520
pH	6.5–8.3	More than 8.3	—

[1]Source: Farnham, D. S., R. F. Hasek, and J. L. Paul. 1985. *Water Quality.* University of California Div. Agric. Sci. Leaf. 2995.

[2]TDS (total dissolved solids), SAR (sodium adsorption ratio).

MULCHING

Mulching vegetable crops to improve growing conditions is a time-honored practice that goes back to early agriculture. In the past, mulches were primarily organic in nature and used mainly to conserve moisture, but in the 1960's, with the introduction of new synthetic plastics, the role of mulches in vegetable production expanded considerably. Today, mulches are also used extensively to hasten maturity and to help control weed growth. In the home garden, mulching can result in more efficient use of space. Whenever mulches are used to improve the plant environment, higher yields generally result.

PRINCIPLES

A mulch is created when the soil surface is artificially modified by a covering of natural or synthetic materials. The purpose of a mulch is to enhance crop growth by changing the plant's soil and air microclimate. This includes soil temperature, moisture, weed competition, soil structure, and biological activity. Vegetable crops usually grow better when mulched because an extensive root system is allowed to develop undisturbed under the protective covering.

Changes in soil temperature and moisture from mulching are usually the most important factors in determining crop response to mulch. Mulches conserve soil moisture by reducing water evaporation from soil by 50% or more. They also can increase water for crop use by controlling annual grasses and broadleaf weeds. Mulching modifies soil temperatures; organic and light-colored reflective mulches reduce soil temperatures, while black, gray, and transparent mulches increase soil temperatures. Mulches can also reduce fluctuations of both moisture and temperature in the root environment, which may be as important as these other effects on soil water and temperature.

Generally, the effects of mulching are greatest under adverse weather conditions. Warm-season crops such as tomatoes, peppers, melons, cucumbers, and sweet corn respond most favorably to soil-warming mulches applied early in the season. Even when they do not increase yields, mulches can improve crop quality by keeping fruits clean and free from defects.

MATERIALS

Mulch materials can be grouped into two general categories: natural and synthetic. Commonly used natural materials include plant residues such as straw, leaves, corncobs, peanut hulls, and pine needles; animal manures, peatmoss, and wood products such as bark, wood chips, and sawdust. The most popular synthetic materials are the clear and black polyethylene films. Metal foils, paper, and asphalt mulches have also been used in some situations. Aluminum foil mulch has been used on Chinese cabbage and summer squash to repel aphids that spread mosaic viruses.

Organic Mulches

The natural or organic mulches reduce soil temperatures and provide excellent moisture control, if applied 2 inches deep or more around crop plants. Organic mulches can improve soil tilth and enhance biological activity as they decompose and can reduce wind and water erosion. However, these materials are bulky and difficult to handle on a large scale, requiring much labor to apply, and are often unavailable in sufficient quantities for most commercial operations. Consequently, most natural mulches are largely restricted to the home garden (see Chapter 30).

Plastic Mulches

The most popular mulches for commercial vegetable operations are the clear and black polyethylene films (Figure 8.4). Growing vegetables for fresh market on plastic-covered beds has become a standard practice in many vegetable areas.

Figure 8.4. Peppers are being grown on a twin-row bed covered with black plastic mulch.

Florida has about 100,000 acres of commercial vegetables growing under plastic or other mulch materials.

Because of their ability to increase soil temperatures, it is now standard practice to use clear and black plastic mulches with muskmelons and watermelons, and with early plantings of cucumbers, eggplants, peppers, tomatoes, summer squash, and sweet corn. Yields are often higher, and harvest may be 5–10 days earlier than with unmulched plantings. Clear plastic will generally warm the soil about 8–10°F more than black plastic and should be used for the earliest plantings. However, weeds can grow under clear plastic; thus, herbicides are required. Black plastic prevents light penetration and provides effective weed control. The strips of land between the plastic should be kept free of weeds, either by herbicides or by cultivation. Plastic mulch can also reduce fertilizer losses to leaching, increase fumigant effectiveness, provide for more efficient use of water, and reduce fruit losses to rotting.

The plastic mulch film generally used is 4 feet wide and 1.5 mil (1.5 / 1000 inch) thick, although various widths are available. The laying of the plastic film is highly mechanized and can be adapted for bed shaping, laying of trickle irrigation tubing, and planting all in one operation (Figure 8.5). The equipment for application of plastic mulch is readily available and relatively simple. Before any mulch is applied, the soil moisture should be near field capacity since this moisture is critical for early growth and cannot be effectively supplied by rain or overhead irrigation to small plants growing under plastic mulch.

Figure 8.5. Bed shaping and laying black plastic mulch can be done by machine in one operation.

One of the main problems associated with plastic mulch is the removal of the material after its use. On small acreages growers manually remove it by running a coulter down the center of the row and picking it up from each side. Commercial removal equipment is also available. Photodegradable plastic films, which break down under ultraviolet light, are available; however, these are more expensive than standard plastic mulch and have not proven completely effective. Recently, a biodegradable plastic material with a corn starch base that allows soil microbes to use the plastic as a food source is being tested for the waste disposal industry and may be available soon for agricultural use.

ROW COVERS

A recent development in vegetable production is the use of plastic films or other synthetic materials to cover the crop, creating a greenhouse-like microenvironment around the plant. This practice provides several advantages for vegetable production, including early growth enhancement and earlier maturity, higher yields, insect and wind protection, and in certain situations some frost protection.

The original material was clear or translucent polyethylene film, but polyester, polypropylene, and other polymers are now being used. These new materials may be perforated films; lightweight, porous, spun-bound fibers; or woven materials. When supported, usually by flexible wire hoops placed at 5–6 feet intervals in the row, they are called *row tunnels* (Figure 8.6); when applied without any means of support, they are called *floating row covers* (Figure 8.7). This latter method is more applicable to low-growing vine crops, while the former method is more suited to upright plants, e.g., tomatoes and peppers. Both types are often used in

Figure 8.6. Row tunnels extend the growing season and make possible early planting of warm-season vegetables.

Figure 8.7. Floating row covers made of spun-bound polyester are placed on top of muskmelon plants.

conjunction with plastic mulch. In Europe, field covers are used to cover a number of rows in a single swath.

Acceptance of row covers has not been as rapid as the use of plastic mulch, due largely to problems managing the technique. High air temperatures under

Figure 8.8. Hot caps are placed over individual plants.

the cover can stress the crop, inhibiting growth, inducing bolting, or aborting blossoms. These problems have not been as severe with the translucent materials as with clear plastic. As a result, row covers are always ventilated, but even with slitted air vents, clear plastic has produced heat injury.

Fresh market growers may also use other types of covers to protect their early crops, including "hot caps," which are small, individual paper tents placed over each plant (Figure 8.8). These are then removed when temperatures are favorable and before plant growth becomes confined within the cover.

SELECTED REFERENCES

California Fertilizer Association. 1985. *Western Fertilizer Handbook*, 7th ed. Interstate Publishers, Inc., Danville, Illinois.

Erie, L. J., O. F. French, D. A. Bucks, and K. Harris. 1982. *Consumptive Use of Water by Major Crops in the Southwestern United States*. USDA, ARS Conserv. Res. Rpt. No. 29.

Hopen, H. J., and J. W. Courter. 1982. *Mulch for Vegetables*. Univ. of Illinois Coop. Ext. Ser. Hort. Facts VC-20-82.

Kenworthy, A. L. 1972. *Trickle Irrigation: The Concept and Guidelines for Use*. Michigan State Univ. Agric. Exp. Sta. Res. Rpt. 165.

Lorenz, O. A., and D. N. Maynard. 1988. *Knott's Handbook for Vegetable Growers*, 3rd ed. John Wiley & Sons, Inc., New York.

Mansour, N. S. 1989. Using row and field covers on sweet corn and direct-seeded vegetables. In: *Proc. 1989 Illinois Fruit, Vegetable and Irrigation Conv.* Univ. of Illinois Coop. Ext. Ser. Hort. Series 75.

Marsh, A. W., H. Johnson, Jr., L. J. Booher, N. McRae, K. Mayberry, P. Mobray, D. Ririe, and F. E. Robinson. 1977. *Solid Set Sprinklers for Starting Vegetable Crops*. Univ. of California Div. ANR Leaf. 2265.

Marsh, A. W., R. L. Branson, S. Davies, C. D. Gustafson, and F. K. Aljubury. 1975. *Drip Irrigation*. Univ. of California Div. ANR Leaf. 2740.

Nakayama, F. S., and D. A. Bucks. 1986. *Trickle Irrigation for Crop Production: Design, Operation, and Management*. Elsevier, Amsterdam, Netherlands.

Oebker, N. F., and J. R. Kuykendall. 1971. Trickle irrigation in horticultural crops in the desert Southwest. In: *Proc. Nat. Agric. Plast. Conf. 11*.

Pair, C. H. 1976. *Sprinkler Irrigation*. USDA, ARS Leaf. 476.

Scholz, E. W., and E. P. Lana. 1971. *Mulches for Warm Weather Crops*. North Dakota State Univ. Agric. Exp. Sta. Bull. 34.

Takatori, F. H., L. F. Lippert, and J. M. Lyons. 1971. *Petroleum Mulch Studies for Row Crops in California*. Univ. of California Agric. Exp. Sta. Bull. 634.

Wolfe, D. W., and E. Rutkowski. 1987. *Use of Plastic Mulch and Row Covers for Early Season Vegetable Production*. Cornell Univ. Veg. Crops Rep. No. 355.

9

CONTROLLING INSECTS
AND DISEASES

Successful vegetable production requires the effective and economic control of insect and disease pests. The commercial vegetable gardener must produce a quality product that is attractive and safe to the consumer at a minimum cost. Losses in produce yield and quality due to insect and disease damage are unacceptable.

Effective, economic pest control or pest management requires the use of cultural, mechanical, biological, and chemical methods. For best results, a combination of these is usually necessary. Insecticides and fungicides are highly effective in the control of most insect and disease pests, but their use is closely regulated by state and federal agencies and is subject to change even in mid-season. It is imperative that the commercial grower secure the latest recommendations for any pesticide use. Since growers are interested in maximum control at minimum costs, it may be necessary for them to consider a wide range of materials. The home gardener, who usually grows a variety of vegetables, may encounter many pests. A limited number of generally effective pesticides that should be safe to apply, handle, and store may be used.

IMPORTANCE OF PEST CONTROL

Insect and disease infestations in vegetable crops bring about heavy losses through 1) reduced yields, 2) lowered quality of produce, 3) increased costs of production and harvesting, and 4) required expenditures for materials and equip-

151

ment to apply control measures. These losses individually and collectively are important because they reduce the vegetable grower's income and may result in the total loss of a crop.

The insect- and disease-control picture in vegetable production has changed considerably with the appearance of more effective pesticides in the late 1980's. Control measures have become more selective, and yields of crops such as potatoes have increased greatly. The Environmental Protection Agency (EPA), which regulates the registration and use of pesticides on vegetables, sets the tolerances for miniscule amounts of residues that are allowed on a crop at the time of harvest. It is the federal Food and Drug Administration (FDA), however, that enforces these tolerances on fresh vegetables by random sampling and residue analysis at any point during shipping and marketing.

The continual tightening of pesticide regulations by the EPA has resulted in the present tendency for growers to use a minimum of pesticides, and only those that disappear rapidly and are readily biodegradable. Consequently, renewed interest is being devoted to research on biological and cultural methods of control and insect- and disease-resistant cultivars.

GENERAL CONTROL MEASURES

The recommended insecticides and fungicides are by no means the complete and final answer to insect and disease problems arising in vegetable production. It is true that there are chemical controls for practically every disease and insect problem, but pesticides are used only as a last resort and not as the only method of control. Frequently, when the problem arises, there may be no other options, a situation which quickly demonstrates dependance on these chemical tools and lack of knowledge of the basic biology that would permit the use of other control methods.

Several "common sense" practices, when incorporated into the insecticide-fungicide program, will improve yield, increase produce quality, and in the long run, decrease production costs and increase profits. These fundamentals can be found in almost any text devoted to the art and science of vegetable production as well as in publications of the U.S. Department of Agriculture (USDA) and of state extension services and experiment stations. The following are offered for the convenience of the reader:

1. *Plant the best-quality seed.* This means that the seed should be a) disease-free and b) certified when possible.

2. *Select crops that are best suited to your soil and climate.* Because a crop

is not grown in your area does not mean it cannot be grown there, but it usually is a good indication.

3. *Control weeds.* Grass and broadleaf weeds compete strongly with crops for soil moisture and plant nutrients, and they frequently harbor or attract insects which may later attack the crop and may also serve as disease reservoirs.

4. *Control insect pests as needed*, especially leafhoppers and aphids. Several viral diseases are transmitted by insects with piercing, sucking mouthparts.

5. *Select plots of land that are fertile and well drained.* Substandard land will produce substandard yields, while poorly drained areas will invariably result in sparse stands, damping-off, and seed-decay problems.

6. *Use only the best-quality fertilizers.* Soil tests will indicate what fertilizer combination is needed and whether liming is necessary. Fertilizer bargains are seldom found.

7. *Buy plants the same as seed, disease-free and certified* (when possible).

8. *Use disease-resistant cultivars if available.* At present these include culti-vars that are resistant to only a few diseases of specified crops, but the number is increasing. The degree of resistance varies considerably through the range of available cultivars.

9. *When harvest is completed, destroy the remains of annual crops as soon as practical.* Stems, leaves, and roots can serve as disease reservoirs and insect harbors for the following year.

10. *Rotate crops.* Planting the same crop in a field year after year may eventually result in severe soil-borne diseases and insect or nematode infestations. All of these can be held in check to some degree by crop rotation.

11. *Follow recommended planting dates for your area.* Some crops can be planted so they will mature before diseases strike and before or after certain insects begin their attack. Planting dates are usually issued by the individual cooperative extension services or state experiment stations.

CONTROLLING INSECTS

The number of insect pests of vegetable crops is quite long and diversified (Table 9.1). Some insects cause significant damage in all areas where vegetables are grown, while others may be more localized to certain geographical areas. Certain insects are pests for a wide variety of crops, while others are more specific

Table 9.1. Insects Which Commonly Attack Vegetable Crops

Vegetable	Insect Pest
Asparagus	Asparagus beetle, cutworm, thrips, wireworm
Beans	Aphid, bean leaf beetle, corn earworm, cutworm, leafhopper, Mexican bean beetle, root maggot, spider mite, cucumber beetle, western bean cutworm, wireworm, lygus bug, flea beetle
Beets	Beet webworm, blister beetle, cutworm, flea beetle, wireworm, white-fringed beetle grub
Cabbage, broccoli, cauliflower, kale	Aphid, cabbage looper and caterpillars, cutworm, flea beetle, harlequin bug, mole cricket, root maggot, vegetable weevil, white-fringed beetle grub, wireworm
Carrots	Carrot rust fly, leafhopper, vegetable weevil, wireworm
Celery	Aphid, celery leaf tier, cutworm, lygus bug, spider mite
Cucumbers and melons . . .	Aphid, cucumber beetle, leafhopper, leaf miner, pickleworm, spider mite, thrips, wireworm
Eggplants	Colorado potato beetle, cutworm, eggplant lace bug, flea beetle, hornworm, spider mite, whitefly, wireworm
Lettuce	Aphid, armyworm, cutworm, caterpillars, leafhopper, mole cricket, wireworm
Onions	Onion maggot, thrips, wireworm, leaf miner
Peas (garden)	Aphid, pea weevil, alfalfa and celery loopers
Peppers	Aphid, cutworm, flea beetle, hornworm, leaf miner, pepper maggot, pepper weevil, spider mite, wireworm
Potatoes	Aphid, armyworm, blister beetle, Colorado potato beetle, cutworm, European corn borer, flea beetle, grasshopper, leafhopper, mole cricket, plant bug, potato psyllid, potato tuberworm, vegetable weevil, white-fringed beetle grub, white grub, wireworm
Pumpkins and squashes . . .	Aphid, cucumber beetle, cutworm, squash bug, squash vine borer, pickleworm
Spinach	Alfalfa looper, aphid, beet webworm, leaf miner
Sweet corn	Corn earworm, European corn borer, Japanese beetle, wireworm
Sweet potatoes	Sweet potato weevil, wireworm, white-fringed beetle grub
Tomatoes	Aphid, armyworm, blister beetle, Colorado potato beetle, cutworm, drosophila, flea beetle, hornworm, leaf miner, spider mite, tomato fruitworm, tomato pinworm, tomato psyllid, tomato russet mite
Turnips	Aphid, caterpillars, flea beetle, root maggot, vegetable weevil, wireworm, white-fringed beetle grub

in their host range. Many insects feed directly on plant tissue, while others cause damage by sucking out plant fluids.

Effective insect management requires proper identification and a knowledge of the insect's biology and habits. In general, insect pests of vegetables can be divided into six categories: 1) beetles that chew holes in plant foliage; 2) caterpillars and worms that feed on foliage and sometimes on fruit; 3) cutworms, earworms, and borers that tunnel into corn ear tips and various vegetable fruits; 4) soil maggots, grubs, and wireworms that feed inside seeds and on plant roots; 5) aphids, whiteflies, scale, and mites (covered here although not true insects) that feed in large numbers by sucking juices from new foliage; and 6) adult and immature plant bugs that suck plant juices from foliage and fruit. Illustrations and some suggested methods of control of some of the more major vegetable insect pests are given in Table 9.2.

Scouting for Insect Pests

Vegetable producers, or a specialist hired for the purpose, should check or scout their crops every 2 or 3 days, carefully examining them for signs of insect infestation, such as eggs, insect frass, and damaged leaves or fruit. In this way, most insect pests can be discovered and control measures applied before the problem seriously enlarges. In many of the major sweet corn growing areas, commercial growers set out light traps and pheromone traps to monitor the seasonal population levels of corn borers and earworms, respectively.

The value of scouting fields to determine the need and proper time for control applications cannot be overemphasized. A knowledge of the extent of infestation and the stage of insect development will in the long run save the producer time, money, and worry.

Insecticides

Although insect management programs in vegetable crops include cultural, mechanical, and biological methods, insecticides are still the most efficient means of managing most insect pests.

Insecticides used on vegetables can be divided into two broad categories: 1) inorganic compounds and 2) organic compounds. The inorganic insecticides, which include cryolite, and various types of sulfur are generally not used very much. Rather, the organic insecticides make up most of the chemical insecticides used on vegetables today. They consist of botanical compounds derived from plants and plant parts (e.g., pyrethrum and rotenone) and various synthetic organic chemicals, including chlorinated hydrocarbons, organic phosphates, carbamates, and pyrethroids. These last two groups are widely used commercially since they kill a broad spectrum of insects but have relatively low mammalian toxicity.

A list of insecticides for use on vegetable crops is given in Table 9.3. Some of the insecticides are toxic and their use is restricted to certified applicators only.

Table 9.2. Common Vegetable Insects

Insect	Crop	Dust Formula
Aphid	Cabbage Cucumbers Melons Peas Potatoes Tomatoes	5% malathion
Blister beetle	Potatoes Corn Tomatoes Beans	5% carbaryl
Cabbage worms	Broccoli Cabbage Cauliflower Greens	
Corn earworm ($^2/_3$ nat. size)	Sweet corn Tomatoes	5% carbaryl *Bacillus thuringiensis* (Thuricide, Dipel) on tomatoes
European corn borer	Sweet corn	5% carbaryl or 5% carbaryl granules
Striped cucumber beetle	Cucumbers Melons Squash	5% carbaryl
Cutworm	Most garden crops	Carbaryl bait
Flea beetle	Most garden crops	5% carbaryl
Grasshopper	Most garden crops	5% carbaryl

and Suggested Control

Spray Formula	Remarks
2 tsp. 50–57% emulsifiable malathion in 1 gal. water	Apply on foliage when aphids appear. Repeat weekly as needed. 1 lb. active ingredient not recommended for some crops.
2 tb. wettable carbaryl in 1 gal. water	$1\frac{1}{2}$ lbs. per acre on foliage as needed.
Bacillus thuringiensis; follow label directions	Thorough treatment is necessary. Repeat weekly as needed. Begin treatment when worms are small.
Inject $\frac{1}{2}$ medicine dropperful of mineral oil into silk channel as silks start to dry or 2 tb. wettable carbaryl in 1 gal. water	Dust or spray silks with carbaryl every other day for 10 days. Dust or spray tomatoes with carbaryl three or four times at 10-day intervals; begin when first fruits are small.
2 tb. wettable carbaryl in 1 gal. water	Apply insecticide four times at 5-day intervals beginning with egg hatching near mid-June. Avoid early spring plantings. On late corn, dust as for corn earworm.
2 tb. wettable carbaryl in 1 gal. water	Treat as soon as beetles appear. Repeat when necessary.
	At transplanting, wrap stems of seedling cabbage, pepper, and tomato plants with newspaper or foil to prevent damage by cutworms.
2 tb. wettable carbaryl in 1 gal. water	Apply as soon as injury is first noticed. Thorough application is necessary. 1 lb. active ingredient per acre.
2 tb. wettable carbaryl in 1 gal. water	Treat infested areas while grasshoppers are still small.

(Continued)

Table 9.2

Insect	Crop	Dust Formula
Hornworm ($\frac{1}{2}$ nat. size)	Tomatoes	5% carbaryl or *Bacillus thuringiensis* (Thuricide, Dipel)
Leafhopper	Beans Carrots Potatoes Cucumbers Muskmelons	Carbaryl dust
Mexican bean beetle	Beans	5% carbaryl
Potato beetle	Potatoes Eggplants Tomatoes	5% carbaryl
Squash bug	Squash	
Squash vine borer (adult)	Squash	5% carbaryl

Insects are about natural size except where otherwise indicated. Where two drawings are shown, the smaller one is the natural size.

One pound of dust or 3 gallons of spray should be sufficient to treat 350 feet of row.

tb. = tablespoon, tsp. = teaspoon.

Several of the insecticides have limitations in days between application and harvest. This and other information, including directions, cautions, and restrictions, are indicated on the label. Commercial growers must continually stay abreast of insecticide regulations because registration and label changes may be made without notification. Growers should check with their county extension advisor

(Continued)

Spray Formula	Remarks
2 tb. wettable carbaryl in 1 gal. water	Ordinarily, hand-picking is more practical in the home garden.
2 tb. wettable carbaryl in 1 gal. water	Spray or dust once a week for 3 to 4 weeks, beginning when plants are small. Apply to underside of foliage.
2 tb. wettable carbaryl in 1 gal. water	Apply insecticide to underside of foliage. Also effective against leafhoppers on beans.
2 tb. wettable carbaryl in 1 gal. water	Apply when beetles or grubs first appear and repeat as necessary.
2 tsp. 50–57% emulsifiable malathion in 1 gal. water	Adults and brown egg masses can be hand-picked. Trap adults under shingles beneath plants. Kill young bugs soon after they hatch. Certified applicator only.
2 tb. wettable carbaryl in 1 gal. water	Dust or spray once a week for 3 to 4 weeks beginning in late June when first eggs hatch. Treat crowns of plants and runners thoroughly.

or vegetable extension specialist if there is any doubt about the insecticides they plan to use.

Home gardeners should limit their use of the available insecticides to *Bacillus thuringiensis*, carbaryl (Sevin®), and malathion for foliage application, and diazinon for soil insects.

Table 9.3. Some of the Insecticides Registered

Insecticide[2]	Beans	Peas	Broccoli	Brussels Sprouts	Cabbage	Cauliflower	Horseradish	Radishes	Turnips	Onions
Acephate (Orthene)[3]	X	—	—	—	—	—	—	—	—	—
Bacillus thuringiensis[4]	—	—	X	X	X	X	—	—	—	—
Carbaryl (Sevin)	X	—	X	X	X	X	X	X	X	—
Carbofuran (Furadan)[5]	—	—	—	—	—	—	—	—	—	—
Chlorpyrifos (Lorsban)	—	—	X	X	X	X	—	X	—	X
Diazinon	—	—	X	—	X	X	—	X	X	X
Dimethoate (Cygon)	X	X	X	—	X	X	—	—	X	—
Fonofos (Dyfonate)[5]	—	—	X	—	X	X	—	—	—	X
Ethion[5]	—	—	—	—	—	—	—	—	—	X
Esfenvalerate (Asana)[5]	X	X	X	—	X	X	—	—	—	—
Malathion	X	—	X	X	X	X	X	X	X	X
Methamidophos (Monitor)[5]	—	—	X	X	X	X	—	—	—	—
Methomyl (Lannate)[5]	X	X	X	X	X	X	—	—	—	—
Mevinphos (Phosdrin)[5]	—	—	X	X	X	X	—	—	X	—
Mocap[5]	—	—	—	—	—	—	—	—	—	—
Naled (Dibrom)	—	—	X	X	X	X	—	—	X	—
Permethrin (Ambush, Pounce)[5]	—	—	X	X	X	X	X	—	X	—
Phorate (Thimet)[5]	X	—	—	—	—	—	—	—	—	—
Rotenone	—	—	—	—	—	—	—	—	—	—
Terbufos (Counter)[5]	—	—	—	—	—	—	—	—	—	—
Trichlorfon (Dylox)	—	—	—	X	X	X	—	—	X	—

[1]Source: Randell, R. 1991. *Insect Pest Management for Commercial Vegetable Crops*, pp. 163–172. In: K. Steffey (coord.). *1991 Illinois Pest Control Handbook*. Univ. of Illinois Coop Ext. Ser.

[2]Applicators must read the entire, most recent label, and follow all directions, cautions, and restrictions.

[3]All insecticide names in parentheses are trade names.

[4]The trade names are Dipel, Thuricide, and Sok Bt.

[5]Use restricted to certified applicators only.

Insecticide Formulations

Insecticides used on vegetables may be found in one or all of three forms: 1) emulsifiable or flowable concentrates, 2) wettable powders, and 3) dusts. Any single insecticide is usually not found in all three forms. Emulsifiable or flowable concentrates and wettable powders are manufactured to be diluted with water to the desired concentration and sprayed with hand or power equipment. Dusts are almost never used commercially, but rather only by the home gardener, and are used in standard hand and power dusting equipment in the form in which they are purchased. All three forms have their advantages, depending on the

for Use on Vegetables in Illinois[1]

Eggplants	Peppers	Tomatoes	Potatoes	Collards	Kale	Lettuce	Spinach	Swiss Chard	Sweet Corn	Cucumbers	Melons	Pumpkins	Squash	
													Winter	Summer
—	X	—	—	—	—	—	—	—	—	—	—	—	—	—
—	—	X	—	X	X	X	X	—	—	—	—	—	—	—
X	X	X	X	X	X	X	X	X	X	X	X	X	X	X
—	X	—	X	—	—	—	—	—	X	X	X	X	X	X
—	—	—	—	—	—	—	—	—	X	—	—	—	—	—
—	—	X	—	X	X	X	X	X	X	X	X	—	X	X
—	X	X	X	X	X	X	X	X	—	—	X	—	—	—
—	—	—	—	—	—	—	—	—	X	—	—	—	—	—
—	—	—	—	—	—	—	—	—	—	—	—	—	—	—
X	X	X	X	—	—	—	—	—	X	X	X	X	X	X
X	X	X	X	X	X	X	X	X	X	X	X	X	X	X
—	—	—	—	—	—	—	—	—	—	—	—	—	—	—
—	X	X	X	—	—	X	X	—	X	X	X	—	—	X
—	—	—	—	X	X	X	X	—	—	—	—	—	—	—
—	—	—	—	—	—	—	—	—	X	—	—	—	—	—
—	—	—	—	X	X	X	X	X	—	—	—	—	—	—
—	—	—	X	X	—	—	—	—	X	X	X	X	X	X
—	—	—	X	—	—	—	—	—	X	—	—	—	—	—
X	X	X	—	—	—	—	—	—	—	—	—	—	—	—
—	—	—	—	—	—	—	—	—	X	—	—	—	—	—
—	X	X	—	X	X	X	—	—	—	—	—	X	—	—

insect to be controlled, the crop, the terrain, the weather and ground conditions, and the equipment available.

Granulars are another form of insecticide, used mostly for soil insects. Small clay pellets are evenly impregnated with insecticide and can be distributed by aircraft, fertilizer and seeding equipment, or with equipment made especially for granular application.

Biological Control

Microbial insecticides obtain their name from microbes, or microorganisms, which are used to control certain insects. *Bacillus thuringiensis* is a disease-causing bacterium which produces substances toxic to insects. More than 400 species of leaf-feeding caterpillars are known to be controlled by this important insect pathogen. It is sold under several trade names, as a liquid concentrate or a wettable powder, to be sprayed on infested plants. This form of insect control has two advantages: 1) insect predators and parasites are not killed, and 2) no harmful chemical residues remain on the produce at the time of harvest. *Bacillus thuringiensis* is available for home gardeners as well as commercial growers and is very effective for most leaf- and fruit-eating caterpillars.

CONTROLLING DISEASES

As with insect control, disease control is an important phase of vegetable production. Disease-control measures must begin before the disease is observed in the field. In contrast, measures for controlling insects are usually withheld until insects or their damage is observed.

Disease control begins with soil sterilization and seed treatment and continues with applications of fungicides (materials used to kill or control plant diseases) to the growing plant. Even though disease control appears more complicated with the ever-increasing number of new fungicides, the task has actually been simplified. Most vegetable diseases can now be prevented before they strike. Where fungicides have not been applied in time to prevent disease, they may, in some circumstances, be used to decrease the severity of damage after the disease has become established.

Soil Sterilization and Seed Treatment

If possible, the soil should be sterilized to kill fungi, bacterial spores, insect larvae and pupae, and weed seeds. The grower can do this by using a formaldehyde drench, treating with chloropicrin (a tear gas), dipping bagged soil into boiling water for several minutes, or heating the soil with live steam. Where live steam is available, as in steam-heated greenhouses, steam treatment is the most practical method.

For best results, soil sterilization should be combined with seed treatment. While sterilization of the soil will control many soil-borne diseases that begin with seed germination, it will not control those that are seed-borne. These are controlled by coating the seeds with a good seed protectant, either as a dust or as a slurry. Seed treatment is especially important where soil sterilization is not feasible, such as in field seedlings.

Seed can be purchased already treated at the packaging house, and typically all commercial seed is pre-treated. But if not, it can be treated by the grower, usually without any special equipment. Some of the materials commonly used for seed treatment are captan and thiram. Some seed can be hot-water–treated, but this technique, though very effective, is delicate and requires precise time and temperature control.

Fungicides

After seedlings have been transplanted in the field or field seedlings have sprouted and begun to develop, the next stage of disease prevention must be considered. Occasionally, some seedlings such as cabbage and pepper can be dipped in a fungicide solution just before transplanting to provide further protection while the plants are adjusting to climatic and soil changes. The new, automatic seedling transplanting machines have the capacity to add a fungicide to the water that is applied during transplanting.

Best results are obtained when the fungicides are applied before there is any evidence of plant damage to protect the plants during the stage when they are susceptible to pathogens. With some of the newer fungicides, applications can be delayed until disease symptoms appear without seriously affecting the crop. However, with crops whose sale value depends heavily on cosmetic quality or appearance, such as celery and lettuce, this cannot become the practice.

Some of the fungicides approved for use on vegetables are given in Table 9.4. As with insecticides, fungicides are included under EPA regulations. These regulations limit the amount of fungicides that can remain as residue on or in crops at the time of harvest.

Fungicide Formulations

Some fungicides can be applied as either sprays or dusts, but sprays are generally preferable because the films stick more readily, remain longer, and can be applied even during mild breezes. Dusts can be applied only when there is little or no wind. With the older fungicides, only that portion of the plant that has a coating of dust or spray film is protected from disease. This is not the case with the newer systemic fungicides, which are taken into the plant and moved rather uniformly throughout the stems and leaves, thus not requiring the complete coverage of the older fungicides.

Normally, applications must be repeated when the coating or film wears off or is washed off. In common practice, applications are made at 7- to 10-day intervals. In wet weather more frequent applications are necessary for two rea-

Table 9.4. Some Common Fungicides Registered for Use on Vegetables in Illinois[1]

Crop[2]	Benlate®	Bravo®	Dyrene®	Maneb® + Zinc Salt	Manco-zeb®	Botran®
Asparagus	—	—	—	X	X	—
Beans	X	X	—	—	—	X
Beets	—	—	—	—	—	—
Broccoli	—	X	—	—	—	—
Brussels sprouts . . .	—	X	—	—	—	—
Cabbage	—	X	—	—	—	—
Carrots	—	X	—	—	—	X
Cauliflower	—	X	—	—	—	—
Celery	X	X	X	—	—	—
Chinese cabbage . . .	—	X	—	—	—	—
Corn, sweet and pop	—	X	—	X	X	—
Cucumbers	X	X	—	—	—	X
Eggplants	—	—	—	—	—	—
Endive, escarole . . .	—	—	—	—	—	X
Fennel	—	—	—	—	—	—
Garlic	—	X	—	—	—	X
Kale, collards	—	—	—	—	—	—
Kohlrabi	—	—	—	—	—	—
Leek	—	—	—	—	—	—
Lettuce	—	—	—	—	—	X
Melons (muskmelons, honeydews, and watermelons)	X	X	—	—	—	—
Mustard greens	—	—	—	—	—	—
Onions	—	X	X	X	X	X
Parsley	—	—	—	—	—	—
Parsnips	—	X	—	—	—	—
Peas	—	—	—	—	—	—
Peppers	—	—	—	—	—	—
Potatoes	—	X	X	X	X	X
Pumpkins	X	X	—	—	—	—
Radishes	—	—	—	—	—	—
Shallots	—	X	—	—	—	—
Spinach	—	—	—	—	—	—
Squash	X	X	—	—	—	—
Tomatoes	X	X	X	—	X	X
Turnips, rutabagas . .	—	—	—	—	—	—

[1]Source: Eastburn, D. M., and M. C. Shurleff. 1991. *Plant Disease Management for Commercial Vegetable Crops*, pp. 193–202. In: K. Steffey (coord.). *1991 Illinois Pest Control Handbook*. Univ. of Illinois Coop. Ext. Ser.

[2]Applicators must read the entire, most recent label, and follow all directions, cautions, and restrictions.

sons: 1) the fungicide may be washed off by the rain and 2) some disease pathogens survive better during wet or damp weather than during dry conditions.

Antibiotics

Antibiotics are occasionally used in disease control. Strangely enough, they are produced by living fungi. At present, streptomycin is used primarily on bacterial diseases such as bacterial spot on peppers and tomatoes, but in rare situations it is effective against some fungal diseases. It has been recommended for use on seedling beds and on potato seed pieces.

NEMATODES

Nematodes are neither insects nor fungi, but they do injure all vegetable crops to some extent, depending on the crop, the soil type, and the consecutive number of years the same crop has been planted on the same field.

Nematodes are small eelworms, usually less than $1/16$ inch long, that live in and on the roots and surrounding soil of all vegetable crops. One nematode, the root knot nematode, is fairly widespread. It receives its name from the small, distinct galls it causes on the roots of cabbage and other crucifers. These galls vary from the size of a pinhead to 1 inch in diameter.

Nematodes usually feed and produce their young on the roots of a great number of plants. They live in the soil and in decaying vegetable material from one year to the next. The importance of their damage is not yet fully recognized by either growers or research scientists.

These tiny pests can be controlled in two major ways: 1) by including nematode-resistant cultivars or crops in the rotation system and 2) by fumigating the soil. Fumigation is quite expensive and requires highly skilled applicators. Additionally, most of the soil fumigants have been removed from the market either by their manufacturers or by the EPA. When used as a nematicide, the fumigant is applied several inches deep and is allowed to spread evenly through the soil to kill the nematodes. This usually requires several days before the soil can be worked for planting.

TIMING — THE CRITICAL PERIOD

With few exceptions, vegetable crops represent the highest acre investment of all forms of agricultural endeavor. In the value of the harvested crop, they again take the dollar lead. Each year's harvest usually represents an enormous number of worker-hours and a tremendous investment in irrigation equipment, fertilizer, and special planting, harvesting, and processing machinery. Considering the expense and effort involved in preparing a crop for market, it would seem unreasonable to permit an insect or disease pest infestation to lower the market grade or even, as occasionally happens, destroy the crop.

Yet, this very tragedy does occur, not because of the producer's failure to apply pesticides but because of several other factors. These include 1) poor timing of pesticide application, 2) improper selection of pesticide material, 3) unfavorable weather conditions, 4) low rate of application, 5) failure of equipment, and 6) negligence of operator.

Timing of application is the most important and probably the least attended of these factors. Insect and disease pests usually have a time in their development which can be referred to as the "critical period"; that is, a time in which they are most vulnerable to control. The critical period could also be applied to some stage in the growth of the plant, or even to the minimum number of days a material can be applied before harvest, according to EPA (and sometimes state) regulations. When planning insect and disease control, growers should consider carefully all three critical periods.

PESTICIDE LABELS

The label on a pesticide container gives instructions for its use and should be read and followed carefully. Maximum rates suggested should not be exceeded; the insecticide should be applied only to crops that are listed on the label; and the interval between application and harvest should be carefully observed. A record should be made of the product used, its trade name, the percentage active ingredient of the pesticide formulation, the dilution rate, the rate of application per acre, and the date(s) of application.

The "Read the label" cannot be overemphasized with respect to all pesticide applications. The commercial grower must follow a disease-control program that will assure the production of vegetables with no excessive fungicide residues.

Limits on the residues of insecticides and fungicides that can remain in or on raw agricultural commodities are carefully regulated by the EPA. These allowable amounts of pesticide residues on produce are known as *tolerances*. Vegetables marketed with residues exceeding EPA tolerances may be injurious to consumers, may be seized by the Food and Drug Administration, and may cause the grower to be heavily penalized. Many of the pesticides listed in Tables 9.3 and

9.4 will have limitations on the time in days between the last application and harvest.

Growers can have total confidence in the existing pesticide regulations as long as they use pesticides according to the current label and only on the crops specified, in the amounts recommended, and at the times indicated. These regulations are subject to change without notice and do not constitute recommendations for insect and disease control. For precise and timely information, growers should consult their state extension specialists for the latest suggested measures.

Although these regulations were designed primarily to protect the consumer, they also protect the vegetable producer and the pesticide manufacturer. The producer should follow the label directions for rate and time of application, which must appear on every pesticide container. By adhering to the manufacturer's directions, the grower is assured of placing produce on the market that will meet with tolerances established by the EPA. On the other hand, if the grower neglects to follow the label directions, the resulting harvested produce may be seized for having pesticide residues above tolerance. Under these conditions the grower must assume complete responsibility for residues in excess of tolerance. Obviously, it is extremely important to read and follow label directions.

COMBINING INSECTICIDES AND FUNGICIDES

Disease and insect problems frequently occur at the same time. Under such circumstances, both the insecticide and the fungicide may be applied together, in one operation, provided they are chemically compatible. Some materials, however, are not compatible with others. Applying incompatible materials together can reduce control of the insect, the disease, or both. This happens through chemical action or breakdown of the compounds in the spray tank.

To be certain that two materials can be mixed in the same spray application, growers should consult compatibility charts (graphs or tables that show which materials can and cannot be mixed together). They are usually available on request from pesticide dealers or cooperative extension specialists.

SAFE HANDLING OF INSECTICIDES AND FUNGICIDES

All insecticides and fungicides are toxic to both humans and animals to some extent. The persons most likely to encounter these hazards are the spray tank mixers and the applicators.

Mixers and applicators may have pesticides enter their bodies in three ways: by swallowing, by breathing dust or vapors, or by absorbing through the skin. One form can prove just as toxic as the others, but most cases of poisoning occur through skin exposure; individuals may accidentally pour or spill the concentrate on their hands and clothing or they may be wetted with the spray mixture. On rare occasions, persons are poisoned by accidentally eating or drinking pesticide materials that have lost their labels or have been transferred to other containers such as beverage bottles. Unfortunately, children are the most frequent victims of such adult carelessness. Because of this, all pesticides should be kept in their original containers and locked up. If they cannot be locked up, they should be placed well out of the reach of children.

In the handling of any pesticide, 10 general rules apply. Applicators should:

1. Read carefully the label warning statement and directions for use on the container *before* beginning the operation; *use only as directed*.

2. Wear rubber gloves when handling pesticide concentrates.

3. Wash hands before smoking or eating.

4. If clothing becomes saturated with liquid or dust, remove it immediately, take a shower or wash down with a hose, and change into clean clothes, including underwear.

5. At the end of each day's work with pesticides, always take a shower or bath and change all clothing.

6. Fill tanks and hoppers, treat seed, and make dilutions in well-ventilated places.

7. Leave unused pesticides in their original containers with the labels on them.

8. Triple-rinse pesticide containers, puncture to make unusable, and dispose of in an approved sanitary landfill. Paper containers may be burned, depending on local regulations.

9. Store pesticides out of reach of children and animals — preferably in a locked cabinet or storage room.

10. Not apply pesticides when weather conditions favor drift or near dug wells or cisterns.

Warning: Phorate, methomyl, carbofuran, ethion, fonofos, and mevinphos are very effective insecticides, but they are also highly toxic to humans if inhaled, absorbed through the skin, or swallowed. They should be applied only by certified applicators who have the experience, knowledge, and safety equipment necessary to protect all concerned.

SOURCES OF CONTROL RECOMMENDATIONS

By the time any publication on insect or plant disease control reaches the user, it has become outdated by more recent results of research, recommendations, and pesticide regulations. For a specific insect or a disease on a specific crop, the reader should consult more detailed information from reliable sources.

Insect- and disease-control suggestions come from many sources, but the most dependable are issued by the state agricultural experiment stations, the state cooperative extension services, and the U.S. Department of Agriculture. The cooperative extension service is represented by the county agricultural agents and the extension entomologist and plant pathologist. Most control suggestions can be obtained through the local county agent's office. USDA publications not available from the county extension offices can be purchased from the Superintendent of Documents, U.S. Government Printing Office, Washington, D.C. 20402.

SOURCES OF INSECT AND DISEASE IDENTIFICATION

Frequently vegetable producers find insects or diseased plants which they cannot identify. These problems should be carried to the local county extension office or sent to the extension specialists located at the state university.

Insect pests, including immature stages if possible, should be carefully wrapped in soft tissue paper (soft-bodied insects such as caterpillars can be preserved in 70% isopropyl alcohol or rubbing alcohol), packaged in a small bottle, plastic box, or other strong container, and sent by First Class mail to the extension entomologist.

Plant disease specimens should include entire plants, when possible, with the roots wrapped in moist soil, peatmoss, or wet newspaper. They should then be carefully packed in a strong container and mailed First Class to the extension plant pathologist.

A letter should always be attached to the package describing the crop, area, fungicide or insecticide history, location, and type of damage. The more information given the specialist, the easier it will be to identify the specimens.

Note: Any suggestions made here for pest control are summarized from information available in publications of the U.S. Department of Agriculture and state agricultural experiment stations and are presented only as indications of current practices. Readers are reminded that any use made of the control measures suggested here are at their own risk, and they are urged to consult their local cooperative extension service or state experiment station for detailed information concerning the proper pesticides to use and the best ways to control insect and disease pests in their particular locality. Readers are also strongly urged to follow carefully the directions given by the manufacturer on the label of any pesticide to be applied.

SELECTED REFERENCES

"Anonymous." 1985. *Pest Control for the Home and Garden. Insects. Plant Diseases. Vertebrates. Weeds.* British Columbia Ministry of Agriculture, Victoria, British Columbia, Canada.

Eastburn, D. M., and M. C. Shurtleff. 1991. *Plant Disease Management Guide for Commercial Vegetable Crops,* pp. 193–202. In: K. Steffey (coord.). *1991 Illinois Pest Control Handbook.* Univ. of Illinois Coop. Ext. Ser.

Hamman, P. J., and G. McIlveen. 1983. *Destructive Mites in the Garden and Home Landscape.* Texas A&M Univ. Coop. Ext. Ser. Bull. 1-1244.

Libby, J. L. 1977. *Insect Control in the Home Vegetable Garden.* Univ. of Wisconsin Coop. Ext. Urban Phytonarian A2088.

McNab, A. A., A. F. Sherf, and J. K. Springer. 1983. *Identifying Diseases of Vegetables.* Pennsylvania State Univ. College of Agriculture.

Meister, R. T. (ed.). 1991. *Farm Chemicals Handbook.* Meister Publ. Co., Willoughby, Ohio.

Miller, R. L., and M. A. Ellis. 1989. *Backyard Fruit Sprays for Insects and Diseases.* Ohio State Univ. Coop. Ext. Ser. Bull. L-1.

Miller, R. L. (ed). 1988. *Home Vegetable Garden Insect Control.* Ohio State Univ. Coop. Ext. Ser. Bull. 498.

Randell, R. 1991. *Insect Pest Management for Commercial Vegetable Crops,* pp. 163–172. In: K. Steffey (coord.). *1991 Illinois Pest Control Handbook.* Univ. of Illinois Coop. Ext. Ser.

Turney, H. A., and G. McIlveen. 1983. *Insect Control Guide for Organic Gardeners.* Texas A&M Univ. Coop. Ext. Ser.

U.S. Department of Agriculture. 1982. *Common Vegetable Insects.* Picture Sheet No. 9 (in color). Federal Ext. Ser.

Ware, G. W. 1991. *Fundamentals of Pesticides — A Self-instruction Guide,* 3rd ed. Thomson Publications, Fresno, California.

Ware, G. W. 1989. *The Pesticide Book.* Thomson Publications, Fresno, California.

10

POSTHARVEST HANDLING
OF VEGETABLES

E. L. Kerbel*

The nutritional value of vegetables as a vital source of essential minerals, vitamins, and dietary fiber has been well recognized. In addition to these constituents, vegetables also supply fair amounts of carbohydrates, protein, and energy and add color, flavor, and aroma to consumers' diets.

Vegetables are living tissues that are subject to continuous changes after harvest. Because of their characteristics (high-moisture content, large size, rapid rate of metabolism), they can deteriorate rapidly after removal from the plant.

Vegetables have their maximum potential for high quality when harvested. The postharvest treatments they receive determine whether this potential is realized or is lost. It is incorrect to say that quality always decreases after harvest. A mature green tomato has less visual appeal and nutritive quality when harvested than it has days later after it has ripened. However, the degree of quality it attained upon ripening was dictated by its condition when harvested and the treatment it received after harvest. Postharvest practices are designed to take full advantage of a commodity's quality potential and to reduce the rate of quality loss.

Not only must a vegetable be well grown but it also must be harvested at the right stage of maturity, carefully handled and packed, and delivered to fresh market in prime condition. Expedited operations are thus required by growers,

*Assistant Professor, Department of Horticulture, University of Illinois

171

handlers, marketing specialists, wholesalers, and retailers to move produce from the farm to the consumer.

CLASSIFICATION

Vegetables can be classified in a number of ways. A most useful method is to group crops by plant parts because commodities within these groups usually have similar postharvest characteristics (Table 10.1).

Table 10.1. Classification of Vegetables by Plant Parts

Plant Part	Examples
A. Entire plant	Sprouts, potted plants
B. Root	
1. Swollen taproot	Carrots, turnips, radishes, chicory, beets, celeriac
2. Root tuber	Sweet potatoes, cassavas, yams
C. Bulbs	Onions, garlic
D. Stem tuber	Potatoes, Jerusalem artichokes
E. Stem	Asparagus, kohlrabi
F. Leaf	
1. Blade	Leaf lettuce, spinach, chard, endive
2. Petiole	Celery, rhubarb
3. Buds	Lettuce, Brussels sprouts, cabbage
4. Shoots	Green onions, leeks
G. Floral parts	Artichokes, broccoli, cauliflower
H. Fruits	
1. Immature	
a. fleshy	Green peppers, summer squash, eggplants, cucumbers
b. non-fleshy	Snap beans, lima beans, peas, fava beans, sweet corn, okra, cowpeas
2. Mature	
a. fleshy	Tomatoes, red peppers, pumpkins, winter squash, watermelons
b. non-fleshy	Dry peas, dry beans

Leafy and Succulent Vegetables

These vegetables have a relatively low monetary value per unit weight. Most are also of low density so that they take up a lot of volume per unit weight. These two characteristics require that inexpensive packaging, handling, and transportation be used with these crops. With the exception of cabbage, leafy and succulent vegetables are traditionally marketed quickly after harvest.

Although these vegetables are temperate-zone or cool-season crops and thus, with the exception of asparagus, are not subject to chilling injury (a physiological disorder characterized by a variety of symptoms, which occurs when a commodity is subjected to temperatures above freezing but below a minimum threshold temperature value), most of them are more perishable than underground or fruit vegetables. They have a high water content and a large surface-to-volume ratio — characteristics that contribute to their susceptibility to water loss and physical damage.

Underground Vegetables

Because these crops are surrounded by soil during their growth and development and are exposed to soil-borne contamination during harvest and handling, they are subject to bacterial and fungal diseases. Extracting these large, bulky crops from the soil is often accomplished mechanically, which often produces many harvest-related injuries.

Initial storage conditions should encourage wound-healing to limit infection and water loss. Water loss is often minimal because of their large size; however, it can be severe in early harvested crops or in those crops that do not develop an effective barrier to water loss. Many of these crops are storage organs, and renewed growth can be a potential source of loss during long-term storage.

Potatoes are the most important vegetable within this group, both in the world and in the U.S.

Fruit Vegetables

Many vegetables are classified botanically as fruits, i.e., as the products of ripening ovaries and their associated tissues.

Most fruit vegetables are warm-season crops (tomatoes are the leading fresh market vegetable in the U.S.) and are subjected to chilling injury. Exceptions are sweet corn and cool-season crops like fresh peas and fava beans. Most fruit vegetables are not adapted to long-term storage. The exceptions are hard-rind (winter) squash, pumpkins, and dry legumes.

Fruit vegetables picked immature are more susceptible to water loss than those picked mature because of their poorly developed cuticle. Physical damage is a major source of losses in quantity and quality during postharvest handling and marketing.

FACTORS INVOLVED IN DETERIORATION

Biological Factors

Respiration. Respiration is the overall process by which stored plant reserves (carbohydrates, fats, and proteins) are broken down to simple end products with the release of energy in the form of heat. Oxygen is used in this process, and carbon dioxide is released by the commodity. This heat, called vital heat, is always a part of the refrigeration load that must be considered in handling vegetables in cold storage.

Some vegetables have high respiration rates and require considerably more refrigeration than more slowly respiring crops to keep them at specified temperatures. Asparagus, for example, respires approximately 10 times faster than tomatoes.

The rate of respiration is governed by temperature. Head lettuce respires about three times as fast at 50°F as at 32°F. The faster a commodity respires, the greater the quantity of heat generated. The rate of deterioration (perishability) of harvested commodities is generally proportional to their respiration rate. The storage life of crops like broccoli, lettuce, peas, sweet corn, spinach, and watercress, which have relatively high rates of respiration, is short; and that of onions, potatoes, and sweet potatoes, which have low respiration rates, is long.

Cultural and marketing practices can significantly affect respiration and consequently perishability. Root crops marketed with tops have a higher respiration rate than that of the roots alone (e.g., carrots, radishes). Potatoes harvested immature (new potatoes) respire twice as fast as those harvested mature. Cured potatoes and sweet potatoes have a lower respiration rate than non-cured ones.

Ethylene Production. Ethylene is a natural product of plant metabolism and is produced by all tissues of higher plants. Ethylene plays an important role, often deleterious, increasing the rate of senescence and reducing shelflife. Sometimes ethylene is beneficial, improving the quality of the product by faster and more uniform ripening prior to retail distribution.

Ethylene is physiologically active in trace amounts (less than 0.1 ppm). Generally, ethylene production rates increase with maturity at harvest, physical injuries, disease incidence, increased temperature up to 86°F, and water stress. Ethylene is exempted from the requirement of a residue tolerance when used as a plant regulator either before or after harvest.

Compositional Changes. Many changes in composition may continue in vegetable crops after harvest, and these can be desirable or undesirable. Loss of chlorophyll (green color) is desirable in some fruit vegetables, but undesirable in leafy vegetables. Development of red, yellow, and orange colors is desirable in tomatoes, squashes, pumpkins, carrots, and some peppers and muskmelons.

Conversion of starch to sugar can occur at low temperatures (32°–41°F) and can be desirable (parsnips, sweet potatoes) or undesirable (potatoes). On the other hand, sugar to starch conversion is undesirable in peas and sweet corn.

The breakdown of polysaccharides can result in a softening of fruit vegetables and a consequent increase in susceptibility to mechanical injuries. Increased lignin content is responsible for toughening of asparagus and root vegetables. Loss of vitamin content (mainly through water loss), especially ascorbic acid (vitamin C), is detrimental to nutritional quality.

Transpiration or Water Loss. Loss of water from harvested vegetables is a major cause of deterioration in storage. Most fruit and vegetables contain between 80 and 95% water by weight, some of which may be lost by evaporation. This loss of water is known as *transpiration*. Transpiration rate is influenced by internal or commodity factors (morphological and anatomical characteristics, surface-to-volume ratio, surface injuries, and maturity stage), and external or environmental factors (temperature, relative humidity, air velocity, and atmospheric pressure). The rate of transpiration, which must be minimized to avoid loss in salable weight and to avoid wilting and shrivelling of produce, can be controlled by good handling conditions at recommended humidity and temperature.

A moisture loss of 3–8% is enough to cause a marked loss of quality for many vegetables. Roots stored with the tops attached lose water much faster than those with the tops removed. The vitamin C content of green vegetables decreases more readily when they are stored under conditions favorable to wilting.

Condition of Crop. Commodities should be in excellent condition and have excellent quality if maximum storage life is desired. The physical condition of stored vegetables does not improve in storage. Vegetables should be as free as possible from skin breaks, bruises, and other forms of deterioration. Not only are mechanical injuries unsightly, but they also accelerate water loss, provide good avenues for entrance of decay organisms, and stimulate respiration and ethylene production by the commodity, which results in faster deterioration.

Growth and Development. Sprouting of potatoes, onions, garlic, and root crops greatly reduces their utilization value and accelerates deterioration. Sprouting can often be inhibited by preharvest application (2–4 weeks before harvest) of maleic hydrazide (MH-30). Rooting of onions and root crops is also undesirable. Asparagus spears continue to grow after harvest; elongation and curvature (if the spears are held horizontally) are accompanied with increased toughness and decreased palatability. Seed germination inside tomatoes and peppers reduces quality.

Environmental Factors

Temperature. Temperature is the single most important environmental factor that influences the deterioration rate of harvested vegetables. For each increase in 18°F above optimum, the rate of deterioration increases by two- to three-fold. Temperature influences respiration and ethylene production rates, metabolism, moisture loss, compositional changes, development of physiological disorders, growth rate of pathogens, and undesirable growth, such as sprouting of underground crops. For maximum storage life, the minimum safe temperatures for individual or groups of vegetables should be maintained.

Relative Humidity. Relative humidity can influence water loss, incidence of some physiological disorders, uniformity of fruit ripening, and decay development. For most vegetables the optimum relative humidity is about 90–100%. If the humidity of the air in storage rooms is too low, wilting or shrivelling will occur. High humidity is beneficial for wound healing and curing of certain crops.

The relative humidities recommended are those that retard moisture loss and do not favor growth of microorganisms. Condensation of moisture on the commodity (sweating) during storage is probably more important than is the relative humidity of the ambient air in enhancing decay.

Atmospheric Composition. Reduction of oxygen and elevation of carbon dioxide in the atmosphere surrounding a crop, whether intentional (modified or controlled atmosphere storage) or unintentional, can either delay or accelerate deterioration of vegetables. The magnitude of these effects depends on commodity, cultivar, physiological age, maturity, O_2 and CO_2 levels, temperature, and duration of holding.

About 1–3% O_2 is the lowest limit tolerated by most vegetables. Below this, anaerobic respiration may result in the development of off-flavors and off-odors. Vegetables with a wide variety of plant parts differ greatly in their CO_2 tolerance. Differences in susceptibility to elevated CO_2 and reduced O_2 among commodities or cultivars of a given commodity may be due to structural (anatomical, natural barriers within the plant parts) differences rather than metabolic differences. While lettuce is damaged by 1–2% CO_2, spinach tolerates 20% CO_2. Broccoli tolerates 15% CO_2, but cauliflower is damaged by 5% CO_2.

Ethylene. The most important sources of ethylene as an air pollutant during postharvest handling are internal combustion engines, ripening rooms, and ripening fruits. Other sources include decomposing produce, fluorescent ballasts, cigarette smoke, rubber materials exposed to heat or UV light, and virus-infected plants.

Since ethylene found in the environment can reduce the life of vegetables sensitive to it, techniques to remove or avoid its effects are of considerable importance during postharvest handling, storage, and transportation.

Light. Greening due to exposure to light is a problem with potatoes, onions, garlic, and Belgian endive. The amount of chlorophyll that develops depends upon the intensity and quality of light, duration of exposure, cultivar, and crop maturity. Greening is a serious defect in potatoes because it is often associated with the formation of solanine, a bitter and toxic compound.

Sanitation. Maintenance of sanitary conditions is essential for minimizing development of and contamination by decay organisms during postharvest handling operations. Harvesting equipment, field bins, trucks, packinghouse lines, and storage rooms should be maintained clean, and rotted produce should be disposed of promptly.

Air purification is a recommended practice in storage rooms where odors or volatiles may contribute to off-flavors and hasten deterioration.

MATURATION AND MATURITY INDICES

Horticultural maturity can be defined as "that stage at which a commodity has reached a sufficient stage of development that after harvesting and postharvest handling (including ripening), its quality will be at least the minimum acceptable."

A given commodity may be horticulturally mature at any stage of development. In most vegetables optimum horticultural maturity coincides with optimum eating quality. Yet, for many vegetables, the optimum eating quality is reached before full maturity (i.e., full development), e.g., leafy vegetables, immature fruits (cucumbers, sweet corn, green beans, peas), etc. In this case, the problem frequently is delayed harvest which results in overmaturity and consequently lower quality. Fruit vegetables consumed ripe attain their best quality when ripened on the plant. Immaturity in this group results in inferior quality.

The maturity at harvest has an important bearing on the way in which commodities are handled, transported, and marketed and on their storage life and final quality.

Maturity indices for selected vegetables that have been proposed or are presently in use are shown in Table 10.2.

Table 10.2. Maturity Indices for Selected Vegetables

Index	Examples
Heat units during fruit development	Peas, sweet corn
Development of abscission layer	Muskmelons
Drying of foliage	Potatoes
Drying of tops	Garlic, onions
Surface morphology and structure	Tomatoes—cuticle development
	Muskmelons—skin netting
Size	Most vegetables
Color (external)	Most vegetables
Specific gravity	Watermelons, potatoes
Shape compactness	Cauliflower, broccoli
Solidity	Cabbage, lettuce, Brussels sprouts
Internal color structure	Tomatoes—formation of jelly-like material
Tenderness	Peas
Toughness	Asparagus

HARVESTING

When to Harvest

The time of harvest is almost always a compromise. On the one hand, it is desirable to have the commodity at a stage of development (maturity) which will ensure the maximum quality to the ultimate consumer. On the other hand, the commodity must be harvested when it can tolerate the rigors of harvesting, handling, packing, storage, and transportation.

In many vegetables, tenderness and flavor are best before the crop has reached a size that is profitable to the grower and before the commodity has sufficient mechanical rigidity to withstand the rigors of marketing.

Timing of harvest (based on maturity indices) is complicated by the great differences that occur in the rate of development and maturation of individual plants, or organs on the same plant. This variability in maturation and ripening is especially important when once-over mechanical harvesting is used.

Economic considerations, price and demand for a crop, are often even more important factors that affect the decision to harvest.

Hand vs Mechanical Harvest

Even in the U.S., most fresh vegetables are harvested by hand. Only the unique combination of eyes, intelligence, and hands can permit rapid harvest of delicate and perishable materials with minimum loss and bruising. Pickers can be trained to select only those vegetables that are of the correct maturity and to leave produce that is immature, overmature, blemished, or diseased in the field. This saves in the cost of transportation and later grading of the produce and reduces the danger of spreading infection during the handling and packing operations.

With some commodities, mechanical aids can be used in hand harvesting. Belt conveyors are used for some vegetable crops, such as lettuce and melons, to move the harvested commodity to a central loading or in-field loading device. Lights have been used to a limited extent for night harvest of melons.

Mechanical harvest can be used with commodities that can be harvested at one time and are not sensitive to mechanical injury (e.g., some roots and tubers, sweet corn, peas, and snap beans), and with vegetables designed for immediate processing (e.g., pickling cucumbers and processing tomatoes). Although mechanical harvest has the potential for rapid harvest and reduces problems associated with hiring and managing hand labor, it is not presently used for most fresh vegetables because machines are rarely capable of selective harvest; whatever can be shaken, pulled, or beaten off the plant is harvested. Mechanization has increased the efficiency of harvesting, but in many cases it has also increased damage to vegetables.

Temperature Protection

Temperature protection in the field involves shading the harvested vegetables to minimize high temperature exposure and warming of the crops. This may mean moving harvested produce to the shade of plants and bushes while awaiting transport. If natural shade is not available, then portable shading may be needed. Inverting empty containers over the top of stacks of containers can provide some field protection. During periods of very high field temperatures, it may be desirable to avoid harvesting in mid-day.

PREPARATION FOR FRESH MARKET

The purposes of preparing for market are: 1) to eliminate unwanted material, 2) to select items of similar grade, and by this, 3) to improve the value of the marketed portion of the crop. The preparation of vegetables for marketing may be done mostly in the field (Figure 10.1) or in packing sheds or facilities.

Some advantages of field packing are: 1) less material to transport and dispose; 2) fewer handling steps, which results in less damage to the commodity and consequently better quality; and 3) smaller initial cost. Disadvantages of field packing include: 1) less control over quality, 2) more dependence on weather

Figure 10.1. Harvesting and field packing of crisphead lettuce.

than packinghouse operations, 3) large machines needed in the field, and 4) cooling of produce inside field cartons is more difficult than bulk cooling.

In more typical operations, the crop is transported in bins or gondolas to a facility to be packed and graded.

Packinghouse Operations

Preparation for marketing begins with harvesting (maturity selection and some quality control) and, depending upon the commodity, may include some or all of the following subsequent operations:

Receiving. The receiving area should be covered to keep the product cool and to retard deterioration. The crop is then unloaded from field containers onto a conveyor or into a wet dump for conveying to the packinghouse. This can be done with dry dumps, water dumps, or water flumes. Dry dumps can cause considerable product damage. Sanitation with chlorinated agents is important in water dumps and flumes to prevent bacterial or fungal contamination. A conveyor belt then moves the crop to the eliminator for removal of undersized and decaying products, as well as non-crop materials, e.g., leaves, twigs, and stones.

Cleaning. Washing and / or brushing removes soil, spray residues, and other foreign materials from the product surface. The wash water may or may not be chlorinated. Recycled water should always be chlorinated. Air dryers or sponge rollers are then used to remove excess water from product surfaces.

Pre-sizing. When needed, pre-sizers are usually located immediately after the dump and designed to eliminate commodities below a minimum acceptable size.

Trimming. In crops such as lettuce, celery, cauliflower, asparagus, and dry onions, trimming removes unwanted leaves, stems, or roots prior to grading, packaging, and packing (Figure 10.2).

Figure 10.2. A modern broccoli grading and packinghouse.

Sorting. Sorting eliminates defects. Most products are selected based on maturity, shape, color, or some other physical parameter. Some commodities are machine-sorted.

Waxing. The process of covering the surfaces of product units with a coating of food-grade wax reduces water loss through epidermal openings, replaces natural waxes removed during washing and / or brushing, and covers injuries. Wax is generally applied to fruit vegetables such as tomatoes, peppers, and cucumbers, but it may also be used on root crops such as rutabagas. Waxing is also used to improve the cosmetic appearance of the commodity. A fungicide may be incorporated into the wax.

Sizing. Product units are separated into physical sizes (weight, volume, length, diameter, or other parameters). This is mostly done by mechanical or electronic sizers, although many vegetables are still manually sized.

Curing. Some products such as garlic, dry onions, sweet potatoes, and new-crop potatoes are cured after harvesting and prior to storage or marketing. Onions and garlic are cured to dry their necks and outer scales. Sweet potatoes and potatoes are cured to develop suberized layers and wound periderms over cut, broken, or skinned surfaces. Curing helps heal harvesting injuries, reduces water loss, and prevents entry of decay-causing organisms during storage. Curing may be done in the field (garlic, onions), in curing rooms (sweet potatoes), or during transit (new-crop potatoes).

Grading. Products are separated according to market quality (grades) on the basis of color, shape, maturity, or other physical parameters. Currently, there are many attempts to automate separation of a given commodity into various grades and to eliminate defective units. The availability of low-cost microcomputers and solid-state imaging systems has made computer-aided video inspection on the packing line a practical reality. Solid-state video cameras or light-reflectance systems can be used for detection of external defects, while x-ray or light transmittance systems can be used for detecting internal defects.

Packaging. Individual product units are enclosed in individual packages (wraps, bags, sleeves, trays, or other units) that are subsequently packed in master containers. Most materials used for consumer unit packaging are flexible plastic films. Paper bags are also used. Some packaging involves enclosing a single product unit (a head of lettuce or cauliflower, celery), while in other packaging, several product units are enclosed in a single consumer unit (sweet corn, potatoes, radishes, Brussels sprouts, carrots). Packaging is done both automatically and manually at the shipping point or destination market, or both.

Packing. A given count or weight of similar-sized product units is assembled into shipping containers. Counts, arrangements, and weights are often specified in and regulated by the various grade standards and industry codes. Product units can be packed mechanically or by hand. Liners and pads may assist the operation but increase the materials costs. Shipping containers may be bags, cartons, crates, lugs, or bulk bins. Some vegetables are shipped unpacked to markets in bulk trucks or railroad cars.

The purposes of packing are: 1) efficient handling of products; 2) protection of the commodity from physical injury, contamination, and pilferage; and 3) identification of the product, producer, and shipper. When designing packages for horticultural crops, one should consider important factors such as container ventilation to facilitate air flow and achieve heat removal during precooling and refrigerated storage and transport, protection from injuries and water loss, compatibility with existing marketing systems, and cost.

Ripening Initiation. Ethylene gas is commonly applied at the shipping point in order to stimulate faster and more uniform ripening of mature green tomatoes and honeydews. Satisfactory ripening occurs within the range of 59°–77°F, with the rate of ripening increasing with the temperature within this range. Commodities should be treated with ethylene concentrations of about 100 ppm for 18–48 hours. The relative humidity in the ripening room should be maintained between 90 and 95%. Adequate air circulation and ventilation should be provided to ensure good distribution of ethylene within the ripening room and to prevent the accumulation of CO_2, which reduces the effectiveness of ethylene.

COOLING VEGETABLES

Precooling

Cooling vegetable crops immediately after harvest is the best way to maintain high quality. Precooling entails the rapid removal of field heat to lower the temperature of the commodity to the recommended storage temperature before it is stored. Precooling is usually done in a facility that is separate from the cold storage room. The precooling facility is characterized by having a very large refrigeration capacity and the capacity to move the cooling medium rapidly past the commodity.

The packing method will dictate how, and sometimes when, the product is presented for cooling. Packaging materials and design will affect access of the coolant to the product, and pallet stacking patterns will influence coolant flow through and around containers.

Precooling Methods

The technique selected for cooling a particular produce item depends on a wide range of factors, including the rate of cooling desired, the surface-to-volume ratio, the susceptibility to water damage or fungal infection, and the practical requirements of the packaging and handling system. Economic considerations may dictate which cooling method is used.

Room Cooling. This is the traditional technique. Field bins or packed commodities are placed in a cold room and allowed to cool. Typically, cold air is discharged into the room near the ceiling, moves horizontally across the ceiling, and then sweeps past the produce containers to return to the heat exchangers. Room cooling is relatively inexpensive compared to other methods, but too slow for most vegetables.

The efficiency of room cooling can be improved by the use of ceiling jets or fans to increase air velocities. Cabbage and artichokes are primarily cooled with this method, although all vegetables can be room cooled. Room cooling allows produce to be cooled in the same location where it will be stored.

Forced-Air Cooling (Pressure Cooling). This is a much more efficient and rapid method than room cooling because it provides for cold air movement through, rather than around, containers. The system, which creates a slight pressure gradient to cause air to flow through container vents, achieves rapid cooling as a result of the intimate contact between cold air and warm product. With proper design, fast, uniform cooling can be achieved through stacks of pallet bins or unitized pallet loads of containers. It is widely used for fruit vegetables, tubers, onions, garlic, and cauliflower.

Hydrocooling. Hydrocooling is an extremely efficient method for cooling because of the high heat capacity and thermal conductivity of water, which makes it a better cooling medium than air (Figure 10.3).

Two types of hydrocoolers in common use are immersion and spray. In the first type, the product is submerged in cold water. This can create problems

Figure 10.3. Hydrocooling and washing of artichokes.

because of water intrusion into the commodity. Water can enter the crop because of hydrostatic pressure when it is submerged to a depth of more than a few inches. In a spray-type hydrocooler, cold water is sprayed over the crop. In either type, the water must be clean and usually chlorinated to prevent the spread of pathogens.

Hydrocooling is widely used to cool vegetables in bins or in bulk before packing; these vegetables include lettuce, celery, spinach, some green onions, leeks, artichokes, muskmelons, sweet corn, and most temperate-zone crops. Its use is limited for packed commodities because the containers must withstand water soaking. The product must be tolerant of wetting.

Package Icing. Some vegetables are cooled by filling packed containers with predetermined quantities of ice. Package ice may be finely crushed ice, flake-ice, or a slurry of ice and water at 32°F, called liquid ice. With certain products, for example, broccoli, liquid ice is sprayed into the packed boxes (wax- impregnated) to achieve better ice-product contact (Figure 10.4). Package icing requires the use of more expensive, water-tolerant shipping containers.

Package icing is less efficient than forced-air or hydrocooling but is still useful for some root and stem vegetables, Brussels sprouts, and green onions. It is limited to commodities that can tolerate water–ice contact. Top icing and icing in bulk

Figure 10.4. Liquid icing a pallet of broccoli.

inside rail cars have been used with muskmelons, and carrots, and some other root crops.

Vacuum Cooling. Vegetables that have a favorable surface-to-mass ratio, such as leafy vegetables, can be rapidly cooled by this method. It has the advantage that it cools the product throughout the container and throughout the bulk of a well-insulated item such as iceberg lettuce. It is also used to cool cauliflower, celery, and some sweet corn, carrots, and bell peppers. Its use with carrots and peppers is primarily to dry the surface and stems, respectively, to inhibit postharvest decay.

Cooling is achieved by reducing the atmospheric pressure inside a large, steel chamber containing the product. This reduction in atmospheric pressure causes loss of water vapor from the commodities, resulting in cooling. Vacuum cooling causes about 1% product weight loss (mostly water) for each 11°F of product cooling. A patented process called Hydro-Vac®, which adds water in the form of a fine spray during the vacuum-cooling cycle, reduces water loss, and is used in some operations, especially with celery.

STORAGE OF VEGETABLES

The orderly marketing of vegetable crops often requires some storage to balance day-to-day fluctuations between product harvest and sales, and may include some long-term storage to extend the processing and marketing season of some commodities. Table 10.3 shows recommended storage conditions and shelflife expectancy for various vegetables.

Room Cooling and Cold Storage: Two Different Operations

Refrigeration capacity for fast cooling and that for cold storage are quite different. It takes much more refrigeration to cool a commodity than to cold store it. High relative humidity is essential to prevent excessive water loss during cold storage but is not as important during the relatively short cooling period.

Most cold storage facilities use mechanical refrigeration to control storage temperature. This system is based on a liquid absorbing heat as it changes to a gas. The simplest method for doing this is to release liquid nitrogen into the storage environment. This requires a constant supply of refrigerant. This system is used only to a limited extent with highway vans where high nitrogen concentrations and low O_2 levels may also be of value. The more common mechanical refrigeration systems use a refrigerant such as ammonia or one of several kinds

Table 10.3. Recommended Storage Conditions for Selected Vegetables[1]

Vegetable	Temperature		Relative Humidity	Storage Life[2]
	(°C)	(°F)	(%)	
Asparagus	0–2	32–35	95	2–3 weeks
Beans—snap	5–8	41–46	90–95	7–10 days
—lima	3–5	37–41	90–95	5–7 days
Broccoli	0	32	90–95	10–14 days
Brussels sprouts	0	32	90–95	3–5 weeks
Cabbage—head	0	32	95–98	1–6 months
—Chinese	0	32	98–100	2–3 months
Carrots	0	32	95–100	1–3 months
Cauliflower	0	32	95–100	3–4 weeks
Celery	0	32	98–100	1–2 months
Cucumbers	10–13	50–55	95	10–14 days
Eggplants	10–12	50–54	90–95	1 week
Garlic	0	32	65–70	6–7 months
Honeydews	7	45	90–95	2–3 weeks
Lettuce	0	32	98–100	2–3 weeks
Mushrooms	0	32	90–95	3–5 days
Muskmelons	8–10	46–50	90–95	7–14 days
Onions—dry	0	32	65–70	1–7 months
—green	0	32	95–100	3–4 weeks
Peas	0	32	95–98	1–2 weeks
Peppers	8–12	46–54	90–95	2–3 weeks
Potatoes	4	39	90–95	4–8 months
Spinach	0	32	95–98	10–14 days
Squash—summer	7–10	45–50	95	1–2 weeks
—winter	10–12	50–54	60	1–3 months
Sweet corn	0	32	95–98	5–8 days
Tomatoes—mature green	12–14	54–57	90–95	1–3 weeks
—fully ripe	8–10	46–50	90–95	4–7 days
Watermelons	8–12	46–54	90	2–3 weeks

[1]Source: USDA. 1986. Agriculture Handbook No. 66.

[2]These values represent only approximate values and will vary depending on the cultivar and the atmospheric conditions that are present.

of freons, where the vapor can easily be recaptured by a compressor and a heat exchanger, allowing the refrigerant to be continuously recycled.

Alternate Storage Methods

In places where mechanical refrigeration is prohibitively expensive to install and maintain, a range of other techniques is available for storing vegetables. Some of these less sophisticated techniques are still widely used.

Field Storage. Vegetables such as cabbage, potatoes, and most root crops can be stored in the field in trenches, pits, mounds, or clamps. When freezing weather approaches, a well-drained place is selected. The vegetables may be placed in piles surrounded by straw and covered with just enough soil to prevent freezing injury. Ventilation can be provided by a flue placed in the center of the pile, extending it above the cover and running perforated channels across the pile.

Common or Unrefrigerated Storage. These structures can include specially constructed buildings that are often heavily insulated, rooms dug into the ground, cellars, abandoned mines, or human-made caves. These facilities are best used for commodities that can be stored for long periods, such as potatoes, onions, winter squash, and some root crops. These structures are only effective in climates where the ambient temperatures during the storage period are low enough to maintain product quality for a reasonable length of time.

Night Air Storage. In warmer climates a modification of common storage can be used if there is a substantial difference between the day and night temperature during the storage season. The technique used is termed "night air ventilation." The produce is placed in a common store which is well insulated and supplied with a ventilation system to enable air to be drawn into the store and distributed through the produce during the coolest part of the night. This technique is sometimes used to remove field heat and cool produce before refrigerated storage. It could also be used to maintain produce at the proper storage temperature when the nights are cold.

Nighttime cooling is commonly used for unrefrigerated storage of potatoes, sweet potatoes, onions, hard-rind squash, and pumpkins.

High Altitude Storage. High altitude can also be a source of cold. As a rule of thumb, air temperature decreases by 5.5°F for every 1,000 feet increase in altitude. Consequently, it may be possible to store some commodities at high elevations in mountainous areas. Air temperature has the potential of being more than 27°F cooler at high altitudes than at sea level.

TRANSPORTATION

Transportation methods used for moving fresh vegetables from shipping points to destination markets include railroads, trucks, ships, airplanes, and combinations of these, e.g., trailers on flat cars (TOFC), also called "piggy-backs." Over-the-road truck transport now accounts for over 70% of the movement of vegetables in the U.S.

Modes of Transportation

Water Transportation. Water transport is much more energy-efficient than other modes of transportation. For international trade in commodities such as onions and potatoes, sea transportation under refrigerated or ventilated conditions is still the preferred method.

By far the largest portion of vegetables transported by sea now travel in seagoing intermodal "marine" containers (Figure 10.5). These containers are well insulated and may or may not have their own refrigeration capacity. The containers are 20–40 feet in length. Although many feature top air delivery, there is a trend towards containers with bottom air delivery, where the circulation system works with, rather than against, the natural convective flow of air through the load of product.

Figure 10.5. Refrigerated marine containers being loaded into a ship.

Other vessels, many of which ply between Australia, New Zealand, or South Africa and the countries in Europe, are designed to supply cool air to the containers from a centralized refrigerated system on the vessels.

Rail Transportation. In the latter part of the 19th century, ice refrigeration systems were developed for transport of perishables by rail. Ice-bunker cars needed frequent replenishing, and icing stations were developed along major railways. Ice was often harvested from lakes and streams during the winter. Some ice-bunker cars are still operational. Air is circulated through ice bunkers at either end of the car and over the product by electric fans powered from the locomotive. Disadvantages include the need for replenishing the ice and the volume utilized by the ice bunkers.

Diesel-powered refrigerated rail cars are primarily used for long haul (more than 2,000 miles) domestic and Canadian shipments of generally only one commodity, and sometimes two or three. These cars have a large load space (more than 4,000 cubic feet) and weight capacity (more than 100,000 pounds).

In general, rail cars are heavily insulated and fairly airtight, so that a major problem can be providing enough air exchanges to prevent injurious atmospheric modifications in route. Many of the mechanically refrigerated cars, last made in the U.S. in the early 1970's, are inadequately serviced, and no longer able to maintain proper product temperatures throughout. Transportation times range from 6 to 10 days on transcontinental shipments in the U.S.

Piggy-back trailer or flat car (TOFC) transportation of vegetables has been of considerable interest to shippers in recent years. This system uses road-trailers loaded at the railhead onto flat cars and then reconnected to a tractor unit at the destination. The flexibility of containerized truck transportation and the economy of rail transport are thus combined.

Road Transportation. Over-the-road refrigerated truck trailers are now the dominant mode in the distribution of perishables. Most refrigerated trucks are now of the tractor-trailer type, where a separate power train cab (the tractor) hauls a refrigerated road trailer (Figure 10.6). These trailers are of standard dimensions, have a load space of 2,000–3,500 cubic feet, and carry up to 45,000 pounds of produce. Gross weight of the truck is limited by highway load limit regulations to 72,000–80,000 pounds.

Figure 10.6. Refrigerated highway trucks awaiting loading of produce at a refrigerated distribution center's dock.

The refrigeration unit is diesel-powered, and the air circulation pattern is usually lengthwise, front to rear over the top of the load, down the end of the load, and back through and / or under the load. The air circulation capacity is designed for maintaining product temperatures, not for cooling. New containers incorporate a design in which air circulation is from the bottom, along deeper floor sections, to the top.

Trailers are less insulated than rail cars, allowing more conduction of energy across walls, roof, floor, and doors. Recent studies have shown that a very substantial portion of the heat load in summer shipments by truck is the radiant heat from the road surface, whose temperature can be as much as 14°F higher than the air temperature.

Air Transportation. Due to its very high cost, air shipment is limited to highly perishable and valuable commodities, such as flowers, berries, and tropical fruits.

Factors Affecting Temperature Management During Transit

Refrigeration and Air Circulation System. To be effective at maintaining temperatures, a refrigeration system needs forced-air delivery and air-return channels large enough to enable the fans to operate near peak performance. Anything that interferes with this air circulation will reduce cooling efficiency and temperature maintenance.

A thick layer of top ice, 6 inches or greater, over a load of vegetables prevents cold air from cooling the product. Only the top layer of the product which is in contact with the ice is kept cool. In tight loads of produce, the lower layers can warm.

Condition and Features of the Transit Vehicle. Intact sidewalls and insulation, clean floors and drains, refrigeration units properly serviced and maintained (including frequent calibration of thermostats), intact air delivery chute(s), and tight, undamaged doors and seals are essential to proper temperature maintenance.

Shipping Container Design and Construction. Inadequately vented containers, primarily cartons and large polyethylene bags, prevent sufficient air movement around products for effective temperature management, especially in solid, tight loads. Partial collapse of weak containers results in the formation of a solid load mass which completely prevents air circulation through the loads.

Load Patterns and Sizes. Loads must have open-air channels through and around them that are either vertical or horizontal. Loads should be assembled to assure that their rigidity and conformation will be maintained in transit, which is generally achieved by unitizing load units on pallets or slip sheets.

The use of incentive freight rates, in which per package freight cost decreases as load weight increases, has created serious transit temperature maintenance problems in recent years. Incentive rates have resulted in such increases in load size, weight, and tightness that adequate transit temperature maintenance is difficult. In hot or very cold weather, loads should be palletized and pallets loaded away from the sidewalls and floor to prevent excessive warming or freezing in wall or bottom layers of products.

Mixed Loads. Maintaining optimum product temperatures in mixed loads is difficult, especially in loads containing several commodities. Vegetables are generally packed in containers of different sizes and shapes, which are often loaded in different patterns in various parts of a transit vehicle. In mixed loads certain product compatibility factors must be considered. They are:

1. *Temperature compatibility* — Differences in optimum and minimum safe temperatures for products shipped together must be considered. Chilling-sensitive commodities (e.g., tomatoes, bell peppers, summer squash) should not be shipped with products whose optimum temperature is 32°F (e.g., leafy vegetables, many fruits).

2. *Ethylene production and sensitivity* — Care must be taken not to ship commodities that produce large amounts of ethylene (e.g., apples, pears, avocadoes, bananas, certain muskmelons, tomatoes) with commodities that are very sensitive to ethylene (broccoli, carrots, iceberg lettuce).

3. *Product odors* — Some products produce odors (e.g., garlic, onions) which can be absorbed by other products, causing the latter to have an objectionable aroma and less market appeal.

4. *Moisture* — Some products benefit from package ice or high levels of humidity in their ambient atmosphere (e.g., leafy vegetables, sweet corn), while other commodities benefit from intermediate to low humidity levels (e.g., garlic, dry onions).

Often used are compromise transit temperature settings that are designed to protect the most perishable or most valuable commodity in a load.

Thermostats and Recording Thermometers. Accurate temperature control is provided only if thermostats are accurately calibrated and are in an air stream that is representative of the temperature in the air supply load. Thermostats should be calibrated periodically. It is important to make sure the air-return passage is not blocked and adequate air can circulate through and / or around the load. It is the temperature of the commodity that is important, not the temperature of the air circulating around the containers.

Modified Atmospheres

Some vegetables benefit from the maintenance of modified atmospheres in transit vehicles, while other do not. Successful use of modified atmospheres is largely dependent upon the tightness of transit vehicles. In general, some rail cars and newer marine container vans can maintain modified atmospheres. Older or damaged rail cars are usually no longer tight enough.

Over-the-road trucks and TOFC trailers are generally not tight enough or do not remain tight to maintain modified atmospheres. In these vehicles, modified atmospheres can be established and maintained within pallet covers (polyethylene bags) secured to the pallet bases. Some newer trailers have the capability of maintaining desired atmospheres by using liquid nitrogen tanks which are carried in a special compartment.

Accidental or undesirable atmospheric modification can result when air passages, such as floor drains, become plugged with debris or ice, which results in depletion of the internal oxygen supply by the product's respiration. This is a common problem during the winter with rail shipments of broccoli and Brussels sprouts. These crops are commonly shipped with package ice and under top ice. During the winter, water from the melting ice can freeze at drains and seal all vents from the rail car. This problem can be overcome by providing open-air channels to the outside.

QUALITY OF VEGETABLES

Quality is defined as " . . . degree of excellence, relative nature, attribute, trait, or faculty" (*Oxford Dictionary*). Quality of fresh vegetables is a combination of characteristics, attributes, and properties that give a commodity value to humans for food. The connotation is that the important attributes of quality vary according to the individual(s) defining the term.

1. Growers are interested in disease resistance, high yield, uniform maturity, desirable size, and ease of harvest. Postharvest characteristics have not been one of their main interests.

2. Shippers and handlers are concerned with shipping quality and market quality. Hard fruit that can endure inexpensive handling and transport and still maintain high market quality is desirable.

3. Consumers care about appearance, price, and table quality, including texture, flavor, color, and nutritive value.

An effective quality control system throughout the handling steps between harvest and retail display is essential to providing a consistently good-quality supply of fresh vegetables to the consumer and to protecting the reputation of a given marketing label.

Quality Factors

A wide range of characteristics of vegetables is used to determine their quality. Important features differ according to the commodity being tested. These include:

Appearance (visual):	Size: dimensions, weight, volume
	Shape: diameter, length, compactness
	Color: uniformity, intensity
	Gloss: nature of surface wax
	Defects (external, internal): sprouting, rooting, elongation, curvature, seed germination, floret opening, growth cracks, shrivelling, wilting, bruises, cuts, scars, scabs, sunburn, decay, chilling / freezing injury symptoms, and nutritional-related defects
Texture (feel):	External smoothness and softness
	Internal texture: fibrous, tough, juicy, succulent
Flavor (taste and smell):	Sweetness, sourness, bitterness
	Off-flavors and aroma
Nutritive value:	Carbohydrates, fiber, proteins, lipids, vitamins, minerals
Safety:	Naturally occurring toxicants
	Chemical residues, heavy metals

Grade Standards

The objective of the grade standards and their application is to provide quality control of fresh produce. There are U.S., state, industry, and international types of standards.

The first U.S. grade standard (for potatoes) was developed in 1917. There are now more than 150 U.S. grade standards covering 80 different fruits and vegetables. These standards are normally applied voluntarily, except when required under certain state and local regulations, by industry-marketing orders, or for export produce.

The U.S. grade standards include a range of grade names, of which the most important are U.S. Fancy, U.S. No. 1, U.S. No. 2, and U.S. No. 3. The U.S. Department of Agriculture is gradually phasing out an assortment of other grade names such as U.S. Extra No. 1, U.S. Extra Fancy, U.S. Combination, and U.S. Commercial.

The European Economic Community grade standards include the following quality classes: Extra class = superior quality, Class I = good quality, and Class II = marketable quality. These classes are generally equivalent to U.S. Fancy, U.S. No. 1, and U.S. No. 2, respectively.

Application of the Grade Standards

The grade standards are applied by USDA inspectors or the county agricultural commissioners for state standards. In large packinghouses, the inspectors may be permanently assigned. Sometimes the inspectors are seasonal employees hired during peak production for a given crop or location. In other cases inspection may be at the shipping point, or at the terminal market.

Representative samples, or a prescribed number of boxes or packages, are removed at random from a given lot and inspected. Inspectors are trained in the application of the standards, visual aids (color charts, diagrams, photographs, etc.) are used wherever feasible and practical, and objective methods are used whenever possible.

When the inspection is completed, inspection certificates are issued by the inspector denoting the grade standard to which the product conforms. Tolerances (allowances for product outside the grade quality) are set as a certain percentage of the product in the sample.

SELECTED REFERENCES

Ashby, B. H., R. T. Hinsch, L. A. Risse, W. G. Kindya, W. L. Craig, Jr., and M. R. Turczyn. 1987. *Protecting Perishable Foods During Transport by Truck.* USDA Agric. Handbook No. 669.

Burton, W. G. 1982. *Postharvest Physiology of Food Crops.* Longman House, Essex, United Kingdom.

Dennis, C. 1983. *Postharvest Pathology of Fruits and Vegetables.* Academic Press, London.

Duckworth, R. B. 1966. *Fruits and Vegetables.* Pergamon Press, Elmsford, New York.

Eskin, N. A. M. (ed.). 1989. *Quality and Preservation of Vegetables.* CRC Press, Inc., Boca Raton, Florida.

Haard, N. F., and D. K. Salunkhe (eds.). 1975. *Symposium: Postharvest biology and handling of fruits and vegetables.* AVI Publishing Co., Westport, Connecticut.

Hardenburg, R. H., A. E. Watada, and C. Y. Wang. 1986. *The Commercial Storage of Fruits, Vegetables, and Florist and Nursery Stocks.* USDA Agric. Handbook No. 66.

Hultin, H. O., and M. Milner. 1978. *Postharvest Biology and Biotechnology.* Food and Nutrition Press, Inc., Westport, Connecticut.

Isenberg, F. M. R. 1979. Controlled atmosphere storage of vegetables. *Hort. Rev.,* Vol. I, 1:337–394.

Kader, A. A., R. F. Kasmire, F. G. Mitchell, M. S. Reid, N. F. Sommer, and J. F. Thompson. 1985. *Postharvest Technology of Horticultural Crops.* Univ. of California, Coop. Ext. Sp. Pub. 3311.

Lieberman, M. (ed.). 1983. *Postharvest Physiology and Crop Preservation.* Plenum Publishing Corp., New York.

McGregor, M. 1987. *Tropical Products Transport Handbook.* USDA Agric. Handbook No. 668.

Pantastico, E. B. (ed.). 1975. *Postharvest Physiology, Handling and Utilization of Tropical Fruits and Vegetables.* AVI Publishing Co., Westport, Connecticut.

Ryall, A. L., and W. J. Lipton. 1979. *Handling, Transportation and Storage of Fruits and Vegetables.* Vol I: *Vegetables and Melons,* AVI Publishing Co., Westport, Connecticut.

Salunkhe, D. K., and B. B. Desai. 1984. *Postharvest Biotechnology of Vegetables.* Vol. I, CRC Press, Inc., Boca Raton, Florida.

Salunkhe, D. K., and B. B. Desai. 1984. *Postharvest Biotechnology of Vegetables.* Vol. II, CRC Press, Inc., Boca Raton, Florida.

USDA. 1984. *Composition of Foods: Vegetables and Vegetable Products.* USDA Agric. Handbook No. 8-11.

Weichmann, J. (ed.). 1987. *Postharvest Physiology of Vegetables.* Food Science and Technology Series #24, Marcel Dekker, Inc., New York.

Wills, R. H., T. H. Lee, D. Graham, W. B. McGlasson, and E. G. Hall. 1981. *Postharvest: An Introduction to the Physiology and Handling of Fruits and Vegetables.* AVI Publishing Co., Westport, Connecticut.

11

BIOTECHNOLOGY AND
GENETIC ENGINEERING:
NEW DIRECTIONS IN AGRICULTURE

Technology, which is advancing rapidly, will have an enormous impact on plant agriculture in the future, particularly in the area of crop improvement. During the last two decades, advances made in molecular biology and molecular genetics have made possible novel approaches being applied to improve crop quality and increase production.

Today, it is possible to manipulate the *genome* (the total complement of genetic material) directly at the molecular level. As a result, desirable genes from wild species and other plant species and genera can be introduced into crops which previously were extremely difficult to improve by conventional plant breeding techniques. Such manipulation of genetic material is popularly referred to as *genetic engineering* or *biotechnology*.

GENETIC ENGINEERING

Although biotechnology and genetic engineering are sometimes used interchangeably, biotechnology has a considerably broader meaning. Simply defined, *biotechnology* is the application of biological science to help solve economically and socially important problems. *Genetic engineering* is more specific and involves modifying DNA (deoxyribonucleic acid, the genetic matter of heredity), and then incorporating the restructured DNA into a suitable host for the purpose of changing its heritable characteristics.

By this definition, much of biotechnology is based on genetic engineering. The techniques used in genetic engineering include tissue and cell culture, anther culture, protoplast fusion, recombinant DNA, micro-injection, and somaclonal variation. It is important to recognize that genetic engineering is not a replacement for traditional plant breeding methods, but rather it complements other breeding techniques. Genetic engineering allows the production of genetic combinations that are not possible by normal means.

Tissue and Cell Culture

A necessary step in genetic engineering is learning how to culture single cells or groups of cells rather than whole plants. Tissue culture is a system whereby cells from very small pieces of plants are proliferated on an artificial medium under sterile conditions. Typical sources of plant tissue cultures include embryos, seeds, stems, leaves, shoot tips, root tips, calluses (clumps of cells), single cells, and pollen grains (Figure 11.1).

Figure 11.1. An example of tissue culture is the *in vitro* development of a sweet potato plant. (Photo: courtesy of R. M. Skirvin, University of Illinois)

The techniques of tissue culture and cell culture have advanced to the stage where many species of plants can be regenerated rapidly in test tubes or culture plates. Using these techniques, plants with desired traits can be successfully regenerated from cells that have been transformed to contain desired genes.

Somaclonal Variation

Cell culture techniques can also be used to provide a rapid means of screening cells for a specific trait such as resistance to diseases, herbicides, or environmental stresses such as salt accumulation and temperature extremes. For example, a relatively easy method of selection for herbicide resistance begins with trying to grow plant cells in culture in the presence of a herbicide. Most of the cells will be unable to grow, but one among the millions screened during selection may carry a mutant gene for resistance to the herbicide. This cell will grow and can be recovered from the non-growing cells. Cells that survive the screening can then be regenerated into whole plants.

The above description is an example of somaclonal variation that sometimes occurs when cells are cultured. Although the usual goal of cell culture is to regenerate identical clones, occasionally a cell will exhibit a different genetic makeup, resulting in variability that may be expressed in a desirable trait.

Recombinant DNA

Recombinant DNA, or gene splicing, techniques are used to transfer genetic traits from one organism to another at the molecular level. In this technique (Figure 11.2), foreign DNA that codes for a desired trait is cut out of one organism and spliced into a plasmid (circular DNA molecules found in the bacterium *Agrobacterium tumefaciens*). Enzymes, called restriction enzymes, are used to split the foreign DNA into specific fragments and then to insert the foreign gene segments into the plasmid vector. The "recombined" DNA plasmid is then in-serted into the nucleus of a host cell where it can replicate. Cell clones that have acquired the recombinant DNA must then be isolated from among cells that were not transformed. If regeneration of the host cell is successful, a new plant with the desired characteristics will be formed.

Protoplast Fusion

In this technique, cells from different types of plants or different lines of the same plant can be fused with each other, thus allowing the genetic material (DNA) in the nuclei, mitochondria, and chloroplasts to form new combinations (Figure 11.3). The cell wall, which acts as a barrier that prevents cell fusion, is removed

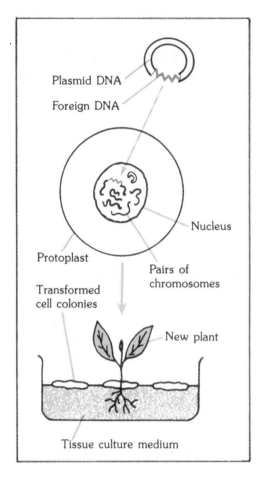

Plasmid DNA

Foreign DNA

Nucleus

Protoplast

Pairs of chromosomes

Transformed cell colonies

New plant

Tissue culture medium

Figure 11.2. In recombinant DNA, or gene splicing, foreign DNA from a donor is "recombined" with a plasmid vector, after which it is inserted into a host cell. (Source: *Illinois Research*, Vol. 25)

by enzymes, resulting in a naked protoplast (a cell after the cell wall has been removed). With the aid of chemical treatments, fusion of protoplasts can be induced. The fused protoplasts must divide by mitosis and establish cell division patterns before a new hybrid plant can develop. If successful, the technique results in the regeneration of a whole plant from the hybrid cell.

Protoplast fusion is useful for transferring genes that are difficult to isolate or that cannot be sexually crossed. However, unlike recombinant DNA techniques, protoplast fusion is not selective since entire gene sets are combined, which may sometimes result in unwanted variation.

Experiments with protoplast fusion have produced hybrids between sexually incompatible species, such as tomatoes and potatoes. This is a good example of one application of genetic engineering that could have horticultural significance in the transfer of chilling resistance from the latter to the former species. Fusion hybrids between carrots and one of their wild relatives have been developed and successfully regenerated.

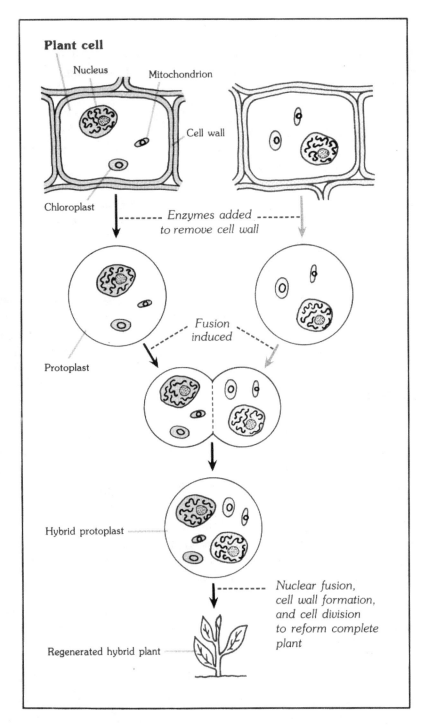

Figure 11.3. Protoplast fusion combines the genetic contents of two cells, after the cell walls have been removed. (Source: *Illinois Research*, Vol. 25)

Micro-injection

It is also possible to put genes into plant cells by micro-injection. Microscopic needles are used to inject DNA segments or whole chromosomes directly into the nucleus of a fertilized egg (zygote). The transformed egg develops into an embryo that matures into a transformed offspring. The process is very selective and transfers traits directly and more precisely than protoplast fusion.

DNA can also be delivered into plant cells by high-velocity microprojectiles. After being accelerated to high velocity, the DNA-coated microprojectiles can pierce cell walls and membranes and enter intact plant cells without killing them. The method of particle acceleration can be by an electric discharge or a modified "gene gun." This technique, although still relatively new, appears to have broad applications, especially since it does not have some of the regeneration problems of protoplast transformation.

Another type of "injection" involves pollen and egg fertilization. Germinating pollen grains are capable of directly absorbing foreign DNA fragments into their cytoplasm. The altered DNA is then carried by the sperm to the embryo sac and introduced into the egg during normal fertilization. The transformed embryo and endosperm develop normally, and the resulting seeds grow into healthy plants.

Plant Regeneration

For genetic engineering to be of value in plant improvement, whole organisms must develop from the transformed cells. If this is to occur, individual cells that have been transformed must develop into embryos. Most of the successful genetic engineering work so far has been with plant species such as carrots and tobacco that can be regenerated fairly easily from either cultured cells or protoplasts. Hundreds of crop species have been regenerated from tissue cultures. However, success in the regeneration of vegetable crops from protoplasts is considerably more difficult and has occurred in relatively few species, including asparagus, cabbage, carrots, eggplants, peppers, and tomatoes.

BIOTECHNOLOGY IN FUTURE
CROP IMPROVEMENT

The potential for genetic engineering in agriculture is enormous, and eventually the new techniques will become standard tools for plant improvement. Accelerating developments in genetic engineering promise to open a whole new era of crop production. Developments in biotechnology will give growers new options in pest control and cultivar selection. Breeders, cytogeneticists, biochemical geneticists, and genetic engineers are working to produce plants that will be far superior to those of today.

Specialized Crop Production

There will be an increase in crops that are more specialized for particular commercial uses. Crops with particular traits such as high protein, oil, and starch, will be developed. The composition of vegetables will be modified to improve the amino acid balance and vitamin content to meet the nutritional requirements of both humans and domestic animals. Researchers have been able to insert a synthetic gene to enhance the protein content of potatoes. When and if this can be bred into a commercial cultivar, a person could obtain the minimum daily protein requirement by consuming only 1.75 pounds of potatoes per day, as compared to 5.5 pounds of presently available cultivars.

Processors will contract with growers for a quality product for specific uses. This already occurs to some extent with potatoes to produce high-quality, disease-tested cultivars, and with tomatoes to improve soluble solids. The industry is testing tomato plants that have been genetically engineered to reduce levels of an enzyme that causes the fruit to soften. This has important implications in postharvest physiology and in extending product shelflife. Advanced hybridization techniques are being used in watermelons to achieve accurate genetic control of fruit size and shape, flesh color, sweetness, and exterior stripping.

Biological Applications

Recent developments in biotechnology show promise in controlling plant viruses, where there are no direct methods of control, as there are for fungi and bacteria. Recombinant DNA techniques are being used to make tomatoes resistant to tobacco mosaic virus. In this work, the gene responsible for producing the protein coat of the virus is taken from the virus and inserted into the crop. Since the transformed plant has the new gene and has already made the protein coat, the virus is unable to replicate itself after infecting the plant, because the sites for its protective coat are already taken up. Cooperative research projects between industry and university scientists are also working to develop a virus-resistant potato. Using cell fusion, USDA scientists have developed hybrid potato plants that contain a natural chemical, leptine, that repels the Colorado potato beetle.

As discussed earlier, genetic engineering will permit the incorporation of resistance to certain herbicides in vegetable crops. Broad-spectrum herbicides will be used to kill all plants except crop species that are resistant to the herbicides. The development of herbicides and other pesticides that biodegrade more rapidly will be emphasized as concern about pesticide residues in the environment increases. A "photodynamic" herbicide that activates on exposure to light is presently being developed.

The morphology or structure of leaves and other plant parts may be modified in the future to make these plant parts less susceptible to predators and organisms carrying disease. It is known that some plants (e.g., alfalfa and quackgrass) excrete compounds that are *allelopathic*, or which inhibit the growth of other plant species. If crop plants can be engineered to excrete substances that inhibit weed growth, fewer herbicides will be required for weed control.

Biological control applications will become more important as they become better understood. Perhaps genetically modified mites and other organisms that eat other pests living on plants will be developed. Bacteria are being developed to suppress insect pests, just as chemicals suppress insects. These "microbial insecticides" produce substances that are toxic to certain insects but safe for beneficial insects and warm-blooded animals. For example, the bacterium *Bacillus thuringiensis* produces a crystal toxin that kills most caterpillar pests. This bacterium is already used worldwide. Also being developed are fungi that contain insect-eating enzymes that are designed to be sprayed on infested farm fields. The enzymes dissolve the insects' protective shell, allowing the fungi to penetrate the insects' bodies. The fungi, commonly found in soil, are known to attack more than 200 types of insects while leaving the crop plants alone.

Genetically engineered bacteria may prevent frost on high-value crops. Scientists studying the mechanism of ice crystal formation in fruits found that a protein produced by bacteria serves as a nucleating point around which water freezes at higher temperatures, thus increasing susceptibility to frost damage. Through genetic engineering, a strain of bacteria has been developed in which the actual gene in the DNA that is responsible for this protein is removed. When a plant is colonized by these "ice-minus" bacteria, it cannot be colonized by other bacteria. This offers the potential of reducing the frost susceptibility of many fruits and vegetables. Although some genetically engineered organisms are available today, existing regulations forbid field testing to prevent their release into the atmosphere.

Plant Breeding

Advances in plant cell and tissue culture have the potential for reducing the time needed to create hybrids. Most vegetable inbreds are able to self-fertilize. This complicates hybridization and necessitates manually emasculating and hand pollinating each plant of one of the seed parents. This process is labor-intensive and costly. Molecular biologists are now able to transform cells of the female parent line to produce plants with infertile pollen. These are used with male plants that have fertile pollen, resulting in seed with a high level of hybridity.

Breeders can rapidly propagate or maintain breeding lines by culturing shoot tips, buds, or pollen grains of designated plants. By using tissue and cell culture techniques, breeders can multiply a single plant into hundreds of plants in a relatively short time. For example, anther culture is relatively simple and is used commonly by seed companies in the development of inbred broccoli and pepper lines.

Genotype Protection

Biotechnology will be useful to plant breeders and to the seed industry for protecting the genotypes developed. A technique known as *restricted fragment length polymorphism* will be useful to identify genotypes and to protect the proprietary rights of plant breeders. This technique will be useful in establishing maps of genes and their linkages. It can be used to test for outcross contamination in seed lots and will save considerable time since it eliminates the need for field testing to identify these outcrosses.

CHALLENGES OF THE FUTURE FOR GENETIC ENGINEERING

Before genetic engineering can be used as a breeding tool, some serious technical problems must be solved. At the molecular and cellular level, it remains difficult to identify genes that code for useful traits such as resistance to disease pathogens and pests.

At present, genetic engineering in vegetables is limited to a few species including tomatoes, peppers, eggplants, carrots, asparagus, and cabbage, and few genes have been identified at the molecular level. Traits such as yield, that are controlled by many different genes, do not lend themselves to isolation or manipulation. The basic biochemical mechanisms that control single gene traits, let alone complex ones, are not well understood. Without this knowledge, the new techniques cannot be applied rapidly and effectively.

Cell selection methods still fall short in selecting for traits such as stalk strength in corn or maturity dates. These traits which are expressed in whole plants are not likely to be seen in cultured cells. Carriers for successful gene transfer are only now being developed.

GLOSSARY OF TERMS USED IN
GENETIC ENGINEERING

Biotechnology — the application of biological science, particularly molecular biology, to solve economically and socially important problems.

Callus — a mass of unorganized cells.

Chromosome — a rod-shaped element in the nucleus of a cell that contain the genetic information of the cell; a collection of genes.

Clone — a group of genetically identical organisms derived from one individual and maintained by asexual means.

Cytogenetics — the area of biology that deals with heredity at the cellular and genetic level.

DNA — deoxyribonucleic acid, a substance of which genes are made and found chiefly in the nucleus of cells.

Enzyme — a proteinaceous molecule that promotes specific chemical reactions in cells.

Gene — the smallest portion of a chromosome that contains the information that determines one or more hereditary characters.

Gene splicing — the technique of inserting new genetic material in a plasmid; used in recombinant DNA.

Genetic engineering — the manipulation of genetic material to modify organisms for specific purposes.

Genome — the total complement of genetic material.

Monoclonal — referring to one specific type of antibody cloned to recognize and attack specific substances.

Plasmid — a circular piece of DNA which is found outside the chromosome in bacteria and which is used for inserting foreign genes into plant cells.

Protoplast — a cell after the cell wall has been removed.

Recombinant DNA — DNA prepared in the laboratory by breaking up and splicing together DNA from different species.

Restriction enzymes — enzymes that behave like a scapel to cut DNA molecules at specific sites.

Somaclonal variation — the genetic change that occurs when cells are cultured.

Somatic hybridization — the fusion of protoplasts of different lines and species, also referred to as parasexual hybridization.

Vector — the agent used to transfer DNA molecules into plant cells, usually plasmids.

SELECTED REFERENCES

The references listed below provide some background information on biotechnology and genetic engineering. Special note is given to the references by J. M. Widholm and L. E. Schrader in *Illinois Research*, which supplied Figures 11.2 and 11.3, respectively. The topics covered in these two articles make excellent reading for persons unfamiliar with genetic engineering.

"Anonymous." 1988. *Genetic Engineering: A Natural Science*. Monsanto, St. Louis.

"Anonymous." 1987. *Of the Earth: Agriculture and New Biology*. Monsanto, St. Louis.

"Anonymous." 1985. Plant biotechnology. Michigan State Univ., *Futures* 4:2–17.

Bliss, F. A. 1984. The application of new plant biotechnology to crop improvement. *HortScience* 19:13–18.

De Wet, J. M. J. 1983. Biotechnology and the future of agriculture. *Illinois Research* 25:3–6.

Facklam, M., and H. Facklam. 1979. *From Cell to Clone: The Story of Genetic Engineering*. Harcourt Brace, New York.

Grierson, D., and S. N. Covey. 1988. *Plant Molecular Biology*. Chapman & Hall, New York.

Klassen, P. 1986. Fighting frost with genetically engineered bacteria. *American Vegetable Grower*, Feb. :25–27.

National Research Council. 1984. *Genetic Engineering of Plants: Agricultural Research Opportunities & Policy Concerns*. National Academy Press, Washington, DC.

Olson, S. 1986. *Biotechnology: An Industry Comes of Age*. National Academy Press, Washington, DC.

Schrader, L. E. 1986. Plant agriculture of the future. *Illinois Research* 28:19–21.

Sink, K. C. 1984. Protoplast fusion for plant improvement. *HortScience* 19:33–37.

Tomes, D. T., B. E. Ellis, P. M. Harney, K. J. Kasha, and R. L. Peterson. 1982. *Application of Plant Cell and Tissue Culture to Agriculture & Industry*. University of Guelph, Guelph, Canada.

Widholm, J. M. 1983. Manipulating plant cells and protoplasts. *Illinois Research* 25:6–8.

Wochok, Z. S. 1987. Status of crop improvement through tissue culture. *Proc. Inter. Plant Prop. Soc.* 36:72–77.

12

PERENNIAL CROPS —
ASPARAGUS, RHUBARB,
AND GLOBE ARTICHOKES

ASPARAGUS

Asparagus is the most important perennial vegetable grown in the U.S. The plant is valued for its edible spring shoots or spears which can be used in fresh, canned, or frozen form. Although 1–3 years are required to establish an asparagus planting, once in production, beds can last up to 25 years. The spears are an excellent source of vitamin A and also contain significant amounts of calcium, phosphorus, riboflavin, and vitamin C. Asparagus can be served in salads, soups, and hot dishes and in combination with various sauces. The whole spears or only the green tips may be used.

CLASSIFICATION, ORIGIN, HISTORY

Asparagus (*Asparagus officinalis*) is a member of the lily family (Liliaceae) and is one of the few vegetables that is a monocot. It is believed to be indigenous to parts of the Union of Sovereign States (USS), the Mediterranean region, and the British Isles. Asparagus was cultivated as a food crop by the early Romans, who also dried the crop for later use. Before being used for food, however, it was highly regarded for medicinal purposes. The plant was brought to America by the early colonists, but it was not until after 1850 that asparagus was planted extensively by commercial growers. The genus *Asparagus* contains over 150 species, including the ornamental asparagus fern.

PRODUCTION AND INDUSTRY

Asparagus is a popular early spring crop for home use and local markets, although the bulk of the crop is grown for processing. Historically, it has been a relatively high-value crop because the major producing regions are located in only a few states.

Asparagus production and acreage have increased in the past 10 years in the western states, especially in California and Washington. Eastern production has tended to decrease, due to old beds having disease problems, imports from other areas, and high labor costs in harvesting. Recently, however, with the introduction of several disease-tolerant and high-yielding hybrid cultivars (see "Cultivars"), this trend has started to reverse.

Production statistics, provided by the USDA Agricultural Statistics Board, are combined for both fresh market and processing since the same fields may be used for each purpose (Table 12.1). Comparing crop statistics for 1989 with those for 1977, harvested acreage, production, and value have increased 15%, 14%, and 86%, respectively. Approximately 94% of the total U.S. commercial acreage (98,510 acres) in 1989 was concentrated in California, Washington, and Michigan. Other leading producing states include New Jersey, Minnesota, Illinois, Indiana, Oregon, and Maryland, with minor production in Arizona, New York, Pennsylvania, and Ohio.

Table 12.1. Harvested Acreage, Production, and Value of Fresh Market and Processing Asparagus in the U.S., 1977 and 1989

State	Harvested Acres		Production		Value	
	1977[1]	1989[2]	1977	1989	1977	1989
			—— (tons) ——		—— ($1,000) ——	
California	30,300	37,500	56,050	54,400	42,775	71,978
Illinois	4,500	800	2,500	650	1,725	900
Michigan	17,300	23,000	9,500	12,650	8,345	14,784
New Jersey	2,300	1,500	1,600	1,900	1,763	2,462
Washington	20,200	32,000	33,350	51,200	21,815	55,074
Other states[3]	11,200	3,710	6,050	3,950	3,826	4,424
U.S.	85,800	98,510	109,050	124,750	80,249	149,622

[1]Source: USDA. 1978. Economics, Statistics, and Cooperatives Service (ESCS), Crop Reporting Board.

[2]Source: USDA. 1990. National Agricultural Statistics Service (NASS), Agricultural Statistics Board.

[3]Indiana, Maryland, Minnesota, and Oregon for 1989; not identified for 1977.

Average asparagus yields vary considerably, depending on location and growing season. In California and Washington, relatively long growing seasons result in average yields of 1.5 tons per acre, as compared to 0.75 ton per acre in other states. Since these values are averages, actual top yields are considerably higher.

There is also considerable asparagus production in Canada and Mexico, and the crop is extensively grown in Europe, the Far East (particularly Taiwan), and in parts of Central and South America. The production of white, or blanched, asparagus is still popular in Europe, although consumption of green asparagus is markedly greater. The high labor requirement for blanched spears has discouraged white asparagus production in the U.S.

PLANT GROWTH AND DEVELOPMENT

Asparagus is a hardy, dioecious (producing male and female flowers on separate plants), perennial herb in which plant growth can be divided into three phases: crown development, spear development, and fern development.

Crown Development

The underground portion of the asparagus plant consists of a network of rhizomes, fleshy roots, and fibrous roots (Figure 12.1). The rhizomes are under-ground horizontal stems that develop from the point of origin of the primary stem. The fleshy roots arise from the rhizomes and function as absorptive and storage organs. The fibrous roots arise from the fleshy storage roots and function primarily in absorbing water and nutrients. Together, the fleshy roots and rhizomes make up the crown, which is the perennial portion of the asparagus plant, and where most of the food material is stored to be utilized in the growth of the spears the following spring.

The rhizomes grow at the rate of about 2 inches a year in a slightly upward fashion, which tends to bring the crowns to the surface after a number of years. The fleshy roots resume growth in late winter or early spring, with new ones being formed each year behind the growing tip of the rhizomes. In old plants, the fleshy roots may extend laterally to a distance of 6 feet or more and downward to a depth of 5 feet. The fibrous roots die back each fall, and new ones develop each spring.

Spear Development

Asparagus spears are edible stems, containing nodes and internodes, which arise from buds developed on the rhizomes the previous summer. Shoot elonga-

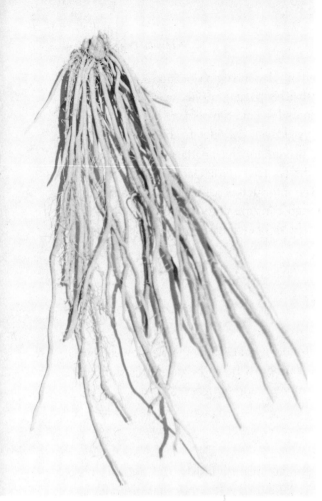

Figure 12.1. The asparagus crown consists of rhizomes and fleshy perennial roots; the spears develop from buds on the rhizome. (Photo: courtesy of Daisy Farms, Decatur, Michigan)

tion begins at the lowest internode, and as the first internodes begin to elongate in rapid succession, the stem elongates, resulting in spear growth. The upper half of each node does not elongate immediately but is pushed above ground by elongation of the nodes beneath it. In the upper part, the nodes are marked by the presence of small, scale-like leaves which overlap, forming the tip. As the tissues of the spear mature, the cells of the pericycle and vascular bundles accumulate lignin compounds that impart toughness to the tissue. Lignification begins at the base, where the cells are older, and proceeds upward toward the tip.

The buds on the rhizome exhibit a type of apical dominance in which a growing bud will repress the development of subsequent buds, and if left undisturbed, only a few shoots will develop. If, however, the spears are cut off as they appear, a continuous succession of shoots will form.

The rate of spear development is greatly influenced by temperature. To grow a 6-inch spear requires over 5 days at 53°F, but only 2 days at 78°F. During periods of warm weather, rapid spear growth can result in a tendency for the spear tips to lose some of their compactness. Cool temperatures increase fiber content of the spear and cause excessive development of anthocyanin pigments, which can give the spears an undesirable purple appearance. Large diameter, good length, compact tips, and low fiber content are desirable features for spear market quality.

Fern Development

The spears, if not harvested, will elongate into ferns 4–6 feet tall. This occurs when the internodes in the tip begin to elongate and secondary branches develop in the axils of the leaf scales. The secondary branches give rise to more side branches, which bear small, leaf-like structures called *cladophylls*. These impart a fine or feathery texture to the shoots and account for its description as a fern.

Flowers and Fruits

The flowers are borne in the axils of the leaves of the side branches. They are small, bell-shaped, and whitish-green. Male flowers are more conspicuous than female flowers. Pollination is by insects, and the fruit consists of small, red berries on female plants.

Female plants are less productive and shorter-lived than male plants. This is attributed to the production of seed in female plants, taking energy and photo-synthate away from the crown. The spears of male plants are more numerous but are usually smaller in diameter than those on female plants. Seed production by female plants can result in problems with volunteer seedlings that compete with established plants and reduce yields.

Carbohydrate Balance

Carbohydrates are manufactured in the above-ground parts of the plant, particularly in the ferns during the growing season. The excess carbohydrate, that which is not used in the growth process, is translocated into the rhizomes and fleshy roots, where it is stored and utilized the following season. When spears are cut in commercial operations, this creates a serious drain on the carbohydrate reserves. A reasonable period of active fern growth is necessary to supply the crown with carbohydrates following the harvest period. As long as the fern is green, it will produce carbohydrates, which are translocated to the crown for storage.

CLIMATIC AND CULTURAL REQUIREMENTS

Asparagus grows best where cool temperatures (75–85°F, day; 55–65°F, night) prevail during the growing season and adequate moisture is available. The high summer temperatures, particularly at night, and mild winters occurring in the southern states do not favor maximum production of spears. Both of these conditions result in depletion of carbohydrate reserves.

Asparagus-growing regions should have a dormant season of 3–5 months, which can be induced either by low soil temperatures (below 50°F) or by drought. The dormant period is critical to preserve the carbohydrate supply used by spears the following season. Asparagus crowns are very hardy and are seldom injured by cold winters. Winter injury is usually restricted to fields where the plant tops have been removed in the fall. In mild regions, such as the Imperial Valley of California, irrigation may be withheld to induce dormancy.

Since an asparagus bed will be in production for many years, choice and preparation of the site is critical. The site should be selected and prepared at least one year before the crop is established so that organic matter can be added, pH adjusted, weeds eliminated, and fertility improved.

Asparagus will not tolerate poorly drained, wet soils. For best results the soil should be well drained, deep, and loose, such as sandy loams. Light sandy and gravelly soils should be avoided because of their low-moisture–holding capacities. Muck soils are not recommended because they are subject to freezing and thawing, which can heave and damage the crowns.

Locations susceptible to late spring freezes should be avoided, and the sites should preferably have no prior history of asparagus production. Since deep planting of crowns is commonly practiced, the soil should be plowed rather deeply. A green-manure crop should be added to the soil in the fall before planting, or wheat or rye sown the previous fall can be plowed under the spring prior to planting.

Asparagus is normally a deep-rooted crop, and in deep, open soils roots will penetrate to a depth of 8 feet or more, extracting water and nutrients. Consequently, on many soils, it does not respond to fertilizers as readily as most other vegetables. Fertilizer recommendations for asparagus vary widely, depending on location, soil type, environmental conditions, and cultural practices.

Prior to planting, it is important to have the soil well fertilized with phosphorus and potassium, since these elements do not move as readily as nitrogen, and efforts to place these down to the feeding roots may be difficult after the plants are established. As a general recommendation, 1,000–2,000 pounds per acre of a 10-20-20 fertilizer (N-P_2O_5-K_2O) in a low fertility soil, and half this amount in a highly fertile soil, should be broadcast and incorporated when the land is prepared for the planting furrows. Additional phosphorus can be banded in the bottom of the furrow at planting, before the crowns or transplants are set.

For established cutting beds, fertility requirements are relatively modest, even when yields are high. Nitrogen (50–150 pounds per acre) should be applied annually, but phosphorus and potassium may not be needed every year and should be adjusted, based on soil tests. Rates of nutrients applied for maintenance fertilization will vary considerably, depending on locale and plant selection. The new hybrids that are being introduced (see "Cultivars") are more vigorous and require higher fertility levels than the traditional open-pollinated cultivars.

The fertilizer can be applied in the spring before spear emergence or after harvesting, or at both times. If available, annual applications of well-decomposed animal manure at a rate of 5–10 tons per acre may be applied and lightly disked in after the cutting season to supplement the mineral fertilizer. Some growers apply some of the nitrogen at this time to stimulate top growth and promote organic matter decomposition.

Asparagus grows well at a soil pH between 6.0 and 7.5 but does not tolerate extremes in soil reaction. One year prior to planting, lime should be deeply incorporated to adjust the pH to approximately 6.8. A liming program should be maintained after planting and throughout the life of the bed.

PLANTING AND CROP ESTABLISHMENT

Three methods are used to start new asparagus beds: transplanting 1-year-old crowns, direct seeding into the field, and transplanting 8- to 12-week-old seedling plants. Transplanting 1-year-old crowns is the most common method, while seedling transplants work well in drier areas like California. Direct seeding in the field

Figure 12.2. Seedling transplants may be used to establish asparagus beds.

is not a common planting method because asparagus seed is erratic in germination and requires considerable expertise to get the plants growing vigorously.

Crowns

In this method, asparagus is propagated by transplanting well-grown 1-year-old crowns in the field. These can be obtained either directly from commercial nurseries or grown from seed by the grower and moved to the field. For smaller plantings, purchasing crowns is generally recommended, but for large acreages, growers usually grow their own. In either case, only the best, healthiest, and most vigorous crowns should be selected for planting in the cutting bed.

Crowns that are purchased directly from commercial nurseries should be 1 year old and certified disease-free stock. Each crown should weigh 2–4 ounces and have a cluster of well-formed and well-distributed buds. Crowns with large roots and two or more bud clusters will start growing more quickly and develop faster. Excessively large crowns should be avoided since the chance of injury is greater when they are dug or planted.

If crowns are produced by the grower, there is less risk of acquiring soil-borne diseases. The grower will also have more opportunity in cultivar selection and availability of a particular seed source. However, considerable time, labor, and expertise are required to dig, sort, and transport the crowns.

When crowns are grown from seed, a light-textured soil with no history of asparagus production should be used to avoid disease problems. The seed is planted in the spring as soon as the soil warms. Seed germination is slow in cool soils, requiring up to 53 days at 50°F and 12 days at 70°F for emergence. Germination may be hastened if seeds are presoaked for 4 days in a waterbath at 85°F, provided planting is not delayed after this treatment. The seed is spaced 2–3 inches apart and covered 1 inch deep. Row spacing should be no less than 24 inches, since thinning is difficult and the crowns are hard to separate after digging if their roots are interwoven.

The crowns should be dug early the following spring and set in the field while they are still dormant. Potato or peanut diggers are commonly used to lift the crowns from the nursery row. Digging should be done carefully to avoid damaging the crowns and to leave 8–12 inches of storage roots. If it is necessary to hold the dug crowns, they should be stored in a dry location at 40°F and 85–90% humidity. At storage temperatures of 32°F, crowns will freeze and significant injury may result if buds have started to germinate. Crowns should not dry out. If stored in large piles without adequate ventilation, they can become overheated.

The crowns are planted in the bottom of a furrow so that the buds are 6–8 inches below the surface level. Initially, the buds are covered with 1–2 inches of soil, and as the shoots grow, the furrow is gradually filled without completely covering the growing spears. In some parts of the country, shallow planting is recommended, especially on heavy soils. Better stands are obtained from shallow planting, but crowns may be injured by disking and freezing so that plants produce small spears.

The spacing for crowns varies considerably in different sections of the country. The final spacing must accommodate equipment such as cultivators, tractors, sprayers, and other general farm implements. Close spacing is often used in home gardens, but commercial plantings should have the rows 4–6 feet apart, with the plants set 10–24 inches in the row. During the early life of a production bed, close spacing will give higher yields but smaller spear size. Over time, however, these differences will decrease. A closer spacing is usually necessary for mechanical harvesting.

Transplants

Asparagus beds can also be established from seedling transplants that are started from seed approximately 3 months before the field is planted (Figure 12.2). After the danger of frost has passed, the seedlings are transplanted in the field in furrows that are gradually filled as the plants grow. Plant spacing is the same as for crowns.

This method can represent a considerable saving in the time, labor, and equipment required to grow and harvest crowns. Also, there is less opportunity to carry *Fusarium* from one field to the next. However, greenhouse space and heat are required, and cost differences between using crowns and transplants may not be great. Seedling transplants are very susceptible to drought stress if irrigation is not provided. Some northern growers use seedling transplants that have been grown in greenhouses in the South.

Direct Seeding

This method consists of direct seeding in the field in a furrow 5–6 inches deep. Seeds are single-spaced 3 inches apart and planted 1 inch deep in the bottom of the furrow. As new growth develops, the furrow is gradually filled in the same manner as crown planting. However, asparagus seed is erratic in germination, and starting plants from seed in the field is generally not recommended. Growers have found that with this method irrigating and controlling weeds may be difficult.

CULTURAL PRACTICES

It is important to maintain healthy fern growth, especially during the late summer and fall when considerable food is stored in the crowns. As long as the plant is green, it will produce carbohydrates which are translocated to the roots for storage. The tops can be left standing over the winter but should be removed and burned in the early spring before any shoot development to reduce insect and disease problems.

Irrigation

The soil around a newly planted crown should not dry out. In the first 2 years, it is very important to avoid moisture stress, particularly during fern development. During this period, 1 inch of water per week is needed for good fern growth and transport of carbohydrates to the developing crown.

Once established, asparagus is very deep-rooted, allowing it to draw water from a large volume of soil and to withstand dry weather. Asparagus plantings in the U.S. normally receive adequate rainfall, except in arid and semi-arid regions in the West and Southwest. In these areas, about 20 inches of water is applied during fern growth following harvest. In established plantings, dry weather during the harvest season appears to have little effect on yield. Rather, the most critical time for moisture stress is after harvest when ferns become large. A good supply of water is needed at this time to maximize transport of carbohydrates from the tops to storage roots. The amount of irrigation water applied should be sufficient to wet the soil to a depth of 2 feet.

Weeds

Since asparagus occupies the same soil for many years, there is a tendency for perennial weeds, such as quackgrass, bindweed, and common milkweed, to be problems. During the initial season, growers control weeds primarily by using cultivations when filling in the furrows. Because relatively few chemicals are labeled for use on seedling plantings, herbicides are of limited value until beds are established.

On established plantings, weed suppression in asparagus entails the use of herbicides in combination with shallow disking or rototilling early in the spring before the spears appear. Cultivation during the harvest season is difficult without injuring the developing shoots, but some growers hill or mound the soil as the harvest season progresses to control weeds in the plant row. During the fern stage, cultivation is difficult because canes can grow rapidly to heights of 5 feet or more.

Beginning the third year after planting, herbicides provide the most effective method of weed control. The two most opportune times to apply herbicides are before the appearance of spears in the spring and again after harvest when all spears have been cut. The list of herbicides currently labeled for use on established asparagus plantings is relatively long. Growers should consult their extension specialists for the most up-to-date information on herbicide application.

Weed problems in asparagus can also arise from volunteer asparagus seedlings from fern-produced seed of female plants. These seedlings compete with the established plants, resulting in small spears and lower yields. Once these seedlings are established, control is very difficult, since they are resistant to most of the asparagus herbicides, and mechanical control measures are not effective. The all-male hybrid cultivars that have been recently developed do not produce seed, so that seedling plants are not a problem with these types.

CULTIVARS

Compared to other vegetable species, there are fewer cultivars of asparagus, and differences between cultivars may not be as well defined. In asparagus, male and female flowers are borne on different plants, resulting in mixing of strains in the field and making it difficult to obtain seed that breeds true. Since the crowns are propagated almost totally from seed, wide variation may appear in any lot of crowns unless special effort is made to isolate the seed-producing plants (females) from the pollen producers (males).

Most of the commercial cultivars currently in use are selections of the open-pollinated cultivar 'Mary Washington,' which gained early acceptance and widespread use as a result of its tolerance to rust, good productivity, and wide adaptability. Some of the selections include 'California 500,' 'Viking,' and 'Waltham Washington.'

In recent years, considerable effort has been made to develop hybrid cultivars especially adapted to cooler climates. Selections include both dioecious and all-male hybrid plants, which are sometimes referred to as "super males" (Table 12.2). The new hybrids have a high level of resistance to rust and *Fusarium* crown rot. Because of their enhanced vigor, the new hybrids can yield 3–5 times more than the 'Mary Washington' types. The all-male plants do not produce seed, enabling the plants to expend their energy on more vigorous crown growth and higher spear production. Another advantage of all-male hybrids is the lack of seeds, which in female plants, produce volunteer seedlings that are regarded as a weed problem in commercial fields.

New asparagus hybrids especially suited to warmer, drier climates have also been developed in the western states. These types are high-yielders in those areas, but when they are grown in colder, more humid climates, yields start decreasing after the third or fourth year.

Table 12.2. Asparagus Hybrid Cultivars and Characteristics

Hybrid Cultivar	Flowering Type	Disease Tolerance	Comments
New Jersey hybrids			
Jersey Giant	All-male	RR, FT[1]	Extremely vigorous; high yields
Jersey Centennial	Dioecious	RR, FT	Widely available; does not start producing maximum yields as quickly as others
Greenwich	All-male	RR, FT	High yields
Rutgers synthetic strains . . .	Mixture[2]	RR, FT	Adapted for production in Northeast
California hybrids			
UC 157	Dioecious	RR	High yields; not recommended for colder climates

[1]RR (rust resistant); FT (*Fusarium* tolerant).

[2]Mixture of dioecious hybrids, or mixture of male hybrids.

As indicated previously, traditional plant breeding methods in asparagus are difficult, and results are often varied. Attempts are being made to propagate genetically uniform clones by tissue culture techniques (Chapter 11). These new methods, however, are relatively expensive and somewhat tedious, and availability in commercial quantities remains severely limited.

INSECTS AND DISEASES

Close attention must be paid to insects and diseases that attack ferns, particularly late in the season when ferns become large and full. During periods of very warm and humid weather, foliage diseases can be very destructive and can cause premature death of the canes.

Insects

Asparagus beetles are the most troublesome insects affecting this crop. The two species involved are the common asparagus beetle (*Crioceris asparagi*) and the spotted asparagus beetle (*Crioceris duodecimpunctata*).

The common asparagus beetle is a shiny, blue-to-black beetle with three large, yellowish, square-shaped spots along each side, and reddish margins (Figure 12.3). The spotted beetle is reddish-orange with six prominent spots on each wing. Both species overwinter in old asparagus growth or in protected locations and emerge as temperatures warm in the spring.

Figure 12.3. The common asparagus beetle *(right)* and the 12-spotted asparagus beetle *(left)* are major insect pests of asparagus. (Photo: courtesy of R. F. Sandsted and L. D. Topoleski, Cornell University)

The common asparagus beetle feeds on the spears and lays eggs near the tip. The larvae feed on the fern and can seriously injure newly established beds and reduce the vigor of a mature stand. There are generally two to five generations per season, depending on location. The spotted beetle lays eggs on the berries where larvae emerge and feed on young tissue, including fern growth. There are usually two generations per season. Control of both species is the same and begins with the destruction of overwintering debris and early application of insecticides, if damage is observed.

The asparagus aphid (*Brachycolus asparagi*) is a potentially destructive pest, particularly in the northwestern states. It is a small, blue-green aphid that feeds on the ferns and is apparently restricted to asparagus as a host. The first winged aphids generally appear about mid-May. Injury symptoms include a marked stunting of fern growth, resulting in a dense clump of bushlike growth, or witches' broom, with a distinctive smokey or dusty cast. The greatest damage is usually on younger plants, which may be killed directly. Older plants show a range of symptoms, from severely weakened plants with few shoots to almost no visible effects. A large number of natural enemies, including ladybird beetles, parasitic wasps, and lacewing larvae feed on the aphid, but the best control is with insecticides.

Grubs, symphylans, and wireworms can also be serious pests on asparagus in certain areas. These insects inhabit the soil and injure the plant by feeding on the roots. Several species of cutworms (spotted cutworm and redback cutworm) cause damage to spears by severing newly emerging shoots below ground or by feeding on the tips. Asparagus miner can damage asparagus when larvae burrow into the base of shoots and provide an entry for *Fusarium* infection.

Diseases

The main diseases of asparagus are rust, *Fusarium* wilt and root rot, and *Fusarium* stem and crown rot. Rust, caused by the fungus *Puccinia asparagi*, appears as red or brown elongated spots on spears, shoots, and fern needles. The disease is usually seen on canes that grow up after harvest and causes the needlelike branches to fall prematurely, giving the plants a naked appearance. This limits the storage of reserve food in the crowns and reduces spear production the following season. It is most destructive in areas of high moisture; heavy dews and warm temperatures particularly favor the development of the disease. Resistant cultivars are available, but the level of resistance may vary. The recently developed New Jersey selections have better resistance to rust than the 'Washington' cultivars. Spraying the unharvested plants with fungicides in the spring and summer may prevent the buildup of inoculum and reduce the severity of the disease. Some growers cut and remove old canes each year to help control rust, although this is not always effective.

Wilt and root rot (*Fusarium oxysporum* f. sp. *asparagi*) and stem and crown rot (*Fusarium moniliforme*) are responsible for a serious disease complex that is found wherever asparagus is grown. Both species inhabit the soil and enter the plant through the fibrous feeder roots. Infection spreads throughout the roots and crown, weakening the plant. In established beds, the disease is usually first noticed when spears turn yellow and become dwarfed and shrivelled. One or two shoots of a crown may be affected while the others are normal, or the entire hill may die. Initially, affected plants are localized, but eventually all plants in a bed may be affected. With *F. oxysporum*, diseased plants possess a large number of dried-out roots, and crowns show a reddish-brown discoloration. With *F. moniliforme*, stem and crown lesions are more prominent. Practical control is to avoid using old asparagus soil, plant only treated material, use tolerant cultivars, and maintain plant vigor through good management practices.

HARVESTING

The initial harvest is normally at the start of the third season, but is limited to no more than 3 weeks. In succeeding years, the harvest season can be increased by 2 weeks each year but should not exceed 6–8 weeks. During the first two seasons, no harvest of spears is made so that all photosynthate is returned to the plant in the production of strong, healthy crowns. However, by using vigorous cultivars and high-quality crowns, some growers may have a brief harvest period of 2–3 weeks beginning the second season.

In general, the length of the harvest period for an established bed is 8 weeks but may vary depending on location and bed vigor. Where the growing season is long and cool, as in California, the cutting season may be longer than in eastern growing areas where the growing season is short. Once beds are established, cutting should continue as long as spear size and growth are vigorous but should be stopped when spear diameter becomes noticeably smaller. Overcutting reduces vigor and productivity and is the major cause of asparagus decline. When beds decline in production, the cutting season should be shortened and cultural practices (fertility, irrigation, pest control) should be started to help plants make more top growth. However, as beds grow older, there is always an increasing proportion of small spears, even in well-tended beds.

When ready for harvest, spears should be 6–10 inches long with tips tightly closed. During cool weather, spears can grow to 10 inches and remain tight, but with warm temperatures, tips open at much shorter spear length. In warm weather, spears must be cut daily and at a shorter height, or they will quickly grow past the market stage.

Asparagus spears are hand-harvested by either cutting or snapping. The spears are usually cut 1 inch below the soil surface with a special V-shaped blade knife. This method tends to increase yields due to heavier spears but also results in an increased percentage of woody, white tissue that must be removed prior to market. The spears should not be cut closer than 2 inches from the crown, or buds on the rhizome may be injured. When snapped by hand, the spear is broken off at or near ground level, usually above the point where the fiber content is relatively high (Figure 12.4). The harvested spear is nearly all green and edible, with very little trimming loss. This method is used for most of the asparagus grown for the local fresh market and roadside market. Some asparagus intended for processing is machine-harvested, but for fresh market, mechanical harvesting has not been economically feasible.

POSTHARVEST HANDLING

Asparagus is one of the most perishable commodities shipped commercially. It has a very high respiration rate, even at low temperatures, and requires special

Figure 12.4. Hand picking asparagus involves snapping off the spears near ground level.

care at all stages of distribution. Once harvested, asparagus quickly loses quality while undergoing marked changes in structure and chemical composition. At temperatures above 40°F, sugars and vitamin C are lost rapidly and coarse fibers develop. It is therefore important to cool asparagus to 40°F or lower, preferably 32–36°F, immediately after harvest, making sure that low temperatures are maintained in transit.

The cut spears are gathered and transported to packing areas where they are washed, graded, trimmed, packed, and cooled. USDA standards provide for two grades, U.S. #1 and #2, based on color, spear diameter, and appearance. Spears of large diameter are generally considered to be of higher quality because they have less fiber content than smaller spears. U.S. #1 asparagus consists of fresh, tender, well-trimmed, and fairly straight spears which are free from decay and damage caused by insects, disease, or breakage. Unless otherwise specified, the spear should have a diameter of not less than 0.5 inch about 1 inch from the butt end and green color not less than two-thirds of the stalk length. USDA standards do not specify a specific spear length, but 7–10 inches is generally used.

The spears are packed either loosely or vertically in bunches in pyramid crates lined with moistened paper to preserve spear quality. Crate size may differ depending on growing region. Western growers use crates containing either

sixteen 1.5-pound bunches or twelve 2-pound bunches. In the East, crates generally contain twelve bunches weighing 2.0–2.5 pounds. If the spears must be held
for 24 hours or longer, or are to be shipped, hydrocooling is the most common
method used today to lower temperature below 40°F.

Asparagus does not hold well and is rarely stored, except for a few days during
those times when the market is over-stocked. For holding periods of 10 days or
less, a temperature of 32°F is best, but for more than 10 days, a temperature of
36°F, or slightly above, is recommended since asparagus may be subject to chilling
injury. A relative humidity of 95% is desirable for storage and transit. The principal
decays of asparagus in storage are bacterial soft rot and gray mold rot.

RHUBARB

Rhubarb (*Rheum Rhabarbarum*) is a member of the buckwheat family and
is grown for its large leafstalks (Figure 12.5), which are cooked and used in sauces

**Figure 12.5. Rhubarb is grown for its fleshy leaf
petioles.**

and in pies and other desserts. The leaf blades, which contain oxalic acid, are poisonous and should not be eaten raw or cooked. The total commercial acreage in the U.S. is less than 1,000 acres and is centered in Washington, Oregon, and Michigan. Most of the crop is used for processing, primarily for use in pies, although a small amount is sold fresh.

PLANT GROWTH AND DEVELOPMENT

Rhubarb is a cool-season perennial plant that emerges from the same crown each year. It grows best where summers are cool and moist and where winters are cold enough to freeze the ground to a depth of 4–6 inches. Temperatures below 40°F are needed to break dormancy and stimulate the production of leaves and petioles. Buds begin to germinate in the spring as temperatures rise above 45°F. The plant does not grow well at temperatures above 80°F, and summer-produced rhubarb is usually of low quality. Foliar growth generally declines during July and August but is renewed in the fall when cooler temperatures prevail. Hot weather results in seedstalk growth, reducing plant vigor. The young shoots are susceptible to frost, but they usually outgrow damage. Similar to asparagus, sufficient foliage growth is required each season to restore food reserves in the crown for the next year's growth.

PLANTING AND CROP ESTABLISHMENT

Rhubarb plants are started vegetatively from crown divisions, which collectively consist of roots and pieces of stems and rhizomes. The divisions may be obtained from commercial nurseries or from large crowns cut into smaller pieces. Each division should have at least two large buds or eyes and a large piece of rhizome. The divisions are planted 3–4 feet apart in shallow furrows on 4-foot centers, making sure that the buds are 2 inches below the soil surface. Some growers use a 4- x 4-foot planting grid, permitting cultivating in two directions. The crowns for dividing and replanting can be dug in the early spring before new growth begins or late in the fall and then stored in a cool, dry place where they will not freeze or dry out. Seeds should not be used for propagation since plants from seeds take much longer to mature and are highly variable.

Rhubarb is very hardy and should be planted in the spring as early as possible, but no later than mid-May or when temperatures are consistently above 60°F. Any deep, well-drained soil that is high in organic matter is suitable. For best results, a cover crop should be seeded the previous fall and plowed in before planting. If available, well-rotted manure at 10 tons per acre can be applied and worked into the soil before planting. A general application of 1,000 pounds per acre of 20-20-20 (N-P_2O_5-K_2O) should be broadcast and disked in prior to planting.

CULTURE

In many respects, rhubarb is grown much like asparagus, and many cultural methods and practices are similar. Rhubarb can tolerate soil pH as low as 5.0 but grows best at 6.0–6.8. Nitrogen is applied each year, usually in two applications, 100 pounds per acre in early spring and 50 pounds per acre in late spring following harvest. This second application is to stimulate top growth. Phosphorus and potassium may not be needed every year, depending on soil test levels. Weed control is primarily by cultivating and mulching. Seedstalks should be removed as soon as they appear, since they inhibit leafstalk production. Once a plant produces a seedstalk, production of petioles declines. The crowns are divided every 7–8 years, or otherwise plants become too thick and produce only slender stalks.

CULTIVARS

Rhubarb cultivars are grouped according to petiole color and resistance to seedstalk formation. 'Canada Red,' 'Ruby,' and 'Valentine' are red-fleshed types, while 'McDonald' has pink petioles, and 'Victoria' is an old, green type. Generally, the red types tend to be smaller than the others. Both 'Valentine' and 'Canada Red' produce relatively few seedstalks, enabling them to be grown in warmer regions.

INSECTS AND DISEASES

The most harmful insect pests are the rhubarb curculio, a rust-colored beetle that bores into the stalks, crowns, and roots, and the potato stem borer. Both insects rely on weeds as alternate hosts (curly dock for the curculio and quackgrass for the stem borer); thus, the best control is to destroy grassy and large-stemmed weeds near the rhubarb field.

The most serious disease of rhubarb is *Phytophthora* crown rot, which attacks the base of the petioles causing them to rot. The best way to control this disease is by using disease-free materials and planting in a well-drained site. In some years, viruses can also affect rhubarb, resulting in small, stunted plants.

HARVESTING AND POSTHARVEST HANDLING

Major harvesting begins the third year after planting, although some leafstalks may be cut in the second season if the plants are established and healthy. The leafstalks are at their prime in early spring. The best-quality rhubarb petioles are deep red, long, thick, and fleshy. The length of harvest depends on plant vigor and may last up to 8 weeks if good stalks are available. Stalks are harvested by pulling the petioles from the plants at the soil line. The leaf blades are usually removed when the petioles are marketed. In areas with long growing seasons, a second harvest may be made in the late summer or early fall if plants are vigorous. However, some leaves should be left on the plants to store up reserves for the next year.

After harvest, the petioles are sensitive to dehydration and wilt easily when exposed to high temperatures and low humidity. Stalks can be stored 2–4 weeks at 32°F and 95% relative humidity.

FORCING RHUBARB

Rhubarb can be used as a forcing crop. Two-year-old crowns can be dug after they become dormant and moved inside for forcing during the winter. Normally, no stalks are removed from crowns in the field that are later to be forced. Crowns are forced at 55–65°F in the dark, in order to avoid chlorophyll development in the stalks. Prior to forcing, low temperatures below 40°F are used to break dormancy. Gibberellic acid sprayed on the crowns can also be used in place of, or in combination with, cold temperatures to break dormancy. All forced rhubarb is sold fresh. After production, the crowns are usually discarded since forcing substantially reduces their vigor.

GLOBE ARTICHOKES

Globe artichokes (*Cynara Scolymus*) are herbaceous perennials that are grown for their edible receptacles and scales, or bracts, of the blossom buds (Figure 12.6). The plants grow to 4–6 feet in height and attain a spread of 5–6 feet. The leaves are thistle-like, giving the plants a coarse appearance.

The origin of the globe artichoke is believed to be North Africa and other Mediterranean areas. The plant was brought to the U.S. by the French settlers in Louisiana, and the Spanish and Italians in California. Today, just about all U.S.

Figure 12.6. Globe artichoke plant, including its edible receptacles and scales of the blossom buds.

commercial production is in California. Worldwide, the major producers are Italy, Spain, and France, with U.S. production accounting for 4% of the world supply.

PLANTING AND CULTURE

Globe artichokes grow best in areas of cool, mild climates. The plants are very sensitive to frost, and temperatures below 30°F will kill the buds. High temperatures lower quality by causing rapid growth, which results in the development of more fiber and increases the toughness of the receptacle and scales. High temperatures also can cause the bud scales to spread apart, rendering the crop unmarketable.

The artichokes are propagated vegetatively, either by rooted offshoots that spring up from the base of the original plants or by divisions from old crowns, with each new section including a stem piece of the original plant. These are planted in the early fall 6 inches deep and covered with soil. Rows are spaced 8–10 feet apart, with plants spaced every 4–8 feet. Plantings generally last 5–8 years. Globe artichokes grow readily from seed, but seedlings tend to be highly variable and are rarely used for propagation.

The plants will tolerate a wide range of soils but grow best on a rich, well-drained loam under irrigation. Fertility requirements are modest since very little of the crop is removed in harvest. Normally, only nitrogen is applied annually. Although it is deep-rooted, moisture is critical to maintain bud quality, and 3–4 acre-feet of water (rainfall and irrigation) is needed each growing season.

After harvest in the late spring or early summer, the plants are cut off at the soil line and irrigation is withheld to induce dormancy. Plants remain dormant for several months until growth is stimulated in the late summer or early fall by fertilizer application and resumption of irrigation. This process allows growers some control of production schedules.

The major insect pests are aphids and plume moths. The aphids cause damage by sucking sap from the underside of leaves, while the larvae of the moths cause serious losses by feeding on the blossom buds. Major diseases affecting globe artichokes are *Fusarium* root rot and *Botrytis*, both of which are most severe during periods of warm, wet weather.

HARVESTING AND POSTHARVEST HANDLING

The crop is ready to harvest when blossom buds have attained maximum growth, but before bud scales begin to spread and show signs of flower opening. The harvest period is relatively long, starting in the fall, when new bud production begins, and peaking in the late spring, when temperatures increase. There is considerable variation in the time of maturity among plants, as well as among buds on individual plants. The terminal buds are the largest (3–5 inches in diameter) and the earliest to mature, followed by the axillary buds (2–4 inches in diameter). Hand harvesting involves cutting the stem about 2 inches below the base of the bud. After the initial year, yields of up to 40 buds per plant may be obtained.

After harvest, the buds are graded for size and quality and then packed in paperboard cartons containing 48–125 buds. The buds can be stored 3–4 weeks at 32°F and 90% relative humidity.

SELECTED REFERENCES

Ellison, J. H., and J. J. Kinelski. 1985. 'Jersey Giant', an all-male asparagus hybrid. *HortScience* 20:1141.

Hiller, L. K., M. Kossowski, and W. C. Kelly. 1974. Factors influencing flowering in rhubarb. *J. Amer. Soc. Hort. Sci.* 99:125–127.

Ingratta, F. 1976. *Growing Rhubarb*. Ontario Ministry of Agric. and Food, Toronto, Ontario, Factsheet 76-044, AGDEX 254 / 13.

Motes, J. E. 1985. *Asparagus Production*. Oklahoma State Univ. Coop. Ext. Ser. Facts No. 6018.

Ryder, E. J., N. E. DeVos, and M. Bari. 1983. The globe artichoke (*Cynara Scolymus* L.). *HortScience* 18:646–653.

Sandsted, R. F., D. A. Wilcox, T. A. Zitter, and A. A. Muka. 1985. *Asparagus*. Cornell Univ. Coop. Ext. Info. Bull. 202.

Sims, W. L., D. D. Souther, and R. J. Mullen. 1987. *Growing Asparagus in California*. Univ. of California ANR. Bull. 21447.

Sims, W. L., V. E. Rubatzky, R. H. Scaroni, and W. H. Lange. 1977. *Growing Globe Artichoke in California*. Univ. of California Div. Agric. Sci. Leaf. 2675.

Takatori, F. H., F. D. Souther, J. I. Stillman, and B. Benson. 1977. *Asparagus Production in California*. Univ. of California Div. ANR. Bull. 1882.

Takatori, F. H., F. D. Souther, W. L. Sims, and B. Benson. 1980. *Establishing the Commercial Asparagus Plantation*. Univ. of California Div. ANR. Leaf. 21165.

Thornton, R., W. Ford, and R. Dyck. 1982. *Washington Asparagus Production Guide*. Washington State Univ. Coop. Ext. Ser. EB 0997.

Zandstra, B. H., and D. E. Marshall. 1982. A grower's guide to rhubarb production. *American Vegetable Grower*, December: 8–10.

13

GARDEN BEANS — SNAP BEANS, LIMA BEANS, AND OTHER BEANS

(SCARLET RUNNER BEANS, COWPEAS, ASPARAGUS BEANS, CATJANG BEANS, GARDEN SOYBEANS, FAVA BEANS, GARBANZO BEANS, MUNG BEANS)

Garden or vegetable beans include three major species within the same genus (*Phaseolus*), along with several minor members of the legume family, Leguminosae. The common "vegetable" bean types are snap beans and lima beans, but there are also other various types of garden beans such as scarlet runner beans, fava beans, cowpeas, and garden soybeans.

By far, the most popular type of vegetable bean is the productive bush green-podded snap bean, which in the past was commonly referred to as *string bean*, because of the tough string-like tissue that developed along one edge of the pod. Today, however, except for some pole types and a few heirloom varieties, almost all modern cultivars of snap beans are stringless.

Beans, in general, are an excellent source of protein, vitamins A and B, and minerals (calcium, phosphorus, and iron). They are low in calories and relatively high in fiber. Beans are a versatile culinary commodity and can be served cold in salads, pickled for use as a relish, or cooked by steaming, boiling, and stir frying. Dry seeds of all species can be eaten after they have been cooked.

SNAP BEANS AND LIMA BEANS

Snap beans and lima beans are very much alike in their growth and development, cultural requirements, and general production. Both are tender, warm-season crops that have climbing and bush forms. Lima beans, however, require a considerably longer growing period (60–110 days) than snap beans (50–70 days). This difference is because lima beans are grown primarily for their enlarged (but not fully mature) seeds, compared to snap beans which are grown for their fleshy, immature pods.

CLASSIFICATION, ORIGIN, HISTORY

Snap beans belong to the species *Phaseolus vulgaris*, which includes a number of different types of beans used in either the green or the mature stage. Those types grown for the immature pods include snap beans and Romano or Italian beans, which produce large, flat pods that have a very distinctive flavor. Other types such as horticultural or "shelley" beans are grown to be shelled for their immature green seeds. Beans grown for their mature seeds, such as red kidney beans, are called dry beans. The widely grown bush forms are classified as *P. vulgaris* var. *humilis*.

Lima beans are generally grouped into large- and small-seeded types. The large-seeded limas (*Phaseolus limensis*) are perennials but are grown as annuals. The bush form is classified as *P. limensis* var. *limenanus*. The small-seeded or baby types are annuals which belong to the closely related species *Phaseolus lunatus*. The small-seeded types are referred to as sieva, or butter, beans. The dwarf or bush form of the small-seeded sieva bean is *P. lunatus* var. *lunonanus*.

Snap and lima beans, and other members of *Phaseolus*, are native to Central and South America, where evidence of beans dates back 7,000 years. Their introduction into the U.S. was through Mexico up into the Southwest, eventually moving east into Florida and spreading into Virginia. The Native Americans, who used beans primarily in the green shell or dry bean stage, showed the colonists how to grow beans among corn, which was probably one of the the first examples of intercropping. From the Americas, beans were introduced in Europe where bean varieties increased dramatically under cultivation.

PRODUCTION AND INDUSTRY

Snap beans are extensively grown both for commercial production and in home gardens in almost all states. Only tomatoes rank higher in popularity among garden vegetables in the U.S.; and after sweet corn, snap beans are the leading commercially grown processed vegetable. Over 80% of the commercial crop is processed and used for canning and freezing.

Statistics for processing snap beans in 1977 and 1989 show that the total acreage in the U.S. has remained relatively constant, while production and value have increased 29 and 58%, respectively, in 1989 (Table 13.1). Most of the production of processing snap beans in 1989 was in Wisconsin (32%) and Oregon (20%), followed by Illinois (9%), New York (8%), and Michigan (7%). Yields per acre in the U.S. average 3.4 tons, with Oregon the highest at 6.3 tons. Fresh market snap bean production (approximately 83,000 acres) is mostly in Florida and California, along with some in New York. After 1981 the U.S. Department of Agriculture discontinued data collection for fresh market snap beans.

Lima bean production for processing is still commercially significant, with most of the acreage in California, Delaware, and Wisconsin. The estimated U.S. total acreage for processed lima beans is 52,000 acres. However, except for some limited production for local use, lima beans for fresh market have almost disap-

Table 13.1. Harvested Acreage, Production, and Value of Processed Snap Beans, 1977 and 1989

State	Harvested Acreage		Production		Value	
	1977[1]	1989[2]	1977	1989	1977	1989
			——— (tons) ———		——— ($1,000) ———	
Arkansas	4,700	—	8,450	—	6,014	—
Illinois	—	24,800	—	82,090	—	17,731
Indiana	—	4,600	—	14,630	—	3,350
Michigan	16,800	21,500	41,300	62,350	5,163	10,350
Minnesota	—	5,900	—	22,660	—	2,515
New York	43,000	25,200	96,100	69,550	14,320	13,075
Oregon	32,500	25,700	140,200	173,990	19,207	30,622
Pennsylvania	5,000	5,700	10,350	14,540	1,681	3,286
Tennessee	13,700	5,200	26,100	9,100	4,340	2,184
Washington	1,700	1,100	4,550	4,790	619	881
Wisconsin	62,700	82,500	185,450	281,330	23,738	42,762
Other states[3]	77,600	46,800	163,400	134,670	21,046	24,623
U.S.	257,740	249,000	675,900	869,700	96,128	151,379
canning	200,250	178,740	519,350	596,890	73,293	101,819
freezing	57,490	70,260	156,550	272,810	22,835	49,560

[1]Source: USDA. 1978. Economics, Statistics, and Cooperatives Service (ESCS), Crop Reporting Board.

[2]Source: USDA. 1990. National Agricultural Statistics Service (NASS), Agricultural Statistics Board.

[3]Alabama, California, Delaware, Florida, Georgia, Idaho, Maryland, Missouri, New Jersey, North Carolina, Ohio, Oklahoma, South Carolina, Texas, Utah, Virginia for 1989; not identified for 1977.

peared. This is mainly due to consumer reluctance to shell fresh beans and also to the very stringent production requirements for fresh market limas.

In comparison to most other vegetables, beans are a relatively inexpensive crop to grow, since much of the production is highly mechanized, particularly the harvest. The worker-hours to produce and harvest 1 acre of snap beans decreased from 132 in 1939, to 15 hours in 1977, to approximately 9 hours in 1987. This compares to 8 worker-hours for peas, 20 worker-hours for potatoes, and over 50 worker-hours for onions and lettuce.

PLANT GROWTH AND DEVELOPMENT

Seedling Germination and Development

Beans are propagated entirely from seed. The embryo consists of the embryonic root (radicle), the lower stem (hypocotyl), two seed leaves (cotyledons), and the first true leaves (plumules). By the time of seed maturity, there is little or no endosperm, and the reserve food materials are located primarily in the cotyledons. The seed coat includes the tissues (integuments) that envelop the embryo and the area where the seed is attached to the pod (hilum).

During germination the radicle emerges from the seed first and establishes the primary root (Figure 13.1). Elongation of the hypocotyl forces a hypocotyl bend or arch through the surface of the ground. When the hypocotyl is exposed to light and straightens out, it pulls the cotyledons upward through the soil. The unfolding and shrinkage of the cotyledons and the expansion of the plumules aid in the shedding of the seed coat.

Any of the preceding parts may be injured before or during germination, resulting in failure of germination or reduced vigor and delayed seedling development. Injury to the seed coat results in leaching food materials from the cotyledons or may permit entry of disease organisms that bring about seed rot. Separation of the cotyledons from the axis, or cracking, reduces the food supply to the developing seedling. Loss of the plumules results in reduced vigor and delayed germination. Injury to the hypocotyl causes an angular crook, or "knee," in the lower stem.

Growth Patterns

Beans have three general growth types: 1) bush (determinate), 2) runner or pole (indeterminate), and 3) half-runner (semi-determinate). Runner beans seem to have been the original form. Bush types are fairly recent, probably resulting

Figure 13.1. Development of snap bean from germination to early plant establishment: 1) radicle, 2) hypocotyl, 3) hypocotyl arch, 4) cotyledons, 5)
taproot, 6) lateral roots, 7) root hairs, 8) cotyledonary node, 9) unifo-
liate leaves, 10) terminal bud, 11) axillary bud, 12) nodes, 13) trifoli-
ate leaves, and 14) nodules.

from mutations of runner types. The bush types are used for quick production,
while the runner types are slower growing but produce more beans per plant.

Bush beans, or determinate types, grow 1–2 feet high and have a short
central stem of six or seven nodes that terminates in a flowering raceme. Several
strong laterals arise from the main stem and also terminate in racemes. Additional
flowers are borne in the axils of leaves on the laterals. The flowers appear in close
sequence and pods mature together, making the plant well suited for machine
harvesting (Figure 13.2).

Runner, or indeterminate, beans have a main stem that can grow up to 10
feet or more in a twining fashion and does not terminate in a raceme. There is
little branching, although occasionally one or more laterals may develop in the
axils of the first true leaves. Racemes are borne in the axils of the leaves, but due
to the continuous growth pattern, flowers and fruits will be in various stages of
development on the plant at the same time.

Figure 13.2. On determinate plants, pods mature together.

Half-runner, or semi-determinate, beans have short- or medium-length vines with some branching, but like the bush types, stems terminate in flower racemes.

Flowers and Fruits

Bean flowers consist of racemes, which may contain up to 12 individual flowers. Stamens and pistils are enclosed in two petals called "keels," and flowers are primarily self-pollinating. Flowering habit is classified as day neutral, although some cultivars may flower sooner under short days.

The fruits are pods that develop from the ovary and style. Snap bean pods are generally 3–8 inches long and 0.25–0.75 inch narrow. Some may be fleshy or rounded and others slender or flat. Pods vary in color, with green or yellow most common; beans with yellow pods are often referred to as wax beans. Pod fiber development increases with seed maturation and varies with cultivar. In older cultivars, a tough, string-like tissue develops along one edge of the pod, but this has been eliminated in newer cultivars.

Snap bean seeds vary in size (0.25–0.5 inch), shape (globular- to kidney-shaped), coat color (white, yellow, green, purple, red, brown, black), and number per pod (4–12). Lima bean pods are generally curved and oblong and contain from two to six seeds, ranging in size from 0.25 to 1 inch (Figure 13.3). The seed

Figure 13.3. Lima bean pods are generally curved and oblong, and contain from two to six seeds.

coat color in lima beans is usually white, cream, or light green, although other colors (red, purple, brown) may occur.

Roots

Beans develop a highly branched taproot system that grows to a depth of 3–4 feet. Being legumes, bean roots have nodules which contain bacteria (*Rhizobium* sp.) capable of converting free nitrogen from the atmosphere to chemically combined nitrogen, which can be used by the plant. However, relatively small amounts of nitrogen are actually "fixed" in this way, and inoculation of beans with *Rhizobium* has generally not proven effective.

CLIMATIC AND CULTURAL REQUIREMENTS

Beans are tender, warm-season vegetables that will not tolerate frost. Adequate moisture and warm, but not hot, temperatures are important for rapid growth, good pod set, and early maturity. Lima beans, particularly the large-seeded types, are more sensitive to environmental extremes than snap beans.

For rapid, uniform emergence, bean seeds should be planted in warm soils. Soil temperatures for best seed germination range from 60° to 85°F, with an optimum of 80°F. If beans are planted in cool, wet soils, germination will be delayed, and seeds may rot. For example, at a soil temperature of 77°F, snap bean germination is 97% and emergence takes 8 days; at 59°F, germination is also 97% but takes 16 days; at 86°F, seed emergence occurs in 6 days but the percentage germination decreases to 50%. Below 50°F and above 95°F, the percentage germination for snap beans and lima beans is extremely poor.

Beans grow best at air temperatures of 70–80°F. Pod set may be adversely affected if air temperatures exceed 90°F or are less than 50°F during the blossoming period. The combination of high temperatures and low humidity favor the dropping of flowers. Hot, dry winds will cause flowers to abort. With many of the large-seeded lima bean cultivars, fruits will fail to set at temperatures above 80°F and relative humidity less than 65%. This severely limits the production of these types to mostly the coastal areas. Excessively damp and rainy weather may also cause blossoms to drop. Bean cultivars vary a great deal in response to weather conditions, and growth tests should be conducted for a given locality.

Sandy to clay loam and muck soils are used for growing beans, but good yields are seldom produced on very heavy soils. Light soils that drain and warm quickly in the spring are best for early plantings. Beans prefer mildly acid soils (pH 5.5–6.5) and do poorly under alkaline conditions, where manganese deficiencies may occur.

Fertility requirements for beans are relatively modest. Beans are in the group of vegetables least responsive to fertilizers. Nitrogen rates vary (40–75 pounds per acre), depending on soil type and management practices. Higher nitrogen rates are applied to crops on sandy soils and those grown with high plant populations. Phosphorus and potassium fertilization is based on soil test results. A standard practice is to band some of the fertilizer with the seed at planting. However, beans are extremely susceptible to salt damage, and fertilizers should not come in contact with roots. To avoid injury, no more than 75–100 pounds per acre of nitrogen plus K_2O should be banded with the seed. Excessive nitrogen can cause vigorous vine growth, at the expense of pod production, and can delay maturity. Beans are very sensitive to boron and can suffer significant yield reductions if boron levels exceed 1 part per million in irrigation water.

PLANTING AND CROP ESTABLISHMENT

Beans are commonly direct seeded in rows for easy cultivation (Figure 13.4). Seeding rates vary, depending on seed size, percentage germination, irrigation, and row spacing.

The traditional plant spacing for bush snap beans consists of rows 2.5–3.0 feet apart with seven to nine plants per foot or row for irrigated fields and six to eight plants per foot of row for dryland. With the recent development of new multiple-row harvesters that allow for close rows to be used, bush snap beans are being grown using high-density plantings consisting of rows 12–24 inches apart with three or four plants per foot of row. This high-density culture has increased efficiencies and yields but requires 50% more fertilizer and better control of

Figure 13.4. Beans are grown as a row crop, which allows for easy cultivation.

weeds and disease. Bush-type lima beans are normally spaced at 2.5–3.0 feet between rows with three or four plants per foot of row. High-density plantings are not used for limas.

Pole cultivars of snap beans and lima beans may be planted either in rows or in hills. If rows are used, seeds are planted every 6–12 inches, with the rows 3–4 feet apart. The hills are spaced 3–4 feet apart each way and contain five or six seeds, which are later thinned to three or four plants. In each case, some type of support and training system (trellises, cages, etc.) is required.

Bean seeds are generally planted 0.5 inch deep in heavy soils and 1.5 inches deep in sandy soils. Shallow planting will improve germination, if adequate moisture is available. Bean seeds should be handled carefully since physical damage to the seed can decrease germination and reduce seedling vigor. Very dry seed is prone to injury in handling and to differential swelling of cotyledons during germination, which can cause poor and uneven germination. Seed from dry storage should be conditioned at 60% relative humidity for 1–2 weeks before planting.

Only seed grown in regions where seed-borne diseases do not exist or can be controlled should be used. Most of the seed is produced in semi-arid regions of California and Idaho. Low humidity and limited rainfall are unfavorable for the development of seed-borne diseases such as bean blight, anthracnose, and mosaic. The use of resistant cultivars and seed treated with a fungicide is generally practiced.

CULTURAL PRACTICES

Weeds

Annual grasses are the main problem with snap beans planted early in the growing season. An effective weed control system consists of a preplant-incorporated or preemergent material which will prevent grass competition with the early growth of the young bean seedlings. In the later planted beans, broadleaf weeds become more of a problem, and a broadleaf herbicide is needed.

For lima beans, which have a longer growing period than snap beans, a longer period of weed control is needed. A commonly used system is a preplant-incorporated treatment of a grass herbicide plus a broad spectrum herbicide as a preemergent or overlay treatment. The use of a postemergent herbicide may be used to control broadleaf weeds that develop later in the season.

Herbicides should be used to control most weeds, but some cultivation will be required. Cultivation should be shallow, since many of the feeder roots are near the surface. Beans are very susceptible to injury from cultivation after the plants begin to flower. Cultivating or working among the plants when the foliage is wet should be avoided because anthracnose and other fungus spores are easily spread under wet conditions.

Irrigation

Beans are a moderately deep-rooted crop in which a constant supply of moisture is critical to maximize yields and quality and to maintain uniformity. The plant may use as much as 0.2 inch of water per day during hot weather and peak growing periods. A shortage of moisture during flowering can cause blossoms and pods to drop. Deformed pods can result from water stress due to low soil moisture or excessive transpiration.

Soil moisture should be maintained in the upper half of the available soil moisture range. In California, irrigation requirements range from 12 acre-inches for a spring crop of snap beans to 18 acre-inches for beans grown in the fall. For processing snap beans on sandy soils in Wisconsin, 1 inch of water every 5 days is applied from planting to bud formation; after which, 1.25 inches of water is applied every 5 days up until 2 or 3 days before harvest.

CULTIVARS

A wide choice of snap bean cultivars is available (Table 13.2). These are

Table 13.2. Selected Cultivars of Snap Beans

Cultivar	Days to Maturity	Pod Characteristics	Seed Color	Uses[1]
Bush Green Pod				
Astro	52	Round, long, slender	White	S, P
Bush Blue Lake 47 . . .	57	Round, long, fleshy	White	P
Bush Blue Lake 92 . . .	52	Round, long, fleshy	White	P
Bluecrop	54	Round	White	M
Cascade	54	Round, fleshy	White	M, P
Eagle	55	Round, long, slender	White	M, F
Early Gallatin	53	Round	White	F
Greencrop	52	Flat, long	White	M
Harvester	54	Round–oval	White	S, G
Spurt	54	Round, long	White	M, S
Strike	52	Round, slender	White	S
Tenderette	54	Round	White	M, S, P, G
Tendercrop	56	Round, fleshy	White	M, G
Provider	50	Round–heart-shaped	Purple	M, S
Bush Yellow Pod				
Goldrush	54	Round, long	White	M, S, P, G
Midas	55	Round, slender	White	M, S, P
Resistant Cherokee . .	50	Oval	Black	M, S, G
Sungold	56	Round	White	M, G
Goldcrop	55	Round	White	M, S, G
Pole Green Pod				
Blue Lake types	63–66	Round	Pure white	G, P
Kentucky Wonder . . .	67	Round	Buff	G
McCasian	64	Flattened oval	Ivory white	G, M
Romano	70	Flattened oval	Tan	G, M, F

[1]General-purpose processing (P), local market (M), shipping (S), canning (C), freezing (F), garden (G).

classified into bush green pod, bush yellow pod, half-runner, and pole. Within each group, there are further divisions according to seed color (white or colored), pod shape (round or flat, fleshy or slender), and use (fresh market or processing).

Most snap bean cultivars are the bush green-podded type. With the development of mechanical harvesters, bush cultivars with concentrated pod set and maturity have generally replaced pole types for canning and freezing, as well as for much of the fresh market. Yellow-podded types are not used as much because they tend to show mechanical injuries and disease spots very clearly. Pole types are limited to the home garden and to the fresh market, where high yields and prices offset the higher cost of production.

Seed color is important to processors who want white or light-colored seed coats, since these present a more attractive product and do not discolor the liquid in the can. However, there are a few cultivars with colored seeds still used for

Table 13.3. Selected Lima Bean Cultivars

	Cultivar	Days to Maturity	Uses[1]	Seed Color
Bush types				
Large-seeded	Fordhook 242	78	FM, P, G	Light green
	Fordhook 169	75	FM, P, G	Light green
Small-seeded	Dixie Butterpea	75	FM, G	White
	Thaxter	70	P	Greenish-white
	Early Thorogreen	66	P	Green
	Henderson Bush	65	FM, G	Pale green
	Nemagreen	70	P	Green
	Bridgeton	70	P	Pale green
Pole types				
Large-seeded	Challenger	90	G	Light green
	King of the Garden	88	G	Greenish-white
Small-seeded	Sieva	80	G	White

[1]Fresh market (FM), processing (P), garden (G).

fresh market and for commercial freezing. Cultivars with fleshy pods are widely used for commercial freezing (cut-pods and French-style slicing) and for general-purpose canning (whole-pods, cut-pods, and French-style slicing). These types tend to form seed and fiber slowly, while the cultivars with slender pods develop seed and fiber more rapidly.

Lima bean cultivars are grouped (Table 13.3) according to growth habit (bush and pole) and seed size (small and large). The bush or dwarf types are used for processing and make up most of the lima beans grown for market. The pole or climbing types are grown mostly in home gardens. Breeding of lima and butter beans in recent years has concentrated on the bush types and has resulted in increased earliness and better tolerance to weather stresses. The large-seeded lima beans are generally more robust than the small-seeded limas but are slower to form seeds in the pods and less tolerant of heat and humidity.

For horticultural beans and Italian, or Romano, beans, bush and pole cultivars are available. Dry bean cultivars are primarily the bush type and typically range in seed size from the large kidney beans to the smaller white, navy, or pea beans.

Processors have strict requirements for specific cultivar characteristics, such as a deep white seed coat and uniform crop maturity, and generally choose their own cultivars.

INSECTS AND DISEASES

Beans have their share of insect and disease problems, although these may differ according to region and season. Bean beetles are the major insect pest. Several bacterial diseases such as common blight, halo blight, and bacterial wilt are problems in the East and South, while viruses and root rots are serious in the West.

Insects

Mexican Bean Beetle. This is a copper-colored and black-spotted beetle (*Epilachna varivestis*) that can be a problem in certain areas. It prefers to feed on vegetable and field beans, but beggar weed is also a common food. The beetles appear before the plants start to blossom, and after feeding for about 10 days, they deposit their eggs. Larvae and adults feed on the underside of the leaves. Turning under vines immediately after harvest helps in control. Chemical control should begin as soon as the beetles appear.

Bean Leaf Beetle. The bean leaf beetle (*Cerotoma trifurcata*) is a small, dark yellow to tan beetle with six black dots on the wing covers. It eats large holes in the leaves, feeding from the underside (Figure 13.5). The eggs are laid at the bases of the plants, and grubs feed on the roots. Control is with several insecticides.

Adult Bean Weevil. The bean weevil (*Acanthoscelides obtectus*) is chiefly a pest of dry beans, including bean seed. The adult bean weevil is a small, dull-colored beetle, while the larva is mostly white. Infested seed should not be used. Seed should be fumigated or treated with a labeled insecticide.

Figure 13.5. The bean leaf beetle eats holes in the leaves, feeding from the underside.

Leafhoppers. Leafhoppers are small, pale green, wedge-shaped insects (*Circulifor tenellus*) that feed by sucking juices from the leaves. Injury appears as curled or crinkled leaves with yellow or brown edges. Severely affected plants will be yellow and stunted. Infestations will occur throughout the season. Control is difficult because of insect mobility, requiring regular applications of insecticides.

Other insect pests of beans vary, depending on location. These include aphids, seed maggots, corn borers, corn earworms, blister beetles, and mites.

Diseases

Anthracnose. Anthracnose is caused by several strains of *Colletotrichum limdemuthianum* and is a destructive fungal disease of snap and field beans in humid regions. Hot, dry weather is unfavorable for the organism, while cool, wet weather promotes disease development. The fungus overwinters in the seed and in bean refuse. Affected areas on pods and stems are recognized by somewhat circular, dark, sunken spots. On lima beans, spots resembling sooty mold develop on leaves and pods. Most cultivars show little resistance. The use of rotations and certified disease-free seed, produced in dry climates, is very effective in controlling the disease.

Bacterial Blight. Several different bacteria can infect beans, causing significant damage. The most prevalent are common blight (*Xanthomonas phaseoli*) and halo blight (*Pseudomonas phaseolicola*). Common blight first appears on leaves as small, water-soaked spots which enlarge and form brown lesions with a narrow, yellow margin. On pods, water-soaked, sunken lesions occur, which turn brownish-red with age.

Halo blight will have similar symptoms, but with a characteristic large, yellow halo around the individual spots. Both organisms overwinter in seed or plant debris. Damp weather favors the development of both diseases; however, common blight is favored more by high temperatures, while halo blight increases under low temperatures. Control measures consist of using disease-free seed and planting beans in a 3- or 4-year rotation. Copper fungicides are only partially successful against bacterial blights.

Rust. Although rust (*Uromyces phaseoli*) is fairly widespread over the eastern U.S., and also along the Pacific Coast, it is only troublesome in some years. The disease is most common on mature plants. It is especially destructive on leaves, appearing as small, chlorotic, pale spots which enlarge and become covered with red rust spores. Cultural practices are important in rust control; a 3- or 4-year rotation is recommended, and all bean refuse should be plowed under after harvest. Fungicides will provide good control if treatments are made in the early stages of the disease.

Sclerotinia White Mold. The characteristic symptom of white mold (*Sclerotinia sclerotiorum*) is a white, cottony growth near the base of the stem, which may also appear on pods. The disease will generally start in wet weather and when plant growth covers the space between the rows. Infection will kill some plants and severely reduce yields of those plants with only pod infections. The disease is favored by high humidity and temperatures between 60 and 70°F. A rotation of 3 or 4 years is recommended for control; however, sunflowers, potatoes, and sugar beets should not be used since they are very susceptible to white mold. Fungicide application at early and full bloom will provide good control of the disease.

Bean Mosaic Virus. Common bean mosaic (BV-1) and a variant strain (NY-15), bean yellow mosaic (BV-2), and peanut stunt (PSV) are viruses affecting beans. Symptoms include mottling, curling, crinkling, and malformation of leaves. Occasionally the pods are mottled, deformed, and rough. Diseased plants are often dwarfed and unproductive. The common bean mosaic is seed-borne, while BV-2 and PSV are not. All three overwinter in white clover. BV-2 also overwinters in gladioli. Spread is mainly by aphids and by mechanical transfer from diseased to healthy plants by workers or equipment. Most cultivars developed in the last 20 years are resistant to BV-1, making this virus less of a problem. Resistance to BV-2 and PSV is not yet available. Using clean seed will help control BV-1.

Root Rots. These are a fungal complex (*Fusarium, Rhizoctonia, Pythium*) that should be suspected whenever plants wilt or are stunted with yellow leaves. In addition, plants may have small pods that contain undersized seed. With *Fusarium* and *Rhizoctonia*, reddish-brown cankers affect the roots up to the soil line and often girdle the stem. *Pythium* affects mainly the lower stem. The root rot organisms live on decomposing vegetation, and rotation is very important in their control. Similar to other bean diseases, rotation on a 3- or 4-year cycle should be practiced to prevent buildup of these soil pathogens.

Downy Mildew. Caused by the fungus *Phytophthora phaseoli*, downy mildew is a serious problem on lima beans, especially in the eastern U.S. Symptoms appear as white, downy spots on pods, which may shrivel, turn black, and die. The fungus overwinters in diseased refuse and on infected seed. It grows in wet weather and is rapidly spread by wind. Using well-drained fields and weekly fungicide sprays will control the disease.

HARVESTING

Snap beans are harvested before they reach physiological maturity, approximately 2 weeks after bloom. The pods should be nearly full size, with the seeds still small (about one-quarter developed), with firm flesh and low fiber content. Lima beans require about 30–40 additional days more than snap beans from planting to harvest. Green shell limas are picked when the seeds are nearly full size and the pods green. Dry beans are harvested after the pods are mature and when seed moisture content is approximately 16–20%. Harvesting and handling low-moisture beans (less than 14%) may result in mechanical damage and seed loss.

Bush types, as compared to pole cultivars, mature over a relatively short time and may be harvested in only a few pickings. Machine harvest is used for almost all bush beans for commerce, including many of those grown for fresh market. Determinate plants with concentrated pod set are required. Modern harvesters use a "once-over" destructive harvest, which strips leaves and removes pods from plants. Lima bean harvesters remove pods from vines and shell the beans in one operation (Figure 13.6). Pole beans are not adapted to mechanical harvesting and are picked by hand.

POSTHARVEST HANDLING

Snap beans and lima beans are highly perishable, and rapid cooling after

Figure 13.6. Almost all beans for commercial marketing are machine-harvested.

harvest is important to maintain quality. Following harvest, snap beans and lima beans are washed and culled to remove inferior beans and waste and then packed in hampers, large bins, bushel baskets, or wirebound crates. Before they are placed into storage or transit, the beans are cooled as rapidly as possible by any one of three methods: hydrocooling, vacuum cooling, and forced-air cooling. Hydrocooling is the preferable method since free water helps prevent wilting and shrivelling.

Optimum storage and transit temperatures are 40–45°F for snap beans and 37–41°F for lima beans, with a relative humidity of 90–95%. Under these conditions, the approximate storage life is 7–10 days for snap beans and 5–7 days for limas.

Both snap beans and lima beans are cold-sensitive, and some chilling may occur even at recommended storage temperatures. At temperatures below 37°F for a few days, either in transport or in storage, severe chilling injury will occur in snap beans and in shelled limas. Chilled beans will develop spotting (russeting) and surface pitting 1–2 days after removal to warm temperatures. Overall, the loss in quality from chilling injury is considerably less than that from normal deterioration at higher temperatures, so growers and processors routinely use cold storage for their beans.

Dry beans are stored at 40–50°F and a relative humidity of 40–50%. Under these conditions, they have a storage life of 6–10 months. If beans have a moisture content below 14%, the relative humidity should be 70% to increase seed moisture content and to avoid seed coat cracking during storage and marketing.

MINOR BEANS

SCARLET RUNNER BEANS

Scarlet runner beans (*Phaseolus coccineus*) are widely grown in North America, not so much for their food value but rather for their ornamental blossoms. However, in Europe these beans are highly valued for their edible, immature pods, much like snap beans. A white-runner cultivar, 'Dutch Caseknife,' is popular for both its white, cream-colored blossoms and its delicious long, broad, slightly curved pods.

Like other beans, scarlet runner beans are native to Central America and grow best in warmer regions or during the summer months in more temperate climates. The plant develops a central twining vine that will reach a length of 10 feet or more.

COWPEAS (SOUTHERN PEAS), ASPARAGUS BEANS, AND CATJANG BEANS

Several different types of beans belonging to *Vigna unguiculata* are grown and used as vegetables in the U.S. These include common cowpeas, or southern peas (*Vigna unguiculata*), asparagus beans (*Vigna unguiculata* subsp. *sesquipedalis*), and catjang beans (*Vigna unguiculata* subsp. *cylindrica*). All are warm-season annuals that are very sensitive to cold weather and are seldom planted in the northern part of the U.S.

Cowpeas

Common cowpeas, or southern peas, are the most important of the group and are grown in many areas of the South and Southwest, where they are preferred over snap and lima beans because of their resistance to heat and insects. They are grown much like snap beans, although they are more susceptible to cold weather and are planted later than snap beans. Plants are tall and erect or semi-erect and twining, with pods 3–12 inches long held on stalks above the foliage. Modern bush types mature in about 55–75 days from planting in warm soil. Pods may be picked as green shell beans or may be left on the plant and used as dry peas.

The various kinds of cowpeas may be distinguished by pod type and color, and pattern of seed coat. These include the "purple hull" types (red to purple pods), the cream types (seeds are creamed-colored when cooked), and the black-eyed types (the seeds have a colored "eye" around the hilum). Each kind contains a large number of cultivars and strains. Within each, there is also what is known as a crowder type, in which seeds are tightly crowded in the pod. The black-eyed types (*V. unguiculata* subsp. *unguiculata*) are used extensively as culinary vegetables. In parts of Texas and California, black-eyed peas are grown as a field crop to supply the demand for the dry product.

Asparagus Beans

Asparagus beans, also known as yard-long beans (Figure 13.7), are grown mostly for their edible, immature pods of extraordinary length (12–36 inches long). Some consider the asparagus bean to be a late-maturing runner type of cowpea. The plant is an annual trailing vine. The pods can also be left on the plant and harvested as either green shell beans or dry beans. The seeds are kidney-shaped, about 0.25–0.5 inch long.

Figure 13.7. Asparagus beans, or yard-long beans, are grown mostly for their immature, fleshy pods, but they can also be used as green shell or dry beans.

Catjang Beans

Catjang beans prefer semi-arid tropical conditions and are seldom grown outside Florida. The plants are erect or semi-erect and are harvested for their immature pods, which contain small, spherical seeds. Catjang beans are of limited commercial importance in the U.S.

GARDEN SOYBEANS

The garden or edible soybean (*Glycine Max*) is a close relative of the cowpea and is grown principally for shelling and eating in the green seed stage. The plants look much like the field-type soybeans, except that the garden types are generally shorter and earlier maturing. The plants are bushy, about knee-high, slender, and furry. Flowers are usually self-pollinated. The short, downy pods contain two or three seeds, which are rich in oil and protein.

Garden soybeans are a warm-season crop, which grow slower than either snap beans or lima beans and require from 75 to over 170 days for maturity. However, they are not as sensitive to frost as are garden beans and may be planted earlier. Soybeans are short-day plants and very sensitive to photoperiod; the time to maturity depends upon the daylength and cultivar. In the U.S., cultivars are grouped into nine maturity groups according to photoperiod requirements, each for a particular latitude. Cultivars to be grown in the North are earliest in maturity and are adapted to longer days, while cultivars to be grown in the South are adapted to shorter days.

Soybeans as a green vegetable should be harvested when the seeds are fully grown and still succulent, before they have hardened. The young beans resemble young lima beans, but they have a richer, nutlike flavor. If allowed to dry, the seeds can be roasted.

FAVA BEANS

Fava beans (*Vicia Faba*), sometimes called broad beans, are a minor crop in the U.S., except in parts of California where they are fall-planted as cover crops in orchards. The plants are erect and fairly tall with heavy, stiff stems. The glossy green pods are about 7 inches long and contain five or six large seeds, which are used as green shell beans or dried for storage. Broad beans have narrow growing requirements and need a fairly long, cool to moderately warm growing season. In certain areas along the Pacific Coast, they may be planted in the fall and grown through the winter for a spring crop.

GARBANZO BEANS

Garbanzo beans (*Cicer arietinum*), or chickpeas, are grown commercially as a dryland crop in central California. The plants are erect and bushy, growing to a height of 2 feet. Garbanzo beans need warm temperatures and mature in about 100 days after planting. The numerous short pods, each of which contains two or three seeds, are harvested with a combine when dry. The cream-colored, marble-sized cooked garbanzos are often seen in restaurant salad bars.

MUNG BEANS

Mung beans (*Vigna radiata*) are best known for their use in the dry seed stage to produce bean sprouts. The plant is bush type in growth habit, is fairly erect, and grows to about 2 feet tall. Cultural and climatic requirements are similar to those for cowpeas. Plants are very susceptible to cold temperatures and are grown almost totally in the South. About 100 days are required from seeding to maturity. Pods are slender, about 4 inches long, and can be cooked and eaten in the green stage or harvested when mature and used for dry seed.

SELECTED REFERENCES

Curwen, D., and E. E. Schulte. 1978. *Snap Beans — Green and Wax.* Univ. of Wisconsin Coop. Ext. Ser. Prog. A2328.

Fletcher, R. F., R. Tetrault, and A. A. McNab. 1976. *Growing Snap Beans for Processing.* Pennsylvania State Univ. Agric. Ext. Ser. Cir. 564.

Kaplan, L. 1981. What is the origin of the common bean? *Econ. Bot.* 35:240–254.

Mansour, N. S., and H. J. Mack. 1978. *Recommendations for Commercial High Density Snapbean Production.* Oregon State Univ. Coop. Ext. Cir. 952.

Nuland, D. S., H. F. Scwartz, and R. L. Forster (eds.). 1983. *Dry Bean Production Problems.* North Central Region Ext. Pub. 198.

Rutledge, A. D. 1975. *Commercial Snapbean Production.* Univ. of Tennessee Agric. Ext. Cir. 823.

Sandsted, R. F., R. B. How, A. A. Muka, and A. F. Sherf. 1974. *Growing Dry Beans in New York State.* New York State Col. Agric. Coop. Ext. Info. Bull. 2.

Seelig, R. A. 1982. *Lima Beans. Fruit & Vegetable Facts & Pointers.* United Fresh Fruit and Vegetable Association, Alexandria, Virginia.

Seelig, R. A., and C. Lockshin. 1979. *Snap Beans. Fruit & Vegetable Facts & Pointers.* United Fresh Fruit and Vegetable Association, Alexandria, Virginia.

Silbernagel, M. J. 1981. *Garden Bean Fact Sheet.* National Garden Bureau, Sycamore, Illinois.

Silbernagel, M. J. 1986. Snapbean Breeding, pp. 243–282. In: M. J. Bassett (ed.). *Breeding Vegetable Crops.* AVI Publishing Co., Westport, Connecticut.

Sims, W. L., J. F. Harrington, and K. B. Tyler. 1977. *Growing Bush Snap Beans for Mechanical Harvest.* Univ. of California Coop. Ext. Ser. Leaf. 2674.

14

COLE CROPS — CABBAGE, BROCCOLI, CAULIFLOWER, AND RELATED CROPS

(BRUSSELS SPROUTS, KOHLRABI, CHINESE CABBAGE)

The group of vegetables (cabbage, broccoli, cauliflower, Brussels sprouts, collards, kale, kohlrabi) collectively known as *cole crops* are all members of the species *Brassica oleracea*. The label *cole* given to these vegetables is derived from the Latin *caulis*, meaning "stem" or "stalk." As a group, they are very similar culturally and taxonomically, belonging to the mustard family (Cruciferae).

All are cool-season, hardy, dicotyledonous plants with origins along the maritime areas of Europe, including the Mediterranean and Asia Minor. The flowers of all crops in the family have four sepals and four petals shaped in the characteristic form of a cross; the family name *Cruciferae* in Latin means "cross bearers." Plant species in the family are capable of synthesizing mustard oils, or related compounds, which give the plants a very characteristic flavor and aroma.

Although collards and kale are members of the cole crops, they are used primarily as "greens" and for convenience are discussed in Chapter 24 along with the other vegetable greens. In addition, Chinese cabbage, a closely related member of the *Brassica* genus (*B. Rapa*) with similar cultural requirements to these crops, will be included in this chapter.

CABBAGE

Cabbage is the most important member of the cole crops. The plant is grown for its fleshy leaves, which may be served boiled, raw (cole slaw), or fermented (sauerkraut). It is more tolerant of warm temperatures than the other cool-season cole crops and can be grown during the summer in many regions. Cabbage is fairly nutritious and ranks higher than tomatoes but lower than spinach in mineral content.

CLASSIFICATION, ORIGIN, HISTORY

Cabbage is classified as *Brassica oleracea* (Capitata group). For more than 3,000 years, cabbage has been used as a food crop, although initially it was probably utilized more for medicinal purposes. The ancient Greeks held it in high esteem, and their fables claim its origin from the father of their gods. Present-day cultivars most likely originated from wild nonheading types found along the chalky coasts of England and northwestern France, where the Romans or Celts may have introduced them from the coastal regions of the Mediterranean Sea. Cabbage was common throughout Europe by 900 A.D. and was introduced into the U.S. around the 16th century by the early colonists.

PRODUCTION AND INDUSTRY

Cabbage is a leading vegetable crop in the U.S., both for fresh market (98,000 acres) and for processing (11,000 acres). Some commercial cabbage is produced in nearly every state and is available year round. Florida, Texas, California, and North Carolina lead in fresh market production during the winter and spring, while New York, New Jersey, and Michigan are the main producers for fresh market in the summer and fall.

A large percentage of the fall cabbage is stored and sold during the winter and early spring, or until the new crop from the southern states appears on the market. Recently, however, the acreage grown in the North for storage has decreased due to increased production of winter cabbage.

Leading states for sauerkraut production are Wisconsin, New York, and Ohio. Average yields are approximately 12 tons per acre for fresh market cabbage and 21 tons per acre for processing, although top yields may be considerably higher.

Worldwide, cabbage is very popular and is grown extensively in eastern Europe (USS, Poland, Romania) and the Far East (China and South Korea). The

Chinese are more familiar with the Chinese cabbage and the mustards than with the hard-heading forms used in the U.S. and Europe.

PLANT GROWTH AND DEVELOPMENT

Cabbage is a herbaceous biennial that is grown as an annual. The edible plant can be thought of as an enlarged terminal vegetative bud. There are several different types of cabbage, including round, pointed, flat, red or green, and savoy (see "Cultivars").

Vegetative Development

During its vegetative development, the plant produces a succession of leaves that are out-spreading, borne on a stem with extremely short internodes. The internodes remain short, but new leaves incurve and overlap, eventually forming a compact head (Figure 14.1). Leaves are broad, round, thick and relatively fleshy, heavily veined, and covered with a waxy surface. Under certain environmental conditions, such as excessive moisture and high nitrogen, the cycle can be repeated several times, beginning with the splitting of the first formed head. The

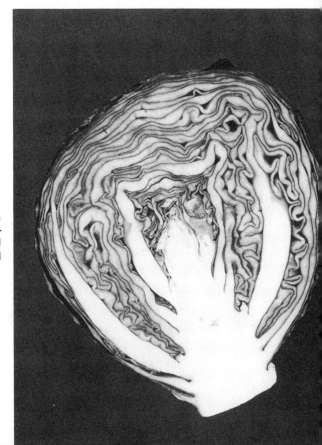

Figure 14.1. The cabbage head consists of a short, compressed stem surrounded by growing leaves and resembles an enlarged terminal bud.

stem then elongates with new out-spreading leaves, followed by the formation of another head. Several heads have been observed to form in this fashion.

Reproductive Development

The reproductive stage is characterized by rapid growth of the compressed stem through the elongation of the internodes. Modified out-spreading leaves will form along the elongated stem, followed by the development of a terminal raceme type of inflorescence. Flowers exhibit moderate to high self-incompatibility. Flowering in cabbage, as well as in other cole crops, is not photoperiod-sensitive. The fruits are slender pods called *siliques*.

Premature Seeding

Cabbage can be induced by low temperatures to send up a flower-seedstalk (bolting) during the first growing season. Usually exposure for over a month to temperatures of 40–50°F is required to cause this transition. The lower the temperature, the shorter the induction period. The longer the period of exposure, the higher will be the percentage of plants producing seedstalks.

However, for cold temperatures to be effective, plants must have passed the juvenile stage. Generally, plants with three or four true leaves or with stems larger than pencil size are considered in their post-juvenile period and are susceptible to low temperatures. Cultivar differences influence premature seeding, with the Copenhagen types more subject to bolting than the Wakefield and other types.

CLIMATIC AND CULTURAL REQUIREMENTS

Cabbage is a hardy, cool-season crop that does best under uniform, cool, moist conditions. It will, however, stand wide variations in temperature. Optimum monthly mean temperatures for growth and quality are 60–65°F, with a minimum of 40°F and a maximum of 75°F. Well-hardened plants will withstand temperatures as low as 20°F for short periods. Generally, young plants can tolerate cold and hot temperature extremes better than older plants.

Cabbage will grow in most soils with adequate moisture and good fertility. For fall, summer, and early winter plantings, cabbage does best on the heavier loams, while for the late winter and spring crops, sandier loams which drain better and are naturally warmer are preferred. Muck, or organic, soils are not recommended for the early plantings since they are slow to warm up in the spring.

Cabbage grows best at pH 6.0–6.8, although some growers prefer to use a slightly alkaline pH if club root is a problem and the disease cannot be controlled by crop rotation. Fertility requirements are relatively high, since cabbage belongs to the group of vegetables very responsive to fertilizers. Usually, part of the nitrogen may be applied as a sidedressing, but all the phosphorus and potassium are applied prior to planting. Excessive nitrogen should be avoided since this can lead to loose heads and rapid secondary growth, which may cause heads to split open. In susceptible cultivars, excessive growth rates due to high nitrogen application can promote the occurrence of tipburn (see "Physiological Disorders"). Early plantings respond well to starter fertilizers high in phosphorus. Along with the other cole crops, cabbage has medium to high requirements for most micronutrients.

PLANTING AND CROP ESTABLISHMENT

Commercial plantings of cabbage are started from either transplants or direct seeding in the field. Processing cabbage is usually direct seeded, while the fresh market crop may be started by either method. Field seeding is less expensive and permits higher populations than transplants but requires more expertise and attention to ensure a full stand. Both methods are highly mechanized, reducing planting costs considerably.

Transplants

In the North and most cooler regions, the early cabbage crop is grown from transplants started in the greenhouse or in cold frames 4–6 weeks before planting in the field or from transplants grown in the South that are shipped north in the spring. For summer plantings and late cabbage, transplants can be grown in field nurseries. If well hardened, plants for the early crop can be transplanted before the danger of frost has passed. Medium-sized stocky plants are best; however, to avoid bolting in early plantings subject to cold temperatures, growers usually use small, hardy plants with no more than three or four fully developed leaves (Figure 14.2).

The plant rows are commonly spaced 2–4 feet apart, with plants set 12–18 inches apart in the row for early plantings and 18–24 inches apart for late plantings (Figure 14.3). In-row spacings are generally less for the "Jersey" and "Copenhagen" types and more for large domestic cultivars and "Flat Dutch" types. Closer in-row spacings tend to produce smaller heads but larger yields per acre.

Figure 14.2. In northern regions, cabbage transplants are used for the early crop.

Figure 14.3. Cabbage is being transplanted into four rows. In northern areas, early cabbage is usually grown from transplants so plants do not mature in hot weather.

Direct Seeding

This method is used for late summer and fall crops in the North and can be used throughout the year in areas favorable to germination and early plant growth. Field seeding on sandy soils requires moist conditions, and irrigation is necessary to ensure stands. On heavier soils, stands can usually be obtained without irrigation when rainfall is well distributed. Before seed is planted, the land should be well-settled by rains or irrigation.

The seed can be planted by precision seeders (0.5–1.5 pounds seed per acre) or drilled (3 pounds seed per acre). Sized seed is used with precision planters, but even then, some growers will overseed slightly and later thin to a desired plant stand. The seed is given shallow covering (0.5–0.75 inch deep), especially on heavy soils. Plants are thinned to the final spacing when they are almost to transplanting size (2–4 inches tall), but before crowding occurs. Plants direct seeded in the field usually mature 2–3 weeks before transplanted cabbage of the same age.

Prior to planting, seeds are given a hot water soak (122°F for 25 minutes) to destroy black rot, black leg, and *Alternaria* disease organisms. This is generally done by the supplier who should also test the seed and certify that it is free of black rot. Because hot water treatment may reduce germination, some growers prefer to soak the seed in a 0.2% thiram solution for 24 hours at 86°F. Seeds should also be dusted with thiram or captan prior to planting for control of damping-off.

CULTURAL PRACTICES

Weeds

Cabbage seedlings do not compete well with weeds, and early weed control, especially on direct-seeded plantings, is important. Preplant-incorporated herbicides provide good control of annual grasses, but broadleaf weeds may be a problem and may require cultivation. Deep cultivation should be used only when plants are small because cabbage has an extensive, but shallow root system. Fall and spring crops generally need more cultivation than winter crops. When plants start to head, cultivation should be discontinued.

Irrigation

Because of its waxy leaf surface, cabbage is relatively drought-tolerant, and supplemental irrigation is often unnecessary in humid regions, except on sandy soils. A crop will require from 15 to 25 inches of water per season. The consumptive use of water by the plant increases up to the time of heading, and correspondingly, the need for more frequent irrigations increases with plant development. Water should be applied by furrow or subsurface irrigation since sprinkler irrigation will wet leaf surfaces, which is conducive to the spread of black rot and *Alternaria*. Cabbage heads may be subject to bursting or splitting when dry weather is followed by rains or when irrigation causes an uneven moisture supply during heading.

CULTIVARS

Cabbage cultivars are generally grouped into "types" or "classes," based on a classification established in 1915, but still in use today. The outstanding characteristics of this grouping and some specific examples are shown in Table 14.1 and Figure 14.4, respectively.

Hybrid cultivars are widely available today, and due to their superior performance, particularly in uniformity of head type and maturity, they have largely replaced the older open-pollinated cultivars. In the selection of cultivars, the primary factors to be considered are intended market use, season of the year to be planted, and appearance. Other cultivar characteristics include:

> *Days to harvest* — Early cultivars require 80–95 days, from seeding to harvest; main-season and late cabbage require 100–115 days.
>
> *Shape* — Shapes range from conical, to round, to oblate (flat). For fresh market, the choice depends on consumer preference.

Table 14.1. Classification of Cabbage Types

Type	Characteristics
Wakefield (pointed)[1]	Small, pointed heads; early-maturing; cold-tolerant, resistant to bolting.
Copenhagen Market (domestic)	Round, medium–large head; early-maturing; prone to bolting from cold temperatures; also used for main-season and fall crops.
Flat Dutch (domestic)	Large, flat, very solid heads; cultivars vary in resistance to bolting and days to maturity.
Danish Ballhead (Danish) . . .	Round–oval, medium-sized head; relatively late-maturing; intolerant of cold temperatures; excellent for storage.
Savoy	Medium–large, flat–globe-shaped heads; crinkly leaves; superior fresh market quality.
Red	Round, medium-sized heads; reddish-purple leaf color.
Alpha (domestic)	Round, very small heads; early-maturing.
Volga (domestic)	Flat–globe-shaped, medium-sized heads; late-maturing.

[1]Some markets also classify cabbage into five distinct types: Pointed, Danish, Savoy, Red, and Domestic (which includes Copenhagen Market, Flat Dutch, Alpha, and Volga).

Figure 14.4. Cabbage can be classified into groups such as Wakefield types (A), Copenhagen Market types (B, C, D), Flat Dutch types (E, F), and Danish Ballhead (G, H).

Weight — The weight of heads will vary from 2 to 12 pounds. In general, the weight increases as days to maturity increase. For fresh market, the preference is for 3- to 5-pound heads, while heavier heads are preferred for processing.

Color — Cultivars range in color from green, to bluish-green, to red. There are variations within each category that affect cultivar attractiveness.

Size of core — Core refers to the stem portion of the head. A small core is preferred, since stem tissue is less desirable than leaf tissue.

Longstanding — Cultivars vary in their capacity to remain in marketable condition over a satisfactory length of time before splitting. Early cultivars are generally not as longstanding as late cultivars.

Disease resistance — Most cultivars available are resistant to *Fusarium* yellows.

Savoying — Some cultivars have crinkled (savoy) leaves. These types are attractive in appearance and popular at roadside markets, and are sometimes used as ornamentals in landscaping.

Resistance to premature seeding — Strains highly resistant to bolting can be bred.

INSECTS, DISEASES, AND PHYSIOLOGICAL DISORDERS

Crucifer vegetables are subject to many of the same insect and disease pests. The most destructive insects to cabbage are various kinds of cabbage worms, along with aphids, thrips, and root maggots. The most serious diseases affecting cabbage are the seed and soil-borne organisms including black rot, black leg,

Alternaria, club root, and yellows. Internal tipburn is a complex physiological disorder which causes significant losses to growers in some years.

Cabbage Insects

Cabbage Worms. The cabbage looper, imported cabbage worm, and larvae of the diamondback moth can cause considerable damage to cabbage by chewing holes in the leaves and heads of cole crops. The worms are light green to dark green and feed from the undersides of the leaves. The adults are gray, brown, and white moths commonly seen around the plants. Each species requires approximately 6 weeks to complete a generation. Control is with chemical and biological (*Bacillus thuringiensis*) measures.

Aphids. Cabbage aphids (*Brevicoryne brassicae*) are small, green, sucking insects that have a waxy covering similar to the cabbage leaves. Aphid damage causes leaves to curl or cup. Timeliness is important in the control of aphids, and plants should be treated before the insects are established and before the leaves start to cup. Several effective insecticides are available to control these pests.

Cabbage Maggots. The maggots (*Hylemya brassicae*) are white larvae that feed on the roots, severely limiting water uptake. As a result, plants will wilt during the day but return to normal over the night. Damage is usually most severe early in the season when cool and moist soil conditions are conducive for egg laying by the adult fly, which deposits eggs close to the stem. Effective control is with an insecticide soil drench or application with transplant water. Preplant broadcast application or band treatment of insecticide at planting also is effective.

Thrips. Thrips are small, wingless insects that have become a serious pest on cabbage in some areas, particularly in northern growing areas such as New York. They damage the plants by their rasping feeding habits on the leaves. Although several species may be present, most of the damage has been attributed to the onion thrip. These insects have many host crops, and chemical control is not always effective, especially once these insects get deep into the head. Less susceptible cultivars are available for processing cabbage but not for fresh and stored cabbage.

Cabbage Diseases

Black Rot. Caused by the bacterium *Xanthomonas campestris*, black rot appears at any stage of plant growth. The disease is first indicated by a yellowing of the leaves along their outer portions and a blackening of the veins. The chlorosis appears as a V-shaped area, with the base of the V pointed at the midrib. Later, plants show dwarfing and one-sided heads. If the disease attacks the plant early, no head will form. The organism is carried over on the seed and residues of infected plants. The use of clean seed, crop rotation, and sanitation are control measures.

Black Leg. Black leg is caused by the fungus *Phoma lingam*. A dry rot, it attacks the stems of young plants, causing dark, sunken areas. The entire plant wilts, and the dead leaves adhere to the stem. Black leg is more active than black rot at lower temperatures and occurs most frequently in cool, humid conditions. Control is similar to that for black rot.

Alternaria. Several species of *Alternaria* affect crucifers. The disease is characterized by dark brown or black spots on leaves and stems consisting of concentric rings. Velvety mold usually covers the spots during moist periods. Conidiophores and conidia appear on the spots. The disease is most severe in wet weather and warm temperatures (90–95°F). It can be most destructive in storage and during transit, and heads should be handled carefully to avoid bruising. The disease is seed-borne and overwinters in diseased plant debris. Control is by seed treatment and fungicide application.

Club Root. Club root (*Plasmodiophora brassicae*) attacks the roots, causing characteristic swellings. Initially, aboveground symptoms are difficult to distinguish, but later, leaves turn pale green or yellow, and plants may wilt during the day and recover at night. Plants will be stunted and eventually die. The disease is most prevalent in fields of high moisture, acid pH, and warm temperatures. Control is by rotating crops, keeping soil alkaline (pH 7.2), maintaining good sanitation, and using disease-free transplants.

Yellows. This disease is caused by a soil-borne fungus (*Fusarium oxysporum*) and is most severe under high temperatures. The foliage turns yellow, progressing from the lower leaves upward, and plants have a sickly dwarfed appearance. Similar to black rot, there is also some discoloration of vascular tissues. The affected tissues turn brown and fall off, and eventually plants die. Use of resistant cultivars is the best control method.

Physiological Disorders

Internal Tipburn. Cabbage plants may be affected by a non-biotic disorder known as internal tipburn, which consists of a breakdown of the plant tissue near the center of the head. Affected tissues become dry and papery and eventually turn brown or black. The area may be narrow along the margins of one or two leaves, or quite extensive.

The exact nature of the disorder is not known, although calcium nutrition, plant–water relations, and growth rate are involved. It is most prevalent during periods of rapid growth and when transpiration in the plant is restricted. Fast-maturing and high-yielding cultivars are generally most susceptible. Calcium mobility in the plant is involved, since affected tissues have very low levels of this element, even in soils well supplied with calcium. Control of tipburn is often difficult, but maintaining adequate and uniform moisture supply is most effective in preventing its occurrence.

HARVESTING

Cabbage for fresh market is usually harvested when heads reach full size for the particular cultivar (Figure 14.5). The plant should be allowed to mature into a firm, white head before harvesting. The head is cut by hand on the stem just below the head, leaving two or three green wrapper leaves attached (unless damaged or worm eaten) to protect against bruising injury (Figure 14.6). Over-mature heads are more prone to split open, especially if plants were subjected to moisture fluctuations prior to harvest.

Fresh market fields may be harvested several times, as heads often mature at different rates. Many growers use pallet boxes for both field harvest and storage

Figure 14.5. Well-grown, uniform cabbage close to harvest.

Figure 14.6. Hand harvest of fresh market cabbage.

containers to reduce the amount of handling involved until ready for shipping. Processing cabbage is harvested when heads are mature and when tonnage is highest. The processing crop is harvested once-over, usually by machine. Unless diseased, split or damaged heads are included in the harvest.

POSTHARVEST HANDLING

Successful storage of cabbage requires a good cultivar, freedom from disease or injuries, a temperature of 32°F, and a relative humidity of 98–100%. The humidity must be kept quite high, or the harvested product will wilt very quickly. If stored under the proper conditions, late cabbage should keep for 5–6 months and early cabbage 1–2 months. Cultivars belonging to the Danish class generally store best. Cabbage should not be stored with fruits like apples, since ethylene concentrations of 10–100 ppm may cause loss of green color and leaf abscission.

BROCCOLI AND CAULIFLOWER

CLASSIFICATION, ORIGIN, HISTORY

Broccoli and cauliflower are two closely related cole crops, for which some confusion has occurred regarding their classification, both genetically and historically. For many years, distinctions between the two were not recognized, and botanists tended to lump the two together.

As generally used today, broccoli refers to sprouting broccoli, also known as Calabrese or Italian broccoli, and is classified as *Brassica oleracea* (Italica group). It should not be confused with heading broccoli, which in effect is a late or overwintering type of cauliflower. Cauliflower is classified as *B. oleracea* (Botrytis group). It can be found in two forms: the early or snowball types and the late or winter types.

Although there is still confusion on the exact origin of both crops, the generally accepted view today is that cauliflower evolved from sprouting broccoli, which initially originated from various wild types of leafy cabbage from southern Europe and the eastern Mediterranean. In the U.S., broccoli was introduced by early immigrants from southern Europe but was relatively little known until about 1920 when Italian farmers in northern California began to ship their product to eastern markets.

PRODUCTION AND INDUSTRY

Among the cole crops, cauliflower has the most exacting climatic and cultural requirements, which limit its commercial production to a few favored localities. In the North, it can be grown as a spring or fall crop, while in the South and West, it is mainly grown in the winter and early spring. Broccoli is less exacting than cauliflower but requires more attention than cabbage. It is grown commercially in all parts of the U.S., although most of the crop is produced in California. Recently, broccoli has acquired renewed popularity from advertising campaigns extolling its excellent nutritional qualities; consequently, its production has increased in many southern and eastern areas of the U.S.

Of the total U.S. crop in 1989, fresh market production made up roughly 80% of the broccoli and 85% of the cauliflower grown (Table 14.2). The total area harvested in the U.S. in 1989 was 138,450 acres for broccoli and 67,700 acres for cauliflower. For each crop, the leading state is California, which produced 90% of the broccoli and 77% of the cauliflower. The Rio Grande valley of Texas is becoming a leading producer of broccoli and cauliflower for the winter fresh market. Other leading states for cauliflower production include Arizona, Oregon, New York, and Michigan.

Although the U.S. is the world's largest producer of broccoli, other major growing areas are Italy, northern Europe, and cooler regions of the Far East. World

Table 14.2.   U.S. Production Statistics for Fresh Market and Processing Broccoli and Cauliflower in the U.S., 1989[1]

State	Production			
	Broccoli		Cauliflower	
	F. Market	Processing	F. Market	Processing
	(tons)			
California	489,600	120,000	268,900	33,000
Arizona	27,000	—	39,100	—
Other states[2]	20,650	18,450	24,650	26,230
U.S.	537,250	138,450	332,650	59,230
Total	675,700		391,880	

[1]Source: USDA. 1990. National Agricultural Statistics Service (NASS), Agricultural Statistics Board.

[2]Oregon, Texas for broccoli; Michigan, New York, Oregon, Texas for cauliflower.

leaders of cauliflower production are China and India, followed by France, Italy, the United Kingdom, and the U.S.

PLANT GROWTH AND DEVELOPMENT

Broccoli and cauliflower growth habits are similar. The early plant development is like that of cabbage, consisting of a short stem and a rosette of leaves. However, sometime thereafter, elongation of the internodes begins, and at a certain point the terminal axis proliferates into numerous branches.

In broccoli, the terminal end of the stems and the proliferated branches thicken, becoming succulent, and together with their compact groups of un-opened flower buds make up the initial marketable product (Figure 14.7). The plant is generally regarded as an annual and a period of cold temperatures is not required to induce flower bud initiation; although flowering is hastened by exposure to low temperatures. When the terminal inflorescence is removed, side shoots, which have been retarded by apical dominance, develop into smaller inflorescences that are marketable.

Cauliflower is grown for its white head, called a *curd* (Figure 14.8). In the early or snowball types, the curd consists of highly branched, prefloral, undifferentiated shoot apices. In the late or winter types, the curd is much like the flower head in broccoli and consists of true flower primordia and terminal stem tissue. The late types are true biennials and require exposure to cold temperatures for

Figure 14.7. In sprouting broccoli, the market-able head consists of tightly packed, immature green buds and thick, fleshy flowerstalks.

Figure 14.8. The marketable part of cauliflower is called the "curd" and in the snowball types consists of highly branched, undifferentiated, terminal ends of shoot apices.

curd formation. The early types are generally annuals, or sometimes biennials, and do not require cold temperatures to induce curd formation.

CLIMATIC AND CULTURAL REQUIREMENTS

Moderately uniform cool temperatures are best for growth and quality of cauliflower and broccoli. Too much heat can prevent plants from heading. While still vegetative, plants have some frost resistance, but freezing temperatures can cause considerable damage once buds and inflorescences have formed. Large or old plants of cauliflower and broccoli are likely to pass prematurely into the generative stage if exposed to cool temperatures (below 50°F) after field planting, resulting in smaller than normal heads called *buttons*.

The optimum temperature range for curd and flower head formation is 57–68°F. Above 68°F, quality is poor, and above 77°F heads may not form. In particular, cauliflower curd formation is very sensitive to temperature extremes, which may cause several different types of market defects. At temperatures near 32°F, freezing injury to the shoot apices may result in no curd development. High temperatures may cause the plant to regress into vegetative growth and cause bracts or small leaves to develop in the curd. Also, high temperatures during curd development may result in loss of compactness and development of ricey curds.

Soil and fertility requirements for broccoli and cauliflower are similar to those for cabbage. Both broccoli and cauliflower have a relatively high requirement for molybdenum. A molybdenum deficiency is most likely to be encountered on acid soils with pH below 5.5. In the early stages, the deficiency shows up as crinkling and mottling and marginal leaf scorching. In the later stages, plants will have a deformed growing point and poor growth of the leaf laminae, resulting in a characteristic "whiptail" appearance of the leaves. A molybdenum deficiency can generally be corrected by liming, foliar fertilizer applications, or seed treatment.

PLANTING, CROP ESTABLISHMENT, AND CULTURAL PRACTICES

Similar to cabbage, plantings of broccoli and cauliflower may be established by either transplanting or direct seeding in the field, if climate permits. Transplants are used mostly in areas of relatively short periods of favorable weather. In California and much of the West, just about all the commercially grown broccoli and cauliflower is direct seeded on raised beds, and later thinned at an early age.

In northern and eastern regions, transplants are commonly used, although some direct seeding is practiced for late summer and fall crops.

The spring crop should be planted early enough to allow the plants to mature before hot weather begins. For early plantings, small transplants should be used, or plants are likely to button. Spacing is variable, ranging from 20 to 36 inches between rows and from 8 to 24 inches between plants, depending on cultivar, equipment, and planting date. Up to the time of flower head and curd formation, the handling of the crop (seed treatments, transplanting procedures, fertility, irrigation, pest control) is generally the same as for cabbage.

As the heads or curds appear in cauliflower, they should be protected from full sunlight, which tends to discolor the white curd to a creamy yellow, reducing market quality. Early-maturing cultivars must be protected from sun injury by tying the long outside leaves loosely over the forming heads. Late-maturing cultivars usually have an abundance of foliage and are self-blanched by the incurving of the inner leaves.

CULTIVARS

Broccoli

Broccoli cultivars differ in days to maturity and may be classified as early, medium, or late, according to their response to time of planting. Early cultivars are adapted for planting during the period from late winter to early summer for harvest from late spring to early fall. When seeded or transplanted in the early spring, early cultivars will mature rapidly enough to produce crops before the onset of hot weather. They also may be seeded in the summer for harvest in the fall. Cultivars of medium maturity are seeded in the summer and early fall for harvest in the late fall and early winter. Late cultivars are adapted to areas where broccoli can be grown throughout the winter to be harvested in the late winter and early spring.

Another important characteristic that distinguishes broccoli cultivars is the size of the flower head, including the ability to form side shoots. For fresh market, larger heads are preferred, while for freezing, smaller heads are used. In order to extend their marketing period, pick-your-own and roadside market growers prefer types which continue to produce side shoots over several weeks.

Other important cultivar characteristics include shape, color, compaction, and size of floral buds of the inflorescence head, ability of buds to resist opening when at harvest maturity, and disease resistance. In recent years, much breeding work has been done to develop hybrids of uniform maturity that produce a single large head, both qualities necessary for mechanical harvest. Because of their superior performance in many of these characteristics, hybrids comprise over 80% of the commercial crop.

Cauliflower

In comparison to other cole crops, the number of cauliflower cultivars is relatively small, but a large number of strains is available. Cultivars can be grouped into two general types: early or snowball cultivars and late or winter cultivars. The snowball types are the most popular and are grown in all regions. As indicated, the late types are true biennials and require cold temperatures to form a head. The plants are difficult to grow and will become large in size and will not form heads if the plants are too small during cold weather to be vernalized. These types generally require a much longer growing period to mature and are seldom used in the U.S.

Similar to broccoli, cultivar choice depends mainly on days to maturity, along with size, shape, and compactness of the curd, foliage cover, and productivity and tolerance to curd defects under adverse conditions. Open-pollinated cultivars still dominate, although hybrids with better uniformity of maturity have been introduced.

INSECTS, DISEASES, AND PHYSIOLOGICAL DISORDERS

The common insect and disease pests of broccoli and cauliflower are similar to cabbage. Many disease problems can be reduced if broccoli and cauliflower are grown in a 4- to 5-year rotation with other non-cruciferous crops. In addition to "whiptail," another physiological disorder sometimes found in broccoli and cauliflower is "hollow stem." On soils deficient in boron, symptoms appear as curling and rolling of the leaves, deformed foliage, brown curds or brown flower buds, and hollow stem centers. Although boron deficiency has been shown to cause hollow stem, all hollow stem is not caused by boron deficiency. Sometimes a hollow cavity will also develop in the stem just below the base of the curd or inflorescence, which is attributed to a very rapid growth rate from excessive nitrogen.

HARVESTING

Broccoli is harvested while the inflorescence is still immature and compact, and before the individual flower heads open. Overmature heads develop tough, woody fibers in the stems, making the product unmarketable. The terminal or central head is first to develop and is cut with 6–10 inches of stem remaining.

Most broccoli is still hand-harvested because present cultivars do not mature uniformly. This condition may necessitate four to six cuttings over a 1- or 2-month period. Secondary heads are sometimes harvested if cost-effective.

Cauliflower is harvested by hand as soon as the curds have attained marketable size but before they become discolored, loose, and ricey. Marketable heads should be cut with three or four whorls of leaves. These should be trimmed long enough to leave a circle of petioles to protect the head. In broccoli and cauliflower, the introduction of F_1 hybrids has resulted in greater uniformity in maturity and has reduced the number of cuttings to harvest the crop. In the future, hybrids should allow for greater use of non-selective mechanical harvesting.

POSTHARVEST HANDLING

Broccoli is highly perishable and should be cooled immediately after harvest, usually by packed ice or hydrocooling, and maintained at 32°F and 95–100% relative humidity. Under these conditions, it may be stored for 10–14 days, but generally as briefly as possible in order to maintain its deep green color and firmness. Use of film wraps can increase storage life. Similar to cabbage, broccoli should not be stored with fruits, such as apples and pears, that produce large quantities of ethylene which can cause yellowing of buds.

Cauliflower can be stored up to 3–4 weeks at 32°F and 95–98% relative humidity. Cooling can be by either vacuum cooling or hydrocooling. Freezing injury may occur at 30.6°F, resulting in discoloration and softening of the curd. For much of the cauliflower that is not usually held in cold storage, packing in crushed ice will aid in maintaining freshness. Both broccoli and cauliflower should be handled carefully during and after harvesting to protect the heads from bruising and dirt, which can markedly reduce storage life.

BRUSSELS SPROUTS

Brussels sprouts are one of the numerous cultivated forms in the *Brassica* genus derived from the wild cabbage, and are classified as *B. oleracea* (Gemmifera group). The name comes from the city of Brussels in Belgium, where the plant may have originated and was extensively grown. Today, it still is very popular throughout northern Europe where much of the crop is used for fresh market. In the U.S., 90% of the commercial crop is produced in California where it is grown primarily for freezing.

The plant is a nonheading cabbage whose early development is similar to that of cabbage. The rosette form, however, is soon lost, and instead of producing a head of over-wrapping leaves enclosing a terminal bud, it produces a series of lateral buds or sprouts in the form of miniature heads in the axils of the leaves along a single unbranched stem, usually 2-3 feet tall (Figure 14.9).

In most respects, the cultural requirements of Brussels sprouts up to harvest are similar to those for fall or late cabbage. They require a somewhat longer growing season than late cabbage and must therefore be planted in the seedbed or in the field fairly early. In order to shorten the growing season, transplants are commonly used. The plants are very hardy and will withstand a light freeze. Cool temperatures during sprout development are important for compact quality buds. Some say that a light freeze during sprout maturation enhances taste.

Brussels sprouts are susceptible to all insects, diseases, and physiological

Figure 14.9. Brussels sprouts produce a series of small lateral buds
in the axils of the leaves.

disorders that affect other cole crops. To help control pests, the seedbed should be well-drained, and the field for growing the crop should not have been in cabbage or other crucifers for 3-4 years prior to planting.

Harvesting begins when the sprouts are firm and well developed, usually 1-2 inches in diameter. For fresh market, several successive harvests by hand are usually taken from the same plant during the season. The sprouts are harvested in succession as they mature, starting from the base of the plant. The upper sprouts continue to develop as the lower ones are removed. In harvesting, the lower leaves below the sprouts are broken away, and the sprouts are cut off close to the stem.

The processing crop is harvested in a single operation. For once-over harvest, the set of sprouts can be concentrated by treating the plants with SADH (succinic acid-2,2-dimethylhydrazide). Alternatively, the plants can be topped, to remove the growing point and promote the maturity of small sprouts at the top of the stem. This should be done when the lower sprouts are approximately 0.5 inch in diameter. In this way, a full stem of uniform sprouts will develop in about 4 weeks, so that the crop can be harvested mechanically. New hybrid cultivars selected for more uniformity in bud production are being used.

The crop can be kept in storage for 3–5 weeks, at 32°F and 95–100% relative humidity. Similar to cabbage and broccoli, Brussels sprouts should not be stored with fruits that emit ethylene, which can cause leaf yellowing and abscission.

KOHLRABI

Kohlrabi is classified as *Brassica oleracea* (Gongylodes group). The plant is grown for its turnip-like enlargement of the lower stem that may be eaten either raw or cooked (Figure 14.10). Although the crop has limited production in the U.S., it is an excellent vegetable that has a mild taste similar to the turnip and is more common in Europe where it is used for human consumption as well as stock feed.

The plant is a cool-season biennial but is grown as an annual. It makes its best growth between 60 and 70°F and is subject to vernalization and bolting at

Figure 14.10. Kohlrabi is grown for its thickened bulb-like lower portion of stem.

temperatures below 45°F. For good quality, growth must be uniform, rapid, and continuous. High temperatures check growth, causing the stem to become tough and stringy. It is grown mostly as a fall or winter crop but can be grown during the spring in northern areas. It is grown much like cabbage and is usually direct seeded in the field, although transplants may be used for the spring crop in northern areas.

Kohlrabi is a quick growing crop (55 days from seeding to harvest), which should be harvested when the swollen stem is 2–3 inches in diameter and before it becomes tough and woody. The stem can be cut just above the ground or can easily be pulled by hand. When the plants are prepared for market, the roots are cut off and the plants tied in bunches with the leaves still attached, or sold in bulk.

CHINESE CABBAGE

There are several different types of Chinese cabbage, all probably native to China and eastern Asia. The two most common types in the U.S. are pe-tsai, classified as *Brassica Rapa* (Pekinensis group), and pak-choi, classified as *B. Rapa* (Chinensis group). The former produces an elongated head, much like cos lettuce (Figure 14.11), while the latter is a nonheading form resembling Swiss chard or celery, with its rosette of oblong, shiny, dark green leaf blades and thick, white petioles. Both types are used as salad or cooked vegetables. Pak-choi is closely related to mustard and is also known as mustard cabbage or Chinese mustard.

Chinese cabbage is generally a cool-season annual, sometimes a biennial, which does best when grown under daily average temperatures between 55 and 70°F. Cultural requirements for Chinese cabbage are similar to those for the cole crops. The plant is sensitive to both cold temperatures (40–50°F) and long days to induce flowering. Photoperiods of 15–16 hours or more for 4–5 weeks will cause flowering in the crop. This limits the production of the Chinese cabbage in most parts of the U.S. to the fall, or in winter in the South, so that the crop can mature under short days.

The plant requires a rich, well-drained, moist soil. Crops may be started from transplants or direct seeded in the field. Transplants are generally used for spring crops, while fall plantings are most often direct seeded (0.5 inch deep). In the latter method, the seed is usually drilled in rows, and the plants later thinned to the desired stand, according to the size of the mature crop.

The crop is ready to harvest when the heads are fully developed (65–100 days) or when nonheading leafy types have reached marketable size (35–60 days). Pe-tsai is harvested by cutting off the entire head at ground level and removing the outer leaves. For pak-choi, the entire plant may be cut at ground level or the individual leaves removed for multiple harvests.

Figure 14.11. Pe-tsai is the heading type of Chinese cabbage.

Standard cultivars of the leafy types are 'Crispy Choy,' 'Pac Choy,' and the slow bolting 'Lei Choy.' Cultivars of pe-tsai include the traditional 'Michihli' (elongated head) and 'Wong Bok' (shorter head), and the newer F_1 hybrids 'Jade Pagoda' (tall head), and 'Springtime,' 'Summertime,' and 'Wintertime' (short, compact heads).

SELECTED REFERENCES

"Anonymous." 1983. *Major Diseases of Crucifers.* Asgrow Seed Company, Kalamazoo, Michigan.

"Anonymous." 1985. *Integrated Pest Management of Cole Crops and Lettuce.* Univ. of California Div. ANR. Pub. 3307

Becker, R. F. 1971. *Cabbage: Tipburn and Other Internal Disorders.* New York Agric. Expt. Sta., New York Food and Life Sci. Bull. 7.

Dickson, M. H., and D. H. Wallace. 1986. Cabbage Breeding, pp. 395–432. In: M. J. Bassett (ed.). *Breeding Vegetable Crops.* AVI Publishing Co., Westport, Connecticut.

Nieuwof, M. 1969. *Cole Crops, Botany, Cultivation, and Utilization.* Leonard Hill Books, London.

Ryder, E. J. 1979. *Leafy Salad Vegetables.* AVI Publishing Co., Westport, Connecticut.

Sackett, C. 1975. *Kohlrabi. Fruit & Vegetable Facts & Pointers.* United Fresh Fruit and Vegetable Association, Alexandria, Virginia.

Seelig, R. A. 1971. *Broccoli. Fruit & Vegetable Facts & Pointers.* United Fresh Fruit and Vegetable Association, Alexandria, Virginia.

Seelig, R. A. 1969. *Cabbage. Fruit & Vegetable Facts & Pointers.* United Fresh Fruit and Vegetable Association, Alexandria, Virginia.

15

ROOT CROPS – CARROTS, BEETS, AND RELATED VEGETABLES

(HORSERADISH, PARSNIPS, RADISHES, RUTABAGAS, TURNIPS, JERUSALEM ARTICHOKES)

Root vegetables include carrots, beets, parsnips, radishes, rutabagas, turnips, horseradish, and Jerusalem artichokes. Of these, carrots and beets are the most widely grown, while the others are of minor commercial significance. These crops are grown for their enlarged fleshy roots, which actually consist of both root and some stem tissue. From the lower part arises the absorbing roots, and from the upper part arises the stem and leaves. All grow best in cool weather and have similar cultural requirements. All are biennials, except radishes, which are either annuals or biennials, and horseradish and Jerusalem artichokes, which are perennials.

CARROTS

CLASSIFICATION, ORIGIN, HISTORY

Carrot (*Daucus Carota* var. *sativus*) belongs to the parsley family (Umbelliferae), which also includes celery, parsnips, and parsley. About 60 species of *Daucus*, many of which are wild types, have been described. The cultivated forms belong to the subspecies *sativus*.

Historically, carrots were used primarily for medicinal purposes, and their use as a food crop dates back to only the 16th century. The initial types had purple roots, and the reddish-orange carrot did not appear until much later. From their center of origin and initial domestication in middle Asia, most likely Afghanistan, carrots spread under Arab influence to the eastern Mediterranean, and by the 12th century were being grown in Spain. Roots which varied in size, shape, and color were developed. Yellow types gradually replaced purple types, and by the mid-1700's, reddish-orange carrots were being grown in Germany, the Netherlands, and England. The crop was grown in Virginia and Massachusetts by the early colonists and soon became popular among the Native Americans.

Carrots are an excellent source of vitamin A (carotene is the precursor of vitamin A) and a good source of vitamins B_1, C, and B_2. Superior quality is associated with high sugar levels, mild taste, and a deep orange color.

PRODUCTION AND INDUSTRY

Carrots are grown commercially for both fresh market (68%) and processing (32%), as well as extensively in the home garden (Table 15.1). The crop is produced year-round in the U.S.; summer production (California, Michigan, Wisconsin) makes up approximately 25% of the crop, fall production (California, Washington, Michigan) 35%, winter production (California, Florida, Texas) 20%,

Table 15.1. Harvested Acreage, Production, and Value for Fresh Market and Processing Carrots in the U.S., 1989[1]

State	Harvested Acres	Production		Value	
		F. Market	Processing	F. Market	Processing
		——— (tons) ———		——— ($1,000) ———	
Arizona	1,400	11,900	–	3,737	–
California	57,600	767,800	125,000	210,377	8,088
Colorado	1,400	26,600	–	4,442	–
Florida	9,400	47,000	–	15,040	–
Michigan	6,800	48,900	34,380	12,225	1,822
Minnesota	1,800	16,650	16,200	2,498	1,037
New York	2,600	6,200	51,000	3,323	3,351
Oregon	1,300	20,500	16,910	6,150	734
Texas	9,900	66,150	18,000	18,522	954
Washington	6,800	36,950	126,850	7,760	6,647
Other states[2]	5,100	5,600	104,320	3,136	7,343
U.S.	103,600	1,054,250	492,660	287,210	29,976

[1]Source: USDA. 1990. National Agricultural Statistics Service (NASS), Agricultural Statistics Board.

[2]New Jersey, Ohio, Wisconsin.

and spring production (California, Florida, Texas) 20%. The leading producing state is California, which grows about 58% of the crop, followed by Washington (11%), Texas (5%), Michigan (5%), New York (4%), and Florida (3%). Average yields are quite variable, ranging from 28 tons per acre in Washington and Oregon to 5 tons per acre in Florida.

Worldwide, major producing nations include the USS, China, the U.S., Japan, Poland, and France.

PLANT GROWTH AND DEVELOPMENT

The carrot is a biennial that is grown as an annual for its root, which accumulates starches and sugars. The edible root is actually an enlarged taproot that includes stem, hypocotyl, and root tissue (Figure 15.1).

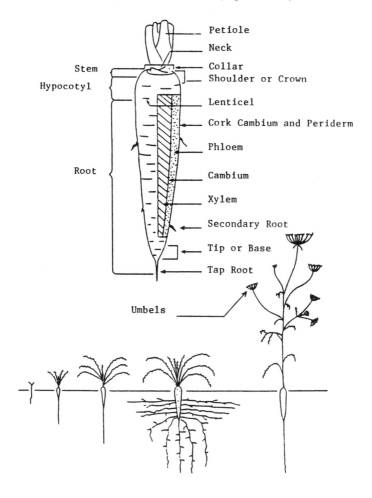

Figure 15.1. Growth, development, and anatomy of a carrot.

In the seedling stage, the tissues present in the root from the center outward are the xylem, cambium, phloem, pericycle, endodermis, cortex, and epidermis. As growth begins and thickening occurs, the tissues of the cortex and epidermis are sloughed off. A cork cambium arises in the pericycle and produces a periderm consisting of several layers of cork cells on the surface. At harvest, the mature root consists of two distinct regions, the inner core containing mostly secondary xylem and pith and an outer core consisting of secondary phloem and periderm.

High-quality carrots are those with a relatively large outer core, since sugars are higher in the phloem than in the xylem. Although the total percent of sugar does not increase much during development, there is a shift from the glucose to the sucrose form, resulting in an increase of sweetness with age. Carotene, the constituent that gives carrots their characteristic orange color and vitamin A activity, is highest in the older cells of the cortex. It increases rapidly with age during the early development and less rapidly in the later part of the season.

Carrots develop a deep, extensive, absorbing root system, with depths down to 30–36 inches. Initially, the absorbing roots develop rather slowly, but as the edible taproot enlarges, it gives rise to a large number of absorbing lateral roots.

The stem consists of a small, plate-like crown that develops from the plumule. In the vegetative stage the internodes fail to elongate, but during the second year, the plate-like stem starts to grow and forms branches 2–4 feet high which bear the flowers in compound umbels. The seed is a very small, dry, indehiscent, one-sided fruit. Seed germination is epigeal (the cotyledons rise above the soil surface) and relatively slow. The cotyledons are narrow and erect, giving little shade and protection to the hypocotyl.

CLIMATIC AND CULTURAL REQUIREMENTS

The carrot is a cool-season vegetable in which temperature extremes, especially during early seedling development, can limit growth and substantially reduce yields. For optimum yield and quality, including color development, carrots grow best at temperatures of 59–65°F. As temperatures increase, roots become shorter and less tapered; when temperatures become cooler, roots tend to become long and pointed. Low temperatures (below 50°F) decrease carotene production, resulting in poor color development, which is a problem with winter-grown carrots in certain areas of the South. Conversely, prolonged high temperatures bring about strong flavor and coarse roots. Exposure of young post-juvenile plants to low temperatures for several weeks can cause premature flowering later in the season.

Soils for carrot production should be deep, loose, well-drained sandy loams or loams with a slightly acidic reaction. The edible roots may become misshapened as a result of poor soil structure or obstructions such as stones, clods, or trash. If carrots are grown on heavy soils, they are likely to produce abundant leaf growth and forked roots. However, in dry areas where soil moisture can be accurately regulated by irrigation, silt loams and heavy soils can be used to produce high-quality carrots. Because of their light textures, muck soils can also be used, although roots tend to be rougher than on light mineral soils. Manure should be well decomposed or composted before application, since it has been shown that the liquid portion of manure apparently stimulates branching of the roots.

Fertility requirements for carrots are relatively modest and will vary with locality, intended market use, and cultural factors, including soil type. Nitrogen requirements range from 50 pounds per acre on dark-colored mineral soils to 150 pounds per acre on some light, sandy soils. A sidedressing of nitrogen is often applied to maintain foliage during the season, but care must be taken to avoid excessive top growth. Phosphorus and potassium rates are based on soil test results. In many western growing regions, potassium is rarely used, due to high levels of potassium in the soil.

Because carrot seedlings are salt-sensitive, fertilizer rates should not exceed 150–200 pounds per acre banded in the row. Important micronutrients include boron, copper, and manganese. Copper deficiencies are usually confined to acid, highly organic, or muck, soils and may cause poor color development in roots. Boron and manganese may be needed on alkaline, sandy soils.

PLANTING AND CROP ESTABLISHMENT

Carrot plantings are begun entirely from seed, and stand establishment is a major concern in commercial production. The seed is small and generally slow to germinate. Optimum soil temperatures for seed germination range from 50°F (93% emergence in 17 days) to 85°F (95% germination in 6 days). Above 86°F, seed germination decreases rapidly. Seedling growth is quite weak, and soil crusting can severely interfere with germination, causing poor stands. The soil in the seedbed should be well pulverized so that it will readily conduct soil moisture from below the seed, yet not puddle and crust during heavy rains.

Plant spacing greatly affects root shape and development. Increased spacings result in large roots and are used mostly for the processing crop. Since the cost of hand thinning is prohibitive, seeding rates must be as accurate as possible. The seed is usually planted with a standard vegetable seeder with a scatter shoe that spreads the seed thinly in a 3- to 4-inch band to eliminate thinning. Single rows are spaced 15–20 inches apart, with seedlings planted to a stand of sixteen to twenty-four plants per foot of row for fresh market and five to eight plants per foot of row for processing. Raised beds (8 inches high) increase the depth of tilled soil and are frequently used to improve root shape and smoothness. The beds are 20 inches wide and spaced on 40-inch centers and usually contain two rows. By using precision seeders and coated seed, some growers are planting four-row beds, with the rows spaced 2–4 inches apart.

The seed is planted 0.25 inch deep on heavy soils and 0.5 inch deep on sands. Shallower planting may be used in irrigated seedbeds. The time of planting varies, but seed may be planted as soon as hard freezes are over in the spring.

CULTURAL PRACTICES

Weeds

Carrot seedlings grow slowly, so weed control, particularly during the early part of the growing season, is necessary. However, weeds are difficult to control by machine cultivation while plants are small, and hand weeding is too expensive in commercial plantings.

There are several herbicides available that will control weeds until the carrot foliage is large enough to shade weed seedlings in the row. A long-time standard that provides excellent control is the use of herbicidal oils such as Stoddard solvent. This material is used as a postemergent spray after carrot seedlings have their first true leaves but not later than the four-leaf stage. Preemergent herbicides give good control of annual grasses and some broadleaf weeds. Postemergent herbicides are applied when carrot seedlings are 4–5 inches tall to control small, emerged annual weeds.

Generally, conventional shallow cultivation will take care of weeds between the rows. At the last cultivation, a little soil is hilled over the tops of the roots to help reduce greening. On sandy soils, some growers allow early weeds to grow and act as wind breaks when the carrot seedlings are small and then later they kill the weeds with a selective postemergent herbicide.

Irrigation

Carrots require an abundant and well-distributed water supply. Even in humid areas where irrigation is not normally used, supplemental sprinkler irrigation can increase yields, especially on soils with low water-holding capacity. Dry weather followed by wet weather is conducive to cracking of roots.

The amount of irrigation water depends on factors such as soil type, rate of evaporation, and amount of water in the soil at planting. Generally, the total amount of water needed, including that in the soil at planting, plus rainfall and irrigation, ranges from 18 to 36 acre-inches per crop. In cooler areas where evaporation is moderate, the equivalent of about 1 inch of water per week should be applied at 10-day intervals, amounting to a total of 18–24 inches of water. In warmer and dryer regions, water application should be heavier or more frequent, or both, amounting to about 30–36 inches. On muck soils that are kept wet by a high water table, the water table should be maintained 30–36 inches below the soil surface to allow for adequate soil aeration.

CULTIVARS

Carrot cultivars may be grouped according to the shape and length of the root and by intended market use. When grouped by shape and length, carrot cultivars fall into four categories, or types: Danvers, Chantenay, Nantes, and Imperator (Figure 15.2). These four groups along with their F_1 hybrids make up the large majority of important carrot cultivars in the U.S.

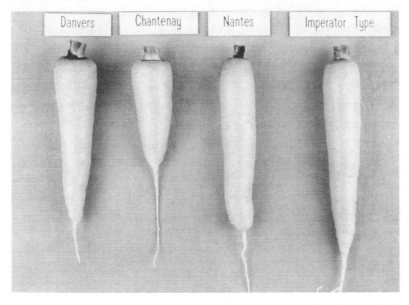

Figure 15.2. **Carrot types and characteristics: Danvers, roots medium–long, pointed or conic tips, broad shoulders with root tapering noticeably to the tip; Chantenay, roots medium–short, blunt tips, broad shoulders with root tapering to the tip; Nantes, roots medium–long, rounded tips, generally slender and cylindrical along the whole root; Imperator, roots long, slender, and pointed, tapering slightly to the tip.**

In most seed catalogs and grower guides, carrot cultivars are generally grouped into processing and fresh market. The Chantenay, Danvers, and Nantes types make up most of the processing cultivars, where uniformity and intensity of interior color, strength of petiole attachment, resistance to premature flowering, and high yields are required. Most of the fresh market cultivars are derived from strains of Imperator types, where uniformity of color and shape is important. Some Nantes and Danvers types are used as home garden and market cultivars.

INSECTS AND DISEASES

Insects

The major insect problems are with carrot rust flies and leafhoppers. The rust fly (*Psila rosae*) causes damage in production areas of the Northeast and in the Pacific Northwest from larvae burrowing into roots. Satisfactory control can usually be achieved by the use of insecticides in the seed furrow at planting for the first brood of maggots and a foliar application of insecticide to control the second generation maggots.

Leafhoppers, by their feeding activity, are vectors of aster yellows, a very serious disease of carrots in some years. The insects can be controlled by several insecticides, if applied when they appear. In areas of heavy infestation, seedling protection from leafhoppers is very important, and spraying should begin at the first-leaf stage.

Other insect pests of carrots which may be problems in localized areas are aphids, cutworms, carrot weevils, and mites.

Diseases

Aster Yellows. Referred to as "carrot yellows" in some areas, this is a mycoplasma disease spread by the six-spotted leafhopper. Infected plants have a pale yellow cast and a heavy concentration of very fine rootlets on the taproot. The most practical means of control is to eradicate leafhoppers and to keep down weeds in surrounding fields that serve as nesting sites for the insect vectors.

Leaf Blight. Alternaria and Cercospora are soil-borne fungal diseases that infect wet foliage, causing dead spots on leaves. In the major production areas of California, *Alternaria* is very serious during the fall when warm days and cool nights favor disease development. Symptoms are most severe on older leaves on a maturing crop, giving a scorched appearance. Control is by early application of fungicides.

Other Diseases. Bacterial blight, *Sclerotinia*, and powdery mildew are other diseases which damage the foliage. *Sclerotinia* also causes roots to rot. Seed decay and damping-off can decrease plant stands, and seeds should be treated with a fungicide before planting.

Root dieback (*Pythium irregulare, P. ultimum*) and cavity spot (*P. violae*) are two soil-borne fungal diseases that have recently been found to cause serious losses in major production areas of California by making roots unmarketable. The former disease kills the young taproot, causing new roots to develop and the taproot to become forked and stubby. It is usually a problem in late summer when soil temperatures are high. Cavity spot is favored by cool soil temperatures and results in small lesions on the taproot, which later become infected with other organisms, causing roots to rot. The best method of controlling both diseases is soil fumigation.

HARVESTING

In order to assure quality, carrots for fresh market are harvested before plants reach full maturity, while those for processing are allowed to grow longer in the season in order to maximize yields. The smaller-sized roots used for fresh market are more tender, milder in flavor, and more uniform in appearance than the larger roots for processing. Average days to harvest range from 70 days for some fresh market cultivars to over 100 days for some processing types.

Nearly all carrots for fresh market and processing are machine-harvested, except those that are marketed with the tops left on (Figure 15.3). In the same operation, mechanical harvesters undercut the roots, loosening them from the soil, lift the plants by the tops, and then separate the roots from the tops.

Those roots harvested with the tops are called bunch carrots, while those without the tops are called bulk carrots. Most carrots for market are now topped, which greatly reduces water loss from the roots and increases storage life. However, many fresh market buyers prefer green tops left on the roots since this presents a more attractive product. Carrots to be marketed with the tops left on are undercut by machine but pulled by hand and bunched.

POSTHARVEST HANDLING

Under proper conditions, carrots store well, and large portions of the crop,

Figure 15.3. Bunch carrots for fresh market are pulled by hand.

both fresh market and processing, are stored during the fall and winter. Cold storage at 32°F with high humidity (98–100%) gives best results. When harvested for storage, carrots should be relatively mature. They should be handled carefully to avoid bruising, which causes them to be very susceptible to storage diseases such as gray mold and various soft rots. Prompt removal of field heat and protection from freezing are important.

Mature topped carrots can be stored up to 7–9 months, while immature bunched carrots can usually be held no more than 2–3 weeks. If promptly cooled by hydrocooling and packed in polyethylene consumer bags, immature topped carrots can be held 4–6 weeks. Sometimes top ice is used with bagged, precooled carrots. Bitterness may develop in roots if carrots are stored with other produce, such as apples and pears, that release ethylene. Controlled atmosphere storage in carrots has not been successful.

BEETS

CLASSIFICATION, ORIGIN, HISTORY

Along with spinach and Swiss chard, beets (*Beta vulgaris*) belong to the goosefoot family (Chenopodiaceae). Beets are generally classified into two major groups, based on the edible part. Those beets grown mainly for their fleshy roots belong to the Crassa, or garden, group, and include yellow beets and the common table, or red, beets. Those kinds grown as leafy vegetables belong to the Cicla group, and include leafy beets and Swiss chard. Sugar beets and mangels belong to the same species as the garden beets.

The beet is native to Europe, North Africa, and West Asia. Though the ancients knew about the beet, they did not cultivate it until the 3rd century A.D. The first extensive records of beet culture are from the 16th century. The Germans and French became interested in beets around the year 1800, and since that time many improved types have been developed.

The roots of table beets can be served boiled, pickled, and in salads. The tops may be used much like spinach, as leafy greens for salads or boiled.

PRODUCTION AND INDUSTRY

Major commercial production of beets is limited mainly to Wisconsin and New York, where approximately 8,500 and 4,000 acres for processing are grown, respectively. About 100,000 tons are processed annually in Wisconsin, with 60% of the roots less than 2 inches in diameter. Texas leads in fresh market production, although the total acreage is relatively small. Other areas of beet production include California, Michigan, New Jersey, and Ohio. Average yields range from 12 to 15 tons per acre for processing and from 8 to 10 tons per acre for fresh market. In addition to its use as a food crop, there is also some beet production for pigment extraction for food coloring purposes. Worldwide, Germany and France are leading producers of beets.

PLANT GROWTH AND DEVELOPMENT

The plant is a herbaceous biennial, although grown as an annual, which forms a large storage root and leafy top the first year. The edible portion of the root consists of alternating circular bands of conducting and storage tissues (Figure 15.4). The bands of storage tissues are relatively broad and dark, while those of conducting tissues narrow and light. The contrast in color between alternating bands is known as zoning, which varies greatly between cultivars and within a cultivar. The substance responsible for color development in beets is betaine, which may be suppresed at high temperatures, resulting in a marked increase in zoning under hot weather. Numerous fibrous roots arise in close proximity to the enlarged storage root and function in nutrient and water absorption. These may extend down to 2–3 feet.

The stem is short and plate-like. The leaves are simple and arranged in a

Figure 15.4. Zoning in beet roots consists of alternating bands of storage and conducting tissues.

closed spiral on a part of the stem called the crown. The leaves vary in color from dark green to red and may be eaten as a vegetable green (see Chapter 24). The second year, the plate-like stem elongates, and flowers and seeds are produced. The so-called seed is really a dried fruit which contains from two to six seeds, making up a seedball.

CLIMATIC AND CULTURAL REQUIREMENTS

Beets are a cool-season crop that can tolerate mild frosts and light freezes. Seeds germinate over a wide range of soil temperatures (40–85°F), but optimum germination occurs between 65 and 75°F. Although beets grow well in warm weather, highest quality occurs in cool temperatures (55–70°F) where growth is rapid and uninterrupted, zoning is reduced, and sugars are relatively high. Temperatures below 50°F for 2–3 weeks when plants have several true leaves will induce seedstalks to develop later in the season.

Soil requirements for beets are similar to those for carrots. Heavy clay soils or soils that crust can reduce seedling emergence. Beets are sensitive to very acid soils, and soil pH should be adjusted to 6.5 or higher for maximum yields.

Fertilizer rates on mineral soils for nitrogen, phosphate (P_2O_5), and potash (K_2O) usually range from 75 to 150, 50 to 150, and 100 to 300 pounds per acre, respectively, depending on soil type, cultural practices, and soil tests. On lighter soils, some of the nitrogen may be sidedressed 4–6 weeks after planting. Less nitrogen and more potash are usually needed on muck soils.

Perhaps more than any other vegetable crop, beets are high users of micronutrients, especially boron. A deficiency of this nutrient may result in the physiological disorder known as *black spot*, which can make roots unfit for canning and fresh market (see "Physiological Disorders"). A boron deficiency is most likely to occur in alkaline soils high in calcium and is promoted by dry conditions. A common practice is to apply boron in the broadcast fertilizer or over the row at planting. Other important micronutrients include iron, manganese, copper, and molybdenum.

PLANTING AND CROP ESTABLISHMENT

The crop is propagated primarily from seed, although some growers may use transplants for their very early fresh market crop. The seedballs are usually planted 0.5–1.0 inch deep, in rows 12–24 inches apart, at rates ranging from 8 to 10 pounds of seed per acre for fresh market beets to 15–25 pounds of seed per acre for processing beets. Maximum yields can be obtained with high-density plantings; however, crowding can result in small roots with flat sides. Since seedballs contain several seeds and hand thinning is expensive, accurate seeding rates are important, especially for the fresh market crop. Even so, some hand thinning may be required for beets grown for fresh market in order to obtain a final stand of ten to twelve plants per foot of row. For processing, thinning is seldom practiced and processors usually pay a premium price for small-sized beets, so close spacing (fifteen to twenty plants per foot of row) is desirable.

Beets can be planted 4–6 weeks before the average last frost date. In the major production areas of Wisconsin and New York, beets for market production are planted from early April to late July, while for processing, the main planting period is late May through July.

CULTURAL PRACTICES

Beets have a moderately deep root system, and irrigation is usually not required for most commercial production, except on sandy soils or in dry regions. In California, growers apply around 18 inches of water per crop. Use of irrigation allows growers to increase plant populations, resulting in the more desirable small-sized roots.

Beet seedlings do not compete well with weeds, and effective weed control requires the use of herbicides and cultivation. Combination herbicides for annual grasses and broadleaf weeds are used in commercial plantings. However, beets are very sensitive to some herbicides; early seedling growth can be stunted and stands reduced from these chemicals, especially on very light soils. On sandy soils, in particular, extra care is needed when preplant herbicides are used. Shallow cultivation is usually necessary to keep down weeds. Rolling or deer track cultivators are effective when beet plants are very small.

CULTIVARS

Compared to other vegetables, the number of commercially important beet cultivars is relatively small. Several criteria are reflected in cultivar selection. These include days to maturity, root shape and ability to hold shape, root color, foliage color and length, intended use, surface smoothness, and degree of zoning (Table 15.2). Some new cultivars have a monogerm seed (one seed per seedball), which is very desirable for precision planting.

Table 15.2. Selected Beet Cultivars and Root Characteristics

| Cultivar | Days to Maturity | Root | | Comments[1] |
		Shape	Color	
Cardinal	60	Globe	Bright red	Processing; roots hold shape
Croby Green Top . . .	58	Oval	Dark red	Home garden; bunching; distinctly zoned
Detroit Dark Red	60	Globe	Dark red	Processing, market, home garden; main-season crop
Early Wonder Green Top	58	Oval	Purple-red	Bunching; greens; tops hold color
Gladiator	54	Globe	Bright red	Early; processing
Redpack	68	Globe	Dark red	Processing; little interior zoning
Ruby Queen	55	Round	Bright red	Processing, market, home garden; holds shape

[1]These are open-pollinated types that make up most of the commercial production, although several hybrids are available.

INSECTS, DISEASES, AND PHYSIOLOGICAL DISORDERS

Insects

The principal insect pests of beets are cutworms, leafminers, flea beetles, and aphids. Cutworms can cause damage to seedling plants by chewing them off at the soil line. Leafminers are small, white maggots that burrow into the leaves. These are problems mainly on beets for bunching and those where the tops are to be used. Flea beetles chew tiny holes in the foliage. Insecticides are usually effective in controlling these insect pests.

Diseases

Cercospora leaf spot is the most common disease of beets, causing circular lesions with reddish-brown margins on the leaves. The disease is most severe later in the season under warm, humid conditions. Weekly sprays with fungicides at the first sign of symptoms will control the disease.

A disease complex (*Aphanomyces, Pythium*) consisting of seed rot, seedling damping-off, and root rot of older plants affects beets. Seed rot and damping-off may be problems, especially in early plantings. Seeds should be treated with fungicide prior to planting. Planting in well-drained soil and rotating with cereals and grasses will help in controlling this complex.

Physiological Disorders

As indicated, beets deficient in boron may develop *black spot*, which is characterized by irregular, black spots throughout the interior of the root. Black spots may also form on the surface of the root, usually at the point of greatest circumference. As the roots mature, the external spots develop into large, dry, black cankers. Dead areas and cavities may form along cambial rings within fleshy roots. Beets already affected by *black spot* are predisposed to *Rhizoctonia* dry rot.

HARVESTING AND POSTHARVEST HANDLING

Beets are usually harvested when they have reached their desired size. For fresh market, roots will generally range from 1.25 to 2.5 inches in diameter. For processing, beets are usually harvested when 60% of the roots are less than 2 inches in diameter and 40% are over 2 inches in diameter. This ratio, however, will vary, depending on whether the product will be diced, sliced, or used whole. Root size is controlled primarily by spacing and cultivar, and not by maturity date. Fresh market beets are generally harvested 55–80 days after planting, while those for processing are usually ready 90–110 days after planting.

Harvest and handling methods for beets are very similar to those for carrots. Beets for processing and those for fresh market bulk pack are harvested and topped by machine. Fresh market beets to be marketed with tops on are usually pulled by hand, graded according to size, and bunched with three to six roots per bunch.

Beets under proper conditions can be stored for relatively long periods. At 32°F and 98–100% relative humidity, topped beets can be stored for 4–6 months, while bunched beets will keep for about 10–14 days. Beets should not be stored in large bulk, in order to remove respiratory heat. Cool-cellar storage can also be used, if humidity is kept sufficiently high to prevent shrivelling.

HORSERADISH

CLASSIFICATION, ORIGIN, HISTORY

Horseradish (*Armoracia rusticana*) is a well-known garden perennial that has nothing to do with either horses or radishes. It belongs to the Cruciferae family and is a near relative of cabbage, turnips, and mustard. The name supposedly came from an English adaptation of its German name *meerrettich*, which is translated "mareradish."

The plant is native to southeastern Europe, where the roots and leaves were used for food, condiments, and originally for medicinal purposes. Today, it is grown for its enlarged taproot (Figure 15.5), which is used as an appetizing condiment for meats and fish. Its unique characteristic pungent aroma and taste comes from the sulfur compound allyl isothiocyanate. If exposed to air or stored improperly, horseradish loses its pungency rapidly after it has been ground or processed.

PRODUCTION AND INDUSTRY

In general, horseradish is a highly specialized and relatively expensive crop to produce, requiring much hand labor. More than 75% of the U.S. crop is produced on about 1,200 acres in southwestern Illinois in the Mississippi River Valley in the area known as the "American Bottoms." About 80% of the product goes directly to the processor for grating and grinding. Yields of horseradish roots

Figure 15.5. Although a perennial, horseradish is grown as an annual for its large root, which is processed for use as a condiment.

average 2–4 tons per acre, although some growers may harvest up to 6–8 tons per acre. Other areas of horseradish production include northern California, Wisconsin, Washington, Pennsylvania, and parts of southern Ontario.

PLANT GROWTH AND DEVELOPMENT

Although it is a perennial, horseradish is grown as an annual, with roots harvested each year. The early development of the plant is concentrated in foliage growth, in which a large whorl of coarse-textured leaves arise from the crown. The taproot starts to grow in midsummer, but makes its largest amount of growth in late summer and fall when temperatures are cooler. The taproot, which matures with the first killing frost, is pale yellowish–brown and relatively smooth. The internal flesh is white and leathery. Horseradish roots exhibit a distinct polarity; small branch roots, or sets, arise from the distal end of the taproot and are used as propagating material for the next year's crop (Figure 15.6).

Figure 15.6. Horseradish is vegetatively propagated with small branch roots from the previous year's growth.

CLIMATIC AND CULTURAL REQUIREMENTS

Horseradish grows best in regions which have warm temperatures during the early part of the season when the plant is making foliage growth and cooler weather in the second part of the season in the late summer and fall when the taproot is developing rapidly. It generally does not grow well in the South except at higher elevations.

The plant will grow in most soils except deep, sterile sands and shallow clays with a hardpan subsoil. The best crops are grown on rich, moist, deeply tilled, friable loams or sandy loams, like those found in the part of Illinois along the Mississippi River bottoms. On poor or sandy soils, roots are highly branched, generally small, and of poor quality.

Although a crop will remove large amounts of nutrients from the soil, it generally does not require high fertilizer rates, since it is a relatively long-season crop and has a rather deep root system for absorbing nutrients. Plants should have a continuous supply of nutrients and moisture during the summer months in order to promote vigorous foliage growth. The use of animal manure is decreasing, and growers now rely almost totally on commercial fertilizers. Nitrogen rates range from 100–150 pounds per acre, while phosphorus and potassium are applied according to soil tests. Excessive nitrogen should be avoided, since this can result in too much top growth and highly branched irregular roots. Like other crucifers, horseradish has a high requirement for boron.

PLANTING AND CROP ESTABLISHMENT

Horseradish is vegetatively propagated from sets or secondary roots from the previous year's crop. These increase in diameter to become the current year's marketable taproots.

The 1-year-old secondary roots are selected from the large primary roots after they are harvested and as they are being trimmed for market. The sets should be 6–18 inches long, 0.5–0.75 inch in diameter, and fairly straight. They are stored overwinter in commercial coolers, outdoor pits, or cold cellars.

At planting the following spring, the sets are placed in furrows 4–5 inches deep, at spacings 18–24 inches apart in each furrow, and covered with soil. Furrow spacing can vary from 30 inches to 36 inches apart, resulting in populations of 7,200 to 11,600 plants per acre. Prior to planting, the sets are given a slanting cut at the bottom ends and a square cut at the top or crown ends, in order to determine proper root placement. Experience has shown that the sets are best planted with the top ends slightly higher, at a 45-degree angle, than the bottom ends. Planting can be done either by hand or with tomato transplanters.

CULTURAL PRACTICES

Commercial production practices have been highly developed. Irrigation is generally not required on bottomland ground, but it may be needed on lighter upland soils, especially during August and September. Weed control is a particular problem since there are very few herbicides labeled for use on horseradish. Growers must use mechanical and hand cultivation for the major part of their weed control program.

In order to obtain straight roots with few side shoots, growers sometimes use a procedure known as "lifting." This involves lifting the top or crown end of the main root out of the soil, stripping off the side roots and all but the main crown leaves, and then replacing the root and covering it with soil. This is usually done twice during the season, when the leaves are 6–10 inches tall and again about 6 weeks later. The practice, however, is expensive since it must be done by hand, and many growers no longer use it since most of the roots to be processed will be grated and ground. Some growers will also prune the tops during the season to induce the plant to put most of its energy into the production of the root.

CULTIVARS

Horseradish cultivars are very few, and commercial production is largely confined to 'Common,' 'Big Top Western,' and 'Swiss.' The 'Common' cultivar has broad, crinkled leaves and produces roots of high quality, but is very susceptible to turnip mosaic virus and white rust diseases. The 'Big Top Western' cultivar has large, upright, smooth leaves. It is resistant to white rust and tolerant of turnip mosaic. 'Swiss' has smooth leaves and is moderately susceptible to both white rust and turnip mosaic virus. The names 'Bohemian' and 'Maliner Kren' are sometimes used by commercial growers in referring to the smooth-leaf and crinkled-leaf types. Growers with the ability to save healthy plants tend to develop their own strains by selecting high-yielding plants adapted to their local conditions.

INSECTS AND DISEASES

Insect and disease problems are relatively few. Flea beetles and beet leafhoppers are the most serious insect pests and cause injury by feeding on the young shoots as they emerge through the soil. The diseases white rust (*Albugo candida*), turnip mosaic, and brittle root are of major importance. The first two cause extensive leaf damage, which prevents normal root growth and results in reduced yields. Brittle root, caused by the spiroplasma *Spiroplasma citri*, is the most serious disease of horseradish. The disease is transmitted by the beet leafhopper and causes an internal browning in the vascular tissue of the root. Starch accumulates in the roots which snap easily when bent. In the West, curly-top virus may affect plants and is spread by leafhoppers. In some years, *Verticillium* wilt and nematodes may be troublesome.

HARVESTING AND POSTHARVEST HANDLING

The horseradish root makes its best growth during the cool weather of autumn, and harvest should not begin until after the tops have been killed by frost. Roots are lifted from the soil with either a modified potato digger or a heavy plow. The roots are then loaded by hand onto a flatbed wagon. To facilitate harvest, tops that have not been killed by frost may be mowed down about 7–10 days before the roots are dug.

The harvested roots can be placed in plastic bags and stored over the winter in pits, cool cellars, or barns; or they may be left in the ground over the winter and harvested in early spring. Roots to be held for summer use should be placed in cold storage at 30–32°F and 98–100% relative humidity. Horseradish that is dug when the roots are still actively growing does not store as well as that when roots are conditioned by cold weather before harvest. Prior to storage or before going to the processor, the small lateral roots to be used for planting stock for the next season are removed and stored. Generally, for fresh market and most processing, the roots are marketed as they are harvested.

PARSNIPS

Parsnips (*Pastinaca sativa*) are a relatively little known root crop that are grown for their long, tapered taproot that resembles a white carrot (Figure 15.7).

Figure 15.7. Parsnips are a cool-season crop grown for their long, tapered roots. (Photo: courtesy of Charles Voigt, University of Illinois)

They are a member of the Umbelliferae family which also includes carrots, celery, and parsley.

The plant is native to the eastern Mediterranean and was known to the early Greeks and Romans who used it for food and medicinal purposes. It was brought to the U.S. by the colonists and was cultivated in Virgina and Massachusetts in the early 17th century.

The crop is not extensively grown in the U.S., with Pennsylvania, Illinois, California, and New York the major producing states. Parsnips are more popular in northern Europe in Germany and in parts of Asia.

PLANTING AND CULTURE

Plant development and crop cultural requirements are much like those for carrots. Although a biennial, parsnips are grown as an annual. They are a cool-season crop that is not as heat tolerant as carrots and should be grown in areas of relatively cool summers; best growth is made at 60–65°F. The crop will withstand freezing if left in the field. Some consider them a winter crop because their sweet, nutty flavor is not fully developed until almost early winter when the roots have been exposed to near-freezing temperatures.

The plants have a long growing season, requiring 100–120 days from seeding in the spring to harvest in the late fall or early winter. Seeds are relatively slow to germinate, even at optimum temperatures (14 days at 68°F). The seeds are usually planted in rows 15–18 inches apart for hand cultivation and 24–30 inches apart for mechanical tillage, and covered to a depth of 0.5 inch. After emergence, plants are thinned to three to six per foot of row. If plants are too far apart, the roots become large and fibrous, while crowding plants produces smaller, more tender roots.

Soil requirements and seedbed preparation are similar to those for carrots and beets. Smooth roots and good stands are difficult to obtain on heavy soils. Since the growing season is long, fertilizer rates are usually slightly lower than are required for carrots, under comparable conditions. Irrigation requirements, weed control, and insect and disease management are similar to those for carrots. Parsnip seed is short-lived; thus, fresh, certified seed should be used each year.

HARVESTING AND POSTHARVEST HANDLING

The roots are usually left in the ground until the late fall and sometimes throughout the winter. They may be dug by hand or loosened with a plow and lifted by hand. The roots attain a length of up to 12 inches, and care must be used in digging so as not to break them. When freezing occurs, it is not practical to leave the roots in the ground because of the difficulty in digging them when needed.

At the time of harvest, the roots are high in starch. Exposure to low temperatures (32°F), either in the field or in storage, results in conversion of this starch to sugars, causing an increase in sweetness and market quality of the roots.

The storage methods for parsnips are similar to those for most root crops. The roots may be stored in a cellar, in an outdoor pit, or left in the ground over the winter until they are needed. Cold storage requirements (32°F, 98–100% relative humidity) are nearly the same as for topped carrots, and roots may be stored up to 4–6 months. The main storage problem is shrivelling from moisture loss, which may be lessened with the use of ventilated polyethylene films and liners.

RADISHES

CLASSIFICATION, ORIGIN, HISTORY

The radish (*Raphanus sativus*) is an easy-to-grow and widespread vegetable that can usually be found in most home gardens. It is a member of the Cruciferae family and as such has a characteristic pungent aroma and taste. The cultivated forms can be grouped into two general types: the very common, rapid-growing, quick-maturing types known as spring radishes; and the less common, slower-growing, late-maturing types known as winter radishes.

The radish dates back to about 2000 B.C. when it was cultivated in Egypt. Western Asia is thought to be its place of origin. The Greeks were especially fond of radishes, as were the Romans who probably introduced radishes to many parts of northern Europe. The plant did not reach England until the early 16th century, and by the early 17th century, it was being cultivated in the U.S.

PRODUCTION AND INDUSTRY

Although grown extensively in home gardens, radishes are a minor commercial crop in the U.S. Commercial production is primarily with the early spring types. The major producing areas are Florida and Ohio, where much of the crop is grown on muck soils, and in parts of southern California.

Radishes are a very efficient crop to produce since all the production steps are mechanized and the growing time for spring types is very short, usually 3–5 weeks. The winter types are more important worldwide, particularly in the Far East, where they are pickled and used with rice, and are one of the leading crops in annual tonnage.

PLANT GROWTH AND DEVELOPMENT

The radish is grown as an annual for its enlarged fleshy taproot, which also consists of some stem tissue. The stem is a short crown, and when the plant produces seed, the stem elongates and forms the flowerstalk. The leaves are simple and lobed and arise in a rosette from the center of the crown. The absorbing root system is not very extensive, with most of the roots 2–8 inches long. The fleshy taproot varies considerably among cultivars in size, shape, color, and texture of the flesh.

The radish is a hardy, cool-season crop that can withstand subfreezing temperatures. Optimum growth occurs at average monthly temperatures of 60–65°F. Hot weather generally decreases quality. If growth is checked from hot weather, roots will become pithy and pungent. Plants can go to seed quickly when grown under high temperatures.

The spring types grow quickly and mature in a relatively short time (20–30 days), but root quality deteriorates rapidly. These types are annuals with relatively small roots that are mildly pungent. Winter radishes, which are biennials, grow slower (50–90 days to mature), have larger roots, and store better than spring types. The winter types are usually planted to mature in the fall but can be grown over the winter in mild climates. The winter types have very characteristic strong flavors.

PLANTING AND CULTURE

In northern areas, production is mainly in the spring and fall, while winter plantings are used in the South; in regions of cool summers, radishes can be grown almost year-round. To obtain successive harvests, seed is usually planted at 7- to 10-day intervals. Spacing of harvests can also be obtained by cultivar selection.

Radishes grow on a wide range of soils. For irrigated plantings, sandy loams are generally best, while heavier soils are generally used for dryland crops. Muck soils are used in some areas and are especially well suited for summer production since they are usually well supplied with moisture and provide a cool growing medium. Good crops have been obtained from mid-summer plantings in Ohio on muck soils; however, the best quality occurs when the seed is planted in mid-June to mid-July for a fall crop so that the roots mature in cool temperatures. The soil must be well drained and should be thoroughly prepared to provide a smooth seedbed to get uniform depth of planting and even seedling emergence.

The seed is drilled 0.5 inch deep in rows 8–10 inches apart to give populations of twelve to eighteen plants per foot of row. In the West, growers furrow irrigate plants on raised beds consisting of two or more rows. Some seed is also sown broadcast. The increased use of irrigation has allowed the use of greater plant populations up to three or four seeds per inch of row. The use of graded seed with precision planters ensures uniform seeding rates and eliminates the need for thinning. The larger winter types are usually thinned to four to six plants per foot of row.

Since plant growth is rapid, a fertile soil is needed. On muck soils, more potassium and less nitrogen should be used. Less fertilizer is needed if the crop follows one that has been heavily fertilized. Pest problems are similar to those of other crucifers. Insect pests include root maggots, flea beetles, and aphids. *Alternaria*, downy mildew, club root, and *Fusarium* wilt are major diseases of radishes.

HARVESTING AND POSTHARVEST HANDLING

Roots are harvested when they are of usable size and relatively young. Harvest procedures are similar to those for carrots. Multiple-row mechanical harvesters dig and pull the plants from the soil, remove the tops, and load the roots in bins. Plants to be marketed with tops on are pulled by hand. Bunching is used mostly for local market. Long-rooted cultivars are bunched in four's and fives's, while round and globe-shaped cultivars are tied in bunches of six to twelve roots.

Radishes remain in edible condition for only a short period of time before they become pithy and pungent. They should be cooled quickly to 40°F or below; hydrocooling is effective in this regards. At 32°F and 95–100% relative humidity, topped radishes can be held for 3–4 weeks, while bunched roots will generally keep no longer than 1–2 weeks. Winter radishes are handled and stored in much the same way as topped carrots and at 32°F should keep 3–4 months. Nearly all spring radishes are topped and prepackaged in plastic bags for retail sale.

RUTABAGAS AND TURNIPS

Rutabaga and turnip are two closely allied species in the Cruciferae family, which are very similar in their cultural and culinary characteristics; consequently, they are sometimes confused for each other. Both are frost-hardy, cool-season biennials that are grown as annuals for their enlarged fleshy taproot. Like other Brassicas, the two crops are native to northern Asia. It is generally thought that the rutabaga probably evolved from a cross between cabbage and turnip. Both are grown extensively in northern Europe, Canada, and Asia, but U.S. production is limited to Wisconsin, Minnesota, and Washington. Turnips are also grown for their leaves, which when young and tender make for excellent greens, either raw or cooked.

Although closely related, the plants are very distinguishable by their foliage and roots. Rutabagas, also known as "Swede turnips," are classified as *Brassica Napus* (Napobrassica group); turnips are classified as *Brassica Rapa* (Rapifera group).

Rutabagas have smooth, fleshy, bluish-green foliage, while turnip leaves are usually green, thin, rough, and hairy. Rutabaga roots (Figure 15.8) are round, larger, and firmer than those of turnip, which tend to be more flattened and range in shape from spherical to elongated and conical. Whereas turnip roots have little or no neck and a more distinct taproot, rutabaga roots are thick with leafy necks. The roots of both crops may have either white or yellow flesh, but commercially, rutabaga roots are generally yellow while those of turnips are white. The exterior color of rutabaga roots is generally tan-yellowish, while turnip roots range from white to tan and often have purple in their upper parts.

Both crops make their best root growth under low temperatures, and planting schedules are timed for roots to mature during cool weather. Turnips mature in 60 days, and in the North can be grown as a spring or fall crop; the fall crop is generally of higher quality and can be stored for winter use. Rutabagas take

Figure 15.8. Rutabaga roots are larger and firmer than those of turnips.

about 4–5 weeks longer to mature and are generally grown in the North as a fall crop only. In the South, both crops can be grown during the fall, winter, and early spring. Prolonged exposure of post-juvenile plants to low temperatures will induce seedstalks to form later in the season.

Cultural requirements are very similar to those for carrots and beets, although turnips and rutabagas are not as exacting as these other crops. Both are grown as row crops with larger spacings used for rutabagas (30-inch rows, 4–8 inches between plants) than with turnips (rows 12–24 inches apart, 2–6 inches between plants). High fertilization rates are sometimes used to stimulate rapid development for spring plantings but are not so important in the fall. On some soils boron may be required. Disease and insect pests are similar to those for cabbage.

Turnip and rutabaga roots are of the best quality when they are medium-sized; turnips should be 2–3 inches in diameter, rutabagas 3–5 inches in diameter. Topped turnip roots are harvested by machine, while bunched roots are pulled by hand. Most of the turnip roots are now topped and packed for retail sale in transparent film. Rutabaga roots are pulled by hand and trimmed. Turnip greens are harvested 4–6 weeks after seeding.

Rutabagas and topped turnips require the same storage requirements (high humidity and cool temperatures) as topped carrots. If harvested in good condition, roots should store well for 4–6 months. Waxing with paraffin is used for those roots going to market to reduce moisture loss, but it is not used for long-term storage. The growth regulator maleic hydrazide may be applied to plants in the field before they are harvested to prevent rutabaga roots from sprouting in storage.

JERUSALEM ARTICHOKES

Jerusalem artichokes (*Helianthus tuberosus*) are perennial plants that are cultivated as annuals. They are a member of the sunflower family (Compositae) and are native to North America, where they were widely grown by the Native Americans. The Jerusalem artichoke is not related to the globe artichoke nor does it bear any relationship to Jerusalem.

The plants are grown for their potato-like, fleshy, oblong tubers (3–4 inches long) that may be baked, boiled, or fried. The tubers are knobby and range in color from white to yellow and from red to blue (Figure 15.9). The primary carbohydrate reserve in the tubers is insulin, a polymer of fructose that is of value because it can be utilized by diabetics in lieu of glucose.

The plants can be grown in most parts of the U.S. They grow 4–8 feet in height and resemble sunflowers. The crop is vegetatively propagated by planting the individual tubers 2–3 inches deep, 2–3 feet apart, in rows 3–4 feet apart.

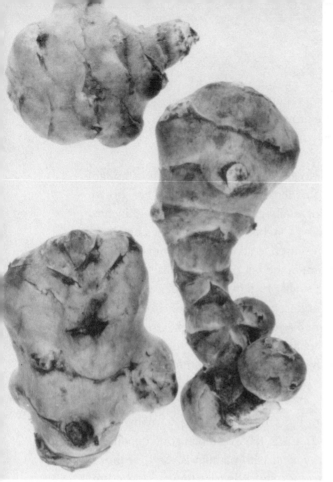

Figure 15.9. The fleshy tubers of Jerusalem artichokes are used in a manner similar to potatoes.

Plantings can be made in the early spring as soon as the soil can be worked. Sandy loams are best; although silt and clay loams give higher yields, the harvest of the tubers is difficult in heavy soils.

Tuberization occurs in the late summer when daylengths decrease. The tubers are ready for harvest in about 5 months after planting, generally when the top growth is killed by frost. Prior to harvest the tops should be removed. If weather conditions permit, the tubers should be dug just before use. In areas where the ground does not freeze, the tubers may be left in the ground and harvested over the winter. In colder regions, the tubers are dug before the soil freezes and stored at 32°F and 90–95% relative humidity. Under these conditions, the tubers may be stored up to 4–5 months. Any tubers that are not harvested will resume growth in the late winter or early spring and may become weed problems.

SELECTED REFERENCES

"Anonymous." 1970. *Commercial Growing of Horseradish.* USDA Leaf. No. 547.

"Anonymous." 1966. *Production of Turnips and Rutabagas.* USDA Leaf. No. 142.

McClurg, C. A., and F. D. Schales. 1982. *Commercial Production of Horseradish.* Univ. of Maryland Coop. Ext. Ser. Pub. HE 127-82.

Murray, J. 1977. *Radishes. Fruit & Vegetable Facts & Pointers.* United Fresh Fruit and Vegetable Association, Alexandria, Virginia.

Murray, J. 1976. *Carrots. Fruit & Vegetable Facts & Pointers.* United Fresh Fruit and Vegetable Association, Alexandria, Virginia.

Rhodes, A. M., J. W. Courter, and M. C. Shurtleff. 1965. Identification of horseradish types. *Trans. Illinois State Acad. Sci.* 58:115–122.

Sackett, C. 1975. *Parsnips. Fruit & Vegetable Facts & Pointers.* United Fresh Fruit and Vegetable Association, Alexandria, Virginia.

Schoenemann, J. A., L. K. Binning, J. A. Wyman, L. G. Bundy, and W. R. Stevenson. 1980. *Commercial Beet Production.* Univ. of Wisconsin Coop. Ext. Ser. Pub. A2347.

Seelig, R. A. 1973. *Turnips. Fruit & Vegetable Facts & Pointers.* United Fresh Fruit and Vegetable Association, Alexandria, Virginia.

Seelig, R. A. 1966. *Beets. Fruit & Vegetable Facts & Pointers.* United Fresh Fruit and Vegetable Association, Alexandria, Virginia.

Whitaker, T. W., A. F. Sherf, W. H. Lange, C. W. Nicklow, and J. D. Radeweld. 1970. *Carrot Production in the United States.* USDA Agric. Handbook No. 375.

Zandstra, B. H., and H. C. Price. 1979. *Red Beets.* Michigan State Univ. Coop. Ext. Ser. Bull. E-1306.

16

CELERY

CLASSIFICATION, ORIGIN, HISTORY

Celery (*Apium graveolens* var. *dulce*) belongs to the parsley family (Umbelliferae), which includes carrots, parsley, and parsnips. It probably developed as a wild marsh plant in its native habitat, extending from Sweden to Egypt and Abyssinia, and in Asia from the Caucasus to India. Celery has also been found growing wild in California, New Zealand, and near the southern tip of South America. Although it was first mentioned as a cultivated crop in France in 1623, celery was used as a medicinal plant centuries before it was used as a food. It is not known when the plant was brought to the U.S., although reference to it in the country was made in 1806.

Celery is grown for its long, fleshy petioles, which are valued for their flavor and texture, although they are low in nutritive content. The fresh product contains approximately 94% water and 6% fiber. It is eaten mainly as a salad crop, but some celery is used in soups and a little is dehydrated. Celery seeds may also be used as a condiment for flavor.

Celeriac (*Apium graveolens* var. *rapaceum*), also known as knob or root celery, is a close relative which is grown for its enlarged root that resembles a turnip (see Chapter 28).

PRODUCTION AND INDUSTRY

Statistics for U.S. fresh market and processed celery production in 1977 and 1989 are presented in Table 16.1. Generally, harvested acreage remained rela-

Table 16.1.   Harvested Acreage, Production, and Value for Fresh Market and Processing Celery in the U.S., 1977 and 1989

State	Harvested Acres		Production		Value	
	1977[1]	1989[2]	1977	1989	1977	1989
			———— (tons) ————		———— ($1,000) ————	
California						
southern	10,900	11,300	314,000	307,950	54,118	89,912
central	9,500	10,500	277,000	422,650	38,068	94,930
Florida	9,900	8,000	160,000	166,000	36,036	52,456
Michigan	2,400	2,800	54,000	53,200	8,854	14,103
New York	550	430	12,000	8,600	1,967	3,165
Ohio	230	400	5,000	9,300	788	2,083
Texas	—	1,900	—	46,100	—	11,617
Washington	280	—	5,400	—	745	—
U.S.	33,760	35,330	822,000	1,013,800	140,576	268,266

[1]Source: USDA. 1978. Economics, Statistics, and Cooperatives Service (ESCS), Crop Reporting Board.

[2]Source: USDA. 1990. National Agricultural Statistics Service (NASS), Agricultural Statistics Board.

tively constant, while production tonnage and value increased 24 and 97%, respectively, in 1989. California (72%) and Florida (16%) are the leading states in commercial celery production. The production in California, which is year-round, is located mainly in the central and southern coastal areas. Florida production is primarily in the winter and spring. Other leading producing states include Michigan and New York for summer and fall production and Ohio for summer.

The production costs per acre are the highest of any vegetable crop, averaging over $3,000 per acre. It costs approximately $1,000 per acre to grow celery and over $2,000 per acre to harvest, pack, and cool the crop. Yields average 29 tons per acre, but they may be as high as 50–60 tons per acre. Most of the crop is produced for fresh market, with a small amount used for processing and packed as celery hearts.

PLANT GROWTH AND DEVELOPMENT

Celery is a biennial which grows vegetatively during the first year, after which it is harvested. The plant is slow-growing and makes most of its growth in the later part of the season. During the first year, the stem develops as a short, compact, lens-shaped plate, which forms a rosette of leaves with thick petioles. The older petioles develop on the outside, while the younger ones form on the inside and comprise the "heart" of the plant. During the second year, following exposure to low temperatures, the short stem elongates to produce a flowerstalk. The plant bears compound clusters of small, white flowers, which produce seeds toward the end of the flowering season. Premature flowering and seedstalk formation (bolting) may occur during the first year if plants are subjected to temperatures below 50°F for 10 or more days. After celery produces a seedstalk, it is no longer marketable.

The thickened petioles, or leafstalks, which comprise the edible part of the plant, make up almost all of the above-ground material (Figure 16.1). The leafstalks consist of epidermis, thin-walled parenchyma tissue, thick-walled collenchyma tissue, and vascular tissue. They are prominently ribbed along their abaxial (outer) length, with considerable differences among cultivars. The thin-walled parenchyma tissue makes up the bulk of the interior of the leafstalk, while the outer ribs are composed mainly of thick-walled collenchyma cells. These cells comprise a mechanically strong tissue and are mainly responsible for its characteristic stringiness.

Figure 16.1. Celery is grown for its thickened petioles or leafstalks that orginate from a compact stem plate.

Celery is considered a shallow-rooted vegetable. The root system consists of a taproot, which is destroyed when the plant is transplanted. The plant then develops a dense, fibrous root system from the compact stem, with most of the roots in the top 6–12 inches of soil. Because of its restricted root system when transplanted, celery is not considered a good forager for either moisture or nutrients. When grown from seed, celery produces a well-developed root system consisting of a taproot, although not deep, with several laterals.

CLIMATIC AND CULTURAL REQUIREMENTS

Climatic requirements are very demanding. Celery thrives best in climates with long, cool growing seasons, especially at night, and where rainfall is well distributed or irrigation is used. Mean monthly temperatures should be 60–65°F with an average maximum of 75°F and a minimum of 55°F. It is intolerant of high temperatures, especially near maturity, which can result in poor growth and strong flavor. Although the plant will withstand light freezes, it can be damaged by cold temperatures.

Because of its high nutrient and water requirements and a relatively shallow root system, celery requires a highly fertile soil with good moisture-holding capacity. A fertile muck or a loose and friable sandy loam high in organic matter is best. In Ohio and Michigan, virtually all celery is grown on muck soil (Figure 16.2). If a cover crop is used, it should be turned under in sufficient time to allow decomposition before planting. The crop does best within a pH range of 6.0–6.6 in mineral soils and 5.5–6.0 in organic soils.

Celery is a heavy feeder and a poor forager, so it requires heavy fertilization. A crop has been shown to remove 280 pounds of nitrogen, 72 pounds of phosphorus, 635 pounds of potassium, and 35 pounds of magnesium per acre. Over 45% of the mineral nutrients are absorbed during the month preceding harvest.

Figure 16.2. Celery growing on muck soil with overhead irrigation.

The kind and amount of fertilizer will vary considerably from region to region, and within a producing area, depending on soil type and native fertility. In California, 200–400 pounds nitrogen per acre, 100–200 pounds phosphorus (P_2O_5) per acre, and 50–400 pounds potash (K_2O) per acre are applied to the crop. In some areas, potassium and phosphorus may not be needed because of high soil levels of these nutrients. In Ohio, potassium rates up to 400–500 pounds K_2O per acre may be used on muck and peat soils, where potassium is often deficient.

In general, the fertilizer recommendation for a given soil should provide a high level of fertility throughout the growing season, and a maintenance application of phosphorus and potassium should be made, regardless of the response to these elements. Nitrogen has the most pronounced effect on plant growth and is usually put on over several applications, while all phosphorus and potassium are broadcast before planting beds are thrown up. For early plantings, extra nitrogen may be needed if the soil is cold and wet. In northern areas, starter solutions are commonly used with transplants.

Celery seedlings are not tolerant of salts, and high salt fertilizers such as KCl (muriate of potash) should be used with care. The plants have a relatively high requirement for boron. Plantings on muck or other organic soils may require copper fertilization. Boron, magnesium, and calcium deficiencies can have significant effects on stalk quality (see "Physiological Disorders").

PLANTING AND CROP ESTABLISHMENT

Celery beds may be started from transplants or by direct seeding in the field. The use of transplants permits easier stand establishment, earlier maturity, fewer irrigation problems during early growth, and lower incidence of bolting in early plantings. Direct seeding is considerably cheaper, and higher plant populations are economically feasible. Occasionally, the labor cost of thinning direct-seeded plantings can offset the labor expense of transplanting.

Transplants

Celery transplants may be grown in the greenhouse, or in other protected structures, or they may be started directly in field beds where climate permits. In northern growing regions, some growers use transplants produced in warmer areas, such as Florida. Plants seeded in the greenhouse or a hotbed are usually started in flats and later transplanted after 4–5 weeks to seedling beds. Plants for the late crop can be seeded directly in outdoor nursery seedling beds and later moved.

When growing greenhouse transplants, growers should start seed 8–10 weeks before the desired field transplanting date. Soaking seeds prior to planting hastens germination. The seeds are planted shallow, and are sometimes sown on the soil surface. Diffuse light and a diurnal temperature fluctuation (85° / 60°F day / night) are sometimes used to increase germination. Celery is a marsh plant, and seeds germinate best when soil moisture is above field capacity. After seedlings emerge, night temperatures should be kept above 60°F so plants do not become vernalized, to lessen the chances of bolting later in the season.

When producing transplants directly in field seedling beds, growers generally start the plants 6–8 weeks before transplanting to the production field. Gel seeding is used to enhance seed germination and seedling vigor (see Chapter 5).

Plants are removed from seedling beds and transplanted to the field when they have attained a height of 4–6 inches and a crown diameter of 0.25–0.50 inch. The plants should be set at the proper depth, not too deep to cover the growing point in the crown. Planting distances and methods vary in different parts of the country. The distance between rows ranges from 30 to 42 inches and between plants in the row 5–8 inches. Prior to transplanting in the field, some growers prune tops for easy handling, but this can sometimes slow root growth. The use of gang transplanters ensures uniform spacing and reduces the cost of planting. Because plants can be damaged by moderate freezes, the crop should not be set in the field too early in the season.

Direct Seeding

In some coastal areas of California, celery is seeded directly in the production beds. However, this method requires extra care and considerable grower expertise to get a good stand. Direct seeding can only be used if irrigation is available to keep the soil surface continuously moist during germination and early growth. Soil crusting is serious with small celery seedlings, so the seedbed should be thoroughly prepared. Seed is sown at a rate of 0.75–1.5 pounds per acre and later thinned to about 6–8 inches between plants when seedlings have four to six true leaves.

CULTURAL PRACTICES

Weeds

Celery grows slowly and is easily injured by weeds, especially during its early development. Weeds also interfere with harvesting operations. Celery roots do not have as much spread as most other vegetable roots and do not compete effectively with weeds. The high-moisture requirement and moisture supply during growth favor weed competition in the crop. In northern areas, annual grasses and broadleaf weeds are the main weed problems.

Herbicides available for use on celery are relatively few. For transplanted crops, postemergent herbicide application 2–3 weeks after transplanting is used to control most annual weeds. For direct-seeded celery, preemergent herbicides are used. Postemergent oil sprays applied after celery is 2–3 inches tall may be used to control emerged annual weeds.

Cultivation is normally required to control weeds and to prevent soil crusting, and it may also be used to reshape and maintain beds. Cultivation should be shallow, especially near the plants, since most of the roots grow near the surface and lie within 6–12 inches of the row. In all cultivation, the surface soil should be left as level as possible; small-tooth cultivators are best.

Irrigation

Celery is a moisture-loving plant, and unless the soil is naturally moist, the application of water is necessary. The moisture supply during the growth of the crop influences greatly its succulence and tenderness. Celery requires about 1–2 inches of water per week to maintain optimum growth and quality. Even on naturally moist muck soils, irrigation may be required to maintain or improve quality.

Soil moisture should be maintained in the upper half of the available moisture range. Celery grown during the summer in California may require a total of 16 irrigations and a seasonal water requirement of 45 acre-inches of water, compared to 11 irrigations and 25 acre-inches of water for a winter crop. Early in the season growers may need to irrigate every 10–15 days, but by the time the crop reaches maturity, the water requirement will be quite high and the crop may need irrigating every third day.

The three systems of irrigation in general use with celery are 1) underground or subirrigation, used principally in Florida, 2) furrow or surface irrigation, most common in California, and 3) overhead-sprinkler irrigation, used in most northern areas. The subirrigation system gives the grower almost complete control of the moisture supply and is used for both irrigation and drainage. Many muck soils and some sandy soils are ditched so that the ditches can be filled for irrigation or drained if necessary by reversing the pumps.

Blanching

Blanching removes the green color in the petioles and is accomplished by excluding light from the leafstalks while plants are still growing in the field. This treatment reduces the strong flavor and makes the leafstalks tender but decreases the vitamin A content. Various methods of covering the developing leaf petioles are used; the most common ones are hilling the plants with soil and shading the plant rows with black plastic or shadecloth (Figure 16.3). Stalks may also be blanched while they are in storage. Self-blanching cultivars have been developed to reduce labor costs. Increasing plant populations can also be used to a limited extent to blanch the crop, since close spacing and crowding of plants may inhibit color development in the stalks. In the past, blanching was popular, but because of the increasing demand for green celery and the expense involved with blanching, it is no longer a common practice.

Figure 16.3. Blanching of celery stalks in the field is done by excluding light from the petioles.

CULTIVARS

Cultivars of celery are generally classified as golden (yellow) or green (Table 16.2). Plant characteristics of commercial importance include growth rate, color, overall appearance, number of petioles, height, heart development, compactness, resistance to bolting, susceptibility to pests and physiological disorders, and field-holding ability. Important petiole characteristics are length, width, thickness, shape, ribbing, brittleness, pithiness, flavor (freedom from bitterness), and tenderness.

The yellow or golden types, also known as self-blanching cultivars, are characterized by their golden foliage. These are generally earlier, less vigorous,

Table 16.2. Types and Cultivars of Celery

Golden Cultivars	Green Cultivars
Golden Plume	**Utah type**
Golden Self-Blanching	
Michigan Improved Golden	Utah 52–70 R
Cornell 619	Utah 52–70 HK
Golden Detroit	Florida 683
	Utah 52–70
	Tall Green Light
	Tendercrisp
	Summer Pascal type
	Summer Pascal
	Giant Pascal
	Slow Bolting type
	Slow Bolting Green No. 96
	Slow Bolting Green No. 12

with thinner petioles, but more sharply ribbed than the green types. They have a well-developed heart, but they tend to be stringy and are generally more inferior in eating and keeping qualities than the green cultivars. The golden types have declined in importance and are produced on a limited scale in certain areas, primarily for specialty markets.

The green celery cultivars are characterized by their green foliage and are generally grouped into classes, or types, such as "Utah," "Summer Pascal," and "Slow Bolting." Within each group, cultivars differ in green color, number of petioles, petiole length, days to maturity, and susceptibility to bolting, stem cracking, and magnesium deficiency. Buyers and shippers refer to all cultivars of green celery generically as "Pascal"; however, when used in the horticultural sense, "Pascal" refers to a specific type of green celery.

The "Utah" types predominate because they tend to have a large number of attractive, well-overlapped petioles and a well-developed heart. Many of today's commercial cultivars are selections from 'Utah 52-70.' Most cultivars of the "Summer Pascal" type have excellent eating quality when properly grown, but they generally lack compactness and have few petioles; they also tend to have poor heart development. Strains of "Summer Pascal" and "Slow Bolting" types are less affected by cold temperatures and less likely to bolt in early plantings.

INSECTS, DISEASES, AND PHYSIOLOGICAL DISORDERS

Celery is susceptible to a wide range of insect and disease problems, as well as several physiological disorders. Many of these can be controlled or lessened in severity by good cultural practices, such as crop rotations, field sanitation, balanced nutrition, and regular spraying programs.

Insects

A number of leaf-eating worms, including cutworms, loopers, marsh caterpillars, leaf miners, and army worms, attack celery. Other serious insect pests include aphids, leaf tiers, tarnished plant bugs, leafhoppers, wireworms, and carrot rust flies. Although many of these may cause serious losses, damage is usually not significant because most of them can be effectively controlled with timely insecticide sprays.

Diseases

Early Blight. Caused by the fungus *Cercospora apii*, early blight first occurs in the seedbed and is transmitted to the field by the young seedlings. It tends to develop in warm weather when humidity is high. The disease first appears as small, circular, yellowish-brown spots on the petioles, which enlarge and eventually assume a grayish appearance. A few enlarged spots are normally sufficient to kill a leaf. Early spraying with fungicides will usually control early blight. The use of hot-water–treated seed (118°F for 30 minutes) is recommended. Since the disease is often introduced on 1-year-old seed, the most effective control is through the use of pathogen-free seed.

Late Blight. Caused by the fungus *Septoria apiicola*, late blight attacks plants in the cooler part of the growing season, in fall, winter, and early spring crops. It is very similar to early blight and first appears as small, yellow areas, being distinguished only by the smaller, more oval spots speckled with black dots. It attacks all parts of the plant above ground. Disease development and spread are favored by moist conditions. The control is the same as for early blight.

Pink Rot. A soil-borne fungus (*Sclerotinia sclerotiorum*), pink rot is a destructive disease in Florida and some northern growing areas, especially in years when cool and moist conditions are favorable for its development. The disease causes damping-off in the seedbed, a light pinkish rot of stalks in the field, and a watery soft rot in transit and storage. The early lesions are light brown with pinkish-brown borders. Eventually, the tissues become water-soaked and very soft. Soil fumigation or spraying with fungicides will help control pink rot in the seedbed and in the field. Field sanitation and careful washing and packing are effective in preventing the disease in transit.

Fusarium Yellows. A soil-borne fungus (*Fusarium oxysporum* f. *apii*), *Fusarium* yellows has recently become a major concern in just about all the celery-growing regions of California, as well as in Ohio and northern areas. Affected plants are severely stunted and yellow. Later, the water-conducting tissues of the plants turn brown, and a black dry rot of the internal crown may develop. It is more prevalent in the summer than in the winter, and no effective control is known.

Viral Diseases. Two significant viral diseases of celery are aster yellows and western celery mosaic. Aster yellows is spread by leafhoppers and causes plants to be stunted with yellow and brittle leaves. The primary method of control is to eradicate the leafhopper vectors. Western mosaic is spread by aphids. Leaves of infected plants exhibit vein clearing followed by mottling and twisting. Plants become stunted. The most effective control of mosaic has been achieved in California by county-mandated 3-week celery-free periods during which all fields must be harvested and no new plantings allowed.

Physiological Disorders

Chlorosis. This is characterized by yellowing of older leaves due to a magnesium deficiency. It can be corrected by spraying magnesium sulfate ($MgSO_4$) at 20 pounds per acre on the foliage every 2 weeks; soil application of magnesium is usually not effective. Most "Summer Pascal" cultivars are fairly resistant.

Cracked Stem. Also called "brown checking," this disorder is first evident by a brownish mottling of the leaf, appearing along the margins. This is accompanied by a brittleness of the petiole, followed by crosswise cracks in the outer layers of the petiole. The tissues surrounding the cracks turn brown. Roots may also turn brown and the laterals die. The disorder is caused by a boron deficiency and is accentuated by high rates of nitrogen and potassium. Soil application of 1–2 pounds of boron per acre broadcast before planting or foliar application of 0.5 pound of boron per 100 gallons of water per acre is effective in preventing the disorder. 'Tall Utah 52-70' appears less affected by this disorder than other cultivars.

Black Heart. This is a calcium deficiency which causes the heart (inner leaves and growing point) to turn black. Bacterial soft-rot organisms invade the affected tissues, resulting in black, water-soaked centers. Occasionally, outer leaves are also affected and may turn yellow. High temperatures, rapid growth, and water stress are associated with this disorder. Large plants are more susceptible, especially with high nitrogen rates, indicating that the disorder may be growth-related. It is more serious in regions where irrigation waters contain high levels of sodium. Calcium chloride (5–10 pounds per 100 gallons of water per acre) or calcium nitrate (5–15 pounds per 100 gallons per acre) sprays directed at the growing point will help control the disorder. Black heart may occur in the field as well as in storage.

Pithiness. This disorder is a breakdown of the thin-walled parenchyma cells that make up the major part of the leafstalk, resulting in soft tissue and a hollow cavity. It usually develops in the outer petioles first and has been attributed to too rapid growth, particularly with high nitrogen rates. Some cultivars are more susceptible than others.

HARVESTING AND POSTHARVEST HANDLING

Celery is usually ready for harvest 100–150 days after transplanting. Plants are normally harvested when they have attained proper size. The hearts or inner leaves enlarge rapidly as the plants mature; therefore, harvest should not be delayed too long. Early celery may be harvested before the plants are full grown in order for growers to take advantage of high market prices.

Celery harvest is labor-intensive and is the major production expense. Normally, the crop is cut, trimmed, and packed in the field. The plants are hand-harvested; each is undercut with a knife just below the stem (Figure 16.4). The trimmers follow the cutters, removing outer unmarketable petioles and any attached roots, and trim the plants to a uniform length by topping the leaf-blade foliage to a specified length. The cut celery plants should be thoroughly cleaned; damaged and discolored leaves should be stripped off and then the plants should be washed with fresh or chlorinated water to remove soil and trash. Washing may

Figure 16.4. Much of the crop is still harvested by hand by undercutting with a knife just below the stem.

be done in the field when the stalks are packed, but in larger operations it is done mostly in packing sheds, where the crop is also inspected for grade.

In some localities, mechanical harvesters are now used. The larger mechanical harvesters may cut 10–12 rows and operate ahead of a "mule train," which trims, washes, and packs the produce (Figure 16.5). Smaller two-row harvesters cut, top, and load celery bunches into trailers traveling beside the harvester for transport to the shed. The small amount of processing celery grown for dehydration or for use in canned and frozen products is usually harvested by machine.

Figure 16.5. A "mule train" trimming, washing, grading, and packing celery in the field.

Most celery is packed into crates because hydrocooling is the common method of cooling the produce for shipment. Paper cartons are used with celery for vacuum cooling (Figure 16.6). Depending on the size of the celery heads, crates are usually packed with two to three dozen heads; or cartons with one to two dozen heads.

Cut celery is very perishable and should be cooled as soon as possible, preferably near 32°F. Hydrocooling involves dunking the packed crates in an ice-water bath until the celery in the center of the crate is below 40°F. Celery for long distance shipment is often packed in corrugated cartons. Celery may also be precooled by refrigerated forced-air cooling. At 32°F, 98–100% relative humidity, and given circulating air, celery can be stored 2–3 months. During extended storage, heads will grow slightly and blanch somewhat.

Figure 16.6. A carton of celery field packed, and eventually to be vacuum cooled.

SELECTED REFERENCES

Paulus, A. O., D. H. Hall, and B. Teviotdale. 1977. *Late Blight of Celery*. Univ. of California Div. Agric. Sci. Leaf. 2982.

Paulus, A. O., D. H. Hall, and B. Teviotdale. 1976. *Pink Rot of Celery*. Univ. of California Div. Agric. Sci. Leaf. 2929.

Ryder, E. J. 1979. *Leafy Salad Vegetables*. AVI Publishing Co., Westport, Connecticut.

Sackett C., J. Murray, and R. A. Seelig. 1977. *Celery. Fruit & Vegetable Facts & Pointers*. United Fresh Fruit and Vegetable Association, Alexandria, Virginia.

Schoenemann, J. A., L. G. Bundy, J. A. Wyman, W. R. Stevenson, and L. K. Binning. 1983. *Commercial Celery Production*. Univ. of Wisconsin Coop. Ext. Ser. A2334.

Sims, W. L., J. E. Welch, and V. E. Rubatzky. 1977. *Celery Production in California*. Univ. of California Div. Agric. Sci. Leaf. 2673.

Zandstra, B. H., S. Honma, and D. D. Warncke. 1980. *Celery*. Michigan State Univ. Coop. Ext. Bull. E-1308.

17

CUCUMBERS

Along with squash, melons, and pumpkins, cucumbers are part of the Cucurbitaceae family and collectively with these crops belong to the group of vegetables known as cucurbits or vine crops. The family (also known as the gourd family) consists of about 96 genera, but only three are of commercial importance in the U.S. These include *Cucumis* (cucumber and muskmelon), *Citrullus* (watermelon), and *Cucurbita* (pumpkin and squash).

Cucurbits are generally annuals that are extremely intolerant of cold weather. They are grown mainly for their fruits, which are derived from a single ovary containing many ovules or seeds. In some parts of the world, flowers and leaves of some species are also used for food. Among vegetable crops, the cucurbits are somewhat different, along with sweet corn, in that they bear different kinds of flowers on the same plant. Most cucurbits are monoecious, producing both male and female flowers separately on the same plant, or andromonecious, producing numerous male flowers to each perfect (bisexual) flower. However, gynoecious (all female) flowers and other forms of sex expression may exist in some species. In each of these, insects serve as the main pollen carriers.

CLASSIFICATION, ORIGIN, HISTORY

The cucumber is classified *Cucumis sativus*. The genus comprises about forty species, including muskmelons, honeydews, and cantaloupes. The cucumber is believed native to India, and evidence indicates that it has been cultivated in western Asia for 3,000 years. From India it spread to Greece and Italy, where the Romans were especially fond of the crop, and later into China. It was probably introduced into other parts of Europe by the Romans, and records of cucumber cultivation appear in France in the 9th century, England in the 14th century, and in North America by the mid-16th century.

PRODUCTION AND INDUSTRY

Cucumbers are both a leading commercial crop and a popular home garden vegetable. Commercial cucumber production includes processing types for pickling and fresh market types for slicing. At one season or another, cucumbers may be grown in all regions of the U.S.

The major portion of the commercial crop in the U.S. is for processing, with Michigan, North Carolina, Texas, California, and Wisconsin the leading states for pickle production (Table 17.1). Processing cucumber yields average about 5 tons per acre in the U.S., and range from 4 tons per acre in the East to over 18 tons per acre in California. Approximately 40% of the pickling crop is fresh-packed,

Table 17.1. Harvested Acreage, Production, and Value for Processing Cucumbers in the U.S., 1977 and 1989

State	Harvested Acreage		Production		Value	
	1977[1]	1989[2]	1977	1989	1977	1989
			——— (tons) ———		——— ($1,000) ———	
California	4,300	4,300	61,800	52,460	7,425	12,958
Colorado	1,600	1,300	17,250	10,560	1,863	1,478
Florida	—	2,700	—	14,310	—	5,223
Indiana	1,400	1,700	9,750	15,810	1,053	2,103
Maryland	2,800	—	19,450	—	2,178	—
Michigan	24,500	24,500	114,000	147,000	12,426	24,696
New Jersey	1,400	670	13,200	4,110	1,742	801
North Carolina	28,000	26,500	72,900	86,920	9,623	19,383
Ohio	6,400	3,700	71,200	39,290	9,398	7,701
Oregon	—	2,400	—	29,350	—	4,813
South Carolina	8,700	11,100	24,950	36,740	3,510	8,009
Texas	5,500	18,100	39,850	67,880	5,557	17,988
Washington	—	1,700	—	17,320	—	3,066
Wisconsin	9,400	6,700	58,550	50,850	7,436	9,356
Other states[3]	29,990	18,800	125,200	70,090	17,033	13,507
U.S.	123,990	124,170	628,100	642,690	79,244	131,082

[1]Source: USDA. 1978. Economics, Statistics, and Cooperatives Service (ESCS), Crop Reporting Board.

[2]Source: USDA. 1990. National Agricultural Statistics Service (NASS), Agricultural Statistics Board.

[3]Alabama, Arizona, Arkansas, Delaware, Georgia, Idaho, Illinois, Kentucky, Louisiana, Massachusetts, Minnesota, Mississippi, Missouri, Nebraska, New York, Tennessee, Virginia, for 1989; not identified for 1977.

15% is refrigerated, and 40–45% is brined. Cucumbers for pickling are usually grown under contract, so profits are directly related to yield per acre.

Florida, the Carolinas, and Texas lead in fresh market production. Average yields for fresh market slicers picked by hand range from 3 tons per acre in parts of the eastern U.S. to over 16 tons per acre in California; top yields can be much higher. Fresh market cucumbers produced early in the marketing season are a high-value crop in most areas of the U.S.

Worldwide, cucumbers are extensively grown, with most of the crop used for fresh market. China leads in production, followed by India, the USS, the U.S., and various European countries. In addition, there is some greenhouse production, particularly in northern Europe and Japan, and to a lesser degree in the U.S. and parts of the Middle East.

PLANT GROWTH AND DEVELOPMENT

Vine Types

Cucumber is an annual with a prostrate vining type of growth, which results from the branching of the main stem into several trailing laterals. Three distinct types of vine growth can occur in the plant: indeterminate, determinate, and compact. Indeterminate vines continue to grow until the plant dies, with the internode length relatively constant throughout the length of the vine. Determinate vines have similar internode length as indeterminate plants but their vines terminate in a flower cluster. Compact vines have considerably shorter internodes than either of the other two types. The growth habits of cucumbers are important in breeding programs that utilize different vine types so that hybrid yields might be increased.

Flowering and Sex Expression

Normally, cucumber plants are monoecious, producing both male and female flowers separately on the same plant. The male (staminate) flowers have very short stems and are borne in clusters of three to five. These are located mostly on the main stem, while female (pistillate) flowers are located on the laterals, as well as on the main stem, and can be recognized by the ovary at the base of the flower which develops into the fruit (Figure 17.1). The male flowers are the first to appear and in considerably larger numbers than the female flowers. Monoecious cucumbers generally go through three phases of sex expression: 1) an initial period when only male flowers are produced, 2) a long period when equal numbers of male and female flowers are borne, and 3) a final relatively short phase when female flowers largely predominate.

Female Flower   Male Flower

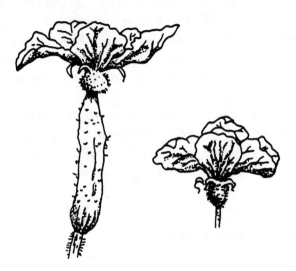

Figure 17.1. The female flower in cucumbers can be recognized by the presence of a miniature fruit at
the base of the flower.

New cucumber types incorporate a gynoecious flowering habit, whereby only female flowers are produced. These hybrids, often referred to as "all-female," tend to be early in maturity, outyield standard cultivars, and produce a concentrated fruit set, making them well suited for mechanical harvest.

Somewhat similar to the gynoecious lines are the predominantly female types, commonly referred to as "PF" cultivars. These hybrids are not completely gynoecious but produce some male blooms. The "PF" expression is more typical of most present-day gynoecious hybrids. The number of male flowers is generally far less than those of monoecious plants but can vary widely, depending on cultivar and environmental conditions. The highly female expression of the hybrid "PF" plants concentrates fruit set so plants are well suited for once-over harvest.

Sex expression in cucumbers can be modified by the use of several chemicals. Silver nitrate and gibberellic acid will promote male blooms on gynoecious plants. The growth regulator ethephon induces female flowering and causes monoecious plants to exhibit gynoecious expression.

Environmental factors can also have significant influences on sex expression in cucumbers. High temperatures and long days favor male blooms, while short days and low temperatures promote female flower development. As a general rule, environmental factors that result in stress to the plant, such as increased plant populations and low moisture, will tend to increase male flowering in "PF" types and will sometimes cause some male flowers to develop in gynoecious lines.

Fruit Set and Development

In monoecious types, fruits are produced progressively at nodes. A developing fruit set at a lower node may inhibit or delay fruits from setting at subsequent nodes. The size and shape of the fruit is usually related to the number of seeds produced by pollination, with each seed requiring one or more pollen grains. In order for normal fruit set and development to occur, pollen from the male flower must be successfully transferred to the female flower. Poor pollination is one of the main causes of fruit abortion, misshapen fruit, or poor fruit set in cucumbers, although other factors may also be involved.

Some cucumber cultivars are able to set fruit without pollination and sexual fertilization. These are known as *parthenocarpic* fruits and are used primarily in greenhouse production. Parthenocarpic fruits do not have seeds, even though occasionally some seeds may be present. In order to obtain normal fruit growth and development, parthenocarpic cultivars must be sprayed with a fruit-setting hormone, such as chlorflurenol. Some newer cultivars contain a gene for parthenocarpy and do not require hormone sprays for fruit set.

CLIMATIC AND CULTURAL REQUIREMENTS

Cucumbers are a warm-season crop, and young plants are easily injured by frost. Average daily temperatures of 65–75°F are most favorable for growth. The ideal growing temperature is 82°F; temperatures above 90°F and below 60°F cause slow growth. High temperatures above 92°F have been implicated in the increase of bitterness in fruit, although there is no data to support this. Conversely, more complaints about bitter cucumbers will generally occur during a cool growing season. The cause of bitterness in cucumbers is more often related to cucurbitacins, which are compounds often found in high levels in wild species.

Cucumbers can be grown on a wide range of soil types, provided they are well drained. A light loamy sand which contains moderate to high amounts of organic matter is best for the early crop. Heavy soils can be used for commercial production, although fruit quality may be adversely affected because of poor drainage. Although cucumbers are fairly tolerant of acid soils, best growth is obtained in the pH range of 6.0–7.0. The young plants are very susceptible to herbicide residues in soils from previous crops, especially triazine residues. Potential growing sites should be checked for herbicide carry-over if the previous cropping history of the sites is not known.

Cucumbers are a quick-growing and succulent crop and must be well supplied with nutrients and moisture for vigorous growth. Fertilizer requirements will vary depending on soil type, native fertility, previous cropping, cultural practices, and yield levels. Machine-harvested gynoecious hybrid cultivars grown for processing, which mature in 40–50 days, require less fertilizer than hand-harvested monoecious cultivars grown for fresh market, which have a considerably longer growing season. The higher plant populations now being used with machine harvest, however, increase fertilizer requirements, so fertility rates for both machine- and hand-harvested plantings may be comparable.

Nitrogen fertilizer recommendations range from about 75 pounds per acre on some heavy, dark-colored soils to 150 pounds per acre for lighter soils. Phosphorus and potassium fertilizer recommendations depend on soil test levels. On sandy soils where leaching is likely to occur, one-half of the nitrogen is applied close to planting, and the remainder is sidedressed in several applications when vines start to fill the rows. To avoid damaging the roots, no more than 40 pounds of nitrogen (or potassium) should be sidedressed at any one time. Where irrigation is used, nitrogen and potassium are sometimes applied through the irrigation system.

The most important micronutrients are zinc and manganese. Deficiencies of these elements are most likely in alkaline soils and under high phosphorus fertility. A standard practice of growers in some regions is to make foliar application of both manganese and zinc 2–3 weeks after seedling emergence.

PLANTING AND CROP ESTABLISHMENT

Cucumbers are propagated from seed and planted when soil temperatures at the 2-inch depth have warmed to 55–60°F, and the danger of frost has passed. Planting dates vary with climatic conditions. The optimum soil temperature for germination is 80–85°F. Planting in very cool soils significantly delays germination, so little benefit is gained from planting too early when soil temperatures are low.

Plant population and spacing depend on the availability of soil moisture and the harvest method. Higher populations are used with destructive machine harvests to maximize yields, but they require more intensive management and grower skill. Pickling cucumbers usually have smaller vines than slicers and are grown at higher populations. With irrigation and machine harvest, populations of over 150,000 plants per acre are used (Figure 17.2). On light-textured soils and no irrigation, machine-harvested plantings will have 30,000–60,000 plants per acre. Plant populations for slicers picked by hand generally range from 7,000 to 20,000 plants per acre.

For hand-harvested crops, the seed is planted with standard corn or bean planters 0.5–1.5 inches deep, and later thinned. Deeper seeding is used on light-textured soils to place the seed in contact with soil moisture; however, too

Figure 17.2. High plant populations up to 150,000 plants per acre, or more, are used with destructive machine harvests to maximize yields, but they require more intensive management and grower skill.

deep seeding may result in delayed emergence and poor stands. Row spacings vary from 30 to 60 inches, with plants spaced 8–15 inches apart. Generally, the wider spacings are used with fresh market slicers.

For machine-harvested crops, precision seeders are used to plant the higher populations, to allow the grower to plant to a desired stand and eliminate thinning costs. Row spacings vary from 12 to 30 inches, with plants 2–6 inches apart. In California, twin-row production on 40-inch beds is used to increase plant populations. The two rows are spaced 12–14 inches apart on the bed, with plants spaced 2 inches apart in the rows. Since there are more plants per acre and more competition between plants, twin-row production requires more precision and closer management.

Fresh market cucumbers (slicers) are sometimes transplanted for early production. Transplants should be grown in specialized containers such as peat pellets or peat pots and should be no older than 3 weeks when set in the field. Special care should be taken so as not to damage roots since this will greatly delay the development of the crop. For early plantings of slicers, row tunnels and plastic mulches have proved very effective in cooler climates for increasing early growth response. A small number of fresh market cucumbers are still planted in hills. With this method, several seeds are planted in each hill and later thinned to three or four plants.

Scheduling Planting Dates

The extensive use of once-over machine harvesting and the need to reduce the number of hand harvests per season make prediction of the date of first harvest important. Processors require a continuous supply of fruits spread out evenly over the season, so as not to have a harvest glut at any one time.

In order to ensure successive harvests, some growers will schedule their planting dates based on the size or physiological age of previously planted cucumber seedlings. As a general rule, later plantings are made when the seedlings from the previous crop have the first true leaf showing between the two cotyledons. This method works reasonably well for the first part of the growing season. Towards the middle of the season, as temperatures rise and growth rate increases, the schedule must be adjusted and subsequent plantings made when approximately 80% of the seedlings of previous plantings have emerged.

Heat unit systems are also used in cucumber production to space planting dates for successive harvests (see Chapter 3). By knowing the number of heat units required to reach first harvest for a crop type and maturity group (early, mid-season, late), a grower can schedule plantings based on heat summations so that one harvest would be finishing as another was about to begin. One system uses a base temperature of 60°F and a ceiling temperature of 90°F. Another system determines heat units by subtracting a base temperature of 55°F from the daily mean temperature. Cultivars differ in heat units required to reach maturity, and some variation may be expected for both location and season.

CULTURAL PRACTICES

Weeds

Weeds must be controlled from planting through harvest for maximum yields and for successful machine harvesting. The most effective weed control program is achieved through a combination of mechanical and chemical methods, along with site or crop manipulation. Fields infested with perennial weeds such as quackgrass and nutsedge or with hard-to-control annual weeds such as ragweed, cocklebur, and morning-glory should be avoided.

Herbicides are used to control weeds when close plantings and high populations make cultivation difficult and where high weed pressures exist. Most herbicides available today tend to provide more effective control on grasses than broadleaf weeds. Usually the best results are obtained by using combinations of herbicides. However, cucumbers are very susceptible to injury from many herbicides, and even at labeled rates of application, the safety margin is relatively narrow.

Timely cultivation can provide effective weed control, where row spacing and vine growth allow. Up until the third- or fourth-leaf stage, close cultivation can be accomplished without undue damage. Once vines start to run, mechanical cultivation should be shallow and not too close to the plant. Hand weed control is sometimes practiced, depending on the size of operation and the availability of labor. When earliness is desired, black polyethylene mulch can be used to increase soil temperatures for fresh market crops, and in the process, control weeds and conserve soil moisture.

Irrigation

Cucumbers require a continuous supply of moisture during the growing season, especially during blossoming and fruiting, when water stress can seriously reduce marketable yields.

Most irrigated production is on sandy soil or on heavy-textured soil in arid climates. Irrigation permits high-density planting and will generally be needed, even on soils of relatively high-moisture–holding capacity, to reach the maximum yield potential as plant populations increase to 100,000 plants per acre or more. Crop moisture requirements range from 15 to 24 acre-inches of water, depending on climate, soil type, plant populations, and market type. On the average, cucumbers need 1 inch of water each week, which may increase to 2 inches per week during hot and dry weather, or if plants are fruiting. In arid areas, furrow irrigation is preferred to reduce evaporation losses, while in humid regions, overhead sprinkler or gun-type systems are used. Where possible, overhead irrigation should be timed to allow leaf surfaces to dry before nightfall. Irrigation should be scheduled so as not to interfere with bee pollination in the mornings during flowering.

Pollination

In most cucurbits, the pollen is rather heavy and sticky, and pollination by insects is required. Honeybees are the principal means of pollination since most other insects are not reliable for adequate pollen transfer. Monoecious cultivars and the newer hybrid "PF" types require one hive of bees per 50,000 plants per acre. When fully gynoecious hybrids become more available, two or three times as many bees may be required. Since no male flowers are produced, these types must be interplanted with monoecious types that produce male and female blooms to ensure an adequate supply of pollen. Approximately 10–15% of the crop should consist of the monoecious pollinator in order to ensure adequate pollination. Seed dealers usually add the male parent of the gynoecious cultivar to the seedlot to serve as the pollinator seed.

Cucumber flowers normally open only one day. Bee activity is generally greatest in the morning up until early afternoon. Wet, cool weather significantly reduces bee activity and is a major reason for poor fruit set in certain years. Overhead irrigation is detrimental to bee activity, and during flowering watering should be withheld until late in the day or at night if possible.

Bee colonies should not be placed in the field before the first female flowers appear. If placed too early, the bees will visit plants in bloom outside the field and will be less effective on the cucumber crop to be pollinated. In experiments with cucumbers for machine harvest, delaying pollination for as much as 12 days resulted in a significant increase in the number of fruits per plant. Generally, colonies should not be set out until about 3–6 days after blooming starts. This ensures that flowering will be sufficiently well along to attract bees and will result in a more concentrated and uniform fruit set. Also, for maximum pollination, bee colonies should have a nearby source of water, preferably within 0.25 mile of the site.

Highly toxic insecticides applied to other crops will kill bees visiting the crop. Bees are attracted to sweet corn when it sheds pollen and are easily killed by carbaryl applied for earworm control. The carbaryl remains highly toxic to bees for several days, since it is mixed with pollen, which bees store in the hive to feed their young. Insecticides should be applied late in the day or at night when there is little or no bee activity.

Contrary to popular belief, cucumbers, melons, and squash will not cross-pollinate with one another; however, cultivars within each species will inter-breed.

CULTIVARS

Cucumber cultivars are usually classified according to their intended use as fresh market slicers, pickles, or greenhouse cucumbers. This classification includes several fruit characteristics such as shape, color, spine type (coarse or fine), spine color (white or black), fruit length/diameter ratio, skin thickness, and surface warts (Table 17.2).

Fruits for fresh market slicing are preferably long, smooth, straight, thick-skinned, with a uniform medium–dark green color. Pickling fruits are lighter green in color, shorter, thinner-skinned, and characterized by a warty surface (Figure 17.3). Fresh market cultivars have fewer spines than processing types. Each type should be cylindrical with blocky ends, although rounded ends are also acceptable for slicers. Greenhouse cultivars should have long, relatively narrow fruits, with rounded ends. Dutch greenhouse cultivars are parthenocarpic with gynoecious expression and high-yield potential, while Japanese greenhouse cucumbers are

Table 17.2. Comparative Characteristics of Various Cucumber Fruit Types[1]

Type	Shape	Green Color	Spine Type	Spine Color	L/D Ratio	Skin Thickness	Warts
Pickling							
Standard	Cylindrical with blocky ends	Lt.–med.	Coarse	White or black	2.6–3.2	Medium	Distinct
Fresh Market							
North American	Cylindrical with blocky or rounded ends	Med.–dark	Coarse	White	3.8–6.0	Thick	Distinct
Greenhouse							
Dutch	Long, rounded ends	Uniformly med.–dark	Fine	White	6.0–7.0	Thin	None or indistinct
Japanese	Long, rounded ends	Med.–dark	Coarse	White	5.0–6.0	Thick	Distinct

[1]Source: Asgrow Seed Company. 1984. *Modern Cucumber Technology*. Asgrow Seed Company, Kalamazoo, Michigan.

mostly monoecious. Unlike those for processing and some slicing, greenhouse types are fairly smooth-skinned.

All commercial cultivars have either white or black spines on the fruit surface, a trait related to fruit maturity. White-spined cultivars are generally slower in their rate of development and retain their green color and firmness longer than black-spined fruits. Cultivars with black spines tend to turn yellow prematurely, especially under high temperatures, and produce larger fruits that soften with maturity. Consequently, black-spined cultivars are used for pickling in regions where sum-

Figure 17.3. Pickling fruits characterized by their cylindrical shape, blocky ends, and warty appearance.

mer conditions are relatively cool. White-spined hybrids have largely replaced black-spined cultivars in warmer growing regions and in areas where once-over machine harvesting is prevalent.

For processing cucumbers, the grower generally has little choice of cultivar since the processor selects and provides the cultivars to be grown. Gynoecious hybrids are grown for just about all machine harvest. These types have also replaced many of the standard monoecious types that were previously used in hand-harvested pickling cucumbers. For fresh market slicers, both monoecious hybrids and gynoecious hybrids are available. Vigor, uniformity, and higher yields are some advantages of hybrids over previous open-pollinated monoecious cultivars. Regardless of how they are to be used, cultivar differences in earliness and disease resistance are also important considerations for cultivar selection (Table 17.3).

INSECTS AND DISEASES

Insects

The principal cucumber insects include aphids, flea beetles, cucumber beetles (spotted and stripped), spider mites, squash bugs, squash vine borers, seedcorn maggots, cutworms, and pickleworms. Generally, all of these will not be serious pests every year. Particular attention must be given to insect activity during the seedling stage when feeding damage by cucumber beetles can quickly defoliate young plants. Early control is essential, particularly with high plant populations. Control of cucumber insect pests can be fairly well obtained by timely insecticide application.

Cucumber Beetles. The striped (*Acalymma vittatum*) and spotted (*Diabrotica undecimpunctata*) cucumber beetles feed on the foliage and later on the fruit. Both can transmit bacterial wilt, and the striped cucumber can also spread cucumber mosaic virus (see "Diseases"). Larvae feed on roots and stems. Both beetles are about 0.25 inch long. The striped cucumber beetle has a black head and black- and yellow-striped wings, while the spotted cucumber beetle has a black head and a yellowish-green body with twelve black spots on its back. The adults appear in the early spring and feed on the cotyledons and new leaves. Rapid germination and seedling development will sometimes allow the plants to outgrow the severity of damage, once vines start to grow.

Pickleworm. This is a destructive insect pest during July and August. The worm is a bright-colored larva with numerous black dots over its body. It is found

Table 17.3. Fresh Market and Processing Cucumber Cultivars

Market Type	Flowering Type	Cultivar	Disease Resistance/ Tolerance[1]	Comments
Slicers	F₁–Gynoecious	Centurian	—	Very early
		Dasher II	1, 2, 3, 4, 5, 6	Early; uniformly dark green
		Gemini	1, 2, 3, 4, 5, 6	Early; short fruit
		Raider	2, 5	Early
		Slicemaster	1, 2, 3, 4, 5, 6	Early; commercial, market, home garden
		Sprint 440	1, 2, 3, 4, 5	Early; large; dark green
		Victory	1, 2, 3, 4, 5, 6	Early; mod. long fruit
	Monoecious	Pacer	2, 5	F₁, medium maturity; deep green; needs spray program
		Poinsett	1, 3, 4, 6	Medium maturity; long-time standard
		Poinsett 76	1, 3, 4, 5, 6	Medium maturity
		Marketmore 76	2, 3, 4, 5	Late maturity; dark green
		High Mark II	2, 3, 5	F₁; medium maturity; greenhouse use
		Sweet-Slice	2, 5	F₁; medium maturity; market, home garden
Pickles	F₁–Gynoecious	Bounty	1, 2, 3, 4, 5, 6	Black spine; long fruit; excellent for brining
		Calypso	1, 2, 3, 4, 5	White spine; dark green; mod. long
		Carolina	1, 2, 3, 4, 5, 6	White spine; medium green; widely adapted
		Flurry	1, 2, 3, 4, 5, 6 (trial)	White spine
		Earlipik	2, 5	White spine
		Peto Triple Mec	1, 2, 3, 4, 5	White spine; widely adapted; strongly gynoecious
		Pioneer	2, 5	Black spine; hand harvest
		Premier	1, 2, 3, 4, 5, 6	White spine; widely adapted; medium green
		Score	1, 2, 3, 5, 6	White spine; medium–dark green

[1](1) Angular leaf spot, (2) cucumber mosaic virus, (3) downy mildew, (4) powdery mildew, (5) scab, (6) anthracnose.

in the southeastern part of the country and in major production areas of North Carolina, but it may be destructive as far north as Michigan and New York. The worms feed on flowers and leaf buds and will tunnel into vines and fruits. They must be killed before they enter the fruits; once they are inside the fruit they will not be found until after the fruit is processed. Weekly insecticide applications should begin at the first sign of damage.

Diseases

A wide spectrum of disease organisms (bacteria, fungi, viruses) can affect cucumbers and cause serious losses. Diseases are best controlled by a combination of resistant cultivars, crop rotation, and preventive fungicide applications. Careful cultivar selection is perhaps the main method of disease control. Cucumbers should be rotated with non-cucurbits for a minimum of 2 years, preferably longer. Following the last harvest, crop residues should be immediately incorporated into the soil. Wet plants should not be worked or handled to help prevent the spread of disease.

Angular Leaf Spot. From the bacterium *Pseudomonas lachrymans,* angular leaf spot causes small, angular, water-soaked or tan-colored spots on the leaves and fruits. The organism overwinters in plant refuse, soil, or seed and is favored by warm, wet weather. Resistant cultivars should be used to help control the disease.

Mosaic. Also referred to as "white pickle," mosaic is a viral disease found in many areas throughout the country. It is characterized by stunting of the plants; mottling, yellowing, and wrinkling of the leaves; and warting and mottling of the fruits. Sometimes plants outgrow symptoms. Mosaic affects other cultivated plants such as muskmelons, squashes, peppers, tomatoes, and celery. The organism also attacks several wild plants, including pokeweed, milkweed, catnip, and ground cherry. It overwinters on roots and seeds and is spread by aphids and striped cucumber beetles. It can also be spread by personnel working among infected plants and then carrying it to new fields. Eradication of wild host plants and control of insect vectors are important in the control of mosaic. Some cultivars are resistant to mosaic.

Scab. Scab is caused by the fungus *Cladosporium cucumerinum* which produces sunken, dark brown spots on the fruits. In moist weather, the spots will be covered with a greenish mold. A gummy substance oozes from the fruits. The leaves and stems may also be affected. The fungus also attacks muskmelons and pumpkins. The disease occurs primarily in the north-central and northeastern states and is favored by cool, moist weather. The organism overwinters in old refuse and on the seed. The best control measures are the fixed copper fungicides, a 2-year rotation, and resistant cultivars.

Bacterial Wilt. This disease is caused by the bacterium *Erwinia tracheiphila* and appears as a progressive wilting of the plant and eventual death. It can be recognized by a sticky, stringy ooze that can be squeezed from the cross section of a diseased stem. The organism overwinters in cucumber beetles and is spread by their feeding on the plant. Dry weather and temperatures of 50–70°F favor beetle migration and feeding. There are no resistant cultivars, and the best preventive measure is to control cucumber beetles with timely insecticide sprays.

In addition to the above diseases, cucumbers may be infected by downy mildew, anthracnose, root knot (caused by nematodes), damping-off, powdery mildew, gummy stem blight, and *Alternaria* and *Cercospora* leaf blights. Downy and powdery mildew are not as widespread as they previously were, since most commercial cultivars are resistant to or tolerant of these diseases. Damping-off is a disease complex (*Pythium* sp., *Fusarium* sp., *Rhizoctonia solani*) similar to that causing root rots in beans (Chapter 13). *Anthracnose, Alternaria,* gummy stem blight, and root knot are also major diseases of melons and are discussed in Chapter 19. Presently, there are no resistant cucumber cultivars for damping-off, gummy stem blight, or leaf blights.

HARVESTING AND POSTHARVEST HANDLING

Fresh market cucumbers are picked by hand. However, for the processing crop, harvest procedures may differ considerably from region to region. In North Carolina, nearly all (90%) of the pickling crop is hand-harvested, while in Michigan the reverse is true, with about 95% of the processing acreage harvested by once-over mechanical methods. Most often the processors will decide the method of harvest. Under some contracts, the processors provide machines and operators, while in others this is the responsibility of the growers.

The slow acceptance of once-over machine harvesting of pickling cucumbers in some areas is generally because the yields do not compare favorably with those obtained by repeated hand harvests. In most areas, however, the cost of labor is making hand harvesting of pickling cucumbers prohibitive. The newer gynoecious cultivars that combine uniform fruit set and maturity with good fruit size are producing better once-over harvest yields. Also, improvements in mechanical harvesters have increased field recovery and decreased damaged fruits. It appears that mechanical harvesting will one day replace hand harvesting for all pickling cucumbers.

For hand-harvested fresh market slicers and pickling cucumbers, fruits are harvested when they have reached the desired market size. For pickling cucumbers this will be at a very immature fruiting stage. Generally, pickling fruits are picked 5–12 days after anthesis (flowers fully open). In warm weather, this may mean a harvest as soon as 32–36 days after planting. By 10–12 days after anthesis, fruits may exceed marketable size (2 inches), especially if temperatures are warm. Fresh market slicers take longer to reach the desired size, and harvest may begin

50 days after planting for some gynoecious hybrids and more than 65 days for monoecious cultivars.

For destructive machine-harvested plantings, a compromise must be made between fruit size and total yields. This is usually decided by the processor. The growers must coordinate harvest time with the processor's capability to handle the crop at the plant.

For multiple harvests, the frequency of picking will depend on the size desired and the weather conditions. Cucumber fruits mature very quickly, especially in warm weather, when they can have a 40% increase in weight in 24 hours. Fruits should not be left on the vine, since oversized fruits will tend to inhibit new fruits to set. Fresh market slicers in the field are generally harvested every 2–3 days. When they are hand-harvested, the growing season in the field may last 100–120 days, or more. Slicers grown in greenhouses may be harvested almost daily. Undersized fruits (less than 0.5 inch) should not be picked. When hand-harvested, fruits should be twisted and snapped off the vine, since pulling results in much vine damage and may uproot the plant.

Grading and sorting of fruit can be done in the field or packing shed. Slicing cucumbers are graded by fruit diameter, length, shape, and color. The fruit should be firm, straight, uniformly smooth, and deep green. The desired length is 6.0–8.5 inches, with a diameter of 1.5–2.5 inches. Standard grades include "U.S. Fancy," "U.S. Extra No. 1," "U.S. No. 1," "U.S. No. 1 Large," "U.S. No. 1 Small," and "U.S. No. 2." Pickling cucumbers are generally graded by fruit diameter into "No. 1" (up to 1.06 inches), "No. 2" (1.06–1.5 inches), and "No. 3" (1.5–2.0 inches). Fruits greater than 2 inches in diameter are called "oversize."

Cucumbers are normally hydrocooled to remove field heat as soon as possible. Fruits ripen rapidly at temperatures above 50°F, resulting in color change from green to yellow. They can be held 10–14 days at 50–55°F and 95% relative humidity. Fruits are subject to chilling injury if they are held longer than 2 days at temperatures below 50°F. Yellowing is accelerated if cucumbers are stored with apples or other crops giving off ethylene. Slicers for fresh market are usually waxed to reduce moisture loss and packed in waterproof cardboard cartons prior to marketing.

SELECTED REFERENCES

"Anonymous." 1984. *Modern Cucumber Technology.* Asgrow Seed Company, Kalamazoo, Michigan.

"Anonymous." 1968. *Growing Cucumbers for Processing.* Asgrow Seed Company, Kalamazoo, Michigan.

Antle, G. G., and C. E. Johnson. 1981. *Slicing Cucumber Graders Manual.* Michigan State Univ. Coop. Ext. Ser. Bull. E-1461.

Binning, L. K., J. A. Wyman, and W. R. Stevenson. 1982. *Pest Control in Commercial Pickling Cucumber Production*. Univ. of Wisconsin Coop. Ext. Ser. Bull. A2358.

Curwen, D., and E. E. Schulte. 1981. *Commercial Pickling Cucumber Production*. Univ. of Wisconsin Coop. Ext. Ser. Bull. A1587.

de Ponti, O. M. B. 1975. Breeding parthenocarpic cucumber (*Cucumis sativus* L.). *Euphytica* 18:101–105.

Hughes, G. R., C. W. Averre, and K. A. Sorensen. 1983. *Growing Pickling Cucumbers in North Carolina*. North Carolina Agric. Ext. Ser. Ag-315.

Motes, J. E. 1977. *Pickling Cucumbers*. Michigan State Univ. Coop. Ext. Ser. Bull. E-837.

Perry, K. B., T. C. Wehner, and G. L. Johnson. 1986. Comparison of 14 methods to determine heat unit requirements for cucumber harvest. *HortScience* 21: 419–423.

Robinson, R. W., H. M. Munger, T. W. Whitaker, and G. W. Bohn. 1976. Genes of the Cucurbitaceae. *HortScience* 11: 554–568.

Seelig, R. A. 1972. *Cucumbers. Fruit & Vegetable Facts & Pointers*. United Fresh Fruit and Vegetable Association, Alexandria, Virginia.

Sims, W. L., and M. B. Zahara. 1978. *Growing Pickling Cucumbers for Mechanical Harvesting*. Univ. of California Div. of Agric. Sci. Leaf. 2677.

Taber, H. G., R. G Hartzler, L. E. Sweets, and D. R. Lewis. 1985. *Cucurbits*. Iowa State Univ. Coop. Ext. Ser. PM-1185b.

Whitaker, T. W., and G. N. Davis. 1962. *Cucurbits*. Interscience Publishers, New York.

18

LETTUCE AND OTHER LEAFY
SALAD VEGETABLES
(ENDIVE – ESCAROLE, CHICORY)

Lettuce, endive–escarole, and chicory are related cool-season crops that can be grouped under the category "leafy salad vegetables." All are grown primarily for their leaves, or more precisely for their tender leaf blades, along with a small amount of petiole and stem tissue, and are used fresh or raw in salads. Although low in food nutrients and food energy, these crops are excellent dietary sources of bulk and fiber. The only one of the group grown on a large scale is lettuce, but commercial production of the others may be significant in certain areas.

LETTUCE

CLASSIFICATION, ORIGIN, HISTORY

Cultivated lettuce belongs to the sunflower family (Compositae) and is classified as *Lactuca sativa*. Under this classification, there are four distinct types of lettuce: looseleaf or bunching lettuce, and three heading types — crisphead, butterhead, and cos or romaine. Each is an annual but differs considerably in form and growth habit.

The garden or cultivated lettuce is closely related to the wild or prickly lettuce (*L. Serriola*), so much so that the two species cross readily. It is widely accepted that *L. sativa* developed from the wild type, although some botanists believe that

341

hybridization may have played a part in the development of both species. Another close relative to cultivated lettuce is *L. virosa*, which along with *L. Serriola* is often used in breeding programs with the garden type.

Lettuce is thought to be native to the Mediterranean area and inner Asia Minor, where it was probably first domesticated along the shores of Egypt, as early as 4,500 B.C. The crop was cultivated throughout the Mediterranean region and was common in much of the Roman Empire. However, worldwide its spread was relatively slow. It was not until the 7th century that the plant was grown in China. Lettuce was brought to the New World by the Spanish explorers and by the 18th century was widely used in the Americas.

Garden lettuce is sometimes referred to, in a generic sense, as leaf lettuce to differentiate it from another type of lettuce known as stem lettuce, or celtuce (*L. sativa* var. *augustana*). This latter kind is a perennial plant grown mainly for its thick, succulent stem, or seedstalk. In contrast to leaf lettuce, stem lettuce is usually cooked for use in stewed and creamed dishes; although on a limited scale, the leaves are sometimes eaten raw. Stem lettuce is not widely grown in the U.S. but is popular in the Far East.

PRODUCTION AND INDUSTRY

Lettuce is one of the leading fresh market vegetables in acreage, production, and value in the U.S., and ranks behind only the potato in each of these categories for all vegetable crops. It is grown commercially in over 20 states and produced for local market and home use in many areas throughout the country. In comparing commercial production statistics for 1977 and 1989, fresh tonnage and acreage increased 34 and 5%, respectively, in 1989, while market value more than doubled (Table 18.1). Because of the constant demand and because there is no way to process excess supply, lettuce prices tend to be extremely volatile.

The leading producing state is California, which accounts for approximately 76% of the U.S. production, followed by Arizona (17%) and Florida (2%). California production is fairly evenly distributed year-round. The Imperial Valley–Blythe area, Salinas-Watsonville, the San Joaquin Valley, and the Santa Maria–Oceano areas are the major growing regions in California. The Arizona crop is grown mostly during the winter and late fall, along with some early spring production, while Florida production is mainly from October to May. Yields in California average 16 tons per acre, compared to 13 tons per acre in Arizona, and 10 tons per acre in Florida. Most of the production in the Midwest is in Michigan (1,100 acres) and Ohio (1,400 acres), while New York (2,400 acres) and New Jersey (2,100 acres) are leading states in the Northeast.

Table 18.1. Harvested Acreage, Production, and Value of Fresh Market Lettuce in the U.S., 1977 and 1989

State	Harvested Acres		Production		Value	
	1977[1]	1989[2]	1977	1989	1977	1989
			——— (tons) ———		——— ($1,000) ———	
Arizona	37,900	50,200	402,050	640,950	61,298	190,130
California	159,700	168,400	2,101,300	2,862,800	303,539	669,895
Colorado	4,300	2,600	50,550	36,400	5,955	9,537
Florida	9,400	8,300	70,250	91,300	18,247	36,155
Hawaii	—	260	—	1,650	—	1,287
Michigan	1,400	1,100	11,900	10,450	2,285	4,464
New Jersey	6,100	2,100	29,850	14,700	5,326	4,528
New Mexico	3,000	2,000	30,000	23,500	5,310	6,251
New York	—	2,400	—	24,600	-	7,134
Ohio	—	1,400	—	8,400	-	4,738
Texas	4,600	2,400	39,350	23,400	6,991	7,582
Washington	1,100	1,400	10,750	20,300	1,591	8,120
Other states	3,980	—	65,650	—	13,954	—
U.S.	231,480	242,560	2,811,650	3,758,450	424,496	949,821

[1]Source: USDA. 1978. Economics, Statistics, and Cooperatives Service (ESCS), Crop Reporting Board.

[2]Source: USDA. 1990. National Agricultural Statistics Service (NASS), Agricultural Statistics Board.

Worldwide, the U.S. leads in lettuce production and consumption. Europe is the next leading producing area, where much of the crop is grown in protective structures, including considerable controlled environment production. Leading European countries include the Netherlands, Italy, France, Great Britain, and Germany. Lettuce has recently gained popularity in Australia and New Zealand, but in many parts of the world, it is still a relatively minor crop.

PLANT GROWTH AND DEVELOPMENT

Seedling Growth and Development

The seed is a dried fruit, or achene, in which the outer layer is made up of the ovary wall, or pericarp. The inner layer is a membrane that encloses the embryo and consists of the seed coat and endosperm. The seed coat is protective in nature, while the endosperm supplies the food reserves to the embryo. By the time the seed is mature, the endosperm is generally used up and the embryo is completely developed. Lettuce seeds have a rest period or dormancy immediately after harvest, which usually disappears within 2 months.

The germination of lettuce seed can be inhibited by high temperatures.

Exposure of seed to temperatures above 77–85°F for 24 hours, in soil or in storage, can induce a dormant period in the seed that may be broken by exposure to cold temperatures. Some cultivars or types are more inhibited at high temperatures than others, but the number affected generally increases as the temperature increases. The butterhead types are the most susceptible to thermal dormancy, while the crisphead and looseleaf types are affected the least. Thermal dormancy in lettuce is believed to be associated with some characteristic of the seed coat or endosperm. When these structures are removed from the seed, the embryo develops normally at high temperatures.

In some cultivars, visible light is required for successful seed germination. Light sources rich in red wavelengths (sunlight) convert a pigment known as *phytochrome* in the seed embryo to a form that promotes the germination processes, while far-red light sources (darkness or low light) convert phytochrome to a form inhibitory to germination. The process is reversible. The cultivar 'Grand Rapids' is very sensitive to far-red light dormancy, while other cultivars are not affected.

The effects of light and temperature on seed germination can interact with each other, as well as with different cultivars, making interpretation of results complex. Chemicals such as kinetin, gibberellic acid, thiourea, and ethrel are used by commercial seed companies prior to shipment to overcome the inhibitory effects of high temperatures and far-red light on lettuce seed germination.

Vegetative Development

Leaf lettuce is an annual which makes approximately 70% of its total growth in the 3 weeks preceding maturity. During the early development, in both looseleaf and heading types, the stem remains quite short, and the leaves are flat or slightly incurved, forming an open rosette. In heading types, the leaves that are formed later curve inwards and become cup-shaped. Each successive leaf curves inside the previous leaf to form a head. The rate of head formation is greatly affected by temperature and generally increases as the temperature increases. If plants start to head prematurely, as is sometimes the case under high temperatures, heads will generally be undersized and poor quality.

Reproductive Growth

When reproductive growth is initiated, the stem elongates, producing a much-branched flowerstalk 2–5 feet tall. With head lettuce, the flowerstalk must break through the head, making the product unacceptable. Reproductive growth may be initiated before the plant reaches a marketable stage, and in heading types this will occur before the head is formed. Premature flowering in lettuce usually takes place when plants are exposed to extended periods of high temperatures, but it may also be induced by long days, or both.

CLIMATIC AND CULTURAL REQUIREMENTS

Lettuce thrives best at relatively cool temperatures, and climatic requirements are precise. Ample sunlight, uniformly cool nights, and plenty of moisture in the soil are essential for well-developed, solid heads. In the South and Southwest, lettuce is grown primarily as an early spring, fall, and winter crop. It can be grown successfully in the summer in northern regions and along the coast in the West or at higher elevations.

Optimum temperatures for growth are 66–73°F during the day and 45–52°F at night. High temperatures, generally above 85°F, are conducive to early seedstalk development and also result in inferior edible quality, including a strong, bitter flavor. At temperatures above 75°F, firm heads are difficult to obtain, and the stems tend to elongate. High temperatures may cause plants to head prematurely, resulting in small, underdeveloped heads. Plants will withstand light freezes, but below 45°F, growth is extremely slow. Well-hardened seedlings will stand temperatures as low as 22°F. As plants approach maturity, they are more easily injured by freezing than when they were younger. Freezing results in the breakdown of epidermal tissues, and injured areas become susceptible to soft rot.

Lettuce can be grown on a wide variety of soil types, depending on irrigation, drainage, and local climatic conditions. The largest commercial acreages are on muck soils, sandy loams, and silt loams. Mucks tend to warm up slower and are used for much of the summer production in the East and Midwest. Sandy loams are used for much of the winter production, while silt loams are best for fall crops when it is desirable to maintain cool soil temperatures. The use of animal manures to increase soil organic matter is declining in practice, due to trucking costs and danger from high salt levels. Instead, growers in western regions commonly use green-manure cereal and legume crops.

Nutrient removal from soils by lettuce is relatively modest, but fertility requirements are generally high because of the plant's limited root system and the necessity for rapid, continuous growth, which is essential for crispness and high quality. Nitrogen is the most important fertilizer nutrient. A crop will remove on the order of 80–120 pounds of nitrogen per acre, but fertilizer recommendations may be higher to account for losses due to leaching and denitrification. Approximately one-half of the nitrogen should be applied prior to planting and the remainder sidedressed later in the season when plants make most of their growth.

A crop of lettuce will remove approximately 12–15 pounds of phosphorus per acre and 120–200 pounds of potassium per acre. Phosphorus and potassium fertilizer rates are based on soil test results and yield levels. On soils that fix phosphorus strongly, up to 350 pounds of phosphate (P_2O_5) may be applied. In many production areas, little or no potassium fertilizer is used, due to high levels of potassium in soils from the high potash content in irrigation water.

Lettuce is moderately tolerant of salts, but in all dry climates excess salts can be a problem. It is estimated that in the Imperial Valley of California each acre-foot of irrigation water applied adds 0.5–1.0 ton of salts. Once the crop is past the seedling stage, lettuce has a fairly high salt tolerance. Lettuce may be grown on some alkaline soils, but for best growth a slightly acid or neutral pH is recommended.

PLANTING AND CROP ESTABLISHMENT

Direct seeding in the field is still the primary method of planting lettuce, but interest in transplanting is increasing. Transplants are used mainly in areas where the climate is suitable but of too short duration for successful direct seeding. While transplanting costs remain high, the introduction of new precision seeding equipment and new seed technologies has markedly improved seed germination. Lettuce grown in greenhouses or other protective structures is usually transplanted.

Seed Germination

The seed is the first factor affecting stand. It must have high percentage germination and vigor. The seed should have no dormancy — postharvest, far-red light, or thermal dormancy. The range of soil temperatures for good seed germination is 40–80°F, with 75°F as an optimum (Table 18.2). At lower temperatures, germination is high, but seed emergence is delayed. The maximum soil temperature for germination is about 86°F, and the minimum around 35°F. The soil should be moist, preferably slightly below field capacity.

Table 18.2. Effect of Soil Temperature on Lettuce Seed Germination[1]

Germination	Soil Temperature (°F)							
	32	41	50	59	68	77	86	95
%	98	99	99	99	99	99	12	0
Days	49	15	7	4	3	2	3	0

[1]Source: Harrington, J. F., and P. A. Minges. 1954. *Vegetable Seed Germination.* Univ. of California Agric. Leaf. 7–54.

Direct Seeding

In the past, lettuce seed was sown or drilled at high rates, up to 3 pounds per acre, and then blocked (removing all plants except small clusters) 10–14 days after planting. As the first true leaves appeared, the seedling clusters were thinned to one plant. However, with this method, thinning costs were high, and the remaining plants were often injured by the hoeing or by crowding. In some cases, thinning costs would make up 50% of the total labor costs for the crop.

Today, precision seeders along with seed coating or pelleted seed are used to direct seed lettuce. New seed technologies, such as osmoconditioning and fluid drilling, are commonly used to improve germination (see Chapter 5). These have reduced seeding rates and eliminated much of the thinning required to establish the crop. Seeding rates have been reduced to 4–6 ounces per acre, and in areas of favorable climate to as little as 1 ounce per acre. In order for the seed to be handled easier and planted more accurately, most lettuce seed is now coated, usually by the seed company. Some growers plant pregerminated seed by fluid drilling. This technique can enhance earliness, time of emergence, percentage of emergence, and uniformity of crops.

Transplanting

The use of transplants is more common in the eastern growing areas than in the western ones and has traditionally been used for the extra early spring crop. Compared to direct seeding, the amount of time needed by plants to grow in the field may be reduced by 14–24 days.

Seedlings are started in greenhouses or other protective structures about 3–5 weeks before transplanting. Plants should be hardened and can be set in the field as soon as hard freezes are over. Transplanting is usually done with a standard cabbage transplanter, which sets the plants to the exact final spacing, eliminating the need for thinning. Newly designed lettuce transplanters now available are used by some growers. Most transplanted California lettuce is by the "Speedling" method, whereby seedlings are grown in cone-shaped styrofoam cells that promote more secondary roots for better plant establishment.

Spacing

Planting distances will affect head development and yields. Close spacing reduces head size and delays maturity but may increase yields. Two plants in one space (doubles) may produce no heads. Looseleaf lettuce, butterhead, and cos cultivars, which produce smaller plants, can be grown with closer spacing than the larger crisphead types.

Systems of planting vary from one- to six-row beds. The most widely used method in the West is the two-row bed (Figure 18.1). The beds are generally 18–22 inches wide and spaced on 40- or 42-inch centers. The plant rows are 3–4 inches from each edge, with 12–14 inches between rows. In-row plant spacings vary, depending on cultivars, ranging from 10 inches for crisphead cultivars to 4 inches for the other types. In eastern and northern regions, lettuce is usually grown in single rows on raised beds or on level ground. The distance between rows may range from 12 to 24 inches, but is generally around 18 inches for crisphead cultivars and 12 inches for other types.

Figure 18.1. Most commercial lettuce is grown on two-row beds and is furrow-irrigated.

Bed height varies with soil type, drainage, and season. Higher beds require more water and take longer to wet. These are generally used in the winter and the spring to provide better drainage and to increase soil temperatures for early planting.

CULTURAL PRACTICES

Weeds

Young lettuce seedlings are susceptible to competition from weeds. The normal practice is to use a combination of herbicides and cultivation. The list of labeled herbicides for lettuce is relatively small, but several selective herbicides against annual weeds and grasses are available. Most acreage is treated before it is planted. Muck soils tend to present more weed control problems than other soil types, since several of the herbicides are less effective on these soils than on mineral soils.

Cultivation is primarily used for weed control. Lettuce plants have shallow root systems, and most of the small roots are near the surface. Cultivating deeper than 2 inches will break off many of these roots and cause serious injury to plants. Cultivator attachments that cut the weeds off just below the surface are usually more satisfactory than cultivator teeth or vertical blades.

Irrigation

For optimum growth and quality, lettuce requires a constant and relatively abundant supply of moisture throughout the growing period. Fluctuations in moisture, especially during the early and later stages of development, are detrimental to plant growth. Too much moisture during periods of high temperatures late in the season can result in loose, puffy heads.

In the western regions, all commercial lettuce is irrigated. The most common method used is furrow irrigation. Sprinkler irrigation is increasingly being used early in the season to help germinate and establish the crop, by preventing soil crusting, maintaining cooler soil temperatures, and leaching out excessive salts. In California, irrigation requirements range from 18 acre-inches of water in the spring and fall along the southern coast to over 27 acre-inches in the Imperial Valley and 30 acre-inches in the Salinas Valley in the summer.

In humid regions, water requirements for lettuce are much less, sometimes as low as 6 inches of water from either rainfall or irrigation for a spring crop. Lettuce grown on muck soils with normal rainfall will generally not require irrigation during the season once seedlings are established. For crops grown on most mineral soils, or on mucks during extended periods of dry weather, irrigation requirements consist of approximately 1 inch of water every 10–14 days before heading and every 7–10 days thereafter. In humid regions, supplemental water is usually applied through a sprinkler system and sometimes by subsurface irrigation on muck soils.

Thinning

Despite the introduction of precision seeding equipment, new seeding techniques, and improvements in seed quality and performance, it is still very difficult to plant lettuce to stand from direct seeding. To compensate for anticipated losses, growers will generally use a slight excess of seed when planting, which later necessitates some thinning. The crop is thinned as soon as seedlings are established, in order to avoid plant injury and to reduce plant competition. Normally this is done when seedlings have their first pair of true leaves.

Most of the direct-seeded lettuce is thinned by hand with either a small hoe or a comparable tool. Because of the expense involved in hand thinning, the trend is towards mechanical thinning. Nonselective types of mechanical thinners have not proven too effective, and selective mechanical thinners using electric, photo, or sound sensors are being developed and tested. These work by having a beam of light, sound, or electrical current interrupted by the plant in the row. The plant is sensed and protected, and the area around the plant is thinned. However, these still are relatively rare in commercial use, and most of the direct-seeded lettuce is still thinned by hand.

CULTIVARS

The crisphead types, or "Iceberg" lettuce, make up most of the commercial leaf lettuce cultivars (Table 18.3). They are characterized by large, solid heads, which usually weigh over 2 pounds and are more than 6 inches in diameter (Figure 18.2). The leaves are brittle and crisp with prominent veins and midribs. The outer leaves are relatively large and medium to dark green in color, while the inner leaves are light in color and tightly folded. These types are very sensitive to heat and may not be adapted to some areas. They tolerate shipping and handling better than other types and make up nearly all the lettuce grown in the western U.S.

Butterhead cultivars, sometimes referred to as semi-heading lettuce, are characterized by smooth, soft, pliable leaves that form a loose head. The veins,

Table 18.3. Lettuce Types and Cultivars

Crisphead	Butterhead	Cos	Looseleaf
Bounty	Bibb	Dark Green Cos	Black-seeded
Calmar	Buttercrunch	Green Tower	Grand Rapids
Climax	Dark Green Boston	Parris Island	Oakleaf
Empire	Summer Bibb	Valmaine	Red Salad Bowl
Great Lakes 659	White Boston		Ruby Red
Green Lake			Salad Bowl
Ithaca			Waldmann's Green
Mesa 659			
Montello			
Pacific			
Salinas			
Sea Green			
Velverde			
Vanguard			

Figure 18.2. A 'Great Lakes' cultivar of crisp-head lettuce.

midrib, and stem are not as prominent as in the crisphead types. Butterhead lettuce is considered to have better table quality and more delicate flavor than crisphead types. Leaves bruise and tear easily, requiring considerable care in handling and shipping. For this reason, they are grown mainly for local markets and often used for greenhouse production. Butterhead lettuce is sometimes referred to as "Boston" or "Bibb," after some leading cultivars.

Cos or romaine cultivars are easily recognized by their long, narrow leaves; upright habit of growth; and long, somewhat loose heads. In some cultivars, the leaves turn inward at the top and the inner leaves become blanched. Cos lettuce is more tolerant of unfavorable weather conditions than either crisphead or

Figure 18.3. A 'Black-seeded Simpson' cultivar of looseleaf lettuce.

butterhead lettuce. Although they are best adapted for local use, some types grown in the winter are shipped to eastern markets.

Looseleaf or bunching cultivars do not form heads (Figure 18.3). They are early, easy to grow, and popular for the home garden. Leaf lettuce is not adapted for long distance shipment and its market life is short. These types are grown primarily in greenhouses in the winter.

Stem lettuce, or celtuce, is not extensively grown in the U.S., and the cultivar 'Celtuce' is the main commercial type available.

INSECTS, DISEASES, AND PHYSIOLOGICAL DISORDERS

Insects

Lettuce is attacked by several kinds of insects. The most destructive ones are six-spotted leafhoppers, wireworms, plant bugs, aphids, whiteflies, and several types of caterpillars. In addition, corn earworms will occasionally attack lettuce during the early stages of growth.

Aphids are the most serious insect pest and can cause physical damage, as well as serving as vectors for lettuce mosaic virus. The caterpillars include loopers, variegated cutworms, and various species of armyworms. The worms hatch from eggs laid by grayish-brown moths. The cabbage looper (*Trichoplusia ni*) begins feeding on the underside of the foliage and eventually develops into a green caterpillar. The beet armyworm (*Spodoptera exigua*) and the yellow-striped army-worm (*S. ornithogalli*) can cause severe seedling damage at the ground by the feeding of emerging larvae. Later generations or older larvae of caterpillars can enter the head, making control difficult. Insecticides give good control if applied early. The bacterial insecticide *Bacillus thuringiensis* is frequently used to control certain caterpillars as a substitute for synthetic insecticides.

Diseases

Bottom Rot. This common fungal disease is caused by the same organism that causes damping-off (*Rhizoctonia solani*). It is most prevalent during wet weather. The plants may be attacked at nearly all stages of growth, and the disease may be present throughout the season. Infection starts at the lower leaves that are in contact with the soil and later progresses into the head. Tissues deteriorate and become brown and slimy. Rotation with crops not susceptible to *Rhizoctonia*, such as sweet corn and onions, is a practical means of control. Growing plants in ridged rows and maintaining optimum fertility also help. Fungicide control measures are not available.

Mosaic. This is a widespread viral disease characterized by mottling of the leaves and stunting of the plants. Early symptoms include badly misshapen cotyledons, and the first true leaves are irregularly shaped and show a green–dark green, blotchy pattern. The disease is spread by aphids and mechanical means, but the primary infection is from infected seed. The use of certified mosaic-free seed and special efforts to control aphids are the best ways of controlling the disease.

Downy Mildew. Downy mildew is caused by the fungus *Bremia lactucae.* Although it is fairly widespread, it is more common in western production areas. The first symptoms appear on older leaves as pale, yellowish-green, blotchy areas on the upper surfaces. On the lower sides, a distinct visible downy or velvety growth occurs on the affected surface. The affected areas enlarge and coalesce. Wild lettuce is a host for the disease organism and should be eradicated from nearby fields. Fungicide sprays and dusts are effective in controlling the disease if applications are started at the first sign of infection.

Lettuce Drop. This is a fungal disease (*Sclerotinia sclerotiorum*) that induces wilting and sudden collapse of the outer leaves. It is particularly common on muck soils during cool periods. The organism causing drop is widespread and attacks many other vegetables, including beans, carrots, celery, cole crops, cucurbits, potatoes, and tomatoes. Loss can occur in transit, in storage, and in market, as well as in the field. No resistant cultivars are available. Crop rotation is recommended with non-susceptible crops such as onions, spinach, and small grains. The newer fungicides may give some control.

Aster Yellows. Caused by a mycoplasma, this disease is a major problem in northern growing regions. Affected plants show yellowing and curling or twisting of young leaves, and later heads may not fill out. The organism overwinters in weeds such as wild lettuce, Queen Anne's lace, and horseweed and is spread by leafhoppers from host plants to lettuce. Insecticides should be used on plants in the field and on weeds in the field and borders to control leafhoppers.

Big Vein. The exact causal agent for this disease has not been identified, although many features of the disease resemble a virus. Symptoms include vein clearing and crinkling and stiffness of outer leaves. Older plants show vein clearing more distinctly, which is due to chlorosis of tissues on both sides of veins. Infected young plants remain small and stunted, and do not produce heads, while older plants make poor-quality heads. The disease is more common in cold, wet soils, during cooler periods. Fungicides and rotations are not very effective in the control of this disease. Some cultivars such as 'Calmar' show some tolerance.

Physiological Disorders

Several abiotic disorders such as tipburn and bolting can affect lettuce in the field. The most common and serious is tipburn, but in some years bolting, or premature flowering and seedstalk formation, can be very severe. Both occur most frequently when plants are exposed to high temperatures.

Tipburn. This disorder is characterized by brown spots along the outer margins of the leaves, which eventually turn brown and later die. The affected tissues show internal breakdown and have low levels of calcium, even though calcium levels in the soil may be quite high. The disorder is more prevalent in hot weather and in periods when plants are growing rapidly. Factors that tend to check the growth rate serve to reduce the amount of injury. Irrigation and foliar calcium sprays may also help reduce the severity of the disorder. Some progress has been made in breeding resistant cultivars. The crisphead cultivars generally have more tolerance than the other lettuce types.

Bolting. Lettuce plants exposed to warm weather (usually above 85°F) are very prone to flower prematurely, making the heads unmarketable. Sometimes the heads may appear normal, but they have an elongated core and stem inside. Long days may induce premature flowering and seedstalk formation, as do most environmental stresses, including hot, dry weather. The crisphead cultivars 'Empire,' 'Ithaca,' and 'Great Lakes 659' are more resistant, but given the proper environmental conditions, most cultivars will bolt.

HARVESTING AND POSTHARVEST HANDLING

Crisphead lettuce should be harvested when the heads are full and firm. Immature heads are spongy and will not withstand shipping and handling. Sometimes the home gardener harvests head lettuce before the heads are fully mature. Butterhead and cos types can be picked as full heads or in the semi-heading stage. Leaf lettuce is harvested as soon as the leaves are large enough, but before they become tough and bitter.

The time required from planting to harvest may differ widely, depending on cultivar, region, and seasonal adaptation. The crisphead types will take considerably longer to reach maturity than other types. When planted in the early spring these will require 70–120 days to reach maturity, compared to 55–70 days for butterhead and cos cultivars and 40–50 days for looseleaf types. However, hot weather will cause all types of lettuce to mature earlier.

Most commercial fields are hand-harvested only once, normally when most of the plants have reached the desired stage. Lettuce is cut with a knife at or slightly below the soil surface. Soiled and diseased leaves are removed before the lettuce is packed. Practically all of the crop is now field packed (Figure 18.4) and vacuum cooled. This has eliminated the need for direct icing and made it possible to use paperboard cartons, which hold two dozen heads drypacked (Figure 18.5). The cartons are mechanically placed in precooling chambers and then transported to a central vacuum cooler, where the temperature at the center of each head of lettuce can be reduced to 34°F in less than 30 minutes. The cooled cartons are placed in precooled refrigerator cars and trucks for shipment to market. Harvest crews, equipment, and coolers are very often provided by the shipper.

Figure 18.4. The crop is hand-harvested, but various types of machinery aid in field packing.

If the crop is in good condition at the beginning of the storage period, and is held at 32°F and high humidity, head lettuce may be kept in cold storage for a period of 3–4 weeks. Looseleaf types respire at about twice the rate of head lettuce and their storage life under optimum conditions is reduced proportionally. Raising storage temperatures to 37°F reduces lettuce storage life by approximately 50%. Freezing injury to mature lettuce can occur quickly, so storage temperatures should not drop below the highest freezing point of the crop (31.7°F).

Several significant postharvest problems can affect lettuce, either in storage or in transit. The most common postharvest problem is bacterial soft rot, which

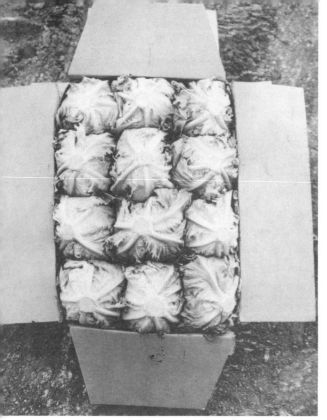

Figure 18.5. A standard lettuce carton contains 24 heads.

results from physical damage and decay of bruised tissue. This is usually not as severe if the crop is stored at 32°F than at higher temperatures.

Another postharvest disorder is russet spotting, which consists of brown spots on the lower midrib of the outer leaves, spreading to the leaf blades. It is caused by ethylene levels in the atmosphere above 0.1 ppm combined with high storage temperatures (above 41°F). The ethylene may be produced by the lettuce itself or may come when lettuce is stored with crops such as apples, pears, and melons, which give off relatively large amounts of the gas.

Lettuce shipped in atmospheres with excessive CO_2 concentrations may develop dark, water-soaked lesions near the leaf base and midrib. This is known as brown stain and is usually intensified when O_2 levels are reduced to around 3%. Pink rib, a pink discoloration along the midrib of the outer leaves, is most severe under high transit temperatures and low O_2 atmospheres. Although tipburn is usually of field origin, occasionally its severity may increase after harvest.

ENDIVE–ESCAROLE

Endive–escarole (*Cichorium Endivia*) closely resembles looseleaf lettuce in growth and appearance. It belongs to the sunflower family (Compositae) and is thought to be native to eastern India. Endive–escarole is commonly used fresh in salads, although it can be cooked as greens. The crop is of minor commercial significance in the U.S., with an estimated total acreage of approximately 10,000. Florida produces about 70% of the crop, followed by Ohio and New Jersey.

The two types, endive and escarole, are very similar. Endive is a loose-headed plant with curled, fine-cut, fringed leaves (Figure 18.6), while escarole is a broad-leaf type or selection of endive. The outer leaves are dark green in color and have a slightly bitter taste, while the inner leaves are lighter in color and milder in taste. However, considerable variation can occur in leaf shape, size, and color; some cultivars develop anthocyanin and will have a red or purple cast. Because of its attractiveness, the fringed-leaved type is more widely grown, and may also be used for garnishing.

Figure 18.6. Curled leaf endive.

The plant is a moderately hardy, cool-season annual or sometimes biennial, which is commercially grown as an annual. It will withstand moderate freezes and is more tolerant of cooler temperatures than lettuce. Rapid, continuous growth is essential for good yield and high quality. Flowering is in response to long photoperiods and low temperatures (vernalization) in biennial types. Long days will also induce bolting, as will most environmental stresses. The plant will produce a seedstalk in hot, dry weather.

The culture of endive–escarole is much like lettuce. Plant growth is best in the mean temperature range of 60–75°F. In most regions, it can be grown as a spring or early summer crop. In the South, it is grown mainly in the winter, while in the North, it is grown in the early spring, summer, and fall.

Commercial plantings are started from transplants, or they may be direct seeded in the field. When seedlings are 1 inch high, they should be thinned or transplanted to 8–12 inches apart. Crowding of plants will cause some blanching of the center leaves, which may be desirable to reduce bitterness associated with dark green leaves. Tying the leaves loosely together over the top of the plant or using some other method to exclude light for 1–2 weeks prior to harvest will result in blanching.

Most cultivars are ready for harvest within 80–100 days, usually when the blanched heads are well developed. Harvesting involves cutting the plants off at the soil surface and then removing diseased, discolored, and / or damaged leaves. The outer leaves are often tough and bitter and may be discarded. The methods used for rapid cooling and handling of lettuce can also be used for endive–escarole.

Cultivars of the fringed-leaf type include 'Green Curled' and 'Salad King.' Some broadleaf cultivars are 'Florida Deep Heart,' 'Broad Leaved Batavian,' and 'Full Heart Batavian.'

CHICORY

Chicory (*Cichorium Intybus*), also known as French endive, Belgium endive, witloof, and succory, is a member of the sunflower family (Compositae) and is native to the Mediterranean region. Although it is a popular crop in Europe, it has limited commercial production in the U.S. The plant has several uses and may be grown for both its roots and tops. The leaves may be used fresh for salads or cooked as greens. The roots can be roasted and ground and used as a coffee adulterant or substitute.

The major part of the commercial crop in the U.S. is grown for forcing. A compact, leafy, terminal bud, called a *chicon* (Figure 18.7), is produced by forcing its growth under controlled conditions from roots previously grown in the field (Figure 18.8). This type of chicory is referred to as witloof or French / Belgium endive and is very popular in northern Europe.

The various types of chicory are similar to endive in growth and appearance. There are annual and biennial forms. The plant produces an open rosette of leaves from a short stem, but some types will form a head when mature while others will remain open. Similar to endive, chicory has a distinctive bitter taste.

The culture of chicory when used for greens is much like that of lettuce and endive. Seeds are sown in the spring in drills 15–18 inches apart. When the plants are established, around the time they have one or two leaves, they are thinned to 6–8 inches apart in the rows. Hot weather will cause seedstalks to form. The tops are usually harvested 60–70 days from planting, when the leaves are about 6–8 inches long. Two to three weeks before harvest, the outermost leaves may

Figure 18.7. Forced chicory is grown for its compact, leafy bud known as a *chicon*.

Figure 18.8. Chicory roots to be forced are grown in the field the previous season.

be tied loosely over the tops of the plants, in the same manner as endive, to reduce the bitter taste.

When the roots are to be used for forcing, the seeds should not be planted too early, otherwise the roots may grow too large or the plants may develop seedstalks, making them unsuitable for forcing. The roots are harvested at the end of the growing season and the tops removed, leaving the growing point of the stem still attached. They are then placed in cold storage (32-40°F) under high humidity for several weeks to vernalize the buds.

The roots are forced in greenhouses, cellars, forcing beds, or other suitable structures. After they are removed from cold storage, the roots are placed tightly together in soil, sand, peat, or hydroponic media. Light is excluded during forcing, which reduces the bitterness and prevents the leaves in the chicon from expanding. Forcing temperatures range from 54 to 68°F. If possible, maintaining cooler temperatures around the tops than the roots will help keep the developing bud tight and compact. The chicons are ready for harvest in about 30 days when they are creamy yellow with tightly folded leaves and about 3–5 inches in length. The chicons are cut off at the base from the roots and handled much the same way as lettuce, while the roots are discarded.

SELECTED REFERENCES

"Anonymous." 1985. *Integrated Pest Management for Cole Crops and Lettuce*. Univ. of California Div. ANR. Pub. 3307.

Gage, M. B., and T. E. Eltzroth. 1983. *1983: The Year of the Lettuce Factsheet*. National Garden Bureau, Willowbrook, Illinois.

Montelaro, J. 1977. *Lettuce and Endive*. Univ. of Florida Coop. Ext. Ser. Circ. 123C.

Pew, W. D. 1977. *Growing Head Lettuce in Arizona*. Univ. of Arizona Coop. Ext. Ser. Bull. A87.

Ryder, E. J. 1986. Lettuce Breeding, pp. 436–472. In: M.J. Bassett (ed.). *Breeding Vegetable Crops*. AVI Publishing Co., Westport, Connecticut.

Ryder, E. J. 1979. *Leafy Salad Vegetables*. AVI Publishing Co., Westport, Connecticut.

Ryder, E. J., and T. W. Whitaker. 1980. The Lettuce Industry in California: A Quarter Century of Change, 1954–1979, pp. 164–207. In: J. Janick (ed.). *Horticultural Reviews*. AVI Publishing Co., Westport, Connecticut.

Schoenemann, J. A., L. K. Binning, J. A. Wyman, E. E. Schulte, and W. R. Stevenson. 1982. *Commercial Lettuce Production*. Univ. of Wisconsin Coop. Ext. Ser. A2340.

Seelig, R. A. 1970. *Lettuce. Fruit & Vegetable Facts & Pointers*. United Fresh Fruit and Vegetable Association, Alexandria, Virginia.

Whitaker, T. W., E. J. Ryder, V. E. Rubatsky, and P. V. Vail. 1974. *Lettuce Production in the United States*. USDA Agric. Handbook No. 221.

Zandstra, B. H., D. D. Warncke, and M. L. Lacy. 1983. *Lettuce*. Michigan State Univ. Coop. Ext. Ser. Bull. E-1746.

19

MELONS — MUSKMELONS, WATERMELONS, AND HONEYDEWS

W. H. Shoemaker*

Melons are members of the gourd family of vegetables, the Cucurbitaceae, also known as the vine crops. There are numerous different types of melons, with the principal ones being muskmelons, watermelons, and honeydews. Other types include cantaloupes, casabas, Persians, and crenshaws. Although there is much diversity among melons, plant habit and culture are very similar. All are warm-season crops and very susceptible to cold injury. Most of the commercial supply is produced in warm areas with long growing seasons, but melons of some type can usually be found in the home garden in nearly all regions of the U.S.

CLASSIFICATION, ORIGIN, HISTORY

Muskmelons and other melons classified as *Cucumis Melo* (honeydews, casabas, cantaloupes, Persians) are treated here as the common melons, to differentiate them from watermelons, which belong to a different genus and species. The melons of *C. Melo* have the ability to cross freely, making classification difficult.

---

*Horticulturist, University of Illinois

There are several subdivisions of the species *C. Melo*, with the Reticulatus group and the Inodorus group the most important in the U.S. The Reticulatus group (*C. Melo*, Reticulatus group) includes all melons with netting. They are also characterized by having a thick, orange flesh, a musky, fragrant odor, and a stem which separates from the fruit at full maturity. Members of this group are the muskmelon (the name describes the aroma) and Persian melon (Figure 19.1). The common use of the term *cantaloupe* for melons in this group by the public and by industry is a misnomer, as the "true" cantaloupe belongs to a different subdivision (*C. Melo*, Cantalupensis group), and few are grown in North America. Although its flesh is somewhat similar to that of the netted melons, the "true" cantaloupe has a medium-sized fruit, with a hard, rough-warty rind, but is not netted.

Figure 19.1. Muskmelons belong to the Reticulatus group, which is characterized by fruits with netting.

Melons in the Inodorus group (*C. Melo*, Inodorus group) include honeydews, casabas, crenshaws, Juan Canaries, and a few others. The flesh of these melons is either white or green, the skin brightly colored, smooth, and covering a hard rind (Figure 19.2). These melons do not have a stem that separates from the fruit, so they are cut from the vine at harvest. This group is sometimes referred to as "winter melons."

The origin of these melons is not well understood, as wild predecessors have not been found. It is believed that their origin may be western Africa or the Middle

Figure 19.2. Melons in the Inodorus group have smooth fruits that cover a hard rind, such as these honey-dews.

East. Dispersal was very early, and historical records are inconclusive. The development of many subdivisions that freely cross indicates a long period of selection.

The introduction of melons into North America appears to have been as early as the 1600's. These probably were muskmelons. As the colonists moved west, melon seed advanced with them. At the beginning of the 20th century, Rocky Ford, Colorado, and Vincennes, Indiana, were major production areas that shipped melons east by rail. At that time honeydew melons were introduced from France to Rocky Ford. The dry climate and long growing season in the West allowed for successful production of those types. Later, California became the major production area for melons because of its superior climate.

Watermelons are classified as *Citrullus lanatus*. The origin of the watermelon is thought to be tropical Africa, although early French explorers recorded the production of watermelons by the Indians in the Illinois River Valley in the early 1600's. These were probably citron melons, closely related to watermelons.

Because of its tropical origin, the watermelon grows well where seasons are warm and long. It is more tolerant of humid conditions than the muskmelon and has traditionally been produced commercially in the Southeast as well as in the Southwest. It is often grown for local sales in all parts of the country, especially where there are coarse soils which warm quickly in the spring.

PRODUCTION AND INDUSTRY

Melons are very susceptible to frost and thrive in hot conditions, so production is greatest in the southern and western states, especially in Florida, Texas,
and California (Table 19.1). Florida leads all states in watermelon production,
followed at a distance by Texas, Georgia, and California. All other sources contribute much less. For muskmelons and specialty melons, the bulk of production
takes place in California, with Texas and Arizona also contributing significant
amounts. Harvest and shipping take place from May to November for all but a
small percentage of the crop. For the rest of the year, December through April,
a significant amount of production by U.S.-based operations takes place in
Mexico, shipping to all major markets. Other imports, most from the Caribbean
and Central America, contribute a minor amount to the U.S. market.

**Table 19.1. Harvested Acreage and Production of Honeydew Melons, Muskmelons,
and Watermelons in the U.S.**

| State | Honeydews[1] | | Muskmelons[2] | | Watermelons[2] | |
	Harvested Acres	Production	Harvested Acres	Production	Harvested Acres	Production
		(tons)		(tons)		(tons)
Arizona	2,100	15,750	6,500	45,350	—	—
California	21,300	202,350	51,300	387,500	7,800	108,000
Florida	—	—	—	—	42,500	393,150
Georgia	—	—	3,800	7,600	27,200	129,500
Texas	6,500	37,400	17,800	101,350	36,000	170,250
Other states	—	—	6,950	52,750	71,000	334,900
U.S.	29,900	255,500	86,350	594,550	184,500	1,135,800

[1]Source: USDA. 1990. National Agricultural Statistics Service (NASS), Agricultural Statistics Board.

[2]Source: USDA. 1981. Economics, Statistics, and Cooperatives Service (ESCS), Crop Reporting Board.

PLANT GROWTH AND DEVELOPMENT

Seedling Germination and Development

Melon seeds require warm conditions for good germination. Soil temperatures need to reach a minimum of 60°F, with an optimum range of 70–95°F.
Under these conditions, melons are quick to germinate and can emerge in 3 days.
After imbibition, the radical emerges and establishes itself. Development of the
hypocotyl (the stem below the cotyledons) pushes the seed through the soil to

emerge. At emergence, the seed coat falls off, and the cotyledons unfold. Occasionally, the seed coat will remain tight (does not split), and the seedling inside will die. This is particularly the case with older seeds whose vigor is reduced.

At emergence, the root system has already begun to develop its highly branched habit, taking up moisture and nutrients for use by the newly developing true leaves. The cotyledons splay open upon exposure to sunlight and begin delivering photosynthates to the developing true leaves and root system. Damage to the cotyledons during the first week of plant growth will set back plant development substantially. Often the plant will recover but is left weak and susceptible to attack or poor conditions during recovery.

Two stages of vegetative growth take place. During the first, growth is upright. After approximately six nodes have grown, side shoots will begin to emerge from the leaf axils at each of those nodes. Though the leader continues to grow, the development of the side branches begins the vining process, eliminating the upright growth and causing the plant to spread in all directions, particularly where there is no competition. In the second stage, vining becomes established, and the plant begins to initiate the reproductive stage.

Flowers and Fruit

Muskmelons are *andromonoecious*, bearing both perfect flowers (hermaphroditic) and male flowers (staminate) on the same plant. Watermelons are monoecious, bearing only male flowers and female (pistillate) flowers. The first flowers, appearing near the crown of the plant, are male flowers. In several days the perfect flowers or pistillate flowers begin to open (Figure 19.3). The flowers are borne singly in the leaf axils and are open for only 1 day. Melons cross-pollinate, and the activity of honeybees greatly enhances pollination and increases production. Fruit maturity of muskmelons takes place 6–8 weeks after pollination, depending on the cultivar. Watermelons are generally about 10 days longer in maturity.

Fruits of melons vary widely in appearance and flavor. By far the most common melons though are orange-fleshed, soft-textured, from 10 to 12% sugar at maturity with a slightly musky flavor. The exterior is netted (referring to a hard, corky surface in a net pattern) and sometimes ribbed. Fruit shape ranges from globular to oblong. At maturity an abscission layer develops where the pedicel attaches to the melon, allowing the melon to be pulled freely from the vine.

Other members of C. *Melo* may have green flesh, as in honeydew melons, or white flesh, as in Juan Canari melons. The exterior appearance can be smooth-skinned and of a variety of colors and shapes. Often these other types do not develop a distinct abscission layer and must be cut from the vine at maturity. All C. *Melo* fruits have a hollow seed cavity in the center of them. Because of the

Figure 19.3. A female (pistillate) flower shortly after fruit set.

close genetic relationship shared by those types, they are crossed freely, and most mixes of characteristics are possible.

Watermelon fruits are very different from those of C. Melo. They are covered with a smooth, hard rind, enclosing a crisp, very juicy flesh. The exterior of the fruits may range from light to dark green and may be striped. The flesh is usually red, although yellow- and orange-colored types are available. The flesh is very sweet, measuring up to 14% brix (soluble solids) at full maturity. Fruit shape ranges from globular types to very elongated types. Fruits may range in weight from 2 to 50 pounds. There is no seed cavity. Normally, each vine will mature one or two full-sized fruits. If more than two melons mature, fruits will usually be small and of poor quality.

Melons have a highly branched taproot system. For muskmelons the roots can grow 18–36 inches deep. Watermelon roots may reach up to 60 inches in depth.

Seedless Watermelons

The seedless watermelon is a modern development with a very limited, albeit growing, niche in the market. Wholesalers are finding a ready market in the service industry, especially among restaurants that are looking for high quality and are less concerned about cost.

The seedless trait is a result of crossing a diploid (2n) parent with a tetraploid (4n) parent. The seed of the fruit from the female parent is a triploid (3n). The plant grown from that seed is unable to develop zygotes; hence, no seed development occurs. However, with pollination from a diploid cultivar, the triploid plant's flowers will set fruit, resulting in a seedless condition. The fruit will contain empty, white pericarps, or seed coats, that should not be confused as seeds (Figure 19.4). Seedless watermelon production is expensive and difficult, a risk that many growers are reluctant to take.

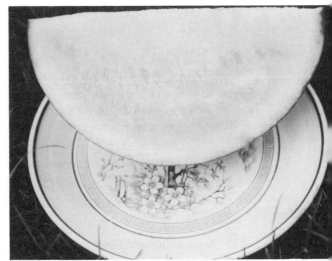

Figure 19.4. Seedless watermelon fruit; note the small, empty seed coats.

Pollination

Thorough pollination is essential to proper fruit development of all melons. Inadequate pollination can result in fruit abortion or distortion of the mature fruit. Growers who rely on natural insect populations to pollinize their crops will not reach maximum production or quality. The size of mature fruit is dependent on the number of fully developed seeds inside the fruit, which is a function of pollination. The more thorough the pollination, the greater the size of the fruit. Growers should provide one or two strong hives of honeybees per acre, centered on blocks of 4 acres.

CLIMATIC AND CULTURAL REQUIREMENTS

Watermelons, muskmelons and other *C. Melo* have similar climatic and cultural requirements. Melons are heat-loving crops and are very susceptible to frost. They need a long growing season of relatively high temperatures. Air temperatures for good melon vegetative growth range from 65 to 90°F. Muskmelons do better at the lower end of the scale (65–75°F), whereas watermelons thrive in warm temperatures (70–85°F).

Though they are somewhat tolerant of short periods of drought, the best production occurs when moisture levels are adequate. The total moisture needed for good melon production is about 15 inches of water per crop. Plants do poorly where excessive moisture and poor drainage are combined. In parts of the country where there is adequate rainfall, melons are usually grown in sandy soils, providing good drainage.

Soils and Fertility

Though melons can thrive in most soils, producers have long known the advantages of growing melons in sandy soils. The chief advantage seems to be the ability of sandy soils to warm quickly in the spring, getting the plants off to a quick start. The vegetative canopy spreads over the soil surface quickly, reducing weed competition and generating more leaf tissue, which provides more support for developing fruit. Sandy soils drain faster, preventing waterlogging and reducing fruit rot diseases.

Melons are not especially heavy feeders, which allows them to thrive in less fertile soils. Still, they respond well to nitrogen fertilization. A moderate sidedressing of nitrogen (25–30 pounds of nitrogen per acre) in addition to the preplant application is important at the time of vine initiation for promoting vegetative growth. Though growers often avoid heavy vine growth to aid harvest operations, good vegetative growth is fundamental to the productivity and quality in melons. Banding phosphate (P_2O_5) and potash (K_2O) works well because of the wider row spacing in melons than in most other vegetable crops.

Watermelons and muskmelons differ in their response to soil pH. Though muskmelons are sensitive to acidic soils, preferring a pH range of from 6.0 to 6.8, watermelons tolerate acidic conditions fairly well and can be grown in a pH range of 5.5 to 6.8. Often, watermelons will be found near the end of a rotation pattern, just before liming is scheduled.

PLANTING AND CROP ESTABLISHMENT

Most of the commercial crop is direct seeded in the field, but for small acreages or where the growing season is short, melons are often started as transplants in the greenhouse or other protective structure.

Direct Seeding

Soil temperatures need to be warm. For watermelons, soil temperatures can range from 70° to 95°F, with 95°F being the optimum temperature for seed germination. The best range of soil temperatures for seeding muskmelons and other *C. Melo* is 77–90°F, with an optimum of 90°F. The minimum soil temperature for adequate germination and uniformity for all melons is 60°F.

Melons are large-seeded crops and the seed can be planted from 0.5 to 1.0 inch deep on heavy soils and from 1.0 to 2.0 inches on light soils. The seeds are drilled at row spacings of 5–8 feet apart for muskmelons (Figure 19.5) and 6–10 feet apart for watermelons. After thinning, in-row spacings are 12–24 inches for muskmelons and 24–36 inches for watermelons.

Figure 19.5. A production field of muskmelons close to maturity.

Transplants

Melons are grouped with those vegetables that require special care when transplanting (see Table 5.4). Transplants should be grown in individual containers such as peat pots, which are planted directly in the ground, or in large plug trays. Container sizes range from 1.5 to 4.0 inches in diameter.

Greenhouse temperatures of 65–75°F during the day are optimum for growing transplants. For seedless watermelons, the temperatures should be 10 degrees warmer. Plants should not be overwatered. The production of transplants takes place quickly, in about 3 weeks, and plants should not be held in the greenhouse past the three-leaf stage. Before being set in the field, melon transplants need to be "hardened off," or slowly adjusted to outside temperatures and wind.

Setting transplants in the field is usually done by machine. Workers sit on the machine and place the transplants in cups which set the plants. The machine then applies starter solution and firms the soil around the plants. A number of machines that vary in the functions they can perform, for example, planting through plastic, are available.

CULTURAL PRACTICES

Plastics

Because of their affinity for high temperatures, melons are perhaps the most responsive vegetable crop to the use of plastics in the field. The use of plastic mulch is commonplace in most melon growing areas, especially in the North. Because plastics generate extra heat, melons respond faster, resulting in more prolific early growth, greater productivity, earlier harvest, and sometimes larger fruit. As the season advances, the advantages of plastic mulch decrease due to the consistent warm temperatures in bare soil. Plastic mulch does not provide frost protection. When plastic mulch is used, wider-row spacing and closer in-row spacing reduces the cost of mulch without reducing population or production potential.

Melons also respond well to the use of plastic tunnels (see Chapter 8), although the results may not be as consistent as with plastic mulch. Higher material and establishment costs, as well as a greater requirement for intensive management, make row tunnels an expensive endeavor. However, early melons are high-value crops, and if managed properly, tunnels can provide greater dividends than plastic mulch alone.

Weed Control

Weed populations can have a significant impact on melon production. The upright growth of many weeds quickly shades out melons, which have a spreading habit. Therefore, control of weed interference is essential to good melon production. Planting in fields in which weed populations are low is a good start. A few herbicides are labeled for melon production, and proper use of these materials can provide selective control of weeds. Plastic mulch will provide weed control in the rows. The use of wide mulch and cultivation between the rows of mulch can reduce weed pressure until vining is well established and a crop canopy is in place.

Irrigation

Because melons are often grown on coarse soils with a low water-holding capacity, irrigation is important. Early in the season, especially if transplanted, the plants have very little root system established and are particularly susceptible to drying conditions. For proper fruit development melons require a consistent moisture supply throughout the season. Water requirements increase as plants come into full bloom and once fruit set has occurred. In California, water requirements for muskmelons vary from 18 inches of water in the inland valleys to 24 inches of water in the Imperial Valley. In Arizona, early muskmelons require about 20 inches of water, compared to 17 inches for a fall crop. Watermelons are more drought-tolerant than muskmelons. Growers in California will generally apply about 15 inches of water to watermelons in a season.

A number of types of irrigation systems can be and are used in melon production. Examples include furrow, sprinkler, and drip irrigation (see Chapter 8). System choice usually involves a whole-farm strategy rather than a system chosen for a crop. However, with wide rows a grower can gain a distinct advantage from using drip irrigation, especially under plastic mulch. Much less drip tubing is needed to supply the crop with adequate water, and less of the field needs to be irrigated.

CULTIVARS

The choice of cultivars for melon production rests largely on the preference of the markets and secondarily on the grower's cultural practices. For instance, in the West the muskmelon of choice is non-ribbed and very heavily netted, weighing 3–5 pounds. In the Midwest and East, muskmelons have distinct ribs, are less heavily netted, and can range from 4 to 8 pounds in weight. This difference has led to the western types of muskmelons being called cantaloupes or "western shipping melons." Though this is botanically incorrect, the practice is well established in the marketplace.

In selecting cultivars, growers must consider disease resistance. In the East, Midwest, and South, there is considerable disease pressure due to high humidity and plentiful rainfall. In many areas where melons have been grown, cultivars without *Fusarium* wilt resistance should not be used.

Muskmelons are common throughout the U.S., but there are other types of melons in the C. *Melo* species that are grown primarily in the West. The crenshaw melon is a large, smooth-skinned cultivar with orange flesh that has a long season. Though grown regionally in other parts of the country, it has poor disease resistance and is difficult to grow. It is shaped like a fig and becomes large, often in excess of 10 pounds. It is very hollow and should be handled gently. Maturity is from 110 to 125 days.

Casaba melons are white-fleshed, globular fruits with a pointed stem-end. The plants are vigorous and coarse with deeply lobed leaves. The fruit color is golden yellow, and the surface of the fruit is hard and covered with longitudinal wrinkles. No abscission layer forms between the stem and the fruit, and maturity takes from 110 to 125 days. Like crenshaws, casabas are susceptible to several foliar diseases.

Persian melons belong in the Reticulatus group but are grown much like other specialty melons. They are globular, lightly netted fruits with a grayish-green color that lightens at maturity. The fruit is orange-fleshed and large (4–7 pounds). An abscission layer will form at full maturity, but for shipping the melons are cut from the vine for earlier harvest. Maturity is from 100 to 110 days.

Honeydew melons are large (4–7 pounds), green-fleshed fruit with a creamy white rind. The rind is smooth-skinned and hard. The plants are also susceptible to foliar diseases. No abscission layer forms at maturity, which occurs about 110–115 days from planting.

INSECTS AND DISEASES

For the melon grower, perhaps the greatest obstacle to producing an abundant, high-quality crop is the struggle against insects and diseases. Soil-borne and foliar fungal diseases are an ever-present threat to plant health, while control of the cucumber beetle seems to be a constant challenge. Although total crop loss is always a possibility, the lack of adequate pest control is more likely to result in reduced plant population, fruit size, and / or quality.

Insects

Striped Cucumber Beetle. The striped cucumber beetle (*Acalymma vittatum, trivittatum*) may be the most serious pest of melon crops in North America. The beetle is attracted to melon plants by cucurbitacin, a compound found in all cucurbits. It will feed on plant tissue and can be especially destructive on young or newly emerged plants. It also is a vector for bacterial wilt (see "Diseases") and some viral diseases. In all parts of the country but the West, the beetle is yellow with black stripes, approximately 0.2–0.3 inch long, and is black on the underside. In the West it is green and black. Control of this insect can be accomplished with the help of several insecticides.

Melon Aphids. Melon aphids (*Aphis gossypii*) congregate in large numbers on the undersides of newer leaves. They are small, green lice that suck sap from the plants and leave honeydew, a sticky exudate that serves as a substrate for molds. High populations can reduce plant vigor or even result in plant death. Selective use of insecticides can control these pests.

Pickleworm. The pickleworm (*Diaphania nitidalis*) is a serious pest of melons in the southern states. The larvae of this moth burrow into ripening fruits, making them unmarketable. Control is accomplished with the use of insecticides.

Diseases

There are a large number of diseases which can infect melon plants. These include bacterial, fungal, and viral pathogens. In recent years environmental (ozone, pollution) problems, nematodes, and nutrient deficiencies have been recognized as contributing factors in the decline of plant health in melon fields. These point out the need for an integrated approach by the growers for maintaining plant health.

For melon growers, rotation needs to be a part of that approach. Though resistance to soil-borne diseases is incorporated into many of the cultivars currently in use, a grower can build up pathogen populations in the field without rotation, contributing to the selection of resistant races of those diseases. The use of rotation, resistance, clean seed, sanitation, control of hosts and vectors, and discriminate use of pesticides all contribute to good plant health and successful production.

Bacterial Wilt. Muskmelons are very susceptible to this disease (*Erwinia tracheiphila*), while watermelons seem somewhat tolerant of it, though they can be infected artificially. Symptoms include the wilting of a few leaves near the end of a vine, then the collapse of the whole vine, and eventually the collapse and death of the whole plant. Often this occurs just as the fruits are nearing maturity. The pathogen is transmitted to the plant by the cucumber beetle during feeding on the plant early in the season. The bacteria enter the wounds from feces left on the plant by the beetle, take up residence in the vascular system of the plant, and eventually build up populations to the point that the vascular system is clogged. Once the plant is infected, there is no control. The beetle, as vector, must be eradicated to control the disease.

Fusarium Wilt. *Fusarium* wilt of watermelons (*Fusarium oxysporum* f. *niveum*) and *Fusarium* wilt of muskmelons (*Fusarium oxysporum* f. *melonis*) are soil-borne fungal diseases. Different pathogens attack each crop but are similar in habit and life cycle. The pathogens can remain in the soil for many years. The plants can be infected and killed as early as the seedling stage. The fungus enters the plant through wounds or cracks in the root system and colonizes the xylem. Once populations are built up, the xylem clogs and the plants wilt. Resistance is the main means of control, especially in conjunction with rotation and the use of fumigants. As several races have emerged, evaluation of cultivar resistance in the grower's fields is important.

Anthracnose. Anthracnose (*Colletotrichum lagenarium*), a fungal disease, can be found infecting all aboveground parts of melons. Foliar symptoms include small, yellow spots that grow rapidly into large, round lesions. Lesions can also be found on petioles, stems, pedicels, and fruits. The fruits will develop large, sunken cankers that make them unmarketable. Rotation and discriminate use of fungicides are important control methods. Some resistance has been found for watermelons.

Powdery Mildew. A foliar fungal disease of muskmelons and other cucurbits, powdery mildew (*Erisyphe chicoracearum, Sphaerotheca fuliginea*) seldom infects watermelon. The disease colonizes leaf tissue during periods of high humidity, appearing first on the undersides of leaves as white, powdery spots, eventually colonizing the leaves. Major control methods are resistant varieties and fungicides.

Downy Mildew. Another foliar fungal disease of both muskmelons and watermelons, downy mildew (*Pseudoperonaspora cubensis*) infects leaf tissue, appearing as pale green angular spots on the upper surface of the leaf. On the undersurface a purplish fungal layer can develop in humid, moist conditions. Again, fungicides and resistance offer the best means of control. Rotation can reduce severity.

Gummy Stem Blight and Black Rot. Gummy stem blight (*Didymella bryoniae*) refers to the stem phase of the disease, and black rot *(Phoma cucurbitacearum)* refers to the fruit phase of the disease. A fungal disease, it can infect the plant at all stages and inflict severe damage, ultimately resulting in death. Watermelons are particularly susceptible at the seedling stage, while muskmelons usually are infected at the leaf nodes of mature plants. On fruits, lesions appear as small, water-soaked spots that grow into large, sunken lesions. The fungus can overwinter in all parts of the country and can be seed-borne. Therefore, clean seed and rotation are important elements of control. Resistance is available, but fungicides are important, even at early stages of plant growth.

Alternaria Leaf Spot. A foliar fungal disease infecting both muskmelons and watermelons, *Alternaria* leaf spot (*Alternaria cucumerina*) appears as small leaf spots on the older leaves near the center of the plant. As lesions grow, concentric rings can be seen as the lesions turn brown. The disease sporulates during warm, humid weather, spreading air-borne spores. Rotation and deep tillage are the first steps in control, followed by fungicide protection. Some resistance is also available.

Viral Diseases (CMV, WMV-1, 2, SqMV). The most serious viral diseases of melons include cucumber mosaic, watermelon mosaic, and squash mosaic viruses. Usually these viral diseases are transmitted by insect vectors, with cucumber beetles and aphids the most serious threats. The symptoms usually develop on new growth and include dwarfing or stunting, wrinkling, and mottling or mosaic of the leaves. Early infection prevents fruit set. Infected fruits can become warted and mottled. The interior quality of fruits on infected vines is unacceptable. A positive identification cannot be made simply by symptom examination. Control of these diseases is accomplished by eradicating insect vectors and alternate weed hosts and by using clean seed.

HARVESTING

The edible quality of melons is closely associated with the sugar content in the fruit. The sugars are manufactured in the leaves and translocated to the fruits. Over half of the final concentration of sugars in the fruit may be accumulated during the last two weeks of fruit ripening. Since there are no starch reserves in the fruit, there is no increase in the sugar content of the fruit after harvest. Therefore, to maximize edible quality, healthy, green vines should be maintained right up to harvest.

Melons should be harvested when their fruits have reached their maximum sugar content. This is normally at full maturity, when the flesh of the fruit is crisp and just beginning to soften and the color is deep and bright. However, market and shipping considerations must be taken into account, and fruits may have to be harvested before they are fully matured.

Determining Maturity and When to Harvest

Maturity of melons differs greatly according to type. Muskmelons and other melons in the Reticulatus group develop a clear abscission layer between the pedicel and the fruit during maturation (Figure 19.6), resulting in complete separation of the melon when the fruit is fully mature.

Figure 19.6. Abscission layer of pedicel on muskmelon fruit.

For the grower, determining when to harvest rests mainly on the specific market. Where melons are direct marketed, the fruit can be allowed to mature to the point where, with a little nudge, the fruit easily separates from the pedicel. This is the "half-slip" stage. Fruit harvested at this stage must be handled gently, cooled quickly, and sold soon. Further maturation will result in an overmature melon.

Some growers harvest a little earlier, at the "quarter-slip" stage, to give them more time to market without seriously reducing quality. At this stage the fruit is just beginning to show a change in color, and the abscission layer has just cracked full circle around the pedicel.

For growers who ship melons, an earlier harvest allows them to handle the fruit more but at the expense of a reduction in quality. Therefore, it is important that the fruit be harvested at the greatest maturity possible to fit into the grower's handling procedure. This can be as late as the "quarter-slip" stage.

For honeydews and specialty melons in the Inodorus group, determining maturity may be more difficult. For most there is no abscission layer that develops. Experience is important, as the criteria used are somewhat subjective. At harvest maturity for honeydew melons, the surface of the melon begins to change color from a lime green to a creamy white. The blossom-end of the fruit will soften slightly (Figure 19.7). At this point the fruit is cut from the vine. With crenshaw melons and other specialty melons, fruit color changes and slight softening also determine maturity.

Watermelons have always had a mystique about them because there is no sure method other than experience, especially with particular cultivars, for determining maturity. Criteria used include the browning of the tendril across the stem from the pedicel of the fruit, color changes on the belly of the fruit, and changes in the pitch of the sound from rapping or slapping the side of the fruit. Growers frequently cut or plug melons to determine the validity of criteria and to familiarize themselves with the characteristics of specific cultivars.

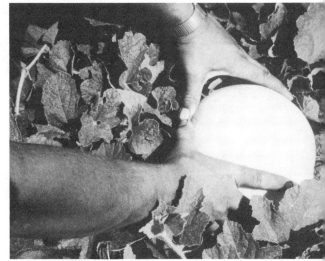

Figure 19.7. Testing the blossom-end of a honeydew fruit for softness.

Harvesting Procedures

Melon harvesting is a labor-intensive procedure, whether it is done on a small scale or a large scale. Melons are picked by hand and then handled in one of several ways for transport. On small acreages the melons are carefully tossed or passed by hand to someone at a wagon or truck in the field who loads the fruit gently. On some farms the fruit may be containerized, as in baskets, at the edge of field lanes before being loaded. Larger acreages use harvest aides with conveyor belts to move the fruit from the picker to the truck (Figure 19.8). In some cases, the melons are windrowed and picked up by a machine which dumps them into a following trailer. The greater the involvement of machine harvest, the greater the need to harvest melons early so that bruising and interior damage do not take place.

Though little field packing is done because of the problems of cooling and cleaning or sanitizing melons, a new innovation which shows promise is night

Figure 19.8. Melon fruits are picked by hand and loaded on the conveyor belts of the harvest aide.

harvesting. Mobile banks of lights are used to illuminate the melons while pickers harvest. This reduces cooling costs and allows pickers to work in more comfortable conditions. An increase in productivity and a decrease in cooling costs offset the cost of energy for the light banks.

POSTHARVEST HANDLING

Cooling is an important part of handling melons after harvest. The postharvest life of a healthy melon is a function of temperature. For growers who direct market or ship short distances, a cooling system may be unnecessary, but significant losses may occur because of unreliable markets and the rapid advance of deterioration. Watermelons have more tolerance of warm temperatures, but all melons need to be placed away from sunlight. Picking as early as possible takes advantage of night cooling and reduces loss to deterioration. Customers will be more satisfied too.

For growers who ship long distance, it is essential to reduce the interior temperature of melons by cooling to 40°F. The methods used to cool melons include hydrocooling, forced-air cooling, and top-icing or package-icing. Hydrocooling uses cold water spilled over the fruits to draw the heat from the melons. Forced-air cooling draws air through containerized fruit to accomplish the cooling. Package-icing involves filling the spaces between the fruits in their containers with ice. A hybrid of hydrocooling and package-icing, slush-icing accomplishes the same thing.

After the melons have been precooled to remove the field heat, they should be held in cold storage until shipped. In general, extended cold storage is little used for melons except to avoid temporary adverse market conditions. Optimum storage temperatures are 36–41°F for muskmelons, 45°F for honeydews, and 50–60°F for watermelons. At these temperatures and 90–95% relative humidity, melons may be held for about 2–3 weeks. However, all melons are sensitive to chilling, and they can be injured if stored for a period of time at temperatures below 50°F.

Ethylene Treatment

Honeydew melons that are not fully ripe at harvest may need an ethylene treatment to complete the ripening process. This can take place at either the shipping or the receiving end of the transport process. The fruits are placed in sealed compartments at 70–80°F and are exposed to ethylene concentration of 1,000 ppm for about 18–24 hours. This treatment is generally not needed for muskmelons and watermelons.

Containers

In the past, melons were shipped by bulk-loading in refrigerated trucks or rail cars. This procedure has changed, and the industry is now turning to containerized shipping.

Watermelons are still often shipped in bulk bins holding from 800 to 1,000 pounds of fruit. However, cartons holding three to five fruits are becoming more common, especially for seedless or icebox types. Muskmelons have traditionally been packed in crates but are now often packed in stylized cartons containing from twelve to thirty fruits. Honeydew melons and other specialty melons are given specialized single-layer cartons containing four to six fruits. Honeydews may also be packed in wooden crates.

SELECTED REFERENCES

Kasmire, R. F. (ed.). 1981. *Muskmelon Production in California*. Univ. of California Div. of Agric. Sci. Leaf. 2671.

Johnson, H., Jr., K. Mayberry, J. Guerard, and L. Ede. 1984. *Watermelon Production*. Univ. of California Div. ANR. Leaf. 2672.

Longbrake, T., J. Parsons, and R. Roberts. 1983. *Keys to Profitable Watermelon Production.* Texas Agric. Ext. Ser., Texas Pub. B-1317.

Morse, R. 1986. Production Methods for Maximizing Muskmelon Quality. *The Vegetable Growers News.* Vol. 40. Virginia Coop. Ext. Ser.

Sackett, C. 1975. *Persians. Fruit & Vegetable Facts & Pointers.* United Fresh Fruit and Vegetable Association, Alexandria, Virginia.

Sackett, C. 1975. *Watermelons. Fruit & Vegetable Facts & Pointers.* United Fresh Fruit and Vegetable Association, Alexandria, Virginia.

Seelig, R. A. 1973. *Cantaloupes. Fruit & Vegetable Facts & Pointers.* United Fresh Fruit and Vegetable Association, Alexandria, Virginia.

20

ONIONS AND
RELATED ALLIUMS
(GARLIC, LEEK, CHIVES, SHALLOTS)

Onions are the main vegetable crop in the genus *Allium*, which also includes garlic, leek, chives, and shallots. The *Allium* genus is classified in the amaryllis family (Amaryllidaceae) and includes about 400 species, with many native to North America. Some species are grown for food, while many others are used for ornamental purposes.

The vegetable alliums are hardy, cool-season crops, most of which produce prominent bulbs, leek being the exception. All are characterized by a unique "onion-like" flavor or pungency. While the onion is the only one of the group grown extensively on a commercial scale in the U.S., the others may be important in certain parts of the country.

ONIONS

CLASSIFICATION, ORIGIN, HISTORY

The onion (*Allium Cepa*) dates back to antiquity. It is mentioned in the Bible and in early Greek literature, and pictures of it have been found on ancient Egyptian monuments. The cultivated species are probably native to central and southwestern Asia, including Iran, Afghanistan, and southwest China. It is thought to have entered Europe by way of Italy, through North Africa. The domestic types were introduced to the U.S. by the early Spanish explorers, and records of the first cultivation of the onion date back to around 1625. The crop was one of the culinary staples of the early colonists, who introduced it to the native Indians.

Onions have many uses and are a major contributor to the U.S. diet. They may be eaten raw, broiled, boiled, baked, creamed, steamed, fried, french fried, and pickled. Onions can also be dried or dehydrated and shredded into flakes.

PRODUCTION AND INDUSTRY

Onions are grown and marketed as two main types: dry bulb onions and green bunching onions. Dry bulb onions are mature bulbs that are usually harvested after the tops have died. Green bunching onions are pulled in the immature stage, when the tops are still green but before the bulbs are enlarged. Dry onions make up most of the crop in the U.S., although on a worldwide scale, the two may be more equal in production. Worldwide, major producing nations include China, India, the USS, Spain, Greece, and Turkey; U.S. production accounts for approximately 7% of the total world crop.

U.S. commercial statistics for dry bulb acreage, tonnage, and value for 1977 and 1989 are presented in Table 20.1. Total acreage and production of dry bulb onions increased 23% and 43%, respectively, while the value of the crop almost tripled in 1989, compared to 1977.

The early or spring crop is produced in the southern and southwestern states and is usually marketed directly, with very little being stored. The late-maturing or summer crop is produced in the northern states and is used for both fresh market and processing. Much of the late crop is put in storage and used over the winter when supplies are lower.

California leads the U.S. in onion acreage and production. Much of the crop is grown in the late summer and used for processing, particularly for dehydration. Texas, which is second in acreage, produces onions mainly during the spring and early summer. Other major late-summer producing states, besides California, include Colorado (13,800 acres), Oregon (13,300 acres), New York (11,200 acres), Michigan (7,900 acres), and Idaho (7,400 acres). Yields per acre in the U.S. are quite variable, ranging from 26 tons per acre in Idaho and eastern Oregon to 10 tons per acre in Texas in the spring and early summer. Since 1977, average yields in the U.S. have increased from 16 tons per acre to slightly over 18 tons per acre in 1989.

Table 20.1. Harvested Acreage, Production, and Value of Commercial Dry Bulb Onions in the U.S., 1977 and 1989

State	Harvested Acres		Production		Value	
	1977[1]	1989[2]	1977	1989	1977	1989
			(tons × 1,000)		*($1,000)*	
Spring						
Arizona	1,400	1,000	31	22	4,644	3,916
California	16,900	7,700	98	154	16,601	34,804
Georgia	—	4,700	—	32	—	17,272
Texas	—	15,000	—	161	—	34,508
Total	18,300	28,400	129	369	21,245	90,500
Summer (non-storage)						
New Mexico	3,200	7,500	52	150	8,008	44,400
Texas	6,800	4,000	94	52	18,420	19,032
Washington	600	1,500	10	26	1,652	9,345
Total	10,600	13,000	156	228	28,080	72,777
Summer (storage)						
California	5,700	—	98	—	16,601	—
Colorado	6,800	13,800	102	276	8,793	58,385
Idaho	5,300	7,400	121	200	9,461	39,230
Michigan	7,100	7,900	105	111	10,584	17,773
Minnesota	840	670	11	8	1,270	1,030
New Jersey	650	—	6	—	973	—
New York	13,300	11,200	203	146	25,367	41,823
Ohio	560	490	11	9	1,151	2,419
Oregon	8,700	13,300	214	336	16,954	67,052
Utah	1,400	1,900	23	42	1,783	6,339
Washington	2,700	6,200	55	140	4,075	26,656
Wisconsin	1,200	1,300	17	24	1,724	3,273
Total	54,250	64,160	966	1,292	98,736	263,980
California[3]	24,500	27,000	423	506	34,220	74,867
Summer total	89,350	104,160	1,389	2,026	161,036	411,624
U.S. total	107,650	132,560	1,674	2,395	182,281	502,124

[1]Source: USDA. 1978. Economics, Statistics, and Cooperatives Service (ESCS), Crop Reporting Board.

[2]Source: USDA. 1990. National Agricultural Statistics Service (NASS), Agricultural Statistics Board.

[3]Source: Summer, primarily processing.

PLANT GROWTH AND DEVELOPMENT

The onion is a biennial plant and one of the few vegetables that is a monocot. It develops a bulb the first year and after exposure to cool temperatures produces a seedstalk.

During germination the cotyledon pushes the embryo through the seed coat. The tip of the cotyledon remains embedded in the endosperm and serves as an absorbing organ through which digested foods are translocated into the growing seedling. The primary root elongates but usually does not form the main part of the root system. This comes from adventitious roots that develop quickly from the stem. The first leaves emerge from a cavity at the base of the cotyledon. The leaves are hollow, tubular structures that emerge from inside the previously formed leaf through a hole in the side of the next older leaf. The stem remains a plate-like structure during the vegetative stage, but will elongate and develop a flowerstalk when the reproductive stage is initiated.

The bulb consists of concentric, swollen leaf bases (Figure 20.1). During the early stages of development, the leaf bases form a slender cylinder. Under proper environmental stimuli, the inner leaf bases swell, forming the bulb, while the outer leaf bases remain thin. Usually several of the innermost leaves fail to develop completely and do not emerge within the previously formed leaf. Should these inner leaves develop in the same manner as the outer leaves, a bulb with a thick

Figure 20.1. Cross section of onion bulb showing concentric, swollen leaf bases.

neck will be formed. As a rule, these bulbs generally do not store well. Buds are developed in the axils of the leaf bases. If one of these is stimulated into growth, a double bulb will form.

As the bulb matures, the outermost leaf bases become dry and papery, forming a protective layer around the bulb. The leaf bases just above the bulb fall over and eventually shrivel and die. Food storage in the mature bulb consists primarily of sucrose. Of particular importance is the presence of a volatile sulfur compound, allyl-propyl-disulfide, which imparts pungency to the onion.

Bulbing in onions is determined by the interaction of photoperiod and favorable temperature for bulb induction. Bulbing occurs above a minimum daylength; and thus is a long-day effect (see Table 3.3). Critical minimum daylengths differ among cultivars, ranging from 12 hours in some short-day cultivars to over 16 hours in some long-day types (see "Types and Cultivars"). Once the critical photoperiod is reached, a further increase in photoperiod will usually hasten bulbing. Short days promote top growth and often inhibit bulb formation.

Bulb initiation is not affected by the age of the plant; however, once bulbing starts, the plant will cease to produce new leaves. Therefore, it is desirable for the plant to have extensive foliage growth prior to bulbing since the size and rate of development of the mature bulb will depend on the size of the plant at the beginning of bulbing.

As a general rule, onions bulb quicker at warmer than at cooler temperatures. Increasing temperatures in the range of 50–85°F will hasten bulbing, provided daylength is favorable. Cold temperatures below 25°F may inhibit bulbing and result in mature plants with very thick and elongated necks.

The fully mature bulb remains in a rest period for about 6–8 weeks, after which further development will begin to take place if environmental conditions are favorable. If the renewed growth is vegetative, a new bulb will be formed. If the renewed growth is reproductive, the growing point will develop a tall, tubular flowerstalk and produce an umbel of flowers at the tip.

Reproductive growth, including seedstalk formation, may be initiated before the bulb matures if plants are subjected to temperatures below 50°F for several weeks. In order for cold temperatures to be effective however, the plant must be beyond the five-leaf stage. Before this size, plants are still in their juvenile stage, and low-temperature induction of flowering (vernalization) will have no effect. Onions grown from sets or transplants are especially susceptible to bolting because they can be vernalized before planting, and also because sets and transplants tend to develop into large plants quickly in the field. Bolting in onions is not induced by photoperiod, as is sometimes believed.

CLIMATIC AND CULTURAL REQUIREMENTS

The onion is a cool-season crop that will grow over a wide range of temperatures. The plant will grow best between 55°F and 75°F. Optimum growth and development occur when temperatures are cool during early development and then warm up near maturity when bulbing is taking place. Above 85°F and below 45°F, growth is poor. The plant is fairly resistant to frost injury, but below 28°F some damage may occur.

Since bulb development is greatly affected by climatic conditions, chiefly daylength and temperature, onion growers must pay particular attention to climate. If a particular cultivar is exposed to daylength photoperiods less than necessary for bulbing, there will be a high percentage of non-bulbous plants. Conversely, if a cultivar is exposed to daylengths longer than required for bulbing while plants are still small, they may be induced to bulb prematurely, resulting in reduced bulb size and low yields. Therefore, growers must exercise care in choosing the appropriate cultivar for their location.

Good onion soil should be friable, fertile, well drained, and have an abundant supply of humus. A heavy soil that bakes and crusts after irrigation is not desirable. Sandy loams and mucks are often used for onion production. Because of their high nitrogen content, good water retention, and ease of management, muck soils are considered best. Soil pH should be in the range of 5.3–6.5 on muckland soils and 6.2–6.8 on mineral soils.

Onions, with their limited root system, respond to fertilizers on most all soils. Fertilizer rates differ widely, depending on soil type and area. Muck soils will generally require less nitrogen and phosphorus but more potassium than mineral soils. On some muck soils, potassium may be a severely limiting nutrient. In some western growing areas, potash may not be needed due to high potassium levels in irrigation waters.

Usually all the phosphorus and potassium can be broadcast and disked in before planting, while nitrogen is applied by various combinations of preplant broadcasting, band application at seeding, and topdressing approximately 4 weeks into the season. Late sidedressing of nitrogen may delay maturity. In California, band placement of fertilizer 4 inches under the row is commonly used for winter production. Although onions are very sensitive to ammonia and salts, there is usually very little damage from banding because the plants do not develop strong taproots.

On muck soils or mineral soils with pH above 6.5, deficiencies of copper, manganese, and zinc may occur. These can be prevented by band application at planting with the respective micronutrient sulfate salt or by several foliar sprays during the growing season. In areas where onions will be grown on a regular schedule, some growers follow a maintenance fertility program by building up soil levels of phosphorus and potassium and then adding smaller amounts of fertilizer each year to maintain approximately 150 pounds P_2O_5 per acre and 350 pounds K_2O per acre in the soil.

PLANTING AND CROP ESTABLISHMENT

Three methods are commonly used to plant and establish the crop: direct seeding in the field, transplants, and planting sets. The latter two methods are used mainly for early plantings when time is a critical factor, but they are more costly than field seeding. Almost all California onion production is direct seeded, but transplants and sets are used in other areas. Many home gardeners prefer sets over the other two planting methods because the plants are quickly established.

Direct Seeding

The primary method used to plant commercial crops of bulb onions is direct seeding in the field. The seed is usually sown on 32- to 40-inch beds, in double rows 8–12 inches apart (Figure 20.2). Single rows on narrower beds (12–18 inches) are sometimes used on sandy soils where fertility levels are difficult to maintain. In some areas, growers are now direct seeding using 4-row, 60-inch beds to cut production costs and to increase plant populations.

Onion seed germinates at soil temperatures above 35°F, but optimum germination is at 75°F. Muck soils, because of their high water-holding capacity, warm up slowly in the spring. To improve drainage and enhance seedling emergence and growth, growers on muck soils seed their onions on 2- to 4-inch raised beds.

Direct-seeded onions generally are not thinned, so uniform spacing by pre-

Figure 20.2. Onions are commonly grown in double-row raised beds.

cision seeding equipment is used. This results in a high percentage of large bulbs. The seed is normally planted 0.25–1.0 inch deep, with the deeper planting used on lighter and drier soils. In northern areas such as Michigan and New York where the crop is grown during the summer, early seeding is important to provide sufficient time for leaves and large plants to develop in the cool spring before bulbing begins in the summer.

Transplants

Dry onions can also be started from transplants, especially for early crops. Medium- or pencil-sized plants are most desirable. These can be grown indoors or in other protective structures and later moved to the fields when the plants are about 6 inches tall. Approximately 8–9 weeks is required to produce good transplants in the greenhouse. Some growers purchase transplants from commercial nurseries in the southern U.S. When using this method, it is important to make sure that the plants have not been vernalized, either in the field or in transit. Before planting, some growers prune back the tops on the transplants to one-half their length to facilitate planting and to reduce dehydration; however, this practice may delay maturity and lower yields.

Due to the high labor requirement for transplanting, starting commercial onions from transplants is costly and is used mainly for early production or for some specific market situation. For example, most Spanish cultivars mature late when grown from seed. In places like Oregon and Michigan, where they are to be used for the early market, these types must be started from transplants in order to obtain early maturity and adequate size and to provide enough time for curing after harvest.

Sets

Sets are small dry onion bulbs produced the previous year. Set onions generally mature 3–4 weeks earlier and tend to yield higher than seeded onions. Commercially, they are used primarily to produce early green onions, but they can also be used for dry bulb production.

Set onions are planted at the same populations as seeded onions. They are planted in a shallow furrow by machine and covered lightly with soil. Although onions grown from larger sets tend to produce higher yields and mature earlier than those produced from smaller-sized sets, they are more subject to splits and doubles and are more likely to bolt. Consequently, smaller sets (less than 0.5 inch in diameter) are used for dry bulb onions, while the larger sets (greater than 0.75 inch) are more suited for green onions, which are harvested before bulb formation begins.

Spacing and Plant Populations

Bulb size and shape are affected by the population density, particularly the spacing within the rows. Depending upon the size of bulbs desired at harvest, in-row spacing will vary from 1 to 4 inches between plants (Table 20.2).

Table 20.2. Seeding Rates and Planting Distances for Onions

Crop	Seed per Acre	Plants per Foot of Row	Spacing Between Rows
	(lbs)		
American or pungent bulbs . .	3–4	8–12	8–24 inches
Sweet Spanish	1–2	3–5	12–24 inches
Green bunching	8–12	20–56 with a scatter shoe	12–18 inches
Onion sets	40–80	solid with a scatter shoe	12–18 inches
Pearl onions	100–120	solid	3–4 inches on multiple-row beds

The sweet Spanish types produce larger bulbs and are planted at wider spacings than the smaller northern storage onions. Wider in-row spacings generally produce larger, smoother bulbs but may delay maturity and decrease total yields, while closer plant spacings produce smaller bulbs but higher yields. For example, optimum yields of pungent yellow bulbs 2.0–2.5 inches in diameter are obtained with plant populations of around 250,000 plants per acre, planted in 16-inch rows with six to eight plants per foot of row. Closer spacings result in higher plant populations, which will generally increase total yields, but the percentage of 2-inch diameter bulbs decreases. Research at Cornell University has shown that to obtain the highest percentage of 2-inch onion bulbs on muck soils, the optimum plant density is 22 to 27 square inches per plant.

Where large- or jumbo-sized bulbs are grown, staggered planting patterns within the rows can be used to allow more room for bulbs to enlarge. Close spacing and overpopulations are not as severe on muck soils, since bulbs can move in the soil when crowded. In mineral soils, bulbs are more firmly embedded and may become misshaped and small if crowded.

CULTURAL PRACTICES

Weeds

Because of their slow growth, small stature, shallow roots, and lack of dense foliage cover, onion seedlings more than most vegetables cannot withstand competition from weeds. Weed pressures anytime before bulb formation will reduce yields. Later in the season, weeds may shade bulbs and keep onions from drying quickly.

Chemical weed control is used extensively in commercial onion production. A good chemical weed control program consists of preemergent grass herbicides to reduce early annual grass weeds and postemergent broadleaf herbicides to control later germinating and emerging weeds. Onion seedlings are very sensitive to injury by some herbicides in the early part of their growth, particularly during the flag stage, which is the period from just after emergence until the time the plant develops three leaves. Application of some broadleaf herbicides after onion emergence or transplanting should be avoided during these times.

Good chemical weed control should eliminate the need for most cultivation, except later in the season when some cultivation between the rows may be necessary. All necessary mechanical cultivation should be shallow to avoid root damage to the shallow-rooted onion crop.

Irrigation

Since the root system is shallow, onions must receive a fairly constant supply of water. Deep muck soils with good moisture retention capacity will produce a good crop without irrigation. On mineral soils, however, irrigation is almost always required. Approximately 15–30 acre-inches of water are needed during the grow-ing season, depending on time of year and location. In drier growing areas and for late crops, water requirements will be higher than in humid regions or for early crops.

In the seedling stage, onions may require approximately 1 inch of water every 7–10 days and 1.5 inches every 7 days during bulbing. When tops start to fall over, irrigation should be stopped. This will allow the crop to mature faster, will help cure the bulbs, and allow the soil to dry out, facilitating undercutting the roots at harvest. Excessive moisture and nitrogen during the growing season will delay maturity and produce bulbs that break down quickly. If the crop is to be stored for any length of time, growers should reduce both.

TYPES AND CULTIVARS

Two different "types" or groups of dry bulb onions are recognized. These consist of the American or domestic onions, and the European or foreign onions, which include the Bermuda and Spanish types. The American types make up about 75% of the dry bulb crop produced in the U.S. and are extensively grown in northern areas. The bulbs are relatively pungent, small to medium in size, up to 2–3 inches in diameter, and oblate- to globe-shaped. Because these types store well, much of the crop is put in prolonged storage for later use.

The sweet Spanish types are large in size (4–5 inches in diameter) and round. These are mainly grown in the Northwest, central California, and Colorado, and are used mainly for fresh market and ring processing. The Bermuda types, including the Grano-Granex onions, are mild-tasting onions which are adapted to the southern latitudes (Texas, New Mexico, Arizona, southern California, and Georgia) for production during the winter. These types are harvested in the spring and early summer but do not store well.

Onion cultivars are classified in several different ways: by skin color — red, white, yellow, brown; by taste — mild (sweet) or pungent; and by shape — round, flat, globe (Table 20.3). Also, since bulbing is a daylength response, onion cultivars can be classified according to the minimum photoperiod required for bulbing: short day (12–13 hours), intermediate day (13–14 hours), and long day (14–16 hours).

Long-day cultivars are adapted for northern growing areas, usually above 35° latitude, where they are seeded or transplanted in the early spring for late summer or fall harvest. Short-day cultivars are adapted for use in areas south of 28° latitude, such as southern Texas, where the crop is planted in the fall and harvested in the early spring. The intermediate types are adapted to regions between 32° and 40° latitude, including central California and the Middle and South Atlantic states. These are planted in the fall for late spring and early summer harvest.

Both the sweet Spanish types and the American types require a long daylength to bulb, while the Bermuda onions are well adapted to grow under the short days of winter. The short-day onions require a long growing season, sometimes up to 180 days, which can be demanding on the plant. As a rule, intermediate- and short-day cultivars require long growing seasons, and in northern production areas should be grown from either sets or transplants.

Today, F_1 hybrids have replaced many of the standard older cultivars in all the major types. The hybrids are vigorous and uniform for bulb shape, size, and maturity and outyield the older open-pollinated cultivars. However, hybrids generally have limited adaptation since they are often developed for a specific area.

Several non-bulbing cultivars of green bunching onions include 'Japanese

Table 20.3. Characteristics of Selected Cultivars of Dry Bulb Onions

Cultivar	Days[1]	Shape	Size	Color	Taste	Storage
Short-day cultivars						
Bermuda Yellow	185	Semi-flat	Medium	Yellow	Very mild	Poor
Crystal Wax	180	Flat	Medium	White	Mildly pungent	Poor
Excel G	182	Semi-flat	Medium	White	Mild	Poor
Granex 429*[2]	165	Globe	Large	White	Mild	Fair
Granex 33*	162	Flat	Large	Yellow	Mild	Poor
Red Creole	190	Semi-globe	Large	Red	Pungent	Good
Texas Grano 502PRR	168	Top-shaped	Large	Yellow	Mild	Poor
Texas Grano 1015Y	175	Globe	Large	Yellow	Mild	Fair
Intermediate-day cultivars						
Australian Brown	180	Semi-globe	Medium	Reddish-brown	Pungent	Good
Pronto S*	195	Globe	Large	Dark yellow	Mildly pungent	Limited
Rialto*	198	Globe	Large	Dark yellow	Mildly pungent	Limited
Granex 429*	180	Globe	Large	White	Mild	Fair
Long-day cultivars						
Benny's Red	112	Globe	Large	Red	Mildly pungent	Limited
Donning Yellow Globe . . .	110	Globe	Medium–large	Yellow	Pungent	Excellent
El Capitan*	110	Globe	Large	Yellow	Mild	Fair
Nutmeg*	100	Globe	Medium	Yellow	Pungent	Excellent
Ontario*	100	Globe	Medium–large	Yellow	Mildly pungent	Excellent
Pronto S*	100	Globe	Medium	Dark yellow	Mildly pungent	Limited
Progress*	95	Globe	Large	Yellow	Pungent	Poor
Ruby	105	Globe	Medium–large	Red	Pungent	Good
Sentinel	105	Globe	Medium–large	Yellow	Pungent	Good
Southport White Globe . . .	110	Globe	Medium	White	Mildly pungent	Fair
Spartan Banner*	105	Globe	Medium	Yellow	Pungent	Good
Sweet Sandwich*	115	Globe	Medium–large	Yellow	Mildly pungent	Good
White Ebenezer	100	Flat	Small	White	Mildly pungent	Poor
White Sweet Spanish	120	Globe	Large	White	Mild	Fair
Yellow Ebenezer	105	Flat	Small	Yellow	Pungent	Poor
Yellow Globe Danvers . . .	100–125	Globe	Medium	Yellow	Pungent	Good
Yellow Sweet Spanish	115	Globe	Large	Yellow	Mild	Fair

[1]Relative days to maturity with approximate daylengths of 12–13 hrs. (short-day), 13–14 hrs. (intermediate-day), and 14–16 hrs. (long-day).

[2](*) Hybrid.

Bunching,' 'White Spanish Bunching,' 'Beltsville Bunching,' and 'Evergreen Bunching.' Since green onions are not used for bulbs, almost any standard cultivar of dry bulb onions can be used as green bunching onions, if harvested at the proper stage. Green bunching onions can be produced from standard cultivars by growing long-day cultivars under short-day conditions to inhibit bulbing. In addition, the Welsh or Japanese bunching onions (*Allium fistulosum*), as well as shallots, can be used as green onions since the mature bulbs are small.

INSECTS AND DISEASES

Insects

Onion thrips and onion maggots are the most serious insect pests of onions. Onion thrips (*Thrips tabaci*) are similar to other thrips that cause damage by rasping the leaf surface and feeding on the sap. In hot, dry conditions, damage may be severe. The injury appears as white or scorched areas on the leaves. Several insecticides are effective in controlling thrips, but they usually require two or three applications.

Onion maggots (*Hylemya antiqua*) are similar to root maggots of cole crops (Chapter 14). They are larvae of a small fly that lays its eggs near the base of the plant. The maggots burrow into the stem and bulb and may feed on the roots. There are usually two or three generations per year. The maggots overwinter in the soil and emerge the following spring. Hot weather will kill eggs, so damage is normally more severe under cooler temperatures. Soil insecticides, applied in the seed furrow or as a soil drench after transplanting, will provide good control.

Other insects that can cause damage are wireworms and leaf miners, and black cutworms in low, wet areas of muck soil.

Diseases

Downy Mildew. Downy mildew (*Peronospora destructor*) is a common foliar disease of onions and is especially destructive in direct-seeded crops. A white to purplish mold develops on older leaves. Tan spots develop and eventually leaves dry up and drop off. The disease is favored by cool, wet weather. Fungicide sprays every 7 to 10 days are effective in controlling the disease.

Pink Rot. This is a soil-borne fungus (*Pyrenochaeta terrestis*) that may infect plants at any age. Since the disease affects roots and bulbs, it may go unnoticed for some time. Roots turn pink, then shrivel and die. Infected plants have 50% of the root system of healthy plants, resulting in significantly reduced water and nutrient uptake. Bulb size and yield are subsequently reduced. Using disease-free material, planting in disease-free soil, and using long rotations of non-related crops can help prevent the disease. Cultivars and hybrids with some resistance to the disease are being developed.

Neck Rot. This is a common fungal disease (*Botrytis* sp.) of bulbs in storage or transit, although some losses may also occur in the field. Infection occurs at the neck or in wounds on the bulbs during or following harvest. Tissues become soft, and a whitish-gray mold develops on the surface of the infected area. Soft rot bacteria often follow, causing bulbs to become foul-smelling and to rot severely. Control measures include proper curing and storing. Bulbs that are well dried, especially at the neck, are less likely to be infected by the disease. Growers should avoid bruising bulbs during harvest and handling.

Onion Smut. Onion smut (*Urocytis cepulae*) is one of the most destructive diseases on northern-grown onions. It is a soil-borne fungus that usually infects during the seedling stage, often before the first leaf has made full growth. Grayish-black streaks appear in the outer bulb scales, leaves, and leaf sheaths. Young leaves become twisted and turn yellow; young seedlings may die. The fungus overwinters in the soil. High soil temperatures are not conducive to growth of the fungus, so the disease is generally not a problem for onions grown during warm weather. Seed should be treated with a protectant fungicide, and crop rotations should be used.

Tip and Leaf Blight. Sometimes referred to as "blast," leaf blight (*Botrytis squamosa*) causes numerous white spots on leaves. The spots may expand, covering large portions of the leaves, which may die starting from the tips. Large areas in the field may be affected. The disease is most common during prolonged wet weather. Foliar fungicide sprays every 7 to 10 days will help in its control.

White Rot. This disease (*Sclerotium cepivorum*) is most prevalent in northern regions when humidity is high. It first appears as yellowing and wilting of leaves. Below ground the bulbs become soft and rotten, and eventually a white mold develops on the bulbs. Although infection occurs in the field, symptoms may not appear until storage. The disease may persist in the soil for a long time. Resistant cultivars and chemical control are not effective. Since the disease is specific to onion or related crops, long crop rotations are the best control.

Purple Blotch. This is a fungal disease (*Alternaria porri*) that first appears as water-soaked spots on leaves that quickly expand and turn brown or dark purple. In wet weather the spots become covered with a brown mold. Affected leaves may break over and die. The disease is favored by long periods of wet, cool weather or during heavy dews. Preventive foliar fungicidal sprays provide the best control.

HARVESTING AND POSTHARVEST HANDLING

Onions for dry bulbs are ready for harvest when the bulbs are mature and the tops are dry. In this condition, yields are generally higher, bulbs can be stored longer, and neck rot (*Botrytis*) is less likely to occur. Onions for green bunching can be harvested from the time they reach pencil size up until bulbing begins.

The exact time of harvest for dry bulbs varies with environmental conditions. Generally, harvest should wait until all the tops are down, but this may not be feasible, especially for the early crop which is sometimes harvested before the bulbs are fully mature when the leaves are still green. In the West and South, harvest during warm weather begins when approximately 25–50% of the tops are down, while under cooler conditions, harvest may not take place until over 50% of the tops have fallen over (Figure 20.3).

To hasten the maturing process, the tops can be rolled down with a light-weight roller when about 10% of the tops have fallen naturally. About 7 days prior to lifting, the bulbs can be undercut with a cultivator or a blade. Both practices facilitate the maturing process by reducing water uptake and growth.

In the harvest operation, the bulbs are lifted and topped, by hand or machine, leaving 1–2 inches of neck on the bulbs to ensure a tight seal after they have dried. Crops intended for long-term storage may have the tops left on. The bulbs are placed in windrows or in slotted bulk bins in the field for 2–3 weeks to cure (Figure 20.4), or they may be harvested into trucks (Figure 20.5) and cured in bulk storage with forced air and a drying temperature of 85–90°F. The bulbs are sufficiently cured when the outer scales are papery and the necks dry and tight. The Spanish types with their soft, tender skins are susceptible to sunburn and should not be exposed to direct sunlight for more than 1–2 hours after harvest. These types should be cured in the shade.

Figure 20.3. Onion bulbs are ready to harvest when the tops are down.

Figure 20.4. After being removed from the ground, onion bulbs are placed in windrows for several weeks for curing.

Figure 20.5. Onion bulbs may be harvested from the windrows and transported to indoor facilities for bulk curing.

Storage of dry bulb onions is best at 32°F and 65–70% relative humidity. The relative humidity is lower than for most vegetables because dampness in storage causes considerable rot and mold growth. High moisture and temperatures may induce new growth. If the crop can be kept cool and dry, and well ventilated, it can be held in common storage for several months. The later-maturing, pungent, globe types, which tend to have more bulb dry matter, can be stored up to 8 months, while the mild or Bermuda types have poorer keeping qualities and can be held for no longer than 2 months; however, these types are usually consumed soon after harvest. The Spanish types are often stored, and if well matured, can keep for 4–5 months. As a rule, bulbs started from sets generally do not store well and should be used soon after harvest.

Onion bulbs are dormant at harvest for a period of 6–8 weeks. However, for any long-term storage, the sprout inhibitor maleic hydrazide is used. This is usually sprayed on the foliage 1–2 weeks before harvest, when the bulbs are mature and the leaves are still green, in order to translocate the chemical down to the bulb. Application of the chemical after most leaves have turned brown will not improve storage. If applied too early before onion bulbs are mature, maleic hydrazide can cause soft, spongy bulbs which break down in storage.

Green bunching onions are highly perishable and are normally marketed promptly. If held at 32°F and packed in polyethylene film to reduce moisture loss, they may be stored up to 3–4 weeks.

ONION SETS

These are small bulbs (0.25–1.0 inch in diameter) grown the previous year that are used as propagating material for dry bulbs and bunching onions. The production of onion sets is very specialized, with a limited number of growers. Much of the crop is produced in a two-county area in Illinois south of Chicago and in parts of Oregon and Colorado. The general methods of culture are similar to those for dry bulbs, except the seed is planted at very close spacing (30 seeds per foot or more) to produce the desired bulb size. The smaller sets (less than 0.75 inch) are used to produce dry bulb onions since they are less likely to bolt. These are grown at closer spacings than the larger sets (greater than 0.75 inch in diameter), which are best used for green onions.

UNUSUAL ONIONS

In addition to dry bulb onions, several very different types of onions are available, usually from certain seed specialists. The multiplier onion or potato onion (*A. Cepa*, Aggregatum group) sends up multiple tops, each of which produces small onion bulbs in clumps. The Egyptian onion or tree onion (*A. Cepa*, Proliferum group) produces bulblets at the tops of stalks instead of flowering. Both types are grown for green bunching. Pickling onions or pearl onions produce small bulbs which are pickled and used as condiments. These are produced from standard cultivars planted at very high populations (Table 20.2).

GARLIC

Garlic (*Allium sativum*) is a hardy perennial, and like onion is a bulbous plant and a monocot. It is grown as an annual for its small bulblets called cloves, which are used both cooked and raw as a flavor component in a wide variety of dishes. Much of the crop is processed into garlic powder, dehydrated flakes, and cloves.

Since it is a specialty crop with limited demand, the industry in the U.S. is concentrated in the hands of a relatively few growers in several states. The commercial acreage committed to garlic fluctuates considerably, ranging from 3,000 acres to over 15,000 acres in some years. California produces most of the garlic grown in the U.S., followed by Texas, Oregon, and Louisiana. The U.S. crop is minor in terms of worldwide production, where the leading producers are the Asian countries of China, South Korea, India, and Thailand.

PLANT GROWTH AND DEVELOPMENT

Garlic differs from the onion in that the bulb is a compound structure composed of several small bulblets called cloves (Figure 20.6). Each clove consists of two mature leaves and a vegetative bud. The outer leaf forms a thin protective covering or sheath around the clove, becoming dry and papery at maturity. The inner leaf has a thickened base and makes up almost the total mass of the clove. Several leaf initials, which form the bud, or clove, for the next season's growth, develop in the axil of the inner leaf. Similar to onion bulbs, garlic cloves are dormant for a period of time after maturity. This varies with the cultivar and external conditions, but temperatures in the range of 45 to 60°F will promote clove germination.

Bulbing in garlic occurs in response to increasing photoperiod and increasing temperature up to 77°F. When exposed to short days and high temperatures, bulbs may not form.

Figure 20.6. Garlic bunched for market; the garlic bulb consists of several white bulblets known as cloves.

CLIMATIC REQUIREMENTS, PLANTING, AND CULTURE

Garlic is a cool-season crop and young plants can withstand heavy frosts and even some light freezing. Climatic requirements are similar to those for onions.

In warmer sections of the country, such as Louisiana and Texas, it is grown over the winter. In California, plantings are usually made between October and January, or in the early spring. The early spring plantings allow the plants to attain sufficient vegetative size during short days, and at the same time be exposed to low temperatures, before long days begin and bulbing is initiated.

The crop is propagated by planting the garlic cloves, which are divisions of the mature bulb. These generally come from the previous year's crop. Bulb development of the following crop is significantly influenced by the storage temperature of the dormant cloves, and bulbs used for propagation should be exposed to cool temperatures (40–50°F) for several months during prior storage. The cloves should not be separated until just before planting, since whole bulbs store better than separated cloves. Large cloves generally give better yields than smaller ones. The cloves are planted singly, 2–6 inches apart, depending on the cultivar, in twin rows 12–16 inches apart, with the distal end up (or base pointing down).

Garlic thrives best on a friable sandy loam; heavy soils should be avoided. The bulbs will be small if the soil is excessively dry and irregularly shaped if the soil is too heavy or compacted. Fertilization, irrigation, and pest management are similar to that used for onions. Irrigation may not be required by crops planted in the fall and grown during the winter.

CULTIVARS

There are early ('Creole,' 'California Early') and late ('California Late,' 'Extra Sweet') cultivars. The early cultivars do not store well and have poorer quality, but they will generally outyield the later ones. 'Creole' is adapted to the hot southern interior of the lower U.S., while the others do well in California and other western states.

HARVESTING AND POSTHARVEST HANDLING

The crop is ready for harvest when the tops bend over and become dry. If the soil is very rich, it may be necessary to break over the tops to speed up maturation, as is sometimes done with onions. The bulbs may be harvested by hand or by machine. Prior to harvesting, the bulbs can be undercut with a tractor-mounted cutting blade to facilitate removing the bulbs from the ground.

After the bulbs are pulled, they are placed in windrows, with the tops covering the bulbs to prevent sunscald. Curing takes about 1–2 weeks, after which the roots are trimmed. In humid areas and during wet weather, shed curing is usually necessary. The bulbs are then graded and bagged. The tops may be left on the bulbs or removed.

Garlic is best stored under similar conditions and practices as used for onions. At 32°F and 65–70% relative humidity, garlic can be stored for 6–7 months. If properly cured, garlic bulbs can be held up to 4 months in well-ventilated common storage. For optimum long-term storage, growers usually apply sprout inhibitors before harvest.

LEEK

Leek (*Allium Ampeloprasum*, Porrum group) is a hardy, cool-season biennial grown as an annual for its blanched sheath of basal leaves, which is used raw or cooked for its mild onion-like flavor. The plant does not form a bulb but instead produces a thick, fleshy cylinder of closely overlapped leaves, similar to that in

Figure 20.7. Leek does not form a true bulb but instead produces a thick, fleshy cylinder of closely overlapped leaves.

green onions (Figure 20.7). Occasionally under long-day conditions, the basal part of the leaves may slightly thicken, resembling a bulb.

Leek is a relatively long-season crop requiring about 120 days from seeding to harvest. It is generally more cold-tolerant than the onion in its early development, but it can be damaged at harvest by frost. In the North and West, the crop is planted in the early spring and harvested in the fall, while in the South and Southwest, it is grown over the winter and harvested in the spring. In some areas of the West, late plantings may be made, which are harvested during the winter.

Where the length of the growing season is not limiting, leek may be started from seed. However, in areas with short seasons, the crop should be started indoors or in some protective structure and later transplanted. The seeds, or transplants, are usually planted in a shallow trench, in order to blanch as much of the fleshy leafstalk as possible by hilling up soil around the plants during the growing season. Under favorable conditions, the blanched edible portion can be 6–8 inches long and up to 2 inches in diameter. Cultural requirements and practices are similar to those for onions.

The crop is ready to harvest once the blanched basal portion of the leaves is at least 0.5 inch in diameter. However, because the plant does not form a bulb, there is no rush to harvest, and growers often wait until the plants reach 2 inches in diameter to pick the crop. Similar to onions and garlic, growers may undercut the plants to facilitate harvest. After the plants are removed from the soil, the roots are cut off, along with all but 2 inches of the green leaf blade, leaving mostly the white sheath of overlapped leaves. The plants can also be left in the ground over the winter but should be harvested in the spring before growth resumes.

After harvest, the crop is promptly cooled to near 32°F by hydrocooling, vacuum cooling, or chilling with crushed ice. If properly handled, leek may keep 2–3 months at 32°F and 95–100% relative humidity. Leek is usually marketed in bunches like green onions.

CHIVES

Chives (*Allium Schoenoprasum*) are cool-season, cold-tolerant perennials. In form and growth habit, they closely resemble the wild onion. The small plants develop into bushy clumps and grow by means of tillering (development of new shoots from the base of the original plant). Unlike the other *alliums*, chives are grown for their tube-like leaves (Figure 20.8), which are valued for their delicate,

Figure 20.8. Chives are composed of clumps of small plants; the leaves of the plants are used for flavoring.

onion-like flavor; the small bulbs are not used. Much of the crop is processed, by being frozen, freeze-dried, or dehydrated.

Overall, chives are a minor crop, with some commercial production in California, Texas, Arizona, and Illinois. They are very popular in home gardens and are often listed in many seed catalogs.

Chives are propagated by seed or from divisions of the compact clumps, keeping ten to twenty bulblets per clump. The plants should be planted where they can remain undisturbed for several seasons. Seeding is the preferred commercial method for starting the crop and is done in early spring. Divisions are made either in the early spring or in the fall. Plants do best if dividing and resetting are done about every 2 or 3 years. Small clumps may be dug and divided in the late fall and moved to cold frames and greenhouses or placed in flowerpots or other types of containers for fresh home use during the winter.

The general care and culture of the crop is similar to that for onions. The leaves are harvested sequentially over the season in several cuttings approximately every 4–6 weeks. Cutting off the leaves appears to stimulate multiplication of the plants. Much of the crop is cut by hand with a knife, but a mechanical harvester, which has recently been developed, is now being used commercially.

SHALLOTS

Shallots (*Allium Cepa*, Aggregatum group) are a perennial crop that is grown as an annual for its cluster of small bulbs or cloves. They have a delicate onion-like flavor and may be grown for their dry bulbs or used in the same manner as green onions. The crop has very little commercial significance in the U.S., with about 1,000 acres in production, mostly in the South.

A plant will produce from two to fifteen bulblets per cluster. The crop is propagated by dividing the bulb clusters and planting individual bulblets, or cloves, 2 inches deep, 4 inches apart, in rows 12–24 inches apart. Warm temperatures and long photoperiods favor bulbing. In the North, shallots are planted in the spring and grown as a summer crop for their dry bulbs. In the South, shallots are grown as a winter crop and used in the same way as green onions. Shallots are very hardy and may be left in the ground over the winter. When they are grown for their dry bulbs, the harvest and handling is similar to that used for onions. Shallots grown for green onions are pulled when their tops are 6–8 inches long and after they have obtained a minimum diameter of 0.25 inch.

SELECTED REFERENCES

Mansour, N. S., H. Mack, and J. Hay. 1979. *Commercial Onion Production in Oregon*. Oregon State Univ. Coop. Ext. Ser. Cir. 817.

Pike, L. M. 1986. Onion Breeding, pp. 357–394. In: M. J. Bassett (ed.). *Breeding Vegetable Crops*. AVI Publishing Co., Westport, Connecticut.

Sabota, C. M., and J. W. Courter. 1979. *Storing Home-grown Onions*. Univ. of Illinois Coop. Ext. Ser. Hort. Facts VC-3-79.

Schmidt, J. C. 1985. *Onions and Related Crops*. Univ. of Illinois Coop. Ext. Ser. Hort. Facts VC-41-85.

Schoenmann, J. A., E. E. Schulte, J. A. Wyman, W. R. Stevenson, and L. K. Binning. 1982. *Commercial Onion (Dry Bulb) Production*. Univ. of Wisconsin Coop. Ext. Ser. A2332.

Seelig, R. A. 1974. *Garlic. Fruit & Vegetable Facts & Pointers*. United Fresh Fruit and Vegetable Association, Alexandria, Virginia.

Seelig, R. A. 1974. *Green Onions. Fruit & Vegetable Facts & Pointers*. United Fresh Fruit and Vegetable Association, Alexandria, Virginia.

Seelig, R. A. 1970. *Dry Onions. Fruit & Vegetable Facts & Pointers*. United Fresh Fruit and Vegetable Association, Alexandria, Virginia.

Sims, W. L., T. M. Little, and R. E. Voss. 1976. *Growing Garlic in California*. Univ. of California Div. Agric. Sci. Leaf. 2948.

Tiessen, H., I. L. Nonnecke, and M. Valk. 1981. *Onions (Culture, Harvesting, and Storage)*. Ontario Ministry of Agric. & Food Pub. 486.

Voss, R. E. (ed.). 1979. *Onion Production in California*. Univ. of California Div. Agric. Sci. Pub. 4097.

Williams, R. D., and J. Montelaro. 1977. *Onion Production Guide*. Univ. of Florida Coop. Ext. Ser. Cir. 176D.

Zandstra, B. H., E. J. Graffius, M. L. Lacy, and D. D. Warncke. 1986. *Onions*. Michigan State Univ. Coop. Ext. Ser. Bull. E-1307.

21

PEAS

CLASSIFICATION, ORIGIN, HISTORY

Garden peas (*Pisum sativum*), also called green or common peas, are a hardy, cool-season, vining annual belonging to the family Leguminosae. They are grown primarily for their fresh, edible green seeds (peas), but they may also be used as a dry-seeded crop. In the South, garden peas are sometimes called "English peas," to distinguish them from southern peas (or cowpeas), which are a warm-season crop more like beans (see Chapter 13) in terms of both culture and climatic requirements.

There are also several other kinds or types of peas (*P. sativum* var. *macrocarpon*), which are grown for their immature pods just as the seeds are developing. These are commonly referred to as edible-podded peas, snow peas, or sugar peas. These types have unpalatable seeds, so they must be used before the peas (seeds) begin to make much development. Commercially, green peas are of much greater importance than podded peas, although the latter types are gaining in popularity as specialty crops.

Peas are believed to have originated in Europe or North Asia. The plants were commonly grown by the ancient Greeks and Romans and were introduced into the U.S. in the early 1600's. Peas have received the attention of plant breeders for many years, and numerous mutant forms have been discovered. Due to the work by Gregor Mendel and others, peas have a special recognized place in the history of genetics and plant breeding.

405

PRODUCTION AND INDUSTRY

Green peas for processing are a leading commercial vegetable in the U.S., with the crop fairly evenly split between canning and freezing.

U.S. commercial statistics for processed pea acreage, tonnage, and value for 1977 and 1989 are presented in Table 21.1. In comparing the data for the 2 years, commercial acreage in the U.S. decreased 10%, while production remained relatively constant, and value increased by 19%. Average yields increased from 1.4 tons per acre in 1977 to 1.6 tons per acre in 1989. The leading producing states are Wisconsin (130,050 tons) and Minnesota (113,500 tons), followed by Washington (99,150 tons) and Oregon (48,080 tons).

Table 21.1. Harvested Acreage, Production, and Value of Processed Green Peas in the U.S., 1977 and 1989

State	Harvested Acres		Production		Value	
	1977[1]	1989[2]	1977	1989	1977	1989
			——— (tons ———		——— ($1,000) ———	
Delaware	8,700	8,100	11,950	9,560	2,760	2,227
Minnesota	65,600	73,700	100,400	113,500	20,180	28,375
New York	5,200	10,600	7,200	16,960	1,786	4,834
Oregon	27,700	34,100	23,000	48,080	4,324	10,578
Washington	70,700	55,700	108,900	99,150	21,889	25,977
Wisconsin	107,500	85,000	146,200	130,050	29,825	29,131
Other states[3]	66,780	49,300	93,950	87,360	20,078	18,841
U.S.	352,180	316,500	491,600	504,660	100,842	119,963
Canning	220,830	155,150	297,200	247,040	61,812	58,646
Freezing	131,350	161,350	194,400	257,620	39,030	61,317

[1]Source: USDA. 1978. Economics, Statistics, and Cooperatives Service (ESCS), Crop Reporting Board.
[2]Source: USDA. 1990. National Agricultural Statistics Service (NASS), Agricultural Statistics Board.
[3]California, Idaho, Illinois, Iowa, Maine, Maryland, Michigan, New Jersey, Pennsylvania.

Once a popular vegetable, fresh peas for commercial production have largely been replaced by processed peas due to the high labor requirements for harvesting and shelling. Because of the limited volume, the USDA Agricultural Statistics Board discontinued reports on green peas for fresh market in 1968. The crop, however, is still very popular for home use and commercially for fresh market sales at roadside stands and pick-your-own operations near large population centers. Dried peas, almost as large a crop as green peas, are grown almost entirely in the dryland wheat–pea region of eastern Washington, Oregon, and northern Idaho.

The U.S. leads the world in the production of green peas, growing over 20% of the worldwide crop. The European fraction accounts for about 45% of the world production, with France, Great Britain, Italy, Hungary, and the USS accounting for much of the crop. Other leading producing nations include India, China, and Australia. Worldwide, dried pea production is greater than that of green peas, since the crop can be easily stored for extended use.

PLANT GROWTH AND DEVELOPMENT

Peas are similar in growth habit to green beans, with both indeterminate (vining) and determinate (bush) types available. The indeterminate, or tall, types have long internodes and set fruit along a long, main stem over an extended period of time. The determinate, or short, types have short internodes and produce stems where flowers develop in a cluster near the end of the shoot and have a concentrated pod set (Figure 21.1). In both types, some branching occurs at the lower nodes. The amount varies with the cultivar, but greatly increases if the terminal growing point is killed. The leaves end in tendrils, which can provide support.

The flowers are similar to those in beans and are self-pollinated. The flowers are borne at the axils, with one, two, or three per node, but often only one

Figure 21.1. Determinate cultivar of peas near maturity exhibiting concentrated fruit set.

develops. The node at which flowering begins is quite consistent for a particular cultivar. The number of nodes to the first flower is an important factor in determining the time to maturity for a cultivar, or for identifying a particular growth stage. For example, eight or nine nodes to the first flower indicates an early cultivar, while later cultivars may have up to sixteen nodes before the first flower. In contrast to beans, the cotyledons of the pea remain below ground during germination. Thus, in effect, two nodes are formed beneath the surface so that the first visible leaf is actually the third node.

The fruit is a pod, or legume, derived from a superior ovary, which contains two rows of ovules that develop into the seeds, or peas (Figure 21.2). The pea seed is large and globular when mature and consists of a thin seed coat that encloses the embryo containing two fleshy cotyledons and a well-developed hypocotyl. As the peas mature, several important changes take place: the peas increase in size and toughness, sugar converts to starch, and in some cultivars cotyledons change in color from green to yellow. In the edible-podded peas, the pod endocarp remains soft and succulent, compared to shelling types, in which the pods become hard and dry at maturity and split open.

Most cultivars have the potential to produce eight to ten peas per pod, but this may not be reached under field conditions. Newer cultivars that may be able to produce up to twelve to fourteen peas per pod are being developed.

Peas develop distinct taproots which may grow 36–48 inches deep. The

Figure 21.2. The fruit is a legume, or pod, which contains the ovules, or seeds (peas).

roots of peas are associated with *Rhizobium* bacteria, which have the capacity to fix atmospheric nitrogen in nodules.

CLIMATIC AND CULTURAL REQUIREMENTS

A cool-season crop, peas do best at temperatures of 50–64°F and should be planted so as not to mature when temperatures are consistently above 85°F. High temperatures increase pod fiber content and seed starch content, and yields drop off rapidly above 75°F. Consequently, the bulk of the crop is grown in northern climates from spring to fall; but peas can be grown in other areas during the cooler parts of the year. In the South and lower California, the crop is grown during the fall, winter, and early spring. The minimum temperature for growth is around 45°F. Although moderately cold-hardy, plants can be damaged by heavy frosts.

Peas are grown on a variety of soils. Two of the most important factors in the selection of a site are drainage and soil structure. Peas germinate slowly in poorly aerated soils, and several root rots become very destructive in wet soils, so good drainage is essential, especially during the early part of the growing season. Sandy loams with clay subsoils are generally preferred for earliness. If well drained, some of the heavier soils, such as clays and loams, produce higher yields than sandy soils, but maturity is later. The soil should be well supplied with organic matter, to improve drainage and to allow better aeration. Studies have consistently shown that organic matter is positively correlated with plant growth, yield, and nodule formation.

Like most legumes, garden peas prefer a slightly acid soil but will not tolerate excess soil acidity. The crop should be grown in a soil with a pH of 5.8–6.8. Peas are especially sensitive to atrazine herbicide residues, and yields can be severely reduced if peas follow corn where more than 1 pound active ingredient per acre of atrazine was used. Generally, 4-year rotations are used, to avoid several root rots caused by soil-borne fungi (see "Diseases").

Peas are less responsive to fertilizers than most vegetables. Nitrogen recommendations are generally low (20–50 pounds nitrogen per acre). This is due to a combination of a short growing season, the ability of peas to fix atmospheric nitrogen, and residual nitrogen from fertilizers and decomposition of soil organic matter. In determinant growth types, excess nitrogen may delay pod set. Phosphorus and potassium rates are based on soil test results.

Peas are sensitive to excess salts during germination, and fertilizer should not come in direct contact with the seed. The fertilizer, up to 200 pounds per acre, is commonly drilled 2 inches below and 2 inches to the side of the seed at planting. When the fertilizer is banded, the potassium rate should not exceed 80 pounds K_2O per acre; any additional potassium or other fertilizer should be broadcast prior to planting. Following periods of heavy rains in the spring, a topdressing of 20–30 pounds of nitrogen per acre may be applied when plants are 4–6 inches tall. Starter fertilizer containing some nitrogen is used for early peas because nitrogen-fixing nodule bacteria are less active in cool, wet soils.

Inoculation

The garden pea, as with other legumes, can be inoculated with a specific legume bacterium to enhance early nodule formation and nitrogen fixation. The nodule-forming bacterium is the same for garden peas, vetch, and Austrian peas. In the past, yield increases were obtained with this practice, and inoculation was common in commercial plantings. However, with the application of nitrogen fertilizers and in soils containing the bacterium, the value of inoculation is questionable. In general, the cost of inoculation is very small, and it may be beneficial to inoculate the seeds before planting if peas have not been grown in the field for more than 5 years.

PLANTING AND CROP ESTABLISHMENT

The crop is started entirely by direct seeding. Grain drills are generally used to plant peas, with seeding rates depending on cultivar.

Peas for processing are of the small vine or determinant types and are normally seeded in rows 6–8 inches apart, at rates to obtain six to eight plants per foot of row (400,000–700,000 plants per acre). For the home garden and much of the fresh market, large vine types are used, with plants seeded 2 inches apart in single rows 2–3 feet apart. Some crops are planted in double rows 8–12 inches apart on beds spaced on 4-foot centers (Figure 21.3). Because of higher returns per acre, some fresh market growers are now using determinate types and higher plant populations (up to 200,000 plants per acre). Although the closer spacing makes walking in the field to hand harvest more difficult, there is usually no reduction in harvest efficiency.

The normal depth of seeding is 1–2 inches, depending on earliness, soil type, and moisture content. Shallow planting is used early in the season when surface soil moisture is adequate and soil temperature is higher closer to the surface. Later plantings are seeded deeper to provide better moisture conditions for germination, which is best in the upper half of the soil moisture range.

Peas can be planted early in the season, once soil temperatures rise above

Figure 21.3. Double-row culture allows for increased plant populations; rows are spaced 8–12 inches apart.

40°F; optimum soil temperatures for germination are 40–75°F. Low soil temperatures increase germination time considerably; at 40°F, seedlings may require more than 30 days to germinate, compared to 6 days at 75° (Table 21.2). Later plantings will mature in less time but will produce lower yields and poorer quality, due to high temperatures at the time of maturity.

To protect against seed rot and damping-off, most growers use seed treated with a commercial fungicide. In areas where seed maggots are a problem, a recommended insecticide may be included in the seed treatment.

Table 21.2. Effect of Soil Temperature on Pea Germination[1]

Germination	Soil Temperature (°F)							
	32	41	50	59	68	77	86	95
%	0	89	94	93	93	94	86	0
Days	—	36	13	9	7	6	6	—

[1]Source: J. F. Harrington and P. A. Minges. 1954. *Vegetable Seed Germination.* Univ. of California Agric. Ext. Ser. Leaf. 7–54.

Heat Units

A heat-unit system (see Chapter 3) is used in commercial pea production to predict relative maturity dates and to schedule planting dates. This system uses 40°F as the threshold or base temperature and 85°F as the maximum temperature.

The daily heat units accumulating during the development of a cultivar are calculated from the daily temperature mean. Heat units accumulate slowly during the cool spring and rapidly as the season progresses. With this information, the expected time of maturity of a cultivar can be determined from the mean temperatures. If the number of heat units per day during harvest are allowed to accumulate between plantings, spacing of harvests can be achieved. This allows the crop to be harvested efficiently and for peas to be processed within a very short time after harvest.

Heat-unit requirements can differ considerably among pea cultivars. In addition, heat-unit requirements for a given cultivar will vary from season to season and area to area, although differences between cultivars remain relatively constant. Processors maintain rigid control of the heat-unit requirements for their specific cultivars, and heat-unit values given for canning and freezing cultivars reflect differences for cultivar and specific geographical area.

CULTURAL PRACTICES

Weeds

Because peas germinate well in cool soils and are planted early in the season before weeds are active, early weed competition in commercial pea production is inherently reduced by the system of culture. In addition, peas are usually grown at high populations and close spacing, which further helps reduce weed competitors. Still, weeds can be troublesome; particularly, Canada thistles, because their buds are hard to remove from shelled peas and greatly reduce the pea grade.

The most effective method to control weeds in pea production is with combinations of preplant, preemergent, and postemergent herbicides. Germinating grasses and annuals are best controlled by the use of preplant-incorporated or preemergent herbicides. Most broadleaf weeds, such as Canada thistle, are effectively suppressed with postemergent herbicides after the peas have germinated. When postemergent herbicides are used, knowing the node of the first bloom for a particular cultivar is important in order to apply the herbicide at the proper growth stage to avoid damaging the crop.

Peas are cultivated only where the rows are far enough apart for cultivation. Since peas develop rapidly, no great amount of cultivation is usually necessary. The cultivation should be shallow to avoid destroying many of the fibrous roots and only frequently enough to destroy weeds.

Staking

With few exceptions, no support is given vines in commercial pea production. Most short and intermediate cultivars are self-supporting. The indeterminate, taller types are generally more productive when supported. Supporting the vines makes harvest easier and keeps pods off the ground. In the home garden, canes or small stakes, set at intervals in the row and overlapping near the top, are used. Wire netting supported by stakes between double rows or inexpensive twine trellis consisting of three to five lines may also be tried.

CULTIVARS

Pea cultivars can be grouped in several different ways, based on plant type (vine growth habit), pod characteristics (size, shape, number), seed characteristics (size, texture, color), and chief use (Table 21.3). Processors usually dictate cultivars, and very often use some of their own.

Plant Type

Cultivars may be grouped into tall (indeterminate), short (determinate), and medium types. The tall types have straight stems with long internodes, while the short types have zigzag stems with short internodes. The short, or determinate, cultivars have a high ratio of pods to vine weight and tend to be earlier, producing pods over a shorter period of time. These types are well-suited for once-over mechanical harvesting and have become the standard for processing, as well as for much of the fresh market crop.

In addition to growth habit, cultivars may be grouped by size of leaves and stipules, color and size of flowers, number of nodes to first flower, number of pods per node, and resistance to disease.

Pod Characteristics

Pea cultivars can be identified by pod size and shape and by the number of pods set at each flowering node. Pod shapes vary between blunt and pointed types. Most cultivars for processing have small- to intermediate-sized pods with blunt ends. Large pods are not adapted to vining machinery. Home garden cultivars may be either large- or small-podded. Cultivars may be single-, double-, or multiple-podded. Generally, the determinate types tend to produce two or more pods at each flower node, while the indeterminate types tend to be single-podded.

Table 21.3. Characteristics of Selected Pea Cultivars

Cultivar	Chief Use(s)	Days to Maturity	Vines	Pods	Pea Size
Green peas					
Green Arrow	Market	68	Medium	Pointed	Small
Sparkle	Garden, market	59	Short	Blunt	Small
Spring	Market	60	Medium	Blunt	Medium
Alderman	Garden, market	72	Tall	Pointed	Large
Dual	Market	71	Medium	Pointed	Medium
Freezonian	Garden, market, freezing	62	Medium–tall	Blunt	Small
Early Frosty	Market, freezing	64	Short–medium	Blunt	Medium
Bolero	Market, freezing	69	Medium	Blunt	Medium
Early Perfection	Canning	65	Medium	Blunt	Small
Early Sweet II	Canning	62	Medium	Blunt	Medium
Greater Progress	Market	60	Short	Pointed	Small
Mars	Processing, freezing	66	Short–medium	Blunt	Medium
Venus	Processing, freezing	62	Short–medium	Blunt	Medium
Knight	Market	62	Medium	Blunt	Medium
Little Marvel	Garden	64	Short	Pointed	Medium
Wando	General-purpose	66	Short–medium	Blunt	Small
Lincoln	Market, freezing	65	Medium	Blunt	Medium
Edible-podded					
Dwarf White Sugar . .	Market, garden	60	Short	Blunt	—
Dwarf Grey Sugar . . .	Market, garden	70	Short–medium	Blunt	—
Sugar Ray	Market	60	Short	Blunt	—
Sugar Daddy	Market	68	Medium	Blunt	—
Mammoth Melting . . .	Market, garden	68	Medium–tall	Rounded	—
Sugar Ann	Market	60	Short	Blunt	—
Sugar Snap	Market, garden	70	Tall	Blunt	—

Seed Characteristics (Surface Texture, Color, Size)

Cultivars can be classified as either smooth-seeded or wrinkle-seeded, which is related to the sugar / starch ratio present in the cotyledon. The smooth-seeded cultivars are more hardy but lower in sugar / starch ratio than wrinkle-seeded types, which hold their sugars longer. Most present-day cultivars are wrinkle-seeded.

Cultivars range in seed color from light green to dark green. Seed color is determined by a single gene which controls the presence or absence of chlorophyll in the seed coat. The dark green types, which have the gene present, are used for freezing, fresh market, and home gardens, while light green cultivars, which lack the gene, are usually preferred for canning.

Seed size differs between cultivars, ranging from less than 0.28 inch to more than 0.40 inch. The smaller-seeded types are preferred for canning because the small seeds are associated with sweetness and tenderness. However, overmature small peas can be just as tough and hard as overmature large peas. The medium to larger peas tend to present a more attractive product and are generally preferred for freezing, fresh market, and home gardens.

Chief Use

Pea cultivars fall into six basic types based on intended use: freezing, canning, market, home garden, edible-podded, and general-purpose. Specific growth, pod, and seed characteristics for a particular use category have already been discussed.

Sugar Snap Peas

These are a type of edible-podded pea, or snow pea, which developed from a cross of a standard pod pea with a mutant. The result was a very crisp, sweet, tender pod pea that can be eaten raw as well as cooked (Figure 21.4). Sugar snaps are characterized by slow development of seeds and pod fiber. Unlike mature pod peas that have unpalatable peas inside, sugar snaps taste like sweet young peas and like tender, sweet edible-podded peas. Since they are a totally edible product, sugar snap peas can produce considerable more product per acre than conventional peas.

Sugar snaps are more difficult to grow than standard green peas and are

Figure 21.4. Podded sugar snap peas have tender, crisp pods, which are edible.

sensitive to adverse environmental conditions. Although they are very susceptible to mildew and spotting under high moisture conditions, they do require irrigation for optimum production. They are very sensitive to overripeness, losing market quality rapidly, and must be harvested within 12–24 hours of maturity. The crop is harvested before the seed enlarges and the pod become fibrous. The more mature the crop becomes, the more susceptible the sugar snaps are to machine damage during harvesting. Getting sugar snaps picked at the right time with the least amount of damage to the raw product is the biggest production problem. Currently, most of the commercial sugar snap pea production is located in eastern Washington and Oregon and southern Idaho.

INSECTS AND DISEASES

Insects

The pea aphid (*Acyrthosiphon pisum*) is perhaps the most widespread and destructive insect pest of peas. The aphid is pale green and larger than most other species of aphids found on vegetables. It feeds on leaves, flowers, and pods, causing reduced fruit set and curling and shrinking of pods. Under favorable conditions, aphid populations multiply rapidly. Insecticides are effective in controlling the aphid, provided treatment is started when the insects are first observed and applications are repeated.

Other insect pests of peas include pea weevils, leaf miners, thrips, seed maggots, spider mites, and several types of caterpillars such as loopers, armyworms, and cutworms. Generally, these insects are usually not a problem every year. Seed maggot problems occur at the time of planting when the larvae attack the seed before seedlings emerge. Pea weevils are snout beetles which become destructive around the time of flowering and fruiting when adults lay their eggs on the pods. Soon after hatching, the larvae burrow into the pods, where they feed and develop into adults. In some regions nematodes may cause some damage to the roots of peas. The only control is to practice rotation and to avoid growing susceptible crops on the land.

Diseases

The most important pea diseases are root rot, *Fusarium* wilt and near-wilt, *Ascochyta* blight, bacterial blight, downy mildew, *Septoria* blight, and powdery mildew. In general, chemical control of most pea diseases is limited, and from a practical standpoint, the best control measures consist of using disease-free seed, seed treatment, resistant cultivars, and crop rotation.

Root rot is perhaps the most serious of the pea diseases. It is actually a disease complex caused by several species of soil fungi (*Aphanomyces*, *Pythium*, *Fusarium*, and *Rhizoctonia*) acting alone or in combination. The disease is hard to detect since it affects the below ground root, but sometimes it may be identified by a discoloration at the base of the stem. There is no definite control for root rot, and no resistant cultivars are available. To combat the disease, good soil drainage, crop rotation (3–5 years), and seed treatment with a recommended fungicide are suggested.

Fusarium wilt and near-wilt are two major wilt diseases of peas, caused by related fungi. Both can be introduced with the seed, and once present, may live in the soil indefinitely. The symptoms are similar, initially consisting of wilting and yellowing of the lower leaves, followed by stunting of plants. Slowly, plants begin to wilt for increasingly longer periods, until they are unable to recover and eventually die. The symptoms are usually more severe on plants infected with *Fusarium* wilt than those with near-wilt, and also tend to occur earlier in the season. The best control is with resistant cultivars.

Bacterial blight and *Ascochyta* blight are seed-borne diseases that can best be controlled by using disease-free seed, preferably obtained from the semi-arid West and Pacific Coast states, along with a fungicide seed treatment. For fungal leaf spots and blights, weekly applications of a fungicide will help control the diseases.

Peas are also subject to attack from several viruses, including pea mosaic, yellow bean mosaic, pea stunt, pea streak, and enation virus. In most of these, infected plants may not die but are severely dwarfed with distorted and stunted pods. There are some cultivars resistant to mosaic but not to other viruses. Since most viruses are carried and spread by aphids, the most effective protective measure is good aphid control.

HARVESTING AND POSTHARVEST HANDLING

Peas are a relatively short-season crop that can be ready to harvest in as few as 57 days in some early cultivars and up to 80 days in some late types. Frequently, growers produce a second crop of peas on the same land after the first crop is harvested.

Garden peas are harvested when the pods are fully green and well developed, but still tender. The seeds should be near full size and should not have begun to harden. The edible-podded types are picked when the pods have reached full length and the seeds are just developing.

The proper stage of growth at harvest is important, since quality depends on tenderness and sugar content of the seed. Although the yields of green peas increase with maturity, quality decreases rapidly if the crop is overmature. As the peas increase in size during maturation, the seed coats and cotyledons of the peas become tougher, and the percent of sugar decreases while starch and proteins increase.

Maturity can be measured in several different ways: by sampling for taste, by the size of the peas in a sample, or quantitatively by tenderness (determined by a tenderometer). High readings indicate overmaturity and an increase in starch, while lower readings indicate more soluble sugars and tenderness.

Peas for processing are harvested with a mowing machine. The processor determines when the peas will be harvested and usually provides the harvesting and hauling equipment. The plants are usually hauled to a vining station where the peas are shelled by machinery. Some viners are self-propelled and harvest the plants from windrows.

Green peas for the fresh market are harvested entirely by hand, making harvest the most expensive operation in producing a fresh market crop. Two or three pickings are usually necessary for determinate types, while indeterminate types will be picked over a considerably longer period.

Rapid handling and removal of field heat are essential to prevent loss of quality after harvesting, especially during periods of high temperatures. Green peas lose much of their sugar content unless they are promptly cooled to 32°F. Hydrocooling is the preferred method for precooling. At 32°F and 95–98% relative humidity, green peas can be stored for 1–2 weeks. If the crop is packed with crushed ice, storage may be extended for about 1 additional week.

MARKETING

Green peas produced for canning and freezing are grown under contracts between growers and processors. Contract terms range widely but generally include price schedules, agreements on planting dates, charges for seed and pest control, cultural practices, and arrangements for harvesting and delivery schedules.

SELECTED REFERENCES

"Anonymous." 1987. *Peas for Canning and Processing.* Asgrow Seed Co., Kalamazoo, Michigan.

Gritton, E. T. 1986. Pea breeding, pp. 283–319. In: M. J. Bassett (ed.). *Breeding Vegetable Crops.* AVI Publishing Co., Westport, Connecticut.

Hagedorn, D. J. (ed.). 1984. *Compendium of Pea Diseases.* Amer. Phytopath. Soc., St. Paul, Minnesota.

Makasheva, R. K. 1983. *The Pea*. Oxonian Press, New Delhi, India.

Mansour, N. S., W. Anderson, and T. J. Darnell. 1984. *Producing Processing Peas in the Pacific Northwest*. Oregon State Univ. Region. Pub. PNW 243.

Meiners, J. P., and J. M. Kraft. 1977. *Beans and Peas Are Easy to Grow*. USDA Agric. Info. Bull. 409: 171–180.

Sandsted, R., R. Becker, and R. Ackerman. 1977. *Production of Processing Peas*. New York State Col. Agric. Cornell Univ. Ext. Info. Bull. 118.

Stevenson, W. R., and J. L. Wedberg. 1980. *Peas — Insect and Disease Control*. Univ. of Wisconsin Coop. Ext. Ser. A2354.

Valenzuela, L. H. 1983. *Edible Pea Pod Production in California*. Univ. of California Div. ANR. Leaf. 21328.

22

PEPPERS

F. J. Sundstrom*

Commercially grown peppers in North America belong to the nightshade family (Solanaceae), and therefore are closely related to eggplants, Irish potatoes, and tomatoes. With one exception, all commercially important pepper cultivars (hot and sweet) belong to the genus and species *Capsicum annuum*. Tabasco pepper, the hot pepper used to produce the internationally marketed tabasco pepper sauce, is the only *Capsicum* grown in the U.S. that belongs to the species *frutescens*. *Capsicum* sp. are not related to black pepper (*Piper nigrum*), the condiment that often accompanies salt at mealtimes.

CLASSIFICATION, ORIGIN, HISTORY

Peppers are classified into different horticultural groups or types based on the wide variation in fruit size, shape, and color (Figure 22.1). The principal groups are:

1. ***Bell group*** — Fruits are large, blocky, and blunt. Fruit color is usually green when immature and red when mature. Both green and red fruits are sold fresh. Red bell pepper fruits have greater concentrations of vitamins A and C, as well as a higher sugar content, than green fruits. Hybrid cultivars

---

*Associate Professor of Horticulture, Louisiana State University

421

Figure 22.1. Examples of different pepper horticultural groups or types: a) bell; b) pimiento; c) chile; d) 'Ancho' (a cultivar of chile); e) cayenne; f) jalapeño; g) banana (an example of the wax group; h) tabasco.

that are gold or yellow at maturity have recently gained significant fresh market popularity. Most, but not all, bell peppers are nonpungent.

Pimientos are a subgroup of the bell pepper group. Pimiento fruits are usually more heart-shaped than typical bell types. They also are nonpungent. Bells are generally marketed fresh, while pimientos are usually processed and used for their intense red color, for example in stuffed olives and processed meats.

2. **Anaheim chile group** — Fruits are smooth, tapering to a point with medium–thick flesh. Fruit color is usually green when immature and red when mature. Most chiles are moderately pungent (with the exception of nonpungent paprika types) and are marketed fresh, canned, processed into sauces, or dehydrated. Paprika describes a product of nonpungent, dehydrated chiles and is not a cultivar. Dehydrated red chile and paprika peppers are often used for their color. 'Ancho' (meaning *wide* in Spanish) is a cultivar of chile that is often stuffed in preparing "chile relleño" recipes.

   Cayennes are a subgroup of the anaheim chile group. Cayenne fruits are more slender and rounder, characteristically wrinkled and irregularly shaped, thin-walled, and highly pungent. They are used in pepper sauces, and the powder is used as a pungent spice.

3. **Jalapeño group** — Fruits are small, with a round, cylindrical shape (almost bullet-shaped), smooth, and with or without a corky network on the skin. The color is green when immature and red when mature. The fruits are very pungent and are sold fresh, canned whole or as slices, or used in pepper sauces.

4. **Cherry group** — Fruits are small and rounded in shape, green when immature and red at maturity. Cultivars can be pungent or nonpungent and are generally pickled and used in salads.

5. **Wax group** — Fruits can be either small or large and are marketed for their yellow color when immature. Pungent and nonpungent are sold fresh, or are pickled.

6. **Tabasco group** (*C. frutescens*) — Fruits are quite small and slender, tapering to a point. They are green when immature and turn red at maturity. Tabasco peppers are the most pungent peppers grown commercially in North America. Immature fruits are pickled, while mature red fruits are used in hot pepper sauces.

Capsicum sp. are thought to be native to Central and South America. In the tropics, peppers are perennials, but they are grown in sub-tropical and temperate zones as annuals. It is believed that Columbus first introduced pungent *Capsicum* to Europe after he returned from the New World. During the Spanish conquest of Mexico, jalapeños were used as barter and to pay taxes. In Europe, peppers acquired immediate popularity as a spice, both in fresh and dehydrated forms, and were often used as a substitute for black pepper.

The spelling and proper usage of words describing peppers is confusing. The word *chile* (not *chilly*, *chili*, or *chilli*) is the native Mexican word used to describe peppers in the pungent anaheim chile group. The Spanish word for peppers is *pimiento*, but in the U.S., this refers to a specific subgroup of nonpungent bell peppers. As the consumer has become more knowledgable concerning the many culinary uses of different peppers, specific subgroup and cultivar names, such as ancho, cayenne, and jalapeño pepper, are now commonly used in fresh market sales.

PRODUCTION AND INDUSTRY

Bell peppers constitute over two-thirds of the total pepper production in North America. Anaheim chile types account for about 15%, followed by pimiento (about 5%), and jalapeño (about 4%). Today, the most commonly used peppers for dehydration purposes are the cayenne, chile, and pimiento types. The increasing popularity of ethnic foods in the U.S., as well as recent medical evidence of the beneficial health effects of pepper consumption, has resulted in an increased fresh market demand for many pungent types.

Sweet bell pepper types are available throughout the year in the U.S. Florida produces in excess of 20,000 acres of peppers and provides fruit from November to July. California (10,000 acres) and Texas (8,000 acres) are the second and third largest producers. Total U.S. bell pepper acreage is about 60,000 acres. Crop yields average about 5 tons per acre. Chile peppers are the most widely grown pungent pepper, and in New Mexico, where the chile plant is the official state vegetable, over 20,000 acres of chiles are grown.

The pungency of peppers is measured organoleptically in terms of Scoville heat units. Nonpungent bell peppers are rated 0, anaheim chile types are rated from around 150 to 2,500, the cayenne and jalapeño groups are rated from about 10,000 to 18,000, and the pungency of the tabasco group is rated at about 40,000 Scovilles. Plant breeders have introduced new pungent cultivars within many groups that may vary from these standards. The pungency of peppers is due to the presence of an alkaloid called *capsaicin*, which is generally concentrated in the placental tissue near the stem end of the fruit of chile types. In cayenne, jalapeño, and tabasco peppers, capsaicin is located throughout the fruit. Many hot pepper sauce producers blend different peppers of various pungencies to produce a satisfactory hot sauce. Capsaicin extracted in its pure form from pepper fruits is used to produce the warmth in some topical analgesic balms and the irritant in mace. It has also been used in sprays as a deer, rabbit, and mouse crop-feeding repellent.

PLANT GROWTH AND DEVELOPMENT

Commercial pepper cultivars are determinate with an erect growth habit. Single stems terminate in a flower bud. Flowers arise from the axils of leaves and branches, generally in the upper canopy as the plant grows. In temperate climates, flowering continues throughout the growing season, and for this reason fruit set is not concentrated. Branches arise from leaf axils, and branching is dichotomous. Leaves of domesticated peppers are simple and alternate and vary in shape from ovate to ovate-lanceolate. Leaves of the wild types are generally smaller and often quite pubescent.

The peduncle position may be pendent, intermediate, or erect. Flowers are self-pollinated, and out-crossing is estimated to be less than 10%. Flowering is day-neutral, but is accelerated under long days and warm temperatures. The fruit is a pod-like berry with seeds borne on the placental tissue within the fruit cavity. Fruit color is normally green when immature, turning yellow, orange, and then red at maturity. Exceptions to normal fruit color development are becoming more common as plant breeders release yellow-, golden-, and even purple-fruited hybrids.

One problem with some peppers is the brittleness of the branches and main stem and the shallow root system. A very heavy fruit load, strong wind, or high soil moisture content may cause severe stem and branch breakage, and even uprooting in crops nearing maturity. Because fruiting is not concentrated and multiple harvests of fresh market peppers by hand are necessary, picking crews must be carefully instructed to avoid seriously damaging the fruit. When severe storm possibilities exist, growers in some production areas will stake plants (in a manner similar to tomatoes) to avoid lodging problems.

CLIMATIC AND CULTURAL REQUIREMENTS

All *Capsicum* sp. are warm-season crops. Due to their tropical origin, they are chilling-sensitive and will not tolerate extended periods of temperatures below 50°F without serious plant metabolic disruptions. Sweet peppers are adapted to mean growing temperatures between 65 and 85°F, but most pungent peppers (cayenne, chile, jalapeño, serrano, and tabasco) are distinctly warm-season crops that grow best in mean air temperatures above 75°F. Sweet types are generally cool summer, spring, and fall crops, while hot types are hot summer crops. Consistent warm (above 70°F) nights are particularly important for the successful production of some pungent pepper types, such as cayenne and tabasco. All peppers are killed by frost.

High temperatures (90°F) will result in flower abortion in sweet peppers but will increase the fruit set of many hot types. Optimum temperatures for pollination of sweet types are between 60 and 77°F, and misshapen fruit may occur (as a result of poor fertilization) if temperatures are greater than 85°F, or less than 60°F. Fruit set of sweet and hot peppers will not occur at less than 60°F. Excessive or deficit soil moisture will cause flower abortion. Peppers are more sensitive to excessive soil moisture than other solanaceous crops.

The seed germination range of bell and other sweet pepper types is between 60 and 95°F, with an optimum soil temperature of about 85°F. Hot pepper seed germination is basically the same as the sweet types. At soil temperatures between 77 and 86°F, bells require about 6 or 7 days to emerge, and tabasco peppers require about 14 days. Seed germination of some pepper types has proved to be very slow and erratic, resulting in poor crop uniformity. Direct-field seeding under cool temperatures (60–65°F) is risky because pepper seed germination is very slow at these temperatures, and seedlings are very susceptible to damping-off organisms. Pepper seed germination and seedling establishment can be stimulated under cool temperatures by seed osmoconditioning (see Chapter 5). Use of pregerminated seed in plug-mix or fluid-drilled seeders has also proved successful under less-than-favorable field seedbed conditions. Seedlings from fluid-drilled pregerminated seeds emerge about 4 days earlier and are significantly heavier than seedlings from untreated or raw seed.

Peppers can be produced successfully in soil of any textural class except heavy clay, provided that there is good internal soil drainage. Peppers are often produced on lighter-textured soils, particularly if an early market is important. Soil acidity should range between 5.5 and 6.8. If soil pH is below 5.5, blossom-end rot and manganese and aluminum toxicities may reduce yields.

Total fertilizer applied to double-row (two rows per bed) bell peppers may be as high as 250 pounds nitrogen (N) per acre, 150 pounds phosphorus (P_2O_5) per acre, and 50 pounds potash (K_2O) per acre. Bells may be sidedressed with nitrogen (40–60 pounds per acre) twice, once after seeding when plants are 6–8 inches tall, and then immediately following first fruit set. Too much nitrogen at flowering may result in flower abortion and spindly, brittle plants. Peppers are a shallow-rooted crop, so care is required when sidedressing. Nitrogen utilization efficiency by bell peppers receiving 200 pounds of nitrogen per acre in a single preplant application and then mulched with black polyethylene was 42% versus

8% for peppers grown with no mulch. When peppers received the same rate of nitrogen, but in split application (1 and 2 months after transplanting), nitrogen utilization was increased to 24%. Yields of No. 1 grade peppers are often greater when black polyethylene mulch is used (Figure 22.2).

Figure 22.2. Bell peppers grown on black polyethylene mulch.

PLANTING AND CROP ESTABLISHMENT

Peppers are established in the field by direct seeding or transplanting. Grower preference usually dictates which method will be used in any one growing area, although in northern-producing states such as Michigan, transplants are generally used. The use of pepper seedlings grown in larger transplant cell sizes results in greater early yields, but not always total crop yields. Florida growers often use black plastic mulch and will plug-mix seed through the plastic. In California, where growers do not have the weed problems found in Florida, peppers are usually direct seeded in unmulched beds.

The seeding rate in warm soils (greater than 75°F) for hot and sweet types is around 2 pounds seed per acre, preferably in clumps of three or four seeds. Bells are often seeded in 2 rows 12 inches apart on beds 38–40 inches apart. They are thinned by hand to a final spacing of 10–12 inches between plants within each row. Some growers believe that single rows are preferable to double rows for disease reasons. Where there are heavy early morning dews, single-row plants dry much earlier than those in double rows. If plant density is too high, crop earliness may be sacrificed.

Direct seeding of tabasco peppers is not recommended unless pregerminated seed in plug-mix or fluid-drilled seeders is used. Tabasco is generally transplanted due to the length of time required for field seedling emergence (around 14 days), even under optimum conditions. The length of the growing season (usually over 120 days following transplanting) dictates the need to produce these peppers only in sub-tropical growing areas.

CULTURAL PRACTICES

Pepper seedlings are comparatively weak with little vigor. Soil crusting within the seedbed can significantly reduce a stand of direct-seeded peppers. Because seedlings are also quite susceptible to damping-off organisms, growers must use seed treated with a protective fungicide, as well as monitoring seedbed moisture carefully. Excessive moisture will increase seedling damping-off problems, and protective fungicides are often applied soon after seedling emergence. *Phytophthora* blight is a serious disease of peppers, resulting in complete losses in some cases. In the greenhouse, media should be thoroughly drenched with a fungicidal solution.

Peppers are shallow-rooted and very sensitive to excessive soil moisture. Field moisture must be carefully monitored, particularly following fruit set. When soil moisture is deficit, blossom-end rot may occur; and under greater moisture stress, fruit abortion is possible. Drip irrigation is used successfully with the crop, particularly if used with plastic mulch. Overhead irrigation may spread serious diseases such as bacterial spot and *Phytophthora* blight.

Because peppers are shallow-rooted, cultivation for weed control must be very shallow and only used when plants are young. Cultivation during later stages of crop growth will likely result in root pruning and a severe check in plant development. Black polyethylene mulch will control weeds in the plant bed, and a light cultivation of the furrows will not damage the pepper root system. Preemergent and postemergent herbicides are also frequently used for weed control and are essential when peppers are grown without mulch.

CULTIVARS

The number of open-pollinated (OP) commercial cultivars of bell peppers grown is as great as the number of hybrids. This is testimony to the availability of superior-performing and inexpensive OP bell types. Hybrid bell pepper seed may be 20 times more expensive than OP cultivars, giving growers good reason to consider alternatives to purchasing hybrid seed. Purple and yellow fruits must be produced from hybrid cultivars, but any OP bell pepper fruit will turn red at maturity (normally about 3 weeks after mature-green fruit would be harvested). Some advantages to using hybrids are increased disease resistance and a wider range of fruit pungency levels.

There are numerous cultivars within each pepper horticultural group or type. Specialty fresh markets for popular ethnic pepper types have dramatically increased. Before selecting cultivars to supply these markets, growers must be aware of specific ethnic fruit preferences. Per capita consumption of fresh and processed hot peppers, such as chiles and jalapeños, has increased significantly and is expected to increase in the foreseeable future.

INSECTS, DISEASES, AND PHYSIOLOGICAL DISORDERS

Most insects and diseases that attack tomatoes also affect peppers. The crop requires constant monitoring to assure that pestilence does not result in economic losses. Peppers are very susceptible to viral diseases, so much so that production is no longer commercially feasible in certain traditional production areas. Many plant breeding efforts are currently focused on increasing pepper viral resistance.

Insects

Aphids. Green peach aphids (*Myzus persicae*) and potato aphids (*Macrosiphum euphorbiae*) injure peppers by feeding in large numbers on the undersides of the foliage. More importantly, both species serve as vectors of many viral diseases. Green peach aphids are resistant to many insecticides, but there are several insecticides that will control them with timely spraying applications. Often, aphid predators keep the number of green peach aphids at a low level.

Cucumber Beetles. Banded and spotted cucumber beetles (*Diabrotica* sp.) feed on the foliage and can defoliate large plants, as well as serve as vectors for some bacterial and viral diseases. The larval stage is known as the southern corn rootworm, which can be very damaging when it feeds on the roots of field and sweet corn.

Leaf Miners. Leaf miner larvae (*Liriomyza sativae*) feed within pepper foliage, creating a characteristic tunnel-like feeding pattern. Contact insecticides are not effective, but systemic chemicals may control the pests.

Pepper Maggots. Pepper maggots (*Zonosemata electa*) are the larvae of a fruit fly species. Eggs are laid through the fruit wall, and the emerging maggots feed within the fruit, causing it to rot. Horsenettle is an alternate host. Applying insecticides after the first appearance of adult flies has proved to be an effective control.

Pepper Weevils. These weevils (*Anthonomus euqenii*) are closely related to cotton boll weevils, but much smaller. Grubs feed on the blossoms and in the fruits, causing some fruits to abort prematurely. The pests are established in most pepper-growing regions in the southern U.S. In western states, they breed during the winter on black nightshade, a weed that should be eradicated around pepper fields. Scheduled spraying of insecticides is effective in controlling pepper weevils.

Cutworms, flea beetles, hornworms, and whiteflies are other insect pests that may cause economic crop losses in peppers.

Diseases

Anthracnose. Also called ripe rot, anthracnose is caused by the fungi *Colletotrichum capsici, C. gloeosporiodides,* and *C. acutatum* and is characterized by circular sunken spots, primarily on red pepper fruits. This fungal fruit rot causes both preharvest and postharvest losses on peppers worldwide. The fungi live on and within the seed coat, and those within the seed coat cannot be killed by seed treatment. Diseased plant residues provide an overwintering source of inoculum. The disease is promoted by moist conditions and high temperatures. Control is by fungicide sprays.

Bacterial Spot. Bacterial spot is caused by the bacterium *Xanthomonas campestris* pv. *vesicatoria.* The disease causes small, dark brown spots on leaves and fruits. The bacteria are seed-borne, and seed and infected transplants are the principal sources of inoculum. Bacteria are spread by splashing water from rain or by overhead irrigation, and disease development is promoted by moist conditions. Antibiotic sprays can be used on seedlings before transplanting, or fixed copper sprays may be used in the field for control.

Damping-off. A serious disease of seedlings, damping-off is caused primarily by the fungi *Rhizoctonia solani* and *Pythium* sp., which form lesions at the soil line, effectively girdling the young plants. These and other damping-off fungi thrive in high-moisture conditions and can be controlled by careful monitoring of soil moisture in the seedbed. Fungicide seed treatments and soil drenches are effective in preventing seedling injury.

Phytophthora Blight. This fungal disease is caused by *Phytophthora capsici* and can affect all parts of pepper plants. Damping-off can occur on young seedlings, while symptoms on older plants include root rot, stem canker, leaf blight, and fruit rot. Warm, wet conditions and overhead irrigation promote disease development.

Southern Blight. Southern blight is caused by the fungus *Sclerotium rolfsii*, which attacks the crown of the plant. Affected peppers wilt suddenly, turn yellow, and then die. This fungus also affects many other vegetable crops in southern growing regions. Drenching the beds with fungicides will provide the best control.

There are numerous viruses that may cause serious crop losses in peppers, including alfalfa mosaic, cucumber mosaic, pepper mottle, potato virus X and Y, tobacco etch and mosaic, and tomato spotted wilt viruses. Symptoms may include leaf mottling, puckering or curling, stem and petiole streaking, deformed or spotted fruit, stunted plants, sudden and complete wilting, and blossom and fruit drop. Reducing insect vector populations and following good sanitation practices are the best control measures.

Physiological Disorders

Blossom-end rot is caused by insufficient calcium availability during fruit development. Calcium availability to the fruit may be reduced by low soil calcium levels, or periodic, but significant, deficit soil moisture conditions that can restrict the transpirational movement of calcium through the plants. Affected areas on one of the lobes on the blossom end of the fruit first appear water-soaked, but soon become dry, light-colored, and papery. Secondary organisms may invade these areas. Cultivars vary in susceptibility to the disorder. The best control is maintaining an adequate supply of calcium to the plant and avoiding periods of water stress.

Sunscald is a result of pepper fruit exposure to long durations of intense sunlight. Exposed areas of the fruit become light-colored, slightly wrinkled, and papery. Secondary organisms may also invade these areas of damaged tissue. Good plant canopy cover will normally provide adequate shade to the fruit and prevent sunscald.

HARVESTING AND POSTHARVEST HANDLING

Bell pepper fruits are harvested at mature-green, yellow, and red or purple stages. Hybrid and open-pollinated cultivars may mature at different rates, but generally fruits reach the mature stage at about 30 days after anthesis, and the mature-red stage at about 50 days after anthesis. Bell peppers destined for the fresh market are harvested by hand because fruits bruise easily.

Fruit set is not concentrated in bell peppers, and multiple hand harvests, typically every 7–10 days, are necessary for maximum yields. Following fresh market harvests, the remaining fruits are often shipped to a processor. A once-over destructive harvest is sometimes used in harvesting peppers for processing. Cayenne (picked red), chile and jalapeño (picked green and red), and paprika and pimiento (picked red) peppers can more easily be mechanically harvested than bells because they do not bruise as readily, and the processor is not as concerned about minor fruit damage. The mature-red fruits of tabasco peppers, used primarily in the production of hot pepper sauces, are selectively harvested by hand in sub-tropical production areas from mid-August until late November.

Ethephon [(2-chloroethyl)-phosphonic acid] can be applied to all pepper types at the mature-green stage to accelerate ripening to the mature-red stage. Premature defoliation may occur when high rates of ethephon are applied in high temperatures. However, the addition of calcium to the spray will usually overcome this problem.

After harvest, bell fruits are graded (Figure 22.3) and frequently run through a hot (128°F) water bath containing 500 ppm chlorine to control bacterial rots. Following this, most bell fruits are sprayed with a wax emulsion prior to being packed to reduce moisture loss during storage. Bell pepper fruits are packed in 25- to 30-pound bushels or cardboard cartons.

Pepper fruits are subject to chilling injury, characterized by pitting of the fruits, if storage temperatures are less than 45°F. At storage temperatures above 50°F, however, further fruit ripening and development of anthocyanin and red

Figure 22.3. An example of U.S. No. 1 grade fruits on left and No. 2's on the right. The primary difference between the two grades is fruit shape.

carotenoid pigments will occur. At these warmer temperatures, bacterial soft rot also becomes a major concern. Pepper fruit quality can be maintained for up to 3 weeks under ideal storage conditions of 45–50°F and 90–95% relative humidity.

SELECTED REFERENCES

Andrews, J. 1984. *Peppers, the Domesticated Capsicums.* Univ. of Texas Press, Austin.

Cannon, J. M., and J. Boudreaux. 1987. *Commercial Vegetable Production Recommendations.* Louisiana Coop. Ext. Ser., Baton Rouge.

Greenleaf, W. H. 1986. Pepper breeding, pp. 67–134. In: M. J. Bassett (ed.). *Breeding Vegetable Crops.* AVI Publishing Co., Westport, Connecticut.

Montelaro, J., and S. R. Kostewicz. 1974. *Pepper Production Guide.* Univ. of Florida Coop. Ext. Ser. Cir. 102D.

Ryall, A. L., and W. J. Lipton. 1979. *Transportation and Storage of Fruits and Vegetables,* 2nd ed. Vol. 1. AVI Publishing Co., Westport, Connecticut.

Sims, W. L., and P. G. Smith. 1976. *Growing Peppers in California.* Univ. of California Coop. Ext. Ser. Leaf. 2676.

Smith, P. G., B. Villalon, and P. L. Villa. 1987. Horticultural classification of peppers grown in the United States. *HortScience* 22:11–13.

Tindall, H. D. 1983. *Vegetables in the Tropics.* AVI Publishing Co., Westport, Connecticut.

Villalon, B. 1981. Breeding peppers to resist virus diseases. *Plant Dis.* 65:557–562.

23

POTATOES

Potatoes are the most important, and perhaps the most widespread, vegetable food crop in the world today. They are cultivated in more than 130 countries that vary in climate and topography. The plant is so adaptable that it grows from below sea level in the Netherlands, to almost 14,000 feet in the Andes, from the Arctic Circle in the north to Tierra del Fuego in the south, and in the arid climates of Australia and Africa. Only in the tropical jungles, where they are seriously depressed by high temperatures and disease, will potatoes not be found under some type of cultivation.

As a food crop, potatoes are used for both fresh market and processing; they are made into chips, dehydrated, canned, frozen, and used for starch and flour. In addition to being a food crop, potatoes are used extensively around the world as livestock feed and in the production of vodka, paste, and dyes. Culled potatoes and surplus potatoes can be fermented into ethyl alcohol (ethanol) and mixed with gasoline as a fuel alcohol source.

CLASSIFICATION, ORIGIN, HISTORY

The potato (*Solanum tuberosum*) is a herbaceous dicot belonging to the nightshade family (Solanaceae). It is a close relative of the tomato, eggplant, pepper, tobacco, petunia, and wild nightshade, but it is not related to the sweet potato. Most of the world's crop, and all potatoes grown in the U.S., belong to the species *S. tuberosum*. The genus *Solanum* contains about 2,000 species, 160 of which form tubers, and 20 of these are cultivated.

The plant is grown for its underground tubers, which are high in carbohydrates or starch. In its native habitat, the potato is a perennial, but in temperate regions, it is grown as an annual. It can persist in the field from one season to the next by volunteer plants which propagate vegetatively by means of the tubers.

The origin of the potato is South America, in the Andean region of Peru and Bolivia, where the crop was cultivated long before the arrival of the Spaniards to the New World in the 16th century. It was introduced to Europe by the returning Spanish explorers and quickly spread throughout the continent. At first it was regarded more as a curiosity than as a cultivated crop. However, by the end of the 17th century the potato was becoming an important food crop throughout Europe, particularly in such countries as Ireland, where it became a staple of the Irish diet, as well as a significant part of the culture. Even today, the potato is referred to as the "Irish" potato, rather than the "South American" potato.

When and how it reached the continental U.S. is not known, but as a food crop it had little significance until the arrival of the Presbyterian immigrants from Ireland in 1718. The crop gained its greatest impetus in this country after 1846, the year the late blight disease destroyed the potato crop in Ireland and caused a great famine. This resulted in the mass emigration of Irish people to the U.S., and along with them the widespread cultivation of the crop in the U.S.

PRODUCTION AND INDUSTRY

In the U.S., potatoes are by far the most important vegetable in terms of the quantities produced and consumed. Per capita consumption in the U.S. in 1989 was 126.2 pounds; 49.8 pounds fresh, 46.1 pounds frozen, 17.8 pounds chips, and 12.5 pounds other. This compares to a total of 202.2 pounds for all other major vegetables.

Potatoes are grown commercially and for home use throughout the U.S. and lead all vegetables in acreage, production, and value. More than half (53%) of the U.S. potato crop in 1988 was marketed in some processed form, including frozen potato products (31%), chips (13%), dehydrated (8%), and canned (1%). Table stock, or fresh market, potatoes comprised about 30% of the total U.S. production. Other uses included seed potatoes (7%) and livestock feed (1%), while shrinkage and other losses amounted to about 8% of the crop. Many growers produce both processing potatoes and fresh market table stock.

Potatoes are grown year-round in the U.S., with the bulk of the harvest (89%) taking place in the fall (Table 23.1). Spring and summer harvests are roughly equal and combined make up about 10% of the crop. Winter production is small and accounts for approximately 1% of the potatoes grown in the U.S. The spring, summer, and winter potato crops are produced mainly in the South and West.

Table 23.1. Seasonal Harvested Acreage, Production, and Value of Potatoes in the U.S., 1988[1]

Season	Harvested Acres	Production	Value
		(tons × 1,000)	*($1,000)*
Winter	11,700	125	46,519
Spring	80,700	886	205,598
Summer	99,400	1,139	147,582
Fall	1,090,300	17,139	1,303,271
U.S.	1,282,100	19,289	1,702,970

[1]Source: USDA. 1989. National Agricultural Statistics Service (NASS), Agricultural Statistics Board.

Most of these go directly to market or into processing. The fall or main crop is produced primarily in the northern half tier of states from Maine to North Dakota, Idaho, and Washington. Most of it is stored for later use. Idaho is the leading state in production, and produces approximately 28% of the U.S. potato crop (Table 23.2), followed by Washington (18%), Maine (6%), Colorado (6%), Oregon (6%), Wisconsin (6%), California (5%), North Dakota (4%), and Minnesota (4%). Average yields increased from 13 tons per acre in 1977 to more than 15 tons per acre in 1988.

Table 23.2. Fall Harvested Acreage, Production, and Value of Potatoes in the U.S., 1988[1]

State	Harvested Acres	Production	Value
		(tons × 1,000)	*($1,000)*
Idaho	347,000	4,986	538,434
North Dakota	135,000	776	98,584
Washington	115,000	3,163	284,625
Maine	80,000	1,100	160,600
Minnesota	74,700	678	85,091
Wisconsin	62,500	1,000	128,000
Colorado	65,600	1,045	149,993
Oregon	45,000	1,037	99,638
Michigan	43,000	472	68,923
New York	32,300	340	61,015
Pennsylvania	20,500	185	28,044
California	47,200	838	153,137
Other states	191,500	2,202	289,671
Total	1,259,300	17,822	2,145,755

[1]Source: USDA. 1989. National Agricultural Statistics Service (NASS), Agricultural Statistics Board.

Worldwide, the USS leads in production and grows about 28% of the crop, followed by China, Poland, the U.S., India, Germany, and France. The annual worldwide crop is estimated at over 340,000,000 tons.

PLANT GROWTH AND DEVELOPMENT

Potato development can be divided into three phases: 1) emergence and early development (predominantly leaf and stem growth), 2) tuber initation, and 3) the period of tuber enlargement and maturation (including the time of maximum vine growth).

Emergence and Early Development

Potatoes usually produce several upright stems that may grow to a height of 3.5 feet. These develop from a small seed tuber or a piece of a larger tuber, referred to as a "seed piece," that was produced the previous year (Figure 23.1). For some time after they emerge, the shoots grow erect and become sturdy stems that form a rather dense bushy foliage. As the plants mature, the stems may recline and ultimately senesce and die. The leaves are compound and alternate, consisting of two to four pairs of primary leaflets, along with a terminal leaflet. Roots arise at the underground nodes of the main stem. Initially, they tend to grow horizontally, but later turn downward. Most will accumulate in the upper 24-inch soil layer, but some may penetrate deeper.

Flowers are initiated in clusters, or cymes, at the top of the plant while the shoots are still erect. The blossoms can range in color from white to purple and may be solid or a combination of colors. In some cultivars, flowers will drop off before they open, particularly under adverse weather conditions. The fruit is a small, green berry, which may contain up to 300 small, flat, oval seeds. However, potato seeds produce plants that genetically vary a great deal from the parent plant, so they are used mainly in breeding programs and are rarely used as propagating material for a commercial crop.

Tuber Initiation and Development

Potato tubers consist of the enlarged or thickened portions of underground stems, commonly referred to as stolons. These arise at one or more nodes of the main underground stems, usually within a week after the above ground shoots emerge. They grow horizontally for several inches and then begin to thicken. Usually the tubers form at the distal end or tip of the stolon but may occasionally develop along the stolon itself.

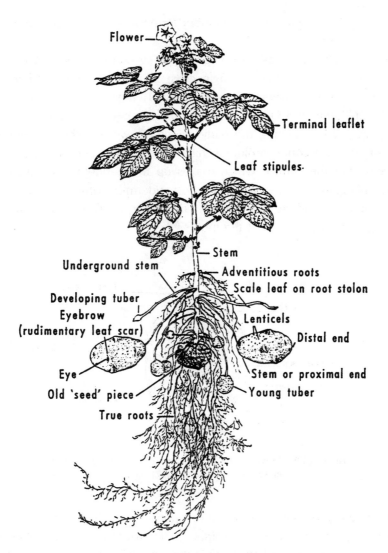

Flower

Terminal leaflet

Leaf stipules.

Stem

Underground stem

Adventitious roots

Scale leaf on root stolon

Developing tuber

Eyebrow
(rudimentary leaf scar)

Lenticels

Distal end

Eye

Stem or proximal end

Old 'seed' piece

Young tuber

True roots

Figure 23.1. Diagrammatic drawing of the parts of a potato plant. The stolons arise from stem tissue, while the true roots arise at the base of the stem. (Source: USDA Agriculture Handbook No. 267)

The tuber represents a storage organ and consists of stored or surplus food materials, mostly carbohydrates, that are in excess of those needed by the plant for its normal growth processes. The initial thickening of the tuber results from rapid cell division, particularly in the center, or pith. By the time the tuber is about 0.5 inch in diameter, most of the new cells have been formed, and further enlargement results primarily from the increase in the size of the cells already formed.

Tubers have all the characteristics of normal stems, including nodes, which are marked by the presence of buds or "eyes." These occur in a spiral pattern on the tuber and usually increase in number from the stem end of the tuber to the seed or distal end.

Anatomically, the tuber is composed of several regions: 1) the epidermis, which is a thin outer layer of single cells; 2) the periderm, or skin, which is composed of several layers of corky cells; 3) the cortex, which is made of secondary phloem; and 4) the medulla or pith, composed mainly of parenchyma tissue (Figure 23.2). During the early stages of swelling, the thin epidermis is sloughed off and a cork cambium is initiated that forms and maintains a layer of cork cells over the surface which makes up the periderm, or skin. As tubers mature, enlargement slows down and the periderm becomes tougher, the starch content increases and the water content decreases, resulting in an increase in the specific gravity (dry weight) of the tubers.

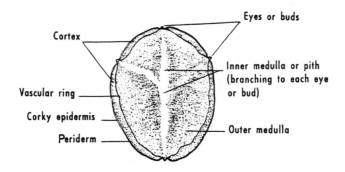

Figure 23.2. Cross section of a potato tuber. (Source: USDA Agriculture Handbook No. 267)

At maturity, the tubers go into a rest period for 1–3 months, depending on the cultivar. During this time the respiration rate drops to a low level. As the tubers emerge from the rest period, the buds in the eyes will germinate and start to grow unless kept dormant by low temperatures or chemical sprout inhibitors.

Shoot / Tuber Relationships

The yield and quality of tubers is directly dependent on an abundant supply of carbohydrates furnished by the foliage to the tubers. It is important during the early part of the season to have vigorous shoot growth in order to build up a large photosynthetic surface for tuber development later in the season. For the first 4–5 weeks after planting, the developing plant will draw on the carbohydrate reserve in the seed piece. However, excessive early shoot growth may result in the seed piece being used up and decaying before the plant is able to support itself.

After tubers are initiated, they are in direct competition for carbohydrates with other parts of the plant. Because the leaves and growing points of the stem are closer to the source of carbohydrates, the tubers receive only that excess portion of the carbohydrates not utilized by the above ground parts of the plant. Therefore, anything that cuts down on photosynthesis or increases the utilization of manufactured carbohydrates in growth or respiration after tubers set retards the growth of the tubers.

Apical Dominance

When the tuber first emerges from the rest period, the eyes may exhibit strong apical dominance. The eye at the seed, or apical, end will inhibit other eyes from sprouting. Consequently, planting whole tubers will usually result in one to three shoots emerging from the apical end. If the apical eye is removed, or if the tuber is cut into seed pieces, the effect of apical dominance is diminished, and each eye (seed pieces usually have one to three eyes) is stimulated to sprout, increasing the number of stalks arising from a single seed tuber. The longer the tuber is kept dormant after the rest period is broken, the more the apical dominance will diminish and the greater the number of sprouts that develop when the tuber is placed in a favorable environment.

CLIMATIC AND CULTURAL REQUIREMENTS

The potato is a cool-season crop that is sensitive to high temperatures, especially during the period of tuber enlargement and development. It is only moderately tolerant of frost and requires a frost-free season of around 100 days.

Temperature and Daylength

The climatic variables of daylength and temperature are the two most important uncontrollable factors influencing the growth and yield of potatoes. In most cases, these will determine in what region and season potatoes can be successfully grown.

As a general rule, optimum tuber production is obtained with a mean temperature range during the growing season of 60–65°F, with a maximum average temperature of 75°F and a minimum of 45°F. High temperatures increase rates of respiration, which decrease the supply of carbohydrates to the tubers. High night temperatures are generally more detrimental to tuber yields than high day temperatures.

Daylength and temperature requirements in potato differ, depending on the particular stage of growth. Long days promote vine and stolon growth, while short days stimulate tuber production. Top growth and stolon growth are greatest at about 77°F. During early plant development, long daylengths and daytime temperatures between 80°F and 90°F and night temperatures near 70°F are most conducive to vine growth. Higher day and night temperatures will result in prolonged vegetative growth and elongated stolons and will delay tuberization.

Tuber initiation is favored by short days, bright sunlight, and moderately low temperatures (59°F). At lower temperatures, top growth and stolon growth are reduced but the initiation of tubers is usually hastened. For the period of tuber enlargement and maturation, tubers develop most rapidly with day temperatures at 70°F and night temperatures below 57°F. Generally, the number of tubers per plant is higher at lower temperatures, but the tuber size will be smaller.

Although considered a cool-season crop, potatoes can be grown successfully at high temperatures, provided a sufficient uniform supply of water is available to meet evapotranspiration demands and night temperatures tend to be moderate. Some of the highest yields are produced in areas such as California, eastern Oregon, and central Washington, where daytime temperatures reach 100°F or more. In these areas, cool night temperatures are critical since they reduce respiration rates.

Soil temperatures also affect tuber yield and quality. Low soil temperatures help in reducing the respiration rate of the tubers. This is especially important when air temperatures are high. Maximum tuber yields occur at soil temperatures of 60°F–75°F. Soil temperatures above 75°F will promote emergence and enhance early stolon growth, but they can reduce tuber yields. Above 84°F, tubers will not form (Figure 23.3). High soil temperatures during the period of enlargement and early maturation may cause internal discoloration.

Soils

Silt loams, sandy loams, and peat or muck soils are best. Soils should be friable (aggregated) and well drained. Good aeration is paramount for potato production. Wet, water-logged soils result in lower yields and enlarged lenticels on the tubers. Excess soil moisture late in the season may encourage vine growth at the expense of tubers. Compacted soils tend to produce misshaped, knobby tubers. If drainage is good, heavy clay soils can be used to grow potatoes by adding large quantities of organic matter. Commercial crops can be grown on porous sandy soils, provided heavy applications of commercial fertilizers are made.

Soil pH should be between 5.4 and 7.0 for best yields, but if scab is a problem, soil reaction should be near 5.0. If scab-resistant cultivars are grown,

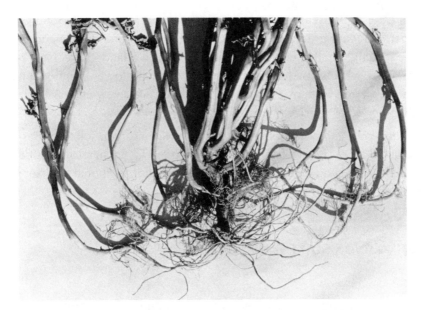

Figure 23.3. **High soil temperatures may inhibit tuberization.**

lower soil pH levels are not as critical. Although potatoes require less liming than most other crops, some lime may be needed in humid regions. Applying lime to the preceding crop or in the fall is usually best.

Summer cover crops turned under in the fall help improve soil aeration and fertility for a potato crop to follow in the spring. Winter cover crops are not well suited for potato production because potatoes are normally planted before the cover crop has time to make any appreciable growth.

Fertility

The potato belongs to the group of vegetable crops having the highest fertilizer requirement. The plant is not a good forager since most roots are in the top layer of soil and extend out to only 2 feet.

On most soils, nitrogen, phosphorus, and potassium will be needed. There may be exceptions, as in the case of some muck soils containing high levels of nitrogen, and some western soils high in potassium. The amount of fertilizer will depend on the available nutrient levels in the soil and on factors affecting the yield potential, such as cultivar, spacing, and environmental conditions. Generally, more fertilizer will be needed for the early crop than for the late crop.

Nitrogen rates can increase up to 250 pounds per acre on some sandy soils. Early in the season, nitrogen is needed to promote vigorous shoot growth. However, too much nitrogen can reduce tuber yields due to excessive vine growth. Later in the season, excessive nitrogen can lower the specific gravity of the tuber, decreasing tuber quality and durability in storage. Nitrogen rates will vary depending on the cultivar: 'Superior' and 'Norland' have high nitrogen requirements, while those for 'Kennebec' are generally lower. Ammonium sulfate often is a preferred source of nitrogen fertilizer since it is very effective in lowering pH, although other fertilizer sources can be used.

Phosphorus and potassium rates are normally based on soil tests. Best results are obtained when most of the fertilizer is banded 2 inches to the side and 2 inches below the seed piece, particularly in cold soils. Additional fertilizer may be sidedressed when plants are about 6 inches tall.

PLANTING AND CROP ESTABLISHMENT

The crop is propagated vegetatively with either small whole tubers or cut seed pieces. Planting small (1–2 inches in diameter) uncut tubers frequently results in a better stand and a heavier set of tubers. There is also less likelihood of spreading disease from the cutting operation. However, whole seed may cost more than cut seed, and sometimes a limited supply is available. When cut seed pieces are used, the cutting operation diminishes apical dominance, which often results in more rapid emergence, more total sprouts, and more uniform sprout development.

Preplanting Procedures

When cut seed is used, the seed piece should weigh about 2 ounces and contain one to several buds, or eyes. A medium-sized tuber can be cut into four to six pieces, with each piece containing one to three eyes (Figure 23.4). Very small pieces having only one eye frequently produce weak plants. If the pieces are cut too large, a large amount of "seed" will be required, thus increasing seed costs. Mechanical cutters are commonly used, but some hand cutting will generally be needed for very large seed pieces.

The seed pieces should be planted as soon as possible after cutting to avoid infection by bacteria and fungi, resulting in seed piece decay. If this is not possible and the cut seed pieces must be held for more than a few days, they should be cured to allow cut surfaces to *suberize* (form a corky protective layer) and heal. Suberization is accomplished by holding the cut seed pieces at 55–65°F, for 3–5 days, in an atmosphere of 85% relative humidity with good ventilation. Many growers synchronize the cutting operation and planting to avoid holding un-

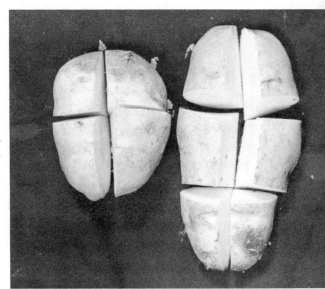

Figure 23.4. Blocky seed pieces with one or more well-developed eyes are used to propagate the crop.

planted cut seed. Seed pieces can be treated with a fungicide dust after they are cut to help prevent decay.

Seed taken from storage should not be planted directly. When tubers are transferred from a cold to a warm environment, they undergo an initial "sweat" period which can contribute to seed decay. Prior to cutting, the tubers should be warmed to 50–60°F for several days.

Freshly harvested tubers are dormant for up to 3 months after maturity and normally will not sprout. If they are used for seed during this time, a treatment to break dormancy may be needed. The seed can be dipped in potassium gibberelate (1–5 ppm) for 5 minutes. In California, high temperature (70–80°F) storage at high relative humidity (80–90%) is used to stimulate sprouting. Other methods to help break dormancy include storing tubers in a modified low oxygen atmosphere, and wounding or cutting the tubers. Each of the above treatments increases the carbon dioxide level inside the tubers, which promotes sprout growth.

Planting

Early potatoes should be planted about 6 weeks before the last spring frost is expected, or when the soil temperature reaches 45°F. Soil temperatures below 40°F at planting may result in delayed emergence and decay of the seed piece. In the South, the major portion of the crop is planted from late fall to late winter. In the northern areas, most planting is usually in May and June, and in March and April in the central states. In western areas, the major plantings are made in the spring and summer for fall crops.

Potatoes are planted with two- or four-row planters. Rows are commonly spaced 30–42 inches apart, with plants spaced 6–16 inches apart within the rows. Production of large tubers is enhanced by wider spacings, and vice-versa. The desired spacing varies, depending on cultivar, planting method, cultural factors such as soil type, fertility, and available moisture, and intended market use.

Whole seed potatoes tend to produce a heavier set and smaller tubers than cut seed, and they are usually spaced further apart in the row to encourage tuber enlargement. Heavy-yielding cultivars such as 'Katahdin' and 'Kennebec,' which tend to produce large tubers and have light set, should be spaced closer in the row to reduce the yield of oversized tubers. In contrast, a cultivar such as 'Norchip,' which tends to have heavy set and small tubers, should be spaced further apart in the row. Wider spacings are best under dry conditions, while the opposite is true with irrigation. Some cultivars, when grown under irrigation, need close spacing to keep tubers from growing too large and to minimize growth cracks and hollow heart (see "Physiological Disorders"). Processors who produce french fries generally desire large tubers, while producers of seed potatoes want tubers less than 3 inches in diameter.

Planting depth varies from 2 inches (between the top of the seed and the soil surface) to 6 inches. The best depth will vary with soil moisture and temperature. Shallow planting promotes faster emergence but may reduce yields, as well as increase the problem of tuber greening due to exposure to light. In the summer, when the soil is hot, shallow planting may result in burning off of sprouts, while deep planting may not allow for sufficient oxygen for adequate seed respiration. In cooler areas the seed is usually planted at a depth of around 2 inches to promote rapid emergence. Deep planting may be used in the early spring when the soil is cold, but it may delay emergence and reduce yields. In the West, where the climate is drier, the seed is planted deeper (4 inches) to provide for better moisture conditions. On heavy clay soils, shallow planting should be used for better drainage. Deep plantings (6 inches) are generally made on muck soils.

Certified Seed

Today, over 70 commercial cultivars are certified. Certification assures the grower of obtaining seed (tubers) true to cultivar and almost free (95–100%) of disease. Most states growing seed potatoes commercially have associations that inspect both field and storage potatoes before certifying the seed stock. Field inspection of the plants is the only reliable way to identify some viral diseases, such as mosaic and leaf roll, which are carried in the tubers. Approximately 25% of the potatoes grown are certified, which far exceeds the amount needed for planting. Using seed from a commercial crop without certification often results in seed with reduced productivity and performance.

CULTURAL PRACTICES

Cultivation and Hilling

Potatoes are grown in ridged rows to provide soil covering to prevent sun greening of developing tubers. Ridging or hilling also promotes stolon growth and facilitates tuber development and harvest. The plants are usually hilled when well developed, but before they come together in the row. Ridging is most beneficial on heavy soils where tubers tend to form at a shallow depth, and with greening-susceptible cultivars such as 'Norchip' and 'Katahdin.' Hilling and cultivation can be combined into one operation.

Cultivation should be held to a minimum and should be practiced as little as possible, especially after plants start to bloom freely and begin to form tubers. Deep cultivations can injure roots and stolons, which can reduce tuberization. With the increased use of herbicides, cultivation is no longer the primary means to control weeds. Except to prevent crusting in heavy soils and for ridging, very little cultivation is needed.

Weeds

Among vegetable crops, potatoes are one of the better competitors with weeds. The most serious weed problems come from perennial species such as bindweed, quackgrass, and milkweed, which are difficult to control chemically. These have to be treated by mechanical and chemical practices before the potato crop is established. For most annual weeds, several effective preemergent broad-leaf and grass herbicides are available. Late in the season some weed problems may arise when herbicides tend to lose their effectiveness and shading by the crop is not sufficient to suppress weed growth. Generally, these weeds can be controlled by chemical dessicants applied just prior to harvest to kill the vines.

Irrigation

Potatoes are grown both with and without irrigation. In many areas of the eastern U.S., potatoes very often receive enough rainfall during the growing season that a good crop can be grown without supplemental irrigation. However, on sands and lighter soils, and throughout the western and southwestern growing regions, irrigation is essential.

For good growth and development, potatoes have a high water requirement. The plants are shallow-rooted and develop a relatively poor root system. A few roots penetrate deeply, but they are not numerous enough to permeate the soil thoroughly at greater depths. Seasonal water requirements range from 20 acre-inches in some humid and coastal regions to 40 acre-inches in the arid valleys of California, Oregon, Washington, and Idaho. Studies have shown that the daily water needs increase linearly until about 2 weeks after maximum vine coverage is reached. During the period of heavy vine growth, potatoes need about 2 inches of water per week. The periods of stolonization and the beginning of tuberization are critical. A deficiency or severe fluctuation in available moisture during the time of tuber formation may result in growth cracks or misshapen tubers, along with initiation of knobby secondary growth. Research from Michigan has shown that overirrigation in the last month prior to harvest can significantly decrease tuber dry matter.

High yields of potatoes are obtained when the available soil moisture is maintained between 50 and 65% throughout the irrigation season. Several methods used to irrigate potatoes include furrow irrigation, sprinkler irrigation (solid-set, wheel-line, overhead center-pivot, hand-move), and subirrigation. Furrow irrigation is popular in the West but is limited to relatively flat land. A common practice is to irrigate daily in alternate furrows. However, most irrigated potato acreage in the U.S. is by sprinkler systems, while subirrigation is used mainly on muck soils.

CULTIVARS

The large number of available cultivars of potatoes differ in time of maturity, yield, appearance, cooking and marketing qualities, and resistance to various insects and diseases. Perhaps more than most other vegetables, potato cultivars must be adapted to the cultural and climatic conditions under which they are to be grown. A cultivar that is good in one geographical area may not do well in another. For example, the cultivar 'Centennial' is grown extensively in Colorado, California, and Arizona, but when it is grown elsewhere, yield and tuber size are inadequate.

Certain cultivars are well suited for particular culinary purposes. Tuber dry matter content is one of the most important measures of quality for best utilization and is measured (with a hydrometer) by the specific gravity or density of the tubers (Table 23.3). Potatoes with a high specific gravity contain more dry matter than those with a low one and are preferred for baking, chipping, dehydrating, and making frozen products, while those with a low specific gravity are preferred for canning. Tuber specific gravity or dry matter is the most important factor influencing the oil content of potato chips. The higher the dry matter, the lower the oil level in the finished product. Potatoes used for boiling are intermediate in their specific gravity measurement.

Table 23.3. Potato Utilization Characteristics[1]

Specific Gravity	Total Dry Matter	Cooked Texture	Best Use
Less than 1.06	Less than 16%	Very soggy	Frying, salads
1.06–1.07	16%–18%	Soggy to waxy	Frying, salads
1.07–1.08	18%–20%	Waxy	Boiling
1.07–1.09	20%–22%	Mealy	Baking, mashing
Over 1.09	Over 22%	Very mealy	Baking, french frying

[1]Source: D. Curwen, K. A. Kelling, J. A. Schoenemann, W. R. Stevenson, and J. A. Wyman. 1982. *Commercial Potato Production and Storage*. Univ. of Wisconsin Coop. Ext. Ser. A2257.

The cultivars listed in Table 23.4 account for most of the U.S. crop. 'Russet Burbank', released by Luther Burbank around 1880, is still the most important potato cultivar. It has excellent baking quality and because of its large, long, cylindrical shape and high specific gravity is a top choice for frozen french fries

Table 23.4. Brief Description of Selected Potato Cultivars

Cultivar	Season	Tuber Color	Use[1]	Resistant to[2]	Susceptible to[2]
Atlantic	Midseason	Cream	C	S, VW, GN	HH, ID
Centennial	Medium late	Russet	FM		
Chipbelle	Medium late	White	C, FM	PVX, GN	HH
Goldrus	Midseason	Russet	FM, F		G
Irish Cobbler	Early	Cream	HG	MM	
Katahdin	Late	White	S, FM, P	MM, BR	S, G
Kennebec	Late	Cream	C, F, P	MM, LB	S, VW
Monona	Midseason	White	C, FM	VW	LB
ND 146-4R	Early	Red	FM	LB, S	
Norchip	Midseason	White	C, S, P	S	LB, EB, VW, G
Norgold Russet	Midseason	Russet		S	HH
Norland	Early	Red	CN, FM		LB
Rhinered	Midseason	Red	FM	S, VW	
Russet Burbank	Late	Russet	S, B, F	S	LB, EB, VW
Russet Norkota	Midseason	Russet	S, FM, F	S	
Russet Sebago	Late	Russet	S	S, LB	
Sangre	Midseason	Red	FM	S	EB, LB, VW
Sebago	Late	White	S, C	S, LB	
Sincoe	Medium early	White	C, FM	S, MM, LB, GN	R, LR
Superior	Medium early	White	S, C, FM	S	LB, VW
Yukon Gold	Medium early	Yellow	F, FM	MM, LR	

[1]C (chips), FM (fresh market), HG (home garden), S (storage), P (processing), F (fries), CN (canning), B (baking).

[2]S (scab), VW (*Verticillium* wilt), G (greening), GN (golden nematode), HH (hollow heart), ID (internal discoloration, PVX (potato virus X), MM (mild mosaic), BR (brown rot), LB (late blight), EB (early blight), R (*Rhizoctonia*), LR (leaf roll).

and flakes. However, the 'Burbank' is quite susceptible to both early and late blight, and a costly spray program is usually necessary.

'Kennebec' is a USDA selection that makes up about 18% of the total seed acreage. It is a high-yielding cultivar that should be grown at close spacing to avoid oversized tubers. Along with 'Superior', it is considered a general-purpose potato satisfactory for baking, boiling, or frying, although both cultivars are mostly used for chipping. Other leading cultivars for chips are 'Norchip' and 'Monona', since they tend to have high total solids.

'Katahdin', also a USDA release, is usually boiled or baked fresh. It makes up a major portion of the northeastern crop, especially in Maine. Along with 'Russet Burbank', 'Sebago', and 'Superior', it tends to have a relatively long dormant period and is one of the better storing cultivars. There are also available yellow-flesh cultivars, such as 'Yukon Gold' and 'Saginaw Gold', which have been accepted in certain markets.

INSECTS, DISEASES, AND PHYSIOLOGICAL DISORDERS

Insects

More than 25 species of insects are injurious to the potato, but most of these are seldom seriously destructive over a great area. However, there are several insect pests that cause varying amounts of damage in most production areas.

Colorado Potato Beetles. The most destructive and widespread insect of potatoes is the Colorado potato beetle (*Leptinotarsa decemlineata*). The adult beetles are thick-bodied, dark yellow–brown with black stripes. The larvae are reddish-orange and have two rows of black spots along their sides. Both adults and larvae feed on foliage, eating irregular holes in the leaves. Plants can be completely defoliated if beetle populations are not controlled. Adults overwinter in the field. The best control is with insecticide sprays.

Flea Beetles. The tuber flea beetle (*Epitrix tuberis*) and the potato flea beetle (*E. cucumeris*) can be serious pests of potatoes, particularly early in the spring. The adults are small, shiny, black beetles that overwinter in the soil and feed on emerging potato seedlings. The adults chew small, round holes in potato leaves, while the larvae feed on roots and tubers. Control of flea beetles is by good sanitation and clean culture to reduce weed growth and by the use of insecticides.

Leafhoppers. The potato leafhopper (*Empoasca fabae*) and the aster leafhopper *(Macrosteles fascifrons)* are small, grayish-green, jumping, wedge-shaped insects that suck juice from the undersides of leaves, causing the tips to turn brown and the edges to curl upward. During feeding, adults and nymphs secrete toxins, resulting in the characteristic "hopperburn." Both species have numerous alternate hosts, and the best control is with insecticides. The aster leafhopper is also the vector of the mycoplasma causing purple top wilt.

Aphids. The small, green peach aphid *(Myzus persicae)* and the larger potato aphid *(Macrosiphum euphorbiae)* feed on potatoes by piercing and sucking juices from the leaves. At low levels of infestation, aphids will not produce significant direct damage, but severe infestations will cause plants to wilt. However, aphids can cause a great deal of indirect damage; both species are vectors of several viral diseases, including potato leaf roll.

Potato Tuberworms. Potato tuberworms *(Phthorimaea operculella)* are pinkish-white caterpillars, each approximately 0.25 inch long. They mine the leaves and stems and burrow into the tubers. Late potatoes and those in storage are more frequently attacked than the early crop. Hot, dry weather in the field and the accumulation of potatoes in warm storage encourage infestation. The tuberworm is more of a problem in southern areas, but it may be found in northern states as well.

Other Insects. In addition to those in the preceding list, numerous other insects can cause damage to potatoes. These include blister beetles, white grubs, wireworms, armyworms and loopers, plant bugs, nematodes, corn borers, and vegetable weevils. Many of these are specific to certain regions, and losses are usually not widespread.

Diseases

The potato is subject to a great variety of fungal, bacterial, viral, and mycoplasmal diseases. Some of these cause serious losses wherever potatoes are grown, while others are more localized. Because many of the most important diseases are seed-borne, it is standard practice for growers to use disease-free seed and seed treatments when they are planting the crop. The following potato diseases are generally the most important and widespread.

Early Blight. Caused by *Alternaria solani*, early blight appears on the leaflets as large, grayish-brown spots, usually showing concentric light and darker markings resembling a target. As the spots enlarge, they coalesce and finally destroy the entire leaf. The lower leaves are infected first and eventually turn yellow and dry up as the disease moves up the plant. The disease can also affect the tubers, causing surface brownish-purple lesions. The fungus overwinters in tubers, plant debris, and the soil. Control involves using a 2-year rotation and spraying with fungicides.

Late Blight. Historically, the late blight fungus (*Phytophthora infestans*) has been the most serious foliage disease of potatoes. It appears as water-soaked, circular to irregular, brown spots on the leaves. The spots enlarge, killing the leaflet and eventually the leaf and stem, and the entire plant. Spores may spread to tubers, causing irregular, reddish-black discolorations that penetrate into the flesh. Infected seed tubers are the primary source of inoculum. Infection requires moisture and average temperatures below 80°F. The best methods of control include destroying cull piles, using clean seed, spraying with fungicides when conditions are favorable for blight, and using resistant cultivars. Vines should be killed 2 weeks before the potatoes are dug, to allow tubers to mature and infected tubers to be recognized and discarded.

Scab. Scab, caused by the fungus *Streptomyces scabies*, is characterized by superficial or deeply pitted corky lesions on infected tubers. The fungus lives in the soil and on infected tubers. Neutral or alkaline soils and dry conditions favor the disease development. Control measures include using resistant cultivars, reducing soil alkalinity, and maintaining uniform moisture.

Black Leg. This is a seed-borne bacterial disease caused by *Erwinia atroseptica*. Diseased plants take on a yellowish-green color. Black, watery lesions develop at the base of the stem of affected plants. Tuber infection usually begins at the stem end, causing a black, slimy rot. The disease is spread by infected tubers, and plants may be infected at any age from soil inoculum if they are wounded. Control measures include using disease-free seed, treating seed, handling and working around plants carefully, and roguing infected plants.

Ring Rot. Ring rot, caused by the bacterium *Cornybacterium sepedonicum*, affects tubers as well as plants. The lower leaves of infected plants turn yellow and curl. Plants may wilt during the day but recover at night. Wilting increases as foliage symptoms develop. Infected tubers show a characteristic yellowing or browning in the vascular ring at the stem end. Secondary rots usually follow and destroy the tuber. The bacteria do not overwinter in the soil in cold climates but become established the following season when infected tubers are planted. The disease is highly infectious and is easily spread by equipment and machinery. Control measures consist of planting only disease-free seed, planting whole seed, and disinfecting equipment and machinery before using.

Mosaic Diseases. Potato mosaic is caused by potato virus X and appears as a mottling of the leaves. Another virus, potato virus Y, causes rugose mosaic, with mottling and crinkling of leaves. Severely infected plants may die prematurely. These diseases are carried from year-to-year in seed tubers. In the field, they are spread by insects, principally the potato aphid, which carries sap from infected to healthy plants. Control is by planting certified seed, eliminating or suppressing aphids, and roguing infected plants.

Leaf Roll. With this viral disease, plants are usually stunted and pale green. The leaves of infected plants roll upward and become thickened, brittle, and off-color. Symptoms develop first on the lower leaves and progress upward. Generally, leaf roll will reduce yield more than potato mosaic, but less than rugose mosaic. The disease is spread by the green peach aphid and carried in infected tubers. Control measures are the same as for mosaic.

Physiological Disorders

Several disorders of potatoes are physiologic or abiotic in nature, due primarily to environmental factors or physical damage adversely affecting plant growth.

Greening of tubers occurs when tubers are exposed to light, either in the field or in storage, resulting in the formation of chlorophyll. Green flesh is bitter and will affect the flavor of the cooked tuber. This comes from an alkaloid compound, solanine, that may be toxic if eaten. Smooth, white-skinned cultivars tend to be more susceptible than other types. To prevent this, tubers should be well covered with soil in the field by hilling and must be stored in the dark.

Hollow heart is the development of cavities of various sizes in the center of the tubers, usually brought about by irregular growth patterns. This occurs when a period of slow growth, often induced by moisture stress or low temperatures, is followed by a period of rapid growth. Cultivars that set large tubers tend to be more susceptible than others.

Bruising of tubers by rough handling during harvest or storage results in a disorder known as "blackspot." This is characterized by numerous, small, discolored areas beneath the tuber skin, with few or no outward signs. Tubers that have relatively immature skin, such as some of the early-crop potatoes that are often harvested before plants are mature, are most susceptible to blackspot.

HARVESTING AND POSTHARVEST HANDLING

The early-crop potatoes harvested in the winter, summer, and spring in the southern and western U.S. are generally stored briefly, if at all. They usually go directly to the fresh market or processing before the tubers are fully mature so that growers can take advantage of favorable prices. In contrast, the main or fall crop produced in the northern half of the U.S. is harvested at a more mature stage. The major portion of the crop is stored and marketed over a period of several months.

Vine Killing

Vine killing is an essential step in the production of potatoes for storage, to improve tuber storage quality. The vines should mature and die before harvest so that the skins of the tubers will be well suberized, thus decreasing the likelihood of skinning and bruising. Also, if the vines are not dead, there is a chance that spores of late blight will be transferred from the vines to the tubers, where they may later produce severe rot in storage. Vine killing also tends to facilitate harvest and in some circumstances may be used to control tuber size.

Most cultivars require 10–14 days from vine killing operations to the time when skins are firm and well suberized. However, if weather conditions are cool and cloudy, or if vines are large and vigorous, more time may be required. Conversely, if plants are stressed, such as by high temperatures, low moisture, or disease, less time is generally needed.

In the past, vines would often die by natural causes before harvest. However, now, with more effective methods of pest control and better fertility and irrigation practices, this is generally no longer the case, and vines may remain green right up to harvest. This has made the practice of killing the vines before harvest necessary. Mechanical vine beaters or chemical dessicant sprays are most often used for this purpose. Mechanical beaters with rubber or steel flails do a good job but usually cover only two rows at a time. Chemical dessicant sprays using several different materials can be applied with regular 4- to 12-row sprayer equipment. In some areas, propane gas is used to burn vines, although this method is decreasing in practice.

Harvesting

Potato tubers should be harvested before the ground freezes, preferably before soil and tuber temperatures drop below 45°F. The crop should be handled as gently as possible during harvest and storage since a substantial loss can occur from mechanical damage to tubers.

Almost all commercially grown potatoes are now harvested mechanically. Machines range from one-row potato diggers to elaborate two-row mechanical harvesters that dig the tubers and convey them directly to low-level trailers or trucks to minimize movement and bruising (Figure 23.5). Early potatoes that go

Figure 23.5. The commercial crop is mechanically harvested with two-row harvesters.

directly to fresh market are frequently washed in chlorinated water for cleaning and disinfecting.

Storing

Potato storage is a significant part of potato production, since the greater part of the crop is held for later use. Good storage should prevent excessive loss of moisture, development of rots, growth of sprouts, and accumulation of sugars. This latter condition occurs in storage from the conversion of starch to sugar in tubers stored under cool temperatures. It is detrimental to the quality of processing potatoes, since high sugar levels tend to result in dark-colored processed products.

The storage operation can be divided into three phases: curing, holding, and removing. Initially, tubers should be held at 55–60°F with high relative humidity and good ventilation for 2–3 weeks. These conditions promote the healing of cuts and bruises. Following this treatment, the tubers should be placed in the holding period for extended storage. During this phase, potatoes for seed or table stock should be held at 38–40°F. Potatoes for processing are held at higher temperatures to prevent the accumulation of reducing sugars. Tubers for chipping are usually held at 50–55°F, while those to be processed as either frozen or dehydrated are stored at 42–45°F. In each case, high relative humidities (90–95%) are required to minimize weight loss, and good ventilation or air circulation should be supplied to provide oxygen for the respiring tubers.

The final phase in potato storage is the removal period. If tubers are kept at prolonged low holding temperatures, it may be necessary to give them a warming treatment of 50–60°F for 2–3 weeks before removal from storage. This treatment is needed to recondition tubers to reduce damage from subsequent handling and to reverse changes of starch to sugar that may have occurred during the holding period.

Sprout Inhibition

After harvest, tubers undergo a rest period for 1–3 months, depending on the cultivar, during which time they will not sprout. This is followed by a dormant period when tubers are able to sprout if the conditions are favorable. Usually this occurs when temperatures rise above 39°F, and particularly around 59°F. This range is very close to the holding period temperatures, especially for chipping potatoes, making them very susceptible to sprouting in storage.

Several chemical sprout inhibitors may be used to prevent sprout development in tubers stored longer than 2 months. The two most common ones are maleic hydrazide and CIPC (isopropyl N-[3-chlorophenyl] carbamate). Maleic hydrazide is sprayed on the green foliage 2–4 weeks before harvest to allow sufficient time for it to be translocated to the tubers. CIPC is applied after harvest when tubers are in their holding period during storage. Cold temperatures will also inhibit sprouting, but they are not feasible in storage since they convert starch to sugar, reducing tuber quality for processing.

MARKETING

Potato growers usually sell through cooperatives or central packing sheds because volume buyers want a uniform quality pack in dependable quantities. Most of the larger producing areas attract buyers from large markets who purchase potatoes at assembling and shipping points. Attractive packaging promotes sales. Potatoes are sold in 50-pound fiberboard boxes or paper or mesh bags, in 3-, 5-, 10-, and 15-pound plastic film or mesh consumer bags, and more frequently in 100-pound burlap bags.

The shift from fresh market potatoes to processed products has changed the structure of the potato market. Sizeable quantities are now grown under contractual arrangements between growers and processors. In some instances, these pre-season arrangements on prices have insulated the response in potato prices from changes in seasonal supply. Also, inventories of frozen and dehydrated potatoes have had an impact on the prices received for fresh potatoes.

SELECTED REFERENCES

Burton, W. G. 1989. *The Potato*, 3rd ed. Longman Scientific & Technical, Essex, England (copublished in the U.S. with John Wiley & Sons, New York).

Chase, R. W. 1981. *Potatoes*. Michigan State Univ. Coop. Ext. Ser. Bull. E-1526.

Curwen, D., K. A. Kelling, J. A. Schoenemann, W. R. Stevenson, and J. A. Wyman. 1982. *Commercial Potato Production and Storage*. Univ. of Wisconsin Coop. Ext. Ser. A2257.

Hooker, W. J. (ed.). 1981. *Compendium of Potato Diseases*. Amer. Phytopath. Soc., St. Paul, Minnesota.

Lana, E. P. 1976. *Potato Production in North Dakota*. North Dakota State Univ. Coop. Ext. Ser. Bull. 26.

Li, P. H., and C. J. Weiser. 1985. *Potato Physiology*. Academic Press, New York.

Rhoades, R. E., and M. Rogers. 1982. The potato. *National Geographic* 161:668–694.

Rich, A. E. 1983. *Potato Diseases*. Academic Press, New York.

Seelig, R. A. 1972. *Potatoes. Fruit & Vegetable Facts & Pointers*. United Fresh Fruit and Vegetable Association, Alexandria, Virginia.

Smith, O. 1977. *Potatoes: Production, Storing, Processing*, 2nd ed. AVI Publishing Co., Westport, Connecticut.

Thorton, R. E., and J. B. Sieczka (eds.). 1980. *Commercial Potato Production in North America*. Potato Assoc. of America, Orono, Maine.

24

SPINACH AND OTHER LEAFY VEGETABLE GREENS

(COLLARDS, KALE, CHARD, MUSTARDS, NEW ZEALAND SPINACH, DANDELIONS)

"Greens" refers to those vegetables grown for their leafy portions for use in both cooking and salads. As a group, they are recognized for their high mineral and vitamin content; recently, they have gained new popularity from nutrition-conscious consumers.

All but one of these vegetables are cool-season crops with very similar cultural requirement, the exception being New Zealand spinach, which is intolerant of frost and thrives in hot weather. The only one produced on a relatively large commercial scale is spinach, while the others are more specialty crops that are important in certain geographical areas and are popular in some specialty markets. Although collards, kale, and mustards are cole crops, belonging to the Cruciferae family (Chapter 14), they are used primarily as greens and are placed in this vegetable classification. In addition, turnip greens and beet tops can be included with the vegetable greens, although they are grown and utilized primarily as root crops and are discussed in Chapter 15.

SPINACH

CLASSIFICATION, ORIGIN, HISTORY

Spinach (*Spinacia oleracea*) belongs to the goosefoot family (Chenopodiaceae), which also includes beets and chard. It is thought to be native to Central Asia where it was probably first cultivated by the Arabs, who later introduced it into North Africa. From there it was brought to western Europe through Spain by the Moors around the year 1100 A.D., eventually spreading to the rest of Europe by the 15th century. The date of its entrance into the U.S. is not known, but records indicate that it was commonly grown in the early 1800's.

PRODUCTION AND INDUSTRY

Spinach is the most important vegetable green grown in the U.S. Among vegetable crops it ranks second only to broccoli in total nutrient concentration. Consequently, the crop, especially the fresh market types, has become more popular, due to the rising demand for fresh green salads in U.S. diets.

The processing crop, which accounts for most of the total U.S. production (about 74%), is used for canning, freezing, and puréed baby food (Table 24.1). For the past several years, fresh market production has tended to increase slowly, while that for processing has remained relatively constant. Although it is not as intensively grown as some of the more major vegetables, spinach is an important crop to occupy the land for only a short period of time in between plantings of other vegetable crops.

The leading states for fresh market spinach production in the U.S. are Texas and California, which produce almost three-quarters of the crop. California also leads in the production of processing spinach, producing over 50% of the crop. Most of the processing spinach is grown during the winter, while fresh market production is more uniformly distributed over the winter, spring, summer, and fall. Average yields range from 7 tons per acre in California to 4 tons per acre in some Atlantic Coast states, and 3 tons per acre in Texas. However, these are averages, and good growers will generally get considerably higher yields, very commonly up to 12 tons per acre for processing and 8 tons per acre for fresh market.

Production and harvest costs per acre of spinach are low, primarily because of highly mechanized practices. Spinach requires less labor than any crop except green peas and sweet corn for processing. The labor input for spinach is now estimated at around 15 worker-hours per acre for the fresh market crop and 12 worker-hours per acre for processing.

Table 24.1.   Harvested Acreage, Production, and Value for Fresh
Market and Processed Spinach in the U.S., 1980[1]

Season	Harvested Acres	Production	Value
		(tons)	*($1,000)*
Fresh Market			
Winter			
California	900	7,000	3,066
Texas	4,600	13,800	7,728
Spring			
California	1,000	7,000	2,674
New Jersey	3,500	6,050	2,735
Maryland and Virginia . .	700	2,700	1,301
Summer			
California	800	6,200	2,616
Colorado	1,100	4,300	2,477
Fall			
California	850	6,150	3,025
New Jersey	600	2,200	1,214
Texas	1,800	3,950	2,631
Processed			
Winter			
California	9,400	82,910	7,197
Other states[2]	4,050	28,440	2,688
Spring[3]	5,720	35,030	3,454
Fall[4]	2,470	18,470	1,806
Total			
Fresh market	15,850	59,350	29,467
Processed	21,640	164,850	15,145
U.S.	37,490	224,200	44,612

[1]Source: USDA. 1980. *Agricultural Statistics.* Statistical Reporting Service.

[2]Florida, Maryland, Texas.

[3]Arkansas, Delaware, Maryland, New Jersey, New York, Oklahoma, Tennessee, Virginia, Wisconsin.

[4]Arkansas, California, Delaware, Maryland, Oklahoma, Tennessee, Washington.

PLANT GROWTH AND DEVELOPMENT

Spinach is an annual that grows to maturity in about 30–50 days. The plant is usually dioecious, producing male and female flowers on separate plants; although rarely, some monoecious plants (having both male and female flowers on the same plant) may develop in certain cultivars. The dioecious types produce two different kinds of male plants: "extreme males" and "vegetative males." The extreme male plants are small with very little vegetative development and tend to bolt (produce flowers) quickly. The vegetative male and female plants are slower to flower and produce considerably more foliage, making them the preferred plant types for commercial production. Consequently, the extreme males have been fairly well eliminated from commercial strains by selection.

The plant goes through two stages of development: a vegetative stage and a reproductive stage. In the vegetative or rosette stage, the plant has a single stem in which the internodes are extremely short. The leaves, which may be smooth or savoyed, arise in a whorl around the stem, forming a rosette of foliage (Figure 24.1).

The reproductive stage is initiated by the elongation of the stem, which breaks apart the rosette and forms a branching flower-seedstalk. This is usually in response to long days and warm temperatures and marks the end of its marketable life. With respect to flowering, spinach is a long-day plant, with critical daylengths ranging from 12–15 hours, depending on the cultivar. The change from vegetative to reproductive growth is conditioned by temperature and is usually accelerated by exposure to cold temperatures followed by high temperatures. Once the critical photoperiod is reached, spinach will go to seed rapidly with increasing photoperiods and warm temperatures. Cultivar differences are important, with some cultivars producing bolters more rapidly than others.

Figure 24.1. Spinach is grown for its tender leaves, which form a compact rosette on a short stem.

CLIMATIC AND CULTURAL REQUIREMENTS

Spinach is a hardy, cool-season crop that does best at temperatures of 60–65°F. Although it withstands hard frosts and temperatures as low as 20°F, growth is depressed below 35°F. The crop can be overwintered in areas of moderately cold climates, such as the Middle Atlantic states. In some northern areas, spinach can also be overwintered if provided with some protective covering. The plant is very intolerant of warm temperatures above 77°F, which in combination with long days causes plants to bolt, quickly destroying market value.

Spinach grows well on a wide range of soils but generally does best on a fertile sandy loam well supplied with organic matter. Sandy soils are preferred for winter and early spring crops. Muck soils have a high water-holding capacity but tend to warm up slowly. These produce some of the highest yields and are widely used for main-crop and processing spinach.

The crop is very sensitive to acidic conditions and grows slowly on acid soils. A soil acidity test should be made before the crop is planted. For optimum growth, the soil pH should range from 6.0 to 7.0. If the pH is too high, manganese is frequently unavailable, which results in leaf yellowing. Spinach has a high tolerance of saline conditions; consequently, it does well in areas of the West and Southwest where soils may be quite alkaline. The crop is very susceptible to air pollution, including ozone and sulfur dioxide emittants, which cause speckling and marginal necrosis on leaves.

For a relatively short-season crop, spinach requires a high level of fertility, especially nitrogen. Fertility requirements vary — nitrogen (N) 60–125 pounds per acre, phosphorus (P_2O_5) 50–200 pounds per acre, and potassium (K_2O) 50–300 pounds per acre, according to soil type, previous management, soil tests, and season. Early spinach will usually require larger amounts of fertilizer than main-season or fall crops. Higher amounts of potassium are recommended for the eastern peat and muck areas. Spinach is more responsive to boron than most vegetables and requires a relatively high level of this nutrient. On muck or organic soils, all fertilizers are usually broadcast and worked into the soil before planting. More frequently, on mineral and sandy soils, split applications are made. For very early plantings, all of the fertilizer should be applied at planting.

Recently, there has been concern by consumers about high nitrate levels in spinach and other leafy vegetable greens, which could present a potential health hazard to humans from nitrites in the diet. High levels of nitrate in the crop are strongly influenced by the amount and source, and the time and method of nitrogen fertilization. Studies have shown that sidedressing some of the nitrogen to a growing spinach crop or using ammonical fertilizer sources can result in lower nitrate concentrations in leaves than when all the nitrogen is broadcast before planting or when fertilizing with nitrate sources. Fertilization regimes using nitrification inhibitors, such as 2-chloro-6-[trichloromethyl]pyridine (nitrapyrin), in combination with ammonium fertilizers have been used to lessen nitrate accumulation in spinach. Also, spinach cultivars can vary considerably in their ability to accumulate high levels of nitrate.

PLANTING AND CROP ESTABLISHMENT

Spinach is planted so as to allow the plants to grow and mature in cool weather. In the South and Southwest and in areas of California, the crop is seeded from September until early February. In the Middle Atlantic states, the crop is planted from February until April, and again later during September and October. In northern areas, very early plantings are made as soon as the soil can be worked in the spring, usually before the last frost, and again in the fall. In Colorado and along the Pacific Coast, where much of the crop is grown during the summer, field seeding begins in the spring and continues through August.

All spinach is direct seeded in the field. The seed is planted in narrow rows 5–20 inches apart at close in-row spacing of 4–20 plants per foot of row, on raised beds (2–8 rows) or flat on the ground. Generally, wider spacings and raised beds are used more for the hand-harvested market crop, while closer spacings and flat rows are used for processing spinach. In California and Texas, where much of the crop is furrow-irrigated, almost all production now is on raised beds.

As a rule, the commercial crop is not thinned and the in-row spacing is usually adjusted by the rate of seeding and planting method. If the plants are crowded, they become leggy and much of their growth is in stem tissue, reducing marketable yields. The savoy types of spinach, which are primarily used for fresh market, produce larger plants and are spaced farther apart than the smaller smooth-leaf types.

Where the seed is drilled, seeding rates range from 12 to 20 pounds of seed per acre. When using raised beds, many growers now use seed treatments and precision seeding methods, such as sized seed and specialized belt seeders. This reduces seeding rates to 4–8 pounds per acre and closely regulates in-row spacing, which allows the establishment of discrete rows and eliminates the need for thinning. In some areas, spinach is planted with a standard vegetable seeder with a scatter shoe which spreads the seed thinly in a 3- to 4-inch band. Broadcasting of seed, a common practice years ago, is rarely used today.

Spinach seeds can germinate at low temperatures, permitting very early plantings. As soil temperatures decrease, the percentage of seed germination generally increases, but seedling emergence will be delayed. For example, at a soil temperature of around 41°F, seed germination is 96%, but emergence takes about 23 days; at 68°F, seed germination decreases to 52%, but seedlings emerge in about 6 days. The optimum range of soil temperatures for seed germination is 45–75°F, with a minimum of 35°F and a maximum of 85°F.

CULTURAL PRACTICES

Irrigation

The spinach plant is shallow-rooted, with most roots contained in the top 2 feet of soil. The crop requires uniformly moist soil throughout the growing season in order to maintain continuous growth. Shortage of soil moisture very often magnifies the adverse effects of high temperatures.

In California and the Southwest, a crop of spinach will require around 9–12 inches of water. The first irrigation is usually applied immediately after planting to speed up germination and emergence. A second application may be necessary within 3 or 4 days if the soil dries too quickly. Between emergence and harvest, one to three irrigations will usually be required, depending on soil and climatic conditions. Fields are irrigated mostly by flooding (border method) or by the furrow method. In the flooding method, the rows are flat, while with furrow irrigation the plants are grown on raised ridges or beds.

In the East, irrigation may not be necessary, except on sandy soils. However, when rainfall is inadequate and irrigation is needed, water may be applied in 1-inch increments every 7–10 days. Most irrigation is by overhead sprinklers, except on muck soils where subsurface irrigation is sometimes used.

Weeds

The increasing acreage of machine-harvested processing spinach requires that weeds be effectively controlled. Weeds can complicate harvest operations, and the presence of weeds in processing spinach may cause rejection of the crop.

Most weed problems are with large-seeded broadleaf weeds for which there is no fully safe and effective chemical control. The crop usually matures in 40–45 days, so shallow cultivation on the beds between rows, along with grass herbicides, is standard practice to control most weeds. Normally two to four cultivations will be required during a growing period. Studies from Texas have shown that for most herbicides, preplant incorporation affords better weed control than broadcast postplant application.

CULTIVARS

Spinach cultivars can be classified into either prickly-seeded or smooth-seeded types and also into savoy-leaved (wrinkled leaves) or smooth-leaved (flat leaves) types (Table 24.2). Most commercial cultivars are of the smooth-seeded type, which are much easier to handle and plant accurately.

Table 24.2. Important Characteristics of Selected Cultivars of Spinach

Cultivar	Chief Use[1]	Season (Days)	Long-standing	Leaf Type	Resistance to			
					Heat	Cold	Mosaic	Mildew
Bloomsdale Dark Green	H, M, S, C, F	40	Med.	Savoy	No	Med.	No	No
Bloomsdale Long Standing	H, M, S, C, F	42	Yes	Heavy savoy	Fair	Med.	No	No
Bounty	M	42	Yes	Semi-savoy				Yes
Chesapeake Hybrid . . .	F	40	No	Semi-savoy	No	Good	Yes	No
Dixie Market	M, C, F	37	Med.	Savoy	—	Med.	Yes	Yes
Hybrid 7	H, M, S, C, F	39	No	Semi-savoy	No	Med.	Yes	Yes
Hybrid 424	H	38	Med.	Smooth	—	Med.	—	Yes
Hybrid 612	M	43	No	Savoy	—	Med.	Yes	Yes
Hybrid 621	H, M, C, F	40	No	Savoy	—	Good	Yes	Yes
Melody	H, M	45	Yes	Semi-savoy	Fair	Med.	Yes	Yes
Packer	M, C	39	Yes	Savoy	—	Good	—	Yes
Seven R Hybrid	C, F	37	No	Semi-savoy	No	Exc.	Yes	Yes
Viking	S, C, F	45	Yes	Smooth	Fair	Med.	No	Yes
Virginia Savoy	M, S, C, F	39	No	Savoy	No	Med.	Yes	Yes

[1]H (home), M (market), S (shipping), C (canning), F (freezing).

The savoy types tend to be larger and are preferred for fresh market. The savoying of the blade is considered to enhance the appearance, as well as long distance shipment, by reducing losses due to anaerobic respiration. The smooth-leaved cultivars are used mostly for processing, because the leaves are easier to wash. Recently, some semi-savoyed types have been used for both fresh market and processing into frozen packs. Cultivars for processing are usually selected by the processors.

Cultivars vary in their resistance to bolting and the length of time they will remain in the vegetative stage after reaching market maturity. This characteristic is known as "longstanding." Flowerstalks in canned or frozen spinach are objectionable, and culling during processing increases expenses.

Other desirable qualities for spinach cultivars include dark green, thick, tender leaves; mosaic (blight) and mildew (blue mold) resistance; cold resistance (for where the crop is grown during winter or overwintered for spring harvest); a high percentage of blade / petiole; and days-to-harvest, which is usually in the range of 35–50 days. Erect growth form is preferred in cultivars for mechanical harvest. High-yielding F_1 hybrids are now used in much of the commercial production.

INSECTS AND DISEASES

Insects

The most severe insect damage occurs from insect feeding on leaves, which results in unsightly blemishes, making the crop unsalable. The two major insect pests of spinach are aphids and leaf miners. Aphids (*Myzus persicae*) or plant lice cause injury by sucking the juice from the foliage and by transmitting mosaic disease from infected to healthy plants. Spinach leaf miners (*Pegomyia hyoscyami*) damage the crop by feeding inside the leaves between the leaf surfaces. The entire leaf may be destroyed or otherwise rendered unmarketable.

In addition, seed corn maggots, cutworms, grasshoppers, and flea beetles can occasionally cause damage. Leafhoppers may carry the curly-top virus. Effective control of insect pests can usually be obtained with one of several insecticides. Because the spinach plants grow close to the ground in a tight rosette, insecticides should be applied as early as possible, before leaves become compacted.

Diseases

Spinach is subject to a number of diseases, including damping-off, mosaic, downy mildew, and *Fusarium* wilt. It is seldom that all of these are severely injurious in any given region on the same crop.

Damping-off. Damping-off (*Pythium*) and closely related rots (*Rhizoctonia*) of germinating seeds are largely responsible for poor stands, and in the past for the necessity of high seeding rates. However, high plant populations are no longer feasible due to the high costs for thinning. The disease can sometimes be controlled or lessened in severity by seed treatment with an appropriate fungicide.

Mosaic. Mosaic, commonly known as blight, is a virus complex caused by cucumber mosaic virus (CMV) and one or more other viruses. It is fairly widespread and sometimes causes serious losses. In the early stages, the young center leaves turn yellow and cease to grow. Later, all growth stops and the larger leaves become mottled and turn brown and eventually die. Insects, especially aphids, carry the virus from plant to plant. The most practical control method is to grow resistant cultivars, although most resistance is poor above 80°F.

Downy Mildew. Also known as blue mold, downy mildew is a fungal (*Peronospora effusa*) disease that can cause serious losses in cool, wet weather. The disease first appears on the undersides of leaves, where irregular patches of grayish mycelia will be found. Later the upper surfaces of the leaves turn yellow. The disease spreads rapidly under favorable damp conditions, and whole fields of spinach can be quickly ruined. Resistant cultivars and hybrids are available. When the disease appears, fungicide sprays can usually suppress its spread.

Fusarium Wilt. This is a fungal disease (*Fusarium solani*) that causes young plants to appear yellow and stunted, while older plants may wilt and fail to recover. Air temperatures above 72°F or soil temperatures above 70°F are very conducive to the development of the disease. The fungus can live in the soil for several years. Growing spinach during cool weather and using crop rotation are practical and the best means of control.

Other disease problems in spinach of a more local or regional nature may arise from *Heterosporium* leaf spots, curly-top virus, and white rust. The former is a widely distributed fungal disease that is most severe on winter crops grown under cold, wet conditions. It first appears as small, brown spots that increase in size and number on both sides of the leaves. There is no specific control except to use good cultural practices and to maintain vigorous, healthy plants.

Curly-top is a virus that is spread by the beet leafhopper. It causes young leaves to become crinkled, deformed, and reduced in size. The plants usually turn yellow and die. Control can only be effected by eliminating the insect vector, since nothing can be done after the plant is infected.

White rust (*Albugo occidentalis*) is a major foliar disease of winter-grown fresh market spinach in Texas and other regions of the Southwest. Breeding for resistance is difficult, since resistance appears to be controlled by several genes. The most effective control program should include the use of fungicides, rotation of crops, and the best available levels of resistance among commercial cultivars.

HARVESTING

Spinach is ready for harvest when it has reached edible size but before there is extensive yellowing, breakage, or other types of deterioration, including seedstalk development. The processing crop is usually harvested when foliage growth is at a maximum. For fresh market use, the time of harvest depends on the market, as well as on the size and condition of the plant. When the price is high, growers may harvest medium-sized plants having only five to seven fully matured leaves, but if the price is low, growers may decide to wait, allowing plants to continue growing. However, after a seedstalk begins to form, the plant is no longer marketable, so high value is placed on longstanding cultivars.

The majority of the crop is harvested during the winter and the spring. In the southern states and in areas of milder climates, such as California and the Middle Atlantic states, the harvest period extends from early November until the following April. In northern sections, harvest occurs during the fall, late spring, and early summer.

Most of the commercial crop is machine-harvested. This includes just about all the spinach for processing, as well as much of the fresh market crop used for loose packaging, in which the leaves are handled in bulk. Mechanical harvesters cut or mow the plants about 1 inch above the soil surface. Very often under short-day conditions, multiple harvests, sometimes up to four or five cuttings, can be made from plants that have been cut above the growing point.

Fresh market spinach to be bunched and tied is still mostly hand-harvested. The stem is cut below the crown at the taproot with a knife, hoe, or other cutting implement. Unsightly and dead leaves are removed. Trimming is done in the field or in packing sheds. The crop may need to be washed, but for long distance shipping, the practice may be omitted since it can hasten decay. Plants harvested for fresh market are usually allowed to wilt slightly before being handled and hauled, in order to minimize the breakage of leaves.

POSTHARVEST HANDLING AND MARKETING

Spinach is very perishable and can be stored for no more than 10–14 days. The crop should be cooled as rapidly as possible to 32°F and placed under a relative humidity of 95–100%. Crushed ice, hydrocooling, and vacuum cooling are satisfactory methods for cooling spinach. Controlled atmospheres of 10–40% carbon dioxide and 10% oxygen have been found to reduce yellowing and to improve quality.

The crop is marketed in much the same manner as other vegetables. Volume buyers prefer to purchase from standard packing sheds or assembly points. Spinach for market is packed in bushel baskets, hampers, and crates. For long distance shipping, top ice is used, and the crop is usually transported by refrigerated truck. Consumers prefer clean, stem-trimmed spinach in standard-sized cellophane bags. The sealed transparent packages help prevent wilting and allow gaseous exchange for maintenance and quality.

COLLARDS

Collards are members of the crucifer family (*Brassica oleracea*, Acephala group) and are a nonheading or looseleaf type of cabbage (Figure 24.2). They

Figure 24.2. Collards are a nonheading form of cabbage grown for their fleshy leaves.

are very popular in the South where they are used as a winter green. The plants are biennials, although grown as annuals, which form rosettes of smooth, thick, bluish-green leaves that can be boiled or fried. The plants grow to a height of 2–4 feet and are hardier than cabbage to cold and heat. Although they are grown year-round, collards are essentially a cool-season crop that does best when grown in the fall and winter. Most of the U.S. commercial production is located on the Maryland coast southward into the southeastern and Gulf states.

The culture of collards is very similar to that for cabbage (Chapter 14). Field plantings may be started either from transplants or from seed. The plants are spaced 12–24 inches apart in rows 3–4 feet apart. The crop is affected by the same disease and insect pests problems as cabbage.

The leaves are harvested sequentially as they approach full size (usually 75–90 days after seeding), but before they become tough and woody. This results in a tall bare stalk with a tuft of succulent leaves at the top. Staking is frequently necessary to hold older plants upright. Collards may also be harvested when the plants are younger (6–12 inches tall) by cutting off the whole rosettes at ground level.

KALE

Closely related to collards, kale (*Brassica oleracea*, Acephala group) can also be described as a winter-hardy, nonheading cabbage that is used as a winter green throughout the South. The plants are biennials but are grown as annuals for their much-curled and succulent leaves (Figure 24.3). Similar to collards, kale is a cool-season crop which does best when planted in the late summer or early fall for late fall and winter use. Cool weather, and even a light freeze, late in the season improves the eating quality of both kale and collards.

Figure 24.3. Kale is very similar to collards with curly, succulent leaves.

Two types of kale are grown in the U.S. One type, known as "Scotch," has a much-curled and crumpled foliage of grayish-green color. The other type, called "Siberian," is less crinkled and is bluish-green. Both types have dwarf and tall forms, with the dwarf forms most popular.

Culture and management are generally the same as for cabbage. Kale has a short season, usually requiring 40–50 days from seeding to harvest, and should be harvested before the plants become large, when the leaves become tough and fibrous. Quickly grown plants tend to be less fibrous and more tender than slowly grown plants. Either the entire plant can be cut at ground level or selected outer leaves can be taken. In the latter method, the inner leaves and growing point should be left to allow for additional harvests. Like spinach and other leafy greens, kale and collards are highly perishable and should be quickly cooled to remove field heat, by crushed ice, hydrocooling, or vacuum cooling. At a temperature of 32°F and 95–100% relative humidity, they can be held for no longer than 2 weeks.

CHARD

Chard, or Swiss chard (*Beta vulgaris*, Cicla group), is a member of the Chenopodiaceae family and is closely related to beets, although it is grown for its foliage instead of its roots. The plant develops large, fleshy leafstalks, which may be white, green, or red, and large, broad, green leaf blades (Figure 24.4). The leaf blades are prepared like spinach, and the midribs or stalks may be cooked in a manner similar to asparagus.

The plant is a cool-season biennial that tolerates hot temperatures fairly well. In the South and areas of mild winters, chard is planted in the fall up through

Figure 24.4. Chard is grown primarily for its broad leaf blades; the stalk may also be used.

early spring. In colder areas, it is planted from early spring until midsummer. Most often the crop is started from seed, but transplants can be used. The culture of chard is practically the same as that of beets (Chapter 15), except that the plants grow larger and need to be thinned to at least 4–6 inches apart in the row. Cultivars are distinguished primarily by midrib color, ranging from white to burgundy red.

The crop is ready to harvest in about 60 days after planting. The outer leaves are harvested as they develop, with care taken not to injure the growing point. Commercial growers very often cut off all leaves above the growing point. In either case, sequential harvests are made over a period of several weeks to 2 months. The leaves are marketed bunched and tied, like other greens.

MUSTARDS

Mustards are a popular processing and home garden crop for greens and salads in certain areas of the U.S., particularly the southern states. They are composed of several different species in the Cruciferae family. White mustard (*Brassica hirta*), leaf mustard (*B. juncea*), and spinach mustard (*B. Rapa,* Perviridis group) are grown for their young, tender leaves which have a characteristic flavor. Black mustard (*B. nigra*) is grown for its pungent seeds, which are made into the popular yellow table mustard. The crop may also be used for oils, soaps, and lubricants.

Mustards resemble spinach in growth habit and culture. All are hardy, cool-season, annual plants in which the foliage forms a compact rosette on a short stem. The leaves on some types may be extremely curled, while in others the leaves are smooth (Figure 24.5). The crop is generally sown for greens very early in the spring for use in the late spring or early summer, and in the fall for winter greens. In the South and in places of mild winters, they may be grown over the winter. Hot weather will cause plants to bolt quickly. The seed is sown in drills 12–24 inches apart, and the plants are thinned 4–5 inches apart as they become crowded. Successive plantings can be made at 10-day intervals to provide a continuous season's supply.

Processors favor smooth-leaved, dark green, and long-standing types. 'Florida Broadleaf' is a popular smooth-leaved type but bolts very rapidly, thus limiting its use by processors in the spring. 'Southern Giant Curled' is a leading curled-leaf cultivar, which is resistant to bolting. A relatively new cultivar is 'Slobolt', which is slow bolting and has smooth, dark green leaves, resulting in an excellent canned product.

Mustard is ready for harvest in about 40–50 days after being sown. The entire plant may be cut off, or the individual leaves may be pulled. The crop can be

Figure 24.5. A plant of curled leaf mustard.

sold and marketed in loose hampers, or it can be tied together in bunches weighing 1–3 pounds.

NEW ZEALAND SPINACH

New Zealand spinach (*Tetragonia tetragoniodes*) is both a green and a salad vegetable grown for its succulent leaves and branch tips, which are used in the same way as spinach, mainly in home gardens. New Zealand spinach is not a true spinach and differs markedly from "true" spinach in growth habit and climatic requirements. The chief similarity between the two plants is in flavor.

New Zealand spinach is an annual belonging to the carpetweed family, Tetragoniaceae. It differs from true spinach in that it grows into a large, much-branched, spreading plant 3–4 feet across and 1–2 feet tall (Figure 24.6). Unlike spinach, it is a warm-season crop only moderately tolerant of frost and light freezes.

The crop can be started from seeds planted in warm, protected seedbeds in the late winter and transplanted later after the frost-free date, or it can be seeded directly in the field where climates permit. In either case, plants require relatively wide spacing, usually 1–2 feet apart in rows 3–5 feet apart. The plants are ready to harvest as soon as they are large enough and the tender tips, 3–4 inches long,

Figure 24.6. New Zealand spinach develops into a large, spreading plant grown for its succulent leaves and branch tips that are used in the same way as spinach. (Photo: courtesy of the National Garden Bureau)

can be removed. This stimulates new growth, so harvesting can continue until cold weather in the fall. Frequently, when grown for market, the entire plants may be cut off about 2 inches above the ground.

DANDELIONS

Dandelions (*Taraxacum officinale*) are members of the sunflower family, Compositae, grown for their leaves which are used as spring greens in either cultivated or wild form. The plants are hardy perennials that grow best at cool temperatures. Similar to spinach and other greens, dandelions develop rosettes of leaves, from which a hollow flowerstalk rises, followed by a characteristic bright yellow flower (Figure 24.7). Wild and cultivated types vary a great deal in growth characteristics, as well as flavor.

When grown under cultivation, plants are usually direct seeded outside in 12- to 15-inch rows and thinned to 8–12 inches apart in the row. The crop is grown much like spinach and is ready to harvest in about 60–95 days after seeding, when plants are a satisfactory size. The taproot is cut just below the crown, with the leaves still attached. Plants may be left in the ground for harvest the following spring before they flower. Some growers blanch the inner leaves by tying the outside leaves over the plant in order to reduce bitterness.

Figure 24.7. Dandelion is a perennial herb grown for its rosette of leaves. (Photo: courtesy of Burpee Seeds)

SELECTED REFERENCES

Daniello, F. J., R. R. Heineman, R. K. Jones, and M. C. Black. 1984. *Efficacy of Selected Fungicides in Controlling Foliar Diseases of Spinach.* Texas Agric. Exp. Sta. PR-4258.

Lamont, W. J., Jr. 1985. *Spinach.* North Carolina State Univ. Ext. Ser. Leaf. 17.

Longbrake, T., S. Cotner, J. Larsen, and R. Roberts. 1973. *Keys to Profitable Spinach Production.* Texas A&M Coop. Ext. Ser. Fact Sheet L-1076.

Nieuoff, M. 1969. *Cole Crops, Botany, Cultivation, and Utilization.* Leonard Hill Books, London.

Ryder, E. J. 1979. *Leafy Salad Vegetables.* AVI Publishing Co., Westport, Connecticut.

Sackett, C. 1975. *Dandelions. Fruit & Vegetable Facts & Pointers.* United Fresh Fruit & Vegetable Association, Alexandria, Virginia.

Sackett, C. 1975. *Spinach. Fruit & Vegetable Facts & Pointers.* United Fresh Fruit & Vegetable Association, Alexandria, Virginia.

Seelig, R. A. 1974. *Collards. Fruit & Vegetable Facts & Pointers.* United Fresh Fruit & Vegetable Association, Alexandria, Virginia.

Seelig, R. A. 1974. *Swiss Chard. Fruit & Vegetable Facts & Pointers.* United Fresh Fruit & Vegetable Association, Alexandria, Virginia.

Vandemark, J. S., and J. W. Courter. 1978. *Vegetable Gardening for Illinois.* University of Illinois Coop. Ext. Ser. Cir. 1150.

25

SWEET CORN

CLASSIFICATION, ORIGIN, HISTORY

Sweet corn (*Zea Mays*) is a member of the grass family (Gramineae) and represents a sugary form (subspecies *saccharata*) of maize. It is considered to be a mutant of field or dent corn in which a sugary gene prevents or retards the normal conversion of sugar to starch, resulting in a sweetish kernel at the immature stage.

In addition to sweet corn, other principal types of maize include flint, flour, dent, and popcorn. Each is characterized by differences in the quality, quantity, and pattern of stored food material (endosperm) in the kernel. Flour or soft corn (subspecies *amylacea*) has kernels which have soft starch throughout. Flint corn (subspecies *indurata*) has hard starch endosperm and possesses good storage and germination qualities. Dent corn (subspecies *indentata*) has endosperm characteristics of each of the above two. The center is soft and floury, while the sides of the kernel are flinty. Because of the soft core, the apex of the kernel shrinks on drying, resulting in a dented crown. Popcorn (subspecies *everta*) has small, pointed kernels with thick skin, or pericarp. Upon heating, steam is trapped until the kernel explodes, exposing the white endosperm.

The exact origin of corn is not clear, although it is known to be one of the few vegetable crops native to the New World, most probably Central America. Remains of maize cobs have been uncovered from caves in the Tehuacan Valley in southern Mexico that date back 7,000 years. Corn was grown extensively by the Native Americans in pre-Columbian time and formed the foundation of many of their cultures. The crop was taken to Europe by Columbus on his return voyage in 1493. In the U.S., the sweet form of maize was cultivated by the early colonists around 1780 and was recognized as a major crop by 1820.

PRODUCTION AND INDUSTRY

Sweet corn is one of the most important vegetable crops in the U.S., in terms of acreage, production, and value, for both fresh market and processing. The crop is grown commercially in over 25 states, and for local markets and in home gardens throughout the country. Although sweet corn is probably the most visible form of maize, it represents less than 2% of the total corn crop.

Approximately 79% of the commercial sweet corn crop produced in the U.S. in 1989 was for processing and 21% for fresh market (Table 25.1). The processing crop is used for both canning (57%) and freezing (43%). The leading states for processing production are Wisconsin (27%) and Minnesota (22%), followed by

Table 25.1. Harvested Acreage, Production, and Value of Fresh Market and Processed Sweet Corn in the U.S., 1989[1]

State	Harvested Acres		Production		Value	
	F. Market	Processed	F. Market	Processed	F. Market	Processed
			——— (tons) ———		——— ($1,000) ———	
Alabama	3,300	—	8,250	—	2,706	—
California	17,500	—	100,650	—	32,409	—
Colorado	3,000	—	21,750	—	5,394	—
Connecticut	4,000	—	12,800	—	5,888	—
Delaware	—	6,300	—	34,400	—	2,363
Florida	49,700	—	260,950	—	88,201	—
Idaho	—	20,200	—	182,000	—	10,538
Illinois	5,100	36,100	21,950	202,520	8,209	13,468
Maryland	—	4,600	—	24,100	—	1,767
Massachusetts	7,800	—	33,150	—	13,260	—
Michigan	11,800	—	40,100	—	14,035	—
Minnesota	—	106,700	—	650,870	—	40,029
New Jersey	8,600	—	26,650	—	9,487	—
New York	24,800	27,700	99,200	110,800	29,958	6,737
North Carolina	3,800	—	12,350	—	3,903	—
Ohio	10,700	—	45,500	—	12,831	—
Oregon	2,400	45,500	13,800	394,940	5,630	31,793
Pennsylvania	17,100	2,000	72,700	9,780	30,389	528
Texas	2,500	—	6,250	—	1,738	—
Virginia	2,000	—	10,500	—	3,318	—
Washington	2,500	51,200	15,000	470,530	3,810	35,054
Wisconsin	—	152,000	—	810,160	—	51,040
Other states[2]	—	12,150	—	59,240	—	3,950
U.S.	176,600	464,450	801,550	2,949,340	271,166	197,267

[1]Source: USDA. 1990. National Agricultural Statistics Service (NASS), Agricultural Statistics Board.
[2]For processing, Indiana, Iowa, Michigan, Virginia.

Washington (16%), Oregon (13%), Illinois (7%), Idaho (6%), and New York (4%). Leading fresh market producing states are Florida (33%), California (13%), and New York (12%). The Florida production is mainly in the spring and fall, with a small amount grown in the winter. New York and the eastern production is entirely in the summer, while in California the crop is grown in both spring and summer.

The growing and harvesting of sweet corn is highly mechanized, requiring considerably less labor than most other vegetables. This is particularly true for processing sweet corn where the labor requirement, next to peas, is the lowest among commercial crops, requiring less than 12 worker-hours per acre. Yields average approximately 6 tons per acre for processing and 4 tons per acre for fresh market. With irrigation and good management, however, yields can reach 9 tons per acre for processing and 6 tons per acre for fresh market.

PLANT GROWTH AND DEVELOPMENT

Sweet corn is a monoecious annual grass, whose development and anatomical structures are unique among vegetable crops. The plant develops a single dominant stem headed by a male inflorescence called a tassel (Figure 25.1). The female inflorescence, or ear, is a lateral flowerstalk which terminates one of the side branches. The cob is the receptacle bearing the ovaries (the future kernels) and the styles, or silks. The husks are leaves, mostly sheath. The kernels are fruitlets in which the plant stores food primarily as sugar and starch. Each kernel develops from an individual flower. The silks are the stigmas and elongated styles of the individual fruitlets that develop into the kernels.

Between planting and tassel initiation, the primary developmental activity is the growth of the main stem and the production of leaves. The growth of the main stalk results from the elongation of the internodes. Depending on the genetic potential of the cultivar and environmental influences, one or more lower side shoots may develop into suckers or tillers.

In a midseason cultivar, the initiation of the tassel occurs about 21 days after planting, generally when about seven leaves are visible and the growing point is still underground. At this stage, the number of leaves of the main stalk is fixed (although some have yet to appear), and the plant has switched from vegetative to reproductive development. The tassel in a fairly well-developed state appears in the whorl of leaves. Elongation of the internodes results in further growth of the stem and separation of the leaves.

After the stem has reached its full height, the first male flowers in the tassel open and release pollen. Pollen is shed from the tassel and is carried by air currents to the silks over a period of several days. Pollination may begin 3–4 days before

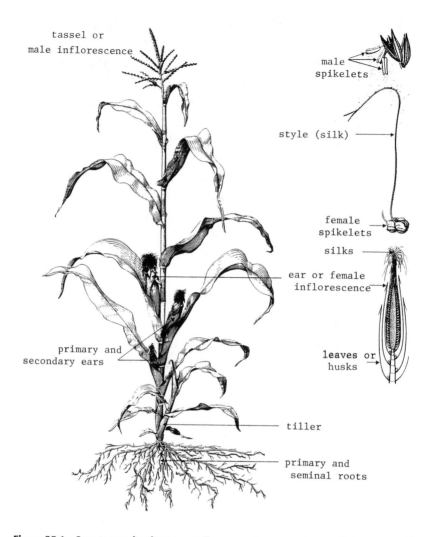

Figure 25.1. Sweet corn develops as a tall, monoecious annual grass. (Source: E. Haflinger. 1979. *Maize*. CIBA-GEIGY, Basle, Switzerland)

the silks appear, and up to 50,000 pollen grains may be available for each silk. The silks remain receptive to pollen for about 9 days. Improper pollination, resulting from drying and killing of pollen grains or silks in high temperatures or from pollen not shedding in cold temperatures, will result in failure of kernel development and incomplete tipfill.

Following pollination, the ear elongates and rapidly develops. Sugars move into the developing kernels from other plant parts. The first ear is normally initiated at the top side shoot of a group of side shoots in the middle of the plant. This ear will usually depress the development of ears below it; however, the depressive effect may not be total and several other ears may form, although they rarely reach marketable size. As the ear matures, the kernels increase in size and pass through four stages of maturation: pre-milk, milk, early dough, and dough (see "Harvesting and Postharvest Handling").

Seed

Compared to most other vegetable species, the corn plant already has a "head start" in that the seed, or kernel, contains a sub-miniature corn plant with most of the organs and features already present (Figure 25.2).

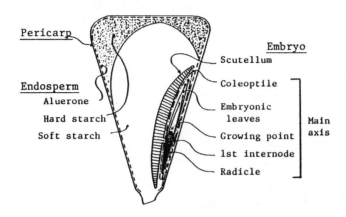

Figure 25.2. Corn kernel anatomy showing the pericarp, endosperm, and embryo.

The seed is composed of three principal parts: the pericarp, endosperm, and embryo. The pericarp is the protective surface layer and consists primarily of the ovary wall. The endosperm makes up the bulk of the seed and functions as a source of food materials for the growing embryo. The embryo consists of the scutellum and the main axis. The scutellum is attached to the endosperm. During germination it produces enzymes that digest the starch of the endosperm and make it available to the growing axis. The main axis contains the plumule, which consists of four or five embryonic leaves and the growing point ensheathed in a tubular structure called the *coleoptile*. The primary root at the lower end of the main axis never really develops and is of minor importance. Adventitious roots arise directly above the point of attachment of the scutellum to the main axis and form the main portion of the root system.

Environmental Influences

The overall effect of temperature on the growth of sweet corn is complex and changes from one developmental stage to another. In general, the higher the temperature between 40 and 90°F, the greater the rate of growth and the shorter the time necessary for the plant to reach a particular stage of development. A cultivar planted in late summer in Florida may take 60 days to reach maturity, but the same cultivar planted in winter can take almost twice as long. Temperature can also affect plant growth by altering the number of leaves produced during certain developmental stages. Plants grown in warm temperatures will generally have higher leaf counts for a particular developmental stage than those grown in cool temperatures (Table 25.2).

Table 25.2. **Effect of Temperature from Fifth Leaf Stage to Tassel Initiation on the Development of 'Golden Cross Bantam' Sweet Corn**[1]

	Cool Temperatures	Warm Temperatures
Day and night temperatures[2]	55–70°F	80–95°F
Leaves appearing during treatment . . .	1.5	3.3
Total leaves	15.2	17.8
Days to tassel initiation	20	21
Days to pollen shed	48	47

[1]Source: C. Y. Arnold. 1969. Sweet corn development as affected by environment and by inherent differences among hybrids. *Illinois Research*, Winter.

[2]Plants were grown in the greenhouse up to the fifth leaf stage, transferred to plant growth chambers until tassel initiation, and then returned to the greenhouse. While in the growth chambers, plants had 14 hours of light and 10 hours of darkness.

Flowering in sweet corn cultivars can be markedly affected by daylength. Generally, plants flower sooner under short days than long days. Cultivars adapted to the tropic latitudes, where days are shorter, will stay vegetative when grown under the long days of summer in temperate regions. By the time of tassel initiation, the growing point, which is normally underground, may be well above ground, and the plant may reach a height of 10–12 feet. Conversely, cultivars adapted to long days and cooler temperatures will generally not do well when grown under short days and warmer temperatures.

CLIMATIC AND CULTURAL REQUIREMENTS

Sweet corn is a warm-season crop which, depending on the cultivar, requires a frost-free season of 65–110 days. The optimum mean temperature range for growth is 70–86°F. Although the shoot and leaves are easily damaged by frost, the plant may survive the injury since the growing point remains below ground during a large part of its development and is protected. The minimum threshold temperature for growth is around 50°F. Cold night temperatures will depress plant growth rate and extend the time required to reach maturity. Contrary to widespread belief, hot nights do not favor corn growth but rather serve to reduce dry weight added during the day from increased respiration.

A wide variety of soil types can be used to grow sweet corn. Growers for the early market usually plant on well-drained, light, mineral soils, while those for the late market select heavier soils. Peat and muck soils are also used to grow sweet corn in some parts of Florida. The best yields and highest quality generally take place at a soil pH of 6.0–6.8, although the crop grows well over a fairly wide pH range (5.5–7.5). Sweet corn fits well into most crop rotations and should be grown on the same land only once every 3 or 4 years.

Sweet corn has a relatively high nutrient requirement. Sufficient nutrients should be available early in the life cycle of the crop in order to ensure rapid, uninterrupted growth. Nutrient deficiencies that develop when the crop is young frequently can be corrected by sidedressing.

Nitrogen recommendations vary, depending on soil type, climatic conditions, cultivar, and cultural practices. Fresh market growers try to maintain high soil nitrogen levels throughout the season, since many consumers want sweet corn with long, dark green husks and long ears. Nitrogen rates may range from 75 pounds per acre on silty clay loams to over 200 pounds per acre on highly leached sandy soils. In some organic soils, nitrogen may not be applied except under prolonged cold weather conditions when very little soil nitrogen may be made available. Slower-growing (early) plantings and closer plant spacings will require higher rates of nitrogen fertilizer.

Phosphorus and potassium fertilization is usually based on soil test results, and in some areas of the West may not be needed. Generally, all the phosphate along with some of the nitrogen and potash may be applied at planting. However, if the fertilizer is banded with the seed, the total amount of nitrogen plus potash (K_2O) should not exceed 80 pounds per acre to avoid salt damage to seedlings. The remaining nitrogen and potash can be supplied in several sidedressings. If the crop is irrigated, nitrogen can be applied several times during the growing season through the irrigation system. When grown on limey subsoil areas, sweet corn is sensitive to zinc deficiency, and growers should add zinc sulfate to their fertilizer regime.

PLANTING AND CROP ESTABLISHMENT

Sweet corn is direct seeded in the field. The plant does not transplant well, although there have been some attempts at using transplants to decrease the time to harvest. Plantings of individual cultivars are usually made in four- to eight-row blocks, in order to ensure successful pollination. In the past, fields were planted at twice the recommended rate and later thinned to stand. Today, most growers use multiple-row precision corn planters to plant to final stand. Growers generally allow for an 80–90% field germination rate under good field conditions.

The seeds are planted in rows 2–4 feet apart at plant spacings of 6–18 inches apart in the row. Plant populations and seeding rates depend on several factors, including the time of planting, cultivar, and cultural practices such as the availability of irrigation. Ear size and appearance are improved slightly at wider row and plant spacing, but the number of marketable ears per acre may be reduced. Overcrowding may result in short ears and lack of tipfill.

As a general rule, the earlier the seed is planted or the colder the soil, the greater is the rate of seeding. Also, small- or single-ear types, such as some of the early cultivars, are usually planted at closer spacings than the larger midseason cultivars, which sometimes bear two ears. Recommended populations range from 16,000 plants per acre for some medium-sized midseason cultivars to around 24,000 plants per acre for early cultivars. Higher populations have increased yields without affecting ear size. When grown under irrigation, some early, single-ear cultivars can be successfully grown at populations as high as 30,000 plants per acre. If irrigation is not available, populations will generally be around 15,000 plants per acre. Seeding rates normally range from 8 to 14 pounds of seed per acre.

The crop can be seeded as soon as soil temperatures reach 50°F at a depth of 2 inches. Seed emergence will vary from 20 or more days in cool soil (50°F) to as few as 4 days in warm soil (75°F). Seeds are normally planted 1 inch deep on heavy soils and up to 2 inches deep on lighter soils. Deep plantings may interfere with germination and prevent emergence if soil crusting occurs following hard rains. Shallow plantings will result in faster emergence in cold soils, provided adequate soil moisture is present.

Scheduling Planting Dates

To secure a continuous supply of sweet corn throughout the growing season, growers may use several different systems: 1) the same cultivar may be planted at 10-day intervals; 2) early, midseason, and late cultivars may be planted at the same time; and 3) a system based on growing degree days or heat units may be used for scheduling of successive plantings. The former two methods are probably best in the home garden, while for commercial plantings a combination of all three is used.

The heat-unit concept (see Chapter 3) takes into account the effect of temperature on the rate of sweet corn development. Although early sweet corn plantings usually require more days to mature than later plantings, both will require approximately the same number of heat units to reach maturity. In corn, heat units are based on night temperatures above 40°F, day temperatures above 50°F, and a maximum temperature of 86°F. Sometimes with irrigation, the upper temperature limit is raised to 92°F. By taking the expected accumulation of heat units between desired harvest intervals and allowing the same to accumulate between planting intervals, growers can space planting dates to provide properly a regular succession of harvest dates. To use heat units effectively, growers must know the heat-unit requirements for the cultivars planted. This information is usually available from the seed supplier.

Field Covers for Early Plantings

Several different types of covering material, ranging from clear plastic to spunbonded polyester (see Chapter 8), are commonly used to enhance germination and speed maturity of early plantings of sweet corn. These do not require mechanical support but are applied as a soil covering or mulch. Germination can be enhanced dramatically when soil temperatures beneath the covering are increased; also soil crusting is prevented. Although frequently total yields may not be affected, maturity dates can be increased by 10 to 14 days when these materials are used with early plantings.

The seed is planted in single or double rows before the covers are laid. With clear plastic, slits or holes should be made in the plastic to increase air circulation and to avoid leaf scorch from high temperatures. When seedlings press on the covering or when temperatures become too hot, the covering should be removed or split to allow plants to grow above the material.

CULTURAL PRACTICES

Irrigation

The plant has a shallow, fibrous root system, with most roots in the surface 2 feet of soil. A few roots penetrate deeply, but they are not numerous enough to permeate the soil thoroughly at greater depths. Consequently, it is necessary to keep adequate soil moisture in the surface 2 feet of soil, especially for the first part of the growing period. Drought stress will result in delayed maturity and uneven harvest.

Sweet corn requires 12–25 acre-inches of water. The rate of water use increases with plant development up until the time of pollination. Water deficiency during any period of the plant's development can reduce yields, but drought stress during tasseling and silking is the most detrimental and will cause improper pollination and poor tipfill. Supplemental irrigation or rainfall totaling at least 1 inch per week is required at this time. When corn leaves become tightly rolled in the morning, this is a sign that water is needed immediately.

Either furrow or sprinkler irrigation may be used to irrigate sweet corn. Thorough but infrequent watering is recommended. Rates and timing of irrigation depend on soil types, temperature, relative humidity, and rainfall.

Weeds

A variety of annual and perennial weeds, including broadleaf and grassy species, infest sweet corn fields. Particularly troublesome are the perennial grasses such as quackgrass (in northern growing areas of the U.S.) and johnsongrass (in central and southern regions). These species grow by underground rhizomes and are able to compete very strongly with corn.

The primary method of controlling weeds is with herbicides. The triazine herbicides (atrazine, cyanazine) are widely used since sweet corn is tolerant of them, while many of the most prevalent broadleaf and grassy weeds are killed. However, these materials can persist in the soil and cause injury to other crops (soybeans) grown the following season. The chloroacetamide herbicides (alachlor, metolachlor) strongly suppress the growth of weedy grasses. These materials, when used at planting along with the triazine herbicides, give excellent broad-spectrum broadleaf and grass weed control. The thiocarbamates herbicides (EPTC and butylate) are not very effective on certain broadleaf weeds but give good control of annual grasses and problem perennial grassy weeds such as nutsedge and quackgrass. In addition, postemergent applications of 2,4-D are very effective in controlling emerged broadleaf weeds.

The use of cultivation to control weeds has declined. It is now of greatest value in those instances where the control of annual weeds with herbicides is inadequate. Cultivation early in the season also helps in destroying or disrupting the root or rhizome system of hard-to-control perennial weed species. Sweet corn lends itself to cultivation later in the season to control those weeds which have escaped herbicide action. However, after the crop is 24 inches tall, there is considerable risk of root pruning.

CULTIVARS

More cultivars of sweet corn are available to growers than of any other vegetable crop. Just about all cultivars now used are hybrids, resulting in better vigor, higher yields, and more uniformity. Many of the standard sweet corn cultivars have been replaced by the newer high-sugar corns, which have substantially higher levels of sucrose in their kernels than standard cultivars.

Sweet Corn Quality

Sweetness, tenderness, creamy texture, and low starch content are four parameters of sweet corn quality. The sweet corn kernel stores sugar, starch, and water-soluble polysaccharides in the endosperm. The sweetness of the kernel at the eating stage is primarily due to sugar accumulation, while the characteristic creamy texture is due to the accumulation of water-soluble polysaccharides. The three principal sugars in sweet corn kernels are sucrose, glucose, and fructose, with sucrose the most important. As the kernels pass from the edible stage (20 days post-pollination) to the dry mature stage, the sugars are converted into starch. The standard sugary cultivars have between 10 and 15% sugar at harvest, compared to elevated sugar levels of 25–35% at harvest in the high-sugar types.

Sweet Corn Genes

The genetic makeup of a cultivar will determine how sweet, tender, and creamy the kernels are likely to be at maturity. In addition to the normal sugary (*su*) gene, several other mutant genes are available which impart considerably higher sugar levels in the kernels. These new high-sugar corns fall into two genetic types: sugary enhanced, commonly called "se corn"; and shrunken-2s, generally referred to as "supersweets" or "extra-sweets" (Table 25.3).

Sugary. The standard sweet corn cultivars have kernels that contain the *su* gene, which is responsible for moderate levels of sugar. This gene also causes the endosperm to be high in water-soluble polysaccharides, resulting in a creamy texture of the kernels. However, there is a rapid conversion of sugars to starch as the kernels mature, resulting in a rapid loss of quality. In seed catalogs, these types are sometimes referred to as "normal," "traditional," or "sugar" cultivars.

Sugary Enhancer. In 1967, an *su* corn line was identified at the University of Illinois which was extremely sweet at the eating stage. Sucrose levels in this line were found to be about two times higher than that in standard sweet corn lines, while water-soluble polysaccharides were comparable. Genetic analysis showed that the elevated sucrose level was due to a single recessive gene acting in combination with the *su* gene. The gene was termed *sugary enhancer* (*se*) and the genotype is abbreviated *su se*, but is commonly known as *se.*

Table 25.3. Sweet Corn Classifications[1]

Names and Designators	Genetic Types	Description	Example Cultivars
I. Sugary Mutants			
A. Standard sweet corn	Full *su*	Sweetness and tenderness vary within a narrow range	Gold Cup, NK199, Silver Queen, Butter and Sugar
B. Augmented sugary			
Partial shrunken synergistic	Full *su* and half *sh2*	Sweeter than standard, less than full shrunken, generally crisp	Sugar Loaf, Honeycomb, Intrepid Synergistic, Sugar Time
Partial sugary enhanced	Full *su* and half *se*	Sweeter than standard, less than full sugary enhanced, creamy	Golden Sweet EH, Kandy Korn EH, Paramount, White Lightning
Augmented sugary enhanced plus shrunken	Full *su* and partial *sh2* + *se*	Sweeter than standard and partial *sh2*, or *se* but less than full *sh2* or *se*	Symphony
Full sugary enhanced	Full *su* and full *se* (100% modification)	Sweeter than standard, less than full shrunken, but more creamy	Miracle, Remarkable, Double Treat
II. Other Mutants			
A. Full shrunken, extra-sweet, supersweet	Full *sh2* (no *su*)	Sweeter than standard, crisper, but less creamy	Illini Xtra Sweet, Florida Staysweet, Sucro, Dinner Time
B. Combined gene, ADX	Full *ae* + *du* + *wx* (no *su*)	High sugar levels, similar to full shrunken types	Pennfresh ADX
C. Brittle	Full *bt* (no *su*)	Sweeter than standard, and similar to full sugary enhanced	Hawaiian Super-sweet

[1]Source: J. W. Courter and A. M. Rhodes. 1982. A classification of vegetable corns and new cultivars. *Proc. 1982 Illinois Vegetable Growers Schools.* Univ. of Illinois Hort. Series 31.

In *se* corns, sugars are converted to starch at the same rate as standard sweet corn; however, because they contain more sugar, *se* corns remain sweeter for a longer period of time after harvest than normal sweet corn. Unlike some other high-sugar corns, *se* types contain high levels of water-soluble polysaccharides, which give their kernels the creamy texture of standard sweet corn.

Shrunken-2. A gene known as "shrunken-2" (*sh2*) was identified in a field corn that contained more sugar than was found with standard sweet corn. This gene was called "shrunken," since the dry seed was light in weight and had a shriveled appearance. Today this gene is used extensively in many high sugar or "supersweet" cultivars, where it produces kernels with sugar contents two to three times higher than in standard sweet corn and with much slower conversion of sugar to starch at maturity.

Unlike *se* corn, the supersweet types are single gene mutants containing the *sh2* gene, but not the *su* gene. The seed coat of the kernels is relatively tough, giving these types a somewhat crisp texture. Also, the endosperm of the *sh2* kernels tends to be low in water-soluble polysaccharides, making the kernels less creamy and more watery than in other sweet corns. These types generally have poor seedling vigor under cold or water stress conditions, and yields tend to be lower than standard sweet corn cultivars.

Augmented Corns. In the development of the high sugar corns, various combinations (or genetic models) of the *su, sh2,* and *se* genes have been developed. In the "augmented types," the standard sugary corns are modified or augmented with either the *sh2* or the *se* gene, or both. This modification may be partial, occurring in about 25–44% of the *su* kernels, or in all kernels. The taste sensation is sweeter than in standard sweet corn with little detectable difference in texture. The hybrid seeds resemble and germinate similar to standard sweet corn seeds.

Other Genes. In addition, other genes have been used to make sweet corn sweeter, such as one called brittle (*bt*) and also a gene combination called "ADX." In the ADX types, high sugar levels, similar to those in the "extra-sweet" kernels, are obtained through the combined effects of three different genes: the amylose extender gene (*ae*), the dull gene (*du*), and the waxy gene (*wx*). However, for both ADX and *bt* types, few commercially acceptable cultivars are currently available.

Isolation of Plantings

It is important for growers to know the genetic type of their cultivars in order to avoid cross-pollination among different types, which can result in undesirable starchy corn. Cultivars of the same genetic type may be planted next to each other without a problem of cross-pollination. The *sh2, bt,* and ADX cultivars must be isolated from each other and all other corns since cross-pollination will make their kernels starchy. Conversely, pollen from these types will make *su* and augmented sweet corns starchy. Kernels of most augmented types, including *se* corn, may be transformed into normal sugary if cross-pollinated with standard cultivars, although their pollen will have no effect on normal sweet corn.

Isolation is usually attained by separating different types by either distance or time. A separation distance of 250 feet between incompatible types will generally be sufficient to minimize cross-pollination effects. If this is not possible, isolation may be provided by scheduling planting times to allow a minimum of 14 days between tasseling and silking dates of different cultivars. Planting a susceptible cultivar upwind from one that could contaminate it will enhance each of the above isolation methods.

Maturity and Kernel Color

Sweet corn cultivars may also be classified according to maturity (early, midseason, or late) and kernel color (yellow, white, or bicolor). The time required for maturity will range from about 65 days in early cultivars to 110 days for late ones. The early cultivars generally produce small marketable ears, while the later cultivars tend to be larger, with some producing two ears per plant.

White and bicolor cultivars are popular for local marketing. In the same way that cross-pollination can adversely affect kernel sugar content, it is necessary to have sufficient isolation to maintain the color of white and bicolor corn. Pollen from yellow cultivars will cause yellow kernels to appear in white cultivars and reduce the number of white kernels in bicolor corn. However, pollen from white cultivars will have no effect on yellow or bicolor cultivars.

INSECTS AND DISEASES

Insects

The principal insect pests of sweet corn are the corn earworm, European corn borer, and corn rootworm. Numerous other insects may cause damage to sweet corn, but usually on a smaller scale. Among these are aphids, fall armyworms, seed maggots and beetles, wireworms, grasshoppers, flea beetles, leafhoppers, and sap beetles.

Corn Earworm. The corn earworm (*Heliothis* zea) is destructive to a number of vegetables, but its damage is most severe on sweet corn and tomatoes. The worm is the larva of a light grayish–brown moth and appears as a greenish-brown–striped caterpillar with a brown head. The species overwinters in the southern U.S. and migrates into northern growing areas in the late spring and early summer. The moths lay eggs singly on the corn silks, where the larvae feed in the whorl and on ear tips. After the larvae reach maturity, they drop to the ground and pupate in the soil, and up to four generations may occur in a year. The insects should be controlled with chemicals in the whorl stage, from silk emergence until about 2 weeks later.

European Corn Borer. The European corn borer (*Ostrinia nubilalis*) is perhaps the most widespread and destructive insect pest of corn. The borer is the larva of a night-flying moth, which emerges from field debris in the early spring and lays eggs on leaf surfaces. The borers appear as small, white worms with black heads and may grow up to 1 inch long. The young larvae feed on the leaf surfaces, collars, and whorls and then bore into the stems. Feeding may also occur in the ears. The insect usually goes through two generations a year, but damage is usually most severe from the first brood, especially on early plantings. Several effective insecticides are available and should be applied during silking and egg laying, and before the insect bores into the stem.

Corn Rootworm. Three species of corn rootworms cause damage to sweet corn: northern rootworm (*Diabrotica longicornis*), southern rootworm (*D. undecimpunctata howardi*), and western corn rootworm (*D. virgifera*). The larvae are small, white worms, about 0.5 inch long, with black heads. They hatch in the early spring from eggs that have overwintered in the soil and feed on the roots of plants. Adult beetles emerge from the soil later in the season and feed on foliage, silks, and pollen, thus interfering with normal pollination. The northern and western rootworms will have only one brood per year, while their southern counterpart may go through several generations. Annual crop rotation and soil insecticides applied over the row at planting are the best methods of control.

Diseases

Bacterial Wilt. Also referred to as Stewart's wilt, bacterial wilt (*Bacterium stewartii*) develops inside the water-conducting tissues and produces wilting about the time plants silk. Infection may appear as long, tan streaks on lower leaves. Plants will be stunted, and young plants may die. The bacteria are carried over in the bodies of flea beetles and in the seed. Cucumber beetles and flea beetles serve as vectors for the disease. Mild winters favor large flea beetle populations and increase the incidence of the disease. Using resistant cultivars and spraying insecticides for the beetles in the spring are the best control measures.

Smut. Caused by the fungus *Ustilago maydis*, this disease produces puffed-out, fleshy growths on the ears and stems. Inside these areas are compact masses of black spores that disperse when broken open. Hot, dry weather favors the disease development. Infections may occur throughout the growth period, and young plants may be killed. The pathogen overwinters in the soil, thus crop rotations and field sanitation help to control the disease. Tolerant cultivars are available.

Leaf Blights. The major fungal leaf blights infecting sweet corn are northern leaf blight (*Helminthosporium turcicum*) and southern leaf blight (*H. maydis*). Both cause leaf lesions which appear as linear water-soaked areas that change to a straw-yellow color on drying, giving the foliage a streaked or scorched appearance. The two can be distinguished from each other since the northern leaf blight lesions are considerably larger (1–6 inches long) than those of the southern leaf blight (0.5–1.0 inch long) and tend to occur more on lower leaves. Both are carried over on infected crop residues and are favored by damp conditions, although the southern leaf blight prefers warmer temperatures than its counterpart. Generally, northern leaf blight occurs toward the latter part of the season, so yield losses are seldom severe. For both, disease control is mainly by using resistant cultivars and crop rotations. Fungicide application is usually necessary with the southern leaf blight and should be started at the first sign of the disease.

Leaf Rust. This is a common fungal disease (*Puccinia sorghi*), which usually appears around tasseling time. Masses of oval, reddish-brown pustules develop on all parts of the plant, but especially the leaves, resulting in loss of photosynthetic capacity. Seedling infection may also occur, causing defoliation and stunting. The disease is favored by cool, damp conditions, so late plantings are likely to be more susceptible to infection. Resistant cultivars and fungicide application are the best control measures.

Maize Dwarf Mosaic (MDM). MDM is a serious viral disease that may affect plants at any age. Infection is usually more severe in late plantings than in early ones. Symptoms initially occur in the youngest leaves as irregular light / dark green mosaic patterns that develop into mottled streaks. Older plants will have a yellow appearance and be severely stunted. Multiple ear shoots may arise but have poor development and fill. The virus overwinters in weedy grasses, especially johnsongrass, and is carried to corn by several aphid species. There is no chemical control, but the use of tolerant cultivars and the eradication of johnsongrass will reduce disease incidence.

HARVESTING AND POSTHARVEST HANDLING

As discussed, the quality of fresh sweet corn at harvest depends to a large extent on kernel texture and flavor, which are directly related to the sugar and polysaccharide content of the endosperm. At optimum edible maturity, high-quality sweet corn contains 70–75% moisture and high sugar concentration.

The proper stage of ear maturity at harvest is critical to market quality. As the ear matures, the kernels pass through four stages of maturation: pre-milk, milk, early dough, and dough. In the pre-milk stage, kernels are small, and their juice is clear and watery. From this the kernels pass into the milk stage, where they become large and plump and their juice becomes milky. While in the milk stage, kernels are sweet since sugars are still relatively high. However, in a relatively short time, usually less than a week, the kernels pass into the early dough and dough stages, during which the pericarp becomes tough and sugars are changed to starch.

The ears should be harvested when the kernels are early in the milk stage, when the juice is turning from clear to milky. Under normal temperature conditions, this will be around 18–21 days after first silking. However, if temperatures during the latter part of the growing season have been warmer than normal, the desired maturity may be reached 18 days or less from silking. With many cultivars, growers have found that when silks first become dry and the ears feel plump, the proper maturity has been reached.

The crop is usually harvested when about 70% of the ears have reached the desired maturity and have filled out. All the processing acreage and part of the corn for fresh market is machine-harvested. Multiple-row harvesters cut the stalks at the ground, remove the ears, and transfer them to bins or trailers (Figure 25.3). For the fresh market crop, self-propelled packing lines or "mule trains" move through the fields and sort, grade, and pack ears that have been hand-pulled by workers on the harvester (Figure 25.4). For local markets, the crop should be picked daily, preferably in the early morning.

After harvest, the eating quality of sweet corn decreases rapidly. The sugars decrease and the starch increases, and this change is directly proportional to temperature. The loss of sugar is about four times as rapid at 86°F as at 32°F. At 86°F, 60% of the sugars may be converted to starch in one day as compared to only 6% at 32°F. In addition, water is lost from the kernel through transpiration, causing denting in the kernel, while the pericarp continues to toughen with time.

Once the crop is harvested, field heat must be removed as rapidly as possible to slow the respiration rate. Precooling sweet corn to 32°F will maximize quality retention. However, even at this temperature sweet corn loses flavor and texture fairly rapidly. Hydrocooling has traditionally been the preferred method for cool-

Figure 25.3. Machine harvest of processing sweet corn.

Figure 25.4. A "mule train" used in harvesting and packing fresh market sweet corn in the field.

ing, since this adds water to compensate for some water loss. Vacuum cooling and slush ice may also be used for precooling. Generally, at 32°F and 95–98% relative humidity, sweet corn can be stored for no longer than 5–8 days.

SELECTED REFERENCES

Arnold, C. Y. 1969. Sweet corn development as affected by environment and by inherent differences among hybrids. *Illinois Research*, Winter.

Courter, J. W., and A. M. Rhodes. 1982. A classification of vegetable corns and new cultivars for 1982. *Proceedings 1982 Illinois Vegetable Growers Schools*. Univ. of Illinois Hort. Series 31.

Haflinger, E. (ed.). 1979. *Maize*. CIBA-GEIGY, Basle, Switzerland.

Hall, R. H. 1968. *Sweet Corn. Fruit & Vegetable Facts & Pointers*. United Fresh Fruit and Vegetable Association, Alexandria, Virginia.

Kaukis, K., and D. W. Davis. 1986. Sweet corn breeding, pp. 475–519. In: M. J. Bassett (ed.) *Breeding Vegetable Crops*. AVI Publishing Co., Westport, Connecticut.

Sims, W. L., R. F. Kasmire, and O. A. Lorenz. 1978. *Quality Sweet Corn Production*. California Agric. Ext. Ser. Leaf. 2818.

Sprague, G. F., and J. W. Dudley (eds.). 1988. *Corn and Corn Improvement*. American Society of Agronomy, Madison, Wisconsin.

Taber, H. G., R. G. Hartzler, L. E. Sweets, and D. R. Lewis. 1985. *Sweet Corn. Iowa Commercial Vegetable Production*. Iowa State Univ. Coop. Ext. Ser., Pm-1185a.

Zandstra, B. H., A. L. Wells, and D. G. and Z. R. Helsel. 1983. *Sweet Corn*. Michigan State Univ. Coop. Ext. Ser. Bull. E-1673.

26

SWEET POTATOES

Sweet potatoes are one of the most important food crops in tropical and sub-tropical countries, as well as in the southern U.S. The crop is grown throughout the world from 40°N to 30°S latitude, under highly contrasting production systems. It is a major carbohydrate source for millions of people, especially in developing nations. The plant is grown for its edible tuberous roots that contain about 27% carbohydrate and high concentrations of vitamins A and C, calcium, and iron. Fresh sweet potatoes provide about 50% more calories than Irish potatoes.

The roots are usually eaten boiled or baked, candied with syrup, or puréed. They also can be used for canning, dehydrating, flour manufacturing, and as a source of starch, glucose, syrup, and alcohol. The tuberous roots can also be used as feed for livestock. Older vines are sometimes used as fodder for cattle, swine, and fish. Because of their vining growth habit, some cultivars have ornamental value as groundcover or in hanging baskets and planters.

CLASSIFICATION, ORIGIN, HISTORY

The sweet potato (*Ipomoea Batatas*) is a native of tropical America and is the only important food crop in the morning-glory family (Convolvulaceae). The plant is a cultigen that is not found in the wild state, and its ancestory is not well known. It is a perennial herb that is grown as an annual in cultivation. There are several hundred cultivars of the sweet potato, and great variation is encountered between cultivars in form and growth habit.

Sweet potatoes were grown in the New World long before Columbus

495

arrived. Early explorers carried the plant to Spain and other sub-tropical and tropical countries, and early writers mentioned different cultivars and colors. The plant has been grown in Virginia for nearly 300 years. The sweet potato was used in the tropical South Pacific islands long before being introduced in North America, and was probably carried there along ancient trade routes. The name *batatas* was used by the Native American Indians in referring to this vegetable.

Sweet potatoes that are used for human consumption are referred to as "food types," to distinguish them from those used for feed and industrial purposes. The food types may be divided into soft-fleshed and firm-fleshed cultivars. The former are sweeter and softer and have moist orange to deep orange flesh. These types are commonly used for baking and are often mistakenly called yams, although the true yam belongs to a different group of plants in the genus *Dioscorea*. The term *yam* is still commonly used in the South for this crop. The firm-fleshed, or dry, types have yellow skins with white, yellow, or light orange flesh. These are used mostly for boiling and frying. The yellow- and orange-flesh types are popular in the U.S., while many tropical cultivars have white flesh.

PRODUCTION AND INDUSTRY

The sweet potato is grown extensively in the South, where it is a main carbohydrate food, similar to the Irish potato in more northern sections. It is grown commercially from New Jersey southward and westward. Commercial acreage declined from 256,000 acres in 1959, to 112,00 acres in 1977, and to almost 90,000 acres in 1988 (Table 26.1). For the corresponding period, production decreased from 1,240,200 tons in 1959 to around 600,000 tons in 1977 and 1988. The leading states in sweet potato production are North Carolina (39%), Louisiana (22%), and California (11%). Other leading producers are Georgia, Texas, Alabama, South Carolina, and Mississippi. Average yields vary considerably; in North Carolina, sweet potato production averages 7 tons per acre (300 bushels per acre), compared to about 5 tons per acre in Louisiana.

The major sweet potato production areas in the world include the continents of South America, Africa, and Australia, the countries in Mediterranean Europe and the Malay Archipelago, and the countries of India, Japan, New Zealand, China, and the U.S., primarily in the southeastern and Gulf coastal regions. Africa has the largest tropical acreage, but China is the largest producer, accounting for over 80% of the total worldwide production.

Table 26.1. **Harvested Acreage and Production of Sweet Potatoes in the U.S., 1977 and 1988**

State	Harvested Acres		Production	
	1977[1]	1988[2]	1977[1]	1988[2]
			(tons)	
Alabama	5,300	6,800	22,550	39,100
Arkansas	1,600	—	6,100	—
California	7,800	7,100	58,500	60,350
Georgia	5,500	5,200	24,750	41,600
Louisiana	27,000	17,000	121,500	123,250
Maryland	1,600	900	12,400	6,750
Mississippi	8,000	3,500	34,000	17,500
New Jersey	2,400	2,300	12,600	8,650
North Carolina	33,000	34,000	222,750	221,000
South Carolina	2,300	3,900	10,450	19,500
Tennessee	2,800	800	14,000	3,600
Texas	9,500	7,400	45,150	25,900
Virginia	5,600	900	35,000	5,650
U.S.	112,400	89,800	619,750	572,850

[1]Source: USDA. 1978. *Agricultural Statistics,* Economics, Statistics, and Cooperatives Service (ESCS), Crop Reporting Board.

[2]Source: USDA. National Agricultural Statistics Service (NASS), Agricultural Statistics Board.

PLANT GROWTH AND DEVELOPMENT

The sweet potato is a tender, warm-season vegetable that grows as a perennial in tropical and sub-tropical climates, and as an annual in temperate regions. The plant arises from adventitious buds on fleshy roots. It develops into branching, prostrate vines with heart-shaped leaves that quickly cover the soil. Feeder roots can develop on vines that come in contact with the ground. The blossoms are like those of the morning-glory, although flowering is uncommon in the northern and central portions of the U.S.

The root system is adventitious (except in plants grown from seed) and arises from seed potatoes, stems, and cuttings. The adventitious roots form a fibrous root system, but some roots will enlarge and thicken greatly to form several fleshy roots. A plant will have from four to ten of these tuberous roots, depending on cultivar and growing conditions (Figure 26.1). The tuberous roots may vary from fusiform (tapering at both ends) to globular in shape, and may be smooth or ridged. The periderm, or skin, varies among cultivars and can be white, orange, red, purple, or brown. Flesh color is also variable, with white, yellow, orange, and reddish-purple the most common. Secondary roots can develop on the tuberous roots.

Figure 26.1. A hill of sweet potato roots.

If subject to the proper conditions, the fleshy roots may produce adventitious shoots called "slips." The slips develop adventitious roots of their own and become small plants attached to the original root. These are used commercially as the propagating material for the production beds.

The slips exhibit a form of apical dominance and are usually restricted to the crown or stem (proximal) end of the original root. This significantly reduces the number of slips that can be produced from the original root. However, if roots are subjected to high temperatures for a period of time (see "Planting and Crop Establishment"), apical dominance can be reduced and slip production increased.

CLIMATIC AND CULTURAL REQUIREMENTS

Sweet potatoes thrive in the warmer portions of the U.S. from New Jersey to Texas. The optimum mean growing temperature is around 75°F. Warm days and nights are essential, and the crop does very well under relatively hot conditions. Growth is restricted in cool weather (59°F), and the plants are damaged by chilling injury at temperatures below 50°F. For full plant development, there must be a frost-free growing period of 4–5 months.

Although the plant does well on a wide range of soil types, the best soils for sweet potato production are deep soils of intermediate texture, such as a sandy loam, with a clay subsoil. Light-textured soils generally produce roots with smoother skins than heavy-textured soils. Very light soils tend to produce long, slender roots. Silt loams usually give good results, but heavy clay loams often cause rough and irregular-shaped roots. Soils high in organic matter (over 2%) are generally not suited for sweet potato production. These tend to produce a high percentage of rough or cracked roots that are damaged by scurf (see "Diseases").

Good drainage is essential for growing sweet potatoes. Wet soils have poor aeration, which causes roots to be large, misshapen, often cracked, and rough skinned. This necessitates the crop being grown on raised ridges to provide for good soil drainage in many regions.

Sweet potatoes are moderately heavy feeders and must be well supplied with nutrients for optimum yields. Production field recommendations call for around 90–100 pounds of nitrogen per acre, 30–80 pounds P_2O_5 per acre, and 60-180 pounds K_2O per acre. Phosphorus and potash rates will vary based on soil test results. The basic application of fertilizer may be put on before, during, or shortly after transplanting, or in split application, combining any of these times. In North Carolina, the fertilizer application is commonly divided between a preplant broadcast application, and two sidedressings during the season. In Georgia, some growers band all the fertilizer before planting, at the time the beds are formed, while other growers band one-half the fertilizer in two side bands at planting and the remainder to each side of the row when the vines are 12 inches long.

Compared to most other vegetable crops, sweet potatoes are more tolerant of acid soils. The optimum pH range is between 5.5 and 6.2. A soil more acid than 5.0 should be limed to bring the reaction within this range.

PLANTING AND CROP ESTABLISHMENT

The crop is vegetatively propagated, either by transplants called "slips" or by vine cuttings. The first method is most common in sub-tropical areas and temperate zones, notably the U.S. Vine cuttings are used in the tropics and in parts of the lower South. Large growers generally produce their own seed stock, while small growers often purchase their propagating material from a commercial source.

Slips

The slips are small plants that are produced from small- to medium-sized (0.75–1.5 inches in diameter) parent seed roots of the previous crop in hotbeds filled with sand or in nursery beds. The slips form when the parent roots develop adventitious shoots and roots when they are placed under warm, moist conditions. Each parent root produces up to fifteen slips, although they do not all develop at the same rate.

The roots are planted about 1 inch apart in a hotbed or other type of bed and covered with 1–2 inches of sand or light soil. A deep layer of soil delays the sprouting of newly bedded potatoes. The seed roots should be free from disease, clean, vigorous, and true to type for the cultivar. Prior to bedding, the seed roots can be given special presprouting treatments to increase the earliness and number of slips produced. Roots are held at 80–90°F with high humidity for several weeks or until sprouts appear. This treatment helps overcome proximal dominance in seed roots and results in two to three times more seedling plants. Cutting seed roots in half before bedding also increases the number of sprouts produced.

As sprouts begin to appear, another 1 inch of sand is applied. This is repeated as sprouts grow. At pulling time, there should be approximately 4–5 inches of sand or soil over the parent potatoes to ensure long (8–12 inches), stocky, well-rooted slips. Plants reach transplanting size in approximately 6 weeks and should have six to ten well-developed leaves (Figure 26.2). The slips are pulled from the parent plant by hand, making sure each slip has sufficient root material (Figure 26.3). Generally, two or three harvests of slips may be made from the original root.

Figure 26.2. Sweet potato plants for transplanting; the plant on the left is too small for easy handling.

Figure 26.3. Slips are drawn by hand, and only plants that have formed good roots are taken. (Photo: courtesy of F. J. Sundstrom, Louisiana State University)

Several types of propagating beds may be used in producing slips. In warmer sections, unheated open field beds (Figure 26.4) or cold frames are commonly used, while in more northern areas, slips are started in heated beds (Figure 26.5) to provide as long a growing season as possible. In some regions, the field beds

Figure 26.4. In warmer regions of the South, sweet potatoes are usually bedded in open field beds. (Photo: courtesy of F. J. Sundstrom, Louisiana State University)

Figure 26.5. In northern regions, slips are produced in heated hotbeds.

are covered with plastic in the form of row tunnels. Sprouts develop best in beds at a soil temperature of 75–80°F, and the covering should be removed when soil temperatures reach 85°F to avoid heat damage. High temperatures increase the rate of growth but produce soft, weak plants. Covered beds may need to be ventilated on bright, sunny days to control temperatures. Unheated beds may need covering on very cold nights, as plants are easily injured by frost.

Vine Cuttings

Another method of propagation is by cuttings taken from vines from an early planting of slips. Apical cuttings are preferred because they tend to give better growth and yields than cuttings from basal or middle portions. The cuttings are usually 12–15 inches long with seven or more nodes. The bottom leaves are removed to facilitate planting and crop establishment.

This method is relatively inexpensive, but it requires a long season, such as in the tropics and the lower South. Vine cuttings are fairly resistant to adverse conditions, and they do not transfer disease and nematodes, which is sometimes a problem when slips are used.

Field Planting

Slips and vine cuttings are set in the field when the soil is warm (above 65°F) and all danger of frost is over. The distance between rows (32–48 inches) and the spacing within the row (8–18 inches) depend on such factors as time of planting, cultivar, soil type, and fertility. The size of sweet potato roots is controlled more by spacing in the row than width of row. Large cultivars such as 'Porto Rico' need more space than those with shorter vines. Close spacing is desirable on rich, fertile soils, since it tends to reduce the number of large roots and to increase marketable yields. Highest economic yields of best grade roots for fresh market are generally attained with 12-inch plant spacing in 42-inch rows. Late cultivars are usually planted at wider plant spacings than early cultivars.

Sweet potatoes are planted on broad-topped ridges 8–10 inches tall, which provide good runoff from heavy rainfall. Small acreage plantings are usually set by hand, but for large areas, crops may be transplanted by drag and precision types of transplanters.

CULTURAL PRACTICES

Weeds

In the production of sweet potatoes, a combination of cultivation and herbicides is generally used to control weeds. Effective weed control is important during the early part of the growing season when the plants are getting established but before the vines have grown extensively. Several row cultivations are usually made before the vines interfere with the cultivators. Once the vines spread to cover the ground, they will normally suppress most weed growth.

Herbicides are used to control weeds early in the season, to reduce the amount of cultivation, and to maintain weed control between the period when vines start to run and before vine growth is extensive. Several herbicides are available for the control of annual grasses and broadleaf weeds. State extension weed specialists can help growers select the correct materials and methods for local conditions.

Irrigation

The sweet potato is considered to be a moderately drought-tolerant crop. The plants develop a deep root system down to about 6 feet. After they are established, sweet potatoes can withstand severe drought, but a moisture stress during storage root formation may reduce yields. Moisture is considered adequate when rainfall or rainfall plus irrigation provides about 1.0–1.5 inches every 7–10 days. In Louisiana the average daily water requirement for sweet potatoes early in the season is around 0.1 inch per day and increases to 0.25 inch per day in midsummer.

Irrigation is usually not required in the warm, humid regions of the South and Southeast because rainfall is consistent enough to supply adequate moisture throughout the growing season. However, during dry periods supplemental irrigation may be needed in these areas to maintain uniform moisture. In the drier areas of the Southwest and West, irrigation is required and is usually supplied by surface or overhead irrigation. A commercial crop in California will require around 18 inches of irrigation water. Overwatering should be avoided since it is likely to result in overgrowth of vines and may lead to oversized and misshapen or cracked roots. Irrigation should be withheld during the last 3–4 weeks before harvest to avoid the development of cracks and oversized roots and to condition the roots for harvest and handling.

CULTIVARS

Important characteristics for food types include attractiveness of skin and flesh colors, uniformity of root shape, flavor and texture of flesh, vitamin and nutritional content, and productiveness. For feed and industrial uses, cultivars should have high-yielding capacity; high solids and carbohydrates, including starch content and recovery; and superior propagative and storage properties. Some of the more important soft-fleshed cultivars include 'Centennial,' 'Georgia Red,' 'Julian,' 'Jewel,' 'Jasper,' 'Nemagold,' and 'Goldrush.' Some firm-fleshed cultivars are 'Nugget' and red and yellow Jersey strains. Leading nonfood cultivars are 'Pelican Processor' and 'Whitestar.'

Variability of Cultivars

Since sweet potatoes are propagated asexually, it would be expected that cultivars would be extremely uniform. This is not the case, however, and many growers have reported variability among hills of plants derived from a single root. A cultivar that fits a certain description at a particular time may produce different types after a few years. For example, yellow- and red-skinned potatoes may occur on the same plant. Roots produced from these various types may differ in yield, size, and maturation period. Differences in chemical composition and cooking quality may also occur. The problem is so severe in the field that growers claim that many cultivars "run out" after several years of culture.

This kind of variability in sweet potatoes has been attributed to mutations. Sweet potato cultivars are very heterogenous and genetically unstable. They mutate at a much higher rate than most other crops. Mutations occur with different frequencies for different traits. Unfortunately, most of the mutations observed in sweet potatoes are detrimental, resulting in inferior roots.

Selection by Growers

In many growing regions, the sweet potato seed stock is badly mixed, and it is not uncommon to find roots of more than one cultivar in the same market package. Growers must be very selective of their seed potatoes, particularly if they were saved from roots produced the previous growing season. Selection is done in the field at harvest time so that the entire plant can be examined. The vigor of the plant; the yield, size, and shape of the roots; and the resistance to disease are given careful consideration. The grower should have an ideal plant in mind and then select the hills (crowns) that most nearly meet that ideal.

Several methods of selection may be used. In ordinary hill selection, all of the selected hills are pooled and used for propagation the following year, without regard for the future performance of each hill. In another method, known as the "hill-to-row" method, each hill is planted separately in a row for further study and selection. Hills that do not maintain the standards of the parent hills are eliminated. A third method is the "tuber-unit" method, in which seed is saved only from "units" (plants produced from a single seed root) that maintain the desirable characters. This method is based on the potatoes within the hill varying just as much as the hills within the strain. None of these methods requires annual selection of plants from the main field, since after the initial selections are made, all further efforts are confined to the seed plants.

Certified Seed Potatoes

It is best for growers to use certified sweet potato seed stock which has been carefully examined for varietal characteristics. Certified seed is the second crop produced from foundation seed. Several states maintain sweet potato seed certification programs that ensure that seed stocks are true-to-type and disease-free. In North Carolina, certified seed stock is produced by seed growers under production guidelines established by the North Carolina Crop Improvement Association.

In most years, however, there is not usually sufficient certified seed for the entire sweet potato crop. Many growers are required to develop and maintain their own seed program and integrate this into their own commercial production program.

INSECTS AND DISEASES

Insects

Sweet potatoes are usually free from very serious insect attacks. The most destructive insect pest is the sweet potato weevil (*Cylas formicarius elegantulus*), which causes serious damage from Texas to Florida. The adult insect is a slender snout beetle about 0.25 inch long. The larvae tunnel through the vines to the roots and often riddle the sweet potatoes. The weevil overwinters in roots left in the ground and in sweet potatoes in storage. Other host plants include members of the morning-glory family. Control measures consist of soil dusting with insecticides, cleaning up fields after harvesting, disposing of the crop as soon as possible after roots are dug, using clean seed, growing plants as far away as possible from infested fields, and disinfecting storage facilities.

Other insect pests that occasionally attack this crop are cutworms, flea beetles, striped blister beetles, wireworms, and whiteflies. These are usually not serious pests, although in certain years they can cause significant damage.

Diseases

A number of serious diseases can significantly reduce sweet potato yields and quality. These can occur in the field, in storage, and during marketing and handling. Losses during storage may be severe as a result of soft rots and other diseases that predispose the roots to secondary infections. General measures for disease control in sweet potatoes include selecting cultivars with multiple resistance, using certified plants, and rotating sweet potato plantings with other crops on a 3–4 year cycle.

Black Rot. This fungal disease (*Ceratocystis fimbriata*) is generally considered to be the most destructive field disease of sweet potatoes. It can occur during propagating, in fields, and on roots in storage. All parts of the plant below ground are affected. In the early stages, foliage appears yellow and sickly, and black spots or cankers develop on the underground parts of the stem and roots. Infection very often increases in storage. The fungus overwinters on dead vines or other decayed vegetable matter in the soil and infects sweet potatoes by contact. Slips from diseased plants are usually infected.

Selecting disease-free seed and disinfecting roots with a fungicide dip just prior to planting helps in controlling the disease. A 3-year rotation will decrease the accumulation of disease material in the soil. Spring and fall selections help to eliminate diseased roots.

Stem Rot. Also called yellow blight or *Fusarium* wilt, stem rot (*Fusarium oxysporum f. batatas*) is a destructive field disease in most regions. The fungus enters through the roots, and the foliage of infected plants turns yellow. The vascular system is usually invaded, and dark-colored lesions develop in the stem. The vines wilt, and eventually the entire plant collapses and dies. Sprouts produced from infected roots are likely to be diseased. Similar to black rot, the fungus can live for several years on decaying vegetation in the soil. Cultivars show a marked difference in susceptibility to this disease. Control measures are similar to those for black rot.

Scurf. Caused by *Monilochaetes infuscans*, scurf is commonly found wherever sweet potatoes are grown, although losses are usually not as severe as those caused by other diseases. The fungus lives in the soil and can be carried on slips. It causes no apparent injury above ground but produces a brown to black surface discoloration of the roots that is restricted to the skin. Affected roots lose water and become shriveled and dried, even in fairly humid storage conditions. The use of disease-free seed and the treatment of seed with fungicide are the main preventive measures. Infected soil should not be planted for at least 3 years.

Soft Rot. Also called ring rot and collar rot, soft rot is caused by the same fungus (*Rhizopus stolonifer*) that causes bread mold. It is a storage disease that enters the sweet potato through breaks in the skin caused by careless handling. Decay usually begins in wounded tissue at one end of the potato and progresses rapidly throughout the root. The initial symptom is a soft, watery, stringy condition. Loss of water later produces a dry, shriveled appearance, resembling a dry rot. A rotting sweet potato may infect surrounding roots. The soft rot organism is ubiquitous and therefore impossible to exclude from storage houses. Proper curing and handling are the best preventive measures.

Nematodes. Several species of root-knot nematodes (*Meloidogyne* sp.) cause galling, or knots, on feeder roots, and roughing and cracking of tubers. Above-ground parts of the plant appear stunted, sickly, and yellow. On hot days, vines will wilt. Lesion nematodes cause irregular, dark, sunken areas on the surface of the tuber. Nematicides used in seedbeds and in the field give the best control, although these chemicals are few in number and tend to be expensive. Cultivars 'Nemagold' and 'Jasper' are resistant, while 'Porto Rico' and Jersey strains have moderate resistance to root knot.

Root Rot. Root rot (*Phymatotrichum omnivorum*) is also called Texas root rot and is caused by the same organism that causes root rot in cotton and alfalfa. Although its distribution is limited to the southwestern U.S., once the disease gets into a field, an entire crop may be destroyed. Root rot causes a firm, brown rot, that results in the complete destruction of the tuber. Infection produces a brown discoloration within the above-ground stems. The fungus overwinters in the soil and on seed sweet potatoes. No satisfactory control is known, although it is killed by hard freezes. Rotation with grasses, corn, and other cereals helps to prevent infection since these crops are not affected by the disease.

Leaf Diseases. Fungal leaf diseases, such as white rust, leaf blight, and *Septoria* leaf spot, may occur during the growing season but very often are not serious enough to justify control measures.

Storage Diseases. In addition to soft rot and black rot, other storage diseases include surface rot, Java black rot, dry rot, internal cork, and some field diseases that continue to develop in storage. Careful handling, proper curing, and favorable storage conditions will prevent storage diseases from getting started. Storage houses must be thoroughly cleaned and disinfected to keep rots to a minimum.

HARVESTING AND POSTHARVEST HANDLING

Harvesting

Sweet potatoes do not mature or ripen as most other crops, and roots will continue to grow as long as the vines remain green. The crop is harvested when the highest percentage of roots reach the desired size. Generally, roots attain the highest yields and best quality at around 130–150 days from planting. Soil temperatures below 50°F will injure the crop, and roots should be harvested before soil temperatures get cold. After the vines are dead, field losses increase considerably, as decay may spread from the vines into the roots.

The bulk of the sweet potato crop is harvested in the fall, with most of it being stored for later use. Earlier harvests made in the summer are usually directly marketed. With very early digging, increased market prices are necessary to offset reduced yields and lower quality of roots.

A variety of methods may be used to harvest sweet potatoes. The methods used in digging and handling greatly influence subsequent storage and market quality. The sweet potato root has a thin skin that is easily broken and flesh that is readily cut and bruised. The crop should be handled as little as possible. Injuries provide opportunity for the entrance of decay organisms and constitute grade defects.

Roots to be picked by hand are most commonly dug with either modified moldboard turnplows or large middlebusters. Modified chain-type Irish potato diggers are also used to dig sweet potatoes (Figure 26.6) but can result in

Figure 26.6. A modified chain-type Irish potato digger may be used to dig sweet potatoes. (Photo: courtesy of F. J. Sundstrom, Louisiana State University)

excessive skinning of roots. Most growers try to dig sweet potatoes when the soil is dry, making it easier to dig and handle roots. The roots are usually permitted to dry slightly after they have been dug from the soil (Figure 26.7).

Whichever system is utilized, some method of vine cutting or vine removal from the crown of the rows is necessary. Vines become tangled around the equipment, interfering with the digging of the roots. Vines also may hide roots, increasing the number of unrecovered marketable tubers. The vines can be cut or removed before the roots are dug, or as part of the digging operation itself. Various types of equipment such as fixed knives, colters (cutting wheels), and disks can be attached to the diggers. In a separate operation prior to the digging, vines can be removed by tractor-operated, rotary-type mowers.

Figure 26.7. After being dug or plowed out, the roots may be placed in rows and permitted to dry slightly.

Mechanical harvesters that will cut vines and dig, remove, and load roots into bins are now available. Labor requirements are greatly reduced with these. However, harvester operators must be careful to avoid damaging the roots as they move through the machine.

Curing and Storing

Proper curing and storing allows growers to market sweet potatoes the year-round. Under the proper environmental conditions, sweet potato roots can be stored up to 12 months.

Prior to storing, the crop should be cured by holding roots for 4–7 days at 80–85°F and 85–90% relative humidity. Curing promotes the formation of cork layers on wounded surfaces, which heals cuts, bruises, and skinned areas on roots, thereby preventing decay. It also lessens shrinkage and weight loss during storage and improves cooking quality. During curing, sweet potatoes may lose up to 5% of their weight. Curing should begin as soon after harvest as possible and is especially important for sweet potatoes harvested during a period of cold weather.

Some sweet potatoes are marketed as uncured. These are usually the early potatoes that are directly marketed. In some cases, these may be cured just for a brief period to help set the skin.

After curing, the temperature should be lowered to 55–60°F by ventilating with outside air, and the relative humidity should be maintained at 85–90%. Under these conditions, most cultivars can be stored for 4–7 months, and some can keep up to almost a year. A weight loss of about 2% will occur in storage, as well as some transformation of starch to sugar.

Being a tropical crop, sweet potato roots are susceptible to chilling injury at temperatures below 55°F. This results in the discoloration of the flesh, internal breakdown, and off-flavors when cooked. Uncured roots are more susceptible to chilling injury than cured ones. Temperatures above 86°F can stimulate the development of sprouts and an increase in pithiness of roots.

Sweet potatoes are usually stored in nonrefrigerated commercial or farm warehouses. Bulk bins, slatted crates, boxes, or baskets may be used as containers and should be arranged to provide adequate ventilation. Some facilities are designed to cure and store in the same room, or in the same building.

MARKETING

Sweet potato roots are usually washed and graded and sometimes waxed before being shipped to market. Waxing does not prolong shelflife and is done only if requested by the buyer. Roots are often treated with a fungicide to reduce decay during marketing. The product is marketed in consumer-perforated film bags or overwrapped trays, and in mesh bags.

Most of the crop is marketed through sales brokers and shipping point buyers. Selling brokers are located near production areas and arrange sales between grower-shippers and terminal market buyers.

SELECTED REFERENCES

Barber, J. M., P. Colditz, and D. M. Granberry. 1979. *Growing Sweet Potatoes in Georgia*. Univ. of Georgia Coop. Ext. Ser. Bull. 677.

Edmond, J. B., and G. R. Ammerman. 1971. *Sweet Potatoes: Production, Processing, Marketing*. AVI Publishing Co., Westport, Connecticut.

Jones, A., P. D. Dukes, and J. M. Schalk. 1986. Sweet potato breeding. In: M. J. Bassett (ed.). *Breeding Vegetable Crops*. AVI Publishing Co., Westport, Connecticut.

Kostewicz, S. R., and J. Montelaro. 1975. *Sweetpotato Production Guide*. Univ. of Florida Coop. Ext. Ser. Cir. 97C.

Steinbauer, C. E., and L. J. Kushman. 1971. *Sweetpotato Culture and Diseases*. USDA Agriculture Handbook No. 388.

Wilson, L. G. 1980. *Growing and Marketing Quality Sweet Potatoes*. North Carolina Agric. Coop. Ext. Ser. AG-09.

27

TOMATOES

CLASSIFICATION, ORIGIN, HISTORY

The tomato (*Lycopersicon Lycopersicum*) is a member of the nightshade family (Solanaceae), along with the pepper, eggplant, and potato. Botanically, it is classified as a fruit, since it is developed from an ovary, although it is commercially recognized and treated as a vegetable. Included in the genus are several known wild forms of tomato (*L. pimpinellifolium, L. hirsutum, L. peruvianum*) that have been very useful in breeding programs for disease and insect resistance.

The tomato is native to tropical America, most likely in the region of the Andes Mountains in Peru and Bolivia. The wild types generally have small fruits, about the size of a cherry or slightly larger. The larger-fruited forms were developed from the wild state by the pre-Columbian Aztecs and Incas, who cultivated tomatoes long before the discovery of the Americas. Mexico is thought to be the region of domestication. Seeds were taken back to Italy by the returning explorers, and the plant quickly found favor in the warm Mediterranean climate. From there, tomatoes moved to northern Europe, and eventually to the U.S. by the late 1700's.

In its history, there has been considerable prejudice against using the tomato as a culinary vegetable. The British thought it to be poisonous or to be the fruit of evil spirits, while the French associated it with love, referring to it as the "love apple." People knew that it was related to certain poisonous members of the nightshade family, such as belladona and mandrake. Perhaps because of this, the crop was slow to gain popularity in the U.S., and it was not until about 1835 that the tomato became generally cultivated for culinary purposes in this country. Extensive commercial production in the U.S. did not come about until the latter part of the 19th century.

For culinary purposes, the tomato is one of the most versatile vegetables — it can be baked, stewed, fried, juiced, pickled, puréed, processed into catsup or sauces, or used fresh in salads. Its nutritional value is modest, as it ranks sixteenth among vegetables in relative concentration of vitamins and minerals. However, because of the quantities consumed, it is the largest contributor among vegetable crops of nutrients to the per capita U.S. diet.

PRODUCTION AND INDUSTRY

Tomatoes are one of the most popular vegetable crops for both fresh market and processing in the U.S., as well as being the most commonly grown vegetable in the home garden. The estimated total acreage harvested for commercial tomatoes in the U.S. in 1989 was approximately 460,000 acres, with a net value of almost $1.8 billion and a total production of 11.3 million tons (Table 27.1). In terms of cash receipts, commercially grown tomatoes were second only to potatoes in 1989. The amount of time, land, and money devoted to tomatoes in the home garden is impossible to estimate.

The processing crop accounted for approximately 69% of the commercial acreage and 84% of the production in 1989, but only 35% of the commercial value. Conversely, fresh market tomatoes made up only 16% of the total commercial production, but accounted for almost 65% of the total commercial value. These figures reflect some of the differences between processing and fresh market tomato production. Although the same species, processing tomatoes and fresh market tomatoes are distinct crops in regard to many aspects of production and marketing.

Fresh market tomatoes are grown for the wholesale, retail, and supermarket trade. Yields in the U.S. in 1989 averaged 13 tons per acre, with growers in Virginia and South Carolina averaging over 20 tons per acre. Depending on location, climate (length of growing season), and cultivar, and with irrigation, top yields of fresh market tomatoes can be over 40 tons per acre. The demand for the crop has expanded dramatically. In comparing commercial production statistics for 1989 with 1977, acreage, production, and value for fresh market tomatoes increased 14, 84, and 184%, respectively.

Fresh market tomatoes are grown year-round in the U.S. The leading fresh market–producing states are Florida and California, which account for 51 and 28% of the total U.S. production, respectively. Production in Florida is in the fall, winter, and spring, while in California the fresh market crop is grown mostly in the summer and fall, plus a small amount in the spring. Other areas of spring production include the southeastern states, as well as Texas and Arkansas. Sum-

Table 27.1. Harvested Acreage, Production, and Value of Fresh Market and Processed Tomatoes, 1989[1]

State	Harvested Acreage		Production		Value	
	F. Market	Processed	F. Market	Processed	F. Market	Processed
			——— (tons) ———		——— ($1,000) ———	
Alabama	2,700	—	16,200	—	7,290	—
Arkansas	1,000	—	7,000	—	4,956	—
California	38,400	276,500	499,200	8,585,330	239,616	569,207
Colorado	—	190	—	3,610	—	343
Delaware	—	470	—	3,650	—	327
Florida	60,200	—	918,050	—	739,948	—
Georgia	2,700	—	27,000	—	12,960	—
Hawaii	250	—	2,750	—	3,047	—
Indiana	1,400	7,800	10,850	157,560	5,859	12,447
Louisiana	340	—	1,550	—	1,178	—
Maryland	2,600	970	16,250	12,310	7,995	1,096
Massachusetts	550	—	6,200	—	7,440	—
Michigan	2,500	5,400	12,500	132,840	6,300	9,671
New Jersey	5,100	3,000	21,700	31,590	13,454	2,799
New York	2,500	1,900	21,250	35,400	16,023	3,292
North Carolina	1,300	—	12,350	—	3,804	—
Ohio	2,700	17,500	19,600	391,300	14,465	30,208
Pennsylvania	4,000	1,700	40,000	35,360	17,120	3,306
South Carolina	3,600	—	70,200	—	24,851	—
Tennessee	3,600	—	25,200	—	12,600	—
Texas	2,800	—	12,600	—	4,763	—
Virginia	3,000	—	54,750	—	39,858	—
Other states[2]	—	5,420	—	95,520	—	7,417
U.S.	141,240	320,850	1,795,200	9,484,470	1,183,527	640,113

[1]Source: USDA. 1990. National Agricultural Statistics Service (NASS), Agricultural Statistics Board.

[2]For processing, Florida, Illinois, Iowa, South Carolina, Texas, Virginia.

mer production ranges from Georgia up into the more northern states. This diversification of producing areas in the spring and summer reduces the risk of losses due to bad weather and expands the available supply during these times.

Prices for commercially grown fresh market tomatoes tend to be down in July and August, since summer retail demand is reduced considerably by home-grown tomatoes. In contrast, winter production is concentrated in Florida and is more subject to variations in weather, causing uncertainty in the available supply and considerable fluctuations in prices.

Processing tomato production is heavily concentrated in California, which produces about 91% of the processing tomatoes grown in the U.S., followed by Ohio, Indiana, and Michigan. The major growing areas in California are in the Sacramento and the San Joaquin valleys, in addition to parts of the coastal areas and some southern counties. In comparing commercial production statistics for 1989 with 1977, the acreage of processing tomatoes decreased 7%, while production and value increased 22 and 29%, respectively. Yields of processing tomatoes in the U.S. average almost 30 tons per acre, but in some parts of California, growers may produce over 60 tons per acre.

Greenhouse production of tomatoes during cold weather is a highly specialized operation, requiring a high degree of technical management. Once a sizeable industry in places like Ohio and Indiana, it has declined dramatically since the mid-1970's due to high heating costs and increased winter importation from Mexico.

Worldwide, tomatoes are extensively grown, including considerable production in developing countries. The U.S. leads the world in total production, producing about 15% of the crop. The USS and China also grow large quantities of tomatoes, and together produce about one-quarter of the world total. The Mediterranean Basin countries such as Spain, Italy, Portugal, Greece, Turkey, and Israel produce a fairly large supply of processing tomatoes. Much of the crop produced in Mexico during the winter is exported to the U.S. for fresh market use.

PLANT GROWTH AND DEVELOPMENT

The tomato is a herbaceous perennial in its native habitat but is usually grown as an annual in the U.S. since it is easily killed by frost before it can complete its first year. The plant should have a vigorous, uninterrupted juvenile stage during which flowering is delayed to allow development of a strong vegetative structure before fruits set.

Vine Types

Three different growth habits or vine types can occur in tomato; these are indeterminate types, semi-determinate (semi-erect) forms, and determinate (bush) types. With the indeterminate types, three or four leaves are usually produced between flower clusters. The primary shoot dominates side shoot development, so there is much less branching than in determinate types. The shoot does not end in a flower cluster but continues to grow until killed by frost or by some other factor.

The determinate types produce flower clusters with only one or two leaves between them. After several clusters have been established, the shoot terminates in a flower cluster. This forces side shoots to develop from axillary growing points, which repeat this pattern. The branches of determinate plants terminate their growth at approximately the same distance from the crown, and flowering is concentrated in a shorter period of time than in indeterminate types. Consequently, determinate types tend to be compact and symmetrically circular, as compared to the sprawling growth pattern of the indeterminate types.

The semi-determinate types have vine characteristics that are intermediate between the other two. These will generally have several lateral flower clusters, but stems will also terminate in flower clusters.

In general, variations in characteristics such as the number of nodes before a branch terminates in a cluster, the amount of apical dominance in the indeterminate types (which influences the number and size of the side branches), the length of the internodes, and the tendency of the stems to grow erectly or procumbently, give rise to a variety of vine patterns, including some quite compact and dwarf growth habits in newer cultivars.

Flowering and Fruit Development

Unlike most plants, the flower clusters in tomatoes occur along the stems, and not at the nodes or leaf axils. Tomato flowers are medium in size and contain both male and female parts. The anthers are united in the form of a hollow cylinder or tube. The style is short and the stigma is wholly enclosed within the anther tube. Pollen is shed toward the center of the tube onto the stigma. This general arrangement makes tomatoes primarily a self-pollinated crop, mostly by wind shaking and with relatively little opportunity for outcrossing. However, in some species, such as *L. peruvianum*, which have long styles that protrude beyond the anther, some cross-pollination may take place.

The number of flowers comprising an inflorescence may vary from four to twelve or more, but not all of these will set fruit. Within the same inflorescence, fruits may not develop at the same time, and it is not unusual to have small fruits, open flowers, and buds in the same cluster. If internal or external conditions are not favorable, the plant will shed its flowers before setting fruit (see "Climatic and Cultural Requirements"). This is usually due to unsuccessful or incomplete pollination. Tomato flowers must be adequately pollinated to avoid fruit defects, since the fruits must have a full complement of seeds for normal development.

The tomato fruit develops from the ovary and is composed of several irregularly shaped carpels. The outer walls form a continuous fleshy band around the outside of the fruit, while the inside walls radiate outward from a central core, or placenta, which has two or more cavities, or locules, containing the seeds (Figure 27.1). As the fruit matures, the inner matrix of the locules softens into a gelatinous mass, or locular jelly, and sugars tend to increase and acids decrease. Other components of fruit quality, such as color, total solids, pH, solids / acid ratio, viscosity, vitamins, and flavor change with the relative maturity of the fruit.

Mature fruits may be red, pink, orange, yellow, or white. Most commercial

Figure 27.1.   A cross section of a mature fruit showing the locular cavities containing the locular jelly and seeds.

cultivars are red or pink. Fruit color is due to pigments; the green color of fruits
is due to chlorophyll, red to lycopene, orange to carotene, and yellow to xantho-
phyll. As fruits mature, lycopene increases and chlorophyll decreases. Generally,
carotene reaches maximum development before lycopene, resulting in a gradual
shift from orange to red in fruit color as fruits ripen. The optimum temperature
range for lycopene development is 70–75°F. The production of this pigment drops
off rapidly above 80°F and is almost nil above 90°F. Carotene, however, develops
readily at high temperatures, so fruits that ripen in hot weather will generally have
a distinct orange color.

CLIMATIC AND CULTURAL REQUIREMENTS

Tomatoes are warm-season plants which require a frost-free period from
about 80 days in some determinate cultivars to over 120 days in indeterminate
types. Optimum growth occurs at a daily mean of 65–75°F, but even at this
average, extremely cool nights or hot days can be deleterious. Growth stops at
a maximum temperature of approximately 95°F and a minimum of 53°F. Tomato
tissues freeze at 30°F, and prolonged exposure to below 50°F kills the plants.

Temperature markedly affects flowering and fruiting by tomatoes, primarily
due to its effect on pollination. With most cultivars, average maximum day
temperatures above 90°F and night temperatures above 70°F during anthesis can
reduce fruit set. There is now considerable evidence that night temperatures are

the critical factor affecting fruit set, with an optimum range of 59–68°F. Some cultivars will set fruit under high night temperatures (80°F), although most do not. High day temperatures, especially in conjunction with low humidity, can destroy pollen. Low temperatures also decrease fruit set by reducing the production and viability of pollen. Hot, drying winds will cause flowers to drop. Other conditions that may cause flowers to drop include insufficient light, excessive nitrogen, moisture stress, and insect and disease injury.

Tomatoes will grow on a wide range of soils. A light, warm, well-drained, and fertile soil is best suited for early fruit production and high quality. Loams and clay loams have a greater water-holding capacity and are better suited to a longer season of production when high yield rather than earliness is of prime importance. Soil reaction for best production is in the pH range of 5.5–7.5.

The tomato is listed with those vegetable crops giving high response to fertility. Perhaps more than any other vegetable crop, growers must use good judgement in fertilizing tomatoes with nitrogen, especially with determinate types for once-over harvest. Sufficient nitrogen should be available for early vegetative growth and early fruit development and then to maintain plant vigor. The crop should run out of nitrogen at harvest time. Excessive nitrogen causes secondary growth and non-uniformity and will delay maturity and reduce yields. A complete fertilizer containing part of the nitrogen and all of the phosphorus and potassium should be applied before planting, and the remaining nitrogen sidedressed after the plants are established.

For determinate tomatoes, nitrogen fertilization ranges from 30 to 100 pounds per acre, depending on soil type, planting method, and harvest method. In general, 25% less nitrogen is needed with direct-seeded crops than with transplants. Some of the early-maturing determinate cultivars may require more nitrogen than late-maturing ones to obtain fast plant growth before fruit setting occurs. Fresh market indeterminate types require 120–175 pounds of nitrogen per acre, with 75–100 pounds of nitrogen applied preplant and the rest side-dressed at 2- to 3-week intervals starting at fruit set.

Phosphorus and potassium are usually applied according to soil tests. Early plantings of direct-seeded tomatoes may show better seedling vigor if phosphate is banded with the seed.

PLANTING AND CROP ESTABLISHMENT

Tomatoes can be started either by direct seeding in the field or from transplants. Crops to be harvested mechanically are usually direct seeded. However, where earliness is desired and when expensive hybrid seed is used, transplanting may be preferred.

Direct Seeding

Crop establishment from direct seeding in comparison to transplanting can result in a considerable savings in time and labor costs, greater chance of disease-free seedlings, and more flexibility in cultivar selection, plant populations (close spacing without extra costs), and planting schedules. However, in spite of these advantages, some growers have been reluctant to use direct seeding for stand establishment, mainly because of difficulties in seedling emergence and problems in weed control due to ineffective herbicides.

Nearly all processing tomatoes in California are direct seeded, as well as most of the main-season processing crop in the Midwest (Ohio, Indiana, Michigan, Illinois). Field seeding is also used for much of the fresh market tomato crop in Florida, and a good part of it in California's Imperial Valley and the Modesto, Delta, and Salinas regions.

Several different cultural systems may be used for direct-seeding tomatoes, including raised beds or flat planting, single-row or twin-row planting, and single-seeded or clump planting. Clump planting involves seeding two to six plants in a clump, which grow and develop as a single plant (Figure 27.2). Generally, there is no sacrifice in yield, and this system eliminates the need for thinning. Twin-row culture requires more precision and closer management but generally gives higher yields, due to an increased fruit accumulation rate and more uniform ripening than single rows. However, with more plants per acre, plant competition is greater, and vine training and use of herbicides are essential with twin-row culture. Generally, the planting method depends on the grower, as well as on field conditions, equipment, and experience.

Plant spacing depends on equipment, vine size, soil type, and cultural system (beds or flat, single rows or twin rows, single-seeded or clumps). Crowding may result in delayed maturity and poor concentration of fruit set. Common spacings include one- or two-row beds on 5- or 6-foot centers, with twin rows spaced 12–16 inches apart, or a single row in the middle of the bed. Spacing between plants in the row for processing tomatoes ranges from 6–9 inches for single plants to 9–12 inches apart for clumps. In-row spacing for fresh market tomatoes consists of 18–24 inches between plants for large-vined types and 12–16 inches apart for small-vined types. Modern precision seeders using sized or pelleted seed will plant to the desired in-row spacing, eliminating the need for most thinning.

Generally, the seed can be planted about a month before the last average spring frost, provided the soil temperature at the 1-inch depth is above 55°F. Planting in cold, dry soil can delay emergence for as long as 20–30 days. The

**Figure 27.2. Two to six tomato seedlings will form a clump
but develop as if a single plant.**

normal seeding depth is 0.5–1 inch, except in dry soils where 2 inches can be used. Shallow planting results in more uniform emergence but increases the chances of seeds drying out. Problems from soil crusting can be prevented by the use of anticrustants such as vermiculite and timely irrigation sprinkling.

Some of the acreage for direct-seeded fresh market tomatoes is started from plug mixes using pregerminated seed (see Chapter 5). A machine prepares the beds, applies the fertilizer, fumigates and applies herbicides, and lays polyethylene mulch. After about 5 days a plug-mix seeder burns holes in the mulch through which a seed mix is placed and covered with vermiculite to prevent drying. The mix contains a slow-release fertilizer, sphagnum peat moss, water, and seed. Plants are thinned to their final spacing once seedlings become established.

Transplanting

In many areas it is standard practice to use transplants instead of direct seeding for early plantings and when growing high value fresh market tomatoes. For fresh market tomatoes, transplanting is probably the best planting method for northern and high altitude growing areas.

Growers normally use bare-rooted transplants for processing and transplants grown in containers for fresh market (Figure 27.3). The plants may be produced by the grower, bought from commercial plant producers, or supplied by the processor. Generally, 6–8 weeks is required to produce large plants. Early plantings can be started in the greenhouse and later moved to transplant beds. For later plantings, the seed can be sown directly outdoors in nursery beds. The plants are ready for transplanting when they have four to six true leaves and when stems are about pencil size. Before transplanting, the plants should be hardened so they will be able to withstand field conditions with as little shock as possible.

In the South, transplants are grown directly in the field and later shipped to northern areas. They can be grown on a large scale and handled efficiently by machinery. This method is used mostly with transplants for processing tomatoes. When plants reach transplanting size, they are pulled and hauled to the packing shed, sorted, and bunched according to size. The roots of each bunch are dabbed with wet peat moss and wrapped in paper to prevent drying. The bunches are packed in wooden crates containing 2,000–3,000 plants and shipped in refrigerated trucks to northern growing areas.

The plants are set by single- or multiple-row transplanting machines, so that the roots and lower parts of the stem are covered with soil. Spacing and plant populations vary according to the same factors as for direct seeding (vine size,

Figure 27.3. Transplants for fresh market and the home garden are usually container-grown plants, while transplants for processing crops are generally bare-rooted.

soil type, cultural practices, etc.). Early, small-vined types can be grown in twin-row beds. Generally, the plants grow slowly at first, then as temperatures moderate, they produce roots on the covered part of the stems and grow rapidly.

CULTURAL PRACTICES

Tomatoes for fresh market are grown either as bush-type on the ground or supported to hold fruits off the ground. Those grown on the ground are primarily for mature-green harvest, while fruits supported off the ground are marketed as "vine-ripe" or breaker tomatoes. All processing tomatoes are grown in bush culture and are harvested by machine when ripe (Figure 27.4).

Figure 27.4. Bush culture is used for all processing tomatoes, as well as for some fresh market production.

Irrigation

Sufficient moisture should be present for germination or quick recovery of transplants. Most tomatoes are planted in moist soil or planted dry and irrigated up. Rapid early growth is essential for good yields. Plants may never recover from water stress during their early development. The use of water by the plant increases until the fruit load is developed. Water requirements in California for a tomato crop will vary from 12 to 18 inches in coastal areas and from 24 to 48 inches for summer crops in inland valleys. Moisture stress during flowering will cause blossoms to abort. Similarly, moisture stress during fruit development may result in a high incidence of blossom-end rot.

Tomatoes are a relatively deep-rooted crop, whose roots can extend to a depth of 6 feet. Irrigation should contact the entire root system. Most acreage is irrigated by furrow and sprinkler systems. In California most processing tomatoes are furrow-irrigated. Sprinklers are used mainly to establish the stand, particularly to prevent soil crusting which can hinder emergence, but the importance of keeping fruits dry limits sprinkler use during the last half of the season. When the crop is to be machine-harvested, the last irrigation should be applied early enough to allow the soil to dry so that harvesting equipment can work the field. Generally, this will be 1–2 weeks before harvest, depending on soil texture, harvest season, and weather conditions. Drip irrigation is used by some fresh market growers and has resulted in yield improvements over conventional sprinkler and furrow irrigation.

Weeds

If weeds are permitted to grow, they not only rob tomatoes of moisture and nutrients but also become hosts for diseases and insects that attack the crop. Weeds such as foxtail and nutsedge can interfere with harvest operations. Tomato seedlings do not compete well with weeds. However, once the crop is established and the canopy cover is sufficient, weed pressures are usually not as severe.

A combination of chemical methods and cultivation is usually needed to control weeds, as well as to maintain bed shape. For transplanted tomatoes, effective preemergent herbicides are available. Most weed control problems in tomatoes are with the direct-seeded crop, since tomato seedlings are sensitive to many herbicides and the choice of effective chemicals is very limited. Perennial weeds may pose a problem, but these should be controlled in the rotation before tomatoes are planted. Where earliness is desired, black polyethylene mulch can be used as an alternative to herbicides to control annual weeds, as well as to conserve moisture and increase soil temperatures.

Supporting and Pruning

Some fresh market growers will make extra effort to support and prune their plants. This is to keep fruits off the ground and help control diseases. Although quite labor-intensive, the training of plants will frequently result in an increase in marketable fruit, easier harvesting, and reduced injury to plants when multiple harvests are being made. This practice is most profitable when a long harvest is possible and when there is uniform fruit production over the season. In home gardens or where space is limited, training tomato plants vertically will save space.

The most common method of pruning and training tomatoes is to prune them to one-, two-, or three-stemmed plants by pinching off the lateral branches as they appear in the axils of each leaf and then to tie each plant to a 5-foot stake driven into the ground about 3 inches from the plant. Plants may also be grown in wire cages (Figure 27.5) or trained onto a trellis consisting of several strands of string or wire running on each side of stakes from one to another. Plants are then tied to the string or wire between the stakes. The large indeterminate plant types develop long vines and set fruit over a long period of time and are best suited for stake or trellis culture.

CULTIVARS

Hundreds of cultivars of tomatoes are available both for commercial growers and for home gardeners. They range widely in fruit size, shape, color, plant type, disease resistance, season of maturity, and market use (Table 27.2). Some cultivars produce well under one set of conditions but may be poorly adapted to others. Most fresh market growers have individual preferences and use cultivars that have performed well in the past. Processors usually have their own cultivars.

Figure 27.5. Cage culture being used for fresh market tomatoes.

Table 27.2. Description of Various Tomato Cultivars

Cultivar	Chief Use(s)	Season	Plant Type[1]	Diseases Resistant to[2]	Fruits Size	Shape
Better Boy F₁	Home	Medium	I	FW, VW, N	Med.–large	Globe
Burpee's Big Boy F₁	Market	Medium	I	VF	Medium	Round
Campbell 1327 . . .	Market	Medium	D	VW, FW, cracking	Large	Flat, globe
Dombito F₁	Greenhouse	Med. early	I	FW, cracking	Large	Round
Earlypak 707	Shipping, canning	Med. early	D	VW, FW	Medium	Globe
Empire F₁	Market, shipping	Medium	D	VW, FW	Large	Oblate
Glamour	Market, home	Med. early	SI	Cracking	Medium	Flat, globe
Heinz 722	Processing	Medium	D	VW, FW	Small	Pear
Heinz 1350, 1439 .	Market, home	Early	D	VW, FW, cracking	Medium	Flat, globe
Heinz 2653	Processing	Early	D	VW, FW	Medium	Blocky
Jet Star F₁	Market	Early	I	VW, FW	Large	Flat, globe
Jubilee	Market	Medium	I	—	Large	Globe
Jumbo F₁	Greenhouse	Medium	I	VW, FW	Large	Globe
Morton Hybrid F₁ .	Market	Early	I		Medium	Flat, globe
Mountain Price F₁ .	Market, shipping	Med. late	D	VW, FW	Large	Globe
New Yorker	Market	Early	D	VW	Medium	Globe
Pik Red F₁	Market, shipping	Early	D	VW, FW, N	Large	Globe
Red Cherry	Home	Early	I		Small	Globe
Roma VF	Processing	Early	I	FW, VW	Small	Pear
Rutgers 39	Market	Med. late	I	VW, FW, cracking	Medium	Flat, globe
Spring Set F₁	Market	Early	D	VF	Large	Round
Supersonic F₁	Market	Medium	I	VW, FW, cracking	Large	Flat, globe
Traveler 76	Shipping	Med. early	I	FW	Large	Flat, globe
VF 134–1–2	Processing	Early	D	FW, VW	Small	Long, globe
UC 82	Processing	Med. early	D	FW, VW	Medium	Blocky
UC 204	Processing	Early	D	FW, VW	Small	Blocky

[1](D) determinate, (I) indeterminate, (SI) semi-determinate.

[2](FW) *Fusarium* wilt, (VW) *Verticillium* wilt, (N) nematodes.

Fresh market cultivars are no longer only indeterminate types but include determinate plants as well. Tomatoes for shipment should have fruits that are smooth, fleshy, medium-sized, highly colored, and solid enough to withstand transportation. Processing cultivars should have well-colored, firm fruits and plants with enough foliage to shade the fruits (Figure 27.6). Fruits must stay harvestable and usable for 3 weeks after ripening. Machine-harvested cultivars must have small, determinate vines, concentrated fruit set, and uniform ripening. In addition, canners require processing fruits to have certain measures of quality, including total solids over 6%, pH below 4.35, a solids / acid ratio of 15, a sugar / acid ratio of 8.5, and high viscosity for pastes. Several processing cultivars that have a "jointless" character, in which the stem on the fruit has no joint, have been developed. This allows the stem to separate cleanly from the fruit and to adhere to the plant, decreasing puncture damage to fruits during harvest and handling.

Figure 27.6. A typical mechanical-harvested cultivar; fruits should have high solids and be sufficiently firm and tough-skinned to withstand machine and bulk handling.

INSECTS, DISEASES, AND FRUIT DISORDERS

The range of potential pest problems and non-biotic disorders is similar in both fresh market and processing tomato crops. However, the capacity for damage and possible control may differ, depending on climate, cultural factors, and cultivar selection.

Insects

The major insect pests on tomatoes are cutworms, aphids, flea beetles, leaf miners, wireworms, fruitworms, hornworms, leafhoppers, cabbage loopers, and mites. Flea beetles, cutworms, and wireworms can damage seedlings and reduce stands. Leafhoppers have the potential to be particularly damaging since they are the vectors of the curly-top and aster yellows viruses. Later in the growing season, several types of worms are the main pests by feeding on foliage and fruits. Of these, hornworms and fruitworms are the most widespread and most damaging.

Hornworms. Two species (*Manduca quinquemaculata* and *M. sexta*) of hornworms feed on tomatoes. These are large, green worms that have a conspicuous "horn" or spike at the rear of their body. Hornworms are heavy feeders of the leaves and can quickly defoliate the plant, leaving only the stems. Control measures should start at the first sign of feeding. Hornworms can spread to the fruits where they can cause significant damage to market quality.

Fruitworms. Tomato fruitworms (*Heliothis* zea) are perhaps the most destructive insect pest of tomatoes. These insects are greenish-brown–striped caterpillars that eat into the fruit from the stem end, and there feed from the inside. The small caterpillars can move from fruit to fruit, and up to 50% of the crop may be destroyed. Infested green fruit usually ripens prematurely and can easily be detected. Fruitworms are also a destructive pest of sweet corn, when they are known as corn earworms (see Chapter 25).

Diseases

Tomatoes are attacked by a wide spectrum of diseases (fungi, bacteria, viruses, nematodes), which may cause low yields, poor quality, or complete destruction of the crop. Some diseases may affect the entire plant, while others damage only the foliage or fruit.

Fusarium Wilt. This disease, caused by a soil-borne fungus (*Fusarium oxysporum*), is one of the most widespread of the tomato diseases. It is characterized by a yellowing, wilting, and progressive dying of the leaves from the base of the plant upward. Single shoots are usually affected first, giving a one-sided effect. Also, a brown discoloration will occur just under the surface of the stem. The disease is most serious during warm weather, since the fungus is most active when soil temperatures are between 75 and 85°F. Many cultivars that are resistant to *Fusarium* wilt are available.

Verticillium Wilt. Also a soil-borne fungus (*Verticillium* sp.), this disease produces symptoms very similar to those of *Fusarium* wilt. It first appears on lower leaves that turn yellow, and gradually wither and fall off. Some vascular discoloration occurs. However, unlike *Fusarium* wilt, all branches are affected, and the disease is more prevalent in cooler weather. Some slight wilting of shoot tips may occur during the day. Plants are stunted but usually live through the season. Planting resistant cultivars is the best method for controlling the disease.

Bacterial Wilt. Bacterial wilt is caused by the soil bacterium *Pseudomonas solanacearum*, which enters the roots through wounds. It is characterized by the sudden wilting of plants with no signs of leaf yellowing. The interior of the stems close to the ground will become water-soaked and will eventually turn brown. The disease is most common at temperatures above 75°F and can be a serious problem on transplants grown in southern areas. Control is effected by the use of disease-free plants and by the rotation of crops.

Early Blight. The spores of this fungus (*Alternaria solani*) may be in or on the seed or may carry over in the soil. The disease can occur at any stage of development on stems, leaves, and fruits, but it is generally observed most often on the lower older leaves as small, dark brown spots, which often enlarge into circular spots with dark, concentric centers. Spots similar to those on the leaves may appear on the stems, and dark, sunken, leathery spots will form on the fruits. The disease is favored by humid weather and air temperatures above 75°F. Regular application of fungicide sprays gives the best control.

Late Blight. Caused by the same fungus (*Phytophthora infestans*) that attacks potatoes, late blight affects both leaves and fruits. Leaves of infected plants first develop greenish-brown or black water-soaked patches, often starting at the tips and enveloping whole leaflets. A white, downy mold will appear along the margins of the affected area and on the undersides of the leaves, and the disease spreads rapidly. Water-soaked spots may occur on fruits, and become brown and wrinkled. Cool, wet weather favors disease development. Control measures are the same as for early blight.

Septoria Leaf Spot. This fungal (*Septoria lycopersici*) disease first appears as small, water-soaked spots on the leaves. The older spots have brownish borders with grayish centers. Damp conditions and air temperatures of 60–80°F promote the growth and spread of the pathogen. When conditions are favorable for disease development, using fungicide sprays will help control the disease.

Bacterial Spot. Bacterial spot is caused by the bacterium *Xanthomonas vesicatoria*, which is carried on the surface of seeds. Infected areas on the leaves and stems show small, irregular, dark green spots, which have a greasy appearance. These spotted areas dry out, and affected leaves eventually turn yellow and fall off. Blossom infection may cause flowers to abort. Sometimes the greatest damage is to green fruits, which develop black, scab-like spots and become distorted. Warm, moist conditions favor disease development, and bacteria spread rapidly with splashing rain, entering the plant through stomata or open wounds. Like most bacterial diseases, it is difficult to control, but rotating on a 3-year basis, using disease-free material, and not working among plants when the foliage is wet will minimize its occurrence.

Anthracnose. Anthracnose, another soil-borne fungus, primarily affects fruits. Early symptoms appear as small, slightly sunken, water-soaked, circular spots on ripe fruits. The spots enlarge, become more sunken, and often develop target-like markings. Warm, moist conditions promote disease development. Infections may take place at any stage of development, but symptoms appear only after the fruits reach maturity. For control, fruits require early protectant fungicide sprays.

Bacterial Speck. One of the major diseases affecting tomato fruits is bacterial speck (*Pseudomonas tomato*). Infection results in numerous small, slightly raised, black specks appearing on fruit surfaces. These spots lose their surrounding green color, leaving white zones on fruits. Numerous spots render fruits unmarketable for fresh market. The disease may also affect leaves and stems, causing black specks, and yellowing of surrounding tissue. The pathogen is ubiquitous, and infection occurs most readily under cool, wet conditions. The chief measures of control are hot water seed treatment, use of disease-free seed, and crop rotation.

Bacterial Canker. The bacteria (*Corynebacterium michiganense*) that cause this disease colonize the water-conducting tissues of the plant. The first sign of the disease is a curling downward of the lower leaves, which begin to wilt and die. Pale streaks and spots appear on the stems and leaf veins, and later crack open and form cankers. A diseased stem lesion shows a mealy-looking layer of bacteria-filled tissue. Affected fruits are spotted with small, white specks; later they have brown spots encircled with a white ring. The bacteria are carried on or in the seed and can remain in the soil for up to 2 years. The disease is favored by wet conditions and warm temperatures. Control measures are the same as for other bacterial diseases.

Viral Diseases. Tobacco mosaic, cucumber mosaic, and spotted wilt are viruses that affect tomatoes. The symptoms are typical of many viral diseases; infected plants may be stunted, with curled and malformed leaves, and reduced yields. The viral diseases are important because of the large number of perennial weeds that serve as host plants. The diseases are highly infectious and are readily spread either by insects or by cultural operations (tobacco mosaic is not spread by aphids).

Root Knot. A malformation of the roots, ranging from small swellings to large galls, is caused by the feeding activity of nematodes. The damage results in a reduced capacity for water and nutrient absorption by roots, causing leaf yellowing and plants to wilt during the day. The nematodes can be starved out by rotating for 2–3 years with corn, oats, cowpeas, or peanuts.

Fruit Disorders

In addition to parasitic diseases, tomatoes can also be affected by a number of nonparasitic disorders, which often involve fruit deformities and secondary rots. These are usually the result of plant response to adverse environmental conditions and are not infectious. Control or correction of these abnormalities generally entails providing the proper environment, such as shading fruits, or it may require changing cultural practices, such as watering and fertilization schedules. However, in some cases the exact nature of the disorder may not be known, or there may be genetic and physiological interactions involved, making correction very difficult.

Blossom-end Rot. A breakdown of tissues, characterized by a dark brown, leathery rot, may occur at the blossom end in developing fruits. The exact cause is still unclear, but it appears to be associated with a calcium deficiency in the affected tissues, most commonly due to fluctuations in moisture supply, heavy nitrogen fertilization, or damage to roots, which causes restricted water uptake. It occurs most commonly on plants that have grown rapidly and then are subject to moisture stress. In some cases using cultural practices that increase moisture supply or spraying fruits with calcium nitrate before the disease appears will help control the rot.

Sunscald. When green fruits are exposed directly to the sun, a light patch will develop on the exposed area, which later will blister. The affected tissues may be invaded by secondary decay-causing organisms. Any factor that causes a premature loss of leaves will increase the chances for sunscald.

Growth Cracks. If expansion of the outer wall of the fruit cannot keep pace with the enlargement of the inner tissues, growth cracks, or breaks in the fruit surface, may appear. There are two types of cracking: radial and concentric growth cracks. The former type starts at the calyx end and radiates out over the surface of the fruit. The latter type occurs in concentric circles around the top of the fruit. Growth cracks are usually the result of extreme changes in the growth rate of the fruit, due to moisture fluctuations. Cultivars differ considerably in their susceptibility to this disorder.

Catfacing. The growth of the fruit may be distorted at the blossom end, resulting in scar tissue with deep indentations extending into the fruit. The exact cause is not known, but any factor (low night temperatures, 2,4-D injury, heavy nitrogen fertilization) that disturbs the development of the pistil contributes to its occurrence.

Puffiness. Poor pollination may result in off-shaped fruits. Also, the locular jelly may not completely fill the locular cavity. The fruits may show flat surfaces and not be firm; thus they are known as "puffy."

Blotchy Ripening, Graywall, Green Shoulder. These are ripening disorders that in some years can be severe and economically important. Blotchy ripening appears externally as areas of yellow or orange discoloration on the fruit surface intermixed with normal red areas. The discoloration may be random over the surface or confined to the fruit shoulder. Internally, a whitish discoloration of the pericarp and placenta tissue may appear, and in severe cases, brown lignified strands occur in the outer pericarp.

Graywall symptoms are grayish-brown discolorations seen through the outer fruit wall that may appear on small, immature, green fruit, as well as on ripe fruit. The areas may become slightly depressed and rough, and severe browning may occur internally.

Green shoulder develops a green-yellowish color in the fruit shoulder, and the fruit wall may be coarse in texture.

For each of the above disorders, cultivars may differ greatly in susceptibility. Although the exact cause for blotchy ripening and graywall is not known, potassium nutrition, sunlight, and temperature have been implicated in their occurrence.

HARVESTING

Fruits generally ripen 6–8 weeks from fruit set (Figure 27.7). Ripening is mainly a function of temperature, and fruits will require less time to ripen during summer harvests when temperatures are high than at other times. The optimum temperature for ripening of mature-green fruits is 68°F. The lowest temperature at which ripening occurs, with good color and flavor development, is 55°F. Above 81°F red color formation is inhibited, and fruits turn orange-yellow.

Maturity at harvest is important to fruit composition and quality and can usually be related to the color of the fruit (Table 27.3). Immature fruits are green and are characterized by lacking the typical jelly-like material in the internal cavities. In immature fruits, the seeds are not fully developed and can be cut easily when the fruits are sliced with a sharp knife. Mature fruits have attained full size when the entire surface is red or white with no green color visible. The seeds are well developed and do not cut when the fruits are sliced and the pulp around the seeds has formed a jelly-like consistency in all of the cavities.

The degree of ripeness at which tomatoes are to be harvested depends on the purpose for which they are grown and the time, distance, and method of

Figure 27.7. Tomato plant showing good set of fruit.

shipping and marketing. For long distance shipping, fresh market tomatoes should be picked at the mature-green stage or the breaker stage and be allowed to ripen during transit. Fresh market tomatoes for roadside retail sales are picked at a more mature stage, usually from the breaker stage onward (Figure 27.8). Vine-ripened fruits look and taste best but do not have the firmness to stand up well for most

Table 27.3. Stages of Maturity in Tomato Fruits

Fruit Stage	Description
Immature-green	The seeds are not fully developed, there is no locular jelly surrounding the seeds, the fruit color is pale green, and the flesh is hard.
Mature-green	The fruit is fully grown, the light green color at the blossom end has changed to a yellow-green cast, the seeds are surrounded by locular jelly, and the flesh is hard.
Breaker	About one-quarter of the surface at the blossom end shows some pink color.
Pink	About three-quarters of the surface is pink, and the flesh is firm.
Full-ripe	The fruit is nearly all red or pink, and the flesh is still firm.
Over-ripe	The fruit is fully colored, and the flesh soft.

marketing processes. Processing tomatoes are harvested when fully mature in order to optimize chemical measures of quality such as total color, solids, pH, solids / acid ratio, viscosity, vitamins, and flavor. For home use, tomatoes may be left on the plants until they are fully colored, if the average daily temperatures are 75°F or below. At higher temperatures, the fruits should be picked at the breaker stage and ripened at 70°F.

If the grower is attempting to hasten or increase uniformity in ripening, the chemical growth regulator ethephon may be used. When applied to tomatoes, ethephon results in an increase in ethylene generated by the fruit, triggering the ripening processes. The chemical has little or no effect on immature fruits and is usually applied to mature-green fruits for processing tomatoes and to breaker or pink fruits for fresh market tomatoes. Although ethephon initiates ripening, it has little effect on the rate of ripening, which is mainly a function of temperature. The average time to harvest after treatment ranges from 14–21 days with processing tomatoes to 5–6 days with fresh market tomatoes. If it is applied under stress conditions or high temperatures, there is the possibility of foliar injury including some defoliation.

Practically all tomatoes grown for processing in California and increasing amounts in other regions are harvested mechanically by sophisticated harvesters (Figure 27.9). These machines cut the plants slightly below ground level, lift and shake the plants on a conveyor, separate the fruits from the vines, and deliver the fruits to a side trailer. Some harvesters electronically sort the fruits by color, although a work crew is present to cull fruits for other defects.

Machines for harvesting fresh market tomatoes have also been used success-

Figure 27.8. Fruits harvested at the breaker stage packed for market.

Figure 27.9. Most processing tomatoes are now mechanically harvested.

fully, but commercially fresh market tomatoes are primarily harvested by hand. Hand picking reduces physical damage to the fruit and permits selectivity according to maturity as well as defects. Frequently, the cost of harvest by tomato pickers paid on an incentive basis is competitive with machine-harvesting cost.

POSTHARVEST HANDLING AND MARKETING

Tomatoes may go to the packing house from the field partially culled or straight run. They are usually handled in boxes that can be lifted and emptied readily. Packing-house operations may include unloading, weighing, checking, cleaning, drying, waxing, sorting, grading, sizing, wrapping, packing, lidding, and loading onto freight cars and trucks. Many shippers have ripening rooms where immature tomatoes are exposed to ethylene gas. However, fruits beyond the breaker stage do not benefit from supplemental ethylene because their ripening processes have already been initiated by their own ethylene. Small growers may grade and pack their tomatoes on their farms.

Tomatoes can be kept in storage for only a comparatively short time. For mature-green fruits, a temperature range of 57–61°F is probably best for slowing ripening without increasing decay problems, and fruits can be stored up to 3 weeks. Pink fruits will tolerate lower temperatures and can be held up to a week at 50°F. Prolonged holding of ripened tomatoes at low temperatures (below 41°F) or high temperatures (above 81°F) will result in loss of color and firmness. When it is necessary to hold ripened tomatoes for as long as possible, they can be held at 35°F up to 3 weeks, but there will be a considerable decrease in quality, with little or no shelflife.

Most of the tomatoes for processing are grown under contract with prices based on grade standards, the competitive market situation, and different receiving procedures among companies. Both wholesaler and retailer play a role in supplying fresh market tomatoes to the consumer. Upon arrival at the receiving point, the fruit is inspected. Other operations depend on how and where the tomatoes are to be marketed.

SELECTED REFERENCES

"Anonymous." 1971. *Controlling Tomato Diseases.* USDA, Farmers Bull. 2200.

Collin, G. H. 1975. *Tomato Color Defects.* Ontario Ministry of Food and Agriculture, Factsheet AGDEX 257 / 25, Ontario, Canada.

Conway, K. E., J. E. Motes, and R. Campbell. 1981. *Common Diseases of Tomatoes. Part I. Diseases Caused by Fungi.* Oklahoma State Univ. Coop. Ext. Ser. Facts 7625.

Conway, K. E., J. E. Motes, and R. Campbell. 1981. *Common Diseases of Tomatoes. Part II. Diseases Caused by Bacteria, Viruses and Nematodes.* Oklahoma State Univ. Coop. Ext. Ser. Facts 7626.

Conway, K. E., J. E. Motes, and R. Campbell. 1981. *Common Diseases of Tomatoes. Part III. Diseases Not Caused by Pathogens.* Oklahoma State Univ. Coop. Ser. Ext. Facts 7627.

Courter, J. W., J. M. Gerber, and L. L. Hill. 1982. *Training Tomato Plants.* Univ. of Illinois Coop. Ext. Ser. Hort. Facts VC-22-82.

Gould, W. A. 1983. *Tomato Production, Processing, and Quality Evaluation,* 2nd ed. AVI Publishing Co., Westport, Connecticut.

Johnson, H. G., and F. L. Pfleger. 1977. *Nonparasitic Disorders of Tomato.* Univ. of Minnesota Coop. Ext. Ser. Fact Sheet 14.

Kretchman, D. 1980. *Ohio Guidelines for Production of Machine-harvested Tomatoes.* Ohio State Univ. Coop. Ext. Serv. Bull. 647.

Magoon, C. E. 1969. *Tomatoes. Fruit & Vegetable Facts & Pointers.* United Fresh Fruit and Vegetable Association, Alexandria, Virginia.

Morse, R. 1982. Optimizing flowering and fruit set in tomatoes. *American Vegetable Grower,* August: 34–35.

Rick, C. M. 1978. The tomato. *Sci. Amer.* 239:82,84–87.

Sims, W. L., and R. W. Scheureman. 1981. *Mechanized Growing and Harvesting of Fresh Market Tomatoes.* Univ. of California Div. of Agric. Ser. Leaf. 2815.

Tigchelaar, E. C. 1986. Tomato breeding, pp. 135–171. In: M. J. Bassett (ed.). *Breeding Vegetable Crops.* AVI Publishing Co., Westport, Connecticut.

Toscano, N. C., E. R. Oatman, and R. A. Van Steenwyk. 1980. *Insect and Nematode Control Recommendations for Tomatoes.* Univ. of California, Div. of Agric. Ser. Leaf. 21138.

Wott, J. A., and J. Chamberlain. 1980. *Tomatoes.* Purdue Univ. Coop. Ext. Ser. HO-26.

28

OTHER VEGETABLES — EGGPLANTS, PUMPKINS AND SQUASHES, OKRA, SALSIFY, CELERIAC, FLORENCE FENNEL, ORACH, PARSLEY

A number of vegetables of lesser general economic importance are discussed in this chapter. Some, such as eggplants, pumpkins, and squashes, are fairly widespread and still have significant production in some areas of the U.S. Others, such as okra, are grown on a limited scale in fairly specific geographic regions. Despite their minor status, these vegetables are important to some growers and to those consumers who use them. Many are sold by market gardeners and commercial growers in certain areas as specialty crops, and many can be found in home gardens.

EGGPLANTS

The eggplant, also known as "Guinea squash," is a member of the nightshade family (Solanaceae), along with the tomato, pepper, and potato. The plant is grown for its purple fruits that are usually baked, broiled, or fried.

The common large-fruited forms (*Solanum Melongena* var. *esculentum*) are believed to have originated in India, with a possible secondary center of origin in China for the small-fruited types. The plant was probably introduced into southern Europe during the Moorish invasion of Spain and eventually spread north. It was brought to the Americas by the Spanish explorers, but up until the 20th century, the plant was used in the U.S. more for ornamental purposes than for human consumption.

Eggplants are grown commercially in only a few states, but they are produced for local markets and in home gardens in many areas. They are considered a minor vegetable commercially, and the U.S. Department of Agriculture discontinued recording production statistics for the crop in 1981. Commercial acreage in the U.S. is estimated at around 4,000 acres, with Florida and New Jersey as the leading production states. Yields average about 9 tons per acre. Many of the eggplants used in the U.S. during the winter and early spring are produced in Mexico. Although several different types of eggplants are grown around the world, they are not considered a major crop except in Asia, where the plants are grown on a fairly wide scale in China, India, and Japan.

PLANT GROWTH AND DEVELOPMENT

The eggplant is a perennial that is cultivated as an annual. It develops bushy plants that grow erect to about 2–4 feet tall. Growth is indeterminate. The fruit is a pendent, fleshy berry that can be oval, round, or oblong, 2–8 inches in diameter. The epidermis or skin of the fruit is thin and smooth. The fruit is mostly fleshy placenta, in which the seeds are embedded in a mass of spongy tissue. Most cultivars today have purple fruits, although colors may range from yellowish-white to red, and to blackish-purple.

CLIMATIC AND CULTURAL REQUIREMENTS

Eggplants are warm-season crops that require a growing season of 100–140 days with high average day and night temperatures. Day temperatures of 80–90°F and night temperatures of 70–80°F are considered optimum. The plants are more susceptible to injury by low temperatures than are tomatoes or peppers. Temperatures below 65°F may result in poor growth and fruit set.

Well-drained, fertile, sandy loams with a pH of 5.5–6.5 are best. Fertility recommendations vary with soil type. On the average, about 100 pounds per acre of nitrogen should be applied. Because of its relatively long growing season, one or two additional sidedressings of nitrogen (25 pounds per application) may be necessary. Phosphorus (P_2O_5) and potash (K_2O) rates are based on soil test results and are similar to those for tomatoes.

PRODUCTION AND CULTURE

Eggplant seeds germinate slowly, and young plants are very susceptible to adverse temperature and moisture conditions. Consequently, commercial and home garden plantings are usually started from transplants. In northern regions, the seeds are sown in greenhouses or other structures about 8–10 weeks before the plants are to be set outdoors. In the South, the seeds are started in outdoor plant beds from June to August for the fall and early winter crop and in February and March for the spring crop.

When seedlings are 4–5 inches tall, they are transplanted to pots or cells (2 inches or larger in size), or spaced 4 inches apart in the plant beds. This allows the young plants to be lifted with a block of soil around their roots when they are transferred to the field, minimizing transplanting shock (Figure 28.1). Plants should be hardened at 65–70°F for several weeks prior to transplanting. After the soil has warmed and all danger of frost has passed, the plants are transplanted in the field. Plants are usually spaced 18–24 inches apart, with rows 3–5 feet apart.

Figure 28.1. To minimize transplanting shock, eggplants are transplanted with a block of soil around their roots. The stocky plant on the right is preferable to the spindling plants grown in the smaller containers on the left.

If hot caps or other protective coverings are used, the field planting date may be moved up 10–12 days. In Florida and other areas, black and clear plastic mulch is used extensively to increase yields and promote earliness.

Eggplants develop a moderately deep root system (down to 4 feet) and respond well to irrigation during periods of drought and high temperature. Moisture stress during flowering and fruit set can reduce yields considerably. In dry climates, up to 18 inches of water will be required to produce a commercial crop.

Frequent shallow cultivations are used to control early weeds before plants become large. Since eggplants are a long-season crop, herbicides are also used to control weeds.

Insect pests include flea beetles, aphids, Colorado potato beetles, leaf miners, lacewings, and mites. Flea beetles cause tiny holes in the leaves, and damage can be severe if unchecked. These can be controlled by timely application of insecticides.

Diseases affecting eggplants are *Verticillium* and *Fusarium* wilts, *Phomopsis* blight, damping-off, *Phytophthora* fruit rot, and powdery mildew. *Verticillium* causes yellowing, wilting, and then death of plants. *Phomopsis* blight causes girdling of young plants at the soil level and brown leaf lesions. Fungicides and crop rotation provide the best disease control. Also, blossom-end rot, a physiological disorder, can cause considerable fruit damage in some years.

CULTIVARS

Open-pollinated and hybrid eggplant cultivars differ in size, shape, and color of the fruit, as well as season of maturity. Most cultivars grown in the U.S. are the purple, oval-fruited, large types ('Dusky,' 'Black Magic,' 'Black Beauty,' 'Epic'). Also grown are the smaller, elongated, slender fruits, known as the "Oriental" types, including 'Ichiban,' 'Tycoon,' and 'Long Tom.' Most cultivars reach maturity 80–90 days after transplanting.

HARVESTING AND POSTHARVEST HANDLING

The fruits are harvested when they reach marketable size. They should be firm, and the outside color glossy purple (Figure 28.2). Overmature fruits are spongy and seedy. Loss of their glossy color and dark-colored seeds are signs of overmaturity. Fruits can be harvested up until the first frost and should be picked as they mature to ensure continued fruit set.

Harvesting is done by hand; the fruits are cut from the vines, with the calyx, or cap, and a short piece of stem left attached to each fruit. Careful handling is required because fruits bruise easily, which can result in significant surface disfiguration.

Eggplant fruits are sensitive to chilling injury below 50°F and deteriorate rapidly at warm temperatures, so they are not adapted to long storage. Pitting,

Figure 28.2. The fruit is ready to harvest when it is full size and firm and still has its glossy purple color.

surface bronzing, and browning of seeds are symptoms of chilling injury. Symptoms may not become pronounced until after the fruits are removed from low temperatures. Chilled fruits are susceptible to *Alternaria* decay when they are returned to room temperatures.

Eggplants are sold for distant as well as for local markets. Because the fruits do not keep well, they are stored only for incidental movement to market. Fruits can usually be held no more than 7–10 days at 46–54°F and 90–95% relative humidity.

PUMPKINS AND SQUASHES

CLASSIFICATION, ORIGIN, NOMENCLATURE

Pumpkins and squashes belong to the family Cucurbitaceae (gourd family), which also includes cucumbers, honeydew melons, muskmelons, and watermelons. The vegetables comprising pumpkins and squashes (and some gourds) are made up of four species of the genus *Cucurbita*, namely *C. Pepo*, *C. maxima*, *C. moschata*, and *C. mixta*.

The nomenclature of this group, however, is greatly confused. The species botanical characteristics have not been followed in distinguishing squashes and pumpkins, and current terminology is based largely on culinary characteristics. For example, the terminology of *summer squash* and *winter squash* bears no

Table 28.1. Classification of Pumpkins, Squashes, and Gourds

Cucurbita Species	Pumpkins	Summer Squash	Winter Squash	Gourds and Ornamental Squash
C. Pepo	Field and pie pumpkins Naked-seeded pumpkins Miniatures	Yellow (crookneck) (straightneck) Scallop Marrow (zucchini) (cocozelle)	Acorn Fordhook	Gourds
C. maxima	Decorative or jumbo pumpkins		Hubbard Banana Delicious Orange marrow Buttercup Kindred	Turban
C. moschata	Large cheese and crookneck pumpkins		Butternut	
C. mixta	Cushaw		Cushaw	

relation to the season when they are grown, but rather to the state of maturity of the fruit when utilized. Table 28.1 summarizes the classification of the various vegetable species that make up squashes and pumpkins (and some gourds).

Summer Squashes. Commonly C. Pepo, summer squashes are eaten in the immature stages when the rinds are very soft. Consequently, they are harvested when immature and do not store well. These types include the yellow summer squash (crooknecks and straightnecks), scallop squash, and zucchini (Figure 28.3).

Winter Squashes. These are harvested in the mature fruit stage when the rinds are hard. They are used as feed for livestock, as a table vegetable, or as an ingredient in pies. Winter squashes usually have flesh of mild flavor and fine texture and are suitable for baking. They store well for use throughout the winter, especially the hard-shelled types, such as Hubbard squash. All species of Cucurbita comprise winter squashes and include acorn, Hubbard, butternut, banana, and delicious types.

Pumpkins. These are edible fruits of Cucurbita species that are used when ripe as forage or for human consumption, mostly as an ingredient in pies. The flesh is often coarse and strong flavored and hence is not generally served as a baked vegetable. Although the name pumpkin is applied to all species of Cucurbita, most pumpkins are C. Pepo and C. moschata.

A large diversity in size, shape, and color of cultivars exists among the four

Figure 28.3. There are many types of squash, with different fruit shapes and colors. (Photo: courtesy of United Fresh Fruit and Vegetable Association, Alexandria, Virginia)

pumpkin species. The small types (4–6 pounds) are grown mostly for cooking and for baking in pies; the naked-seeded types for their seeds, which can be roasted and used for snacks; the intermediate (8–15 pounds) and large (15–25 pounds) cultivars for cooking and jack-o'-lanterns; the jumbo or mammoth types (50–100 pounds) for exhibit purposes; and the miniature cultivars for specialty markets.

Gourds. The name *gourd* is commonly applied to certain warm-season vine crops that are closely related to pumpkins and squashes. The fruits are hard-shelled and are used primarily for decorative purposes and for making utensils. The yellow-flowered gourds are found in *C. Pepo*, while the turban gourds and ornamental squash are *C. maxima*.

Squashes and pumpkins are of western origin. Long before Columbus came to the New World, these crops were widely distributed in both North and South America and were extensively used by the people of the Americas for receptacles, utensils, and food.

Although they are indigenous to the Americas, the specific origin of the *Cucurbita* species differs. *C. moschata* is believed to have originated in Central America or northern South America, and *C. maxima* in the Andes Mountains of

Argentina, Bolivia, and Chile. Both *C. Pepo* and *C. mixta* are probably of North American origin, most likely northern Mexico and the southwestern U.S.

PRODUCTION AND INDUSTRY

The members of the genus *Cucurbita* are considered minor vegetables, and consequently their production statistics are normally not reported by the U.S. Department of Agriculture. However, these crops are commonly found in most home and market gardens. Pumpkins and squashes are extensively canned and can be used for stock feed and for ornamental purposes. In addition, the blossoms of pumpkins and squashes may be dipped in batter and fried as a delicacy.

The states most important in the production of pumpkins are Illinois, New Jersey, California, Indiana, New York, Ohio, Michigan, and Pennsylvania. For commercial processing pumpkins, Illinois is the leading producing state with about 7,000 acres. Average yields of processing pumpkins in the U.S. vary considerably; in Illinois yields average around 24 tons per acre, compared to 35 tons per acre in California. Top yields of processing pumpkins can reach over 40 tons per acre.

Winter squashes are grown mainly in the northern half of the U.S., with production occurring primarily in the late summer and fall. Significant acreages of winter squashes are located in New York, New Jersey, Michigan, and Massachusetts. The summer types are grown throughout the U.S., with about 6,000 acres in both Florida and California.

PLANT GROWTH AND DEVELOPMENT

Squashes and pumpkins are annuals that are usually trailing vines with tendrils. Three to eight laterals rise from nodes near the base of each stem. In most types, the stems grow to a length of several feet, and in a few species may extend outward to 40–50 feet. Some of the summer squashes (*C. Pepo* var. *Melopepo*) develop bushy plants. In these, the internodes are shorter and tendrils are absent.

The flowers in *Cucurbita* are borne singly in the leaf axils and are very conspicuous with bright yellow petals. The flowers are generally monoecious. The female flowers are easily recognized by the enlarged ovary at their base (Figure 28.4). The staminate (male) flowers are generally more numerous than the pistillate (female) flowers and usually appear first, although under some conditions (low temperatures and short days), pistillate flowers predominate. In some hybrids of summer squash, female flowers develop before the male flowers.

Pollination is by insects, mostly honey bees. Stigmas are receptive for a

Figure 28.4. Squash stem showing male (right) and female (left) flowers; note the enlarged ovary at the base of the female flower.

period of about 24 hours. New fruits may enlarge for a short time, but if not adequately fertilized, they will usually abort. Crossing among plants of the same species is very general. For example, zucchinis will cross with acorn squashes or pumpkins, but the taste, shape, and color of the fruits will not be affected unless the seeds are saved and grown the following year. Interspecific hybridization is possible and used for plant breeding purposes. Crossing between certain species combinations (*C. moschata* x *C. Pepo*, *C. moschata* x *C. maxima*) can occur. Contrary to popular opinion, squashes and pumpkins do not cross with muskmelons, watermelons, and cucumbers.

CULTURE AND PRODUCTION

Climatic and Cultural Requirements

The culture and production of squashes and pumpkins are similar to other vine crops (Chapters 17 and 19). Squashes and pumpkins are warm-season vegetables that are easily injured by frost. However, they will do better in cooler climates than will either melons or cucumbers. For successful production, a warm, frost-free period of 80–140 days is required for pumpkins and winter squashes. Summer squashes are harvested shortly after bloom and require 40–60 days to produce marketable fruits. Sunny, dry weather is especially important for successful pollination by honey bees and the development of mature fruits.

Almost any good, well-drained soil will grow pumpkins and squashes. It should be well supplied with organic matter and a uniform moisture supply. In general, soil type is not critical if each is properly handled and fertilized. A light, fertile soil that warms up quickly is desired for summer cultivars for the early market. Heavy soils are best for cultivars grown during the late summer and fall. A soil pH range of 5.5–7.5 is satisfactory, and extremely acid soils should be avoided or limed.

The amount of fertilizer required varies with fruit yield, soil, and culture (irrigated vs. dryland). Irrigated sandy soils will require more fertilizer than dryland loams. Additional nitrogen (and potassium on sandy soils) is usually applied when vines start to run. In some areas, growers supply part of the fertilizer along with the irrigation water in several applications during the growing season.

Field Planting

Like other cucurbits, squashes and pumpkins are somewhat difficult to transplant, and most crops are direct seeded in the field. Seeds are planted after the danger of frost is over, since germination is very slow in cool soils and because young plants are easily injured by cold temperatures. Optimum soil temperatures for seed germination for pumpkins and squashes are 70–95°F, with a minimum of 60°F and a maximum of 100°F.

In some cooler regions, summer squash for early market may be transplanted; however, special care is required. The seeds are usually planted in individual 3-inch containers to allow seedlings to be transplanted without disturbing the roots.

The bush and small-vined types of squashes are planted 18–36 inches apart in rows 4–6 feet apart. The large-vined types of squashes, and pumpkins for fresh market, are spaced 2–5 feet apart in rows 6–8 feet apart.

Pumpkins for processing are planted 12–18 inches apart in 30-inch rows. Then, depending on plant stand, entire individual rows may be cultivated out in order to establish a plant density of around 3,500 plants per acre. Experience has shown that this results in the optimum number and size of pumpkin fruits for maximum yields and efficient harvest. This system is used with open-pollinated pumpkin cultivars, which account for about 90% of the processing crop. However, with hybrids, the high cost of seed makes this impractical, and more traditional plant seeding is used.

Production Practices

Cultivation, weed control, irrigation, and pest control are managed similarly to other vine crops. Like these other crops, plastic mulch is sometimes used with summer squashes to increase early yields.

The major insect pests of pumpkins and squashes are cucumber beetles (spotted and striped), vine borers, and squash bugs. Cucumber beetles may cause serious damage to emerging seedlings by feeding on the new leaves and by serving as vectors of bacterial wilt. Around the time vines start to run, vine borers and squash bugs appear and feed on foliage. For each of these, excellent control can be achieved with timely insecticide applications.

Pumpkins and squashes are susceptible to most common vine crop diseases. These include several leaf blights, wilts, and fruit spots and rots. Squash mosaic is caused by several viruses and can be quite destructive in some years. Control measures are generally effected with a combination of using resistant cultivars (when available), crop rotation, and preventive fungicide applications.

Pumpkins and squashes, being monoecious, require bee activity for successful pollination and good fruit set. Poor pollination results in excessive blossom drop and poorly shaped fruit. Local bees are usually not numerous enough to provide adequate pollination; thus, outside colonies must be brought in. One strong hive of honeybees per acre should be placed in the field just as female blossoms appear.

HARVESTING AND POSTHARVEST HANDLING

Summer squashes are harvested usually 2–8 days after anthesis (40–60 days after planting), when the fruits are very immature and the rinds are soft. The size of the fruits usually depends on market preference. Generally, fruits are harvested when they are 4–8 inches long and 2 inches in diameter for most elongated types, and 3–4 inches in diameter for scallop squashes. Fruits grow rapidly, especially in warm weather, and may need to be picked almost daily. As fruits mature and approach full size, the shell begins to harden and quality decreases rapidly. At each harvest all fruits should be picked, because if allowed to mature on the vine, they tend to reduce the production of subsequent fruits.

Winter squashes and pumpkins are usually harvested when fully mature (80–140 days after planting). The fruits should be full size and a deep color with the hard rinds. Winter squashes are usually harvested all at one time. If they are to be stored for winter use, winter squashes and pumpkins should be harvested before they are exposed to frost, since even slight freezing results in some tissue damage, giving decay organisms a point of entry into the fruits.

Care must be taken harvesting and handling fruits, especially when the fruits are immature. The soft skin of immature fruits bruises easily, resulting in brown and discolored blemishes on exterior surfaces and permitting the entry of decay organisms. Some growers require that pickers wear gloves when harvesting summer squashes to avoid surface injuries from fingernails.

Due to mechanical damage during machine handling, all squashes and pumpkins for fresh market, including Halloween pumpkins, and many of the squashes for processing are harvested by hand. Processing pumpkins and some squashes are machine-harvested. The fruits are placed in windrows and then loaded into large trucks in the field (Figure 28.5).

Figure 28.5. Processing pumpkins are machine-harvested, but fresh market pumpkins, including Halloween and decorative types, are picked by hand.

The hard-shelled squashes, like Hubbard squash, are well adapted for long storage. Other winter squashes and pumpkins can be held for extended periods, if properly handled. Squashes store best if fully mature. After they are harvested, fruits are sometimes cured for about 10 days at a temperature of 80–85°F and a relative humidity of 80%. This practice promotes healing of mechanical injuries and also ripens immature fruits, so they store better.

Unlike most other vegetables, winter squashes and pumpkins require warm temperatures (50°F) and fairly dry conditions (50–70% relative humidity) during storage. Butternut squash is especially sensitive to chilling injury, which usually occurs in the field at temperatures above freezing (35–45°F). The damage, which appears as a pitting of the shell, is not apparent until much later, usually after the fruit is in storage.

If in good condition, Hubbard squash can be stored for 6 months or more, acorn squash 5–8 weeks, pumpkins 2–3 months, and butternut squash 2–3 months. Summer squashes, because of their soft shell, are quite perishable and can be stored no longer than 1–2 weeks at 41–50°F and 95% relative humidity.

OKRA

Okra, or gumbo (*Abelmoschus esculentus*), is a popular home garden vegetable in the South, belonging to the mallow family (Malvaceae). The edible portion of the plant is its immature pods, which are used in soups and stews, or as a fried or boiled vegetable. In soups, they impart a flavor and a glutinous consistency known as gumbo.

Okra is thought to be of Asiatic origin, most likely in Ethiopia and the upper Nile region of Sudan. Early records of okra date back to 12th century Egypt. It came to the Americas with the African slaves, who used the pods extensively in their cooking. The crop is of minor importance in the U.S., with practically all the commercial production in the southern states, including Texas and Arkansas.

The plant is a tender annual that grows upright to a height of 3–7 feet. It has a half-woody stem and many short branches. Flower buds develop in the axil of each leaf above the six to eight most basal leaves. As the stem elongates, the hibiscus-like flowers open one at a time. The fruit is a pod (one pod per blossom), usually ridged, that grows to 8 inches in length and 1 inch in diameter (Figure 28.6). The pods are green or purplish-green when immature, but they develop into dark brown capsules when mature.

Cultivars of okra may be classified as dwarf, intermediate, or tall, according to the height of the plants. Okra may also be classified according to pod length and whether pods have distinct lengthwise ridges or are smooth. Most commonly used cultivars have spineless pods and range in color from creamy white to dark green.

Okra is a very tender plant that grows best in hot weather (temperatures above 85°F), especially in regions with warm nights. Almost any good garden soil can be used to grow okra, provided it is well drained since the plant is intolerant of prolonged wet conditions. Fertility practices vary with the specific area and soil type. For most garden soils, 500–1,000 pounds of a 5-10-5 fertilizer per acre should produce good yields. In most areas, rainfall is sufficient to provide adequate moisture, but in drier regions irrigation may be needed.

The crop is direct seeded in the field, as soon as the soil warms up (70–95°F) and all danger of frost has passed. The seed is planted thickly (or sometimes drilled) on slightly raised rows spaced 2.5–4.0 feet apart. When the plants are established, they are thinned so that dwarf cultivars are spaced 12 inches apart, and larger cultivars are 18–24 inches apart. Okra seeds have hard seed coats,

Figure 28.6. Okra plant showing immature pods in leaf axils.

and soaking seeds in a water bath (110°F) for 1–2 hours prior to planting improves germination. For a continuous supply of pods throughout the long season, growers in the lower South may make successive plantings at 6-week intervals.

The cultivation of okra is about the same as for any other cultivated crop. Shallow cultivation near plants will keep down weeds. Insect pests, generally few, are many of the same ones related to cotton, including the cotton bollworm, corn earworm, and cotton aphid. The plant is very susceptible to nematodes and *Verticillium* wilt. Other disease problems include *Rhizoctonia, Phytophthora,* and *Pythium,* under wet conditions, and *Fusarium* and *Cercospora.*

The crop is ready for harvest in about 45–60 days after it has been planted. The pods should be picked (usually cut) while they are tender and immature (2–3 inches long). This will usually be 4–6 days after flowering. They must be picked often, sometimes daily in hot weather. All pods should be removed, which induces the plants to keep producing new fruits. Large pods become tough and woody. Plants will continue to bear until frost.

SALSIFY

Salsify (*Tragopogon porrifolius*) is a hardy biennial that is grown for its edible, long, fleshy, white taproot, produced the first year. It is commonly known as the "oyster plant" or "vegetable oyster" because of its flavor when cooked in soups and other ways. It is a member of the Compositae (sunflower) family and is a native of the Mediterranean area. The tapered taproot grows to 1 foot in length and 1–2 inches in diameter. The tops tend to spread out rather than grow upright, giving the plant a somewhat distinct appearance. Although relatively unknown in the U.S., salsify makes an excellent garden vegetable or specialty crop.

The culture of salsify is very similar to that of parsnips (see Chapter 15). Seeds are planted at close spacing in the early spring in rows 18–36 inches apart. After germination, plants are thinned to about 2–4 inches apart. A long growing season (about 110 days) is required for full development. Roots are ready to harvest in the late fall. Some growers like to delay harvest until after several hard frosts because cold temperatures tend to increase the sweetness of the roots. Salsify is winter-hardy and in most regions roots can be left in the ground and harvested throughout the winter. The same methods used for storing other root crops apply to salsify.

CELERIAC

Celeriac (*Apium graveolens* var. *rapaceum*) is grown for its enlarged root that develops at the groundline (Figure 28.7). The white interior of the root tastes like celery and can be grated or sliced and used raw in salads or cooked in soups

Figure 28.7. Celeriac roots add seasoning to soups and stews, or they can be used fresh in salads.

and stews. The plant requires a long growing season (120 days) and in most areas is usually started indoors and later transplanted to the field. The swollen roots can be used at any time after they are big enough. The late summer crop may be stored for winter use. In mild regions, the roots may be left in the ground and covered with a protective mulch, such as straw or leaves, and harvested over the winter.

FLORENCE FENNEL

Florence fennel (*Foeniculum vulgare* var. *Azoricum*) is a cool-season crop related to celery and celeriac that is grown for its enlarged, flattened leafstalks. The plants grow about 2 feet tall and resemble celery, producing leafstalks that overlap at the base.

For a summer crop, seeds are sown in rows in the spring; for an autumn and winter crop in the South, seeds are sown toward the end of the summer. After germination, the plants are thinned to about 6 inches apart. When the leafstalks have grown to approximately 2 inches in diameter, the plants may be blanched by mounding up soil around their bases. Plants are ready for harvest in about 75–85 days after they have been planted, before the petioles become tough and stringy. The plants should not be confused with common fennel, which is used as an herb.

ORACH

Orach (*Atriplex hortensis*), also called mountain spinach, is a cool-season vegetable grown in some intermountain regions of the U.S. as a substitute for spinach since it can be grown during times when spinach readily bolts. The plant is grown for its large, ovate leaves that develop on the upper portions of its tall stalks (6–8 feet high) throughout the season. Orach is drought-resistant and easily grown. Seeds are planted 10–12 inches apart in the early spring in rows 18–24 inches apart. In general, its culture is similar to that of spinach.

PARSLEY

Parsley (*Petroselinum crispum*) is a biennial that is usually grown as an annual. It is native to Europe and is a relative of celery and parsnips. Parsley is one of the universal garnishes and is used for flavoring salads, soups, and stews. The plant is also valued as an ornamental and may be grown in pots and other containers, as well as in the garden.

There are two types of parsley: one with fibrous roots and very curled or crinkled leaves, the other with plain leaves and fleshy roots. The curly-leaf type is used for its leaves, while the flat leaf or Italian parsley is grown for both its leaves (Figure 28.8) and its fleshy roots that are used for flavoring soups and stews.

Figure 28.8. Parsley leaves bunched for market.

Parsley is started from seeds, which are small and slow to germinate. Soaking the seeds overnight induces quicker germination. Plants are more resistant to cold than to heat. Young plants are small and quite delicate and require protection and frequent watering to prevent crop damage from drying.

Because of their tender nature while young, plants are frequently started in cold frames or hotbeds. Under favorable conditions, parsley can be started in the open. In the South, the crop is grown mostly in the fall, winter, and spring; the summer heat being too severe for production June through August. In the North, parsley is grown in the field in the spring, summer, and fall, and in greenhouses, cold frames, and hotbeds during the winter.

The plants can be grown on 6-inch centers. The entire top is clipped off to thicken the crown of leaves on well-established plants. Leaves may be harvested throughout the growing season, and the entire plants harvested at the end of the cropping cycle.

SELECTED REFERENCES

"Anonymous." 1968. *Growing Pumpkins and Squashes.* USDA, Farmers Bull. 2086.

Montelaro, J., and S. R. Kostewicz. *Squash Production Guide.* Univ. of Florida, Coop. Ext. Ser. Cir. 103C.

Robinson, R. W., H. M. Munger, T. W. Whitaker, and G. W. Bohn. 1976. Genes of the Cucurbitaceae. *HortScience* 11:554–568.

Sackett, C. 1975. *Okra. Fruit & Vegetable Facts & Pointers.* United Fresh Fruit and Vegetable Association, Alexandria, Virginia.

Sackett, C. 1975. *Squash. Fruit & Vegetable Facts & Pointers.* United Fresh Fruit and Vegetable Association, Alexandria, Virginia.

Seelig, R. A., and C. Magoon. 1978. *Eggplant. Fruit & Vegetable Facts & Pointers.* United Fresh Fruit and Vegetable Association, Alexandria, Virginia.

Vandemark, J. S. 1990. Pumpkin production. *Proceedings 1990 Illinois Specialty Growers Convention.* Univ. of Illinois. Coop. Ext. Ser. Hort. Series 81.

Whitaker, T. W., and G. N. Davies. 1962. *Cucurbits.* Leonard Hill Books, London.

Yamaguchi, M. 1983. *World Vegetables.* AVI Publishing Co., Westport, Connecticut.

29

CONTROLLED ENVIRONMENT
VEGETABLE PRODUCTION

Controlled environment agriculture (CEA) is a total concept of modifying the natural environment for optimum plant growth. It incorporates the manipulation of air and root-zone temperatures, relative humidity, radiant energy (light), air velocity, atmospheric concentration of carbon dioxide, root-zone oxygen concentration, and nutrient and moisture supply to control crop growth. The aim of CEA is to achieve independence of climate and weather and to allow crop production in areas where the natural environment limits or prohibits plant growth.

In the context of today's commercial vegetable industry, the greenhouse is the primary structure in CEA because it affords the most practical opportunity to make environmental modifications (Figure 29.1). CEA encompasses all the various systems and practices of controlled plant growth, ranging from hotbeds and plastic row tunnels (see Chapter 8), to hydroponic greenhouses and growth rooms, to completely enclosed, artificially lighted commercial "plant factories," in which crops are produced without soil, herbicides, or insecticides and grown under 1,000-watt, high-intensity discharge, sodium vapor lamps, never seeing the light of day.

Today, CEA is also finding application in space with the National Aeronautics and Space Administration (NASA). Scientists are developing a working model of a specially designed space growth chamber, or "salad machine," that will be used in orbiting space stations to provide a variety of fresh vegetables for astronauts on long-duration missions.

From the standpoint of commercial vegetable production, CEA requires a significant investment in capital, labor, and grower skills. This necessitates that

Figure 29.1. Modern controlled environment complex with inflated plastic roof.

crops be of high economic value and yields substantially higher than those for conventional open-field production. CEA is one of the most intensive forms of agriculture known and offers some of the greatest challenges in the production of food crops.

HISTORY, SCOPE, AND IMPORTANCE

CEA is not a new concept. High-quality vegetables and other crops have been produced in controlled environments, such as greenhouses, for centuries. The very early stages of CEA date back to between 14 and 37 A.D. when the Romans used talc window coverings to extend plant growth beyond its normal season. By using artificially heated glass enclosures to protect their citrus trees from the cold, growers in northern Italy during the Middle Ages were able to grow citrus all year along some of the lakes by taking advantage of the bright sunlight. By the end of the 15th century, CEA production was centered in the maritime areas of northern Europe. The Dutch, in particular, developed year-round greenhouse production to make the most intensive use of their limited arable land.

It was not until the middle 1800's that development of CEA began in the

U.S., when hotbeds were used for seedling production. By the late 1800's, structures for the production of several crops began to appear regularly.

In the early 1900's, it was estimated that 100 acres of protective greenhouse coverings were used to produce winter vegetables. The area around Cleveland, Ohio, became a major center for greenhouse vegetable production. Prior to the development of modern efficient transportation systems, this region supplied just about all the fresh tomatoes in the eastern U.S. during the late fall and winter, and by the mid-1900's there were over 700 acres of greenhouse tomatoes in Ohio alone.

However, due to the rising energy and capital costs of greenhouses and growing systems, the area in the U.S. devoted to greenhouse vegetable production has declined from 1,029 acres in 1969 to 855 acres in 1974, and most recently to less than 500 acres in 1987 (Table 29.1). Another factor influencing the decline in vegetable greenhouse production is the year-round availability of fresh produce, with California, Florida, Texas, Arizona, and Mexico supplying much of the winter vegetable production. In some regions of the U.S., greenhouse growers have switched from vegetables to higher-value foliage and bedding plants.

Table 29.1. Leading U.S. States in Area and Value of Greenhouse Vegetable Production in 1982 and 1987

State	1982[1]		1987[2]	
	Area	Value	Area	Value
	(sq. feet)	*($1,000)*	*(sq. feet)*	*($1,000)*
California	3,472,784	6,610	5,493,066	13,545
Ohio	5,972,067	8,516	3,959,018	7,715
Florida	1,421,201	3,676	2,816,228	11,634
Pennsylvania	574,593	954	766,598	2,066
Colorado	46,876	53	614,742	753
New York	455,104	619	522,762	2,122
Texas	608,790	925	471,778	936
Virginia	117,628	255	405,408	303
Hawaii	2,713,648	2,755	368,758	513
North Carolina	379,845	453	356,794	616
Kentucky	246,944	583	354,068	818
Michigan	653,601	816	343,447	463
Massachusetts	288,210	383	324,054	588
New Jersey	170,770	237	319,265	787
Other states	3,651,613	5,687	3,100,561	8,582
U.S.	20,773,674	32,522	20,216,547	51,441

[1]Source: U.S. Department of Commerce, Bureau of the Census. 1982. *Census of Agriculture*, Vol. I, Part 51, U.S. Summary.

[2]Source: U.S. Department of Commerce, Bureau of the Census. 1987. *Census of Agriculture*, Vol. I, Part 51, U.S. Summary.

This trend, however, may have started to reverse, and the vegetable greenhouse industry appears to be on the rise, primarily in the southwestern states, where it is more economical to grow greenhouse vegetables because of lower energy and labor costs. Fresh produce transportation and distribution in the U.S. is very good, and growing areas no longer have to be near major population centers. Improved technology in environmental control and greater heating and cooling efficiencies have helped moderate production costs. Similarly, new technology from the perspective of plant culture and handling have increased CEA production efficiency markedly.

CEA, in particular the greenhouse vegetable industry, still remains strong in many parts of the world. In countries such as Spain, Italy, and Portugal, and throughout northern Europe, where fresh vegetables are scarce and expensive for much of the year, the industry is still growing. European production is year-round, compared to that in the U.S. in which production is normally concentrated during the winter months. In the area around the Persian Gulf, and in other desert coastal regions, CEA is used to supply fresh vegetables where outdoor production is not possible. In Japan, where arable land is scarce, CEA has become a very important segment of the agricultural industry.

PRINCIPAL CROPS GROWN

The high capital cost of CEA dictates that the crops produced must be of high value. In general, almost any vegetable crop, within certain limitations, can be grown in a greenhouse or other structure, provided it is profitable. The vegetables grown must have a high yield and demand a premium price. For example, greenhouse tomato production averages about 150 tons per acre, compared to 12 tons per acre for field-grown fresh market tomatoes.

The principal vegetable crops produced under CEA are lettuce, tomatoes, and cucumbers. The lettuce grown is primarily the looseleaf and butterhead types which have shorter seasons than crisphead cultivars (Figure 29.2). Cucumbers of the European type (gynoecious and parthenocarpic) are becoming more important in CEA (Figure 29.3). The fruits of these have edible skin, are seedless, and reportedly do not cause gaseous discomfort. Tomato cultivars used in CEA are primarily "beefsteak" types that have been specifically developed for CEA production. Their fruits are large and yields are equal to or above'those of standard fresh market tomatoes. The plants are strongly indeterminate in their growth habit, which allows the fruit to be harvested over an extended period.

Other crops that are being grown with CEA include various salad greens (dandelions, watercress, and water spinach), green peppers, eggplants, and as-

Figure 29.2. Butterhead types of lettuce are commonly grown in greenhouses.

sorted herbs (basil, mint, rosemary, thyme, chives, sage, parsley, and tarragon). Many greenhouses in southern and western states specialize in the production of vegetable transplants, particularly lettuce, tomatoes, peppers, eggplants, cabbage, broccoli, and cauliflower. In central California, a highly automated green-

Figure 29.3. Gynoecious and parthenocarpic cucumbers have unique fruit characteristics and are widely grown in controlled environment agriculture.

house industry to grow and transplant lettuce to the field has recently developed. CEA has also expanded into a new specialty area producing plant plugs. These are seedlings grown in small cells of a large tray that are used as transplanting material for commercial field production (see Chapter 5).

ENVIRONMENTAL CONTROL

In CEA, the factors that influence the environment need to be continuously monitored and controlled. The main environmental factors relevant to CEA for plant growth include temperature, humidity, radiation, and ambient carbon dioxide concentration.

The amount of control is determined by the type of facility and the profitability of the crop. Completely enclosed indoor facilities, independent of climate and weather, represent a more intensive form of CEA than greenhouses. While a typical commercial greenhouse may produce 10 times more lettuce yield per acre than a field operation, a completely enclosed facility will need to produce 5 to 10 times more lettuce than a greenhouse to pay for considerably higher operating expenses.

Temperature

Plants tolerate a range of ambient temperatures, but for optimum growth and quality, most crops have relatively narrow temperature requirements (Table 29.2). For a given species, different cultivars may respond differently to ambient temperature. Production guidelines (Wilcox, 1981) for greenhouse lettuce growing in a nutrient film system recommend an air day temperature of 60–65°F, a night temperature of 45–50°F, and a root-zone temperature of 60–75°F.

Control of temperature in the root zone is as important as control of ambient temperature, since plant growth and other physiological changes may be manipulated by altering temperatures in the root environment. It is now recognized that if roots are kept warm, the air temperature can be significantly reduced. By

Table 29.2. Optimum Growing Temperatures for
Greenhouse Crops

Crop	Day Temperature	Night Temperature
	(°F)	(°F)
Cucumbers	70–80	70
Lettuce	60–70	45–55
Tomatoes	65–75	60–65

lowering air temperature during the dark period while still maintaining root temperature, growers may reduce greenhouse heating costs, particularly during the winter months. Conversely, by maintaining cool root-zone temperatures, growers may successfully grow plants such as lettuce in the summer when ambient air temperatures exceed 90°F. Root-zone heating is usually installed in the growing medium, such as soil or nutrient solution. Some modern hydroponic CEA facilities are able to increase root-zone temperatures in the winter and cool the root environment in the summer with heat exchangers used on their nutrient solution.

Day and night temperatures are regulated by heating and cooling, depending on outside temperatures. Heating is accomplished primarily by burning fuels and transferring the heat to air or water inside the growing area. Fan-coil space heaters attached to polyethylene ducts that distribute the heat evenly in the house are most common. To reduce high greenhouse energy costs by heating with fossil fuels, some facilities are now using, or testing, alternative heating sources such as solar heating, industrial waste heat, and geothermal energy.

Cooling in greenhouses is accomplished by convective or evaporative cooling. Convective cooling, such as fan and natural ventilation, can at best only reduce the inside temperature to that of the outside environment, and is adequate only in cool climates. Evaporative cooling systems, such as pad and fan cooling, move air through a wetted pad area into the house and cool it by evaporation. Forced air is required to pull the air through the pads into the house. The amount of cooling depends on the relative humidity of the ambient air — the lower the level, the greater the cooling. A fairly new technique for evaporative cooling is a high-pressure fog system that creates a very fine mist system in which the very fine water droplets evaporate easily, reducing the air temperature.

In completely enclosed facilities, refrigeration is the primary source of cooling in the summer. This can be very expensive due to high electricity costs. Cooling in the winter uses the heat sink of the outside air, although during warm periods some refrigeration may also be needed.

Radiation

Artificial light appears to have limited application in most greenhouse situations because of cost. However, in some areas it is used for seedling production and also for supplemental lighting under low-light conditions in the winter to speed up growing time and promote crop uniformity. In the Midwest, normal grow-out time (days after transplanting to harvest) to produce a 6-ounce head of lettuce in the greenhouse is 24 days in the summer and 48 days for an 8-ounce head in the winter. With supplemental lighting provided by HID (high-intensity discharge) sodium vapor lights, the grow-out time in winter can be reduced to 30–36 days.

In completely enclosed facilities, high amounts of artificial lighting are required (Figure 29.4). Utility expenses in these systems may be quite high, amounting to more than one-third of all fixed operating costs, with electricity accounting for 90% of the total.

Figure 29.4. In perhaps the most intensive type of controlled environment agriculture, spinach is being grown in a completely enclosed indoor facility. (Photo: courtesy of PhytoFarms, DeKalb, Illinois)

Carbon Dioxide

The enrichment of the air with carbon dioxide (CO_2) above ambient levels (310–350 parts per million) has been shown to have a stimulating effect on plant growth. Plants use CO_2 in photosynthesis during the daylight hours, and most species have a higher photosynthetic rate under increased CO_2 levels if no other factors are limiting.

CO_2 enrichment has been found to be beneficial to lettuce and tomatoes under low light conditions. Cucumbers also respond favorably to CO_2 but usually under high light conditions. A CO_2 concentration of 1,000 parts per million (ppm) is considered standard for greenhouse enrichment, although for some sensitive crops, such as basil and other herbs, and for plants in the seedling stage, this may be too high, and growth may be depressed. During periods of high temperatures and high light intensity, plant response to CO_2 may increase and optimum levels may be considerably higher than 1,000 ppm for short durations.

Sources of CO_2 are compressed gas, dry ice, and combustion products of burned fuel. Care must be taken in the selection of fuel sources so that no contaminants that will depress plant growth are present.

Relative Humidity

Plants do well under a wide range of humidity. Although low humidity can cause plant drying or wilting, this is generally not a problem in controlled environments, which usually have a higher degree of humidity inside than outside, because of plant transpiration and evaporation. High humidity is normally required in seedling rooms but can increase the incidence of disease in production houses. Humidity is controlled by proper ventilation and adequate air distribution within the system.

GROWING SYSTEMS

Various types of cultural systems are used in CEA. These can be divided into two broad categories: substrate culture and solution culture. Substrate culture is the use of some type of solid medium or substrate for the roots to grow in. In solution culture, no solid medium or substrate is used; instead, plant roots are immersed or suspended freely in water or some type of nutrient solution.

Hydroponics, a term coined in the early 1930's, traditionally means growing plants in aerated water that contains all the essential nutrients. However, in a more generic sense, *hydroponics* describes a technique of growing plants in a soilless or inert medium in which essential elements are supplied in a nutrient solution. This latter description is more appropriate for commercial CEA, where hydroponics is used in both solution and substrate systems.

Hydroponic systems can be classified as either open or closed systems. If the nutrient solution is used only once in a one-way passage through the medium, it is described as an open system. A common example of an open system is the drip-irrigation method to apply fertilizers (see Chapter 8). If the nutrient solution is reused by recirculation, it is referred to as a closed system. The use of sand or gravel beds in a closed system is one of the oldest of all commercial soilless systems, dating back to the 1930's. Today, however, its use on a commercial scale is limited.

Substrate Culture

When a substrate is used as a rooting medium, it can be natural, artificial, or a mix of the two. Natural substrates include sand, gravel, peat, sawdust, pine bark, and soil. Artificial substrates include perlite, vermiculite, rockwool, and polystyrene.

Soil is being used less and less in CEA, and most greenhouse growers now use, or are changing over to, soilless media. Soil-based materials tend to have more problems with disease, salinity, and poor drainage than soilless media. In particular, problems with root diseases with soil requires considerable soil preparation, including steam sterilization, before planting.

Sand, gravel, and vermiculite are standard rooting media used in most soilless substrate hydroponic systems. Recently, however, there has been increasing interest in growing vegetables in polyethylene bags containing peat mixed with vermiculite or some other soilless material (Figure 29.5). Nutrients may be supplied either in solution by a drip irrigation system or in dry form, or a combination of the two. Known as "bag culture," this technique is becoming the most com-

Figure 29.5. Tomatoes are being grown in "bag culture"; notice the drip system being used to apply the nutrient solution.

monly used soilless substrate system for greenhouse tomatoes and cucumbers in the U.S. and in European countries.

Another substrate being used more and more in CEA production is rockwool. This synthetic fibrous material is chemically inert and has a high water retention capacity. The material wets very easily and has a very good air / oxygen content. Tomatoes and cucumbers are normally grown in individual rockwool slabs that are irrigated with a drip irrigation system supplying the nutrient solution. For lettuce, smaller individual cubes that are usually submersed in the nutrient solution are used (Figure 29.6). Rockwool is also used in bag culture and as a medium in seedling germination. A disadvantage of rockwool, however, is that it is not biodegradable, and the amount of spent material can present a disposal problem in larger facilities.

Figure 29.6. Lettuce seedlings are being started in rockwool cubes soaked in a nutrient solution.

Solution Culture

Solution culture, also referred to as water culture or hydroculture, can be divided into three cultural systems: 1) aeroponics (misting roots), 2) nutrient film technique, and 3) deep flow technique. All are characterized by bare-rooted plants. Aeration is critical for healthy root growth, especially for crops such as cucumbers that develop large root systems and are grown at warm temperatures.

Aeroponics involves growing plants with all or parts of their roots suspended in air and spraying them from time to time with nutrient solution or water. It is a very efficient system for utilizing space, and is better suited for lettuce than for tomatoes or cucumbers. Several different designs are possible and systems can become quite elaborate. In a vertical system, the crop is cultured in layered or inclined panels or trays that support the plants in an arcway design. Attempts to commercialize the technique have not been successful, and it is used mostly for research and demonstration purposes.

The nutrient film technique (NFT), developed at The Glasshouse Research Institute in England in the 1970's, utilizes a flowing, recirculating stream of water that bathes the roots in a continuous thin layer or film of nutrient solution. The plants grow in slightly sloping troughs or gullies lined with plastic. The nutrient solution flows down the gradient, covering the roots, and then drains back into a holding reservoir. Increasing or decreasing the slope of the trough controls the rate of flow of solution over the roots, and hence the oxygen supply to the roots. Plants are usually started in rockwool blocks that are covered with the plastic lining to keep the roots in the dark. The NFT hydroponic system is used extensively for the commercial production of tomatoes, lettuce, and cucumbers.

In contrast to NFT, the deep flow technique (DFT) entails growing plants with their roots immersed in a deep, recirculating, continuously aerated nutrient solution. Troughs, pools, plastic containers, or several other types of holding structures can be used. There are various modifications of DFT, including floating "rafts" of polystyrene with perforations to support plants over a pool of nutrient solution.

CULTURAL MANAGEMENT

It is not possible to describe in detail the specific cultural practices required to grow the various crops for all the different soilless systems in CEA. The discussion that follows highlights some of the general management practices used in tomato, cucumber, and lettuce CEA production.

Nutrient Solutions

Nutrients are applied in the form of water-soluble fertilizers. The basic solutions used, in general, are a modified type of Hoagland's solution. Solutions usually contain all the nutrient elements required for plant growth. The concentration of the specific nutrients varies according to the type of crop, medium, and specific growing system used. Also to be considered is the stage of plant growth. For example, some hydroponic recipes recommend increased levels of nitrogen and potassium during fruiting in tomato and cucumber crops to maintain vigorous plant growth and fruit development.

Continuous monitoring and evaluation of the nutrient solution is required throughout the cropping cycle. In closed systems, the nutrient solution must be replenished or adjusted periodically, depending on the rate of uptake of the individual nutrients. Differences in the rate of absorption of the various nutrients by roots can result in a build-up of some elements and a depletion of others in the nutrient solution. In open systems, the nutrient content (as well as the solution pH) is adjusted before application. This lends itself to precise control of the nutrient solution composition in response to different stages of plant growth.

In addition to the solution formulation and concentration, other factors to consider are solution pH and water quality. As plants grow, the pH of the solution will generally increase. Regular adjustment of the pH with acid will be required to maintain the pH between 5.5 and 6.5 for most crops. In some areas, the concentration of some elements such as calcium, magnesium, sodium, sulfate, chloride, and bicarbonate in the water source can be high enough to adversely affect plant growth. Usually these can be neutralized with special water treatments including filtration, ion-exchange resins, and precipitation with other chemicals.

Tomatoes

Most growers produce their own transplants. Depending on the time of year and light conditions, the time to grow tomato transplants varies from 4 to 8 weeks. Generally, tomato seedlings are ready to be transplanted when they reach a height of about 4–6 inches.

Indeterminate cultivars are used for tomato CEA production. They are trained to a single stem and up a string or wire by pruning out the lateral shoots, and wrapping the stems around the string or wire hanging from an overhead wire support system (Figure 29.7). Pruning and training are high-labor operations in tomato culture.

Tomatoes have perfect flowers, but because of lack of wind and insects, compared to outdoor conditions, some form of pollination has to be provided. Many growers use a mechanical vibrator which is placed on the base of each flower cluster to shake out the pollen. In areas where pollen shed is more profuse and light conditions are good, air-blast blowers can shake the plants to facilitate pollination (Figure 29.8). Since all flowers in a cluster do not open at the same time, it is necessary to repeat the pollinating procedure as new flowers open on the cluster. During cloudy weather, flower development is slowed and pollen shed may be significantly reduced.

Greenhouse tomatoes are usually harvested with more color than those from the field. Fruits can be picked from the time color begins to develop until it reaches the full pink stage. Generally, fruits require about 46 days from pollination to the start of ripening. The later the stage of color at harvest, the more care must be

Figure 29.7. Greenhouse tomatoes are trained up string suspended from an overhead support wire.

Figure 29.8. Pollination of greenhouse tomatoes with an air-blast blower.

taken in handling to avoid fruit bruising and damage. Handling and storage procedures are similar to those for field-grown fresh market tomatoes (see Chapter 27).

Cucumbers

The general culture of cucumbers in CEA is similar to that of tomatoes. The plants are very sensitive to environmental factors such as low light, cool air temperatures, pollutants, low humidity, low CO_2, poor root aeration, and high-soluble salts.

Approximately 14 days are needed from seed emergence to transplanting. Each plant is trained up a single string or wire suspended from an overhead support wire 7–8 feet above the plant rows. As the plant grows, the main stem is wrapped around or fastened to the support string. All lateral shoots and female flowers are removed on the first 18 inches of stem, since fruits that develop on the lower part of the plant touch the ground and are usually not marketable. The other laterals are allowed to develop and are pruned at two nodes.

The plant is allowed to grow until the main stem reaches the overhead wire support. At this time, the main growing point is removed, and the top two or three laterals are allowed to develop. These are trained in opposite directions over the wire and allowed to grow downward on support strings. Some growers do not remove the growing point after it reaches the top wire; instead, they allow the main stem to grow down support wires and back up again in a circular pattern.

Because each node contains new leaves and new fruit buds, pruning the lateral branches will encourage continuous fruit production. Fruit set and development in the European cultivars (gynoecious and seedless) does not require pollination. Conversely, because pollination causes misshaped fruits, bees should not be allowed in the facility. Fruits are picked when they reach the desired length, usually 12–18 inches long. Depending on cultivar and environmental conditions, fruit production may continue over a period of about 50–75 days.

Lettuce

Lettuce is one of the very successful crops grown under CEA, especially with solution culture systems. The main types of lettuce produced in controlled environments are the butterhead and looseleaf types, although in some areas, crisphead cultivars are also grown.

Lettuce CEA production can be divided into three general stages: 1) germination, 2) transplant development, and 3) grow-out, or the time from transplanting to harvest. The seed is sown in rockwool cubes soaked with nutrient solution. To keep high temperatures from inhibiting germination (thermodormancy), growers place the seeded cubes in special growth rooms at 68°F. Germination normally takes place in 1–4 days. The seedlings remain in the growth room under 18 hours of fluorescent light. When plants have approximately four leaves, normally about 10–14 days after germination, they are transplanted to the seedling nursery. The plants stay in the nursery for about 14 days and then are transplanted to the production (grow-out) range. This process from seeding to final transplanting requires about 28 days. Under low-light conditions, supplemental lighting may be necessary to maintain seedling uniformity and growth.

Grow-out time will range from about 24 days in the summer to over 48 days in the winter. If supplemental lighting is used, grow-out time in the winter can be reduced to about 30–36 days. High temperatures during grow-out can cause bolting and poor quality. Some of the crop is marketed with the roots left on the plants and is known as "living lettuce."

Insects and Diseases

For most CEA production, there is a fairly constant group of insect and disease pests. From a pest management perspective, CEA production presents a situation different from field-grown crops. When plants are grown in a confined environment, the potential for pest problems is higher than in the open. Due to the high value of CEA crops, economic threshold levels of most insect and disease problems will be lower than for field-grown vegetables. The occurrence and severity of insect and disease problems will vary depending on crop, location, and CEA system.

Insects. Traditionally, the major insect pests in CEA are whiteflies, aphids, and spider mites. All are very small insects that remain motionless when feeding, making them difficult to detect by casual observation. All have high reproductive potential, and destructive populations may be reached in a very short time.

Whiteflies (*Trialeurodes vaporariorum*) are found on both upper and lower leaf surfaces. They cause injury by sucking juices from plant tissues, but most damage results from their excreting sticky honeydew that can coat foliage and fruits. A black, sooty mold will develop on the honeydew which may kill that part of the plant and result in loss of economic value for crops. Yield reductions do not usually occur until high populations are reached.

Aphids (several species) are small, sluggish, soft-bodied insects that may damage crops in a manner similar to whiteflies. They also transmit several types of viral diseases which can severely affect yields.

Spider mites (*Tetranychus urticae*) are probably the major insect pest in vegetable greenhouses, and are especially troublesome on cucumbers. They feed on the undersides of leaves and cause damage by scraping or rasping of tissues.

Feeding injury appears as a speckling of the upper leaf surfaces. Symptoms may appear from only a few mites, while severe infestations may kill leaves and petioles. More so than either whiteflies or aphids, spider mites multiply rapidly, and populations can increase to epidemic levels in a very short time.

Other common insect pests in CEA are leaf miners and various types of caterpillars, including cabbage loopers, leafrollers, armyworms, and tomato pinworms. Thrips can damage tomatoes and may transmit spotted wilt. Various types of tiny, black flies (shore flies, fungus knats, and moth flies) can cause problems when plants are grown in solution culture.

A number of chemical and biological control options are available. However, once insect pests become firmly established, strenuous effort is needed to eliminate them. The leaves of tomatoes and lettuce have a natural tendency to cup downward, making control on the undersides of leaves difficult. A number of insect species have developed a high degree of resistance to some pesticides. Spraying or fogging with insecticides is generally effective. For crops to be marketed as "pesticide-free," natural control methods, including introduced parasites, predators, and fungi, are used.

Diseases. Many of the same foliage diseases (gray mold, leaf mold, leaf blights, powdery mildew, and stem rots) that attack tomatoes, cucumbers, and lettuce in the field also may cause significant damage in CEA. They are encouraged by the high humidity common to most CEA environments. The best general control is proper air circulation and heating to maintain the relative humidity below 90%. Using resistant cultivars in CEA will help control common root diseases such as *Fusarium* and *Verticillium*.

A particularly serious disease problem in hydroponic systems is *Pythium*, a fungal disease responsible for damping-off of seedlings and root decay in mature plants. Because the organism is naturally adapted to semi-aquatic environments, it is especially severe in recirculating solution systems. Young plants may be killed, especially at higher root temperatures. This disease can be so destructive that many tomato and cucumber producers have changed from solution culture to some type of substrate culture. Although several species of the pathogen are involved, the two most common are *P. ultimum* and *P. aphanidermatum*. The former is most active under cool temperatures (65–75°F), while the latter is often responsible for warm-temperature root / stem decays. Typical symptoms include yellowish-tan to brown decayed roots, coupled with wilting and stunting of plants.

Control of *Pythium* in recirculating solution systems is very difficult, and exclusion of the pathogen is essential. Maintaining good sanitation, providing optimum growing conditions, and using disease-free transplants are preventive measures. The water source should be checked for possible contamination. In substrate systems, media drenches of a registered fungicide can be used.

ECONOMIC CONSIDERATIONS

Information on the economics of CEA in the U.S. is relatively sparse. This is because of the considerable variation in different facilities, capital costs, cropping patterns, and marketing systems. In general, capital costs are high. Construction costs for a basic greenhouse module may range from $4 to $30 per square foot. In comparison, an all-enclosed, modern, hi-tech system may cost $150 or more per square foot.

Total annual operating costs include fixed expenses (equipment, interest charges, taxes, and insurance) and variable expenses (utilities, fertilizers, pesticides, labor, repairs, marketing, and other items). Utilities and labor are the two greatest operating costs. For example, a 3,000 square foot greenhouse growing tomatoes in the southwestern part of the U.S. can have an annual operating cost of over $11,000.

As indicated earlier, many vegetable CEA facilities have closed because of the energy costs for heating in the winter and cooling in the summer. Although automation and new technology in plant culture and handling have reduced labor costs significantly, energy expenses still remain high. During times of low production, labor costs can be cut back, but a greenhouse must be maintained under the proper growing conditions (temperature, light, etc.) whether it is in partial or total production. Large, industrial facilities may use waste heat or low-cost energy to reduce operating costs, but small facilities generally do not have these resources.

High capital and operating costs must be offset by greater yields and higher prices obtained from CEA production. Fresh market cucumber yields in CEA greenhouses average about 150–175 tons per acre, compared to a field-grown average of approximately 9 tons per acre. Greenhouse tomatoes average around 120–150 tons per acre, compared to about 12 tons per acre for fresh market crops in the field. Since the optimum environment for growth can be provided, crops can be grown to maturity in considerably shorter time in CEA than in the field. Lettuce can be grown from seed to harvest in about 26–32 days in some modern CEA facilties, while outdoors the quickest that lettuce can be grown from seed to harvest is about 42–60 days.

Higher prices are usually obtained because of the superior quality of CEA–grown crops. However, the ability to produce out of season when prices are higher is no longer a significant advantage for CEA, due to the increased availability of field-grown produce during the winter from southern growing regions.

The higher production per unit area will become more important in the future as the population increases and agricultural land and resources decrease. Research and development of structures, coverings, and control systems; parallel developments in new cultivars; innovative cultural practices; and improved nutritional regimes should lead to future growth in the production of food from CEA systems. However, the future of CEA hinges on more efficient heating and cooling systems being developed to reduce production costs.

SELECTED REFERENCES

Bauerle, W. L., and B. A. Kimball. 1984. CO_2 enrichment in the United States. *Acta Hort.* 16:207–216.

Collins, W. L., and M. H. Jensen. 1983. *Hydroponics: A 1983 Technology Overview.* Environmental Research Laboratory, Univ. of Arizona, Tucson.

Cooper, A. 1979. *The ABC of NFT.* Grower Books, London.

Ellis, N. L., M. Jensen, J. Larsen, and N. F. Oebker. 1974. *Nutriculture Systems: Growing Plants Without Soil.* Purdue Univ. Agric. Exp. Sta. Bull. 44.

Farley, J. D., and R. K. Lindquist. 1981. *Greenhouse Tomatoes: Diseases and Insect Control.* The Ohio State Univ. Coop. Ext. Ser. Bull. 674.

Gerber, J. M. 1985. *Hydroponics.* Univ. of Illinois Coop. Ext. Ser. Hort. Facts VC-19-82.

Graves, C. J. 1983. The nutrient film technique. In: J. Janick (ed.). *Horticultural Reviews* 5:1–44. AVI Publishing Co., Westport, Connecticut.

Hoagland, D. R., and D. I. Arnon. 1950. *The Water-Culture Method of Growing Plants Without Soil.* California Agric. Exp. Sta. Cir. 347.

Jensen, M. H., and W. L. Collins. 1985. Hydroponic vegetable production. In: J. Janick (ed.). *Horticultural Reviews* 7:483–558. AVI Publishing Co., Westport, Connecticut.

Johnson, H., Jr. 1980. *Hydroponics: A Guide to Soilless Culture Systems.* Univ. of California Div. of Agric. Sci., Leaf. 2947.

Jones, J. B., Jr. 1983. *A Guide for the Hydroponic and Soilless Culture Grower.* Timber Press, Oregon.

Lindquist, R. K., and R. C. Rowe. 1984. *Greenhouse Cucumbers: Diseases and Insect Control.* The Ohio State Univ. Coop. Ext. Ser. Bull. 718.

Monk, G. J., and J. M. Molnar. 1987. Energy efficient greenhouses. In: J. Janick (ed.). *Horticultural Reviews* 9:1–52. AVI Publishing Co., Westport, Connecticut.

Resh, H. M. 1978. *Hydroponic Food Production.* Woodbridge Press, Santa Barbara, California.

Savage, A. J. (ed.). 1985. *Hydroponics Worldwide: State of the Art in Soilless Crop Production.* International Center for Special Studies, Honolulu, Hawaii.

White, J. W. 1979. Energy efficient growing structures for controlled environment agriculture. In: J. Janick (ed.). *Horticultural Reviews* 1:141–171. AVI Publishing Co., Westport, Connecticut.

Wilcox, G. E. 1981. *European Greenhouse Cucumber Production in Nutrient Film Systems.* Hort. Dept., Purdue Univ. Coop. Ext. Ser. HO-168.

Wilcox, G. E. 1981. *Growing Greenhouse Tomatoes in the Nutrient Film Hydroponic System.* Hort. Dept., Purdue Univ. Coop. Ext. Ser. HO-167.

Wilcox, G. E. 1981. *Lettuce Growing in the Nutrient Film System.* Hort. Dept., Purdue Univ. Coop. Ext. Ser. HO-169.

Wilcox, G. E. 1981. *The Nutrient Film Hydroponic System.* Hort. Dept., Purdue Univ. Coop. Ext. Ser. HO-166.

30

HOME VEGETABLE GARDENING

Gardening can be an interesting, rewarding, healthful, and remunerating hobby in which the entire family can become involved. A home vegetable garden can provide fresh produce and an opportunity to learn about plants and can give much pride and satisfaction. Fresh, home-grown vegetables are generally comparable to or superior in quality to vegetables sold in markets. The home garden can supply a large part of the family diet and can become a source of additional family income. For a relatively small investment of time, energy, and money, the entire family can reap the benefits provided by a home vegetable garden.

PLANNING THE HOME GARDEN

A planting plan should furnish the grower with a record of the cultivars and the succession of crops and should also include the amount of garden space allocated to the various species (Table 30.1). The plan may take the form of a map or a table showing cultivars, row lengths, row spacings, and planting dates. The plants should be grouped so that those with similar cultural requirements and growth habits are placed together in the same section of the garden.

Planning and Arranging

Perennial crops, such as asparagus and rhubarb, should be located to one side of the garden where they will not interfere with day-to-day garden cultural practices. All-season crops, such as potatoes and tomatoes (also cucumbers,

Table 30.1. Planting Plan for the Home Garden

#	Crop				
1.	Sweet corn	Early	Sweet corn	Midseason	3'
2.	Sweet corn		Sweet corn		3'
3.	Sweet corn		Sweet corn		3'
4.	Sweet corn		Sweet corn		3'
5.	Sweet corn	Late	Sweet corn	Late	3'
6.	Sweet corn		Sweet corn		3'
7.	Tomatoes (staked)				4'
8.	Tomatoes (staked)				4'
9.	Tomatoes (staked)				4'
10.	Early potatoes				3'
11.	Early potatoes				3'
12.	Peppers		Eggplants	Chard (Swiss)	3'
13.	Lima beans (bush)				3'
14.	Lima beans (bush)				3'
15.	Lima beans (bush)				3'
16.	Snap beans (bush)				3'
17.	Snap beans (bush)				3'
18.	Broccoli				3'
19.	Early cabbage				3'
20.	Onion sets		This entire area may be replanted after		3'
21.	Onion sets		harvest with crops such as endive,		2'
22.	Carrots		cauliflower, Brussels sprouts, spinach,		2'
23.	Carrots		kale, beets, cabbage, broccoli, turnips,		2'
24.	Beets		lettuce, carrots, and late potatoes		2'
25.	Beets				2'
26.	Kale				2'
27.	Spinach				2'
28.	Peas				2'
29.	Peas				2'
30.	Lettuce	Seeded early	Lettuce	2 weeks later — Lettuce — 4 weeks later	2'
31.	Radishes		Radishes	Radishes	2'
32.	Strawberries				2'
33.	Strawberries				3'
34.	Asparagus			Rhubarb	3'
35.	Asparagus			Herbs	3'
	— 50 ft. —				3'

melons, and parsnips), should be located so as not to interfere with short-season crops such as beans, beets, cabbage, carrots, lettuce, peas, and spinach that usually have successive plantings (succession planting is the growing of one crop, removing it, and then planting another one in its place). Small plantings of very quick-maturing crops such as leaf lettuce and radishes can be made at two-week intervals early in the season, and again later in the season to provide a continuous fresh supply of vegetables. The short-season crops should be grouped together to allow a large section of the garden to be vacated as the plants mature. This permits the preparation of the land and planting of following crops.

Intercropping of vegetables according to their relative maturities and size can make maximum use of garden space. This entails planting early-maturing crops such as beans, spinach, and lettuce between the widely spaced rows of later or long-season crops such as tomatoes and sweet corn (Figure 30.1). The early-maturing crops will not interfere with the growth of the late-maturing ones, and by the time the tomatoes and sweet corn attain considerable size, the early-maturing vegetables will be ready to harvest. This avoids plant-to-plant competition and allows several crops to be grown in almost the same space.

Selecting Vegetables

The kinds and cultivars of vegetables to grow in the home garden will depend on the tastes of the family. Cultivars should be chosen to meet special requirements, such as earliness, succession, adaptability, disease resistance, and productivity. Since most home gardens are limited by space, vegetable selection must take into account plant growth habit. Crops such as muskmelons, potatoes, sweet corn, watermelons, and winter squash require much space and are best suited for a field garden and may not be appropriate for the smaller kitchen garden. Conversely, beets, carrots, chard, lettuce, onions, radishes, spinach, and herbs can be grown successfully in limited space and are often used in container gardens (growing vegetables in containers when adequate ground space is not available).

Agricultural experiment stations or the extension service of state universities can provide information on specific cultivars best suited to particular regions and states. In addition, a nonprofit organization of seed producers known as All-America Selections evaluates new cultivars of vegetables in selected trial gardens

Figure 30.1. Bush beans interplanted with lettuce.

throughout the U.S. The new cultivars are judged against the best cultivars currently available. Those that demonstrate superior performance to existing cultivars over a wide range of soil and climatic conditions are designated All-America Selections (AAS). However, not all new cultivars are tested in this manner, and some cultivars not designated AAS may grow quite well under local conditions.

The home vegetable garden affords an excellent opportunity to grow many hard-to-find and unusual vegetables. Among these are specialty crops, such as ethnic and miniature vegetables, and heirloom cultivars that at one time were popular, but due to cultural and economic reasons are no longer grown commercially. For example, a heirloom tomato cultivar may have excellent taste but requires considerable staking and support. In the home garden, this would generally not be a problem, as would be the case in commercial production.

Location

The success of the garden will depend to a great extent on the site. The location of the house and various other permanent structures largely determines the garden location. Where possible, the garden should have a location that is convenient to the house, particularly the kitchen. The site must afford the maximum amount of sunlight and should be removed from trees and shrubs that could shade the crops. Frost is less likely to injure vegetables on high ground than on low ground or in valleys, and a southern exposure and sandy loam will produce earlier vegetables than a northern exposure and a heavy soil. A level location is best, provided it is properly drained.

Soil

A good garden soil is similar to that used for commercial vegetable production. The soil should be fertile, open, properly drained, and well supplied with organic matter. A sandy loam is usually ideal since it provides for good drainage while still being relatively fertile. Heavy soils should be avoided since they are subject to poor drainage and roots may suffer from lack of good aeration. Planting on raised beds will improve drainage and should be used on clay soils.

Water

The garden should be located close to an abundant and inexpensive supply of water. This is of major importance in semi-arid and arid regions, but water will help the garden almost anywhere. Water is particularly needed when seeds are started or crops are transplanted. In many humid regions, home gardening can usually be successful without irrigating.

Size

The ultimate size for the home garden will depend upon its intended use and the space available. It is important to allow for proper growth of plants, ease of cultivation, and efficient use of space. A surprising supply of vegetables may be obtained from a plot 25 × 25 feet, or even smaller. A kitchen or backyard garden (Figure 30.2) containing approximately 0.25 acre will furnish enough vegetables for a family of five. A field garden may range in size up to 2–3 acres or more. As a rule, the garden should be large enough to produce what is needed, but its size should not allow it to become a burden or a chore.

Figure 30.2. A backyard vegetable garden can supply enough produce for a large part of the season; the trellis system is used to make more efficient use of garden space. (Photo: courtesy of J. C. Schmidt, University of Illinois)

PLANTING AND CROP ESTABLISHMENT

Most vegetables in the home garden are started from seeds or transplants (Table 30.2). Seeding is less expensive and easier than using transplants, but crops require considerable more time to reach maturity. Using transplants not only saves time but also reduces hazards common to seedlings, such as weeds, birds, and

Table 30.2. Vegetable Planting Chart

Vegetable	Seeds or Plants per 100-Ft. Row	Distance Between Plants	Distance Between Rows	Planting Depth
		(in.)	(in.)	(in.)
Artichokes, Jerusalem	40–50 tubers	24–30	36–48	2–3
Asparagus	50 crowns	18–24	36–60	6–8
Beans, bush (lima)	8 oz.	3	18–24	1–1.5
Beans, bush (snap)	8 oz.	3	18–24	1–1.5
Beans, pole	8 oz.	3–4	30–36	1–1.5
Beets	1 oz.	2–3	12–18	0.5–1
Broccoli	50 plants	18–24	30–36	T[1]
Brussels sprouts	50 plants	18–24	30–36	T
Cabbage	75–100 plants	12–18	18–30	T
Carrots	4 oz.	1–2	12–18	0.25
Cauliflower	50–75 plants	18–24	24–36	T
Celeriac	200 plants	6	18–24	T
Celery	150–200 plants	6–8	24–36	T
Chard	2 oz.	4–6	18–24	0.5
Chinese cabbage	0.5 oz.	12–15	24	0.25
Collards	0.5 oz.	12–15	18–24	0.25
Corn, sweet	4 oz.	9–12	24–48	0.5–1
Cucumbers	1 oz.	12 (single) 36 (hills)	48–72	0.5
Eggplants	50–75 plants	18–24	30–36	T
Endive	0.5 oz.	9–12	18–24	0.25
Kale	0.5 oz.	8–12	18–24	0.25
Kohlrabi	0.25 oz.	2–5	18–24	0.25
Lettuce, leaf	0.25 oz.	4	12–18	0.25
Muskmelons	0.25 oz.	8–10	48–72	0.5
Mustard	0.50 oz.	2–4	12–18	0.25
Okra	2 oz.	12–24	12–18	0.5
Onions (plants)	300–400 plants	3–4	15–18	T
Onions (sets)	3–4 lbs.	1–2	15–18	2–3
Onions (seed)	0.25 oz.	2–3	15–18	0.5
Parsnips	0.50 oz.	2–4	18–24	0.5
Peas	1 lb.	1–2	18–24	1
Peppers	50–75 plants	18–24	18–24	T
Potatoes, Irish	10 lbs. tubers	10–12	24–36	4
Potatoes, sweet	75–100 plants	12–18	36–48	T
Pumpkins	1 oz.	48	84–120	1.5
Radishes	1 oz.	0.5–1	12–18	0.5
Rhubarb	25–30 crowns	36–48	36–48	2
Rutabaga	0.25 oz.	6	18–24	1
Salsify	1 oz.	3	24	0.25
Spinach	1 oz.	2–4	12–18	0.25
Squash, summer	1 oz.	24–36 (single) 48 (hills)	36–48	1
Squash, winter	1 oz.	24–36 (single) 48 (hills)	84–120	0.5–1

(Continued)

Table 30.2 (Continued)

Vegetable	Seeds or Plants per 100-Ft. Row	Distance Between Plants	Distance Between Rows	Planting Depth
		(in.)	(in.)	(in.)
Tomatoes	50–75 (staked) 30–50 (caged or groundbed)	18–24 (staked) 24–36 (caged or groundbed)	36–60	T
Turnips	0.5	2–4	12–18	0.2
Watermelons	1 oz.	24–36 (single) 72 (hills)	84–120	1

[1]Normally set in the garden as transplants.

heavy rain. Home gardeners should use transplants when they are trying to avoid cold temperatures early in the season and hot conditions later in the year.

Generally, root crops (beets, carrots, radishes, rutabagas, turnips), beans, peas, cucumbers, spinach, sweet corn, melons, pumpkins, and squashes are started outdoors from seed. Tomatoes, peppers, eggplants, cabbage and its relatives, sweet potatoes, and celery are transplanted. Lettuce and onions can be started either way. Sometimes melons, squashes, and cucumbers can be transplanted but require special care not to disturb the roots. In a few cases, other means are used to start vegetables in the home garden, including crowns (asparagus) and crown segments (rhubarb), sets (onions), cloves (garlic), tubers or tuber pieces (potatoes), slips (sweet potatoes), and roots (horseradish).

CULTURAL PRACTICES

The home garden, like commercial vegetable plantings, should receive the required cultural practices to make it productive and profitable. Seedbed preparation, plant growing, fertilization, cultivation, pest control, and other necessary operations are discussed fully in preceding chapters.

Fertility

Nitrogen (N), phosphorus (P), and potassium (K) are the nutrients most lacking in garden soils. Although commercial vegetable growers adjust their fertilizer applications for each vegetable grown, this is neither practical nor very important for home gardeners. They can ensure adequate fertility by making annual applications of a standard garden fertilizer, such as 10-10-10 (10% each of N, P_2O_5, K_2O). Established vegetable gardens will generally require around 2–3 pounds of garden fertilizer per 100 square feet each year. Lawn fertilizers should not be used on vegetables since they may contain weed killers that will damage the vegetable crops.

All garden soils should be tested for pH. Vegetables generally grow best in slightly acid soils, but a range of 5.8–7.5 is satisfactory for most home gardens.

Manure and Compost

Well-decayed organic matter adds nutrients to the soil, improves soil structure, aids in the growth of beneficial microorganisms, and increases water-holding capacity. In most home gardens, it usually will be necessary to add fertilizers, but a good garden soil to which organic matter is added periodically will often contain most of the nutrients required for growth.

Organic matter is added to garden soil most often in the form of animal manure, compost, and green manure. If available, partially decomposed barnyard manure can be turned under at the rate of 10–20 tons per acre. Poultry or sheep manure may be used but at about half the above rate. At times, animal manure can be expensive and is not always practical. In some areas it is unavailable, while for urban dwellers it may be difficult and messy to apply.

Compost is an effective source of organic matter, as well as a disposal site for garden waste. It is basically decomposed organic matter made from leaves, straw, grass clippings, manure, and any other disease-free waste vegetable matter (Figure 30.3). During the composting process, raw plant materials are converted to compost through the action of microorganisms. The finished compost is soft and loose and smells and feels like freshly plowed soil. Compost can be added to the garden soil, used with soil to grow transplants, or applied as a mulch. Although it releases plant nutrients as it decomposes, compost should not be considered a complete substitute for fertilizer. A compost pile is easily constructed, and detailed instructions for making compost are available from extension publications and numerous gardening magazines.

Another way to add organic matter to garden soils is to grow a green-manure crop (see Chapter 6). Some examples of green-manure crops are sweet clover, alfalfa, and winter rye. These can be sown in the fall and turned under the following spring before they mature.

Organic Mulches

Although organic mulches are not particularly suited for most commercial vegetable operations, they are excellent for most home gardens. Organic mulches improve soil tilth and create a favorable environment for root growth; they keep soil moisture and temperature uniform and have a cooling effect on soil (Figure 30.4). Applied to a depth of 3–4 inches, organic mulches should keep down most

Figure 30.3. A garden compost pile is an excellent source of organic matter, as well as a disposal site for garden waste. (Photo: courtesy of J. C. Schmidt, University of Illinois)

annual weeds. However, most organic materials are bulky and difficult to handle. Some materials, such as straw, hay, and wood byproducts (sawdust, shavings, woodchips), may require additional sidedressings of nitrogen to avoid tying up soil nitrogen and resulting in nitrogen deficiency during their decomposition.

Figure 30.4. Organic materials, such as straw, make excellent mulches for vegetables.

Other types of common organic mulches include grass clippings, leaves, peanut hulls, composts, peat, and animal manures.

ORGANIC GARDENING

Many gardeners prefer to use "natural" pesticides and fertilizers in place of those chemical products manufactured in laboratories and factories. In general, most practices and principles for organic gardening are similar to those for non-organic gardening. Successful organic gardening depends on good fertility; control of weeds, insects, and diseases; and adherence to other established gardening practices.

Fertility

Nutrients for growing vegetables can be supplied from organic materials such as leaves, grass clippings, peat moss, straw, and hay. These materials must be decomposed by microorganisms before their nutrients become available for plants to use. More readily available nutrients may be obtained from compost, manure, sewage sludge, steamed bone meal, dried blood, fish meal, rock phosphate, and hardwood ashes (see Table 6.3). With most of these materials, however, they must be used in quite large amounts to fullfill the total fertilizer requirement for most vegetables. Since organic matter will tend to make soil slightly acid, ground limestone or marl may be needed.

Controlling Weeds and Pests

Filling the space between the rows with straw or other undecomposed material as a mulch will discourage weed growth. A mulch will also keep tomato fruits from contact with the soil and help avoid fruit rots. It will hold and conserve moisture.

Some crops can be grown with relatively little danger from insect and disease pests. These include radishes, lettuce, onions, leeks, shallots, chives, beets, chard, mustard, chinese cabbage, parsnips, salsify, peas, spinach, sweet potatoes, turnips, and most herbs. Very often, tomatoes can be grown without insecticides if the tomato hornworms are hand-harvested.

Some types of biological control are effective against some insects. *Bacillus thuringiensis* will control tomato hornworms, fruit flies, webworms, bagworms, and cabbageworms. Lady beetles may be effective against aphids. Other harmful insects such as striped cucumber beetles and flea beetles are difficult to control without the use of insecticides. Some insecticides such as pyrethrins and rotenone are of vegetable origin. These can be used when pest epidemics threaten, but many manufactured insecticides are both safer to use and more effective than the botanical insecticides.

However, the best method of controlling insect and disease pests in organic gardening is to use superior plants. Hybrid cultivars are generally stronger and heathier than open-pollinated types and have built-in resistance to many diseases. They tolerate air pollution and adverse weather conditions better and usually bloom and produce fruit earlier.

HERBS IN THE HOME GARDEN

Every home garden should contain some herbs that can be used as flavoring or seasoning in cooking and baking. Herbs can be annuals, biennials, or perennials. Most of them should be planted in the perennial section of the garden. The following list contains some of the more common herb species found in home gardens.

Anise (*Pimpinella Anisum*) — seed used in medicines, cooking, and flavoring liquors (annual).

Balm (*Melissa officinalis*) — leaves used for their lemon-like flavor in liquors and medicines (perennial).

Basil (*Ocimum Basilicum*) — clove-flavored foliage used in seasoning meats, soups, and salads (annual).

Borage (*Borago officinalis*) — coarse leaves sometimes used as pot-herbs and for seasoning salads (annual).

Caraway (*Carum Carvi*) — seeds used in making bread, cheese, salads, sauces, soups, and cakes (biennial).

Catnip (*Nepeta Cataria*) — leaves used in making sauces and teas; a mild condiment (perennial).

Chives (*Allium Schoenoprasum*) — leaves used for flavoring (perennial).

Coriander (*Coriandrum sativum*) — seed used in making confections and bread (annual).

Dill (*Anethum graveolens*) — stems and blossom heads used for making dill pickles and seasoning soups (biennial).

Fennel (*Foeniculum vulgare*) — seed used in French and Italian cooking; stems sometimes used raw (biennial or perennial).

Horehound (*Marrubium vulgare*) — leaves used in making tea and medicines and for flavoring sugar candy; supposed to be good for colds (perennial).

Lavender (*Lavandula officinalis*) — flowers, leaves, and stalks used for their pleasant fragrance; also used in medicines (perennial).

Peppermint (*Mentha x piperita*) — green or dried leaves used in seasoning soups, sauces, and meats; also used for flavoring puddings and gelatin desserts (perennial).

Rosemary (*Ceratiola ericiodes*) — aromatic leaves used for seasoning (perennial).

Sage (*Salvia officinalis*) — leaves used for seasoning dressings and strong meats (perennial).

Spearmint (*Mentha spicata*) — green or dried leaves used for seasoning soups, sauces, and meats; also used for flavoring puddings and gelatin desserts (perennial).

Summer savory (*Satureia hortensis*) — green parts used in seasoning meats and dressings (annual).

Sweet marjoram (*Origanum Marjorana*) — leaves used in seasoning soups, meats, and dressings (annual or perennial).

Thyme (*Thymus vulgaris*) — leaves used for seasoning soups, gravies, stews, sauces, and meats (perennial).

SELECTED REFERENCES

Adams, E. B., A. L. Antonelli, D. Bosley, R. S. Byther, S. J. Collman, R. E. Hunter, and R. E. Thornton. 1979. *Home Gardens*. Washington State Univ. Coop. Ext. Ser. EB-422.

"Anonymous." 1984. *The Encyclopedia of Organic Gardening*. Rodale Press, Emmaus, Pennsylvania.

Barber, J. M., P. Colditz, and D. M. Granberry. 1980. *Gardening*. Univ. of Georgia Coop. Ext. Ser. Bull. 577.

Boxer, A., and P. Back. 1984. *The Herb Book*. Octopus Books, Quarry Bay, Hong Kong.

Calvin, C. L., and D. M. Knutson. 1983. *Modern Home Gardening*. John Wiley & Sons, Inc., New York.

Clarkson, R. E. 1970. *Herbs, Their Culture and Uses*. Macmillan, New York.

Cotner, S., and J. Larsen. 1988. *Home Gardening in Texas*. Texas A&M Univ. Coop. Ext. Ser. B-1139.

Erhardt, W. H. 1982. *Home Vegetable Gardening*. Univ. of Maine Coop. Ext. Ser. Bull. 544.

Ezell, D., W. Cook, R. Griffin, and F. Smith. 1982. *Home Vegetable Gardening*. Clemson Univ. Coop. Ext. Ser. Cir. 570.

Gerber, J. M. 1985. *Making Compost for the Garden*. Univ. of Ilinois Coop. Ext. Ser. Hort. Facts VC-6-85.

Harrison, H. C. 1985. *The Vegetable Garden*. Univ. of Wisconsin Coop. Ext. Ser. A1989.

Lerner, B. R., and M. N. Dana. 1985. *Home Gardener's Guide*. Purdue Univ. Coop. Ext. Ser. HO-32.

Naeve, L., and H. G. Taber. 1982. *Planting a Home Vegetable Garden*. Iowa State Univ. Coop. Ext. Ser. V-6-82.

Ray, R., D. Fell, and M. MacCaskey. 1987. *The Complete Book of Gardening*. Oracle Books, Tucson, Arizona.

Reynolds, C. W., and C. A. McClurg. 1982. *Vegetable Gardening in Maryland*. Univ. of Maryland Coop. Ext. Ser. Bull. 220.

Sams, D. W. 1981. *Growing Vegetables*. Univ. of Tennessee Coop. Ext. Ser. Pub. 901.

Schmidt, J. C. 1982. *Vegetable Planting Guide*. Univ. of Illinois Coop. Ext. Ser. Hort. Facts VC-14-82.

Schmidt, J. C., S. B. Grace, and J. M. Gerber. 1985. *Examining the Economics of Home Vegetable Gardening*. Univ. of Illinois Coop. Ext. Ser. Hort. Facts VC-38-85.

Sims, W. L., H. Johnson, R. F. Kasmire, V. E. Rubatzky, K. B. Tyler, and R. E. Voss. 1978. *Home Vegetable Gardening*. Univ. of California Div. of Agric. Sci. Leaf. 2989.

Splittstoesser, W. E. 1990. *Vegetable Growing Handbook — Organic and Traditional Methods*, 3rd ed. Van Nostrand Reinhold, New York.

Taylor, J. L., R. C. Herner, D. C. Cress, H. S. Potter, and D. J. deZeeuw. 1981. *Home Vegetable Gardening*. Michigan State Univ. Coop. Ext. Ser. E-529.

Topoleski, L. D. 1981. *The Home Vegetable Garden*. Cornell Univ. Info. Bull. 101.

Utzinger, J. D., W. M. Brooks, and E. C. Wittmeyer. 1982. *Home Vegetable Gardening*. Ohio State Univ. Coop. Ext. Ser. Bull. 287.

Vandemark, J. S., and J. W. Courter. 1978. *Vegetable Gardening for Illinois*. Univ. of Illinois Coop. Ext. Ser. Cir. 1150.

Webster, R., and A. Kehr. 1978. *Growing Vegetables in the Home Garden*. USDA, H&G Bull. 202.

Webster, R. E. 1974. *Minigardens for Vegetables*. USDA, H&G Bull. 163.

APPENDIX

CAREERS IN VEGETABLE PRODUCTION

Employment opportunities involved with some facet of vegetables are numerous and diversified. Some of the major career areas related to vegetables include production, education, economics, communications, engineering and mechanization, marketing, and food processing.

The demand for technically trained specialists in vegetable-related areas has been high. Many career opportunities require junior college and college degrees, while others, such as university and corporate research positions, demand advanced graduate degrees. Management and business skills are required for many vegetable-related careers, especially those involved with agribusiness. A partial listing of specific career opportunities is presented in Table A.1.

Table A.1.   A Partial Listing of Career Opportunities in Areas Related to Vegetables

Commercial vegetable grower

Consumer relations specialist

Crop consultant

Disease and pest manager

Equipment sales representative

Extension specialist

Farm manager

Fertilizer and chemical sales representative

Financial manager (including broker, analyst, and consultant)

(Continued)

Table A.1 (Continued)

Food researcher

Garden writer, reporter, or editor

Greenhouse manager

Irrigation specialist

Plant breeder

Plant propagator

Postharvest physiologist

Production manager

Quality control specialist

Researcher — USDA, university, corporate

Retail and wholesale sales and marketing representative

Roadside marketer

Seed and bulb sales and marketing specialist

Soil conservationist/environmental specialist

Teacher — high school, junior college, university

Vegetable consultant

SOURCES OF INFORMATION

New developments in the industry, results of current research, and new cultivars are continually being made available. These and other information on vegetables can be obtained in circular and bulletin form from the U.S. Department of Agriculture and the various state experiment stations (Table A.2).

Table A.2. State Agricultural Experiment Stations

State	Address	State	Address
Alabama	Auburn 36830	Delaware	Newark 19711
Alaska	Fairbanks 99701	Florida	Gainesville 32611
Arizona	Tucson 85721	Georgia	
Arkansas	Fayetteville 72701	University Station	Athens 30602
California		Main Station	Experiment 30212
Berkeley Station	Berkeley 94720	Coastal Plain Station	Tifton 31794
Davis Station	Davis 95616	Hawaii	Honolulu 96822
Riverside Station	Riverside 92521	Idaho	Moscow 83843
Colorado	Fort Collins 80523	Illinois	Urbana 61801
Connecticut		Indiana	West Lafayette 47907
State Station	New Haven 06504	Iowa	Ames 50011
Ag. College and		Kansas	Manhattan 66506
Storrs Station	Storrs 06268	Kentucky	Lexington 40506

(Continued)

Table A.2 (Continued)

State	Address	State	Address
Louisiana	Baton Rouge 70893	Ohio	
Maine	Orono 04469	University Station	Columbus 43201
Maryland	College Park 20742	Ag. Research Station	Wooster 44691
Massachusetts	Amherst 01002	Oklahoma	Stillwater 74075
Michigan	East Lansing 48824	Oregon	Corvallis 97331
Minnesota	St. Paul 55108	Pennsylvania	University Park 16802
Mississippi	Mississippi State 39762	Rhode Island	Kingston 02881
Missouri	Columbia 65211	South Carolina	Clemson 29631
Montana	Bozeman 59715	South Dakota	Brookings 57007
Nebraska	Lincoln 68503	Tennessee	Knoxville 37901
Nevada	Reno 89507	Texas	College Station 77843
New Hampshire	Durham 03824	Utah	Logan 84322
New Jersey	New Brunswick 08903	Vermont	Burlington 05405
New Mexico	Las Cruces 88003	Virginia	
New York		Main Station	Blacksburg 24061
State Station	Geneva 14456	Truck Station	Virginia Beach 23455
Cornell Station	Ithaca 14853	Washington	Pullman 99164
North Carolina	Raleigh 27650	West Virginia	Morgantown 26506
North Dakota	Fargo 58103	Wisconsin	Madison 53706
		Wyoming	Laramie 82071

VEGETABLE COMPOSITION

Fresh vegetables are important in human nutrition. When handled properly, they are major contributors of vitamins A and C. Some are good sources of minerals and other vitamins.

As a group, vegetables tend to be low in calories and sodium and high in dietary fiber and potassium (Tables A.3 and A.4). The dark green, leafy vegetables tend to be high in vitamin B_6 and are excellent sources of ascorbic acid (vitamin C) and vitamin A (Table A.5). Carrots and sweet potatoes are particularly high in vitamin A content. Green peppers and most of the cruciferous crops contain the highest levels of ascorbic acid. Kidney beans, lima beans, peas, and sweet corn are good sources of both thiamin and niacin.

Several factors, such as natural variation, postharvest handling and storage, and method of preparation, can affect the composition and nutritive value of vegetables. Leafy vegetables, such as spinach, are especially susceptible to the loss of ascorbic acid (vitamin C) associated with wilting during postharvest handling and marketing. In addition, the ascorbic acid content in vegetables such as cabbage and lettuce is relatively unstable and can undergo oxidation during preparation to other forms that have considerably less vitamin activity. In some types of processing, sodium compounds may be added to vegetables as flavor enhancers.

The optimum postharvest conditions for prolonged storage life are not necessarily the best to maintain the nutritive value. In general, maximum nutrient content in vegetables is retained when vegetables are stored at near freezing temperatures and high humidity.

Table A.3. Proximate Composition in the Edible Portion of Vegetables[1]

Raw Vegetable	Water (%)	Calories (kcal)	Protein (g)	Fat (g)	Carbohydrates (g)	Fiber (g)	Ash (g)
			(100 g of edible portion)				
Roots and tubers							
Beets	87	44	1.5	0.1	10.0	0.8	1.1
Carrots	88	43	1.0	0.2	10.1	1.0	0.9
Parsnips	80	75	1.2	0.3	18.0	2.0	1.0
Potatoes							
flesh	79	79	2.1	0.1	18.0	0.4	0.9
skin	83	58	2.6	0.1	12.4	1.8	1.6
Radishes	95	17	0.6	0.6	3.6	0.5	0.5
Rutabagas	90	36	1.2	0.2	8.1	1.1	0.8
Sweet potatoes	72	105	1.7	0.3	24.3	0.9	1.0
Turnips	92	27	0.9	0.1	6.2	0.9	0.7
Leaf and stem vegetables							
Asparagus	92	22	3.1	0.2	3.7	0.8	0.8
Beet greens	92	19	1.8	0.1	4.0	1.3	2.0
Brussels sprouts	86	43	3.4	0.3	9.0	1.5	1.4
Cabbage	93	24	1.2	0.2	5.4	0.8	0.7
Celery	95	16	0.7	0.1	3.6	0.7	0.9
Chard	93	19	1.8	0.2	3.7	0.8	1.6
Chicory							
greens	92	23	1.7	0.3	4.7	0.8	1.3
witloof	95	15	1.0	0.1	3.2	0.8	0.6
Chinese cabbage							
pak-choi	95	55	1.5	0.2	2.2	0.6	0.8
pe-tsai	94	68	1.2	0.2	3.2	0.6	1.0
Chives	92	25	2.8	0.6	3.8	1.1	0.8
Collards	94	19	1.6	0.2	3.8	0.6	0.6
Endive	94	17	1.3	0.2	3.4	0.9	1.4
Kale	84	50	3.3	0.7	10.0	1.5	1.5
Kohlrabi	91	27	1.7	0.1	6.2	1.0	1.0
Lettuce							
butterhead	96	13	1.3	0.2	2.3	—	0.6
cos	95	16	1.6	0.2	2.4	0.7	0.9
iceberg	96	13	1.0	0.2	2.1	0.5	0.5
looseleaf	94	18	1.3	0.3	3.5	0.7	0.9

(Continued)

Table A.3 (Continued)

Raw Vegetable	Water (%)	Calories (kcal)	Protein (g)	Fat (g)	Carbo-hydrates (g)	Fiber (g)	Ash (g)
	(100 g of edible portion)						
Mustard greens	91	26	2.7	0.2	4.9	1.1	1.4
Onions	91	34	1.2	0.3	7.3	0.4	0.4
Parsley	99	33	2.2	0.3	6.9	1.2	2.3
Spinach	92	22	2.9	0.4	3.5	0.9	1.7
Turnip greens	91	27	1.5	0.3	5.7	0.8	1.4
Flower, fruit, and seed vegetables							
Artichokes	84	51	2.6	0.2	11.9	1.1	0.8
Beans							
lima, green	70	113	6.8	0.9	20.2	1.9	1.9
red kidney	91	29	4.2	0.5	4.1	—	0.5
snap green	90	31	1.8	0.1	7.1	1.1	0.7
Broccoli	91	28	3.0	0.4	5.2	1.1	0.7
Cauliflower	92	24	2.0	0.2	4.9	0.9	0.7
Cowpeas	67	127	9.0	0.8	21.8	1.8	1.6
Cucumbers	96	13	0.5	0.1	2.9	0.6	0.4
Eggplants	92	26	1.1	0.1	6.3	1.0	0.6
Mushrooms	92	25	2.1	0.4	4.7	0.8	0.9
Peas							
edible-podded	89	42	2.8	0.2	7.6	2.5	0.6
green	79	81	5.4	0.4	14.5	2.2	0.4
Peppers, green	93	25	0.9	0.5	5.3	1.2	0.6
Pumpkins	92	26	1.0	0.1	6.5	1.1	0.8
Soybeans, green	68	147	13.0	6.8	11.1	2.1	1.7
Squash, summer							
crookneck	94	19	0.9	0.2	4.0	0.6	0.6
zucchini	95	14	1.2	0.1	2.9	0.5	0.5
Squash, winter	89	37	1.5	0.2	8.8	1.4	0.8
Sweet corn	76	86	3.2	1.2	19.0	0.7	0.6
Tomatoes, ripe	94	19	0.9	0.2	4.3	0.5	0.6

[1]Source: USDA. 1984. *Composition of Foods: Vegetables and Vegetable Products.* Human Nutrition Information Service, Agriculture Handbook No. 8–11.

Table A.4. Mineral Content in the Edible Portion of Vegetables[1]

Raw Vegetable	Calcium (mg)	Phosphorus (mg)	Iron (mg)	Potassium (mg)	Sodium (mg)	Magnesium (mg)
	(100 g of edible portion)					
Roots and tubers						
Beets	16	48	0.9	324	72	21
Carrots	27	44	0.5	323	35	15

(Continued)

Table A.4 (Continued)

Raw Vegetable	Calcium (mg)	Phosphorus (mg)	Iron (mg)	Potassium (mg)	Sodium (mg)	Magnesium (mg)
			(100 g of edible portion)			
Parsnips	36	71	0.6	375	10	29
Potatoes						
flesh	7	46	0.8	543	6	21
skin	30	38	3.2	413	10	23
Radishes	21	18	0.3	191	67	11
Rutabagas	47	58	0.5	337	20	23
Sweet potatoes	22	28	0.6	204	13	10
Turnips	30	27	0.3	191	67	11
Leaf and stem vegetables						
Asparagus	22	52	0.7	302	2	18
Beet greens	119	40	3.3	547	201	72
Brussels sprouts	42	69	1.4	389	25	23
Cabbage	47	23	0.6	246	18	15
Celery	36	26	0.5	284	88	12
Chard	51	46	1.8	379	213	81
Chicory						
greens	100	47	0.9	420	45	30
witloof	18	21	0.5	182	7	13
Chinese cabbage						
pak-choi	105	37	0.8	252	65	19
pe-tsai	77	29	0.3	238	9	13
Chives	81	51	1.6	250	6	55
Collards	117	16	0.6	148	28	17
Endive	52	28	0.8	314	22	15
Kale	135	56	1.7	447	43	34
Kohlrabi	24	46	0.4	350	209	19
Lettuce						
butterhead	—	—	0.3	257	5	—
cos	36	45	1.1	290	8	6
crisphead	19	20	0.5	158	9	9
looseleaf	68	25	1.4	264	9	11
Mustard greens	103	43	1.5	354	25	32
Onions	25	29	0.4	155	2	10
Parsley	130	84	6.2	536	39	44
Spinach	99	49	2.7	558	79	79
Turnip greens	190	42	1.1	296	40	31
Flower, fruit, and seed vegetables						
Artichokes	48	77	1.6	339	80	47
Beans						
lima, green	34	136	3.1	467	8	58
red kidney	17	37	0.8	187	—	21
snap green	37	38	1.0	209	6	25
Broccoli	48	66	0.9	325	27	25

(Continued)

Table A.4 (Continued)

Raw Vegetable	Calcium (mg)	Phosphorus (mg)	Iron (mg)	Potassium (mg)	Sodium (mg)	Magnesium (mg)
			(100 g of edible portion)			
Cauliflower	29	46	0.6	355	15	14
Cowpeas	26	53	1.1	432	4	51
Cucumbers	14	17	0.3	149	2	11
Eggplants	36	33	0.6	219	4	11
Mushrooms	5	104	1.2	370	4	10
Peas						
edible-podded	43	53	2.1	200	4	24
green	25	108	1.5	244	5	33
Peppers, green	6	22	1.3	195	3	14
Pumpkins	21	44	0.8	340	1	12
Soybeans, green	197	194	3.6	—	—	—
Squash, summer						
crookneck	21	32	0.5	212	2	21
zucchini	15	32	0.4	248	3	22
Squash, winter	31	32	0.6	350	4	21
Sweet corn	2	89	0.5	270	15	37
Tomatoes, ripe	7	23	0.5	207	8	11

[1]Source: USDA. 1984. *Composition of Foods: Vegetables and Vegetable Products.* Human Nutrition Information Service, Agriculture Handbook No. 8–11.

Table A.5. Vitamin Content in the Edible Portion of Vegetables[1]

Raw Vegetable	A (IU)[2]	Thiamin (mg)	Riboflavin (mg)	Niacin (mg)	B6 (mg)	Ascorbic Acid (mg)
			(100 g of edible portion)			
Roots and tubers						
Beets	20	0.05	0.02	0.40	0.15	11
Carrots	28,129	0.10	0.06	0.93	0.15	9
Parsnips	0	0.09	0.05	0.70	0.09	17
Potatoes						
flesh	—	0.09	0.04	1.50	0.26	20
skin	—	0.02	0.04	1.00	0.09	9
Radishes	8	—	0.05	0.30	0.07	23
Rutabagas	0	0.09	0.04	0.70	0.10	25
Sweet potatoes	20,063	0.07	0.15	0.70	0.26	23
Turnips	0	0.04	0.03	0.40	0.09	21
Leaf and stem vegetables						
Asparagus	897	0.11	0.12	1.10	0.15	33
Beet greens	6,100	0.10	0.22	0.40	0.11	30
Brussels sprouts	883	0.14	0.09	0.75	0.22	85
Cabbage	126	0.05	0.03	0.30	0.10	47
Celery	127	0.03	0.03	0.30	0.03	6
Chard	3,300	0.04	0.09	0.40	—	30

(Continued)

Table A.5 (Continued)

Raw Vegetable	A (IU)	Thiamin (mg)	Riboflavin (mg)	Niacin (mg)	B$_6$ (mg)	Ascorbic Acid (mg)
			— (100 g of edible portion) —			
Chicory						
greens	4,000	0.06	0.10	0.50	—	24
witloof	0	0.07	0.14	0.50	—	10
Chinese cabbage						
pak-choi	3,000	0.04	0.07	0.50	—	45
pe-tsai	1,200	0.04	0.05	0.40	0.23	27
Chives	6,000	0.10	0.18	0.70	0.18	79
Collards	3,300	0.03	0.06	0.30	—	8
Endive	2,050	0.08	0.08	0.40	0.02	7
Kale	8,900	0.11	0.13	1.00	0.27	120
Kohlrabi	36	0.05	0.02	0.40	0.15	62
Lettuce						
butterhead	970	0.06	0.06	0.30	—	8
cos	2,600	0.10	0.10	0.50	—	24
crisphead	330	0.05	0.03	0.19	0.04	4
looseleaf	1,900	0.05	0.08	0.40	0.06	18
Mustard greens	5,300	0.08	0.11	0.80	—	70
Onions	0	0.06	0.01	0.10	0.16	8
Parsley	5,200	0.08	0.11	0.70	0.16	90
Spinach	6,715	0.08	0.19	0.72	0.20	28
Turnip greens	7,600	0.07	0.10	0.60	0.26	60
Flower, fruit, and seed vegetables						
Artichokes	185	0.08	0.06	0.76	0.11	11
Beans						
lima, green	303	0.22	0.10	1.50	0.25	23
red kidney	2	0.37	0.25	2.90	—	39
snap green	668	0.08	0.11	0.75	0.09	16
Broccoli	3,000	0.07	0.12	0.64	0.16	93
Cauliflower	16	0.08	0.06	0.63	0.23	72
Cucumbers	45	0.03	0.02	0.30	0.05	5
Eggplants	70	0.09	0.02	0.60	0.09	2
Mushrooms	0	0.10	0.45	4.10	0.10	4
Peas						
edible-podded	145	0.15	0.08	0.60	0.16	60
green	640	0.27	0.13	2.10	0.17	40
Peppers, green	530	0.09	0.05	0.60	0.16	128
Pumpkins	1,600	0.05	0.11	0.60	—	9
Soybeans, green	180	0.40	0.18	1.70	—	29
Squash, summer						
crookneck	338	0.05	0.04	0.50	0.11	8
zucchini	340	0.07	0.03	0.40	0.08	9
Squash, winter	4,060	0.10	0.03	0.80	0.08	12
Sweet corn	281	0.20	0.06	1.70	0.06	7
Tomatoes, ripe	1,133	0.06	0.05	0.60	0.05	18

[1]Source: USDA. 1984. *Composition of Foods: Vegetables and Vegetable Products.* Human Nutrition Information Service, Agriculture Handbook No. 8–11.

[2]International Units (IU); one IU of Vitamin A is equivalent to 0.3 microgram of Vitamin A alcohol.

SOURCES OF VEGETABLE SEEDS

Most growers buy their seed in preference to saving it or growing it themselves. Judicious buying of seed requires utmost care, and emphasis should be placed on the ultimate value of the crop rather than on the initial costs of the seed. Cheap seed, if poor, may cost many dollars in reduced yields and extra production practices. However, a high price does not necessarily mean good seed, and very often good seed may be had at moderate, though seldom at low, prices.

It is now common practice for vegetable growers to buy seed produced by commercial seed specialists who offer many different services including: 1) breeding, 2) growing, 3) seed enhancement, 4) wholesale dealing, 5) importing, and 6) distributing, serving commercial growers or home gardeners or both. Commercial seed houses may handle one kind of seed or all kinds of seed, and other merchandise as well. Seed companies must be recognized for quality of seed, dependability, and good service. There are enough good seed houses that grower need not take an undue risk in buying seed from unreliable sources.

Most vegetable seed in the U.S. is produced in the West, largely because of disease and poor curing (drying) conditions in the East. Most of the muskmelon and cucumber seed comes from Colorado and California, while a large part of the sweet corn, pea, and bean seed production is in Idaho and Oregon. Some vegetable seed may be imported from other countries, including Mexico, Japan, Canada, the Netherlands, Great Britain, and Israel. In general, the skill and care of seed producers are far more important for seed quality than is the place of production. Seed growers in the U.S. maintain high-quality seed production, and the seed industry in the U.S. is for the most part self-sufficient.

Table A.6. A Partial Listing of Sources of Vegetable Seeds

Abbott and Cobb, Inc. Feasterville, PA	Agri Seed & Co. Metamora, MI
Agrigenetics Corp. Eastlake, OH	Agway, Inc. Syracuse, NY
American Takii, Inc. Salinas, CA	Asgrow Seed Co. Kalamazoo, MI
Bakker Bros. Twin Falls, ID	George J. Ball, Inc. West Chicago, IL
Bodger Seeds, Ltd. El Monte, CA	Brinker-Orsetti Seed Co. Fresno, CA
W. Atlee Burpee Co. Philadelphia, PA	Canners Seed Corp. Lewisville, ID

(Continued)

Table A.6   (Continued)

Castle Vegtech, Inc. Morgan Hill, CA	Crookham Co. Caldwell, ID
Daehnfeldt, Inc. Albany, OR	DeRuiter Seeds, Inc. Columbus, OH
Ferry-Morse Seed Co. San Juan Bautista, CA	Genecorp, Inc. Salinas, CA
Goldsmith Seeds Gilroy, CA	H & H Seed Co., Inc. Yuma, AZ
Harris Moran Seed Co. Rochester, NY	Hazera Seed, Ltd. Haifa, Israel
Hollar & Co. Rocky Ford, CO	Illinois Foundation Seed, Inc. Champaign, IL
Johnny's Selected Seeds Albion, MA	Leighton Seed Co. Salinas, CA
J. Mollema & Sons, Inc. Grand Rapids, MI	Musser Seed Co. Twin Falls, ID
Neuman Seed Co. El Centro, CA	Nickerson-Zwaan Barendrecht, Netherlands
Northrup King Co. Minneapolis, MN	Park Seed Co. Greenwood, SC
Petoseed Co., Inc. Saticoy, CA	Plant Genetics, Inc. Davis, CA
Royal Sluis, Inc. Salinas, CA	Sakata Seed America, Inc. Morgan Hill, CA
Seed Dynamics, Inc. Salinas, CA	Seedway, Inc. Hall, NY
Sluis & Groot Denver, CO	Stokes Seed, Inc. Buffalo, NY
Sunseeds Hollister, CA	Twilley Seeds Co. Trevose, PA

CONVERSION OF U.S. MEASUREMENTS TO METRIC UNITS

The metric system originated in France in 1790 and spread throughout Europe, Latin America, and the Far East during the 19th century. With the exception of the U.S. and a few other countries, such as Liberia in West Africa, the metric system is the official language of measurements. Even in the U.S., the metric system is being used more and more, but for the majority of the commercial vegetable industry, measurements are still in U.S. units.

Simply defined, the metric system is a decimal system in which the gram (0.002205 pounds), the meter (39.37 inches), and the liter (61.025 cubic inches) are the basic units of mass (weight), length (distance), and volume, respectively. These basic units and their associated units are related to one another based on a scale of 1000 or multiples thereof:

1 millimeter (mm) = 1/1,000 meter (m); 1 centimeter (cm) = 1/100 m
1 kilometer (km) = 1,000 m
1 milligram (mg) = 1/1,000 gram (g); 1 kilogram (kg) = 1,000 g
1 megagram (Mg) = 1,000,000 g, or 1,000 kg
1 milliliter (mL) = 1/1,000 liter (L)

Conversion equivalents of U.S. units to metric measurements are shown in Table A.7. For example, 1 pound in U.S. units is equal to 454 grams in metric units. To convert 6 U.S. pounds to the metric equivalent, multiply 6 by 454, which is 2,724 g, or 2.7 kg. Conversely, to change 2.7 kg into pounds, multiply 2.7 by 2.205, which (after some rounding) is 6 pounds.

Table A.7. Conversion Equivalents of U.S. and Metric Units

Length

1 inch = 2.54 centimeters	1 centimeter = 0.394 inch
1 foot = 0.304 meter	1 meter = 3.28 feet
1 yard = 0.914 meter	1 meter = 1.094 yards
1 mile = 1.609 kilometers	1 kilometer = 0.621 mile

Area

1 inch^2 = 6.452 centimeters^2	1 centimeter^2 = 0.155 inch^2
1 foot^2 = 0.093 meter^2	1 meter^2 = 10.765 feet^2
1 acre = 0.405 hectare (ha)	1 hectare = 2.471 acres

Mass

1 pound = 454 grams	1 gram = 0.0022 pound
1 ounce = 28.4 grams	1 gram = 0.035 ounce
1 pound = 0.454 kilogram	1 kilogram = 2.205 pounds
1 ton = 907 kilograms	1 kilogram = 0.0011 ton
1 ton = 0.907 megagram	1 megagram = 1.1 tons

Volume

1 fl. ounce = 0.0296 milliliter	1 liter = 33.78 fl. ounces
1 pint = 0.473 liter	1 liter = 2.11 pints
1 gallon = 3.78 liters	1 liter = 0.264 gallon
1 bushel = 35.24 liters	1 liter = 0.0284 bushel
1 foot^3 = 28.3 liters	1 liter = 0.0353 foot^3
1 foot^3 = 0.0283 meter^3	1 meter^3 = 35.3 feet^3

Temperature

°F = ($9/5$°C) + 32	°C = ($5/9$°F) − 32

(Continued)

Table A.7 (Continued)

Yield and Rate

1 pound/acre = 1.12 kg/hectare

1 ton/acre = 2.24 Mg/hectare

1 gallon/acre = 9.35 L/hectare

1 kg/hectare = 0.893 pound/acre

1 Mg/hectare = 0.446 ton/acre

1 L/hectare = 0.107 gallon/acre

Water Measurement

1 acre-foot = 0.123 hectare-meter

1 acre-inch = 1.028 hectare-cm

1 hectare-meter = 8.1 acre-feet

1 hectare-cm = 0.973 acre-inch

GLOSSARY

Adventitious — referring to structures arising from other than normal location, for example, roots arising from aerial plant parts.

Aerobic — requiring oxygen, or occurring only in the presence of oxygen

Achene — a one-seeded, dry fruit that remains closed at maturity; common to lettuce.

Allelopathy — the excretion of a chemical by plant roots which is toxic to other plant species.

Alluvial — a stream-laid deposit.

Anaerobic — pertaining to bacteria or other organisms that flourish without free oxygen.

Andromonoecious — producing numerous male (staminate) flowers for each perfect flower.

Angiosperm — any plant of the class having the seed in a closed ovary.

Annual — a plant that completes its life cycle in one year and then dies.

Anther — the pollen-bearing part of a stamen.

Anthesis — the time or process of expansion in a flower.

Apical dominance — the inhibition or control of lateral buds or shoots by terminal buds or shoots.

Axil — the angle formed by a leaf or branch with the stem.

Axis — the central line of any organ or support of a group of organs; a stem, etc.

Biennial — a plant that lives for two years under normal, outdoor conditions, usually flowering and producing seed the second year.

Blanching — excluding light from plants or plant parts, resulting in loss of color.

Bolting — premature flowering and the emergence of a seed stalk.

Buffer — any material that prevents sudden changes in acidity.

Bulb — a subterranean leaf-bud with fleshy scales or coats.

Bulbil — a miniature bulb developed from buds in the axils of leaves, and capable of regenerating a new plant.

Calyx — the outer envelope of the flower.

Cankers — localized lesions on stems that generally result in the corrosion and sloughing away of tissues with the final production of an open wound, exposing or penetrating the wood.

Capsaicin — the alkaloid responsible for the pungency in peppers.

Carbamates — substituted organic nitrogen derivatives of carbamic acid, which may contain sulfur, used as insecticides, fungicides, and herbicides.

Carbohydrate — any of certain compounds composed of carbon, hydrogen, and oxygen.

Carotene — yellow pigment, precursor of vitamin A.

Cellulose — a complex carbohydrate that is resistant to breakdown, constitutes the fundamental structural material of plant cells.

Chlorinated-organic insecticides — also referred to as chlorinated hydrocarbons or chlorinateds, basically the DDT or chlordane group of insecticides which contain chlorine, carbon, hydrogen, and sometimes oxygen.

Chlorophyll — the green coloring matter (pigment) of plants that is central to photosynthesis.

Chloroplast — a plastid containing chlorophyll, developed in cells exposed to light.

Chlorosis — lacking chlorophyll, giving the plants a blanched appearance.

Chromosomes — number of well-individualized units, in the nucleus, that transmit hereditary characteristics.

Cladophyll — a small flattened branch that resembles a leaf or bract; occurs on asparagus spears.

Clove — one of a group of small bulbs produced by the garlic plant.

Controlled environment agriculture (CEA) — the concept of modifying the natural environment for optimum plant growth.

Cork cambium — meristematic tissue of the cortex or phloem from which cork develops.

Corm — the enlarged fleshy base of a stem, bulblike but solid.

Corolla — the inner perianth of distinct or connate petals.

Cotyledon — a seed leaf or first leaf of any embryo.

Cultivar — a horticultural variety that originated under cultivation.

Curd — the creamy head of cauliflower.

Curing — a drying treatment to prepare vegetables for storage.

Cuticle — a continuous layer of structureless, waxy substance that covers the aerial parts of vascular plants except the growing points.

Cutin — a waxy substance that covers most of the aerial parts of vascular plants.

Cytoplasm — a more or less transparent, viscous fluid constituting all of the protoplasm except the nucleus.

Deoxyribonucleic acid (DNA) — the fundamental unit of inheritance in genes.

Determinate — having a growth pattern in which the vegetative parts grow within certain limits.

Dextrin — a shapeless, brownish-white carbohydrate substance.

Dicotyledonous — having two cotyledons.

Diffusion — the passage of molecules or ions in solution from one part of the solution to another, especially through a membrane.

Dihybrid — a cross which involves two character differences.

Dioecious — unisexual, with the male and female flowers on separate plants.

Dominant — a parental character which has the ability to express itself in the resulting hybrid offspring.

Emasculation — the removal of the stamens.

Embryo — an organism in the early stages of development, as before hatching from an egg, or sprouting from a seed.

Emulsifiable concentrate — a liquid formulation of pesticide which contains a surface mixing agent so that water may be added to form a suspension-like system.

Endodermis — sheath, composed of one or more layers of modified parenchymatous cells, that encloses certain fibrovascular bundles.

Endosperm — the stored food supply in a seed.

Enzymes — proteins that act as catalysts for chemical reactions.

Epicotyl — the upper part of the embryo axis above the cotyledons and below the first true leaves.

Epigeal — referring to seed germination in which the cotyledons rise above the soil, for example, beans.

Ethephon — a chemical that breaks down to release ethylene and that promotes ripening.

Family — a division of an order; usually a family comprises two or more genera, but one genus possessing sufficiently distinctive characters may form a family.

Flora — the aggregate of plants growing without cultivation in a country or district, or indigenous to a particular geological formation, as a desert flora.

Floret — a small flower, usually one of a dense cluster.

Fluid drilling — sowing of pregerminated seeds suspended in a protective gel.

Foliar — pertaining to, consisting of, or resembling leaves.

Formulation — the form or concentration of a pesticide usually as purchased.

Fungicide — any substance that kills fungi or destroys their germs.

Gene — that portion of the chromosome which serves to transmit a character from parents to progeny.

Genotype — the constitution of an organism with respect to factors of which it is made up; the sum of all genes.

Genus — a classification group of animals or plants embracing one or more species.

Grower cooperative — an association or group of growers who work together to market their produce.

Gynoecious — producing only female flowers.

Hardening — a preplanting treatment (withholding water, lowering temperature) designed to increase the adaptability of transplants to field conditions.

Herb — a plant with no persistent woody stem above the ground.

Herbicide — a phytotoxic chemical used for killing or inhibiting the growth of plants.

Hermaphroditic — being of both sexes.

Homologous — alike, similar, or same.

Hybrid — the offspring of plants or animals of two genetically diverse genotypes.

Hybridization — the practice of crossing between two genetically diverse genotypes.

Hydrocooling — the process of removing field heat by immersing the crop in cold water.

Hydroponics — the process of growing plants in aerated water containing all the essential nutrients; in a more generic sense, the process of growing plants in a soilless or inert medium in which the essential elements are supplied in a nutrient solution.

Hypogeal — referring to the type of seed germination in which the cotyledons remain below the ground, for example, peas.

Indehiscent — not opening; remaining persistently closed.

Indeterminate — having a growth pattern in which the vine grows continuously until the plant dies.

Inert ingredient — a substance, specifically in a pesticide formulation, which is not active.

Inflorescence — the general arrangement and disposition of flowers on an axis; flower cluster.

Inoculation — the process of improving soils by the introduction of special microorganisms.

Inorganic pesticide — a compound which does not contain carbon as a part of the molecule.

Insecticide — a substance used to destroy or to repel insects.

Internode — the portion of a stem between two nodes or joints.

Keel — the two anterior united petals of a butterflylike flower, such as a bean flower.

Lignin — a substance related to cellulose, which, with it, constitutes the essential part of a woody tissue.

LISA — the acronym for low-input sustainable agriculture; agricultural production based on low-input technology in ways that increase profits and reduce farmers' inputs and environmental hazards.

Longevity — the length or duration of life.

Macronutrient — an essential element required by plants in relatively large amounts (e.g., nitrogen, phosphorus, potassium, calcium, magnesium, sulfur).

Maleic hydrazide — a growth regulator commonly applied to crops to prevent sprouting in storage.

Market gardening — the intensive production of vegetables for local markets.

Marketing — the performance of services to move the produce from producer to consumer.

Micronutrient — an essential element required by plants in relatively small amounts (e.g., iron, copper, manganese, zinc, boron, molybdenum).

Miticide — any substance used to kill mites.

Molecule — a unit of matter, the smallest portion of an element or compound which retains identity in character with the substance in mass.

Monocotyledon — a plant having only one cotyledon or seed leaf.

Monoecious — having both sexes on the same plant.

Mosaic — a disease characterized by mottling of the plant due to spots of light green or yellow on dark green.

Muck soils — highly decomposed organic soils.

Mulch — any substance, such as straw, used to protect roots of plants from heat, cold, or drought, or to keep fruit clean.

Mutation — a hereditary change in the character of an organism.

Mycelium — the vegetative body of a fungus composed of threads.

Necrosis — a physiological disease that causes plant tissue to turn black and decay.

Nematocide — a material that kills nematodes.

Nematode — an eelworm (an unsegmented roundworm) not usually visible to the naked eye, inhabiting soil, water, and plants.

Nucleus — the more or less centrally situated organ of the cell containing the chromatin, known as the hereditary substance.

Olericulture — the science of vegetable production and culture.

Organic pesticide — a pesticidal compound containing carbon in addition to the other elements.

Osmoconditioning — a water treatment to stimulate seed metabolism, but stops short of radicle emergence; also called *priming*.

Osmosis — the passage of the solvent from one side of a membrane to another where the escaping tendency of the solvent on the two sides is unequal.

Ovary — an enlarged basal portion of the pistil containing ovules or seeds.

Ovicide — a chemical compound specifically toxic to the egg stage of arthropods; truly effective ovicides prevent the full development of embryos.

Panicle — a loose, irregular compound inflorescence with pedicellate flowers.

Parenchyma — the fundamental tissue, usually composed of thin-walled cells, making up the bulk of the substance of the leaves, the pulp of fruit, the pith of stems, etc.

Parthenocarpy — fruit set and development without sexual fertilization, resulting in seedless fruit.

Pectin — a neutral substance occurring in many vegetable tissues as part of the sap or cell wall.

Peduncle — a flowerstalk.

Perennial — a plant that lives year after year.

Perianth — the floral envelope, consisting of the calyx and corolla (when present).

Pericarp — in corn kernels, the protective surface layer consisting mainly of the ovary wall.

Pericycle — a thin cylinder of tissue sheathing the vascular tissues.

Periderm — the cortical tissue derived from the phellogen (cork cambium).

Pesticide — a material that kills pests such as insects, fungi, nematodes, weeds, rodents, etc.

Petiole — the stalk or stem of a leaf.

Phenotype — the external appearance of an organism.

Phloem — a part of the conducting tissue of plants, usually thought to be instrumental in the conduction of food and other materials.

Photosynthesis — the process in green plants of capturing radiant energy and transferring it to chemical energy in the form of sugars.

Phytochrome — a reversible photo-sensitive pigment that affects several photomorphogenic processes, including photoperiod response and seed germination in some species.

Pick-your-own — a method of direct marketing in which the customer harvests the produce.

Pigment — a molecule colored by the light it absorbs; for example chlorophyll in plants.

Pistil — the seed-bearing organ of a flower, consisting of the ovary, stigma, and style.

Pistillate — female flower having pistils but no stamens.

Pith — a roughly cylindrical body of undifferentiated tissue in the center of the axis, enclosed by the vascular tissues.

Plastid — a unit of protoplasm.

Plumule — the bud or growing point of the embryo.

Pollen — dustlike male bodies capable of fertilization of ovules.

Pollinate — to transfer the pollen from the stamens to the pistils.

Ppb — parts per billion.

Ppm — parts per million.

Precooling — the process of lowering the temperatures of harvested vegetables before they are stored or shipped.

Progeny — the descendents of a single plant or pair of plants.

Propagate — to cause to multiply.

Protein — any of several organic, nitrogenous compounds.

Protoplasm — the living substance within a cell.

Radicle — the part of the embryo axis that develops into the root.

Receptacle — the more or less expanded or produced portions of an axis which bears the organs of a flower or the collected flowers of a head.

Recessive — pertaining to a character which is subordinate to or masked by a contrasting character.

Residue — the part of a pesticide which remains after application.

Rhizosphere — the immediate zone around the roots of plants.

Ribonucleic acid (RNA) — nucleic acid found in the protoplasm controlling cellular chemical activities.

Root crown — the region in a plant where root and stem join, usually the location of dormant buds.

Rogue (noun) — an off-type or diseased plant.

Rogue (verb) — to remove off-type or diseased plants.

Sclerotium — a compact, waxy or horny mass of hyphal tissue found in certain higher fungi.

Seed — an embryonic plant with its surrounding integuments or coats.

Semi-determinate — having a growth pattern exhibiting both determinate and indeterminate characteristics.

Sepal — a leaf or division of the calyx.

Sheath — a tubular envelope, as in the lower part of the leaf in grasses.

Shoot — the main portion of the plant above ground, including stems, branches, and leaves.

Silique — a slender, pod-like fruit that splits open at maturity, common to the Cruciferae.

Slips — adventitious shoots used as vegetative propagating material.

Specialty crops — minor, mostly non-traditional crops, that are grown on a small scale for a very limited market.

Species — a classification group of plants or animals, subordinate to a genus, and having members that differ only slightly among themselves.

Sperm — a motile, ciliated male reproductive cell.

Spreader — a wetting agent that causes the spray to spread over the leaf surfaces.

Stamen — a pollen-bearing organ of a flower.

Staminate — a male flower having stamens but no pistils.

Sticker — a material added to a spray or dust to improve adherence to the plant surfaces.

Stigma — the part of the pistil which receives the pollen in pollination.

Stipule — an appendage at the base of the petiole of a leaf.

Stolon — a slender, above ground, prostrate stem.

Style — the extended portion of a pistil connecting stigma and ovary.

Suberin — a fatty or waxy substance characteristic of cork tissue.

Sucrose — a non-reducing sugar, formed by joining a glucose molecule and a fructose molecule; common forms are cane or beet sugar, with the empirical formula $C_{12}H_{22}O_{11}$.

Systemic insecticide — a substance which, when absorbed by plants, renders them toxic to insects feeding on them.

Tendril — a slender, clasping outgrowth, such as found on cucurbit or grape plants.

Thermodormancy — inhibition of seed germination by high temperatures.

Tipburn — a physiological disorder characterized by necrosis of outer leaf margins.

Tolerance — the amount of pesticide residue that is permitted by federal regulation to remain on or in a crop.

Toxicity — the capacity of a substance to produce injury; the measure of damage resulting from exposure to a substance.

Translocation — the movement of food or other materials from one part of a plant to another.

Transpiration — the movement of water from the inside of plants out into the atmosphere by evaporation.

Truck farming — the production of special vegetables in relatively large quantities for distant markets.

Tuber — a short, thickened underground stem having numerous buds or eyes.

Umbel — a flower cluster in which the flowerstalks spring from the same point, as in a wild carrot.

Unisexual — of one sex, either male or female; not hermaphroditic.

Vacuum cooling — cooling by evaporation of water from plants under reduced pressure.

Vernalization — the process by which exposure to low temperatures for an extended period is required by some plants for flower induction.

Viability — ability to remain alive.

Virus — small pathogenic particles consisting of a protein sheath and RNA that infect plants.

Vitamins — organic natural substances other than fats, proteins, and carbohydrates, which are required in small amounts for normal metabolism of plants.

Volatile — capable of rapid evaporation in air at ordinary temperatures.

Weed — a plant growing where it is not desired.

Wettable powder — a powder form of an insoluble material so treated that it will readily become suspended in water.

Wetting agent — a compound added to a spray solution which causes it to contact plant surfaces more thoroughly.

Whorl — a group of organs arranged about a stem, arising from the same node.

Xylem — a part of the vascular bundle or conducting tissue used for upward translocation of water and other materials.

Zero tolerance — no amount of the pesticide chemical may remain on the raw agricultural commodity when it is offered for shipment.

INDEX

Abelmoschus esculentus, okra, 33, 549

Abscissic acid, growth inhibitor, 45

Abscission layer, melon harvesting, 375, 376

Acephate, insecticide, 160

Achene, defined, 601

Adult bean weevil, 245

Adventitious, defined, 601

Aerobic, defined, 601

Agrobacterium tumefaciens, 199

Alleles, defined, 57

Allelopathy, 122, 204, 601

All-female, hybrid cucumbers, 325

Allium Ampeloprasum, leek, 31, 400

Allium Cepa, multiplier onion, 31, 398

Allium Cepa, onion, 31, 381

Allium Cepa, shallots, 31, 403

Allium fistulosum, bunching onions, 31, 392

Allium sativum, garlic, 31, 398

Allium Schoenoprasum, chives, 31, 402

Allium spp., onion genus, 31, 381

Alluvial, defined, 601

Allyl-propyl-disulfide, onion pungency, 385

Alternaria leaf blight, cucumbers, 337

Alternaria leaf spot, melons, 375

Alternaria, radishes, 303

Amaryllidaceae, 31
  onion family, 381

Ambush®, insecticide, 160

Anaerobic, defined, 601

Andromonoecious plants, defined, 58, 365, 601

Angiosperm, defined, 601

Angular leaf spot, cucumbers, 336

Animal manure, 100

Annual crops, 36, 601

Annual weeds, 121

Anther, illustrated, 58, 601

Anthesis, defined, 601

Anthocyanin, endive red pigment, 357

Anthracnose
  beans, 246
  cucumbers, 336
  melons, 374
  peppers, 430
  tomatoes, 530

Antibiotic fungicides, 165

Aphids
  asparagus, 221
  cabbage, 264
  lettuce, 352
  melons, 373
  peas, 416
  peppers, 429
  potatoes, 451
  radishes, 303
  spinach, 467

Apical dominance, potatoes, 441, 601

Apium graveolens var. *rapaceum,* celeriac, 33, 551

Armyworms, lettuce, 352

Asana®, insecticide, 160

Ascochyta blight, peas, 417

Asparagus, 209–225
  carbohydrate balance, 213
  classification, 209
  climatic requirements, 214
  crown, development, 211
  crown, illustrated, 212
  crown, planting, 216–217
  cultivars, 219–220
  cultural practices, 217–219
  cultural requirements, 213–214
  direct seeding, 217
  diseases, 222
  fern development, 213
  flowers and fruits, 213
  growth/development, 211–213
  harvesting, 222–223
  history, 209–210
  hybrids, all-male, 219–220
  hybrids, dioecious, 219–220
  insects, 220–222
  irrigation, 218
  origin, 209
  planting/crop establishment, 214–217
  postharvest handling, 223–225
  production/industry, 210–211
  spear development, 211–212
  spear quality, 224
  transplants, 217
  weeds, 218–219

Asparagus beans, 250
Asparagus officinalis, asparagus, 31, 209
Aster yellows
    carrots, 286
    celery, 319
    lettuce, 353
Asteraceae, sunflower family, 31
Atmospheric composition
    modified atmospheres, 193
    role in postharvest
        deterioration, 176
Augmented corns, sweet corn, 489
Auxins, growth hormones, 44
Available water, defined, 44
Axil, defined, 601
Axis, defined, 601

Bacillus thuringiensis, 204, 264
    caterpillar control, 157, 160, 162, 352
Back-crossing, plant breeding
    described, 63
Bacterial blight
    beans, 246
    carrots, 287
    peas, 417
Bacterial canker, tomatoes, 530
Bacterial soft rot, lettuce, 355
Bacterial speck, tomatoes, 530
Bacterial spot
    peppers, 430
    tomatoes, 529
Bacterial wilt
    cucumbers, 336
    melons, 373
    sweet corn, 491
    tomatoes, 529
Bars, plant water uptake
    measurement, 43
Base temperature, heat units, 42
Beans, 233–253
    asparagus beans (yard-long beans), 250
    black-eyed peas, 250
    broad beans (fava beans), 252
    catjang beans, 251
    chickpeas (garbanzo beans), 252
    cowpeas (southern peas), 250
    fava beans (broad beans), 252
    garbanzo beans (chickpeas), 252

garden soybeans, 251–252
lima beans, 234–249
mung beans, 252
snap beans, 234–249
southern peas (cowpeas), 250
Beet armyworm, 352
Beets, 288–294
    Cicla group, 289
    classification, 288
    climatic requirements, 290
    Crassa group, 288
    cultivars, 292
    cultural practices, 291–292
    cultural requirements, 291
    diseases, 293
    harvesting, 293–294
    history, 289
    insects, 293
    origin, 289
    physiological disorders, 293
    planting/crop establishment, 291
    postharvest handling, 294
    production/industry, 289
    root cross-section, illustrated, 290
    zoning, 289–290
Bell pepper, 421–433
Benlate®, fungicide, 164
Beta vulgaris (Cicla group), chard, 31, 289, 472
Beta vulgaris (Crassa group), beets, 31, 288
Bibb lettuce, 351
Bicarbonate, effects on water quality, 143
Biennial
    defined, 601
    crops, 36
    weeds, 121
Big vein virus, lettuce, 353
Biological yield, defined, 39
Biomass, defined, 39
Biotechnology and genetic engineering, 197–207
    biological applications, 203
    future challenges, 205
    glossary of terms, 206–207
    in future crop improvement, 202–205
    micro-injection, 202
    plant regeneration, 203
    plasmid, vector, 199–200, 207
    specialized crop production, 203

techniques, 198–202
    uses in plant breeding, 204–205
Black-eyed peas, 250
Black heart, celery, 319–320
Black leg
    cabbage, 265
    potato, 452
Black rot
    cabbage, 264
    melons, 374
    sweet potatoes, 506
Black spot
    beets, 293
    potatoes, 453
Blanching
    asparagus, 211
    celery, 315–316
    defined, 601
    leek, 401
Blossom-end rot
    peppers, 431
    tomatoes, 531
Blossom parts, illustrated, 58
Blotchy ripening, tomatoes, 532
Bolting (premature flowering)
    beets, 291
    cabbage, 258
    carrots, 282
    celery, 310
    defined, 49, 601
    kohlrabi, 276
    lettuce, 354
    onions, 385
    rutabagas, 305
    spinach, 463, 466
    turnips, 305
Boron
    effects on water quality, 143
    vegetable response, 108
Botran®, fungicide, 164
Bottom rot, lettuce, 352
Brassica Napus (Napobrassica group), rutabagas, 31, 304
Brassica oleracea (Acephala group), collards/kale, 32, 470, 471
Brassica oleracea (Botrytis group), cauliflower, 32, 268
Brassica oleracea (Capitata group), cabbage, 32, 256
Brassica oleracea (Gemmifera group), Brussels sprouts, 32, 274
Brassica oleracea (Gongylodes group), kohlrabi, 32, 276

Brassica oleracea (Italica group), broccoli, 32, 268
Brassica Rapa (Chinensis group), pak-choi, 32, 277
Brassica Rapa (Pekinensis group), pe-tsai, 32, 277
Brassica Rapa (Rapifera group), turnips, 31, 304
Brassica spp., 473
Brassicaceae, mustard family, 31–32
Bravo®, fungicide, 164
Breeder's seed, 70
Breeding, vegetables, 55–68
  chromosome numbers, chart, 60
  flower structure, chart, 60
  improvement, hybridization/ selection, 61–63
  life cycles, chart, 60
  methods, 63–67
  pollination requirements, chart, 60
  propagation method, chart, 60
Brittle root disease, horseradish, 298
Broad beans (fava beans), 252
Broccoli, 267–274
  boron deficiency, 273
  classification, 268
  climatic requirements, 270–271
  cultivars, 272
  cultural requirements, 271
  diseases, 273
  growth/development, 269–270
  harvesting, 273–274
  head, illustrated, 270
  history, 268
  hollow stem, 273
  insects, 273
  origin, 268
  physiological disorders, 273
  planting/crop establishment, 271–272
  postharvest handling, 274
  production/industry, 268–269
  whiptail, 273
Brother-sister mating, cross-pollination, 66
Brown stain, lettuce shipping disease, 356
Brussels sprouts, 274–276
  buds (sprouts), illustrated, 275
  classification, 32, 274

  climatic requirements, 275
  diseases, 275
  growth/development, 274–275
  harvesting, 275–276
  history, 274
  insects, 275
  physiological disorders, 275
  postharvest handling, 276
  SADH (succinic acid-2, 2-dimethylhydrazide), 276
Buffer, defined, 602
Bulb, defined, 602
Bulbil, defined, 602
Bunching onions, 391
Burbank, Luther, potato breeder, 449
Butterhead lettuce, 341–356

Cabbage, 256–267
  Alpha types, 262
  bolting, 258
  classification, 256
  climatic requirements, 258
  Copenhagen Market types, 262–263
  cultivars, types, classes, 262–263
  cultural practices, 261–262
  cultural requirements, 258–259
  Danish Ballhead types, 262–263
  direct seeding, 261
  diseases, 264–265
  domestic types, 262
  Flat Dutch types, 262
  growth/development, 257–258
  harvesting, 266–267
  head development, illustrated, 257
  history, 256
  insects, 264
  internal tipburn, 265–266
  irrigation, 261–262
  looper, 352
  origin, 256
  physiological disorders, 265–266
  planting/crop establishment, 259–261
  pointed types, 262
  postharvest handling, 267
  premature seeding, 258
  production/industry, 256–257

  Red types, 262
  reproductive development, 258
  Savoy types, 262
  transplants, 259
  types, characterized, 262
  types, illustrated, 263
  vegetative development, 257–258
  Volga types, 262
  Wakefield types, 262–263
  weeds, 261
Calcium
  deficiency and disorder, 107
  plant functions, 106
Calyx, defined, 602
Cankers, defined, 602
Cantaloupes, 361
Cantalupensis group, melons, 362
Capsaicin, pepper alkaloid, 424, 602
Capsicum annuum, domestic peppers, 33, 421
Capsicum frutescens, tabasco peppers, 33, 421
Carbamates, 155, 160, 602
Carbaryl, 156, 160
Carbofuran, 160
Carbohydrate, defined, 602
Carbohydrate storage, reproductive phase, 48
Carbohydrate utilization, vegetative phase, 47
Carotene, defined, 602
Carrots, 279–288
  Chantenay types, 285–286
  classification, 279
  climatic requirements, 282
  cultivars, 285–286
  cultural practices, 284–285
  cultural requirements, 282–283
  Danvers types, 285–286
  diseases, 286–287
  growth/development, 281–282
  harvesting, 287
  history, 280
  insects, 286
  Imperator types, 285–286
  irrigation, 284–285
  Nantes types, 285–286
  origin, 280
  planting/crop establishment, 283–284
  postharvest handling, 287–288

production/industry,
280–281
quality, root, 282
root, anatomy, illustrated,
281
weeds, 284
Casaba melons, 361, 372
Catfacing, tomatoes, 531
Catjang beans, 252
Cauliflower, 267–274
boron deficiency, 273
buttons, 270
classification, 32, 268
climatic requirements,
270–271
cultivars, 273
cultural requirements, 271
curd, illustrated, 271
diseases, 273
growth/development,
269–270
harvesting, 273–274
history, 268
hollow stem, 273
insects, 273
origin, 268
physiological disorders, 273
planting/crop establishment,
271–272
postharvest handling, 274
production/industry,
268–269
self-blanching, 272
whiptail, 273
Cavity spot, carrots, 287
Cayenne peppers, 423
Celeriac, 551–552
Cell
components, 56
division, described, 56
reduction division,
described, 57
Cellulose, defined, 602
Center-pivot irrigation, 139
Celtuce lettuce, 342
Cercospora leaf blight, cucumbers,
337
Cercospora leaf spot, beets, 29
Certified applicators, pesticide,
155, 168
Certified seed, 70
potatoes, 446
Chard, 472–473
Chemical
controls, insects, 156
energy, defined, 40
mutation, plant breeding, 61

Chenopodiaceae, goosefoot
family, 31, 288
Chickpeas (garbanzo beans), 252
Chicon, chicory production, 358
Chicory, 341, 358–360
Chile peppers, 423
Chinese cabbage, 277–278
Chitting, 73
Chives, 402
Chlorflurenol, fruit-setting
hormone, 327
Chloride, effects on water quality,
143
Chlorinated-organic insecticides,
defined, 602
Chlorophyll, defined, 602
Chloropicrin, fumigant disease
control, 162
Chloroplast, defined, 602
Chlorosis
celery, 319
defined, 602
Chlorpyrifos, insecticide, 160
Chromosome number
defined, 56
vegetable chart, 60
Chromosomes, role in plant
breeding, 56, 602
Cicer arietinum, garbanzo beans,
32, 252
Cichorium Endivia, endive-
escarole, 31, 356
Cichorium Intybus, chicory, 31, 358
CIPC, potato sprout inhibition, 456
Citrullus lanatus, watermelons, 32,
363
Cladophyll, defined, 602
Classification
by botanical family, 29–33
by edible plant part, 33–34,
172–173
by life cycle, 36–37
by temperature and
hardiness, 34–36
Clove, defined, 602
Club root
cabbage, 265
radishes, 303
Colchicine, in mutation induction,
61
Cole crops, 255–278
cabbage, 256–267
broccoli/cauliflower,
267–274
Brussels sprouts, 274–276
Chinese cabbage, 277–278
kohlrabi, 276–277

Coleoptile, corn, 481
Collards, 470–471
Colorado potato beetle, potatoes,
450
Common asparagus beetle,
220–221
Common blight, beans, 246
Compatibility, pesticides, 167
Compositae, sunflower family, 31
Conservation tillage, 101
Control recommendations,
sources, 169
Controlled environment
agriculture (CEA), defined, 602
Controlled environment
production, 12, 555–573
aeroponics, 565–566
bag culture, 564–565
carbon dioxide (CO_2)
enrichment, 562–563
concept, described, 555
cucumber, culture, 569
deep flow technique (DFT),
566
diseases, 571
economic considerations,
572–573
growing systems, 563–566
gynoecious cucumbers, 558
history, 556–557
hydroponics, defined, 563
industry, overview, 557–558
insects, 570–571
lettuce culture, 569–570
nutrient film technique
(NFT), 566
nutrient solution
management, 566–567
principal crops, 558–560
radiation, supplemental
lighting, 561–562
relative humidity control,
563
solution culture, 565–566
substrate culture, 564–565
temperature control,
560–561
temperatures, optimum for
crops, 560
tomato culture, 567–569
Convolvulaceae, morning-glory
family, 31, 495
Cool-season crops, 35
Copper, vegetable response, 108
Cork cambium, defined, 602
Corm, defined, 602

Corn
  dent, *Zea Mays* var.
    indentata, 31, 477
  earworm, sweet corn, 490
  flint, *Zea Mays* var. *indurata*,
    31, 477
  flour or soft, *Zea Mays* var.
    amylacea, 477
  hybrid process described, 62
  leaf rust, sweet corn, 492
  popcorn, *Zea Mays* var.
    everta, 31, 477
  rootworm, sweet corn, 491
  smut, sweet corn, 491
Corolla, defined, 602
Cos lettuce, 341, 351
Cosmetic quality, vegetable, 163
Cotyledon, defined, 602
Counter®, insecticide, 160
Cover crops, 99
Cowpeas, 250
Cracked stem, celery, 319
Crisphead lettuce, 341
Critical period, pest life cycle, 166
Crop rotation
  use in insect and disease
    control, 153
  use in weed control, 126
  with green manures, 99–100
Cross-pollinated vegetables, 65
Cross-pollination, described, 59
Crowns, asparagus, 216
  globe artichoke, 230
  rhubarb, 226
Cruciferae, mustard family, 31–32,
  255
Cryolite, insecticide, 155
Cucumber beetle
  attractant, cucurbitacin, 372
  control, 334, 372
Cucumber mosaic
  melons, 375
  peppers, 429
Cucumbers, 323–339
  classification, 323
  climatic requirements, 327
  cultivars, 332
  cultural practices, 330
  cultural requirements, 327
  diseases, 336–337
  flower illustrated, 326
  flowering and sex
    expression, 325
  fresh market cultivars, 335
  fruit development, 327
  fruit types, 333
  grading standards, 338

growth/development,
  325–327
gynoecious varieties, 325
harvesting, 337
hybrids, 325
insects, 334–335
monoecious varieties, 325
origin, 323
parthenocarpic fruit, 327
planting/crop establishment,
  328–330
production/industry, 324–325
scheduled planting, 330
seedless, 327
vine types, 325
weeds, 330
yellowing, heat-related, 333
Cucumis Melo (Inodorus group),
  honeydew melons, 32, 361
Cucumis Melo (Reticulatus group),
  muskmelons, 32, 361
Cucumis sativus, cucumbers, 32,
  323
Cucurbita maxima, pumpkins,
  squashes, gourds, 32, 542
Cucurbita mixta, pumpkins,
  squashes, 32, 542
Cucurbita moschata, pumpkins,
  squashes, 32, 542
Cucurbita Pepo, pumpkins,
  squashes, gourds, 32, 542
Cucurbita Pepo var. *Melopepo*,
  bush squash, 32, 544
Cucurbita spp.,
  pumpkins/squashes, 32, 542
Cucurbitaceae, gourd family, 32
Cucurbitacin, cucumber beetle
  attractant, 372
Cucurbits, honeybee pollination,
  331
Cultivar, defined, 602
Cultivar evaluation, published
  results, 67
Cultivars, how to select, 67
Cultivating
  effects on soil moisture and
    temperature, 124–126
  implements and tools, 126
  use for weed control,
    123–124
Cumulated heat units, 42
Curd, defined, 602
Curing
  defined, 602
  onions, 395–396
  potatoes, 455–456
  sweet potatoes, 509–510

Cuticle, defined, 603
Cutin, defined, 603
Cygon®, insecticide, 160
Cynara Scolymus, globe
  artichokes, 31, 228
Cytokinins, growth hormones, 44
Cytoplasm, defined, 603

Dacus Carota var. *sativus*, carrots,
  33, 279
Damping-off
  beets, 293
  cucumbers, 337
  peas, 411
  peppers, 430
  spinach, 467
Dandelions, 475–476
Daughter cell, defined, 56
Day neutral (photoperiod),
  defined, 50
Daylength (*see also* Photoperiod)
  effects on growth, 50–53
  flower-seedstalk spinach, 462
  onion bulbing, 385, 391
  potato development, 442
  sweet corn development,
    482
Degree days, heat units, 42
Deoxyribonucleic acid (DNA),
  defined, 603
Desiccants, potato vine killing, 454
Determinate, defined, 603
Determinate growth
  beans, 237
  cucumbers, 325
  peas, 407
  peppers, 425
  tomatoes, 516–517
Dextrin, defined, 603
Diazinon, insecticide, 159
Dibrom®, insecticide, 160
Dichlorophenoxyacetic acid (*see*
  2,4-D)
Dicotyledoneae, 31
Dicotyledonous, defined, 603
Dicotyledons, 30–33
Diffusion, defined, 603
Dihybrid, defined, 603
Dimethoate, insecticide, 160
Dioecious, defined, 603
Dioecious plants, defined, 58
Dioscoreaceae, yam family, 31
Diploid plants, defined, 61
Direct seeding, 87–94
  asparagus, 217
  beans, 240
  beets, 291

cabbage, 261
carrots, 283–284
celery, 314
cucumbers, 328
lettuce, 346
melons, 369
onions, 387
parsnips, 300
peas, 410–411
peppers, 427
radishes, 303
spinach, 464
sweet corn, 483–484
tomatoes, 520–521
Disease control, general
vegetable, 151–170
Disease identification, procedure,
169
Disease resistance, melons, 371
DNA (deoxyribonucleic acid),
defined, 56
Dominant, defined, 603
Dominant gene, defined, 57
Dormancy, growth inhibition, 44
Downy mildew
beans, 247
cucumbers, 337
lettuce, 353
melons, 374
onions, 393
radishes, 303
spinach, 468
Drift, pesticides, 168
Drill seeding, 89
Drip irrigation, 141
Dyfonate®, insecticide, 160
Dylox®, insecticide, 160
Dyrene®, fungicide, 164

Early blight
celery, 318
potatoes, 451–452
tomatoes, 529
Early-maturing cultivars, flowering
response, 49, 50
Earworms, sweet corn, 490
Economic yield, defined, 39
Eelworms (nematodes), control,
165
Eggplants, 537–541
classification, 33, 537
climatic requirements, 538
cultivars, 540
diseases, 540
fertility, 538
growth/development, 538
harvesting, 540

insects, 540
origin, 537
postharvest handling,
540–541
production/industry, 538
soils, 538
transplanting, 539
Emasculation, defined, 603
Embryo, defined, 603
Emulsifiable concentrate
defined, 603
pesticides, 160
Endive-escarole, 341, 356–358
Endodermis, defined, 603
Endosperm, defined, 603
Enzymes, defined, 56, 603
EPA, pesticide tolerance setting,
152
Epicotyl, defined, 603
Epigeal, defined, 603
Esfenvalerate, insecticide, 160
Ethephon
cucumber sex expression,
326
defined, 603
melon ripening, 379
pepper ripening, 432
tomato ripening, 534
Ethion, insecticide, 160
Ethylene
growth inhibitor, 45
melon ripening, 379
role in postharvest
deterioration, 174,
176–177
Euphorbiaceae, spurge family, 32
European corn borer, sweet corn,
490–491
Evapotranspiration, 134

Family, defined, 603
Fava beans (broad beans), 252
FDA, pesticide tolerance
enforcement, 152
Female flowers
defined, 58
pistillate, 365
Fertilization/pollination, described,
58–59
Fertilizer(s), 111
analysis, formula, ratio, 110
banding, 113
broadcasting, 111
composition, 111, 112
fertigation, 114
foliar application, 114
inorganic, 112

methods of application,
111–114
nitrogen sources, 112
organic, 112
phosphorus requirements,
116
phosphorus sources, 112
potassium requirements, 112
potassium sources, 112
sidedressing, 113
starter solution, 87, 113
Fertility
determining fertilizer rates,
117
soil testing, 114–115
Field capacity, 76, 135
(soil water), defined, 43
Flea beetles
horseradish, 298
potatoes, 450
radishes, 303
Floating row covers, 147
Flood irrigation, 138
Flora, defined, 603
Florence fennel, 552
Floret, defined, 603
Flowable concentrates, pesticides,
160
Flower abortion, peppers, 426
Flowering induction
low temperature, 49
photoperiod, 50
Flowers
parts illustrated, 58
pollination process, 58
Fluid drilling, 93, 603
pregerminated lettuce seed,
347
Foeniculum vulgare var. azoricum,
florence fennel, 552
Foliar, defined, 603
Fonofos, insecticide, 160
Food and environmental safety,
26–27
Forcing
chicory, 360
rhubarb, 228
Formulation, defined, 604
Foundation seed, 70
Fresh market outlets
direct to consumers, 16–17
direct to retailers, 17
direct to wholesalers, 17
Fresh market, production
principal crops, 4
statistics, 3, 5, 6
Frost dates, 90, 91

Fruit vegetables, listed, 172, 173
Fruitworms, tomatoes, 528
Fungicides
    defined, 162, 604
    registered for vegetables,
        164
Furadan®, insecticide, 160
Furrow irrigation, 138
Fusarium root rot
    asparagus, 222
    beans, 247
    radishes, 303
Fusarium stem and crown rot,
    asparagus, 222
Fusarium wilt
    asparagus, 222
    melons, 374
    peas, 417
    spinach, 468
    sweet potatoes, 507
    tomatoes, 528
Fusarium yellows, celery, 319

Garbanzo beans (chickpeas), 252
Garden lettuce, described, 342
Garden soybeans, 251–252
Garlic, 398–400
    climate requirements, 399
    cloves, 398
    cultivars, 400
    growth/development, 398
    planting/harvesting, 399–400
Genes, defined, 56, 604
Genetic variation, 61
Genotype, defined, 63, 604
Genus, defined, 604
Gibberellic acid, cucumber sex
    expression, 326
Gibberellins, growth hormones, 44
Globe artichokes, 228–231
    bracts, buds, illustrated, 230
    classification, 31, 228
    climatic requirements, 229
    cultural requirements,
        229–230
    harvesting, 230
    origin, 228
    plant description, 228
    planting, 229
    propagation, 229
Glucose, in photosynthesis, 40
Glycine Max, 32, 251
Gourds, classification, 542
Gramineae, grass family, 31, 477
'Granex,' hybrid onion, illustrated,
    62
Graywall, tomatoes, 532

Green manures, effect on soil
    organic matter, 99
Green onions, from sets, 388, 397
Green peas, 405–419
Green shoulder, tomatoes, 532
Greening, potatoes, 453
Greens, 459–476
Grower cooperatives, 18, 604
Growth factors, plant
    development, 40
Growth hormones, 44–45
Growth inhibitors, plant
    development, 44
Growth inputs, in vegetable
    quality, 45
Gummy stem blight, melons, 374
Gynoecious
    defined, 604
    flowering habit, all-female
        flowers, 326
    hybrid cucumbers, 334

Half-slip stage, melon harvesting,
    376
Halo blight, beans, 246
Hand-pollination, vegetable
    breeding, 65
Hardening, 83, 604
    transplants, 370
Hardy and half-hardy crops, 35
Harvest index, defined, 39
Harvest mechanization, 23–25
Harvesting, role in postharvest
    deterioration, 178–179
Heat units, degree days, 42
    cucumbers, 330
    peas, 411–412
    sweet corn, 484–485
Herb, defined, 604
Herbicide, defined, 604
Herbicide(s)
    application methods, 129
    classification, 128
    effectiveness, 130–132
    mode of action, 128
    peas' sensitivity, 409
    postemergent, 131
    preemergent (PRE), 130
    preplant-incorporated (PPI),
        130
    selective/nonselective, 128
Hermaphroditic, defined, 604
Hermaphroditic flowers, defined, 58
Heterosis, described, 62
Heterozygous plants, defined, 57
Hollow heart, potatoes, 453
Hollow stem, 273

Home gardening, 13, 575–587
    compost, 582
    crop selection, 577–578
    direct seeding, vegetable
        specifications, 580
    disease control, organic
        methods, 584–585
    fertility practices, 581–582
    herbs, usage, 585–586
    insect pest control, organic
        methods, 584–585
    intercropping, 576–577
    manure application, 582
    mulches, organic, 582–584
    organic fertilizers, 584
    organic gardening, 584–585
    planning, 575–579
    planting/crop establishment,
        579–581
    planting plan, illustrated, 576
    site selection, location, 578
    size, considerations, 579
    soil, characteristics, 578
    succession planting, 576
    transplanting, vegetable
        specifications, 580
    water supply, 578–579
    weed control, organic
        methods, 584
Homologous, defined, 604
Homozygous plants, selection,
    breeding, 57, 64
Honeybees
    insecticide kills, 332
    overhead irrigation effects,
        332
    required for cucurbit
        pollination, 331
    required in melon
        production, 367
Honeydew melons, 361–380
Hornworms, tomatoes, 528
Horseradish, 294–299
    classification, 294
    climatic requirements, 296
    cultivars, 298
    cultural requirements, 297
    diseases, 298
    growth/development,
        295–296
    harvesting, 298–299
    insects, 298
    lifting, 297
    origin, 294
    postharvest handling, 299
    production/industry,
        294–295

roots, marketable, illustrated, 295
sets, propagating, 296
Hot caps, 148–149
Humidity, pollination effects, 60
Hybrid
    corn, process described, 62
    cucumbers, 325
    cucumbers, gynoecious, 334
    cucumbers, honeybee requirements, 331
    cultivars, described, 62
    onion 'Granex,' illustrated, 62
    vegetables, chart listing, 63
    vigor, described, 62
Hybrid, defined, 604
Hybridization, defined, 61–63, 604
Hybrids, listing of vegetable crops, 72
Hydrocooling, 184–185, 604
    beans, 249
    broccoli, 274
    cauliflower, 274
    celery, 320
    cucumbers, 338
    melons, 378
    peas, 418
    spinach, 469
    sweet corn, 493–494
Hydrometer, measuring potato dry matter, 448
Hydroponics, defined, 604
Hypogeal, defined, 604

Iceberg lettuce, 350
Indehiscent, defined, 604
Indeterminate, defined, 604
Indeterminate growth
    beans, 237
    cucumbers, 325
    peas, 407
    tomatoes, 517
Industry, commercial vegetables, 1–28
    exports-imports, 9–11
    farm number and size, 22
    history, 2
    labor management, 25–26
    per capita usage, 7–9
    principal crops, 4
    principal production areas, 4–7
    types of operations, 11–13
    U.S. production statistics, 3–7
Inert ingredient, defined, 604

Inflorescence, defined, 604
Inoculation, defined, 604
Inodorus group, melons, 362
Inorganic pesticide, defined, 604
Insect control, vegetable, general, 151–170
    feeding patterns, described, 155
    identification, procedure, 169
    pest management, 154
    pests, illustrated, 156–158
    pests, listed, 154
Insecticide(s)
    classification, 155
    defined, 604
    dusts, 156, 160
    recommended for vegetables, list, 160
    sprays, 157, 160
Insects, pollination role, table, 60
Internal tipburn, cabbage, 265–266
Internode, defined, 604
Ipomea Batatas, sweet potatoes, 31, 495
Irish potato, 436
Irish potato famine, 436
Irrigating
    frequency and amount, 137
    methods, 138–141
Irrigation
    cucumbers, 331
    lettuce, 346, 349
    melons, 371
    onions, 390
    sprinkler lettuce, 349
Iron
    availability, effect of soil pH, 104, 109
    vegetable response, 108

Jerusalem artichokes, 305–306
    classification, 31, 305
Jalapeño peppers, 423
Juan Canari melons, 365

Kale, 471–472
Keel, defined, 604
Kohlrabi, 276–277

Lactuca sativa, lettuce, 31, 341
Lannate®, insecticide, 160
Late blight
    celery, 318
    Irish potato famine, 436
    potatoes, 452

resistant potato varieties, 55
    tomatoes, 529
Leaf beetles, beans, 245
Leaf blight
    carrots, 286–287
    onions, 394
    sweet corn, 491–492
Leaf miners
    peppers, 429
    spinach, 467
Leaf roll, potatoes, 453
Leafhoppers
    beans, 246
    horseradish, 298
    lettuce, 352
    potatoes, 450–451
    spinach, 467
Leafy salad vegetables, 341–360
Leafy vegetables, listed, 172–173
Leek, 400–402
Legumes, seed inoculation, 410
Leguminosae, pea/bean family, 32–33, 233, 405
Lettuce, 341–360
    classification, 341
    climatic requirements, 345
    cultivars, 350
    cultural practices, 348
    cultural requirements, 345
    direct seeding, 347
    diseases, 352
    growth/development, 343
    harvesting, 354
    insect control, 352
    irrigation, 349
    origin, 340
    physiological disorders, 354
    planting/crop establishment, 346–356
    production/industry, 342–343
    reproductive growth, 344
    seed germination, 346
    temperature requirements, 345
    thinning, electronic sensors, 350
    tipburn, 354
    transplanting, 347
    weeds, 348
Light
    flowering response, 50
    role in postharvest deterioration, 177
Lignin, defined, 605
Liliaceae, lily family, 31, 209

Lima beans, 234–239
  classification, 32, 234
  climatic requirements,
    239–240
  cotyledon cracking, 236
  cultivars, 243–244
  cultural practices, 242
  cultural requirements, 240
  determinant (bush) growth,
    237
  diseases, 246–247
  flowers and fruits, 238–239
  growth/development,
    236–239
  harvesting, 248
  indeterminant (runner, pole)
    growth, 237
  insects, 245–246
  irrigation, 242
  origin, 234
  planting/crop establishment,
    240–241
  postharvest handling,
    248–249
  production/industry,
    234–236
  Rhizobium spp., 239
  roots, 239
  salt injury, 240
  seedling
    growth/development, 236
  semi-determinant (half-
    runner) growth, 238
  vine growth patterns,
    236–237
  weeds, 242
Liming, 104–105
Linear-move irrigation, 139
LISA, defined, 605
Long-day (photoperiod), defined,
  50
Longevity, defined, 605
Loopers/worms
  cabbage, 264
  lettuce, 352
Lorsban®, insecticide, 160
Lycopersicon hirsutum, tomatoes
  (wild type), 513
Lycopersicon Lycopersicum,
  tomatoes, 33, 513
Lycopersicon peruvianum,
  tomatoes (wild type), 33, 513
Lycopersicon pimpinellifolium,
  currant tomatoes, 33, 513

Machine harvesting
  cucumbers, 337

gynoecious hybrid
  cucumbers, 334
  melons, 377
  onions, 395
  potatoes, 454–455
  sweet corn, 493
Macronutrient, defined, 605
Maggots
  cabbage, 264
  onions, 393
  peppers, 430
Magnesium
  enzyme activator, 107
  fertilizer materials, 107
Maize, 477
Maize dwarf mosaic, sweet corn,
  492
Malathion, insecticide, 156, 160
Male flowers
  defined, 58
  staminate, 365
Male sterility, in hybridization, 63
Maleic hydrazide
  onions, 397
  potatoes, 456
  sprout inhibition, 175, 605
Malvaceae, mallow family, 33
Mancozeb®, fungicide, 164
Maneb®, fungicide, 164
Manganese
  availability, effect of soil pH,
    104, 109
  vegetable response, 108
Market gardening, 11, 605
Marketing
  defined, 15, 605
  contractual production, 21
  objectives, 15
  outlets, 16–20
  services, 16
  shifting market
    requirements, 21–22
Mass selection breeding,
  described, 64
Maturity indices, 177–178
Meiosis, defined, 57
Melons, 361–380
  abscission layer in
    harvesting, 375, 376
  Cantalupensis group, 362
  classification, 361–363
  climate requirements,
    367–368
  cultivars, 371–372
  cultural practices, 370–371
  direct seeding, 369
  diseases, 373–375

ethylene treatment, 379
flowers and fruit, 365–366
growth/development 364
harvesting methods, 375,
  377–378
Inodorus group, 362
insects, 372–373
irrigation, 371
night harvesting, 378
origin, 362
planting/crop establishment,
  368–370
plastics, 370
pollination, 367
postharvest handling,
  378–379
production/industry, 364
Reticulatus group, 362
seedling
  germination/development,
    364–365
soils/fertility requirements,
  368
transplants, 369–370
viral diseases, 375
weeds, 370
Messenger RNA, 56
Methamidophos, insecticide, 160
Methomyl, insecticide, 160
Mevinphos, insecticide, 160
Mexican bean beetle, beans, 245
Micronutrient availability
  effect of soil pH, 104, 109
  relative response of
    vegetables, 108
Micronutrient, defined, 605
Mineral absorption, by roots, 43
Miticide, defined, 605
Mitosis, defined, 56
Moisture stress, critical periods,
  135
Molybdenum
  availability, effect of soil pH,
    104, 109
  vegetable response, 108
Monitor®, insecticide, 160
Monocotyledon, defined, 605
Monocotyledoneae, classification,
  30, 31
Monoecious plants, defined, 58,
  365, 605
Mosaic, defined, 605
Mosaic virus(es)
  beans, 247
  celery, 319
  cucumbers, 336
  lettuce, 353

melons, 375
peas, 417
peppers, 431
potatoes, 452–453
pumpkins/squashes, 547
spinach, 467–468
sweet corn, 492
tomatoes, 530
Muck soil
crop usage, 96
defined, 605
onion production, 386, 387
Mulch, 605
Mulching
materials, 144
principles, 144
uses in weed control, 127
Mung beans, 252
Muskmelons, 361–380
Mustards, 473–474
Mutation, defined, 605
Mutations, chemically induced, 61
Mycelium, defined, 605
Mycoplasma, aster yellows,
lettuce, 353

Naled, insecticide, 160
Neck rot, onions, 393–394
Necrosis, defined, 605
Nematocide, defined, 605
Nematode
control, 165
described, 165, 605
peas, 416
sweet potatoes, 507
tomatoes (root knot), 530
Nematode-resistant cultivars, 165
Net photosynthesis, 40, 47
New Zealand spinach, 474–475
Night harvesting, melons, 378
Nitrapyrin, nitrification inhibitor,
464
Nitrification inhibitors, spinach,
464
Nitrite levels, human diet, 463
Nitrogen
crop requirements, 117
fertilizer materials, 112
plant nutrient, 105
Nitrogen-fixing bacteria, seed
inoculation, 410
Nucleotides, defined, 56
Nucleus, defined, 605
Nutrients, plant growth
requirements, 43

Obligate flowering response, photoperiod, 51
Obligate flowering response,
temperature, 49
Okra, 549–550
Olericulture, defined, 29, 605
Onions, 381–404
Aggregatum group, 398, 403
bolting causes, 385
bulbing, photoperiod/
daylength, 385, 391
classification, 381
climatic requirements,
385–386
cultivars, 391–392
cultural practices, 390
direct seeding, 387–388
diseases, 393
fertilization, 386
green, from sets, 388, 397
growth/development,
383–385
harvesting methods, 394
hybrid cultivars, 391
insects, 393
irrigation, 390
long-day/short-day, 392
origin, 381
pearl, 398
photoperiod bulbing, 385,
391
planting/crop establishment,
387–389
production/industry,
382–383
pungency source, 385
seeding rates, 389
sets, planting, 388, 397
short-day/long-day, 392
soils, 386
spacing/plant populations,
389
transplants, 388
water-use curve, 136
weeds, 390
Open-pollinated, 72
Orach, Atriplex hortensis, 552
Organic fertilizers, 112
Organic matter, 98–99
maintenance with animal
manures, 100–101
maintenance with green
manures and cover
crops, 99–100
Organic mulches, 145
Organic pesticide, defined, 605
Organophosphates, 155, 160

Ornamental squashes,
classification, 542
Orthene®, insecticide, 160
Osmoconditioning, 74, 605
Osmosis, defined, 606
Ovary, illustrated, 58, 606
Ovicide, defined, 606
Ovules, defined, 58
Oxalic acid, 225

Package icing, 185
Packinghouse operations, 180–183
Pak-choi, 277–278
Panicle, defined, 606
Parenchyma, defined, 606
Parsley, 552–554
Parsnips, 299–301
classification, 299–300
climatic requirements, 300
harvesting, 300–301
origin, 300
planting/crop establishment,
300
postharvest handling, 301
root, illustrated, 299
Parthenocarpy
cucumbers, 327
defined, 606
Partially cross-pollinated plants, 66
Pastinaca sativa, parsnip, 33, 299
Patterns of plant growth, 46
Peanut stunt virus, beans, 247
Pearl onions, 398
Peas, 405–419
bush (determinate), 407,
410, 413
classification, 405
climatic requirements, 409
cultivars, 413–416
cultural requirements,
409–410
diseases, 416–417
English, 405
garden, 405–419
growth/development,
407–409
harvesting, 417–418
heat-unit requirements,
411–412
herbicide sensitivity, 409
inoculation, 410
insect control, 416
marketing, 418
planting/crop establishment,
410–412
pod characteristics, 413–414
postharvest handling, 418

production/industry,
406–407
seed characteristics,
414–415
shelling process, 418
soil temperature, effect on
germination, 411
southern, 405
sugar snap peas, 415–416
vining (indeterminate), 407,
410, 413
weeds, 412–413
Pectin, defined, 606
Pedigree selection breeding,
described, 64
Pelleted seed, lettuce planting, 347
Pepper maggots, 430
Peppers, 421–433
anaheim chile group, 423
bell group, 422–423
cherry group, 423
classification, 421–423
climatic requirements,
425–426
cultivars, 428–429
cultural practices, 428
cultural requirements,
426–427
diseases, 430–431
growth/development, 425
harvesting, 431–432
illustrated, 422
insects, 429–430
jalapeño group, 423
physiological disorders, 431
planting/crop establishment,
427–428
postharvest handling,
432–433
production/industry,
424–425
tabasco group, 423
wax group, 423
Pepper weevils, 430
Perennial
crops, listing, 36, 209–231
defined, 606
weeds, 121
Perfect flowers, defined, 58
Perianth
defined, 606
illustrated, 58
Pericarp, defined, 606
Pericycle, defined, 606
Periderm, defined, 606
Permanent wilting percentage,
defined, 44

Permethrin, 160
Persian melons, 372
Persians, 361
Pest control, 151–170
recommendations, sources,
169
Pest identification, procedure, 169
Pesticide
application, timing, 165
compatibility, 167
defined, 606
drift, 168
labels, use directions, 166
tolerances, EPA/FDA, 152
Pesticides, safe handling, 167
Petiole, defined, 606
Petroselinum crispum, parsley, 33,
552
Pe-tsai, 277–278
Phaseolus coccineus, scarlet
runner beans, 32, 249
Phaseolus limensis, lima beans, 32,
234
Phaseolus limensis var. *limenanus*,
bush lima beans, 32, 234
Phaseolus lunatus, sieva beans
(butter beans), 32, 234
Phaseolus lunatus var. *lunonanus*,
bush sieva beans, 32, 234
Phaseolus vulgaris, snap beans, 32,
234
Phaseolus vulgaris var. *humilis*,
bush snap beans, 32, 234
Phenotype, defined, 606
Phloem, defined, 606
Phorate, insecticide, 160
Phosdrin®, insecticide, 160
Phosphorus, fertilizers, 112
plant functions, 106
requirements for vegetables,
116
Photoperiod
flowering response, 50
onion bulbing, 385, 391
underground storage organ
formation, 51
Photoperiodic plants, defined, 52
Photoperiodism, defined, 51
Photosynthesis
carbohydrate production, 47
defined, 40, 47, 606
Phytochrome, germination
pigment, 78, 344, 606
Phytophthora blight, peppers, 431
Pickleworm
cucumbers, 334
melons, 373

Pick-your-own
defined, 606
market outlet, 17
Pigment, defined, 606
Pimiento peppers, 423
Pink rot
celery, 318
onions, 393
Piper nigrum, black pepper, 421
Pistil, defined, 606
Pistillate (female) flowers, defined,
58, 365, 606
Pisum sativum, peas, 32, 405
Pith, defined, 606
Plant growth and development,
39–53
flowering, response to light
and photoperiod, 50
flowering, response to low
temperatures, 49
formation of storage organs,
response to photoperiod,
51
growth factors, 40–45
growth patterns, 46–52
growth/quality relationships,
45–46
reproductive growth phase,
48–52
temperature/growth
relationships, 41–42
vegetative growth phase,
47–48
vernalization, 48–50
Plant productivity, defined, 39
Plant variation, 61
Planting dates, determined by
heat units, 42
Plastic, crop coverings, 485
Plastic mulches, 145
melon production, 370
Plastic tunnels, melon production,
370
Plastid, defined, 606
Plowing, 123
Plug-mix seeders, 92
Plumule, defined, 606
Pollen, defined, 607
Pollen storage, examples, 60
Pollinate, defined, 607
Pollination
cucumbers, 331
described, 59
environmental effects, 60
insect importance, chart, 60
melons, 367
pumpkins/squashes, 547

requirements, vegetables,
chart, 60
Polygonaceae, buckwheat family,
33
Polyploid plants, defined, 61
Polysaccharides, sweet corn, 488
Popcorn, *Zea Mays* var. *everta*,
477
Portable pipe irrigation, 140
Postemergent herbicides, 129, 130
Postharvest
compositional changes, 174
factors involved in
deterioration, 174–177
handling, 171–195
Potassium fertilizers, 112
plant functions, 106
requirements for vegetables,
116
Potato onion, 398
Potatoes, 435–457
apical dominance, 441
certified seed, 446–447
classification, 435
climatic requirements,
441–442
cultivars, 448–450
cultural practices, 447–448
curing, for storage, 455
curing, seed pieces, 444
diseases, 451–453
dry matter vs. quality, 448
emergence/early
development, 438
fertility, 443–444
growth/development,
438–441
harvesting, 454–455
hilling, 447
insects, 450–451
irrigation, 447–448
marketing, 456
physiological disorders, 453
plant anatomy, illustrated,
439
planting/crop establishment,
444–446
preplanting procedures,
444–445
production/industry,
436–438
shoot/tuber relationships,
410–411
soils, 442–443
sprout inhibition, 456
storing, 455–456

tuber anatomy, illustrated,
440
tuber initiation, 438
vine killing, 454
weeds, 447
Pounce®, insecticide, 160
Powdery mildew
carrots, 287
cucumbers, 337
melons, 374
Precision seeders, cucumbers, 329
Precision seeding, 89
Precooling, defined, 607
Precooling methods, 183–186
Preemergent herbicides (PRE),
129, 130
Preferential flowering response,
photoperiod, 51
Preferential flowering response,
temperature, 49
Pregerminated seed, lettuce, 347
Preplant-incorporated herbicides
(PPI), 129, 130
Primary plant nutrients, 105–106
Processing markets, 19–20
principal crops, 4
production statistics, 3, 5–6
Progeny, defined, 607
Propagate
defined, 607
vegetative examples, 66
Protein, defined, 607
Protoplasm, defined, 607
Protoplast fusion, 199–201
Puffiness, tomatoes, 532
Pumpkins, 541–549
cheese pumpkins,
classification, 542
classification, 32, 541–542
climatic requirements,
545–546
crookneck pumpkins,
classification, 542
culture, 545–547
cushaw pumpkins,
classification, 542
decorative/jumbo pumpkins,
classification, 542
diseases, 547
field and pie pumpkins,
classification, 542
field planting, 546
growth/development,
544–545
harvesting, 547–548
insects, 547

miniature pumpkins,
classification, 542
naked-seeded pumpkins,
classification, 542
nomenclature, 542–543
origin, 543–544
pollination, by honeybees,
547
postharvest handling,
548–549
production/industry, 544
production practices, 547
soils, 546
storage, 549
Purple blotch, onions, 394
Pyrethroids, insecticides, 155, 160
Pyrethrum, insecticide, 155
Pythium root rot
beans, 247
peas, 417

Quality
defined, 193
grade standards, 194–195
Quantitative flowering response,
photoperiod, 51
Quantitative flowering response,
temperature, 49
Quarter-slip stage, melon
harvesting, 376

Radicle, defined, 607
Radishes, 301–303
classification, 301
climatic requirements, 302
cultural requirements,
302–303
growth/development, 302
harvesting, 303
origin, 301
planting/crop establishment,
302–303
postharvest handling, 303
production/industry,
301–302
spring types, 302
Raphanus sativus, radishes, 32, 301
Receptacle, defined, 607
Recessive, defined, 607
Recessive gene, defined, 58
Recombinant DNA, 199–200, 206
Registered seed, 70
Reproductive growth, 46, 47
Reproductive phase
carbohydrate storage, 48
light effects, 50
photoperiod effects, 50

temperature/vernalization, 48

Residue, defined, 607

Resistant varieties, melons, 371

Respiration
  defined, 40
  role in postharvest deterioration, 174

Restricted-use insecticides, 155, 160, 161

Reticulatus group, melons, 362

Rheum Rhabarbarum, rhubarb, 33, 225

Rhizoctonia root rot, 417
  beans, 247

Rhizosphere, defined, 607

Rhubarb, 225–228
  classification, 33, 225
  climatic requirements, 226
  crown divisions, 226
  culture, 227
  diseases, 227
  forcing, 228
  growth/development, 226
  harvesting, 228
  insects, 227
  oxalic acid, 225
  petioles, illustrated, 225
  planting/crop establishment, 226–227
  postharvest handling, 228

Ribonucleic acid (RNA), defined, 607

Ring rot, potatoes, 452

Ripening, use of ethylene gas, 183

RNA (ribonucleic acid), defined, 56

Roguing, described, 64, 607

Romaine lettuce, 341, 351

Room cooling, 183

Root crops, 279–307
  beets, 288–294
  carrots, 279–288
  horseradish, 294–299
  Jerusalem artichokes, 305–307
  parsnips, 299–301
  radishes, 301–303
  rutabagas, 303–305
  turnips, 303–305

Root crown, defined, 607

Root depth, effect on water requirement, 137–138

Root dieback, carrots, 287

Root knot nematodes, 165, 337, 530

Root maggots, radishes, 303

Root rot
  beans, 247
  complex, peas, 417
  peas, 417
  sweet potatoes, 507–508

Roots, mineral absorption, 43

Rootworms, sweet corn, 491

Rotary hoeing, 123

Rotenone, insecticide, 155, 160

Row covers, 147

Row tunnels, 147

Russet Burbank, potatoes, 449

Rust
  asparagus, 222
  beans, 246
  sweet corn, 492

Rutabagas, 303–305
  classification, 31, 304
  climatic requirements, 304–305
  cultural requirements, 305
  harvesting, 305
  plant characteristics, 304
  postharvest handling, 305

SADH (succinic acid-2, 2-dimethylhydrazide), 276

Safe handling, pesticides, 167

Salinity
  crop tolerance, 142
  effect on water quality, 143

Salsify, 550–551

Scab
  cucumbers, 336
  potatoes, 452

Scarlet runner beans, 249

Sclerotinia
  root rot, carrots, 287
  white mold, beans, 247

Scouting, for insect pests, 155

Scurf, sweet potatoes, 507

Seed
  breeder's seed, 70
  certified seed, 70
  coating, 74–75
  commercial production, 13
  defined, 607
  enhancement, 73
  foundation seed, 70
  germination, effect of soil moisture, 77
  germination, effect of soil temperature, 78
  longevity, 79
  priming, 74
  quality, 70
  registered seed, 70

sizing, 71
thermodormancy, 77
vigor, 73

Seed rot/damping-off, beets, 293

Seed treatment, disease control, 162

Seeding dates, 89

Seeding methods, 89

Seedless cucumbers, 327

Seedless watermelon, triploid, 61, 366

Self-pollinated vegetables, 64

Self-pollination, described, 59

Self-sterile plants, described, 59

Semi-determinate, defined, 607

Senescence, plant, 45

Sepal, defined, 607

Septoria blight, peas, 416

Septoria leaf spot, tomatoes, 529

Sevin®, insecticide, 159, 160

Shallots, 403
  used as green onions, 392

Sheath, defined, 607

Shoot, defined, 607

Short-day (photoperiod), defined, 51

Shrunken-2, sweet corn, 488

Sibling mating, cross-pollination, 66

Silique, defined, 607

Silver nitrate, in cucumber sex expression, 326

Slicers, cucumber types, 329, 333

Slips, defined, 607

Slurry, seed treatment, 162

Smut
  onions, 394
  sweet corn, 491

Snap beans, 234–249
  classification, 32, 234
  climatic requirements, 239–240
  cotyledon cracking, 236
  cultivars, 242–244
  cultural practices, 242
  cultural requirements, 240
  determinant (bush) growth, 237
  diseases, 246–247
  flowers and fruits, 238–239
  growth/development, 236–239
  harvesting, 248
  history, 234
  indeterminant (runner, pole) growth, 237
  insects, 245–246
  irrigation, 242

origin, 234
plant development,
    illustrated, 239
planting/crop establishment,
    240–241
postharvest handling,
    248–249
production/industry,
    234–236
Rhizobium spp., 239
roots, 239
salt injury, 240
seedling
    growth/development, 236
semi-determinant
    (half-runner) growth, 238
vine growth patterns,
    236–237
weeds, 242
Snow peas, 405, 415
Sodium, effects on water quality,
143
Soft rot, sweet potatoes, 507
Soil
    characteristics, 95
    optimum pH ranges, 103
    organic matter, 98
    pH, effect on nutrient
        availability, 100
    preparation, 97
    testing, 114
Soil fumigation, nematodes, 165
Soil sterilization, disease control,
162
Solanaceae, potato or nightshade
    family, 33
Solanum Melongena var.
    esculentum, eggplants, 33, 537
Solanum tuberosum, potatoes, 33,
435
Solid-set irrigation, 140
Somoclonal variation, 199, 206
Southern blight, peppers, 431
Southern peas, 250
Soybeans, garden, 251–252
Specialty crops, 20, 607
Species, defined, 607
Speedling, lettuce transplanting
    system, 347
Sperm, defined, 608
Spinach, 459–470
    classification, 460
    climatic requirements, 463
    cultivars, 466–467
    cultural requirements, 463
    diseases, 467–468

growth/development,
    461–462
harvesting, 468–469
insects, 467
irrigation, 465
marketing, 469–470
planting/crop establishment,
    464–465
postharvest handling,
    469–470
production/industry,
    460–461
weeds, 465
Spinacia oleracea, spinach, 31, 460
Spotted cucumber beetle
    cucumbers, 334
    pumpkins/squashes, 547
Spreader, defined, 608
Sprinkler irrigation, lettuce, 349
Sprouting inhibitors, 175
Spunbonded polyester, crop
    coverings, 485
Squash mosaic, melons, 375
Squashes, 541–549
    acorn squash, classification,
        542
    banana squash,
        classification, 542
    buttercup squash,
        classification, 542
    butternut squash,
        classification, 542
    classification, 32, 541–542
    climatic requirements,
        545–546
    cocozelle squash,
        classification, 542
    culture/production, 545–547
    cushaw squash,
        classification, 542
    delicious squash,
        classification, 542
    diseases, 547
    fertility, 546
    field planting, 546
    fordhook squash,
        classification, 542
    growth/development,
        544–545
    harvesting, 547–548
    Hubbard squash,
        classification, 542
    insects, 547
    kindred squash,
        classification, 542
    marrow squash,
        classification, 542

nomenclature, 542
orange squash,
    classification, 542
origin, 543–544
pollination, by honeybees,
    547
postharvest handling,
    548–549
production/industry, 544
production practices, 547
scallop squash,
    classification, 542
soils, 546
storage, 549
summer squashes, 541
turban squash, classification,
    542
winter squashes, 541
yellow squash, crookneck,
    classification, 542
yellow squash, straightneck,
    classification, 542
zucchini squash,
    classification, 542
Stamen
    defined, 608
    illustrated, 58
Staminate (male) flowers, 58, 365,
608
Starter solutions, 87, 113
Stem rot, sweet potatoes, 507
Stigma
    defined, 608
    illustrated, 58
Stipule, defined, 608
Stolon, 438, 608
Streptomycin fungicides, 165
Striped cucumber beetle
    cucumbers, 334
    melons, 373
    pumpkins/squashes, 547
Style
    defined, 608
    illustrated, 58
Suberin, defined, 608
Suberize, defined, potato seed
    pieces, 444
Subirrigation, 141
Sucrose, defined, 608
Sugar peas, 405, 415
Sugary sweet corn, 487
Sulfur, nutrition, 107
Summer squashes, 541 (*see also*
    Squashes)
Sunscald
    peppers, 431
    tomatoes, 531

Super-sweets, sweet corn, 487
Sweet corn, 477–494
    classification, 477
    climatic requirements,
        482–483
    cultivars, 488
    cultural requirements, 483
    diseases, 491–492
    environmental influences on
        growth, 481–482
    field covers on early
        plantings, 485
    genes, high sugars, 487–489
    genetic classification, 488
    growth/development,
        479–482
    harvesting, 492–493
    insects, 490–491
    irrigation, 485–486
    isolation requirements, 489
    origin, 477
    plant development,
        illustrated, 480
    planting/crop establishment,
        483–484
    postharvest handling,
        493–494
    production/industry,
        478–479
    quality, 487
    scheduling planting dates,
        484–485
    seed (kernel), anatomy,
        illustrated, 481
    weeds, 486
Sweet potatoes, 495–511
    apical dominance, 498
    certified seed, 505
    classification, 495
    climatic requirements, 498
    cultivars, selection, 504–505
    cultural practices, 503–504
    cultural requirements, 499
    curing, 509–510
    diseases, 506–508
    growth/development,
        497–498
    harvesting, 508–509
    history, 495–496
    insects, 506
    irrigation, 503–504
    marketing, 510
    origin, 495
    planting/crop establishment,
        499–503
    production/industry,
        496–497

slips, 498, 499–502
storing, 510
variability of cultivars,
    504–505
vine cuttings, 502–503
weeds, 503
Systemic insecticide, defined, 608

Taraxacum officinale, dandelions,
    31, 475
Temperature
    effects on reproductive
        phase, 48
    flowering response, 49
    optimum
        growth/development
        range, 41
    pollination effects, 60
    role in postharvest
        deterioration, 176, 179
Tender crops, 35
Tenderometer, measuring pea
    maturity, 418
Tendril, defined, 608
Terbufos, insecticide, 160
Tetragonia tetragonioides, New
    Zealand spinach, 33, 474
Tetragoniaceae, carpetweed
    family, 33, 474
Tetraploid (4n) watermelon, 366
Tetraploid plants, defined, 61
Thermodormancy, 77, 608
Thimet®, insecticide, 160
Thinning, using electronic sensors,
    lettuce, 350
Thrips
    cabbage, 264
    onions, 393
Timing, pesticide applications, 165
Tipburn
    cabbage, 265–266
    defined, 608
    lettuce, 353
Tissue and cell culture, 198
Tolerance
    defined, 608
    pesticides, EPA/FDA, 152
Tomatoes, 513–536
    breeding for machine
        harvest, 55
    classification, 513
    climatic requirements,
        518–519
    clump seeding, 520
    cultivars, 525–527
    cultural practices, 523–525
    cultural requirements, 519

direct seeding, 520–521
diseases, control, 528–530
ethephon effects on
    ripening, 534
flowering and fruit
    development, 517–518
fresh market production,
    514–515
fruit disorders, 531–532
fruit maturity stages, 533
greenhouse production, 516
growth/development,
    516–518
harvesting, 532–535
history, 513
insects, control, 527–528
irrigation, 523–524
marketing, 536
nitrogen fertilization
    management, 519
origin, 513
planting/crop establishment,
    519–523
postharvest handling,
    535–536
processing production,
    515–516
production/industry,
    514–515
transplanting, 521–523
vine support and pruning,
    524–525
vine types, 516–517
weeds, control, 524
Total dissolved solids (TDS), 143
Toxicity, defined, 608
Tragopogon porrifolius, New
    Zealand spinach, 33, 550
Translocation, defined, 608
Transpiration
    defined, 608
    role in postharvest
        deterioration, 175
Transplanting, 80–87
    crop adaptability, 86
    growing transplants, 81–83
    hardening, 83–85
Transplants
    asparagus, 217
    cabbage, 259
    celery, 313
    cucumbers, 329
    eggplants, 539
    melons, 369–370
    onions, 388
    peppers, 427
    tomatoes, 521–523

Transportation
    modes, 188–191
    temperature management
        during transit, 191–193
Traveling gun irrigation, 139
Trichlorfon, insecticide, 160
Trickle irrigation, 141
Triploid plants, defined, 61
Triploid (3n) watermelon, 366
Truck farming, 12, 608
Tuber
    defined, 608
    flea beetle, potatoes, 450
    greening, potatoes, 453
    initiation/development,
        potatoes, 438
Tuberworms, potatoes, 451
Turban gourds and squashes,
    classification, 542
Turnip mosaic virus, horseradish,
    298
Turnips, 303–305
    classification, 304
    climatic requirements,
        304–305
    cultural requirements, 305
    harvesting, 305
    plant characteristics, 304
    postharvest handling, 305
Twelve-spotted asparagus beetle,
    asparagus, 220–221
2,4-D, synthetic auxin, herbicide,
    44

Umbel, defined, 608
Umbelliferae, parsley family, 33
Underground vegetables, listed,
    172–173
Unisexual, defined, 608

Vacuum cooling
    broccoli/cauliflower, 274
    defined, 186, 608
    lettuce, 355
    spinach, 469
    sweet corn, 494
Valerianaceae, valerian family, 33
Vegetable
    grade standards, 194–195
    quality, 193–194
    storage methods, 186–188
Vegetative growth, 46, 47
    propagation, examples, 66

Vernalization
    beets, 291
    cabbage, 258
    carrots, 282
    cauliflower, 269
    celery, 310
    Chinese cabbage, 278
    defined 49, 608
    kohlrabi, 276
    onions, 385
    reproductive phase, 48
    rutabagas, 305
    turnips, 305
    vegetable classification, 49
Verticillium wilt, tomatoes, 528
Vicia Faba, fava beans, 32, 252
Vigna radiata, mung beans, 32,
    252
Vigna unguiculata, cowpeas, 32,
    250
Vigna unguiculata subsp.
    cylindrica, catjang beans, 33,
    250
Vigna unguiculata subsp.
    sesquipedalis, asparagus beans,
    33, 250
Vigna unguiculata subsp.
    unguiculata, black-eyed peas,
    33, 250
Viral diseases
    beans, 247
    celery, 319
    cucumbers, 336
    lettuce, 353
    melons, 3758
    peas, 417
    peppers, 431
    pumpkins/squashes, 547
    spinach, 467, 468
    tomatoes, 530
Virus, defined, 609
Vitamins, defined, 609

Warm-season crops, 35
Water
    available, defined, 44
    critical use periods, 134
    crop requirement, 130, 138
    plant growth requirements,
        43
Watermelons, 363, 364, 366–368,
    369, 371, 377, 378, 379 (*see
    also* Melons)

Waxing
    pepper storage, 432
    postharvest operations, 181
    rutabaga/turnip storage, 305
Weed(s)
    chemical control, 127–132
    classifications, 120–121
    competition, 121–122
    defined, 609
    mechanical and cultural
        control, 123–127
Weevils
    beans, 245
    peppers, 430
Western mosaic, celery, 319
Western shipping melons,
    muskmelons, 371
Wettable powders
    defined 609
    pesticides, 160
Wetting agent, defined, 609
Whiptale, cauliflower/broccoli, 273
White pickle, cucumber mosaic,
    336
White rot, onions, 394
White rust
    horseradish, 298
    spinach, 468
Whorl, defined, 609
Winter melons, Inodorus group,
    362
Winter squashes, 541 (*see also*
    Squashes)
Worms/loopers
    cabbage, 264
    lettuce, 352

Xylem, defined, 609

Yams, 496
Yellows, cabbage, 265
Yield
    biological, defined, 39
    economic, defined, 39

Zea Mays, other subspecies, 31, 477
Zea Mays var. *saccharata*, sweet
    corn, 31, 477
Zinc
    availability, effect of soil pH,
        104, 109
    crop response, 108